PHILIP'S

CW00363071

STRE

Nottinghamshire

First published in 1994 by

Philip's, a division of
Octopus Publishing Group Ltd
2–4 Heron Quays, London E14 4JP

Second colour edition 2002
First impression 2002

ISBN 0-540-08128-0

© Philip's 2002

Ordnance Survey®

This product includes mapping data licensed
from Ordnance Survey® with the permission
of the Controller of Her Majesty's Stationery
Office. © Crown copyright 2002. All rights
reserved. Licence number 100011710

Printed and bound in Spain
by Cayfosa-Quebecor

Contents

III **Key to map symbols**

IV **Key to map pages**

VI **Route planning**

VIII **Administrative and Postcode boundaries**

1 **Street maps** at 2½ inches to 1 mile

221 **Town maps** of Chesterfield and Lincoln

222 **Street map of Nottingham city centre**
at 5 inches to 1 mile

224 **Index** of towns and villages

226 **Index** of streets, hospitals, industrial estates, railway
stations, schools, shopping centres, universities
and places of interest

Digital Data

The exceptionally high-quality mapping found in this atlas is available as digital data
in TIFF format, which is easily convertible to other bit mapped (raster) image
formats.

The index is also available in digital form as a standard database table. It contains
all the details found in the printed index together with the National Grid reference
for the map square in which each entry is named.

For further information and to discuss your requirements, please contact
Philip's on 020 7531 8439 or george.philip@philips-maps.co.uk

Symbol	Description
(22a)	**Motorway** with junction number
	Primary route – dual/single carriageway
	A road – dual/single carriageway
	B road – dual/single carriageway
	Minor road – dual/single carriageway
	Other minor road – dual/single carriageway
	Road under construction
	Pedestrianised area
DY7	**Postcode boundaries**
	County and unitary authority boundaries
	Railway, railway under construction
	Tramway, tramway under construction
	Miniature railway
	Rural track, private road or narrow road in urban area
	Gate or obstruction to traffic (restrictions may not apply at all times or to all vehicles)
	Path, bridleway, byway open to all traffic, road used as a public path
	The representation in this atlas of a road, track or path is no evidence of the existence of a right of way
58 / 230 / 237	**Adjoining page indicators**
	The map area within the pink band is shown at a larger scale on the page indicated by the red block and arrow

Symbol	Description
Walsall	**Railway station**
	Private railway station
South Shields	**Metro station**
	Tram stop, tram stop under construction
	Bus, coach station
	Ambulance station
	Coastguard station
	Fire station
	Police station
+	**Accident and Emergency entrance to hospital**
H	**Hospital**
+	**Place of worship**
i	**Information Centre** (open all year)
P	**Parking**
P&R	**Park and Ride**
PO	**Post Office**
Å	**Camping site**
	Caravan site
	Picnic site
Prim Sch	**Important buildings, schools, colleges, universities and hospitals**
River Medway	**Water name**
	River, stream
	Lock, weir
	Water
	Tidal water
	Woods
	Built up area
Church	**Non-Roman antiquity**
ROMAN FORT	**Roman antiquity**

Acad	Academy	Mkt	Market
Allot Gdns	Allotments	Meml	Memorial
Cemy	Cemetery	Mon	Monument
C Ctr	Civic Centre	Mus	Museum
CH	Club House	Obsy	Observatory
Coll	College	Pal	Royal Palace
Crem	Crematorium	PH	Public House
Ent	Enterprise	Recn Gd	Recreation Ground
Ex H	Exhibition Hall	Resr	Reservoir
Ind Est	Industrial Estate	Ret Pk	Retail Park
IRB Sta	Inshore Rescue	Sch	School
	Boat Station	Sh Ctr	Shopping Centre
Inst	Institute	TH	Town Hall/House
Ct	Law Court	Trad Est	Trading Estate
L Ctr	Leisure Centre	Univ	University
LC	Level Crossing	Wks	Works
Liby	Library	YH	Youth Hostel

■ The small numbers around the edges of the maps identify the 1 kilometre National Grid lines

■ The dark grey border on the inside edge of some pages indicates that the mapping does not continue onto the adjacent page

The scale of the maps on the pages numbered in blue is 3.92 cm to 1 km • 2½ inches to 1 mile • 1: 25344

0	¼	½	¾	1 mile
0	250 m 500 m	750 m 1 kilometre		

The scale of the maps on the pages numbered in red is 7.84 cm to 1 km • 5 inches to 1 mile • 1: 12672

0	220 yards	440 yards	660 yards	½ mile
0	125 m 250 m	375 m ½ kilometre		

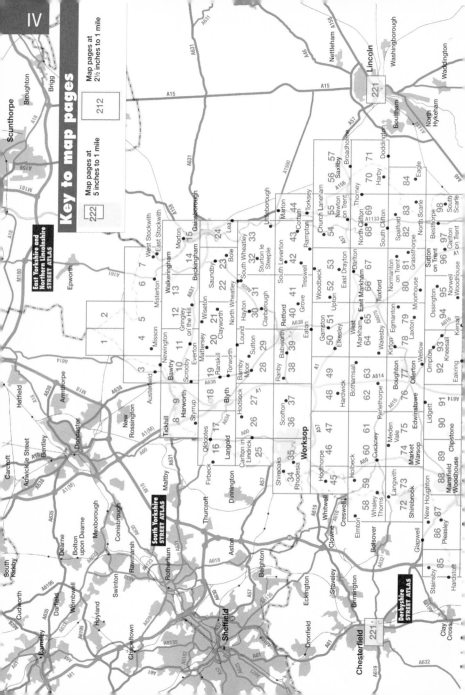

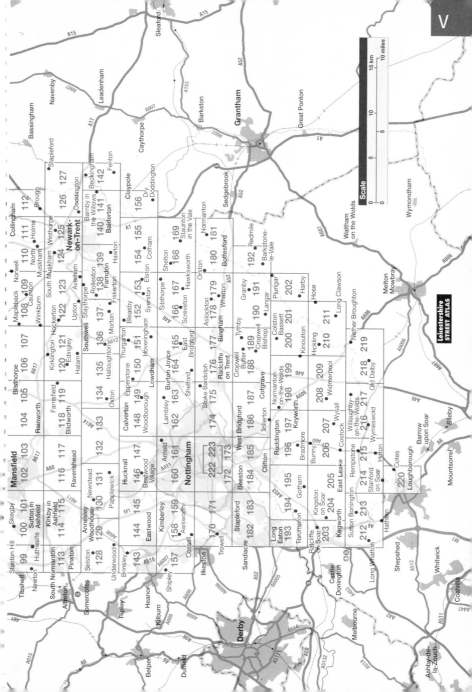

Route planning

Scale

0   5   10   15 km

0   5   10 miles

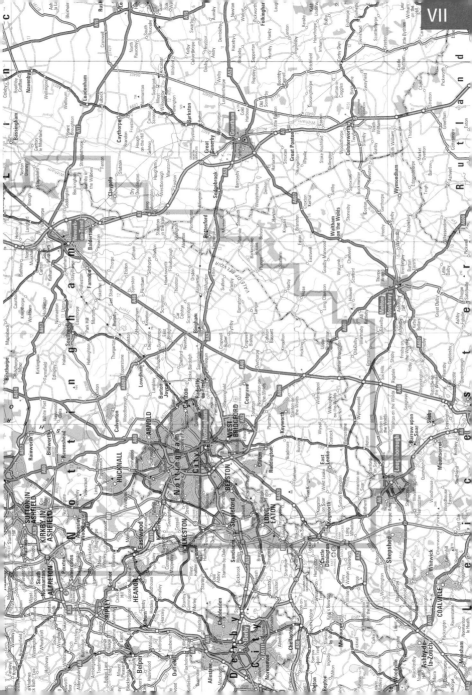

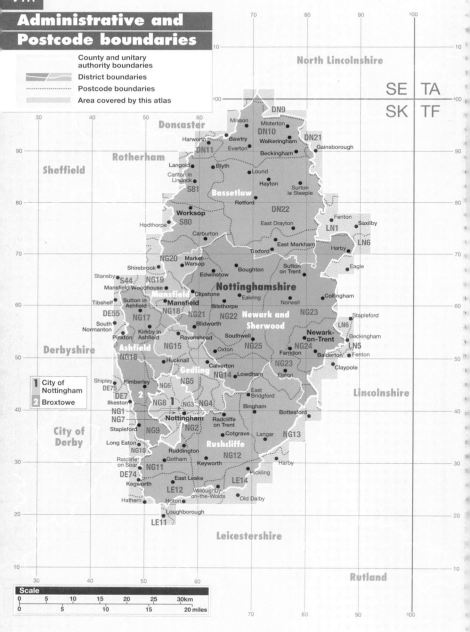

Administrative and Postcode boundaries

County and unitary authority boundaries
District boundaries
Postcode boundaries
Area covered by this atlas

SE | TA
SK | TF

North Lincolnshire

Doncaster

Rotherham

Sheffield

Misson
Misterton
DN9
DN10
Walkeringham
DN21
Harworth
Bawtry
Beckingham
Gainsborough
Everton
DN11
Langold
Blyth
Lound
Carlton in
Lindrick
Hayton
Surton
le Steeple
S81
Bassetlaw
Retford
DN22
Worksop
S80
East Drayton
Fenton
Saxilby
Hodthorpe
Carburton
LN1
East Markham
Tuxford
Harby
LN6
Eagle
NG20
Market
Warsop
Eakring
Collingham
Shirebrook
Boughton
Sutton
on Trent
Stansby
Edwinstow
Clipstone
NG19
Mansfield Woodhouse
Mansfield
Nottinghamshire
S44
Tibshelf
Mansfield
Eakring
Norwell
NG23
Stapleford
DE55
Sutton in
Ashfield
NG18
Bilsthorpe
Newark and
Sherwood
South
Normanton
NG17
NG21
Blidworth
NG22
LN6
Pinxton
Kirkby in
Ashfield
Southwell
Newark-
on-Trent
Beckingham
Derbyshire
Ravenshead
NG15
Oxton
NG25
Farndon
LN5
Balderton
Fenton
Ashfield
Hucknall
Calverton
NG14
Lowdham
Elston
NG23
Claypole
NG16
Gedling
NG5
Shipley
Kimberley
NG6
East
Bridgford
Lincolnshire
City of
Nottingham
DE7
Ilkeston
2
NG8
1
NG3
NG4
Bingham
Bottesford
Broxtowe
NG1
Nottingham
Radcliffe
on Trent
NG7
NG2
Cotgrave
Langar
NG13
Stapleford
NG9
City of
Derby
Long Eaton
Rushcliffe
NG12
NG10
Ruddington
Keyworth
Harby
Ratcliffe
on Soar
Gotham
Hickling
NG11
DE74
East Leake
LE14
Kegworth
LE12
Willoughby-
on-the-Wolds
Old Dalby
Hathern
Hoton
Loughborough
LE11
Leicestershire
Rutland

1 City of
Nottingham
2 Broxtowe

Scale
0   5   10   15   20   25   30km
0   5   10   15   20 miles

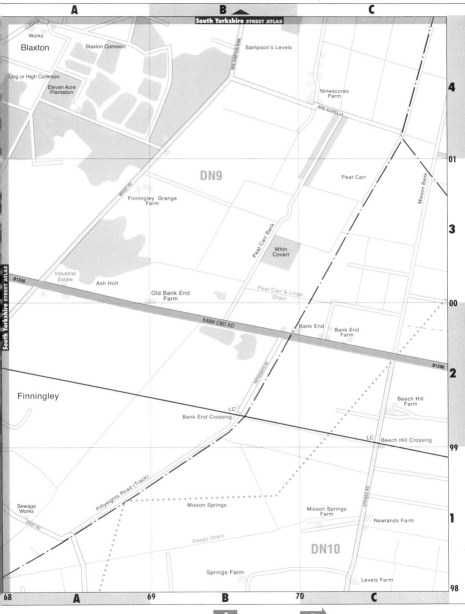

South Yorkshire STREET ATLAS

A   B   C

Works
Blaxton   Blaxton Common   Sampson's Levels

Ling or High Common
                                                        Ninescores
    Eleven Acre   Farm
    Plantation
                                                                        4
                                    NINE SCORES LA

                                                                        01

DN9   Peat Carr

                                                                Misson Bank
        Finninghey Grange
                Farm
                                                                        3
                        Peat Carr Bank

                            Whin
                            Covert

    Industrial
    Estate   Peat Carr & Lings
B1396   Ash Holt   Drain   00
            Old Bank End
                Farm
                        BANK END RD   Bank End
                                                    Bank End
                                                    Farm   B1396
                                                                        2
Finningley
                                                        Beech Hill
                                                            Farm
                        LC
        Bank End Crossing
                                            LC   Beech Hill Crossing
                                                                        99

    Sewage
    Works   Misson Springs
    CROFT RD   Misson Springs
        Fiftyeights Road (Track)   Farm   Newlands Farm
                                                                        1
                Deeps Drain
                                        DN10
        Springs Farm
                                        Levels Farm
                                                                        98

68   69   B   70   C
        A   C

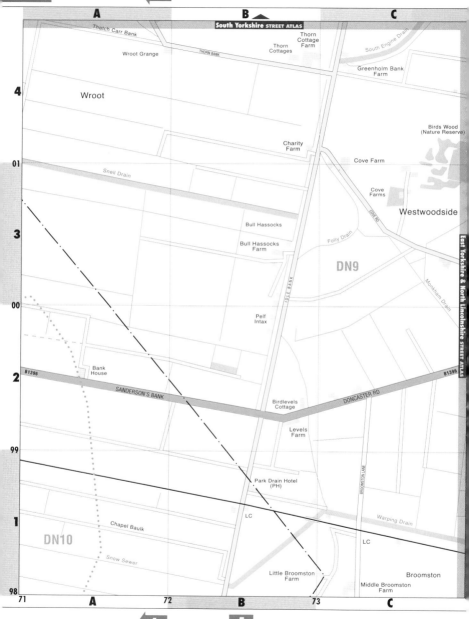

South Yorkshire STREET ATLAS

East Yorkshire & North Lincolnshire STREET ATLAS

A **B** **C**

4

Thatch Carr Bank

Wroot Grange

Thorn Cottages

Thorn Cottage Farm

Greenholm Bank Farm

South Engine Drain

THORN BANK

Wroot

Birds Wood (Nature Reserve)

01

Charity Farm

Cove Farm

Sneil Drain

Cove Farms

Westwoodside

3

Bull Hassocks

Bull Hassocks Farm

Folly Drain

DN9

Monkham Drain

IDLE BANK

COVE RD

00

Pelf Intax

2

B1396

Bank House

SANDERSON'S BANK

Birdlevels Cottage

DONCASTER RD

B1396

BROOMSTON LANE

Levels Farm

99

Park Drain Hotel (PH)

Warping Drain

LC

1

Chapel Baulk

DN10

Snow Sewer

LC

Little Broomston Farm

Broomston

Middle Broomston Farm

98

A **B** **C**

71 72 73

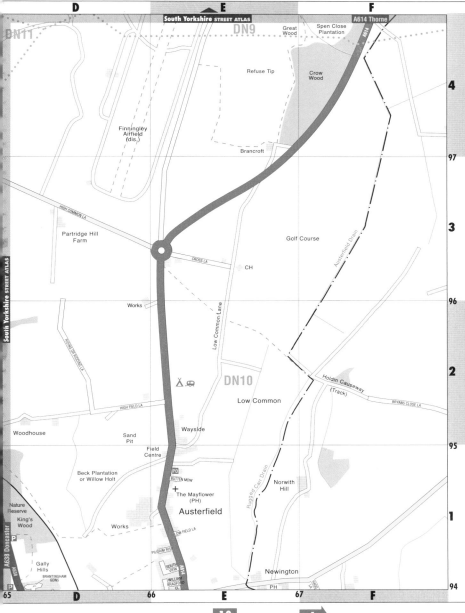

4

DN11

DN9

A614 Thorne

F

D

E

Great
Wood

Spen Close
Plantation

A614

Refuse Tip

Crow
Wood

4

Finningley
Airfield
(dis.)

Brancroft

97

HIGH COMMON LA

Partridge Hill
Farm

Golf Course

Austerfield Drain

3

CROSS LA

CH

Works

Low Common Lane

96

BRIDGEG ROAD

Holdin Causeway

2

HIGH FIELD LA

DN10

Low Common

(Track)

BRYANS CLOSE LA

Woodhouse

Sand
Pit

Wayside

95

Field
Centre

Beck Plantation
or Willow Holt

BUTTEN MOW

Norwith
Hill

Rogers Carr Drain

Nature
Reserve

The Mayflower
(PH)

Austerfield

1

King's
Wood

Works

LOW FIELD LA

A638 Doncaster

PILGRIM RISE

Gally
Hills

SOUTH
VIEW

Newington

BRANTINGHAM
GDNS

WILLIAM
BRADFORD
CL

PH

94

65

D

66

E

67

F

10

4

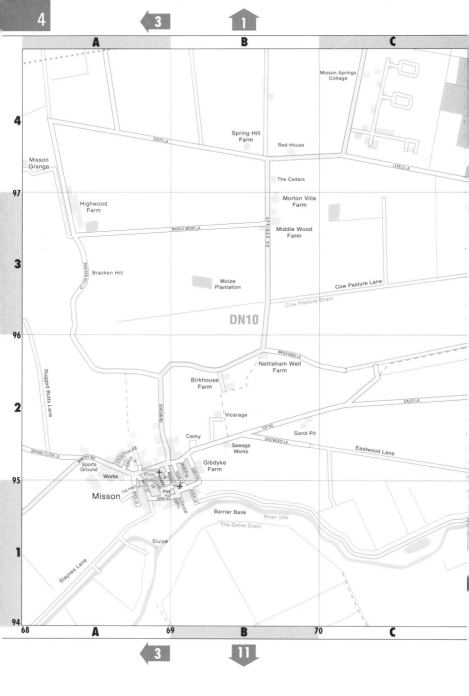

A   B   C

4

Misson Springs
Cottage

Spring Hill
Farm

DEEPS LA

Red House

LEVELS LA

Misson
Grange

The Cedars

97

Highwood
Farm

Morton Villa
Farm

MIDDLE WOOD LA

SPRINGS RD

Middle Wood
Farm

3

BRACKEN HILL LA

Bracken Hill

Moize
Plantation

Cow Pasture Lane

Cow Pasture Drain

DN10

96

BRICKYARD LA

Nettleham Well
Farm

Rugged Butts Lane

Birkhouse
Farm

DALES LA

2

Vicarage

STATION RD

Cemy

TOP RD

Sand Pit

Sewage
Works

EASTWOOD LA

Eastwood Lane

BRYANS CLOSE LA

BAWTRY RD

Sports
Ground

CORONATION AVE

LAUREL CL

Gibdyke
Farm

Works

THE PINFOLD

Misson
Prim
Sch

MIDDLE ST

VICAR ST

MANOR CL

GIBDYKE

95

Misson

BACK LA

HIGH ST

PH

CHURCH ST

NEWLANDS

Barrier Bank

River Idle

The Delve Drain

Sluice

1

Slaynes Lane

94

68   A   69   B   70   C

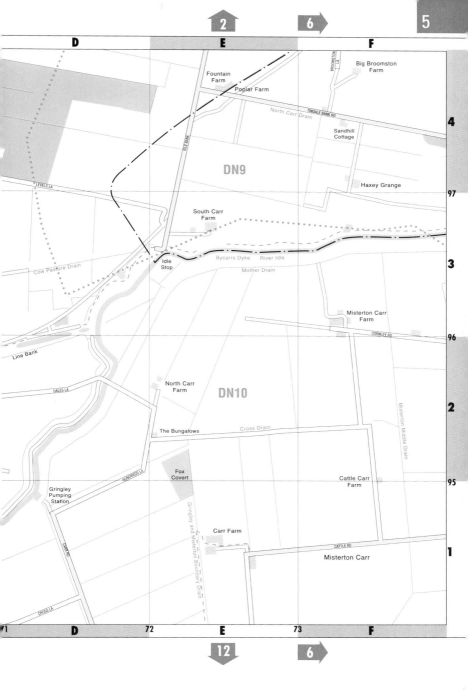

D
E
F

Fountain
Farm

Poplar Farm

Big Broomston
Farm

BROOMSTON LA

TINDALE BANK RD

North Carr Drain

4

Sandhill
Cottage

DN9

Haxey Grange

W LEVELS LA

97

South Carr
Farm

Cow Pasture Drain

Idle
Stop

Bycarrs Dyke   River Idle

Mother Drain

3

Misterton Carr
Farm

CORNLEY RD

96

Line Bank

North Carr
Farm

DALES LA

DN10

Misterton Middle Drain

The Bungalows

Cross Drain

2

Fox
Covert

Gringley
Pumping
Station

HUNDREDS LA

Cattle Carr
Farm

95

Gringley and Misterton Boundary Drain

CARR RD

Carr Farm

CATTLE RD

1

Misterton Carr

CROSS LA

1

D
72
E
73
F

A   **B**   **C**

Warping Drain

Langholme

Langholme Wood

Haxey

DN9

Langholme Farm

4

Langholme

STATION RD

A161

Cornley Farm

TINDALE BANK RD

Langholme Manor

Tindale Bank Drain

Cornley Lane

LC

97

Hunter's Hill

Richmond Farm

North Carr

HAXEY GATE RD

North Carr Farm

3

Mother Drain

River Idle

Haxey Gate Bridge

Haxey Gate Inn (PH)

NORTH CARR RD

Debdhill Farm

Mother Drain Bridge

96

Cornley Farm

Cornley Carr Farm

Debd Hill

HAXEY RD

Cornley

Debdhill Road

2

CORNLEY RD

DN10

New Cemy

White House Farm

Red House

LAUREL AVE

PAPA AVE

95

HOOK LA

BELTON RD

Cattle Farm

Sandholes Lane

CARR LA

CHURCH LA

B1403

CHURCH ST

PO

HIGH ST

A161

WILLOW AVE

OLD LODGE LA

MKT

CHAPEL CL

STATION RD

1

CATTLE RD

MINSTER RD

CHAPEL LA

HILLSIDE AVE

Misterton

Liby

Cooper's Bridge

GRINGLEY RD

Wharf Bridge

Green's Yard

Trent Valley Way

Chesterfield Canal

GROVE WOOD TERR

GROVE LA

DRAY BRIDGE LA

B1403

GRAVELHOLES LA

94

74   **A**   **75**   **B**   **76**   **C**

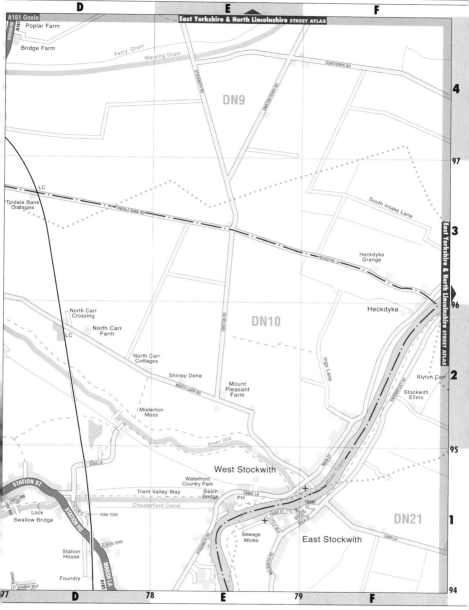

A161 Goole
Poplar Farm

Bridge Farm

Ferry Drain

Warping Drain

GUNTHORPE RD

DN9

STOCKWITH RD

OWSTON FERRY RD

4

97

LC

Tindale Bank
Cottages

TINDALE BANK RD

South Intake Lane

3

HECKDYKE LA

Heckdyke
Grange

96

North Carr
Crossing

North Carr
Farm

LC

DN10

Heckdyke

North Carr
Cottages

Shirley Dene

NORTH CARR RD

OWSTON LA

Mount
Pleasant
Farm

Ings Lane

Blyton Carr

Stockwith
Ellers

RIVERSIDE RD

2

Misterton
Moss

River Idle

95

STATION ST

W SWALLOW
CT

Lock
Swallow Bridge

STATION RD

ANDERSON

SOSS LA

YORK TERR

West Stockwith

Waterfront
Country Park

Trent Valley Way

Chesterfield Canal

Basin
Bridge

PH

CANAL LA

FRONT ST

FRONT
ST

River Trent

MAIN ST

East Yorkshire & North Lincolnshire STREET ATLAS

DN21

1

ALBION TERR

Station
House

Foundry

MARSH LA

A161

GRANGE WLK

STOCKWITH RD

LITTLE LA

Sewage
Works

HIGH KEITH RD

JACK ST

East Stockwith

CARR LA

94

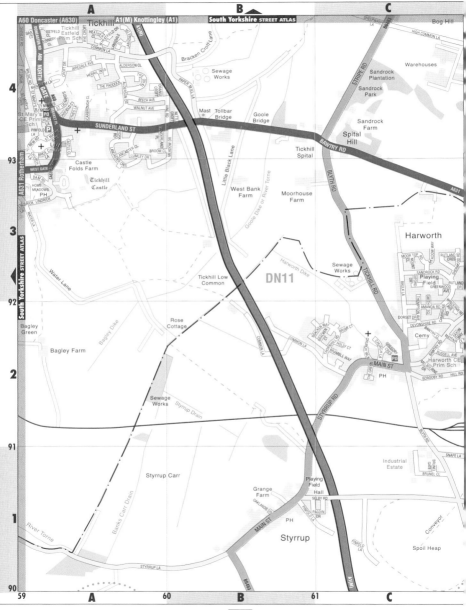

A60 Doncaster (A630) Tickhill A1(M) Knottingley (A1)

Bog Hill

High Common La

Warehouses

Bracken Croft Lane

Sewage Works

Sandrock Plantation

Sandrock Park

Mast Tollbar Bridge

Goole Bridge

Sandrock Farm

Spital Hill

4

SUNDERLAND ST

BAWTRY RD

Tickhill Spital

Castle Folds Farm

Tickhill Castle

West Bank Farm

Moorhouse Farm

93

A631 Rotherham

Little Black Lane

Goole Dike or River Torne

BLYTH RD

Harworth

3

South Yorkshire STREET ATLAS

Water Lane

Bagley Dike

Tickhill Low Common

Harworth Dike

Sewage Works

DN11

TICKHILL RD

Playing Field

Greenwood

Cemy

92

Bagley Green

Bagley Farm

Rose Cottage

COMMON LA

COMMON LA

BRAMBLE WAY

Harworth CE Prim Sch

Main St

PH

2

Sewage Works

Styrrup Drain

STYRRUP RD

Industrial Estate

91

Styrrup Carr

Banks Carr Drain

Grange Farm

Playing Field Hall

SELBY RD

Conveyor

1

River Torne

MAIN ST

PH

Styrrup

Spoil Heap

STYRRUP LA

90

59 **A** **60** **B** **61** **C**

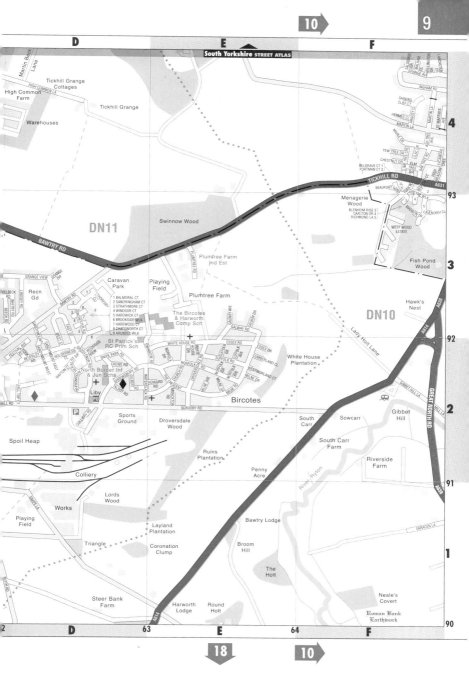

South Yorkshire STREET ATLAS

D **E** **F**

Martin Beck Lane
Tickhill Grange Cottages
High Common Farm
High Common La
Tickhill Grange
Warehouses

South Cliff Rd
Northgate
Lindrick Dr
Grange Rd
Ingham Rd
Shining Cliff Ct
Hermes Ct
Martin La
Arundel St
St Martin's Ave
Maple Gr

4

Yew Tree Dr
Chestnut Dr
Elm
St Saviour's Cres
Sycamore

Belgrave Ct 1
Portman Ct 2

TICKHILL RD
A631

Beaufort Rd
Madison Ct
Cavendish Cl

93

Menagerie Wood
Blenheim Rise 3
Carlton Dr 4
Richmond La 5

West Wood Estate

Bawtry Rd
DN11
Swinnow Wood

Fish Pond Wood

3

Grange View
Grange Dr
Caravan Park
Playing Field
Plumtree Farm Ind Est

Plumtree Rd

Hawk's Nest

DN10

Welbeck
Recn Gd
Beech Rd

Bawtry Rd
Galway Ave
The Bircotes & Harworth Comp Sch
Galway Ave
Galway Rd

Lady Holt Lane

A638

92

St Patrick's RC Prim Sch
Beverley Cl
White House Rd
Essex Rd
Essex Dr
Cumberland Cl
White House Plantation

North Border Inf & Jun Schs
Howard Rd
Crewe Rd
Norfolk Rd
Norfolk Rd
Milne Ave
Milne Rd
Westmorland Ct
Milne Dr

Gibbet Hill La

GREAT NORTH RD
A638

2

Hill Top Ct
Liby
PO
Waterslack Rd
The Crescent
Scrooby Rd

Bircotes

Gibbet Hill

South Carr
Sowcarr

Sports Ground
Droversdale Wood
South Carr Farm
Riverside Farm

Spoil Heap
Ruins Plantation
Penny Acre
River Ryton
Saracen La

91

Colliery
Lords Wood
Works

Bawtry Lodge

Playing Field
Layland Plantation
Triangle
Coronation Clump
Broom Hill
The Holt

1

Neale's Covert

Steer Bank Farm
A614
Harworth Lodge
Round Holt
Roman Bank Earthwork

90

2 **D** 63 **E** 64 **F**

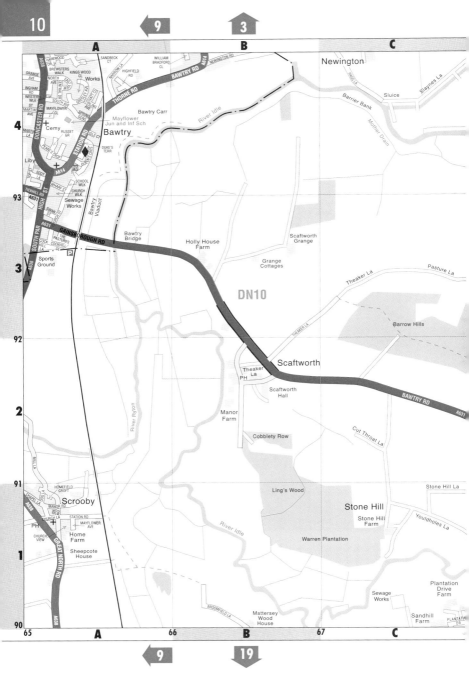

A   **B**   **C**

Newington

RIDGEWOOD DR
BRIDGEWOOD WALK
BREWSTERS WALK
KINGS WOOD
SANDBECK CT
WILLIAM BRADFORD CL
NEWINGTON RD

GRANGE AVE
INGHAM RD
NORTH ... AVE
WESTERN RD
ST MARTIN'S AVE
MAYFLOWER CL
MARTIN ...

Works

HIGHFIELD RD

BAWTRY RD   A614

THORNE RD   A638

Barrier Bank

HILL LA

Sluice

Staynes La

Mother Drain

Bawtry Carr

River Idle

4

Cemy

Mayflower Jun and Inf Sch
RUSSET GR
GOLF CL
SPRINGFIELD

Bawtry

STATION RD
A614
DUKE'S TERR

Lib...

SCOTT ...
WHARF LA

SCHOOL WLK
CHURCH WLK
CHURCH CL

93

A631

TICKHILL RD
HIGH ST
SWAN ...

Sewage Works

Bawtry Viaduct

GAINSBOROUGH RD

SOUTH PAR
A631
A638

THE PASTURES
COCKHILL
COCKHILL

Bawtry Bridge

Holly House Farm

Scaftworth Grange

3

Sports Ground

P

Grange Cottages

DN10

Theaker La

Pasture La

92

Barrow Hills

THEAKER LA

Scaftworth

Theaker La PH

BAWTRY RD   A631

2

River Ryton

Scaftworth Hall

Manor Farm

Cobblety Row

Cut Throat La

91

HOMEFIELD CROFT

MILL LA

Scrooby

MANOR LA
A638

STATION RD
MAYFLOWER AVE

Ling's Wood

Stone Hill La

Stone Hill

Stone Hill Farm

Youldholes La

1

CHURCH LA
PH
CHURCH VIEW

Home Farm

GREAT NORTH RD

Sheepcote House

River Idle

Warren Plantation

Sewage Works

Plantation Drive Farm

90

A638

BROOMFIELD LA

Mattersey Wood House

Sandhill Farm

PLANTATION DR

65   **A**   **66**   **B**   **67**   **C**

D

E

F

4

93

3

92

2

91

1

90

D

E

F

CROSS LA

Black Bank

Green La

Everton Carr Farm

River Idle

Mother Drain

Tch Hill La

Clay Bank La

Magnus Drain

Black Bank Farm

Pasture Farm

Claybank Farm

Everton Carr

DN10

Farm Cottages

Roe Lane Farm

Black Bank Drain

Pasture La

Carr Hill Farm

Roe La

Carr Hill

HARWELL SLUICE LA

Middle Cross La

BURTON HILL LA

Manor Farm

Mansfield Farm

Harwell

HARWELL LA

Tethering La

Oatville

road View Farm

BAWTRY RD

Gordon House

OLD POST OFFICE ST

FERRY LA

CHURCH ST

CHAPEL LA

BREWERY LA

WINDMILL EDGE

CROSS WAY

CARR VIEW

Sewage Works

Everton Cty Prim Sch

LONG MEADOWS

PINFOLD

CROFT FARM CLOSE

Everton

Stone Hill La

PH

Field House

Chesterfield Canal

Haven Croft

GAINSBOROUGH RD

A631

Cemetery

Drakeholes Farm

B6045

Broomhill La

MATTHERSEY RD

Mill La

Pusto Hill La

Rock La

PH

Drakeholes

Youdholes La

Windmill (disused)

Mill Farm

EEL POOL RD

River Idle

LANTATION DR

Sewage Works

REWALL DR

WAVELL CRES

Sewage Works

Pusto Hill Farm

B6045

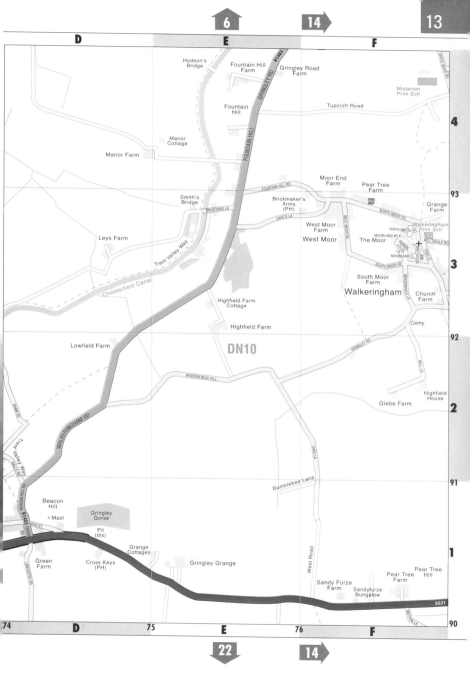

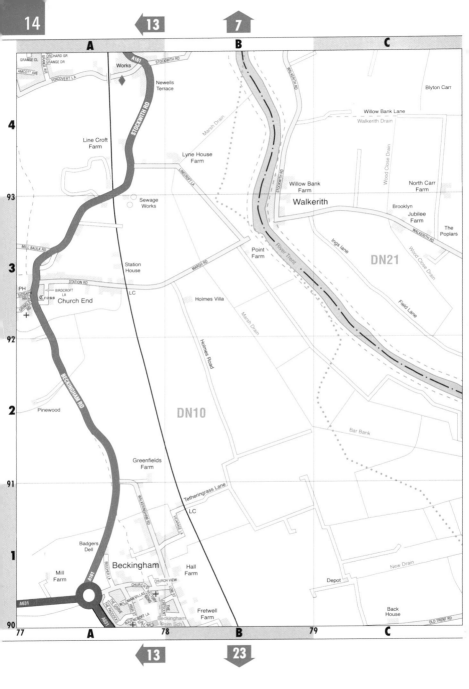

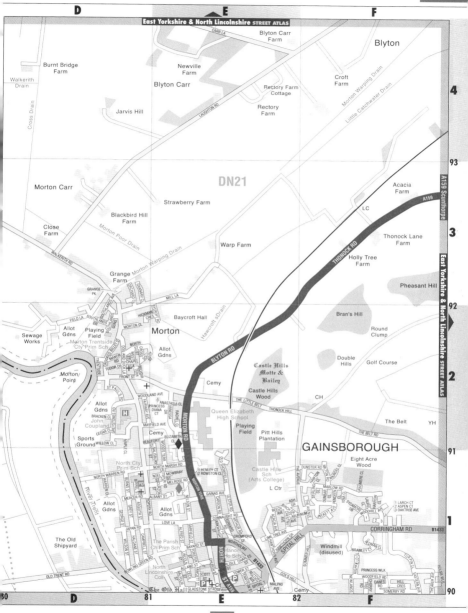

East Yorkshire & North Lincolnshire STREET ATLAS

CARR LA

Blyton Carr Farm

Blyton

Burnt Bridge Farm

Newville Farm

Croft Farm

Walkerith Drain

Blyton Carr

LAUGHTON RD

Rectory Farm Cottage

Rectory Farm

Morton Warping Drain

Little Catchwater Drain

4

Jarvis Hill

Cross Drain

93

A159 Scunthorpe

DN21

Acacia Farm

A159

Morton Carr

Strawberry Farm

LC

3

Blackbird Hill Farm

Thonock Lane Farm

Close Farm

Morton Poor Drain

THONOCK RD

Holly Tree Farm

WALKERITH RD

Warp Farm

Morton Warping Drain

Pheasant Hill

Grange Farm

MILL LA

92

GRANGE PK

FIELD LA

Baycroft Hall

Bran's Hill

Round Clump

Golf Course

Allot Gdns

Playing Field

Morton Trentside Cty Prim Sch

Morton

Hawcroft sDrain

Sewage Works

Allot Gdns

Double Hills

2

Morton Point

CEDAR CLOSE

BLYTON RD

Castle Hills Motte & Bailey

CH

The Belt

YH

Allot Gdns

WOODLAND AVE

ANASTASIA CL

Cemy

Castle Hills Wood

THE LITTLE BELT

THONOCK HILL

Double Hills

91

John Coupland

MAYFIELD AVE

Queen Elizabeth High School

Pitt Hills Plantation

THE BELT RD

Sports Ground

WILLOW CL

Cemy

ELIZABETH

Playing Field

GAINSBOROUGH

Eight Acre Wood

MORTON RD

North Cty Prim Sch

NORTH MARSH RD

NOEL ST

ROWSTON CL

DUNSTER RD

LARCH CT

NORTH WARREN RD

MELROSE RD

GAINAS AVE

Castle Hills Sch (Arts College)

OAKTREE AVE

River Trent

MERCER RD

ALBANY ST

L Ctr

Allot Gdns

Allot Gdns

LOVE LA

CORRINGHAM RD

B1433

The Old Shipyard

The Parish Ch Prim Sch

BAYARD ST

CROMFORD

Windmill (disused)

PRINCESS WLK

North Lincolnshire Coll

SCOTT

WOODFIELD RD

DANES

HILL CRES

OLD TRENT RD

The Old Hall

GLADSTONE ST

STONEWALL

MALPAS AVE

COX'S HILL

Cemy

SPITAL HILL

SOMERBY RD

90

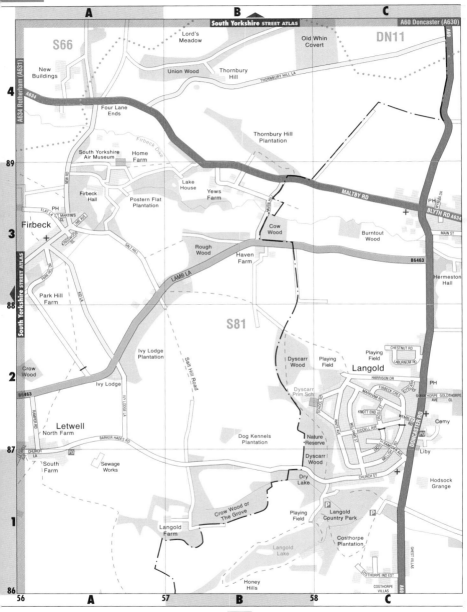

A   B   C

A60 Doncaster (A630)

S66

DN11

Lord's
Meadow

Old Whin
Covert

New
Buildings

Union Wood

Thornbury
Hill

THORNBURY HILL LA

A634 Rotherham (A631)

A634

4

Four Lane
Ends

Firbeck Dike

Thornbury Hill
Plantation

89

South Yorkshire
Air Museum

Home
Farm

MALTBY RD

PH

BLYTH RD A634

Firbeck
Hall

Lake
House

Yews
Farm

Postern Flat
Plantation

NEW RD

Main St

PH
St Martin's

Firbeck

Cow
Wood

Burntout
Wood

FLAT LA
OAK AVE

3

B6463

Hermeston
Hall

KNOLLWOOD RD

SALT HILL

Rough
Wood

Haven
Farm

LAMB LA

PARK HILL RD

Park Hill
Farm

88

S81

Ivy Lodge
Plantation

Salt Hill Road

Dyscarr
Wood

Playing
Field

Playing
Field

CHESTNUT RD

LABURNUM RD

Langold

PH

2

Crow
Wood

B6463

Ivy Lodge

IVY LODGE LA

HARRISON DR

FIRBECK CRES

MARKHAM RD

Dyscarr
Prim Sch

KNOTT END

DONCASTER RD

GOLDTHORPE
AVE

GOLDTHORPE
CL

Cemy

Letwell

North Farm

BARKER HADES RD

Dog Kennels
Plantation

Nature
Reserve

WHITE AVE

WILLIAMS RD

WEMBLEY RD

RIDDELL AVE

PO

Liby

87

CHURCH
LA

South
Farm

PO

Sewage
Works

Dyscarr
Wood

CHURCH ST

SCHOOL RD

MELTON AVE

Hodsock
Grange

1

Dry
Lake

Langold
Farm

Crow Wood or
The Grove

Playing
Field

Langold
Country Park

P

Costhorpe
Plantation

GHEST VILLAS

A60

Langold
Lake

Honey
Hills

COSTHORPE IND EST

COSTHORPE
VILLAS

86

56   A   57   B   58   C

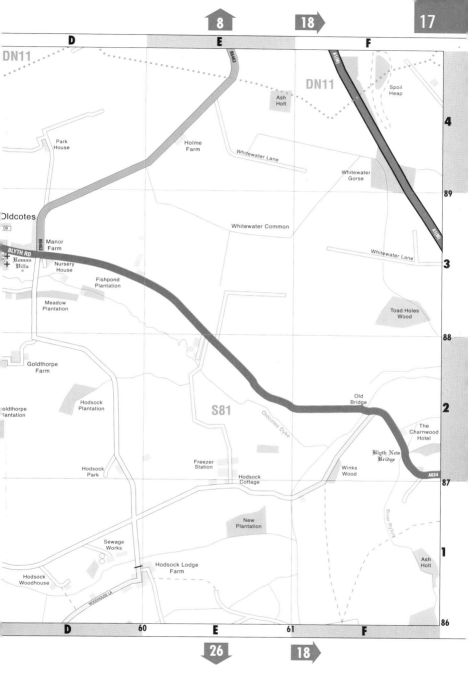

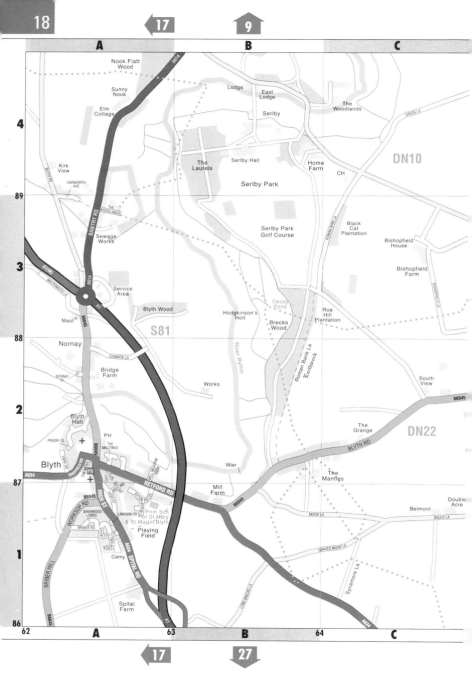

17
9

A B C

Nook Flatt Wood

Sunny Nook

Elm Cottage

Lodge

East Lodge

Serlby

The Woodlands

GREEN LA

4

Kirk View

HARWORTH AVE

BAWTRY RD

THE WOODLANDS

The Laurels

Serlby Hall

Serlby Park

Home Farm

CH

DN10

89

Sewage Works

Serlby Park Golf Course

Black Cat Plantation

Bishopfield House

ROMAN BANK LA

BISHOPFIELD LA

3

A1(M)

WHITEGATES LA

A614

A1

Service Area

Blyth Wood

S81

Hodgkinson's Holt

Decoy Pond

Brecks Wood

Roe Hill Plantation

Bishopfield Farm

Mast

B6045

88

Nornay

COMMON LA

River Ryton

Roman Bank La

Eastthorpe

South View

B6045

NORNAY

Bridge Farm

Works

2

Blyth Hall

PRIORY CL

PH

THE MALTINGS

The Grange

BLYTH RD

DN22

Blyth

A634

B6045

PO

RETFORD RD

MEADOW VIEW

Wier

Mill Farm

B6045

The Mantles

87

WORKSOP RD

HIGH ST

BRISTOLS RD

LAWSON SQ

Prim Sch St Mary & St Martin,Blyth

MOOR LA

Belmont

Double Acre

BAULK LA

SHERWOOD CRES

BRIBER RD

S PIT

Playing Field

A634

SPITAL RD

Cemy

GRAVES MOOR LA

1

BRIBER HILL

B6045

Spital Farm

A1

LONG RIGGS LA

SYCAMORE LA

A634

86

62 A 63 B 64 C

D   E   F

WINSTON GREEN
CUNNINGHAM CL
KEYES CL
KEYES RISE
KEYES CT

DN10

BROOMFIELD LA

GREEN LA

Mattersey Wood

Main Drain

Mattersey Grange

BECK LA

4

Hollins Holt

Lodge Farm

Scrooby Top House

Lodge Court

89

LC

B6045

RANSKILL RD

FIRST BECK LA

MATTERSEY RD

3

ARLNEALL DR

OAKS CL

STONEHILL CL
SOUTH ALL

Ranskill Prim Sch
SPINNEYMEAD

Bridge House

CHERRY TREE WALK

BISHOPFIELD LA

WHITTON CL

PH

RAVENSHILL CL
SAXON AVE

88

PO

+

COMMON LA

Sewage Works

High House Farm

PH

STATION RD

LC
Works

DN22

Antcliff Plantation

2

BLYTH RD   BACK LA

PH

Ranskill

Headlands La

+

Works

Cemy

LINDLEYWOOD
AVE
HUNTSMAN RD

87

The Poplars

PH
Works

HOLDS LA

BLACKSMITH LA

BAULK LA

LOW ST

Moat Farm

Nature Reserve

Works

Works

Torworth

Torworth Crossing

LC

DANESHILL RD

Works

P

Daneshill Piggery

Nature Reserve

1

GREAT NORTH ROAD

A638

A638

Torworth Grange

Daneshill Lakes

Works

86

D   66   E   67   F

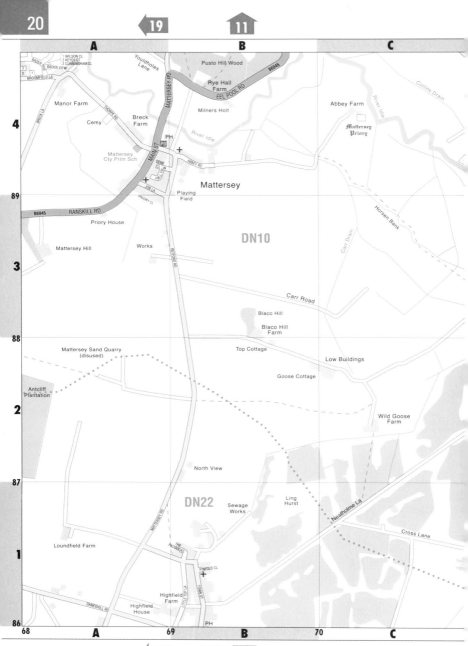

A   **B**   **C**

1 WILSON CL
2 KEYES CT
3 CUNNINGHAM CL

BADER CL
BADER VIEW
BROOMFIELD LA

Youldholes
Lane

Pusto Hill Wood

B6045

Rye Hall
Farm

EEL POOL RD

Manor Farm

BRECK LA

THORPE RD

Cemy

Breck
Farm

Milners Holt

River Idle

Abbey Farm

River Idle

Collins Drain

Mattersey
Priory

4

MAIN ST

PH
RD

MATTERSEY RD

Mattersey
Cty Prim Sch

DENE
CL

HS

ABBEY RD

Mattersey

Horsen Bank

89

B6045

RANSKILL RD

JOB LA

PRIORY CL

RETFORD RD

Playing
Field

Priory House

DN10

Carr Drain

Mattersey Hill

Works

Carr Road

3

Blaco Hill

Blaco Hill
Farm

88

Mattersey Sand Quarry
(disused)

Top Cottage

Low Buildings

Goose Cottage

Antcliff
Plantation

Wild Goose
Farm

2

North View

87

MATTERSEY RD

DN22

Sewage
Works

Ling
Hurst

Nealholme La

Cross Lane

1

Loundfield Farm

THE PADDOCKS

PINFOLD CL

DANESHILL RD

Highfield
Farm

Highfield
House

TITHE LA

TOWN ST

PH

86

68   **A**   **69**   **B**   **70**   **C**

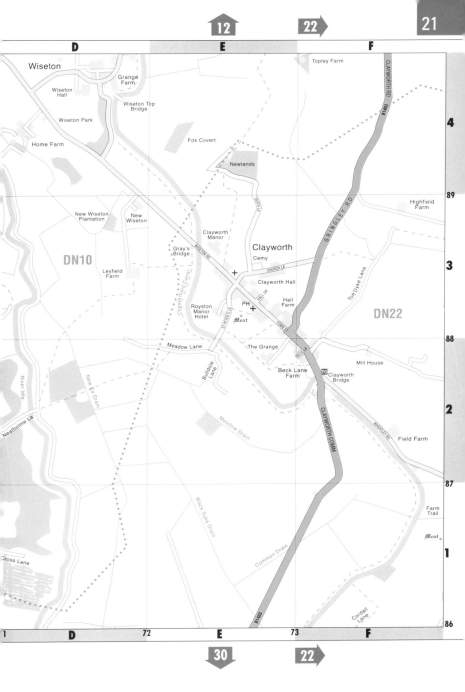

A   B   C

DN10

South Sandy-Furze Farm

WOOD LA

Ash Lea

4

Wood Farm

Beckingham Wood

Tong's Wood

89

Clayworth Woodhouse

Dogholes Wood

Lovers' Lane

3

Saundby Park Farm

Hangman Lane

Trent Valley Way

Wheatley Wood

88

Freeman's Gorse

Wheatley Wood Farm

Walk Lane

2

Wheatley Grange

DN22

87

WHEATLEY RD

Northfield Leys Road

Trough Baulk Lane

A620

1

North Point

Eastfield

GAINSBOROUGH RD

Hayton Castle Farm

Long Plantation

Allot Gdns

WOOD LA

HAUGHGATE HILL

Greenacres

A620

A620

86

74   A   75   B   76   C

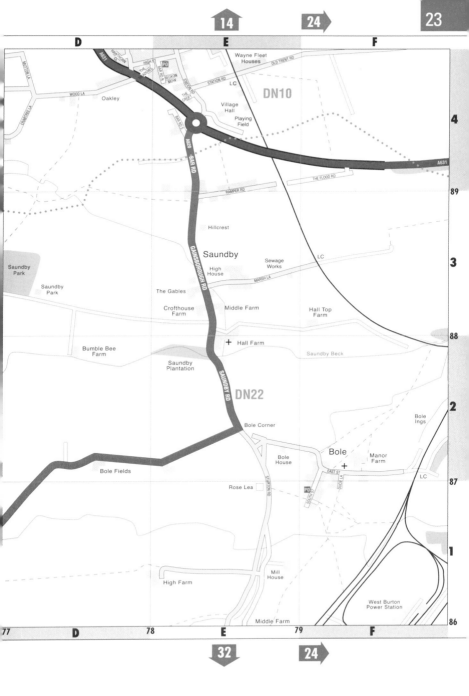

D E F

Wayne Fleet Houses
OLD TRENT RD

WOOD LA

Oakley

THE MOUNT
PO
STATION RD
LC

Village Hall

Playing Field

DN10

4

A631

THE FLOOD RD

89

RAMPER RD

BAR RD

Hillcrest

Saundby

GAINSBOROUGH RD

Sewage Works

LC

3

Saundby Park

High House

MARSH LA

The Gables

Crofthouse Farm

Middle Farm

Hall Top Farm

88

Bumble Bee Farm

+ Hall Farm

Saundby Beck

Saundby Plantation

SAUNDBY RD

DN22

2

Bole Ings

Bole Corner

Bole Fields

Bole House

Bole

Manor Farm

EAST ST

+

LC

STATION RD

Rose Lea

PO

87

Mill House

High Farm

1

West Burton Power Station

Middle Farm

86

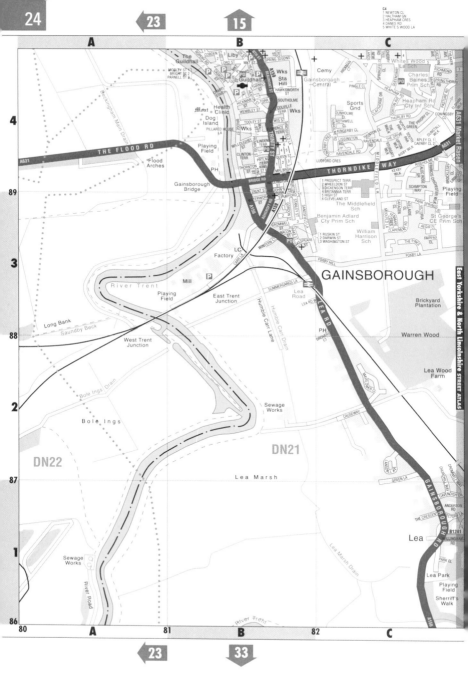

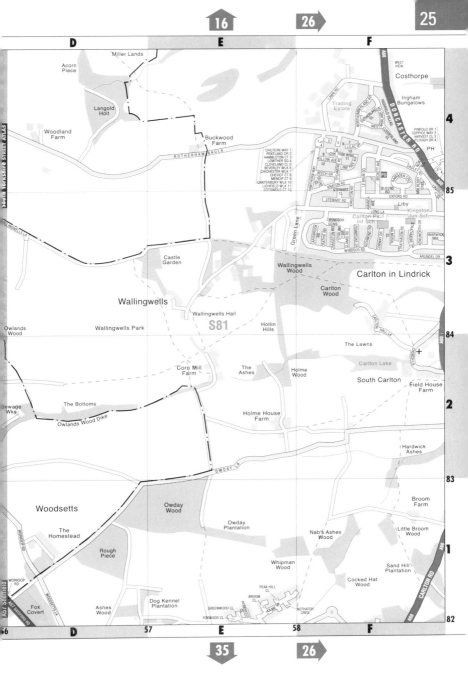

Miller Lands

Acorn Piece

Costhorpe

WEST VIEW

Langold Holt

Ingham Bungalows

Trading Estate

Woodland Farm

PINFOLD DR 1
COPPICE WAY 2
HARVEST CL 3
PLOUGH DR 4

Buckwood Farm

ROTHERHAM BAULK

CHILTERN WAY 1
PENTLAND DR 2
HAMBLETON CT 3
LOWTHER SQ 4
CLEVELAND CL 5
BEVERLEY WLK 6
CHICHESTER WK 7
CHEVIOT CT 8
MENDIP CT 9
CANTERBURY WLK 10
LICHFIELD WLK 11
COTSWOLD CT 12

DONCASTER RD

PH

Liby

Kingston

Carlton Pk Inf Sch

Kingston Jun Sch

WARWICK AVE

Green Lane

Wallingwells Wood

Carlton Wood

Carlton in Lindrick

Castle Garden

Wallingwells

Wallingwells Hall

S81

Wallingwells Park

Hollin Hills

Owlands Wood

The Lawns

Carlton Lake

Carlton Hall La

Corn Mill Farm

The Ashes

Holme Wood

South Carlton

Field House Farm

The Bottoms

Owlands Wood Dike

Holme House Farm

Sewage Wks

Hardwick Ashes

OWDAY LN

Broom Farm

Woodsetts

Owday Wood

Owday Plantation

Nab's Ashes Wood

Little Broom Wood

The Homestead

Rough Piece

Whipman Wood

Cocked Hat Wood

Sand Hill Plantation

CARLTON RD

WORKSOP RD

Fox Covert

Ashes Wood

Dog Kennel Plantation

PEAK HILL CL

GREENWOOD CL

FOXWOOD CL

BROOM

NUTHATCH CRE

D   E   F

Woodleigh

Ash
Holt

Hodsock
ed Bridge

PLANTATION LA

Hodsock
Plantation

Forest Lodge

Damings
Wood

Chestnut
Plantation

S81

Steeple
Plantation

Ford

Pilth
Plantation

Hodsock Manor
Farm

Forest
Farm

Black
Clump

Dewhurst
Plantation

Law Hill
Wood

Willow
Garth

River Ryton

Lower
Flash

DN22

Broom Hill
Wood

Kennels
Wood

Bilby
Farm

Bilby

Firs Farm

Fox
Covert

Bilby Farm

Upper
Flash

S81

Church
Clump

Whin
Hill

Sewage
Works

The Barracks

Motel

SPITAL RD

LONG BRIDGE LA

A1

A634

Jubilee
Farm

A634

TINKER LA

Tinker Lane

BLYTH RD

GREEN MILE LA

A1

4

85

3

84

2

83

1

82

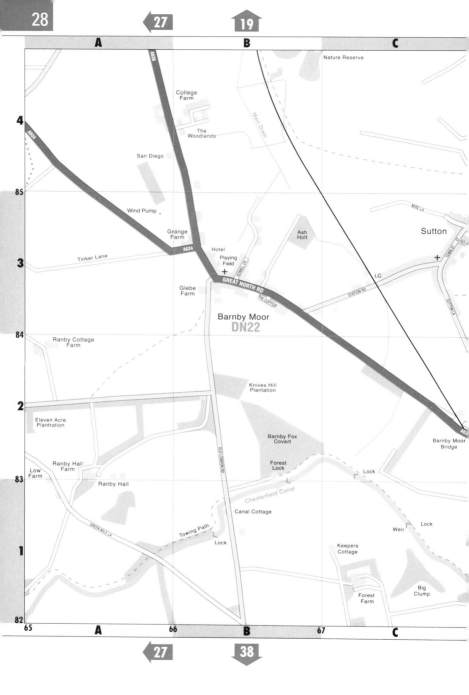

A

B

C

4

85

3

84

2

83

1

82

65

A

66

B

67

C

Nature Reserve

College Farm

The Woodlands

San Diego

Main Drain

Wind Pump

Grange Farm

A634

Tinker Lane

Hotel

Playing Field

Ash Holt

Sutton

MIRE LA

KENNEL DR

GREAT NORTH RD

Glebe Farm

The Cottage

STATION RD

LC

Barnby Moor
DN22

Knives Hill Plantation

Ranby Cottage Farm

Eleven Acre Plantration

Barnby Fox Covert

Barnby Moor Bridge

Forest Lock

Ranby Hall Farm

Low Farm

OLD LONDON RD

Lock

Lock

Ranby Hall

Chesterfield Canal

Weir

Lock

Canal Cottage

GREEN MILE LA

Towing Path

Lock

Keepers Cottage

Big Clump

Forest Farm

A638

A634

A1

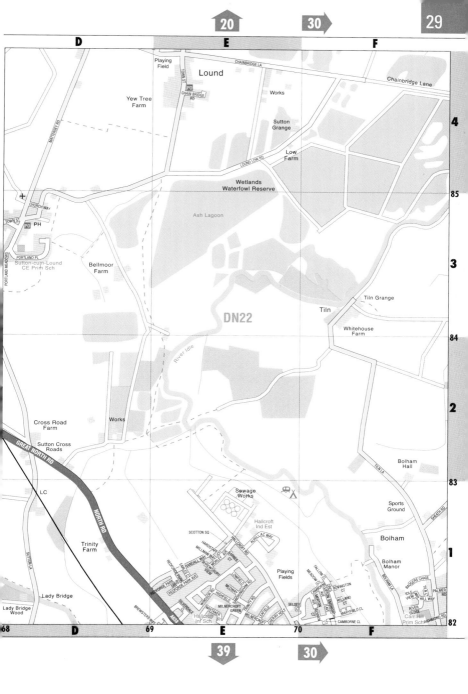

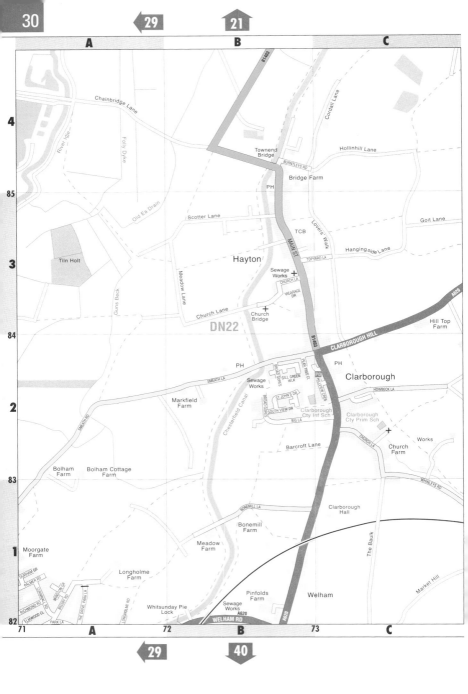

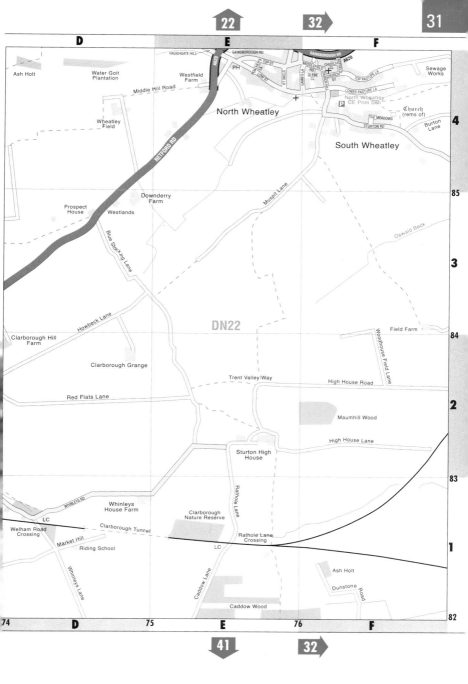

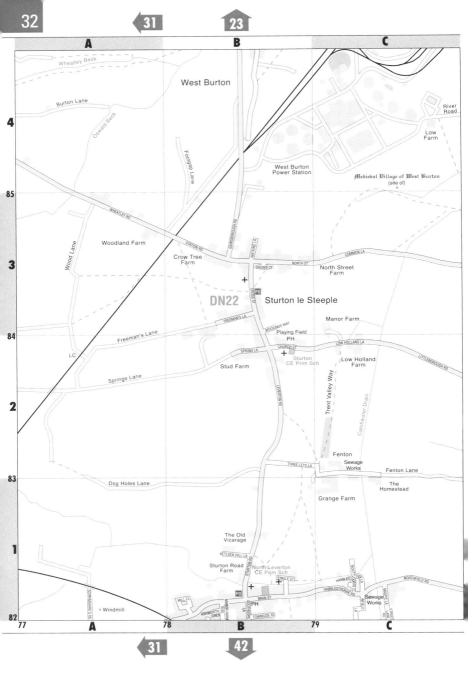

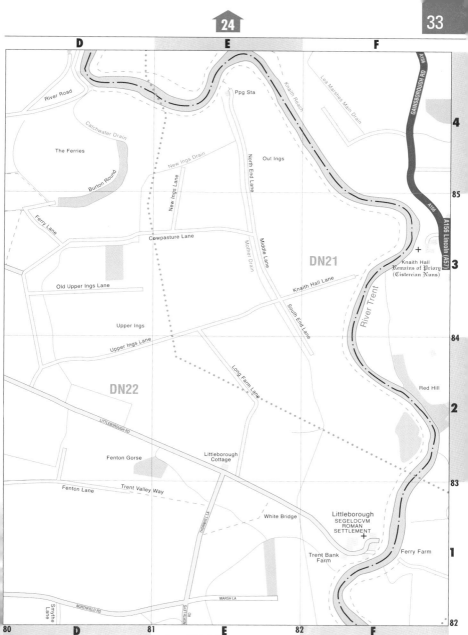

D E F

GAINSBOROUGH RD

River Road

Ppg Sta

Knaith Reach

Leaf Marshes Main Drain

A156

4

Catchwater Drain

The Ferries

New Ings Drain

Out Ings

North End Lane

A156

85

Burton Round

New Ings Lane

Ferry Lane

Cowpasture Lane

Mother Drain

Middle Lane

DN21

A156 Lincoln (A57)

Knaith Hall
Remains of Priory
(Cistercian Nuns)

3

Old Upper Ings Lane

Knaith Hall Lane

South End Lane

River Trent

Upper Ings

Upper Ings Lane

84

DN22

Long Farm Lane

Red Hill

2

LITTLEBOROUGH RD

Fenton Gorse

Littleborough
Cottage

83

Fenton Lane

Trent Valley Way

THORNHILL LA

White Bridge

Littleborough
SEGELOCVM
ROMAN
SETTLEMENT

Ferry Farm

1

Trent Bank
Farm

Smythe
Lane

NORTHFIELD RD

SALTHOUSE DR

MARSH LA

82

80 D 81 E 82 F

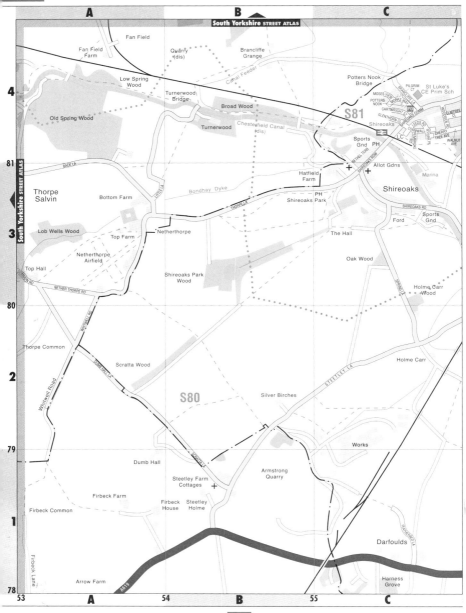

A   B   C

Fan Field

Fan Field Farm

Quarry (dis)

Brancliffe Grange

Canal Feeder

Potters Nook Bridge

PILGRIM CT

St Luke's CE Prim Sch

MOSES VIEW

MONKS ROW

Low Spring Wood

Turnerwood Bridge

POTTERS NOOK

CARTWRIGHT CL

ELMTREE CL

4

Broad Wood

GLENTHORN DR

WOODVIEW CL

Old Spring Wood

Turnerwood

Chesterfield Canal (dis)

S81

Shireoaks

CROMWELL RD

LEEDS RD

CHERRY TREE AVE

WALNUT AVE

Sports Gnd

PH

81

Hatfield Farm

Allot Gdns

Marina

BETHEL TERR

SHIREOAKS ROW

Thorpe Salvin

BACK LA

Bottom Farm

LITTLE LA

Bondhay Dyke

PH

Shireoaks Park

Shireoaks

SHIREOAKS RD

Ford

Sports Gnd

THORPE LA

Lob Wells Wood

Top Farm

Netherthorpe

The Hall

3

Netherthorpe Airfield

Oak Wood

Holme Carr Wood

Top Hall

COMMON RD

NETHER THORPE RD

Shireoaks Park Wood

SPRING

80

Thorpe Common

WHITWELL RD

Scratta Wood

DUMB HALL LA

Holme Carr

STEETLEY LA

2

Whitwell Road

S80

Silver Birches

Works

79

Dumb Hall

SCRATTA LA

Steetley Farm Cottages

Armstrong Quarry

Darfoulds

FRITHWOOD LA

Firbeck Farm

Firbeck House

Steetley Holme

1

Firbeck Common

Firbeck Lane

Arrow Farm

A619

Harness Grove

78

53   A   54   B   55   C

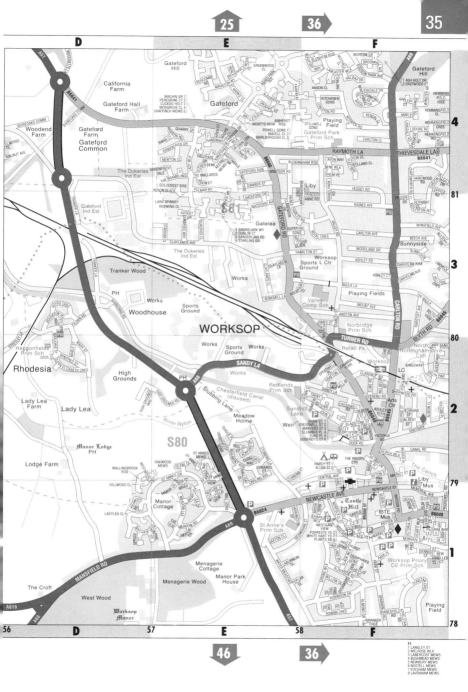

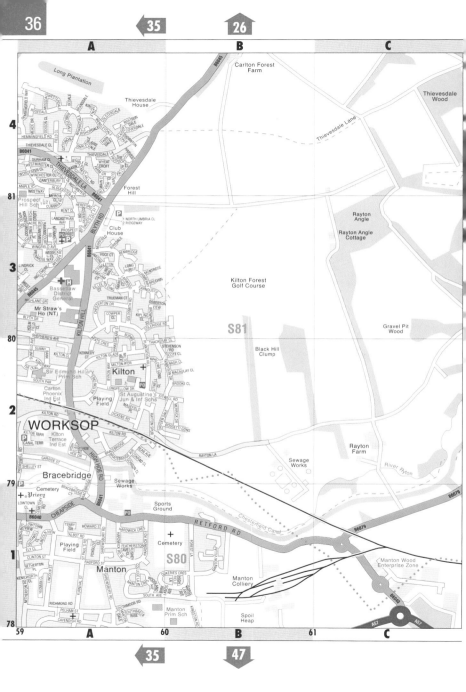

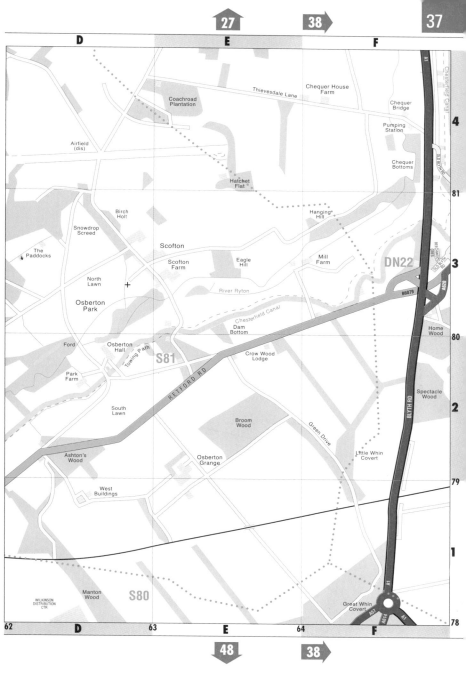

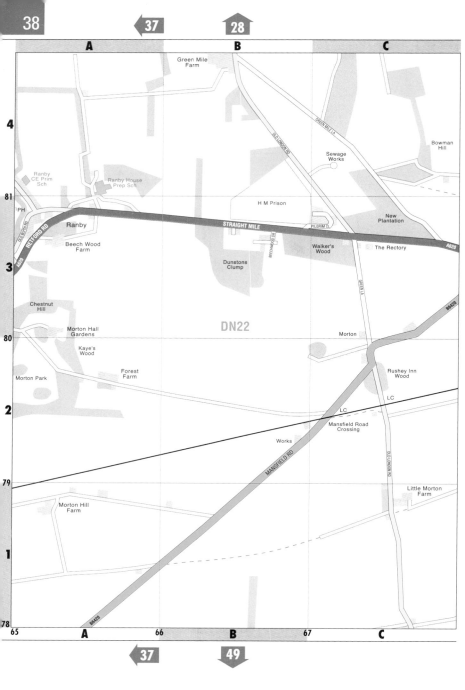

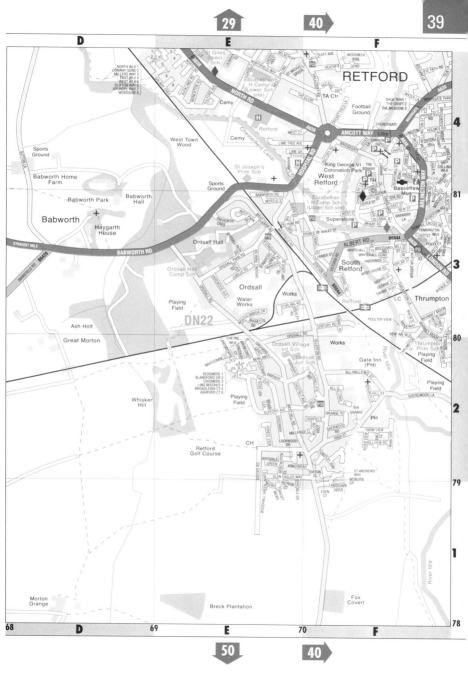

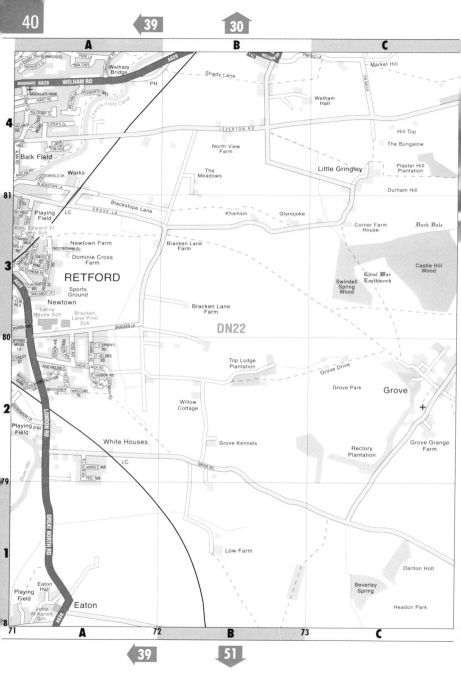

A   B   C

ELMWOOD CL
RIGBY RD
PARK LA
SAVIOUR'S CT   PARK CRFS   LONGMAN RD
WELHAM RD   A620   Welham
Bridge
MOORGATE A620   WELHAM RD   PH
HEXWORTH WAY   Shady Lane   WELHAM
MOORGATE PARK   HIRST RD   PINFOLD LA   Market Hill
HOLDENBY RD   Chesterfield Canal   THE BALK
HOLMES   CLATER'S CL   LEVERTON RD   Welham   Hill Top
4   SPITAL   FERN RISE   Hall   The Bungalow
HILL   PIN RISE   North View
ALMA   Balk Field   Farm   Little Gringley   Plaster Hill
Plantation
RAGLAN ST   CHESTERFIELD DR   Works   The
Meadows   Durham Hill
BLACKSTOPE LA
81   HATFIELD   LC   Blackstope Lane   Corner Farm   Dark Dale
Playing   GROVE LA   Khamsin   Glynojoke   House
Field
KING EDWARD VI   Newtown Farm   Bracken Lane   Castle Hill
Comp Sch   WESTBOURNE CL   Farm   Rival War   Wood
LYNINGTON   CROSS ST   Dominie Cross   Earthwork
HOLLY   RHINO ST   Farm   Swindell
3   CALEDONIAN RD   RETFORD   Spring
RD   STORCROFT RD   Sports   Wood
OAKLANDS LA   Ground   Bracken Lane
ELM   Newtown   Farm
WLK   Lorne   Bracken
House Sch   Lane Prim   DN22
80   WHINNY   Sch   BRACKEN LA
MOOR   RISE AV   ST STEPHEN'S   Top Lodge   Grove Drive
STANLEY   GROVE COACH RD   ST HELEN'S   Plantation   Grove Park   Grove
ST   FIVE FIELDS   RD   Willow   Grove Grange
THE CL   PADDOCK   HADDON RD   Cottage   Rectory   Farm
GROSVENOR   HARCOURT   Plantation
2   GROSVENOR LA   CE   PL   CAVENDISH RD   White Houses   Grove Kennels
Playing   PH   LONDON RD   LC
Field
River Idle   ARNOLD AVE   GROVE RD
79   PEEL AVE

1   GREAT NORTH RD   Low Farm   Darlton Holt
Playing   Eaton   Beverley
Field   Hall   Spring   Headon Park
8   Jamia   Eaton
Al-Karam   A638
Sch
71   A   72   B   73   C

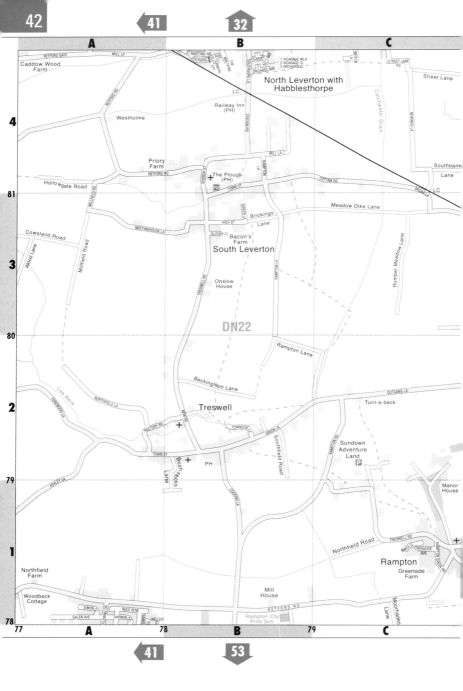

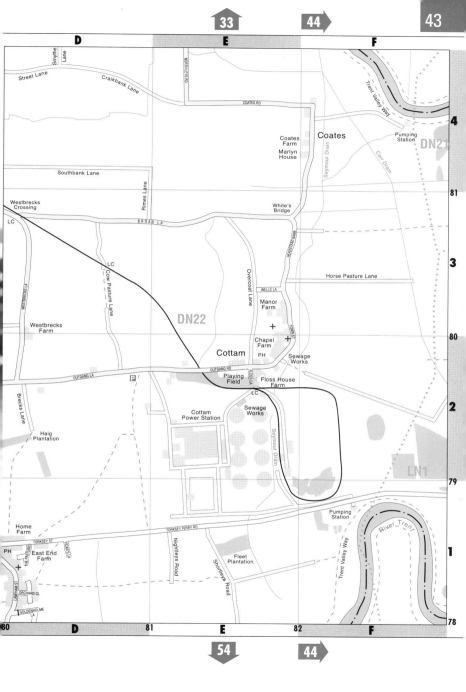

D
E
F

Smythe Lane

Street Lane

Craikbank Lane

NORTHLEYS RD

COATES RD

Trent Valley Way

4

Coates Farm

Coates

Pumping Station

DN21

Marlyn House

Southbank Lane

Rimes Lane

Seymour Drain

Carr Drain

81

Westbrecks Crossing

LC

BROAD LA

White's Bridge

HESSLETON BANK

LC

Cow Pasture Lane

Overcoat Lane

Horse Pasture Lane

3

WELLS LA

WESTBRECKS LA

Westbrecks Farm

DN22

Manor Farm

+

TOWN ST

80

Chapel Farm

+

Cottam

PH

Sewage Works

OUTGANG LA

Playing Field

Floss House Farm

Brecks Lane

P

FLOSS LA

LC

2

Haig Plantation

Cottam Power Station

Sewage Works

Seymour Drain

79

Home Farm

TORKSEY FERRY RD

Pumping Station

Trent Valley Way

River Trent

TORKSEY ST

THE PARK

PH

East End Farm

LANEHAM ST

+

Nightleys Road

Shortleys Road

Fleet Plantation

Trent Valley Way

1

ORCHARD CL

GOLDENHOLME LA

80

81

82

78

D

E

F

A | B | C

A156 Gainsborough | A1500 Gainsborough (A156)

Marton PH
Sewage Works
Cemy
Windmill
Trent Port RD
Trent Port
NTL
Ppg Sta

HIGH ST

A156

THE PADDOCKS
HILLSIDE
THE OLD COURTYARD
A1500
TRENT VIEW
Marton Cty Prim Sch
ADAM WAY
STAFFORD CL
WAPPING LA

STOW PARK RD
Marton Grange

A1500

LC

TILL BRIDGE LA
A1500 Lincoln (A15)

Poplar Farm

4

Sewage Works

DN21

81

Brampton Grange

Marton Moor Farm
LC

3

Bunker's Hill Warren

The Lodge

80

Trent Valley Way
River Trent

Treswell Marsh
Road

Torksey Terminal (dis)

Torksey Viaduct

Manor Farm

LN1

Brampton

West Lawn

CH
Castle Inn (PH)

Ash Holt

Lincoln Golf Course

STATION RD

2

The Grange Farm

Vicarage

79

Caravan Site

MAIN ST

PH
PO
Torksey

Torksey Common

Cemy

Sewage Works
SAND LA

Firs Cottage

1

Firs Farm

A156

Torksey Lock

Caravan Parks

Fossdyke Navigation

78
Ppg Sta

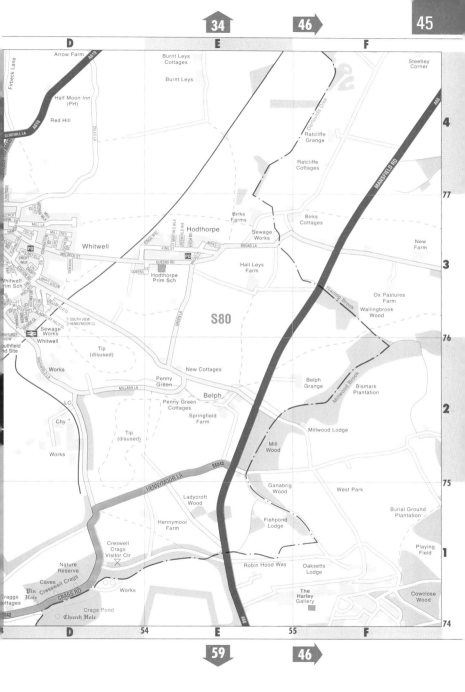

A   B   C

MANSFIELD RD

A60

Worksop
Manor

Manor Park

Hartland
Comp
Sch

SPARKEN

WATER MEADOWS

Portland
Comp
Sch

ASH L

DUNSTAN CRES

4

Hawk's
Nest

Manor Croft

Hawk's Nest
Screed

Pudding Hill
Wood

CASTLE FARM LA

Rock
Cottage

Castle
Farm

77

Oak Wood

Plain Piece

3

BROAD LA

76

Sloswicks
Springs

S80

Manor Hills

South African
Piece

2

Sloswicks
Farm

Hill
Wood

Lodge

Drinking Pit Lane

Robin Hood Way

Duchess' Plantation

Busaco

Wedding Drive

Lord
St Vince
Wood

75

Robin Hood Way

Porter Oaks

Welbeck
Woodhouse

White Stone Piece

St Cuthbert's
in the Woods

White Deer
Park

Lord
Harley's
Wood

Valley
Clump

Lady Harriet's
Plantation

1

Lawn
Wood

Shrubbery
Lake

Hagg Hill

Long Valley

Playing
Field

Welbeck Park

Long Drive
Wood

Wingfield
Wood

Welbeck
College

Welbeck
Abbey

74

56   A   57   B   58   C

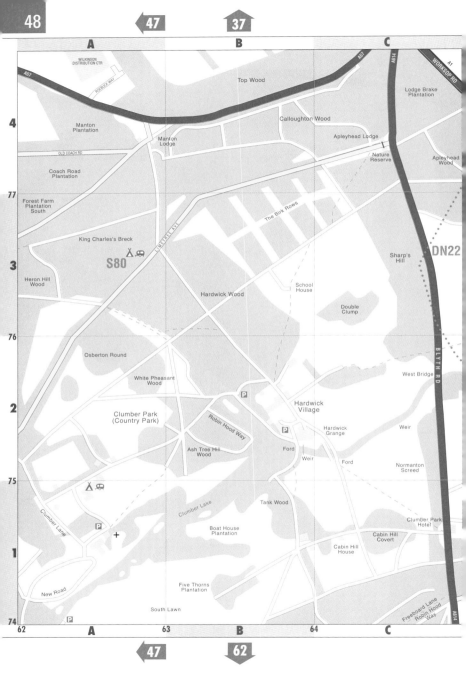

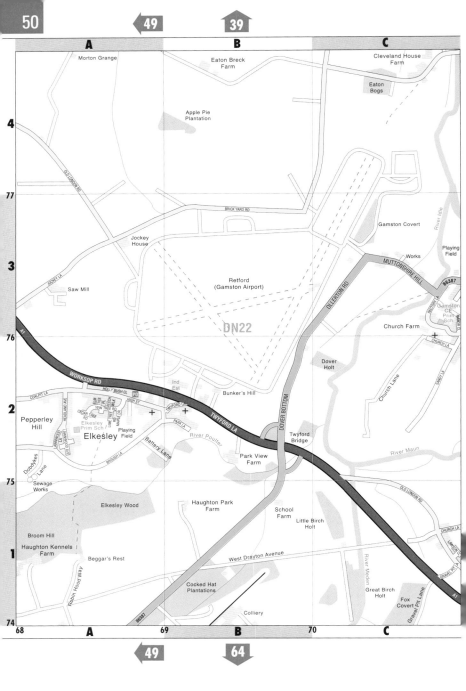

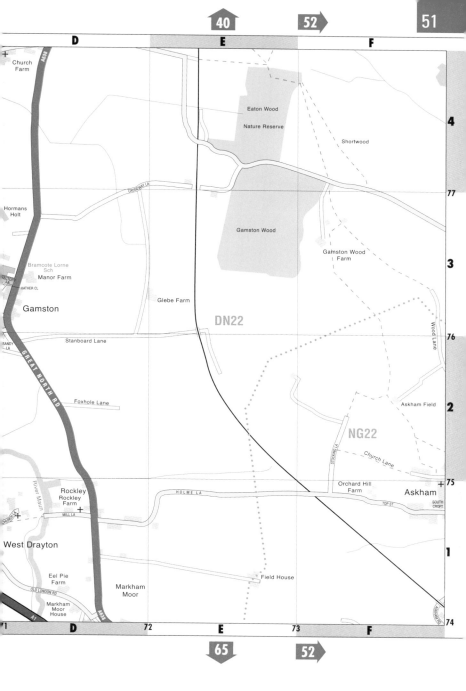

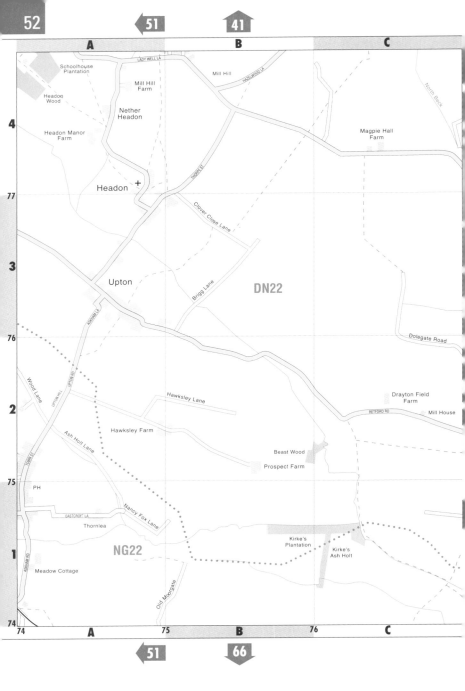

A   B   C

4

Schoolhouse
Plantation

LADY WELL LA

Mill Hill

HAZELWOOD LA

NORTH BECK

Mill Hill
Farm

Headoo
Wood

Nether
Headon

Magpie Hall
Farm

Headon Manor
Farm

THONEX ST

77

Headon +

Clover Close Lane

Upton

Brigg Lane

DN22

3

ASHOLME LA

76

Dolegate Road

Wood Lane

UPTON HILL

UPTON RD

Hawksley Lane

Drayton Field
Farm

RETFORD RD

Mill House

2

Hawksley Farm

Ash Holt Lane

Beast Wood

DON ST

Prospect Farm

75

PH

EASTCROFT LA

Nancy Fox Lane

Thornlea

Kirke's
Plantation

Kirke's
Ash Holt

1

NG22

ASHOLME RD

Meadow Cottage

Old Moorgate

74
74   A   75   B   76   C

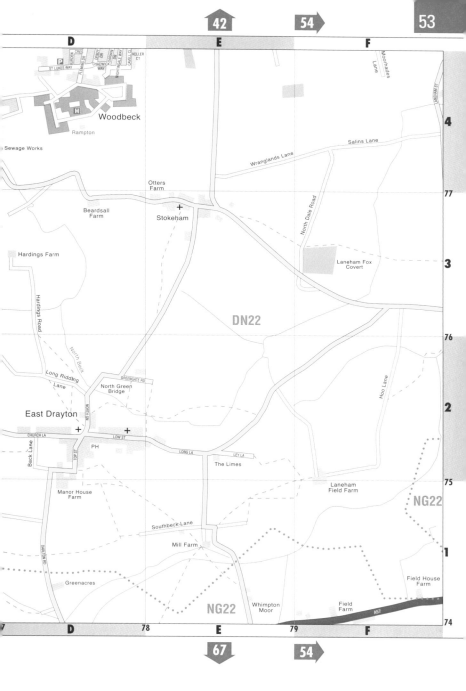

D
E
F

CRES
BIRCHEN
FLEMING DR
DUNCH DR
CHADWICK WAY
DARWIN DR
BRIGHT WAY
RACE WAY
CAVELL CL
KELLER CT
P
ST LUKES WAY

H
Woodbeck

Rampton

Sewage Works

Moorhades Lane

LANEHAM ST

4

Wranglands Lane
Salins Lane

Otters Farm

77

Beardsall Farm
+
Stokeham

North Dale Road

Laneham Fox Covert

3

Hardings Farm

DN22

76

North Beck

Hardings Road

Long Ridding
GREENGATE RD
Lane
North Green Bridge

Hoo Lane

2

East Drayton

+
+

CHURCH LA
NORTON RD
LOW ST
TOP ST
PH
LONG LA
LEY LA

The Limes

Laneham Field Farm

75

Back Lane

NG22

Manor House Farm

Southbeck Lane

Mill Farm

OAKS TON RD

Greenacres

Field House Farm

1

NG22
Whimpton Moor
Field Farm
A57

74

7
D
78
E
79
F

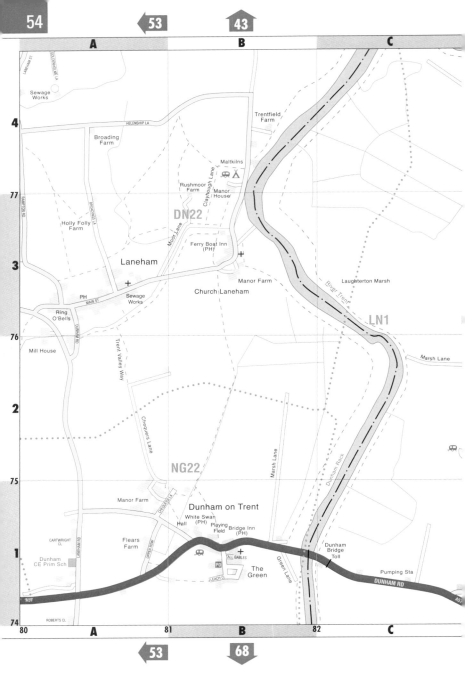

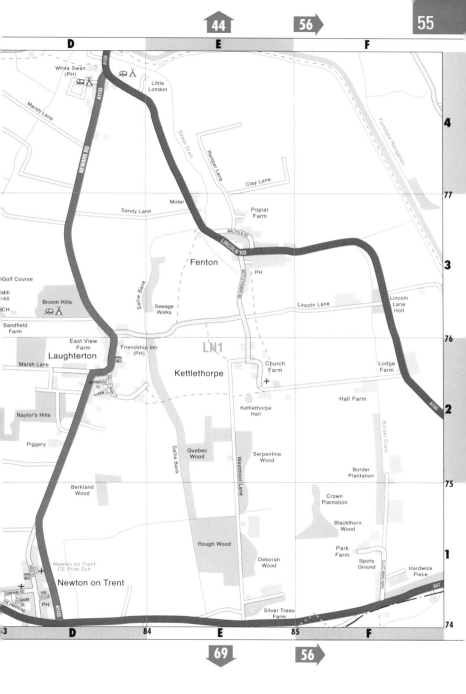

A   B   C

4

Highwood Farm

Saxilby Sykes

77

Highwood Farm

Sykes
Junction

Sykes Farm

3

Hardwick Farm

Works

Foss Dyke
Farm

Manor Farm

LN1

SYKES LA   CHURCH LA

76

Hardwick

LC

Hardwick Wood
Farm

ST ANDREWS DR

WESTERN AV

Highfield
Farm

TORKSEY ST

Orchard Farm

Earthwork

Saxilby

2

Earthwork

WOODHALL CRES

A156

Fossdyke Navigation

75

Green Lane

Sewage
Works

A57

WEST BANK

Drinsey Farm

Whitehouse
Farm

GAINSBOROUGH RD

1

A156

A57

Tom Otter's
Bridge

B1190

DRINSEY NOOK LA

Drinsey Nook

86   A   87   B   88   C

74

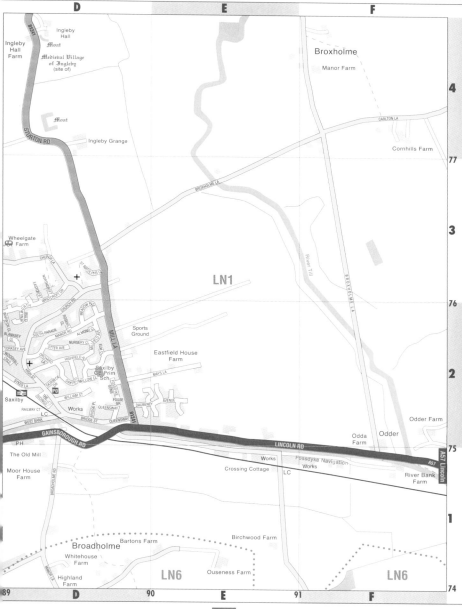

Broxholme

Manor Farm

CARLTON LA

Cornhills Farm

Ingleby Hall

Ingleby Hall Farm

𝔐𝔢𝔞𝔱

𝔐𝔢𝔡𝔦𝔢𝔳𝔦𝔞𝔩 𝔙𝔦𝔩𝔩𝔞𝔤𝔢 of 𝔍𝔫𝔤𝔩𝔢𝔟𝔶 (site of)

STURTON RD

𝔐𝔢𝔞𝔱

Ingleby Grange

BROXHOLME LA

BROXHOLME LA

River Till

LN1

Wheelgate Farm

CHURCH LA

ST BOTOLPHS CL

MEADOW VIEW

MILL LA

Sports Ground

Eastfield House Farm

NORTHOLT

EASTHOLM

WESTCLIFFE DR

CHURCH RD

ALMOND CL

NURSERY CL

MANOR RD

SOUTH PARADE

OTTER AVE

HIGHFIELD RD

ELDER

LILAC

MAY'S LA

Saxilby CE Prim Sch

BLANKNEY AV

TORKSEY AVE

WOODHALL CL

OXFORD

WILLOW CL

FOSSE GR

QUEENSWAY

DAUBENEY

AVENUE

Saxilby

PO

WILLIAM ST

SYKES LA

RAILWAY CT

LC

Works

BRIDGE ST

QUEENSWAY

WEST BANK

GAINSBOROUGH RD

B1241

Odder Farm

Odda Farm

Odder

LINCOLN RD

A57 Lincoln

PH

The Old Mill

Moor House Farm

BROADHOLME RD

Works

Crossing Cottage

Fossdyke Navigation

Works

LC

75

River Bank Farm

Broadholme

Bartons Farm

Whitehouse Farm

Highland Farm

MOOR CL

LN6

Birchwood Farm

Ouseness Farm

LN6

89   **D**   90   **E**   91   **F**   74

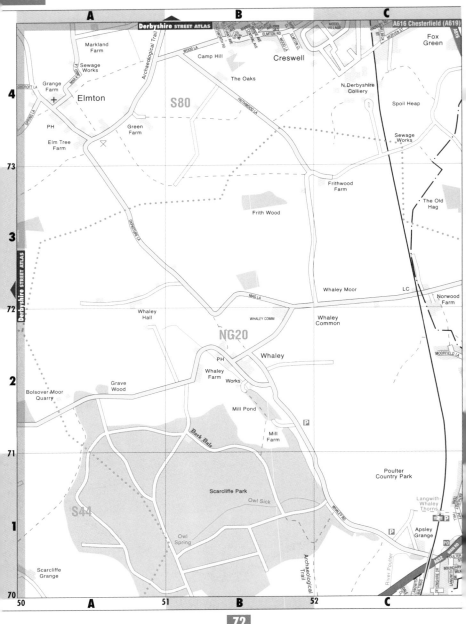

A **B** **C**

A616 Chesterfield (A619)

Markland
Farm

Camp Hill

WOOD LA

Creswell

Fox
Green

Sewage
Works

The Oaks

N.Derbyshire
Colliery

Grange
Farm

Elmton

S80

Spoil Heap

4

Green
Farm

PH

Sewage
Works

Elm Tree
Farm

73

Frithwood
Farm

The Old
Hag

Frith Wood

3

Whaley Moor

LC

Norwood
Farm

MAG LA

72

Whaley
Hall

WHALEY COMM

Whaley
Common

MOORFIELD LA

NG20

Whaley

PH

Whaley
Farm

Works

2

Bolsover Moor
Quarry

Grave
Wood

Mill Pond

Mill
Farm

71

Poulter
Country Park

Dark Dale

Scarcliffe Park

Owl Sick

S44

Langwith-
Whaley
Thorns

1

Owl
Spring

Apsley
Grange

Scarcliffe
Grange

Archaeological Trail

River Poulter

70

50 **A** **51** **B** **52** **C**

Derbyshire STREET ATLAS

WHALEY RD

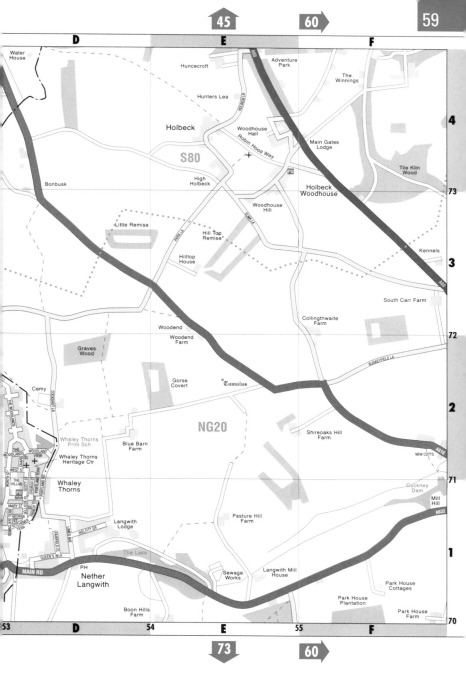

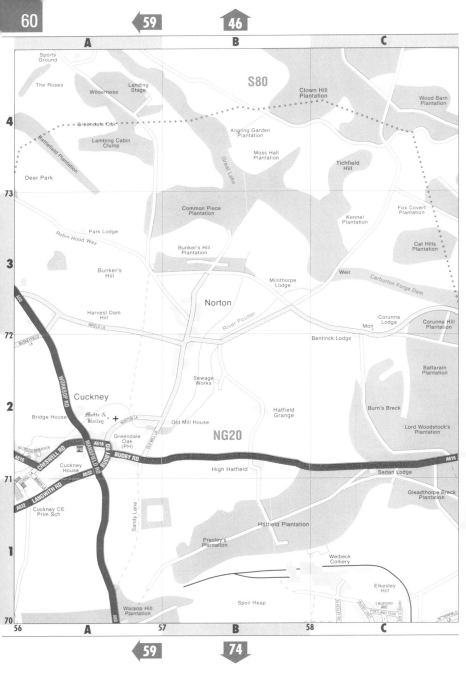

A

B

C

Sports Ground

The Roses

Wilderness

Landing Stage

S80

Clown Hill Plantation

Wood Barn Plantation

4

Greendale Oak

Lambing Cabin Clump

Angling Garden Plantation

Moss Hall Plantation

Tichfield Hill

Battlefield Plantation

Great Lake

Deer Park

73

Common Piece Plantation

Kennel Plantation

Fox Covert Plantation

Park Lodge

Robin Hood Way

Bunker's Hill Plantation

Cat Hills Plantation

3

Bunker's Hill

Minthorpe Lodge

Weir

Carburton Forge Dam

Harvest Dam Hill

INFIELD LA

Norton

River Poulter

Corunna Lodge

Mon

Corunna Hill Plantation

A60

72

BUSKEYFIELD LA

Bentinck Lodge

Battarain Plantation

WORKSOP RD

Sewage Works

Burn's Breck

Lord Woodstock's Plantation

2

Cuckney

Bridge House

Motte & Bailey

NORTON LA

Hatfield Grange

Greendale Oak (PH)

Old Mill House

OLD MILL LA

NG20

GLOBERS RIVERSIDE

CHESWELL RD

MANSFIELD RD

BUDBY RD

BUDBY RD

A616

High Hatfield

A616

Sedan Lodge

A632

BAGGELY LA

Cuckney House

SCHOOL

71

LANGWITH RD

A632

Sandy Lane

Gleadthorpe Breck Plantation

Cuckney CE Prim Sch

Hatfield Plantation

Welbeck Colliery

Elkesley Hill

1

Presley's Plantation

Spoil Heap

1 RUFFORD AVE

PORTLAND TERR

BUSKEYFIELD RD

NETHERFIELD LA

A60

Warsop Hill Plantation

70

56

A

57

B

58

C

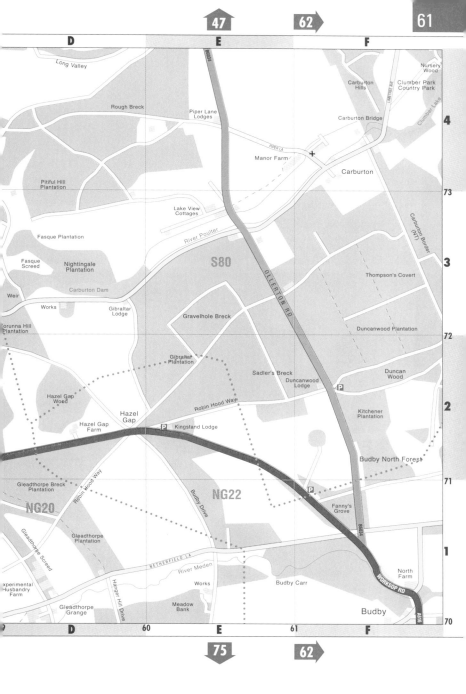

D
E
F

Long Valley

Nursery Wood

Carburton Hills

Clumber Park Country Park

Rough Breck

Piper Lane Lodges

Carburton Bridge

Clumber Lake

LIME TREE AV

4

Pitiful Hill Plantation

PIPER LA

Manor Farm

+

Carburton

73

Lake View Cottages

River Poulter

Fasque Plantation

S80

Carburton Border (NT)

Fasque Screed

Nightingale Plantation

Thompson's Covert

3

Carburton Dam

Weir

Works

Gibraltar Lodge

Gravelhole Breck

OLLERTON RD

Duncanwood Plantation

72

orunna Hill Plantation

Gibraltar Plantation

Sadler's Breck

Duncanwood Lodge

P

Duncan Wood

Hazel Gap Wood

Robin Hood Way

Kitchener Plantation

2

Hazel Gap

Hazel Gap Farm

P

Kingstand Lodge

Budby North Forest

71

Gleadthorpe Breck Plantation

Robin Hood Way

Budby Drive

NG22

P

Fanny's Grove

B6034

NG20

Gleadthorpe Screed

Gleadthorpe Plantation

NETHERFIELD LA

River Meden

1

xperimental Husbandry Farm

Hanger Hill Drive

Works

Budby Carr

North Farm

WORKSOP RD

Gleadthorpe Grange

Meadow Bank

Budby

A616

70

D
60
E
61
F

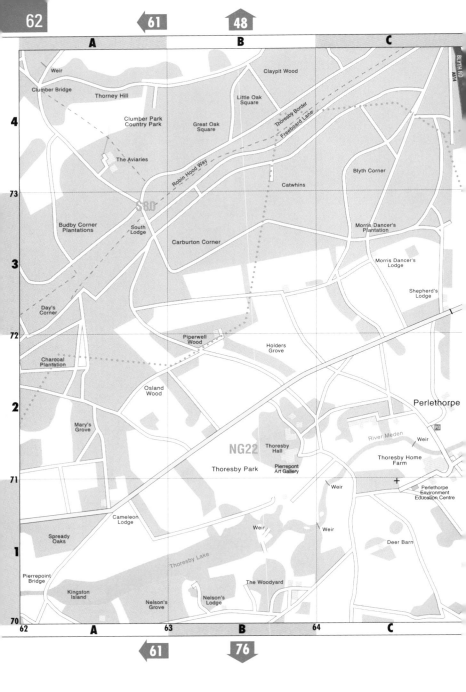

A **B** **C**

BLYTH RD A614

Weir

Clumber Bridge

Thorney Hill

Claypit Wood

Little Oak Square

Clumber Park Country Park

Great Oak Square

Thoresby Border

Freebord Lane

4

Robin Hood Way

Blyth Corner

The Aviaries

Catwhins

73

S80

Budby Corner Plantations

South Lodge

Morris Dancer's Plantation

Carburton Corner

Morris Dancer's Lodge

3

Shepherd's Lodge

Day's Corner

72

Piperwell Wood

Holders Grove

Charcoal Plantation

Osland Wood

2

Perlethorpe

Mary's Grove

River Meden

Weir

NG22

Thoresby Hall

Thoresby Home Farm

Thoresby Park

Pierrepont Art Gallery

71

Weir

+

Perlethorpe Environment Education Centre

Cameleon Lodge

Spready Oaks

Weir

Weir

Deer Barn

1

Thoresby Lake

Pierrepoint Bridge

Kingston Island

Nelson's Grove

Nelson's Lodge

The Woodyard

70

D
E
F

4

Bothamsall

CHURCH LA

RUSHILL LA

MAIN

MEDEN BANK

S80

73

Spittalmoor Forest Farm

River Meden

MEADOW LA

Mill House Farm

Haughton

B6387

Ramillies Plantation

DN22

Conjure Alders

River Maun

Crow Park

3

Gosling Carr

Haughton Warren

72

Pickin's Bridge

BLYTH RD

A614

Middle Ashes

Blackcliffe Hill Plantation

Robin Hood Way

2

Oakham Poultry Farms

Sports Ground

FOREST LA

Forest Lane

NG22

Anthony's Orchard

Whitewater

71

Whitemoor Farm

NEW HILL 1
KENNEDY RISE 2

RETFORD RD

Broom Covert

Robin Hood's Cave

MILL LA

Briers Lodge

PH

1

Henrys Grove

Druids Cottage

New England

Walesby Forest

Breck Cottages

BRAKE RD

BRAKE RD

B6387

The White Lodge

WHITEWATER LA

Whitewater Bridge

70

D
66
E
67
F

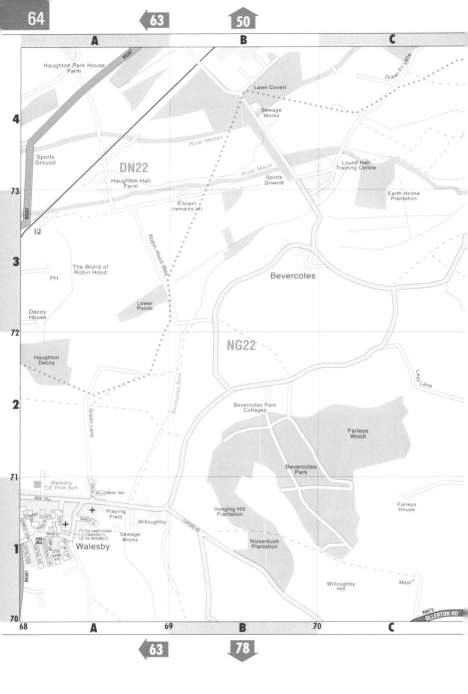

65
52

A **B** **C**

4

ASKHAM RD

A57

Old Moorgate

Playing
Field

PH

HIGH ST

COLLEGE LA

LONG LA

HALL LA

LINCOLN RD

BACK LA

TRINITY
CRES

PLANTATION AVE

TRINITY
CRES

73

MARK LA

CHURCH ST

Markham
Hall

PLANTATION RD

Back Lane

NEWARK RD

HOOKIN

QUAKEFIELD RD

Sewage
Works

High
Brecks Farm

High Brecks
Plantation

Brecks
Plantation

Low Brecks
Farm

BROAD GATE

A57

A6075

Kingshaugh
Ancient Monument
& Royal Manor

Earthworks

Kingshaugh
Farm

3

Darlton Field

Highfields Farm

NG22

72

Darlton Gaps

DARLTON RD

Lodge Farm

Goodhouses
Farm

2

PH

Eastfield
House

Walks of Life
Heritage Ctr

A6075

LINCOLN RD

FLEMING AVE

WELBECK
PL

NICHOLAS

WORDSWORTH

CHARTER CL

HATFIELD CL

HILL CRES

Tuxford
Comp Sch

Tuxford

Park
Cottage

MARNHAM RD

Merryfields
Farm

71

B1164

ASHVALE RD

A1

ASPEN

MASTIN

CHESTNUT
WAY

CAPPS PL

1

LODGE

Sewage
Works

Ashvale

GREAT NORTH RD

Goosemoor
Dyke

A1

B1164

Lodge Farm

Ruddingwood

Peter Barn

70

74 **A** **75** **B** **76** **C**

Medieval Village of Whimpton (site of)

AST

BYRON CL.

BROAD GATE

Darlton

Low Farm

Grange Farm

Farhill Farm

Farhill Lane

Grange Farm

73

Vicarage Farm

Field Farm

WOODCOATES RD

America Farm

Fledborough Beck

3

NG22

Majors Farm

North Farm

Top Farm

GREEN LA

72

Gibraltar

Wells Farm

TAR RD

Woodcoates

2

Crabtree Lane

Station Cottages

71

Babbington Springs Farm

CRABTREE LA

NG23

LC

POLLY TAYLOR'S RD

1

Skegby

SKEGBY RD

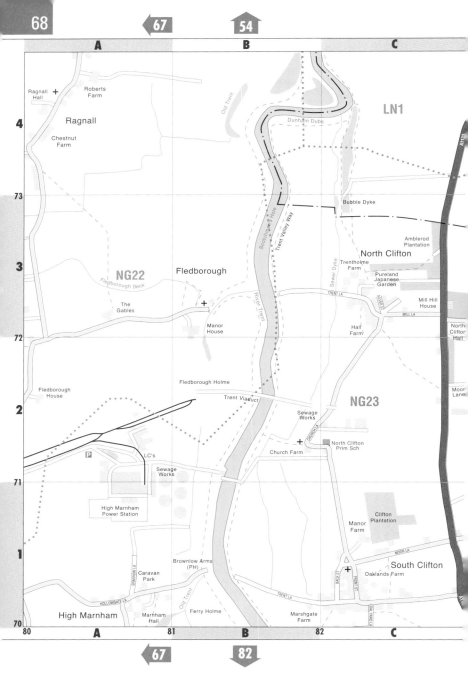

D
E
F

Hall
Farm

A57

Pumping Sta

A1133

HIGH ST

LN1

Thorney
Gate
Farm

Lodge
Farm

Road Wood

BROADINGS LA

4

Thorney

73

Westwood
Farm

+

West Wood

Hawthorn Hill

HOMEFARM LA

3

California
Farm

Northfield Lane

NG23

72

MILL LA

Moor Farm

COTTAGE LA

Carr Wood

Moor LA

Thorney
Moor

BROWN LA

2

Moor Farm

Carr
Farm

Wheatholme Lane

MOOR LA

71

Wheatholme

Moor
Farm

Amblerod
Farm

Wigsley Park

Park Lane

1

Birkland Lane

Rome
Farm

Manor Farm

Birkland Barn

Wigsley Wood

Mill Lane

A1133

70

D
E
F

3

84
85

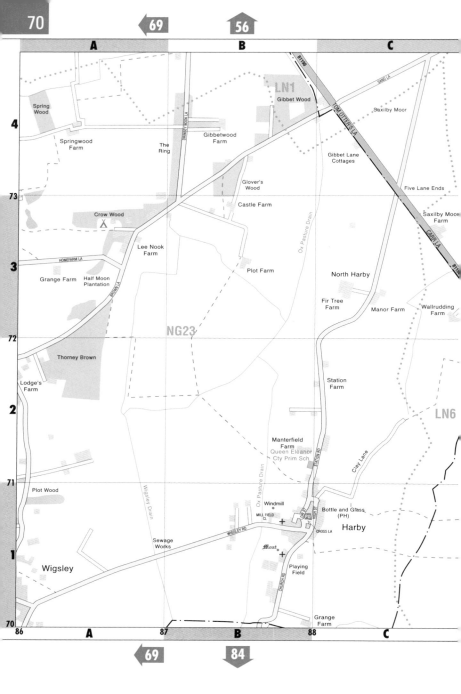

A   **B**   **C**

4

Spring
Wood

Springwood
Farm

The
Ring

Gibbetwood
Farm

LN1

Gibbet Wood

Saxilby Moor

Gibbet Lane
Cottages

Five Lane Ends

Saxilby Moor
Farm

73

Glover's
Wood

Castle Farm

Crow Wood

Lee Nook
Farm

Plot Farm

North Harby

HOMEFARM LA

3

Grange Farm

Half Moon
Plantation

Fir Tree
Farm

Manor Farm

Wallrudding
Farm

NG23

72

Thorney Brown

Lodge's
Farm

Station
Farm

LN6

2

Manterfield
Farm
Queen Eleanor
Cty Prim Sch

Clay Lane

71

Plot Wood

Windmill

MILL FIELD
CL

Bottle and Glass
(PH)

CROSS LA

Harby

Wigsley Drain

Ox Pasture Drain

Sewage
Works

WIGSLEY RD

Moat

CHURCH RD

1

Wigsley

Playing
Field

70

Grange
Farm

Lound Farm

SAXILBY RD

Manor Farm

Broadholme
House

Broadholme
Gorse

Western Plantation

Works

Magtree Hill

Skellingthorpe Big Wood

Old Wood

Carr Farm

Woodbank Farm

Old Wood
House

LN6

Old Wood
Nursery

Skellingthorpe

Old Hag
Wood

JERUSALEM RD

QUEENSWAY

Old Hag
Farm

Ash Lound

Works

Little Sale

Jerusalem
Farm

Birch Spring
Farm

CARR LA

Strunch Hill

Church
Farm
House

KENNEL LA

Doddington
Hall

MAIN ST

B1190

Doddington

Top House
Farm

D

E

F

D

E

F

4

73

3

72

2

71

1

70

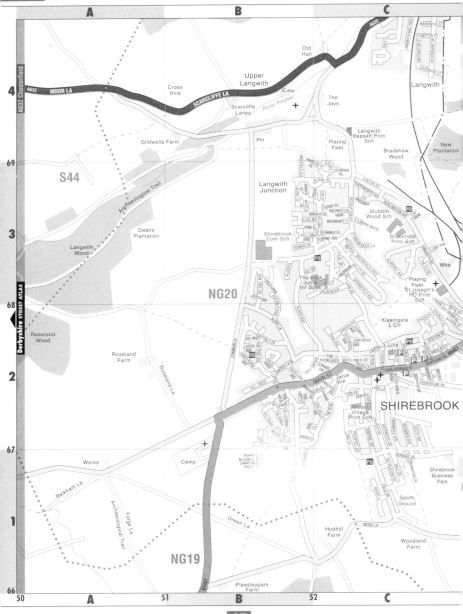

58

A B C

A632 Chesterfield

MOOR LA

Cross Hills

Old Hall

Upper Langwith

SCARCLIFFE LA

Langwith

Scarcliffe Lanes

River Poulter

Cabe

The Jays

Langwith Bassett Prim Sch

Playing Field

Bradshaw Wood

New Plantation

4

69

S44

Gildwells Farm

Langwith Junction

Derbyshire STREET ATLAS

Deans Plantation

Shirebrook Com Sch

Archaeological Trail

3

Langwith Wood

Stubbin Wood Sch

Brookfield Prim Sch

Wks

Roseland Wood

NG20

The Park Jun & Inf Schs

68

Playing Field St.Joseph's RC Prim Sch

Roseland Farm

Kissingate L Ctr

Liby

2

Roseland La

The Rooklands

Mayflower Ct

King Edward St

Main St

SHIREBROOK

Model Village Prim Sch

67

Balkham La

Works

Cemy

POPPY CL
BLUEBELL CL
CAMPION CL
VIOLET CL

Shirebrook Business Park

Forge La

Archaeological Trail

1

Green La

NG19

Hodhill Farm

Woodland Farm

Sports Ground

WOOD LA

66

50 A 51 B 52 C

Pleasleypark Farm

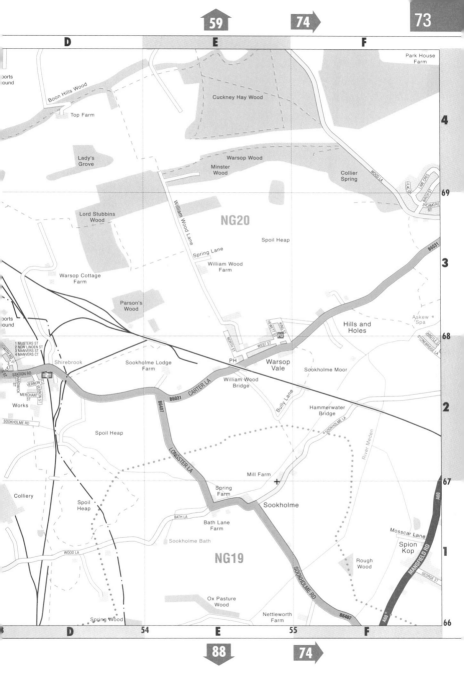

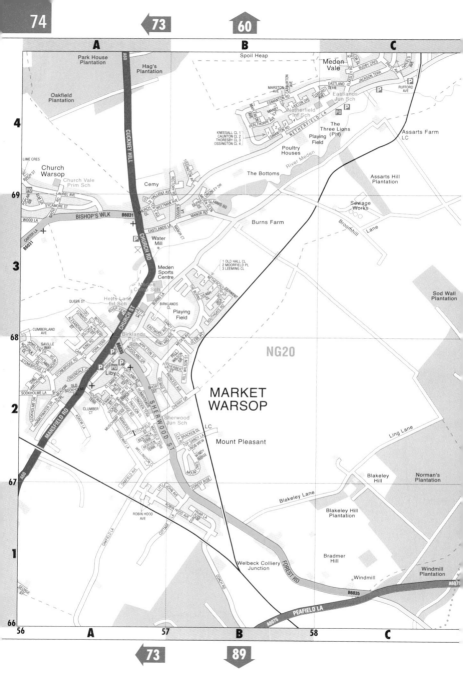

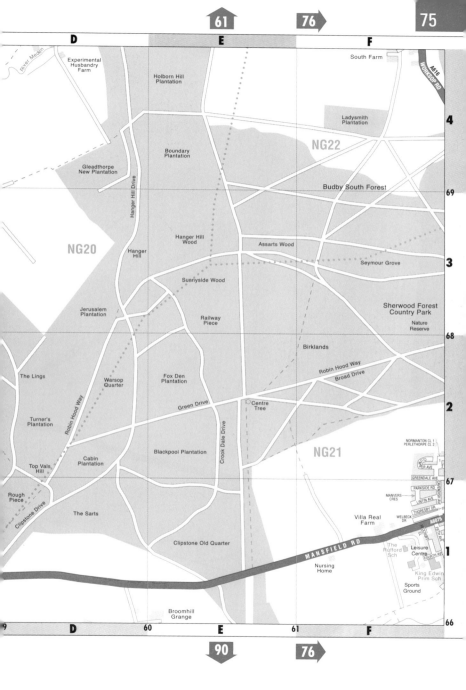

A
B
C

4

Budby
Castle

Wellesley
Plantation

Ceres
Lodge

South Grove

Coronation
Plantation

Proteus
Camp

69

Old Buck
Gates

Thoresby
Park

Clay Pits

WORKSOP RD

3

Ollerton Assarts
Plantation

Stilehollow Plantation

Ollerton Corner

Queen Oak
Plantation

Bilhaugh

NG22

68

Robert's
Plantation

The
"Major
Oak"

Sherwood Forest
Country Park

Spoil Heap

Bursheart
Hill

Robin Hood Way

Visitors
Centre

Birklands

2

SWINECOTE RD

Thoresby Colliery

Nature Reserve

MANSFIELD RD

NG21

Sherwood
Forest
Art and Craft
Centre

Forest
Corner

OLLERTON RD

67

NORMANTON CL

St Mary's
Sch

MAYTHORN GR

Craft
Workshop

Black Hills
Farm

Carr Brecks
Farm

PERLETHORPE CL

PADDOCK CL

GREENDALE AVE

CHURCH ST

Sewage
Works

A6075 MANSFIELD RD

Liby

GREENWOOD AVE

OLD RUFFORD RD

DOVEDALE CL

WEST LA

LYNDS CL

LAMBS LA

River Maun

1

SECOND AVE

FOURTH AVE

Edwinstowe

HIGH ST

BOY LA

WOODHEAD CL

Rainworth Water

FRIEND LA

WELLA

STATION LA

HENTON

CARVER CL

RUFFORD RD

B6034

GAITSKELL CRES

B6030

A614

66

62
A
63
B
64
C

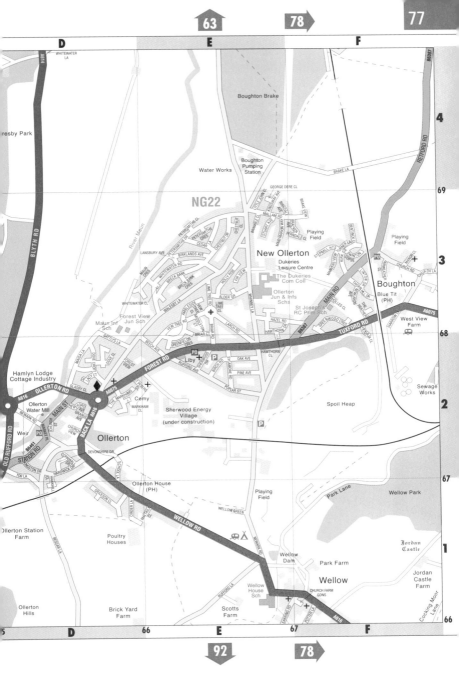

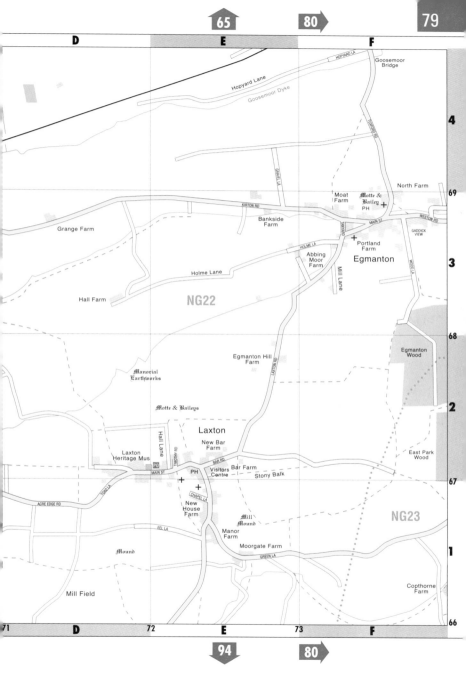

D
E
F

4

Hopyard Lane

Goosemoor Dyke

HOPYARD LA

Goosemoor Bridge

THIEFORD RD

North Farm

69

Moat Farm

Motte & Bailey PH

Main St

Weston Rd

Gaddick View

KIRTON RD

Bankside Farm

GRAVEL LA

HOLME LA

Abbing Moor Farm

Portland Farm

Egmanton

WIGG LA

Grange Farm

3

Holme Lane

TAN YD

Mill Lane

NG22

Hall Farm

68

Egmanton Hill Farm

LAXTON RD

Egmanton Wood

Manorial Earthworks

2

Motte & Baileys

East Park Wood

Laxton

Hall Lane

New Bar Farm

Laxton Heritage Mus

OLD HIGHWAY

BAR RD

Bar Farm

PH

MAIN ST

PH

Visitors Centre

Stony Balk

67

TONG LA

CHAPEL LA

NG23

ACRE EDGE RD

New House Farm

Mill Mound

EEL LA

Manor Farm

Moorgate Farm

Mound

GREEN LA

1

Mill Field

Copthorne Farm

66

D
E
F

71
72
73

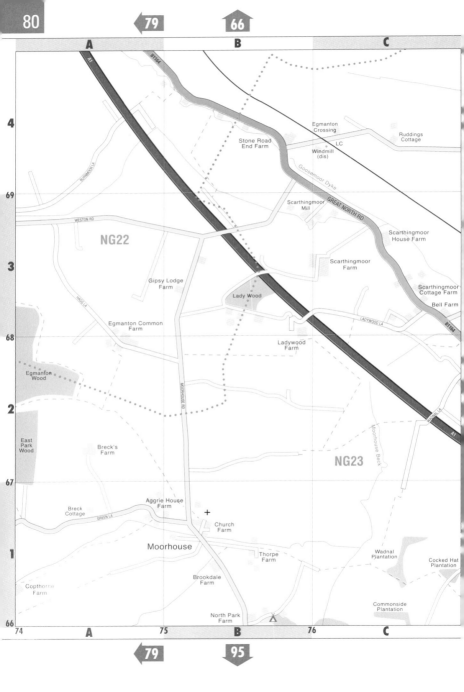

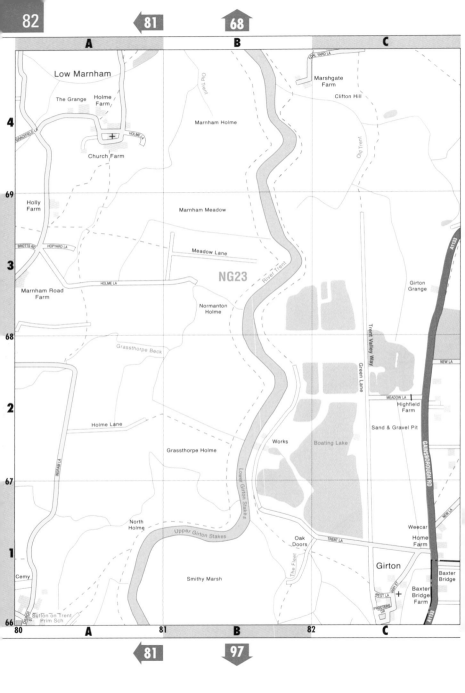

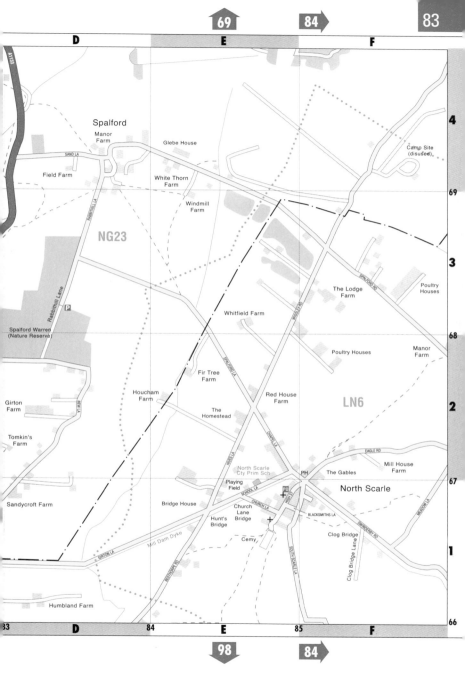

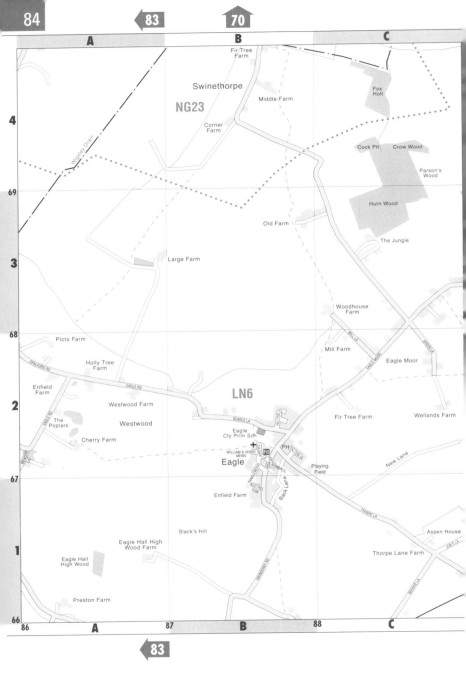

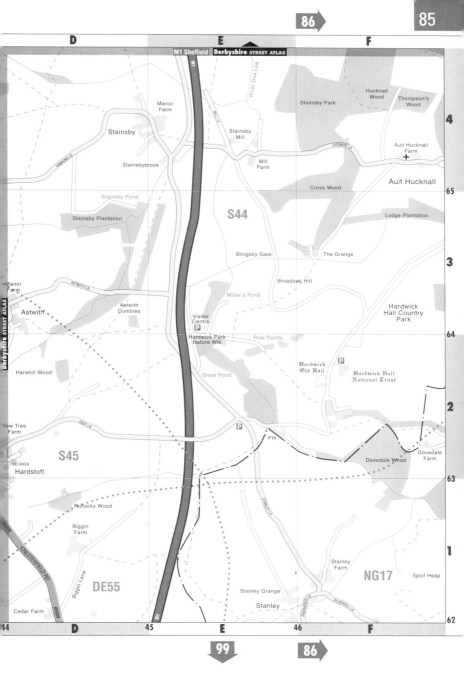

M1 Sheffield **Derbyshire** STREET ATLAS

Manor Farm

Stainsby

Stainsbybrook

Stainsby Pond

Stainsby Plantation

Stainsby Mill

Mill Farm

River Doe Lea

HODMIRE LA

Stainsby Park

Hucknall Wood

Thompson's Wood

Ault Hucknall Farm

Ault Hucknall

Cross Wood

S44

Lodge Plantation

Blingsby Gate

The Grange

Broadoak Hill

HANKINHILL LA

ASTWITH LA

Manor Farm

Astwith

Astwith Dumbles

Miller's Pond

Visitor Centre

Hardwick Park Nature Wlk

Row Ponds

Hardwick Hall Country Park

Harehill Wood

Great Pond

Hardwick Old Hall

Hardwick Hall National Trust

Yew Tree Farm

DEEP LA

S45

THE GREEN

Hardstoft

PH

Dovedale Wood

Dovedale Farm

Ridlocks Wood

Biggin Farm

STANLEY LA

CHESTERFIELD RD

Biggin Lane

DE55

Stanley Grange

Stanley

Stanley Farm

CHERRY LA

SILVERHILL LA

NG17

Spoil Heap

Cedar Farm

Derbyshire STREET ATLAS

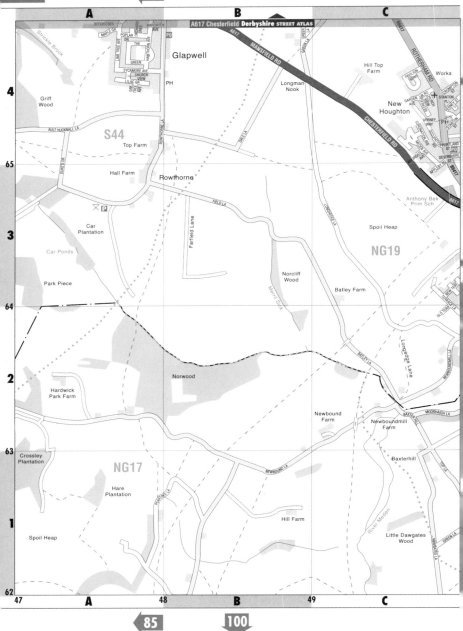

85

A617 Chesterfield **Derbyshire** STREET ATLAS

A **B** **C**

Glapwell

Stickle Brook

BEECH CRES

MAPLE DR

HARDWICK

ORCHARD

CRES

POPLAR

DR

THE

GREEN

LIME TREE AVE

HAWTHORN AVE

SYCAMORE AVE

CHURCH

VIEW

OAK

TREE

AVE

LILAC

GR

PH

PO

MANSFIELD RD

A617

GREEN LA

Longman
Nook

Hill Top
Farm

New
Houghton

ROTHERHAM RD

PAVILION

GARDEN

GR RD

STANTON

ST

A617

Works

PH

PO

CHESTERFIELD RD

A617

4

Griff
Wood

AULT HUCKNALL LA

DUKE'S DR

S44

Top Farm

ROWTHORNE LA

OGLEY LA

65

Hall Farm

Rowthorne

FIELD LA

Anthony Bek
Prim Sch

LANGSIDE LA

Spoil Heap

NG19

3

Car
Plantation

Car Ponds

Farfield Lane

Norcliff
Wood

Batley Farm

64

Park Piece

Meden Sick

Longedge Lane

BATLEY LA

NEWBOUNDMILL LA

THORPE FM

OLD TERRACE

2

Norwood

Hardwick
Park Farm

BAXTER LA

MOORHAIGH LA

63

Crossley
Plantation

NG17

Newbound
Farm

Newboundmill
Farm

NEWBOUND LA

Baxterhill

1

Hare
Plantation

PEARTREE LA

Hill Farm

River Meden

Little Dawgates
Wood

GREEN LA

HIGH FIELD LA

Spoil Heap

62

47 **A** **48** **B** **49** **C**

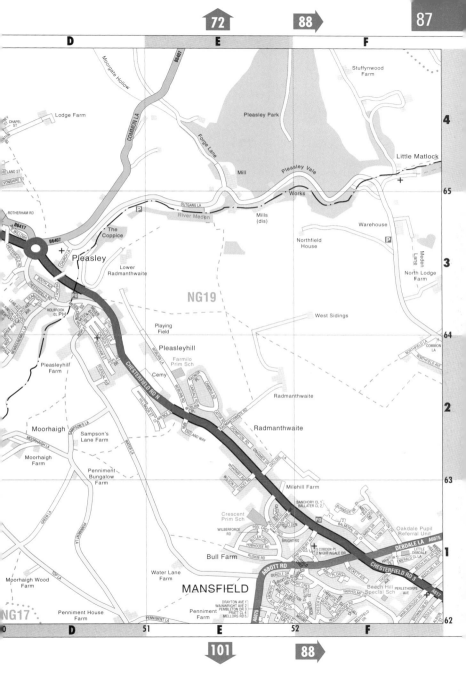

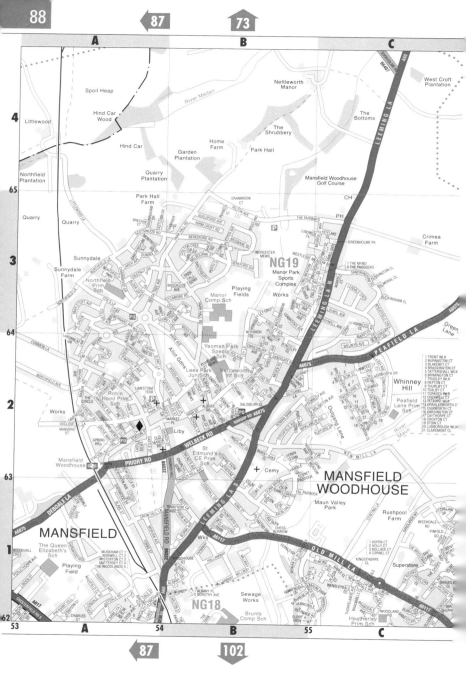

89
75

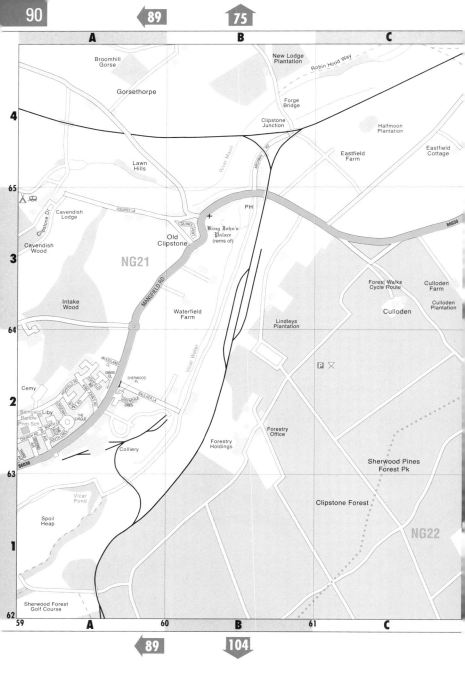

A   **B**   **C**

Broomhill Gorse

New Lodge Plantation

Robin Hood Way

Gorsethorpe

Forge Bridge

Clipstone Junction

Halfmoon Plantation

4

Eastfield Farm

Eastfield Cottage

River Maun

Lawn Hills

65

Cavendish Lodge

Clipstone Dr

SQUIRES LA

SQUIRES CROFT

PH

B6030

Cavendish Wood

Old Clipstone

King John's Palace (rems of)

3

NG21

Forest Walks Cycle Route

Culloden Farm

Culloden Plantation

MANSFIELD RD

Intake Wood

Waterfield Farm

Lindleys Plantation

Culloden

64

WOODLAND CL

DAVIS CL

SHERWOOD PL

Vicar Water

P

Cemy

Samuel Barlow Prim Sch

HIGHFIELD RD

PINE POPLAR RD

SHERWOOD PL

BAULKER LA

GREENDALE DRES

THE CIRCLE

2

Liby

NORTH CR

SOUTH CRES

CHURCH RD

B6030

Colliery

Forestry Holdings

Forestry Office

Sherwood Pines Forest Pk

63

Vicar Pond

Spoil Heap

Clipstone Forest

1

NG22

Sherwood Forest Golf Course

62

59   **A**   **60**   **B**   **61**   **C**

89
104

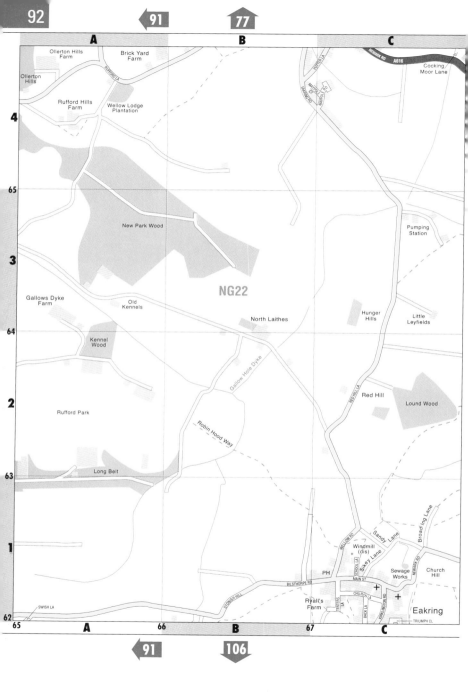

A   **B**   **C**

Ollerton Hills Farm

Brick Yard Farm

Ollerton Hills

Rufford Hills Farm

Wellow Lodge Plantation

RUFFORD LA

POTTER LA

EAKRING RD

MATCHER GATE

NEWARK RD

A616

Cocking Moor Lane

4

65

New Park Wood

Pumping Station

3

NG22

Gallows Dyke Farm

Old Kennels

North Laithes

Hunger Hills

Little Leyfields

64

Kennel Wood

Gallow Hole Dyke

RED HILL LA

Red Hill

Lound Wood

2

Rufford Park

Robin Hood Way

63

Long Belt

Broadfing Lane

1

WILLOW RD

Sandy Lane

SCHOOL LA

Sikey Lane

Windmill (dis)

Sewage Works

NEWTON RD

Church Hill

PH

BILSTHORPE RD

MAIN ST

CHURCH LA

BACK LA

KIRKLINGTON RD

62

SWISH LA

STONISH HILL

TENTERS

Ryall's Farm

Eakring

TRIUMPH CL

65   **A**   **66**   **B**   **67**   **C**

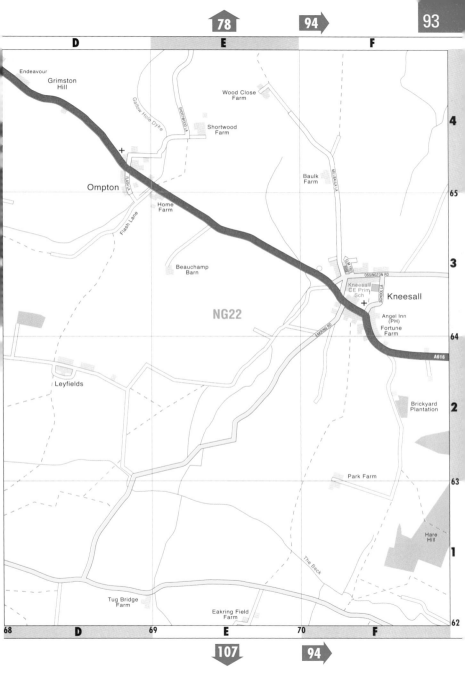

D
E
F

Endeavour
Grimston
Hill

Gallow Hole Dyke

Wood Close
Farm

SHORTWOOD LA

Shortwood
Farm

4

+

BAULK LA

Baulk
Farm

Ompton

FLASH LA

65

Home
Farm

Flash Lane

ELM TREE

Beauchamp
Barn

DISSINGTON RD

SCHOOL LA

Kneesall
CE Prim
Sch

3

Kneesall

+

NG22

Angel Inn
(PH)

Fortune
Farm

EAKRING RD

64

A616

Leyfields

Brickyard
Plantation

2

Park Farm

63

Hare
Hill

1

The Beck

Tug Bridge
Farm

Eakring Field
Farm

62

68
D
69
E
70
F

A

B

C

4

South Field

Knapeney
Farm

Brockilow
Farm

65

Saywood

Kneesall
Wood

Laxton
Wood

Laxton Middle
Wood

3

Kneesall Green
Farm

Hartshorn
Farm

NG22

Mainwood
Farm

64

Victoria
Plantation

High
Wood

A616

Laxton
Lodge

2

Buckshaw
Farm

NG23

63

Kersall
Lodge

Kneesall
Lodge

Woodhouse
Gorse

Woodhouse Common
Farm

1

Mill Lane

Kersall

Cocked Hat
Plantation

A616

62

71

A

72

B

73

C

Manor
Farm

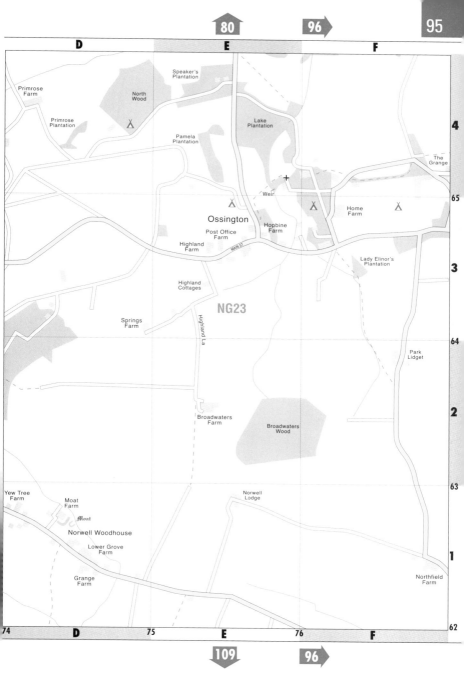

Primrose
Farm

Speaker's
Plantation

North
Wood

Primrose
Plantation

Lake
Plantation

Pamela
Plantation

The
Grange

4

Weir.

65

Ossington

Home
Farm

Post Office
Farm

Hopbine
Farm

Highland
Farm

MAIN ST

Lady Elinor's
Plantation

3

Highland
Cottages

NG23

Springs
Farm

Highland La

64

Park
Lidget

Broadwaters
Farm

Broadwaters
Wood

2

63

Yew Tree
Farm

Norwell
Lodge

Moat
Farm

Moat

Norwell Woodhouse

Lower Grove
Farm

1

Grange
Farm

Northfield
Farm

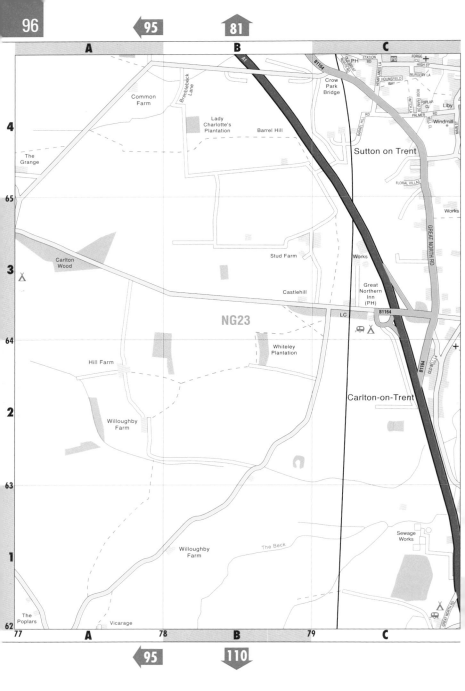

A B C

Crow Park Bridge

Common Farm

Bramblebeck Lane

Lady Charlotte's Plantation

Barrel Hill

Sutton on Trent

4

The Grange

STATION RD

PH

FORGE

HIGH ST

HOUNSFIELD WAY

NURSERY LA

POPLAR

Liby

Windmill

FLORAL VILLAS

65

Works

GREAT NORTH RD

Carlton Wood

Stud Farm

Works

3

Castlehill

Great Northern Inn (PH)

LC

B1164

NG23

64

Whiteley Plantation

B1164

Hill Farm

Carlton-on-Trent

2

Willoughby Farm

63

The Beck

Sewage Works

1

Willoughby Farm

The Poplars

Vicarage

GREAT NORTH RD

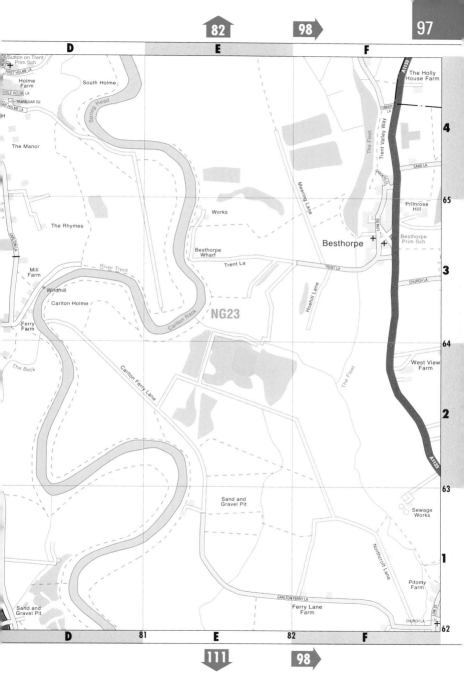

D
E
F

Sutton on Trent
Prim Sch
The Holly
House Farm
Holme
Farm
South Holme
MIDDLE HOLME LA
FIRST HOLME LA
TRAFALGAR SQ
FAR HOLME LA

4

The Fleet
TINKER LA

The Manor
Meering Lane
Works

65

Trent Valley Way
Primrose
Hill
Besthorpe
Prim Sch

The Rhymes
Besthorpe
Wharf
Trent La
Besthorpe
SAND LA

CARLTON LA

River Trent
TRENT LA
CHURCH LA

3

Mill
Farm
Windmill
Carlton Holme
Hoehill Lane
NG23

Ferry
Farm
Carlton Reck

64

The Beck
Carlton Ferry Lane
The Fleet
West View
Farm

2

A1133

Sand and
Gravel Pit
63

Sewage
Works

Northcroft Lane
1

Pitomy
Farm

Sand and
Gravel Pit
CARLTON FERRY LA
Ferry Lane
Farm
CHURCH LA
LORD ST

62

D
81
E
82
F

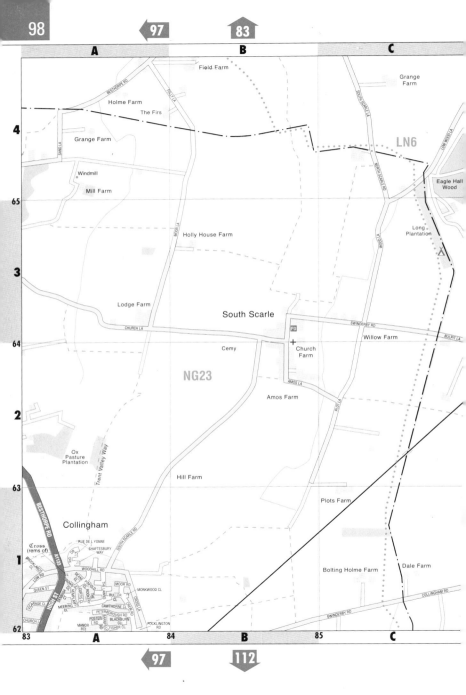

A B C

BESTHORPE RD

Field Farm

Grange Farm

POTT LA

Holme Farm

The Firs

SOUTH SCARLE LA

4

Grange Farm

LN6

SAND LA

LOW WOOD LA

Windmill

Mill Farm

Eagle Hall Wood

65

NORTH SCARLE RD

Long Plantation

MOOR LA

Holly House Farm

WOOD LA

3

Lodge Farm

South Scarle

SWINDERBY RD

CHURCH LA

BULPIT LA

64

Cemy

Church Farm

Willow Farm

PO

NG23

AMOS LA

Amos Farm

RR LA

2

Ox Pasture Plantation

Trent Valley Way

Hill Farm

63

Plots Farm

Collingham

BESTHORPE RD

RUE DE L'YONNE

SHAFTESBURY WAY

SOUTH SCARLE RD

LOW RD

A1133

Cross (rems of)

WOODHILL RD

MOOR RD

MONKWOOD CL

CROSS L

Bolting Holme Farm

Dale Farm

1

CHURCH ST

BRIDON LA

QUEEN ST

BULLER

BAKERY

COLLINGHAM RD

GRANGE CL

MEERING LA

CAWTHORNE CL

SWINDERBY RD

PETERBOROUGH CL

FOSTERS

BLACKBURN CL

POCKLINGTON RD

62

MANOR RD

FISHER CL

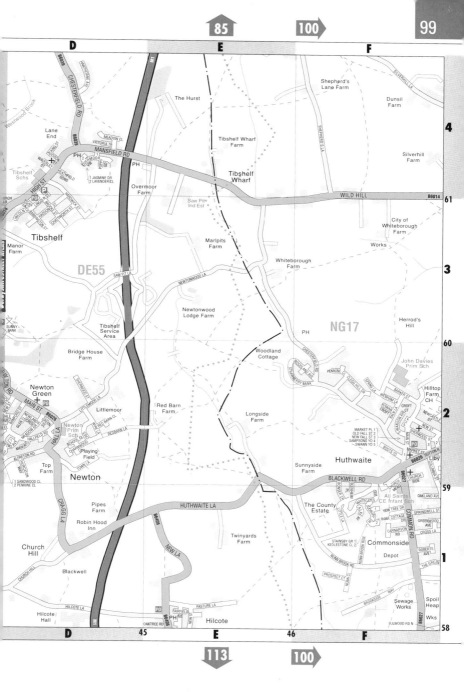

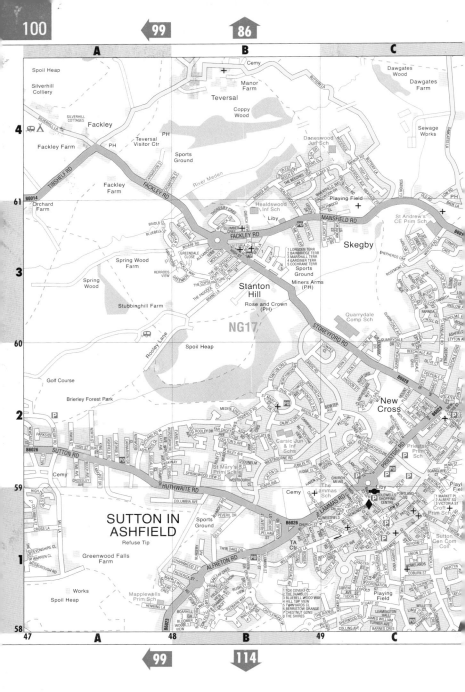

A   B   C

Spoil Heap

Silverhill Colliery

SILVERHILL COTTAGES

Fackley

Cemy

Manor Farm

Teversal

Coppy Wood

Dawgates Wood

Dawgates Farm

Sewage Works

4

Fackley Farm

Teversal Visitor Ctr

PH

PH

Sports Ground

TIRSHELF RD

Daneswood Jun Sch

FACKLEY RD

Fackley Farm

River Meden

Playing Field

61

B6014

Orchard Farm

THORESBY CRES

Healdswood Inf Sch

MANSFIELD RD

St Andrew's CE Prim Sch

B601

Liby

Skegby

SHEPHERDS OAK

Spring Wood Farm

CLUMBER CRES

FACKLEY RD

1 LONSDEN TERR
2 BAINBRIDGE TERR
3 MARSHALL TERR
4 GARDINER TERR
5 COCHRANE TERR

ROSEMONT

3

Spring Wood

GREENDALE CLOSE

HERRODS VIEW

THE COPSE

Sports Ground

Miners Arms (PH)

Quarrydale Comp Sch

FARNDALE

Stanton Hill

Stubbinghill Farm

THE PADDOCK

Rose and Crown (PH)

NG17

STONEYFORD RD

Quarrydale

60

Rooley Lane

Spoil Heap

Golf Course

B602b

Brierley Forest Park

New Cross

B6023

2

P

PARKSIDE

NEWCASTLE

NORTH ST

SUTTON RD

HIGH ST

ASHFORD RD

Carsic Jun & Inf Schs

PRIESTSIC RD

Priestsic Prim Sch

P

PO

B6026

MEDEN BANK

ROOLEY DR

RILEY AVE

DUNELM

JUBILEE RD

PENN ST

SCARCLIFFE ST

Playl Fld

Cemy

HUTHWAITE RD

SPRINGWOOD VIEW LA

WESTBOURNE

Cemy

LAMMAS RD

The Lammas

Liby

IDLEWELLS PORTLAND SHOPPING CENTRE

1 MARKET PL
2 ALBERT SQ
3 VICTORIA ST

Croft Prim Sch

59

COLUMBIA AVE

PEVERIL DR

LOW ST

Sutton Cen Com Coll

SUTTON IN ASHFIELD

Sports Ground

B6026

CHURCH ST

WESTFIELD LA

TA Ctr

THE HOMELANDS

Refuse Tip

CHARNWOOD RD

ALFRETON RD

TWIN OAKS DR

CRASTER ST

CORONATION

Playing Field

1

Greenwood Falls Farm

FREDERICK ST

MAPLE WELLS RD

LEAMINGTON HALL

JAMES WILLIAM TURNER AVE

Works

Mapplewells Prim Sch

BOARHILL

HENNING LA

BLOOMER WOOD VIEW

1 FOX COVERT CL
2 THE DUMBLES
3 BLUEBELL WOOD WAY
4 HILL TOP VIEW
5 TOWNYARDS CL
6 BERRISTOW GRANGE
7 CHESTNUT GDNS
8 THE SHIRES

BARNES CRES

Spoil Heap

B6023

COLLINS AVE

58

47   A   48   B   49   C

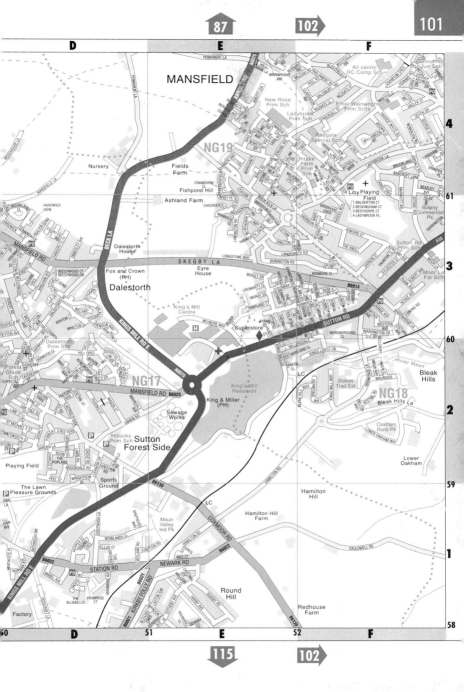

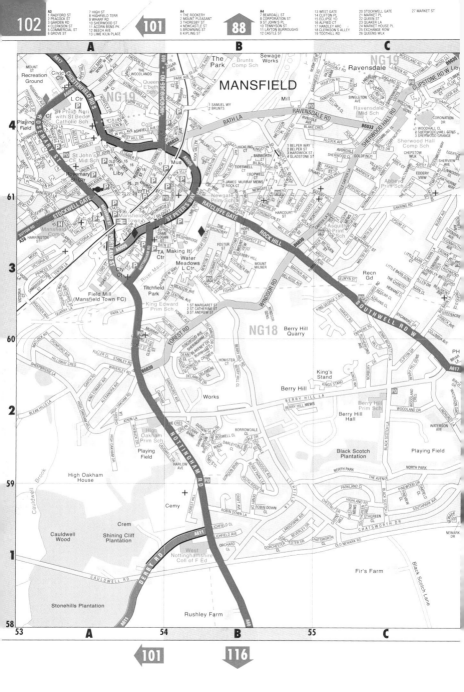

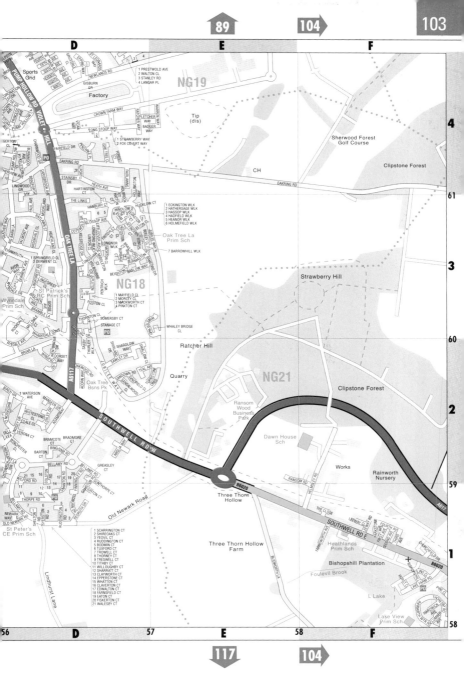

103
90

Sherwood Forest
Golf Course

Birch Row

Clipstone Forest

Brown's
Covert

P

4

EAKRING RD

61

Near Round
Plantation

3

LC

LC

Far Round
Plantation

Black Hill

NG22

Rufford
Colliery

60

NG21

Inkersall Grange
Farm

Rainworth Water

2

Spring
Hill

The Hundred
Acres

Sewage
Works

Watch Hill

59

A617

1

P

Sports
Ground

Rainworth

Python Hill
Jun & Inf
Sch

Rufford Forest
Farm

A617

B6020

KIRKLINGTON RD

KIRKLINGTON RD

NORTH AVE

GARDEN AVE

B6020

LIME TREE

BRECON CL

1 FOREST CL
2 CHEDDAR CL

PH

Liby

WARSOP LA

LITTLE JOHN DR

RUFFORD AVE

HATFIELD CL

AMBER

DENBIGH

WEBSTER

DIAMOND AVE

COOPERS
RISE

THE
SQUARE

BEVERLEY CL

SAPPHIRE CL

58

59   A   **60**   B   **61**   C

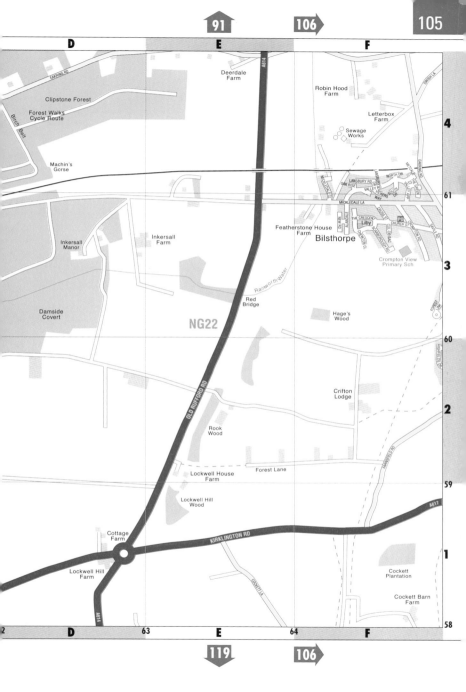

D
E
F

4

LARKING RD
Clipstone Forest
Forest Walks
Cycle Route
Birch Belt
Machin's
Gorse

Deerdale
Farm

Robin Hood
Farm

Letterbox
Farm

Sewage
Works

MARSH LA

MCLEOD CT
LANSBURY RD
OAK RISE
NORTH DR
WITTON CL
VALLEY RD
KEPPEL DR
LARKING RD

61

MICKLEDALE LA

Inkersall
Manor

Inkersall
Farm

Featherstone House
Farm

Liby

NEW RD
AVENUE E
THE CRESCENT
SHERLIN DL
CROSSLEY DL
CL BEAC
CHURCH ST
COMPTON RD
EAKRING RD
SAVER

Bilsthorpe

3

Damside
Covert

Rainworth Water

Red
Bridge

NG22

Crompton View
Primary Sch

Hage's
Wood

FOREST RD

60

Crifton
Lodge

HOPFIELD DR

2

OLD RUFFORD RD

Rook
Wood

Forest Lane

MANSFIELD RD

A614

Lockwell House
Farm

59

Lockwell Hill
Wood

A617

Cottage
Farm

KIRKLINGTON RD

1

Lockwell Hill
Farm

Cockett
Plantation

COCKETT LA

Cockett Barn
Farm

A614

2
D
63
E
64
F
58

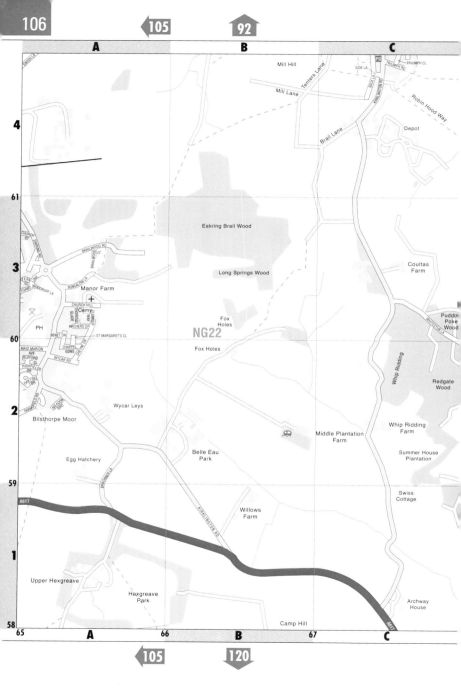

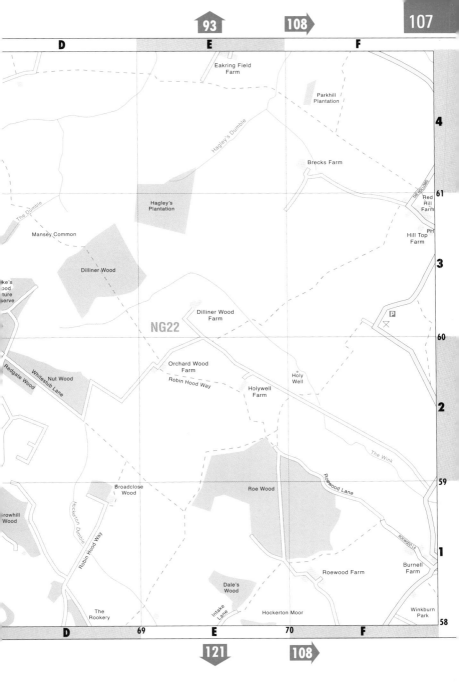

D
E
F

Eakring Field
Farm

Parkhill
Plantation

4

Hagley's Dumble

Brecks Farm

THE SLOUGH

61
Red
Hill
Farm

The Dumble

Hagley's
Plantation

Mansey Common

PH
Hill Top
Farm

Dilliner Wood

3

ke's
ood
ture
serve

Dilliner Wood
Farm

P

60

Orchard Wood
Farm

Holy
Well

Redgate Wood

Whitestub Lane

Nut Wood

Robin Hood Way

Holywell
Farm

2

The Wink

59

Broadclose
Wood

Roe Wood

Roewood Lane

rowhill
Wood

Hockerton Dumble

Robin Hood Way

ROEWOOD LA

1

Burnell
Farm

Roewood Farm

Dale's
Wood

The
Rookery

Intake Lane

Hockerton Moor

Winkburn
Park

58

D
69
E
70
F

NG22

107
94

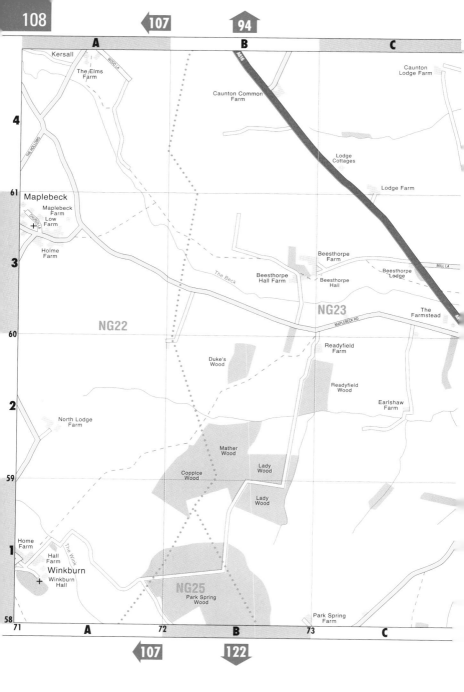

Kersall

The Elms
Farm

WOOD LA

Caunton
Lodge Farm

Caunton Common
Farm

4

THE HOLLOWS

Lodge
Cottages

A616

61

Maplebeck

Lodge Farm

Maplebeck
Farm
Low
Farm

CHURCH LA

Beesthorpe
Farm

MILL LA

Holme
Farm

3

The Beck

Beesthorpe
Hall Farm

Beesthorpe
Lodge

NG23

Beesthorpe
Hall

The
Farmstead

A6

NG22

MAPLEBECK RD

60

Readyfield
Farm

Duke's
Wood

Readyfield
Wood

Earlshaw
Farm

2

North Lodge
Farm

Mather
Wood

Lady
Wood

59

Coppice
Wood

Lady
Wood

Home
Farm

1

Hall
Farm

The Wink

Winkburn

Winkburn
Hall

NG25

Park Spring
Wood

Park Spring
Farm

58

107
122

D   **E**   **F**

School
House
Farm
PH

Highfield
House

Brunk
Wood

4

Southfield
Farm

Park
Wood

Mount
Pleasant

Glebe
Farm

61

Moor La

Watermill
Farm

Mill
Bridge

Flags
Farm

Hill House
Farm

3

Windmill

PH

MILL LA

NG23

The
Woovers

CHAPEL
LA

NORWELL RD

Bathleyford
Bridge

Bathleyhill
Farm

Bathleyhill
Cottages

Dean Hole
CE Sch

TOLNEY LA

MAIN ST

BEANS CL

ADELONE DR

Sewage
Works

The Beck

Winterset La

CAUNTON RD

60

PH

SCHOOL LA

Home
Farm

Holme
Farm

Caunton

NEWARK RD

Hunger
Barn

Newbottles
Plantation

2

Red
Lodge

Worner
Wood

59

Knapthorpe

Middlethorpe
Grange

Dean Hall
Farm

Knapthorpe
Manor

Doncaster's
Plantation

1

OLLERTON RD

A616

Cold Harbour
Plantation

58

D   75   **E**   76   **F**

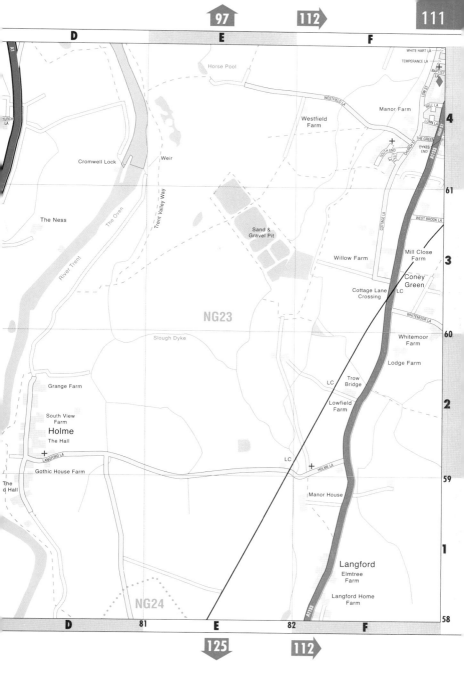

A B C

MANOR RD
LIME TREE CLT
WHITE HART LA
HIGH ST
CREW RD
BARNFIELD RD
TEMPERANCE LA
BAPTIST LA
WINDSOR CL
HEALEY CLT
KINLEY
BREAMER RD
REGENTS CL
PO
John Blows Prim. Sch
Liby
HOOKINS
SWINDERBY RD
CROSS LA
LC
Collingham & Swinderby Crossing
LC

High Park Farm

Valley Farm

THORNTON RD
STATION RD
Breamar Farm
LC
Collingham

LN6

4

Fishpond Plantation

DYKES END
THE PADDOCK
STATION RD
South Collingham Hall

Potter Hill

North Potter Hill Farm

61

GREEN LA
WEST BROOK LA
LC

Potter Hill Spinney

A46

South Potter Hill Farm

North Scaffold Lane

Potter Hill Plantation

3

NG23

HERONS LA
SHORT WHEATLEY LA
Wheatley Hill

South Scaffold Lane

Wheatley Farm

The Woodhey

FOLLY LA

Villa Farm

60

WHITEMOOR LA
WHEATLEY LA
The Havelings

LN6

Brills Hill

2

Brickyard Cottage

NEWARK RD

Brills Farm

BROUGH LA
Field House Farm Cottage

Field House Farm

59

Corner Farm

Norton Bottoms

Turfmoor

The Glebe Farm

Holly Farm

Turf Moor Farm

1

Brough

Church Farm

NORWELL LA
NG24
Danethorpe

Little Danethorpe Farm

A46

BROUGH RD

58

83 A 84 B 85 C

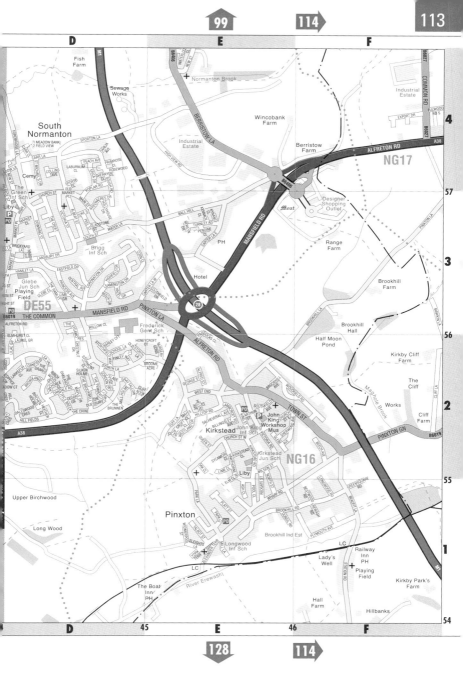

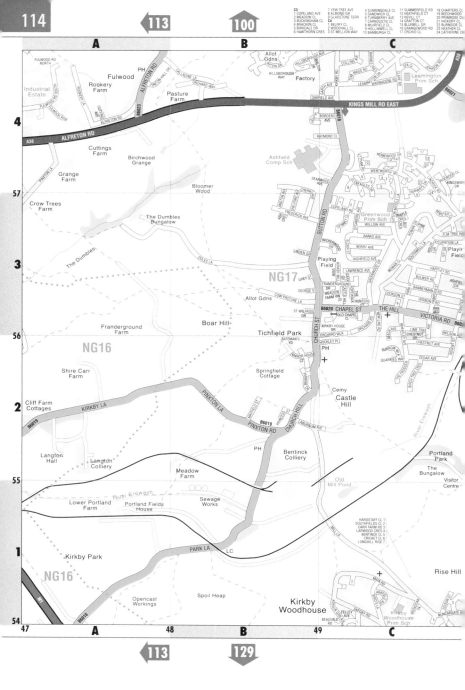

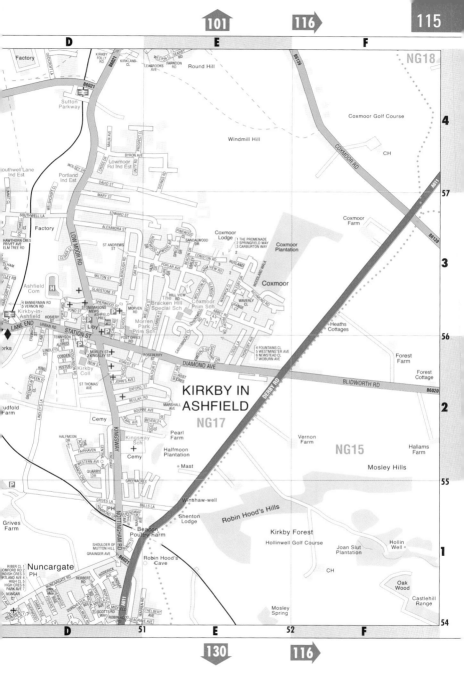

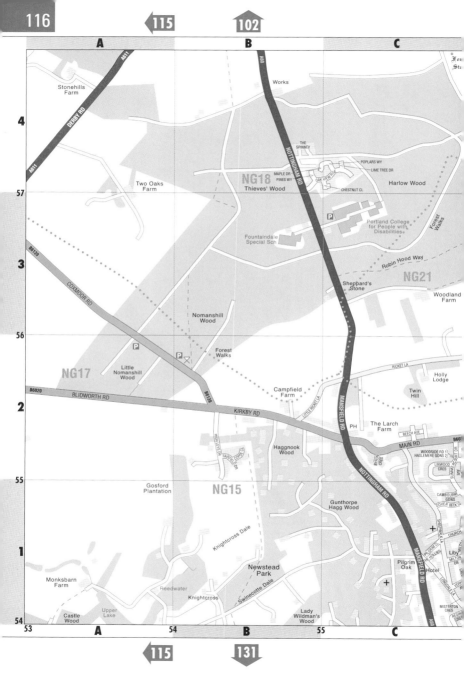

A
B
C

AS11

Stonehills
Farm

DERBY RD

AS11

4

Works

NOTTINGHAM RD

A60

THE
SPINNEY

57

Two Oaks
Farm

MAPLE DR
PINES WY

NG18
Thieves' Wood

OAK VIEW CL

POPLARS WY

LIME TREE DR

Harlow Wood

CHESTNUT CL

Forest
Walks

P

Fountaindale
Special Sch

Portland College
for People with
Disabilities

B6139

3

COXMOOR RD

Robin Hood Way

NG21

Sheppard's
Stone

Woodland
Farm

Nomanshill
Wood

56

P

Forest
Walks

RICKET LA

P

Holly
Lodge

NG17

Little
Nomanshill
Wood

Campfield
Farm

Twin
Hill

B6020

BLIDWORTH RD

B6139

KIRKBY RD

LITTLE BECK LA

MANSFIELD RD

The Larch
Farm

PH

2

BEECH AVE

MAIN RD

B60

Haggnook
Wood

WOODSIDE RD 1
HASLEMERE GDNS 2

HIGH LEYS DR

HAMEL CLOSE CL

55

Gosford
Plantation

NG15

BYRON CRES

NOTTINGHAM RD

LINWOOD
CRES

CAMBOURNE
GDNS

DOVER BECK CL

Gunthorpe
Hagg Wood

Knightcross Dale

+

CHURCH

Pilgrim
Oak

LIBY

1

MILTON

Monksbarn
Farm

Newstead
Park

Reedwater

Knightcross

Swinecote Dale

+

Hotel

MANSFIELD RD

A60

MISTERTON
CRES

Castle
Wood

Upper
Lake

Lady
Wildman's
Wood

54

53

A

54

B

55

C

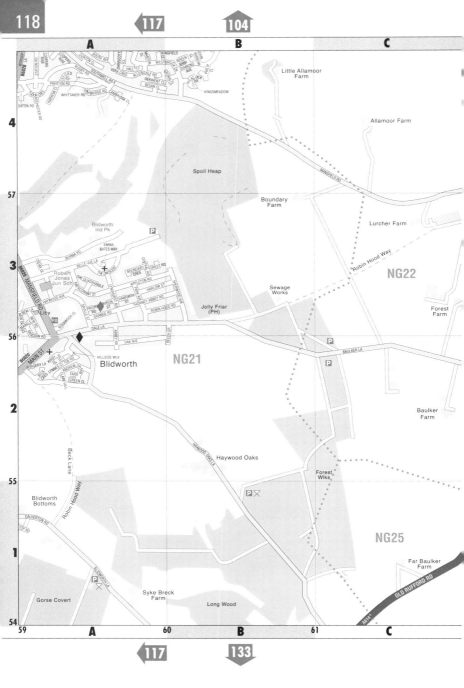

117
104

A

B

C

4

57

3

56

2

55

1

54

59

60

61

South Ave
Southwell Rd E
Anna Cres
Allendale Rd
Derwent Cl
Kingfield Cl
Westby Cl
Green Cl
Diamond Ave
Bevan Cl
Hall
Preston Rd
Whittaker Rd
Bridge Rd
Catherine Cl
Eaton Rd
Manchester Rd
B6020
Kingsmeadow

Little Allamoor Farm

Allamoor Farm

Mansfield Rd

Spoil Heap

Boundary Farm

Lurcher Farm

Blidworth Ind Pk
P
Emma Bates Way
Burma Rd
Belle Vue La
Robert Jones Jun Sch
The Quadrangle
Skinner Rd
Moor La
Forest Rd
Boundary Cres
Appleton Rd
Harlow St
Sherwood Rd
Robin Hood Rd
Sewage Works
Robin Hood Way

NG22

Forest Farm

Library
Haywood Ave
Beck La
Sherwood Cl
New La
Widow Rd
Dale La
Abbey Rd
Oak Ave
Beech La
Jolly Friar (PH)

NG21

Main St
B6020
Surgery La
Andrew Dr
Farm La
Green Cl
Hillside Wlk
Blidworth

P
Baulker La
P

Baulker Farm

Haywood Dale La
Haywood Oaks

Forest Wlks

Beck Lane

Robin Hood Way

55

Blidworth Bottoms
Calverton Rd
Top Rd

NG25

P

Far Baulker Farm
Old Rufford Rd
A614

P
Gorse Covert
Syke Breck Farm
Long Wood

117
133

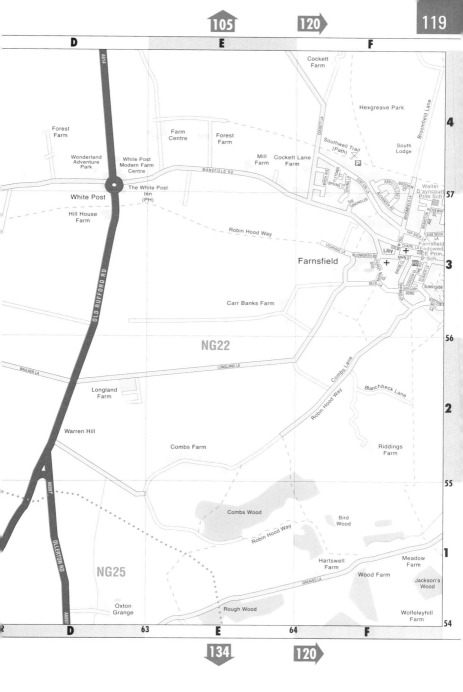

D
E
F

Cockett Farm

Hexgreave Park

Broomfield Lane

4

South Lodge

Southwell Trail (Path)

Forest Farm

Farm Centre

Forest Farm

Mill Farm

Cockett Lane Farm

Walter D'ayncourt Prim Sch

Wonderland Adventure Park

White Post Modern Farm Centre

MANSFIELD RD

57

White Post

The White Post Inn (PH)

Farnsfield Endowed CE Prim. Sch

Hill House Farm

Robin Hood Way

VICARAGE LA

BLIDWORTH RD

MAIN ST

Liby

Farnsfield

3

SUNNYSIDE

Carr Banks Farm

NG22

56

OLD RUFFORD RD

BAULKER LA

LONGLAND LA

Longland Farm

Combs Lane

Blanchbeck Lane

2

Warren Hill

Combs Farm

Robin Hood Way

Riddings Farm

A6097

55

Combs Wood

Bird Wood

Robin Hood Way

1

NG25

Hartswell Farm

Meadow Farm

OLLERTON RD

A6097

Wood Farm

Jackson's Wood

GREAVES LA

Oxton Grange

Rough Wood

Wolfeleyhill Farm

54

D
63
E
64
F

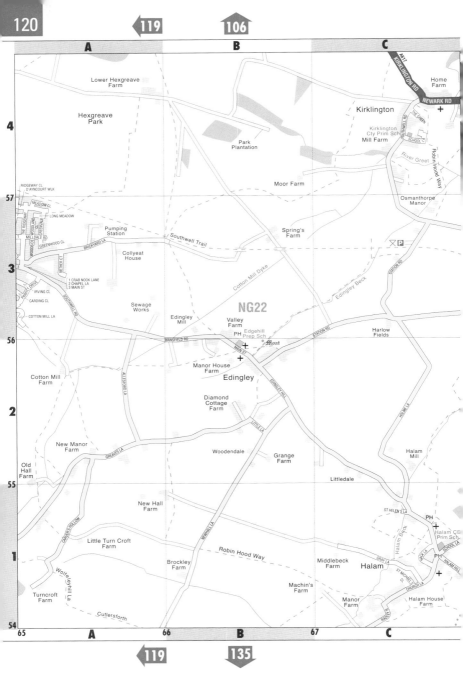

D   E   F

Rodney
Sch
Hall
Farm
Greet
Farm
FB

Hockerton
Road
Farm
Intake La

Hockerton Moor
Wood

Hockerton
Moor
Farm

Winkburn
Park

4

Brickfield
Farm

Hockerton Dumble

NG25

Wyton Lodge
Farm

57

Meadow
Farm

Far Corkhill
Farm

NG22

Cork Hill

A617

3

Goldhill
Cottages

Norwood
View

Middle Corkhill
Farm

Little Corkhill
Farm

56

Goldhill
Farm

River Greet

The Old
Silk Mill

Halam Park La

Robin Hood Way

Maythorne
Farm

Maythorne

2

Halam Osier Beds
Wood

NG25

Chestnut
Farm

55

CH

Norwood Park
Golf Course

Crow
Wood

Maythorn
Orchard

Nurseries
Normanton

Ind
Est

The Hall

Norwood
Park

Lowe's Wong
Anglican Methodist
Jun & Infant Sch

1

Norwood
Hill

Lodge
Plantation

Nurseries

SOUTHWELL

P Liby

Norwood
Park Farm

ALLENBY RD

P

COOKS LA

HALAM RD

WOODLAND VIEW

BURGAGE LA

54

D   E   F
69   70

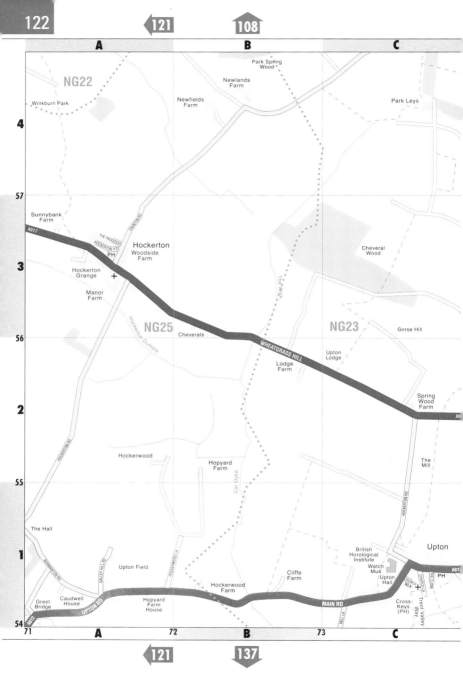

NG22

Winkburn Park

Park Spring Wood

Newlands Farm

Newfields Farm

Park Leys

4

57

Sunnybank Farm

A617

THE PADDOCKS

HOCKERTON HTS

CRINTON RD

PH

Hockerton

Woodside Farm

Cheveral Wood

3

Hockerton Grange

Manor Farm

Hockerton Dumble

NG25

Cheverals

The Wick

NG23

Gorse Hill

56

WHEATGRASS HILL

Upton Lodge

Lodge Farm

Spring Wood Farm

2

A6

HOCKERTON RD

Hockerwood

Hopyard Farm

Car Dyke

The Mill

55

The Hall

NEWINGTON RD

DALLEY HILL RD

Upton Field

HOCKERWOOD LA

British Horological Institute

Watch Mus

Upton Hall

Upton

1

A612

CHURCH LA

THE CLOSE

PH

Greet Bridge

Caudwell House

UPTON RD

Hopyard Farm House

Hockerwood Farm

Cliffe Farm

MAIN RD

MILL LA

Cross Keys (PH)

Trent Valley Way

54

A612

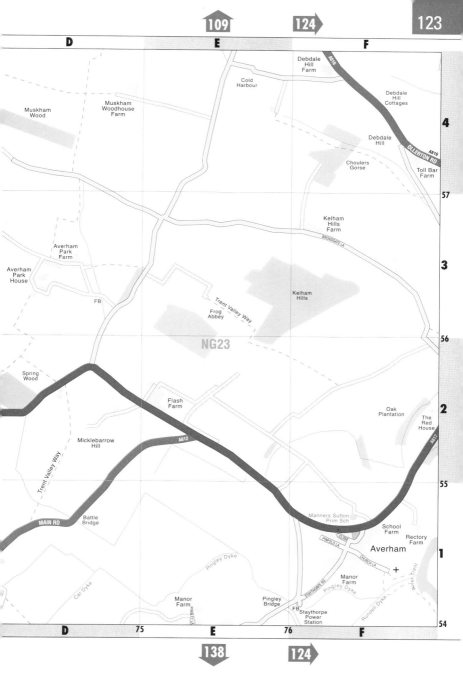

Debdale
Hill
Farm

A616

Debdale
Hill
Cottages

Cold
Harbour

4

Muskham
Wood

Muskham
Woodhouse
Farm

Debdale
Hill

OLLERTON RD

A616

Choulers
Gorse

Toll Bar
Farm

57

Kelham
Hills
Farm

Averham
Park
Farm

BROADGATE LA

3

Averham
Park
House

FB

Trent Valley Way

Kelham
Hills

Frog
Abbey

56

NG23

Spring
Wood

Flash
Farm

2

Oak
Plantation

The
Red
House

Micklebarrow
Hill

A612

A617

Trent Valley Way

55

Manners Sutton
Prim Sch

School
Farm

MAIN RD

Battle
Bridge

CLOSE

PINFOLD LA

Averham

Rectory
Farm

1

Pingley Dyke

CHURCH LA

River Trent

Manor
Farm

Car Dyke

Manor
Farm

PINGLEY LA

STAYTHORPE RD

Pingley Dyke

Pingley
Bridge

FB
Staythorpe
Power
Station

Rundell Dyke

54

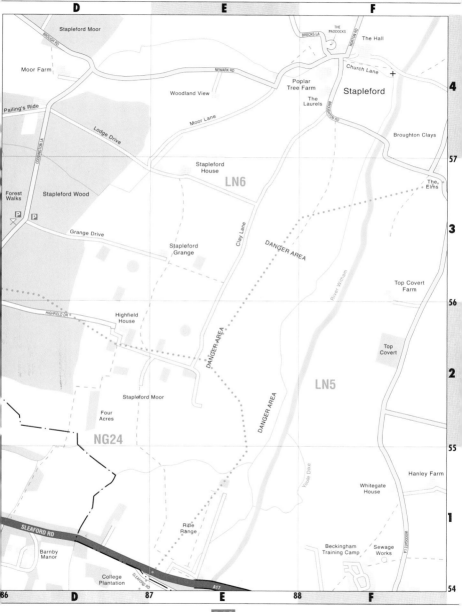

Stapleford Moor

BROUGH RD

Moor Farm

Pailing's Ride

CODDINGTON LA

Lodge Drive

NEWARK RD

Woodland View

Moor Lane

Poplar
Tree Farm

THE
PADDOCKS

BRECKS LA

NORTON RD

The Hall

Church Lane

Stapleford

BROUGHTON RD

The
Laurels

Broughton Clays

4

57

Forest
Walks

Stapleford Wood

Stapleford
House

LN6

Grange Drive

Stapleford
Grange

Clay Lane

DANGER AREA

River Witham

The
Elms

3

HIGHFIELD DR

Highfield
House

Top Covert
Farm

56

DANGER AREA

Top
Covert

Stapleford Moor

Four
Acres

NG24

LN5

DANGER AREA

2

55

Vlous Dike

Hanley Farm

Whitegate
House

WOODHALL DR

SLEAFORD RD

Barnby
Manor

Rifle
Range

SLEAFORD RD

Beckingham
Training Camp

Sewage
Works

1

College
Plantation

A17

54

86

D

87

E

88

F

113

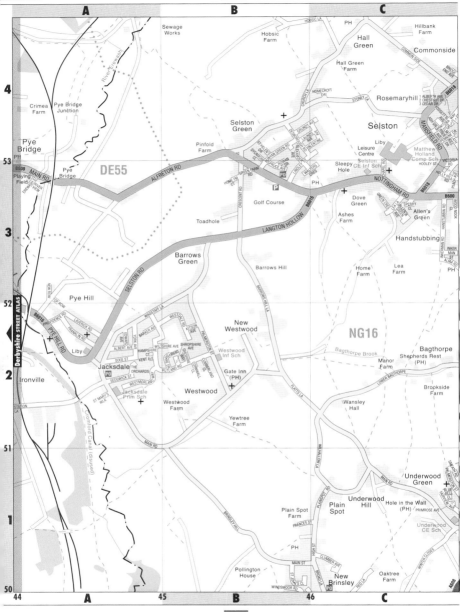

143

D E F

114 130 **129**

Kirkby
Park

Spoil Heap

Bleak Hall
Farm

Annesley
Woodhouse

Cemy

GREENHILL
LA

VICARAGE WAY

Nuncargate

Liby

PO

Kirkby
Lane
Farm

IDGE END
AVE

PARK LA

MANITOBA
WAY

CHAPEL ST

Holly Hill
Prim Sch

PO

Kirkby Park's
Farm

VICTORIA ST

NEWSTEAD CL

Salmon
Farm

DEETLETON
CL

HARDWICK
DR

UPPER
MEXBOROUGH
DR

Boggs
Farm

SALMON LA

NG17

LITTLE OAK DR

CHATSWORTH ALE

VICTORIA RD

OAKDE
GRES
HILLAND
ORES

INWOOD WAY

ANNESLEY LA

ELLAND
ORES

Two Dale
Farm

Cuttall Brook

53

Sherwood
Park

LAKE VIEW DR

Selston
Common

Annesley
Lane End

HILL FULL

Davis's
Bottom

Works

Skegness

PH
Woodnook

NOTTINGHAM RD

WILLOW DR

3

Middlebrook
Farm

Millington
Springs

Home
Farm

A608

52

Alma

ALMA RD

Middle Brook

Middlebrook
Bridge

NG16

MANSFIELD RD

27

KIRKBY LA

Audrey
Wood

WEBSTER LA

2

PH

PH

New
Bagthorpe

SCHOOL LA

MIDDLEBROOK RD

Shipton Hill
Farm

Felley Priory
Farm

William
Wood

Bagthorpe
Prim Sch

Felley Priory
Garden

Felley
Priory

NG15

Bagthorpe
Plantation

ALFRETON RD

LAWRENCE
PARK

SANDHILL
RD

CHURCH LA

OLD CHAPEL LA

BEECH RD

PH

51

DR MORGAN CL

ASHBOURNE CL

WESTBOURNE RD

B600

America
Farm

Friezeland

Felley Mill La S

The
Dumbles

BHARAAN CL

WHEELDON CL

SMALL CL

MAIN RD

PO

Pamela's
Larches

WILSON RD

Underwood

FELLEY MILL LA S

1

CORDY LA

B600

Willeylane
End

Willey
Spring

Greasley Haggs

Felley
Farm

Felley
Mill

Park
Springs

M1

50

Haggs
Farm

D E F

48 49

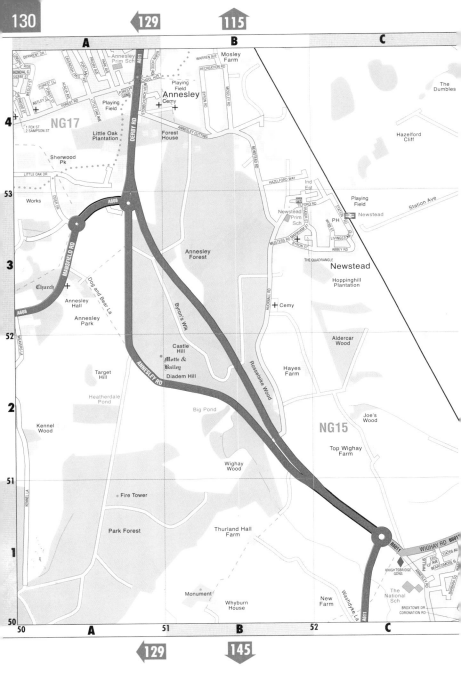

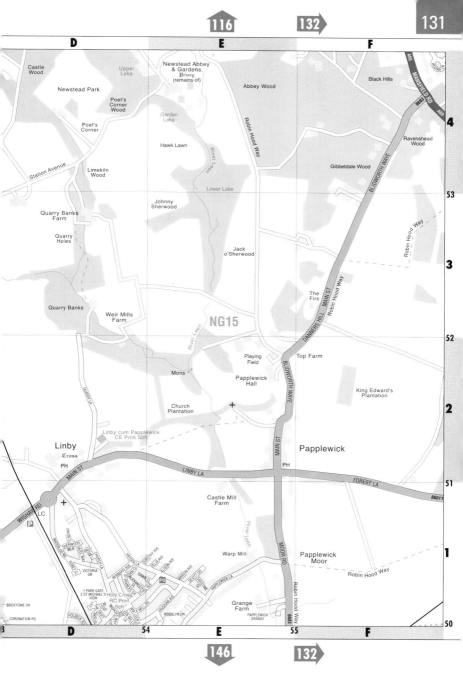

A   B   C

SANDFIELD AVE

REGINA CRES

Ravenshead
L Ctr
P

Blidworth Dale

Appleton Dale

QUARRY LN

HEATHER LA

OLD QUARRY CL

NG21

Playing
Field

Trumper's
Park

Kighill
Farm

Robin Hood Way

KIGHILL LA

GRIVES DR

4

A60

RIGG LA

P ✕

Blidworth
Lodge

53

Sand Holes

LONGDALE LA

Wildman's
Wood

Longdale
Craft Ctr &
Mus

Sand Pit

Longdale
Plantation

Robin Hood Way

3

NG15

52

Barracks
Farm

Papplewick
Pumping
Station

MANSFIELD RD

Forest Farm

Sanse
Woo

2

New
Plantation

Robin Hood Way

NG14

Vincent
Plantation

51

B6011

NG5

FOREST LA

B6011

Seven Mile
Wood

BURNTSTUMP HILL

PH

Stanker Hill
Farm

Robin Hood Way

Burntstump
Country Park

SHERWOOD LODGE DR

Seely CE
Prim Sch

A6

OLLERTON RD

Foxcover
Plantation

SCARLETT HOLLOW

1

PH

H

Park

P

Mast
Sherwood Lodge
Police HQ

Cockliffe Hill
Farm

Cockliffe
House

Sports
Ground

A614

50

Dairy
Farm

The Warren

56   A   57   B   58   C

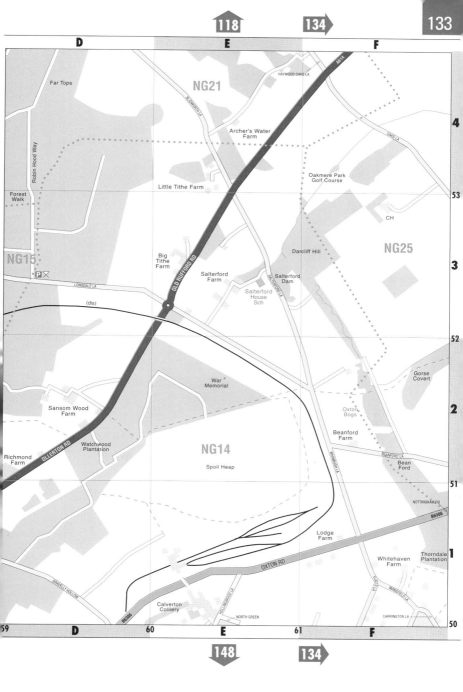

Far Tops

NG21

HAYWOOD OAKS LA

Archer's Water
Farm

OAKS LA

4

Robin Hood Way

Little Tithe Farm

Oakmere Park
Golf Course

Forest
Walk

53

NG15

CH

Big
Tithe
Farm

OLD RUFFORD RD

Darcliff Hill

NG25

P

LONGDALE LA

Salterford
Farm

Salterford
Dam

3

(dis)

Salterford
House
Sch

SALTERFORD LA

52

War
Memorial

Gorse
Covert

Sansom Wood
Farm

Oxton
Bogs

2

OLLERTON RD

Watchwood
Plantation

NG14

Beanford
Farm

BEANFORD LA

Bean
Ford

WRIGHTS LA

Richmond
Farm

Spoil Heap

NOTTINGHAM RD

51

B6386

Lodge
Farm

Thorndale
Plantation

1

OXTON RD

Whitehaven
Farm

LA 131 LA

MANSFIELD LA

BRAMLEY HOLLOW

B6386

Calverton
Colliery

HOLT HINWOOD LA

NORTH GREEN

CARRINGTON LA

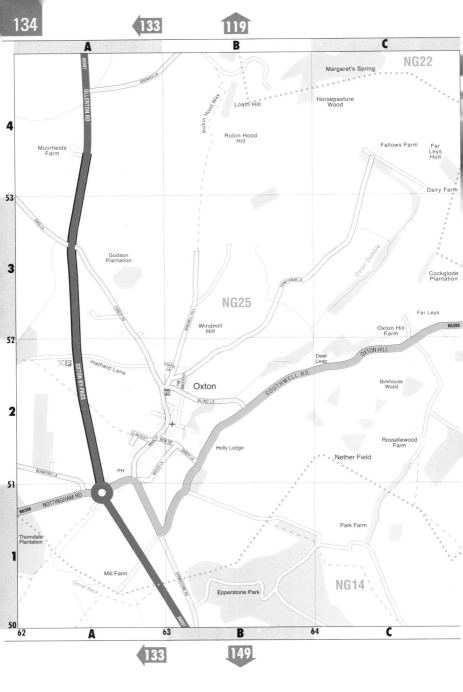

A **B** **C**

NG22

Margaret's Spring

Horsepasture
Wood

Loath Hill

Robin Hood Way

Fallows Farm

Far
Leys
Holt

4

Moorfields
Farm

Robin Hood
Hill

OLLERTON RD

A6097

GREAVES LA

Dairy Farm

53

DAIS LA

Godson
Plantation

Oxton Dumble

Cockglode
Plantation

3

NG25

CONEYKNAB LA

Far Leys

B6386

Windmill
Hill

Oxton Hill
Farm

52

FORREST RD

WINDMILL HILL

Deer
Leap

OXTON HILL

Birkhouse
Wood

Oxton By-Pass

Hatfield Lane

DRAFEL LA

THE WONGLANDS

SOUTHWELL RD

Oxton

BLIND LA

Rossellewood
Farm

2

X P

ELM-CROFT

MAIN ST

NEW RD

Holly Lodge

Nether Field

BEANFORD LA

HAZEL LA

SANDY LA

51

PH

Park Farm

B6386

NOTTINGHAM RD

Thorndale
Plantation

1

Mill Farm

EPPERSTONE RD

NG14

Dover Beck

Epperstone Park

A6097

50

62 **A** **63** **B** **64** **C**

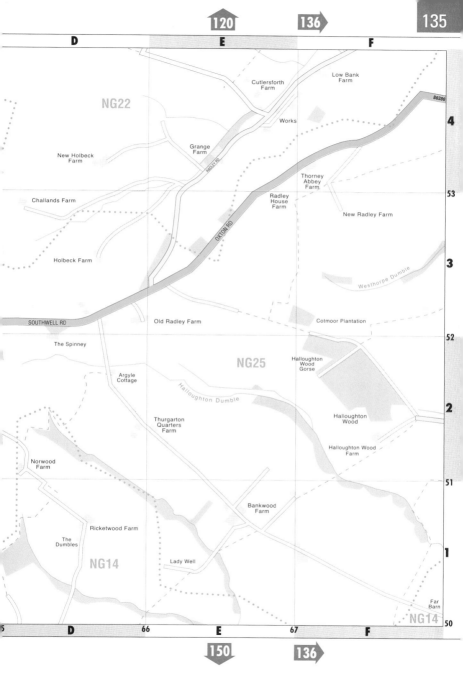

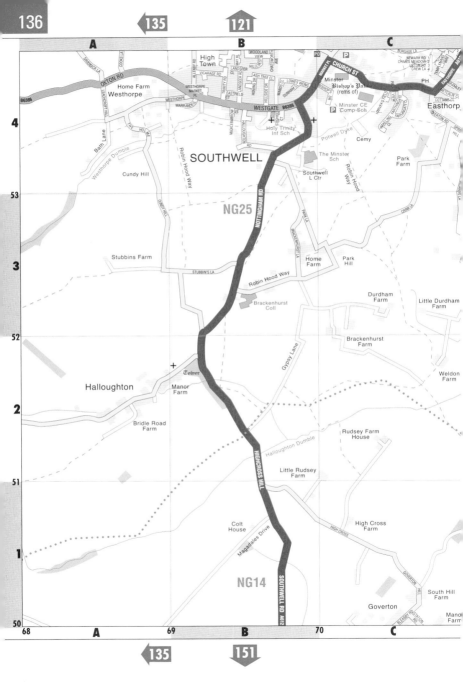

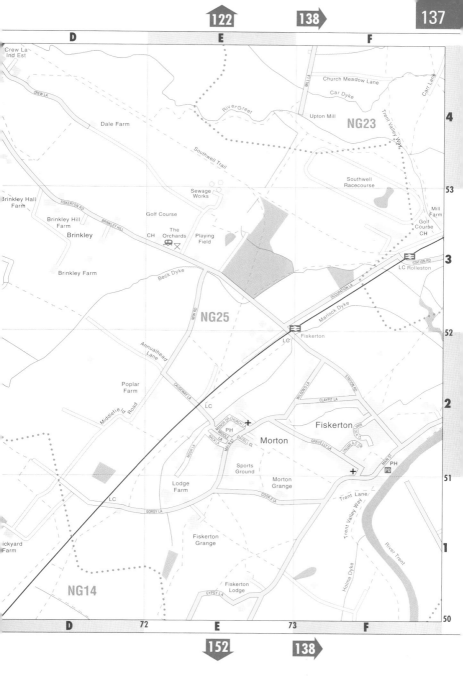

A
B
C

Staythorpe

4

Staythorpe
Power Station

PINGLEY CL

BERRY GDNS

LC

Sports
Ground

Baggerley Rack

53

LC

STAYTHORPE RD

CROFT FARM CL

MANOR
CL

CROFT CL

Greenaway

Rolleston
Gorse

LC

Moats

The Crown Inn
(PH)

3

STATION RD

Rolleston

Runtell Dyke

HOLLM...

Rolleston Field

Ferry
(foot)

The Lazy Otter
(PH)

P

SOUTH CL

WYKE LA

Norwood
Farm

FISKERTON RD

NG23

CHURCH ST

FRIENDS... CL

52

River Greet

Trent Valley Way

Swillow Lane

NG24

WYKE LA

GATE... LANE

ST PETERS...

CRESCENT RD

WEST...

Fiskerton
Mill

OLD HILL CL

2

P

MAIN ST

River Trent

NG25

51

Gawburn Nip

FOSSE RD

1

Gawburn Holt

AD PONTEM
ROMAN FORT
& SETTLEMENT

P

Wharf
Farm

Thorp

Stoke
Hall

The Park

CHURCH LA

A6

50

74
A
75
B
76
C

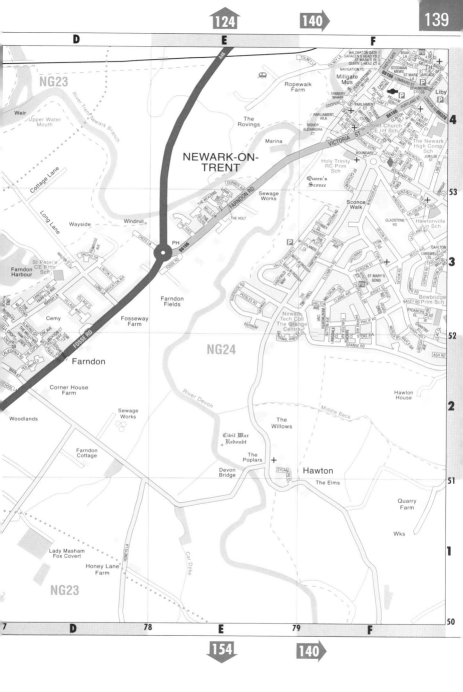

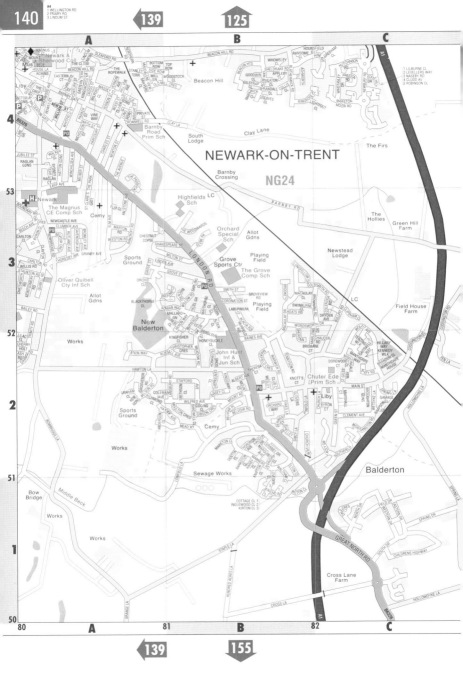

D
E
F

4

Windmill (disused)

Folly House

Hill Farm

Hilltop Farm

Coddington Plantation

Brown's Wood

Golf Course

Manor Farm

Broadsyke Lane

Corporation Plantation

Grove Farm

53

NG24

Slaney Lodge Farm

The Plots Farm

Willow Tree (PH)

Moorhouse

Willow Cottage

Moor Farm

NEWARK RD

Caxton House

BARNBY RD

The Gables

3

Chestnut House

Ivy Cottage

Grange Farm

Fen Farm

Fen Lane

Barnby in the Willows

Bleak House

52

FEN LA

Shire Dyke

2

River Witham

Witham Farm

Holm Lane

51

Holm Barn Farm

NG23

Barnby Lane

HOLM LA

Balderton Crossing

LC

BROAD FEN LA

1

HOLLOWDYKE LANE

OSTER FEN LA

D
84
E
85
F

50

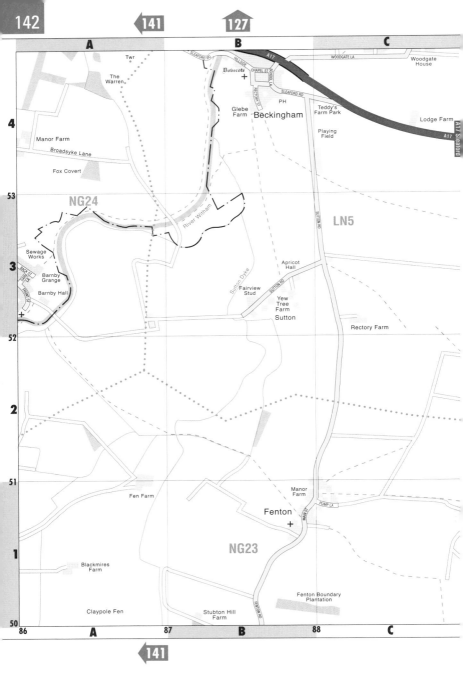

141
127

A   B   C

WOODGATE LA
Woodgate House

Twr

The Warren

Dovecote
Chapel St

SLEAFORD RD
A17

HILLSIDE
SCHOOL LA
RECTORY ST
SLEAFORD RD

PH

Glebe Farm

Beckingham

Teddy's Farm Park

A17 Sleaford

Lodge Farm

4

Manor Farm

Broadsyke Lane

Playing Field

SUTTON RD

LN5

Fox Covert

53

NG24

River Witham

Sewage Works

BACK ST
FRONT ST

Barnby Grange

Barnby Hall

Sutton Dyke

Apricot Hall

Fairview Stud

Yew Tree Farm

Sutton

SUTTON RD

Rectory Farm

3

52

2

Fen Farm

51

Manor Farm

PUMP LA

Fenton

MAIN ST

NG23

1

Blackmires Farm

FENTON RD

Fenton Boundary Plantation

Claypole Fen

Stubton Hill Farm

50

86   A   87   B   88   C

141

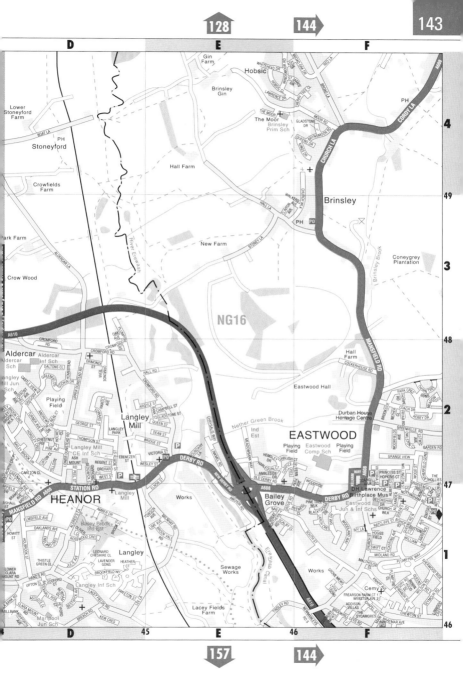

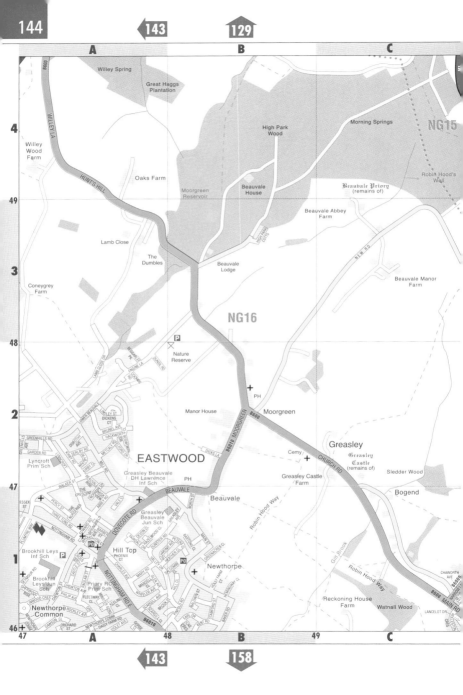

143
129

A **B** **C**

B600

Willey Spring

Great Haggs
Plantation

WILLEY LA

4

High Park
Wood

Morning Springs

NG15

Willey
Wood
Farm

HUNTS HILL

Oaks Farm

Beauvale
House

Beauvale Priory
(remains of)

Robin Hood's
Well

49

Moorgreen
Reservoir

Beauvale Abbey
Farm

NEW RD

Lamb Close

The
Dumbles

Beauvale
Lodge

HIGH PARK LOTTS

Coneygrey
Farm

3

NG16

Beauvale Manor
Farm

P

Nature
Reserve

48

WESTGATE LA

LAMB CLOSE DR

ENGINE LA

DOVECOTE RD

PH

Manor House

B6010 MOORGREEN

Moorgreen

B600

2

LOWES BEVAN
DICKENS
CT

STANLEY ST

BRUNEL AVE

HACKWORTH

EASTWOOD

Greasley

Greasley
Castle
(remains of)

Cemy

CHURCH RD

GREENHILLS RD

DOROTHY
AVE

SEALBY RD

Lyncroft
Prim Sch

GARDEN RD

DICKS LA

Sledder Wood

Greasley
Beauvale
DH Lawrence
Inf Sch

PH

Greasley Castle
Farm

Bogend

BEAUVALE

47

ESSEX
ST

THE
CRESCENT

Beauvale

NORTH ST

Greasley
Beauvale
Jun Sch

Robin Hood Way

PLUMPTRE
CL

NOTTINGHAM RD

PO

HALLWOOD CL

PETERS
CT

GREENHILLS RD

1

Brookhill Leys
Inf Sch

P

Hill Top
PHOENIX
CT

Newthorpe

Gill Brook

Robin Hood Way

CHAWORTH
AVE

Brookhill
Leys Jun
Sch

ROTTINGHAM RD E

Priory
Prim Sch

PO

MARSHALL
AVE

SCHOOL AVE

B6010 MAIN RD

B600

Newthorpe
Common

ORCHARD
ST

B6010

FLEETWAY

Reckoning House
Farm

Watnall Wood

LANCELOT DR

46

47 **A** **48** **B** **49** **C**

143
158

A   B   C

HUCKNALL

NG15

Butler's Hill

Hucknall Golf Course

Hucknall Coll

Baker Brook Ind Pk

Broomhill Park View

Forge Mill GR

Broomhill

The Bowman (PH)

Playing Field

Broomhill Farm

Allot Gdns

Hazelgrove

Butlers Hill Sch

Cemy

Park

Woodford Rd

Playing Field

Leen Valley Way

Mill Lakes Country Park

Cobbler's Hill

Westhouse Farm

Bestwood Village

Broadvalley Farm

Shaft (dis)

Bestwood Country Park

Nature Reserve

Sports Ground

The Duck Ponds

Sports Ground

Robin Hood Way

Moor Rd

River Leen

Allot Gdns

Robin Hood Way

Home Wood

Playing Field

Robin Hood Way

Bulwell Hall Park

City Golf Course

Barker's Wood

Airfield

Farley's Lane

Howden Rd

Mills

Works

NOTTINGHAM

NG6

NG5

Rise Park

Rise Park Prim Sch

Top Valley Sch Liby

Springfield Prim Sch

Hucknall La

Bestwood Rd

1 Colinwood Ave
2 Jenness Ave
3 Crowthorne Gdns
4 Houston Cl

HEXHAM GDNS 1
TITHE GDNS 2
MUIRFIELD RD 3
LYTHAM GDNS 4
MEREGILL CL 5
ECTON CL 6
TERTON RD 7
HELMSDALE GDNS 8
THOR GDNS 9
CARLSWARK GDNS 10

Nottingham Express Transit system
due to open November 2003

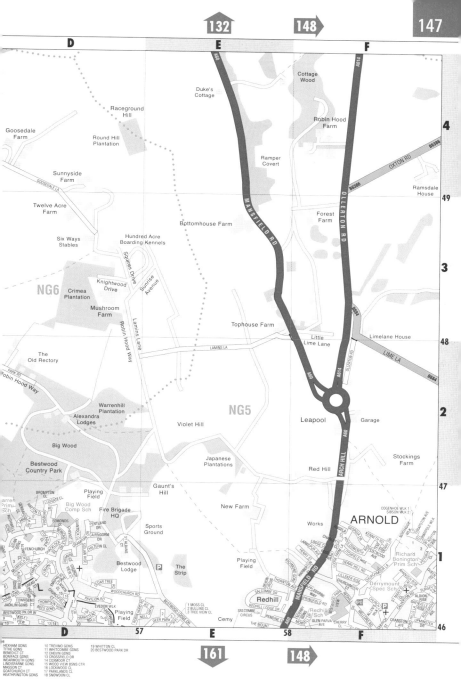

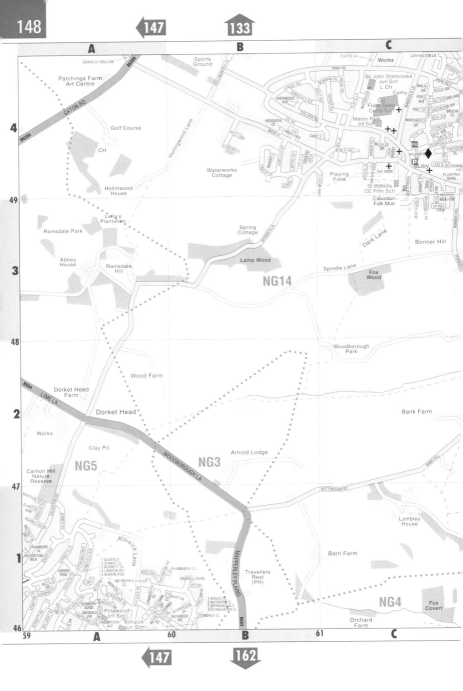

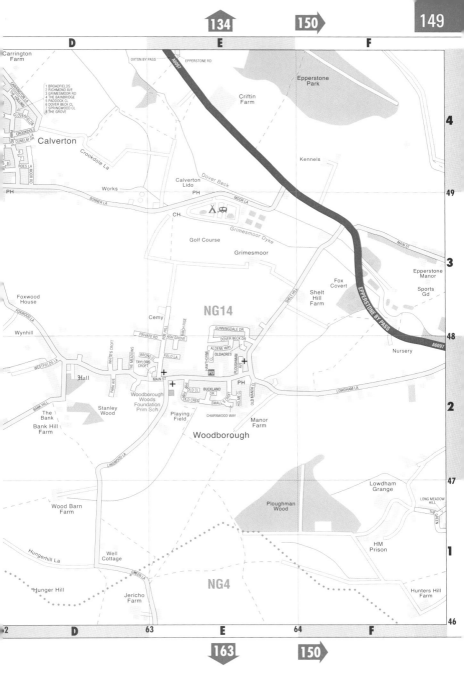

D
E
F

Carrington
Farm

OXTON BY PASS
EPPERSTONE RD

Epperstone
Park

1 BROADFIELDS
2 RICHMOND AVE
3 GRIMESMOOR RD
4 THE BAINBRIDGE
5 PADDOCK CL
6 DOVER BECK CL
7 SPRINGWOOD CL
8 THE GROVE

Criftin
Farm

4

Calverton

CROOKDOLE LA

Crookdole La

Kennels

Calverton
Lido

Dover Beck

PH

Works

BONNER LA

MOOR LA

PH

49

CH

Grimesmoor Dyke

Golf Course

Grimesmoor

MAIN ST

3

Epperstone
Manor

Foxwood
House

Fox
Covert

Sports
Gd

FOXWOOD LA

NG14

SHELT HILL

Shelt
Hill
Farm

Wynhill

Cemy

SUNNINGDALE DR

EPPERSTONE BY PASS

A6097

WESTFIELDS LA

PRIVATE RD

ASH GROVE

RIVER RISE

DOVER BECK DR

48

BANK AVE

WHITE'S CROFT

THE MEADOWS

BROAD
HILL

TAYLORS
CROFT

FIELD LA

ALDENE WAY

OLDACRES

HAWTHORNE

PLOUGHMAN AVE

Nursery

BANK HILL

Hall

MAIN ST

BUCKLAND

PH

LOWDHAM LA

OLD MANOR CL

2

Stanley
Wood

Woodborough
Woods Foundation
Prim Sch

OLD CL
OLD CRES

SMALL'S

HOLME CL

The
Bank

Playing
Field

CHARNWOOD WAY

Manor
Farm

Bank Hill
Farm

Woodborough

LINGWOOD LA

47

Wood Barn
Farm

Ploughman
Wood

Lowdham
Grange

LONG MEADOW
HILL

THE GREEN

Well
Cottage

HM
Prison

1

Hungerhill La

GREEN LA

NG4

Hunger Hill

Jericho
Farm

Hunters Hill
Farm

46

D
63
E
64
F

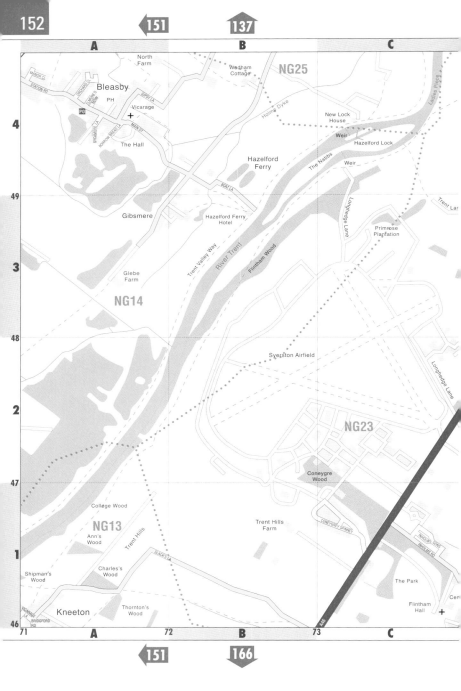

NG25

North Farm

Wadham Cottage

Holme Dyke

New Lock House

Ladies Piece

MANOR CL
ORCHARD CL
STATION RD
Bleasby
ELM'S TING
PH
GIPSY LA
Vicarage
PO
LA THOMPSONS
BORROW BREAD CL
Weir
Hazelford Lock
The Hall
MAIN ST
Hazelford Ferry
The Nabbs
Weir
Trent Lar

4

BOAT LA

49

Gibsmere
Hazelford Ferry Hotel
Longhedge Lane
Primrose Plantation

Trent Valley Way
River Trent
Flintham Wood

3

Glebe Farm

NG14

48

Syerston Airfield
Longhedge Lane

2

NG23

47

Coneygre Wood

College Wood

NG13
Ann's Wood
Trent Hills
Trent Hills Farm
CONEYGREY SPINNEY
BINGHAM RD

1

SLACK'S LA

Shipman's Wood
Charles's Wood
The Park

Flintham Hall

VICARAGE LA
BRIDGFORD RD
Kneeton
Thornton's Wood

46

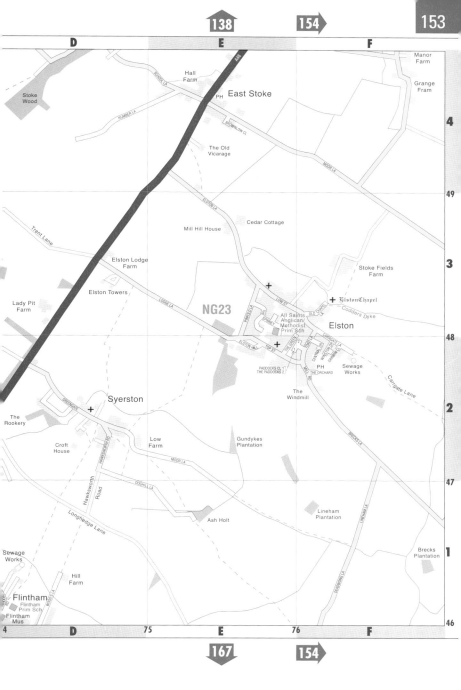

D
E
F

Manor Farm

Hall Farm

Stoke Wood

PH   East Stoke

Grange Fram

SCHOOL LA

A46

4

HUMBER LA

BROWNLOW CL

The Old Vicarage

MOOR LA

49

Trent Lane

ELSTON LA

Cedar Cottage

Mill Hill House

Elston Lodge Farm

Stoke Fields Farm

3

Elston Towers

LODGE LA

NG23

Elston Chapel

Codders Dyke

Lady Pit Farm

LOW ST

OLD CHAPEL

CARTGATE LA

All Saints Anglican/ Methodist Prim Sch

Elston

PRINCE LA

48

ELSTON WAY

TOP ST

PINFOLD LA

CENTRAL DR

LING CL

CHURCH ST

WALSTON'S CL

PH

Cartgate Lane

MILL RD

THE ORCHARD

Sewage Works

PADDOCKS CL 1
THE PADDOCKS 2

The Windmill

GREENDALE

Syerston

BRECKS LA

2

The Rookery

HAWKSWORTH RD

Low Farm

Gundykes Plantation

Croft House

MOOR LA

DOGHILL LA

47

Hawksworth Road

LINEHAM LA

Lineham Plantation

Longhedge Lane

Ash Holt

Brecks Plantation

1

Sewage Works

Hill Farm

DICKMANS LA

Flintham
Flintham Prim Sch
Flintham Mus

46

D   75   E   76   F

A

B

C

4

THORPE LA

Thorpe
Lodge

49

Honies Farm

Car Dyke

3

MOOR LA

NG24

The
Grange

48

River Devon

Manor
Farm

Fox Covert

The Old
Hall Farm

Cotham

2

NG23

Meadow Farm

CROSS LA

Carrgate Lane

Devon Farm

LING LANE

47

Back Dyke

1

Grange Farm

BRECKS LA

Elston
Grange

Station
House

46

77

A

78

B

79

C

140
156

D   E   F

Hundred Acres Lane

Staple Farm

NG24

4

49

Balderton Grange

Cowtham House

Shire Bridge

3

Holmes Farm

Shirebridge Farm

Shire Dyke

Bennington Fen

48

GRANGE LA

Fen Farm

Cotham Thorns

2

Willow Tree Farm

FEN LA

Fen Lane Farms

NG23

47

Red House Farm

Pasture Lodge Farm

Cotham Buildings

Askerton Hill

Bennington Lodge Farm

1

White House Farm

Valley Lane Cottages

VALLEY LA

Middle Farm

Stonepit Plantation

0   D   81   E   82   F   46

GREAT NORTH RD

A1

B6326

169
156

NG24

Balderfields
Sewage
Works

4 Balderfield

BROAD FEN LA

Piggery

SHIRE LA

Well Fen Lane

Liberty Gates
Crossing   LC

Claypole

Cross Lane

Brunts
Farm

Playing
Field

Claypole
CE Prim
Sch

WELL FEN LA
CHAPEL LA
SCOTTS LA
SMITH FIELD CL
KENNEDY CL

Witham View

49

GRETTON
CL

Claypole
Bridge

TOWN ST

PH

MOORS
CL

Mill Road

3

Mill
Farm

48 Weir

River Witham

NG23

Sandhills

STUBTON RD

Hough Lane

LC

LC

DRYFIELD LA

OSIER RD

LC

HINGLEY CL

KA DODDINGTON

2

Holmes Lane

The
Willows

Doddington
Bridge

47

DODDINGTON LA

Bridge Farm

A1

GREAT NORTH ROAD

1

Syke Lane

A1

The Wheatsheaf
(PH)

Manor
Farm

MAIN ST

MANOR HOUSE LA
CLAYPOLE LA
GREEN LA

Long Lane

Red
House
Farm

Coach Road

DENNETT LA

HOUGHAM RD

Dry Doddington

Hill Farm

46 A1 Grantham
83   A   84   B   85   C

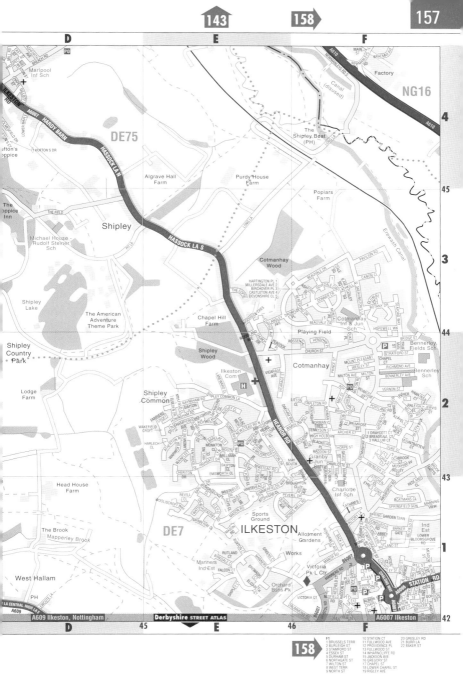

NG16

DE75

Marlpool Inf Sch

Canal (disused)

Factory

Main St

BRAEMAR DR

A610

NORMANTON RD

A610

HARDY BARN

A6007

Lifton's Coppice

THORNTON'S DR

The Shipley Boat (PH)

HASSOCK LA N

Algrave Hall Farm

Purdy House Farm

Poplars Farm

Erewash Canal

The Coppice Inn

THE FIELD

Shipley

HASSOCK LA S

Cotmanhay Wood

Michael House Rudolf Steiner Sch

PIT LA

Shipley Lake

The American Adventure Theme Park

Chapel Hill Farm

HARTINGTON PL 1
MILLERSDALE AVE 2
BIRCHOVER PL 3
CASTLETON AVE 4
DEVONSHIRE CL 5

Cotmanhay Inf & Jun Sch

HOPEWELL WK

Playing Field

Bennerley Fields Sch

Shipley Country Park

Shipley Wood

Ilkeston Com

H

Cotmanhay

Bennerley Sch

Lodge Farm

Shipley Common

ILKESTON COMMON LA

WAKEFIELD CROFT

HARLECH CL

LITTON CL

NEWDIGATE RD

Head House Farm

MONKTON CL

MILLBANK

SKIPTON

CHERITON DR

EMSWORTH CL

REVILL CL

WESTFIELD

Granby Jun

MAY ST BOOTH ST

CHARLOTTE ST

Charlotte Inf Sch

BOATMANS CL

SPRINGFIELD GDN

MANNING VIEW

SPRING GARDEN TERR

BARKER GATE

Ind Est

LOWER BLOOMSGROVE RD

DE7

The Brook

Mapperley Brook

ILKESTON

Sports Ground

Allotment Gardens

Works

RUTLAND ST

West Hallam

PH

Mariners Ind Est

FALCON CL

Victoria Pk L Ctr

Orchard Bsns Pk

VICTORIA GT

MANNERS RD

A6007

STATION RD

CHAUCER ST

ALBION ST

LA CENTRAL HIGH LA E

A609

F1
1 BRUSSELS TERR
2 BURLEIGH ST
3 STAMFORD ST
4 ESSEX ST
5 DURHAM ST
6 NORTHGATE ST
7 WILTON ST
8 WEST TERR
9 NORTH ST
10 STATION CT
11 FULLWOOD AVE
12 PROVIDENCE ST
13 FULLWOOD ST
14 WHARNCLIFFE RD
15 JACKSON AVE
16 GREGORY ST
17 CHAPEL ST
18 LOWER CHAPEL ST
19 RIGLEY AVE
20 GRESLEY RD
21 BURR LA
22 BAKER ST

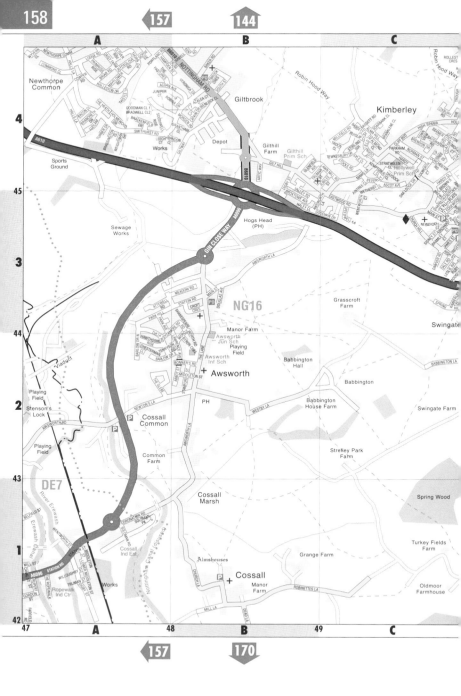

A   B   C

Newthorpe
Common

NOTTINGHAM RD

Giltbrook

Robin Hood Way

ROLLEST
CRES

Robin Hood Way

Kimberley

4

A610

JUNIPER
CT

GOODMAN CL 1
BRADWELL CL2

SMITHURST RD

Works

Depot

Gilthill
Farm

Gilthill
Prim Sch

Gilthill
Farm

STRATHGLEN
CT Hollywell
Prim Sch

P

Sports
Ground

B6010

45

Sewage
Works

GIN CLOSE WAY

A6096

Hogs Head
(PH)

AWSWORTH LA

3

MEADOW RD

STATION RD

CROFT
CRES

P

NG16

Grasscroft
Farm

Swingate

Manor Farm

Awsworth
Jun Sch
Playing
Field

Awsworth
Inf Sch

Awsworth

Babbington
Hall

Babbington

44

Viaduct

PH

Cossall
Common

WESTBY LA

Babbington
House Farm

Swingate Farm

2

Playing
Field

Stenson's
Lock

AWSWORTH RD

P

P

Common
Farm

Streley Park
Farm

Playing
Field

43

DE7

River Erewash

Cossall
Marsh

Spring Wood

CORONATION RD

SOLOMAN RD

1

MILL ST

A6096 STATION RD

WILLOUGHBY ST

TRIUMAN

Works

Cossall
Ind Est

Ropewalk
Ind Ctr

Nottingham Canal (disused)

Almshouses

CHURCH LA

BEAD LA

P

Cossall

Manor
Farm

ROBINETTES LA

MILL LA

Grange Farm

Turkey Fields
Farm

Oldmoor
Farmhouse

42

47   A   48   B   49   C

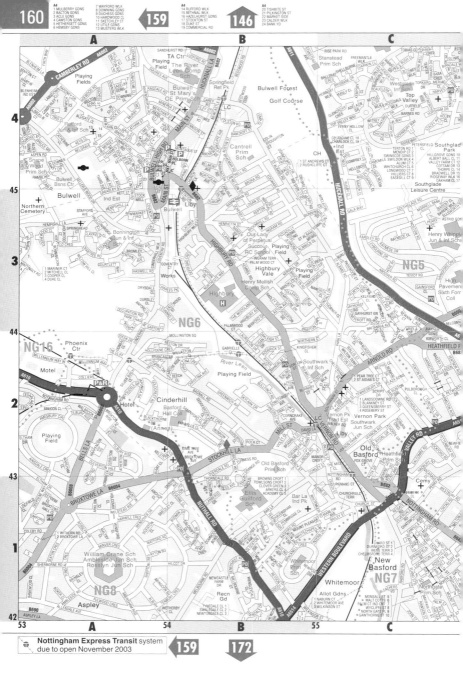

160

A4
1 MULBERRY GDNS
2 BACTON GDNS
3 ACLE GDNS
4 CAWSTON GDNS
5 HETHERSETT GDNS
6 HEMSBY GDNS

7 WAYFORD WLK
8 DOWNING GDNS
9 DUCHESS GDNS
10 HARDWORD CL
11 SKETCHLEY CT
12 LITLE GDNS
13 MUSTERS WLK

159

A4
14 RUFFORD WLK
15 BETHNAL WLK
16 HAZELHURST GDNS
17 STOCKTON ST
18 DUKE ST
19 COMMERCIAL RD

146

A4
20 TISHBITE ST
21 PILKINGTON ST
22 MARKET SIDE
23 CALDER WLK
24 BANK YD

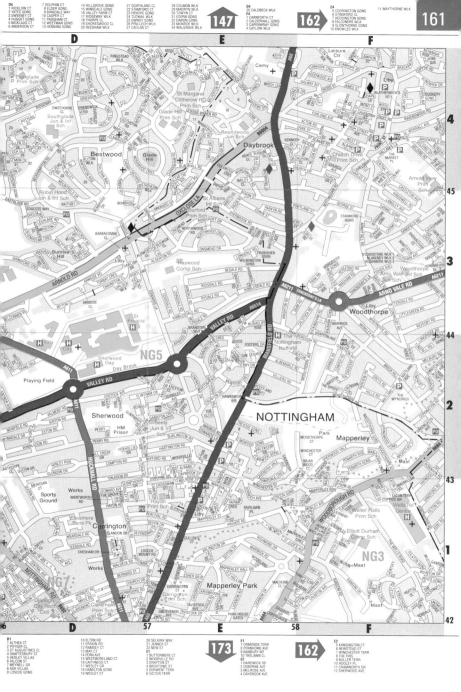

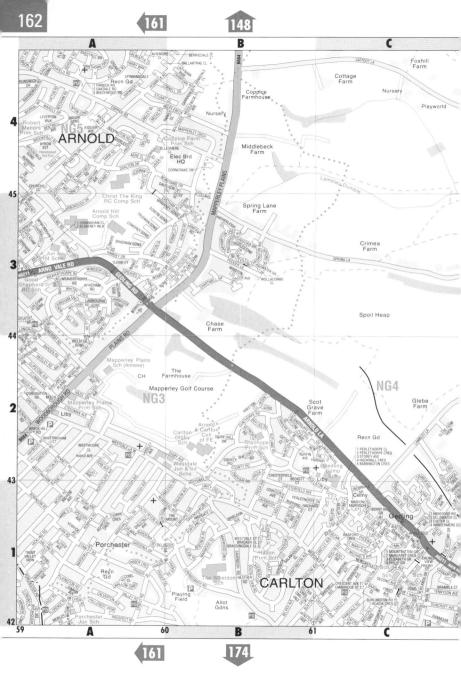

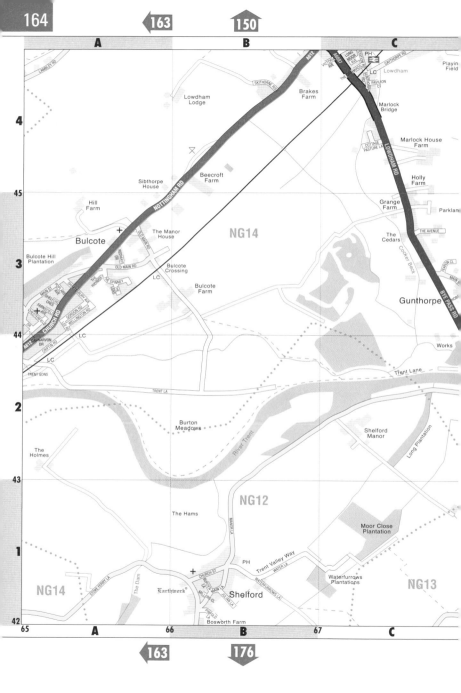

D **E** **F**

HOLME LA

The Old
Vicarage

Manor
House

Caythorpe

Brackenhill

Fernhill
House

Toot Hill

Black Horse
(PH)

HOVERINGHAM RD

Cat Dyke

Caythorpe
House

Watson's
Piece

4

Topfield
Farm

Old Hill

45

NG14

Peck Lane

Bungalow
Farm

Old Hill
Farm

Glebe
Farm

Glebe
Farm

Trent Valley Way

River Trent

Oldhill Lane

Trent Hills

BRAMLEY
CL

3

HOBSON'S
ACRE

Playing
Field

Windmill
(disused)

Mill
Farm

THORPE LEA
ORCHARD DR

STAG CL

Hall

Guntthorpe CE
Prim Sch

BROOK
END

LANE

Occupation Lane

Kneeton Rd

SCHOOL LA

NG13

44

PH

TRENTSIDE

Lock

Manor
Farm

Allotment
Gardens

LANGAR LA

BY PASS RD

Weir

TRENT LA

The
Moorings

MAGSON
CLOSE

DEWBERRY
LA

LAMCOTE
GDNS

CHURCH LA LA

East
Bridgford

2

Works

Cuttle
Hill

PH

CLOSE

HACKERS LA

BROWN'S LA

MILL
FIELDS

Sandfield
House

CLOSES SIDE LA

CASTLE HILL
GDNS

St Peter's
CE Prim Sch

CROSSWAYS

CL

Hill
Farm

PH

BROOKS LA

BRIDLE WAYS

43

KIRK HILL

MAIN ST

FARM LA

BUTT LA

FETTINMAN
LA

A46

LEICESTER
CL

P

Brigdford Street

Trent Valley Way

BURNHAM
CL

SPRINGDALE LA

The
Bungalow

Toll Bar
Farm

BRUNTS LA

Sewage
Works

1

Mill
Farm

A46

A46

Burrow
Fields

Bryejak
House

Woodside
Farm

42

68 **D** **69** **E** **70** **F**

D
E
F

SPRING LA
WELL LA
PH
MAIN ST
Hill Top Farm
TOWN END LA
Longhedge Lane

BESTHORPE RD
Manor Farm
Earthwork
MAIN ST
Sibthorpe
Dovecote
Baxter Lane

4

NG23

Back Dyke

Flintham Grange Farm

CHURCH LA
Top Green

* Moats

Blackford Bridge

NEWFIELD LA

45

CARDGESIDE LA

Portland Oaks

3

Back Dyke

44

Hawksworth

Works

2

HAWKSWORTH RD

NEW DU
The Gutter

Car Dyke Bridge

Yew Tree Farm

TOWN ST

Car Dyke

Manor Farm

NG13

43

The Old Glebe

Scarrington House

+ Thoroton

1

River Smite

Inkerman Plantation

Hall Farm

Holly Farm

42

4
D
75
E
76
F

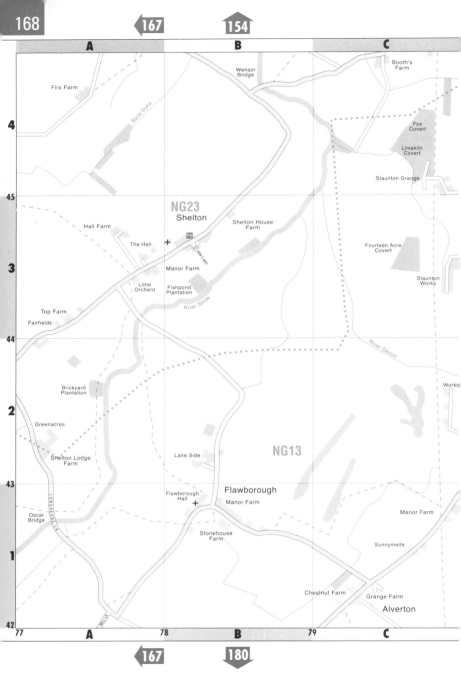

D
E
F

4

45

Costa Hill

3

NG23

44

NG13

2

43

1

42

D
81
E
82
F

Back Dyke

ig Sykes Covert

FER LA

VALLEY LA

Moor Drain

Moor Lane

MOOR LA

Authorpe Farm

Charlton Farm

HIGH ST

Chapelside Farm

Staunton Arms (PH)

Riverside Cottages

Staunton in the Vale

Staunton Park

Jubilee Plantation

Folly Hill

Folly Hill

Follyhill Cottage

NEW RD

VALLEY LA

Staunton Hall

The Rookery

Mar Plantation

The Old Rectory

Kilvington

Waterloo Plantation

Three Shire Oak

Normanton Thorns

Three Shires Farm

Winter Beck

River Devon

Willow Farm

Normanton Lodge

Airfield (disused)

Rowe Farm

Rowe Farm

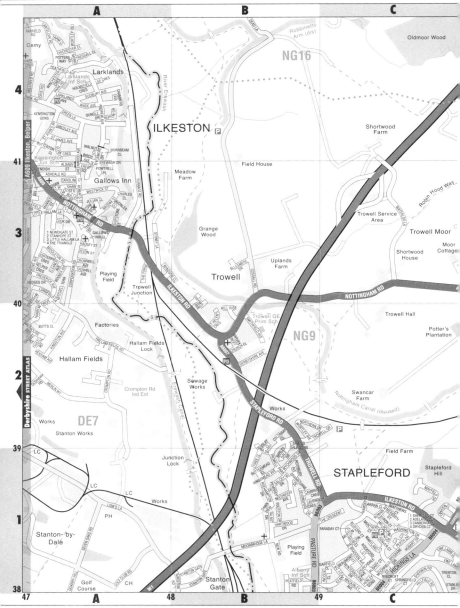

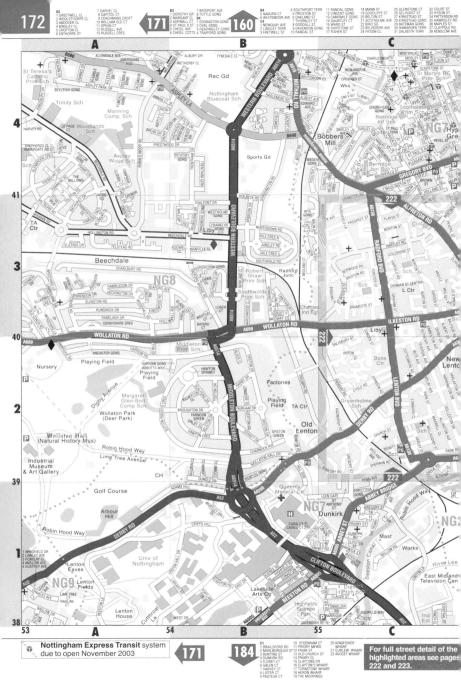

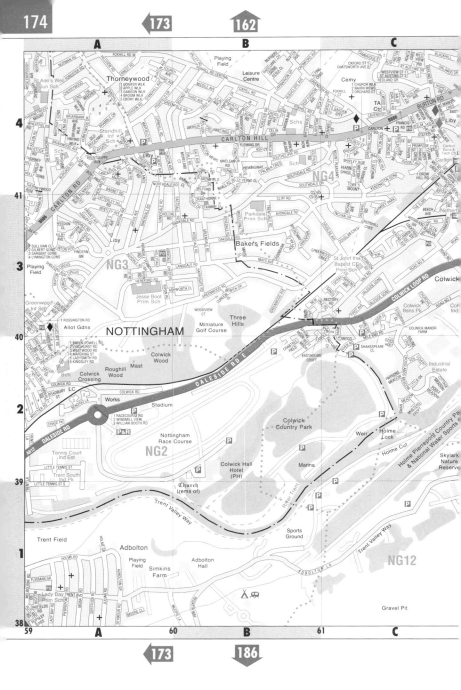

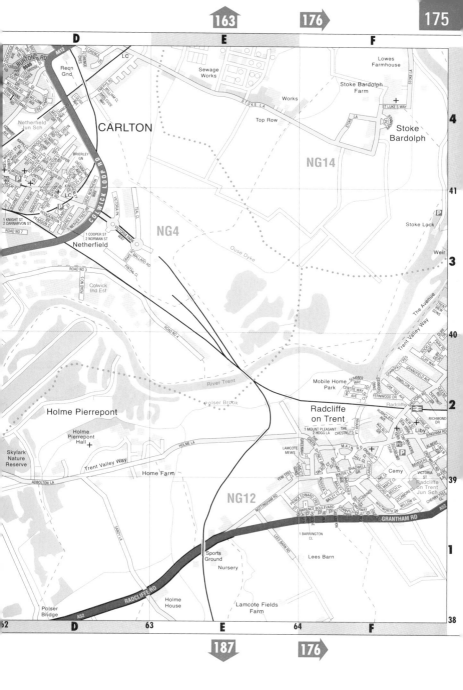

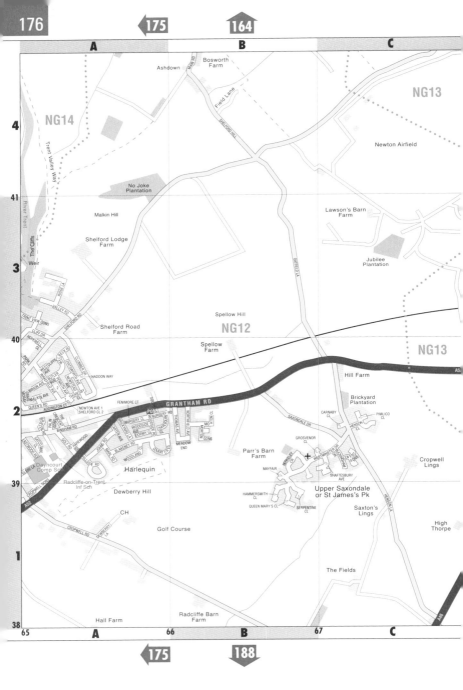

175
164

A **B** **C**

4

NG14

NG13

Ashdown

Bosworth Farm

Field Lane

Newton Airfield

41

Trent Valley Way

No Joke Plantation

Malkin Hill

Lawson's Barn Farm

River Trent

Shelford Lodge Farm

Jubilee Plantation

3

The Cliffs

Weir

Spellow Hill

Shelford Road Farm

NG12

40

Spellow Farm

NG13

HADDON WAY

Hill Farm

2

GRANTHAM RD

Brickyard Plantation

CARNABY CL

PIMLICO CL

HENDON CL

FENIMORE CT

NEWTON AVE 1
SHELFORD CL 2

SAXONDALE DR

NURSERY CL

THOMAS AVE

NORTHFIELD RD

MO TH

MO TH

BINGHAM RD

GROSVENOR CL

WOODSIDE RD

FORMIT CL

SGNS

BLAKENEY RD

WESTMINSTER DR

LINCOLN AVE

GDNS

Parr's Barn Farm

MEADOW END

Cropwell Lings

MEWS

EAST HOUSES

WOODLAND

Harlequin

MAYFAIR

SHAFTESBURY AVE

Upper Saxondale or St James's Pk

GLEBE LA

Dayncourt Comp Sch

Radcliffe-on-Trent Inf Sch

39

HAMMERSMITH CL

Saxton's Lings

CROPWELL RD

QUEEN MARY'S CL

SERPENTINE CL

High Thorpe

Dewberry Hill

CH

Golf Course

The Fields

1

38

Hall Farm

Radcliffe Barn Farm

65 **A** **66** **B** **67** **C**

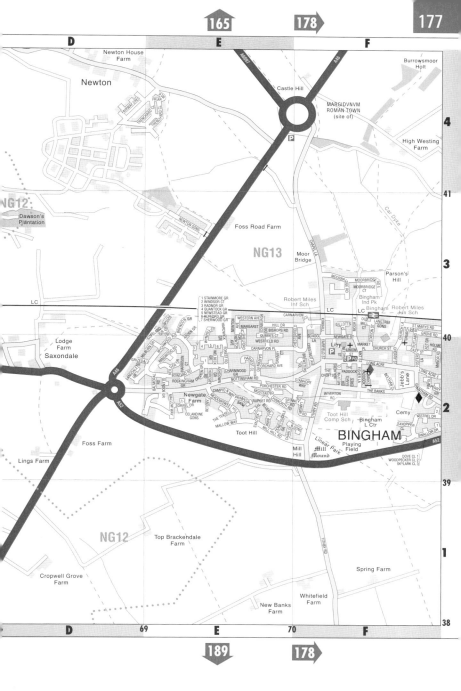

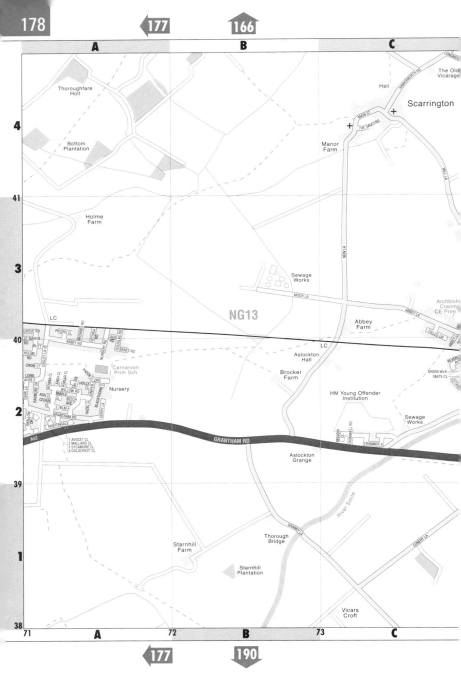

4

41

3

40

2

39

1

38

Thoroughfare Holt

Bottom Plantation

Holme Farm

LC

NG13

Sewage Works

Manor Farm

Hall

Scarrington

The Old Vicarage

Archbishop Cranmer CE Prim

Abbey Farm

GROVE RD
ST MARYS RD
BUTT RD
HOLME RD
CROW CT
LONG ACRE E

PRIORS CL
ABBEY RD

NURSERY RD
DOUGLAS RD
D BANES RD

Carnarvon Prim Sch

Nursery

ASKEW CL
CARDIL CL
TOPHAM CL
WILLOW RD
ASH CL
CEDAR
ELM A
MAPLE
BEECH AVE
HAZEL CL
HOLLY CL
BLACKTHORN
DERRY LA

DARK LA
RAYMOND DR
NIGHTINGALE
GRANTHAM RD

A52

1 AVOCET CL
2 MALLARD CL
3 SYCAMORE CL
4 GOLDCREST CL

GRANTHAM RD

Aslockton Hall

Brocker Farm

HM Young Offender Institution

Sewage Works

Aslockton Grange

GREEN WLK
SMITE CL

BELVOIR
CROMWELL RD
CRAMER A

Starnhill Farm

Thorough Bridge

Starnhill Plantation

Vicars Croft

River Smite

GRANBY LA

GONERBY LA

MAIN ST
THE SAUCERS
HAWKSWORTH RD
LONGHEDGE
NEW LA
MOOR LA
ABBEY LA
FIELD VIEW DR
MILL LA

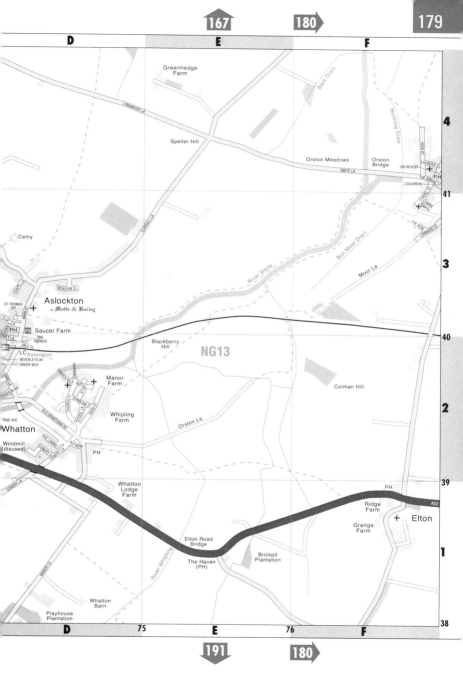

D
E
F

4

41

3

40

2

39

1

38

Greenhedge
Farm

Speller Hill

Orston Meadows

Orston
Bridge

LONGMOOR LA

Back Drain

Northing Drain

HIGH ST

CHURCH ST

SMITE LA

THE GREEN

LOUGHBON

PH

LAUNDER ST

CHAPEL SMITH

THE ROW

LOMBARD ST

Bon Moor Drain

River Smite

Moor La

Cemy

MEADOW CL

CHAPEL LA

MAIN ST

Aslockton

St Thomas
Dr

Motte & Bailey

Saucer Farm

THE SIDINGS

VALE CL

Blackberry
Hill

NG13

Colman Hill

LC Aslockton

BEVERLEYS AV

GREEN WLK

PH

RIVERSIDE

CHURCH WLK

SURF

SCHOOL LA

SUMNER ST

MAIN ST

Manor
Farm

MOOR RD

OLD GRANTHAM RD

TAGE AVE

Whatton

Windmill
(disused)

THE LANINGS

CONERY CT

CONERY LA

IVY ROW

PH

Whipling
Farm

Orston La

Whatton
Lodge
Farm

PH

A52

Ridge
Farm

Elton

MANOR LA

CONERY LA

Elton Road
Bridge

River Whipling

The Haven
(PH)

Brickpit
Plantation

Grange
Farm

Whatton
Barn

Playhouse
Plantation

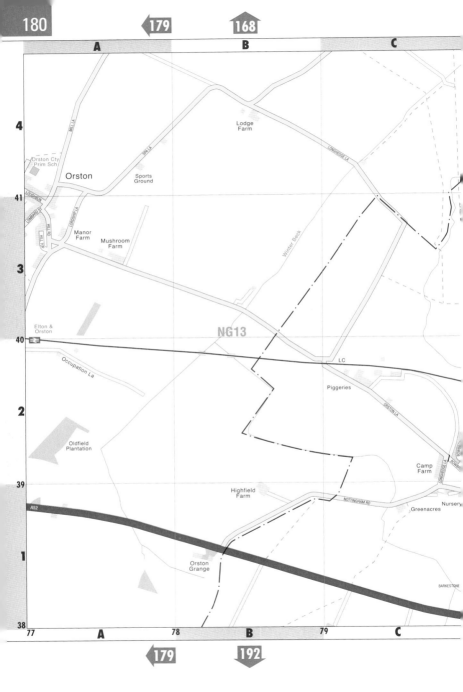

A   B   C

4

Lodge
Farm

LONGHEDGE LA

MILL LA

SPA LA

Orston Cty
Prim Sch

Orston

Sports
Ground

41

LOUGHBON

LOMBARD ST

HILL RD

PK BRIGHT ST

Manor
Farm

Mushroom
Farm

Winter Beck

3

Elton &
Orston

NG13

40

Occupation La

LC

Piggeries

ORSTON LA

2

Oldfield
Plantation

Camp
Farm

LONGHEDGE LA

39

Highfield
Farm

NOTTINGHAM RD

Greenacres

Nursery

A52

1

Orston
Grange

BARKESTONE

38

D E F

4

River Devon

Piggery

Airfield
(disused)

NG23

41

Normanton
Hall

Normanton
House

Peacock
Farm

3

Little Covert
Farm

Normanton

Elm Farm

Home Farm

NG13

40

Sewage
Works

Beacon Hill

2

LC

Rectory
Farm
The
ook

Beckingthorpe

LC
Bottesford

Works

Bottesford

Ford

DEVON LA
STROUD
CT

WYGGESTON
AVE

FLEMING AVE

RUTLAND LA

39

1 WEST END CL
2 NOTTINGHAM RD
3 BOWBRIDGE LA

PO
PH

HAND'S
WLK

ST MARY'S LA

LASTHORPE VIEW

South
View

GRANTHAM RD

WALNUT
RD

SILVERWOOD RD

The
Elms

Manor
Farm

MANOR RD

Easthorpe

River Devon

1

Bottesford
CE Prim Sch

Belvoir
High Sch

JAY'S
CL

BELVOIR AVE

GREEN LA

HOWITT'S RD

Castleview
Farm

CASTLE VIEW RD

MUSTON LA

Corner
Farm

Hospital Muston
Farm

A52

Winterbeck
Bridge

A52

CASTLE VIEW RD

EASTHORPE LA

A52 Grantham

38

0 D 81 E 82 F

Leicestershire STREET ATLAS

170

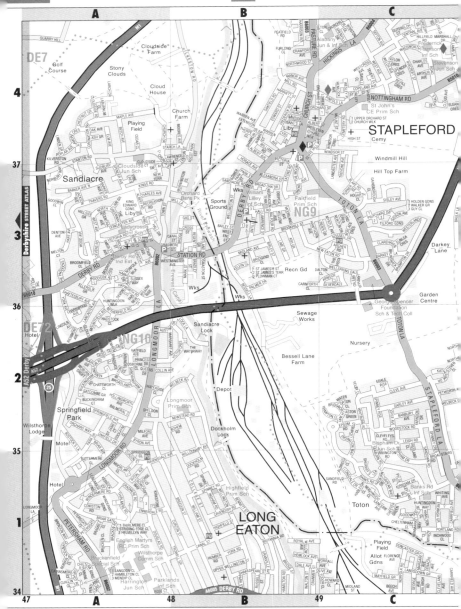

193

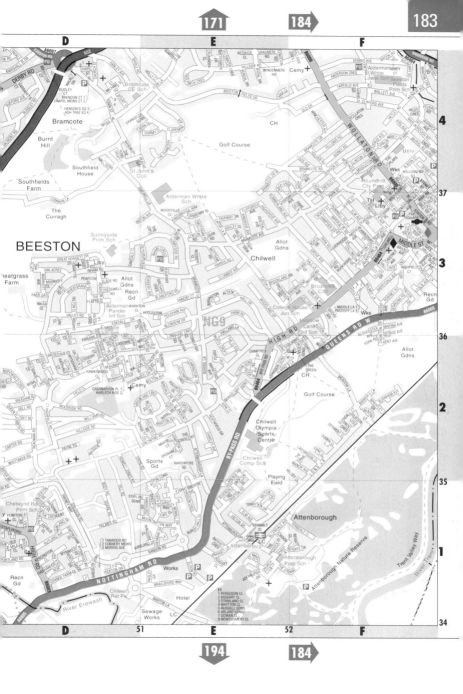

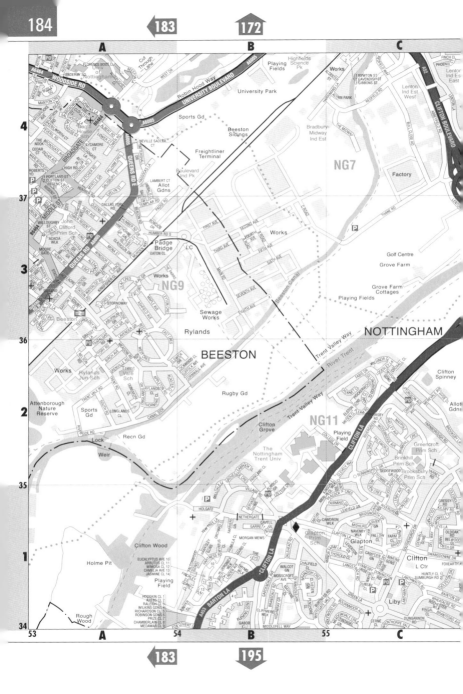

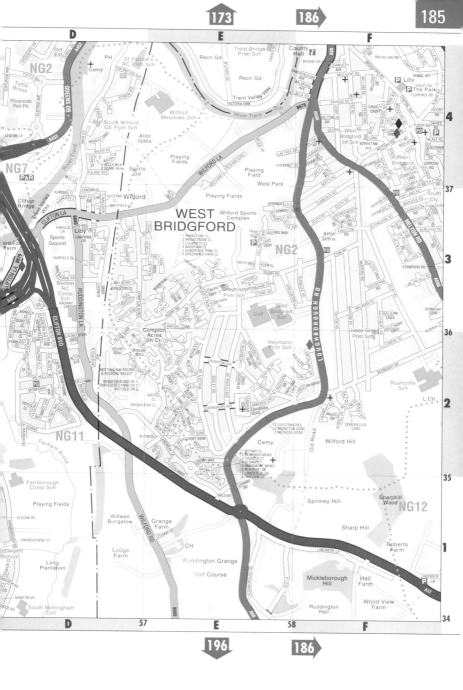

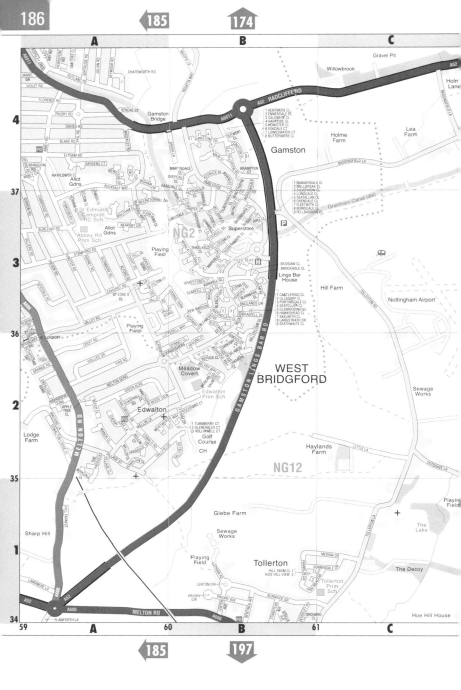

D
E
F

RADCLIFFE RD A52

Holme Pierrepont
CE Sch

NORTHANS LA

4

Bassingfield

Potter Brook

Shepherd's
(PH)

Thornton's Holt
Farm

Sewage
Works

North Farm

Nursery

37

Cotgrave
Place

Grantham Canal (dis)

Cotgrave
Bridge

3

NG12

Peashill Farm

Thurlbeck Dyke

Windmill Hill

36

Sewage
Works

MILLERS HIVES CL

CHICHESTER DR
MOSKINSHIRE CRES

THE OLD
PARK

THE PARK
PINFOLD CL

MILL
MONKINSHIRE
LA
THE FARM CL

EAST RD
CROSS LA

HOLLYGATE CL
GATE

2

HALLS DYKE

CHURCH LA
CROSS

PH
CANDLEBY
CT

BINGHAM RD

COTGRAVE
GATE

THE
PRECINCT
AVONDALE

SCOTLAND
BANK
Liby

ALL
CANDLEBY LA

BARKER HILL LA

RECTORY RD

BROOKGATE CL

Cemy

Sch

BOSTOCK

SEVEN OAKS

CANDLEBY CL

Manvers
Jun Sch

LAMPLANDS

FOSTER

Schs
GREENFIELDS DR
Ash Lea
Special Sch

35

PLUMTREE RD

Cotgrave

WHITE FURROWS

ASH LEA CL

PLUMTREE RD

ASHWORTH
RING LEAS
PARTRIDGE

WOODVIEW

HARTMOOR

WOODGATE

MANNE LEYS

CORN
CL

DALE
CL
WESTRAY

ASHMORE

BRIARWOOD
ASHGROVE

BISHOPS COMM

MILLERS BRIDGE
INGLEBY CL 2

TOFT CL

THE DALES

BONNY MEAD

THE WARREN

SAXON RD

COLSTON CRES

1

COTGRAVE LA

COTGRAVE RD

ollerton
Wood

Hoehill Farm

Clipston

Manor
Farm

Blackberry
Farm

Wolds La

CHURCH GATE

CHURCH GATE

Mill Lane

Brickyard
Plantation

Scotton's
Hill

34

D
63
E
64
F

D
E
F

Newlands

MARGATE RD

GRANBY

RADCLIFFE RD

Cropwell Butler

MAIN ST

BACK LA

OLD SCHOOL HOUSE CL

PH
CARPENTERS CL
THE POSTS
CARPENTERS CL

BUTLER CL

HOE LA

Lower
Brackendale
Farm

NG13

Cemy

TITHBY RD

CROPWELL BISHOP RD

Manor
Farm

Tithby

Holly
Tree
Farm

37

Wiverton
Hall
Farm

GRANTHAM RD

4

3

New
Plantation

Sewage
Works

Meadow Lane

36

Cropwell Bishop

OLD PARK CL
PARKIN CL

MILL ST
ST ETHELDENE

COOPER CL

HALL DR

TRIPLEY CL

HANDEY'S CL

SQUIRES CL
BROWNHILL CL

NEWBERRY CL

THE MALTINGS

ST GILES WAY

MARSHALL CL

WHIPPLING

STOCKDALE CL

TINTAGEL CL

FAIRFIELD

VICAR LA

NOTTINGHAM RD

PH

Cropwell
Bishop
Prim Sch

FERN RD

Spring
Hill

Fern
Hill

Fern
Hill

NG12

LARKE CL
LENTON CL

Home
Farm

Mill Hill

Pasture Lane

Fern Hill
Farm

Ash Holt

Langar
Lane
Covert

Langar
Lane
Bridge

35

2

NEW RD

Old
Brickyard
Plantation

Blue
Hill

COLSTON RD

Colston
Bridge

Home
Farm

Blanches
Gorse

PASTURE LA

Edmondthorpe
Lodge

Winifred
Wood

River Smite

NG13

1

34

D
69
E
70
F

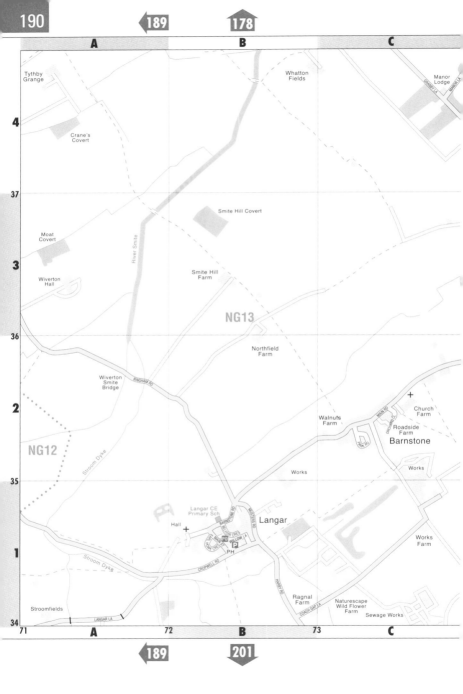

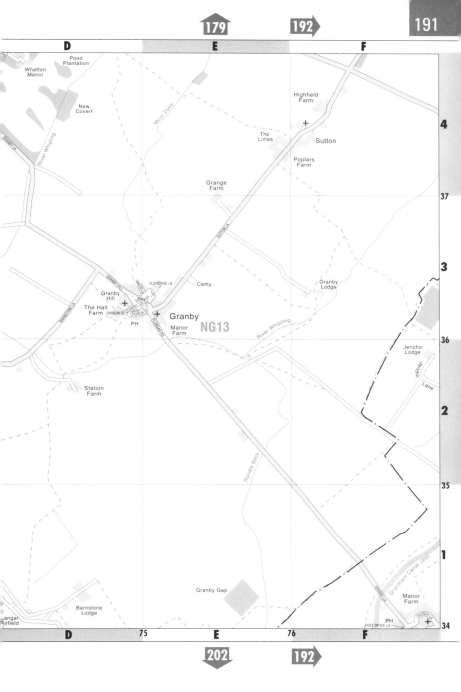

D
E
F

Whatton Manor

Pond Plantation

New Covert

Highfield Farm

4

GRANBY LA

River Whipling

Moor Dyke

The Limes

Sutton

Poplars Farm

Grange Farm

37

SUTTON LA

3

GRANBY HILL

Granby Hill

OLD FORGE LA

Cemy

Granby Lodge

BARNSTONE LA

MAIN ST

GRANBY LA

The Hall Farm

CHAPEL LA

DRAGON ST

CHURCH ST

PH

Granby

Manor Farm

NG13

River Whipling

36

Jericho Lodge

JERICHO LA

Jericho Lane

Station Farm

PERIGAN RD

2

Rundle Beck

35

1

Grantham Canal (dis)

Granby Gap

Manor Farm

angar Airfield

Barnstone Lodge

PH

POST OFFICE LA

CHURCH LA

BARRY LA

34

D
75
E
76
F

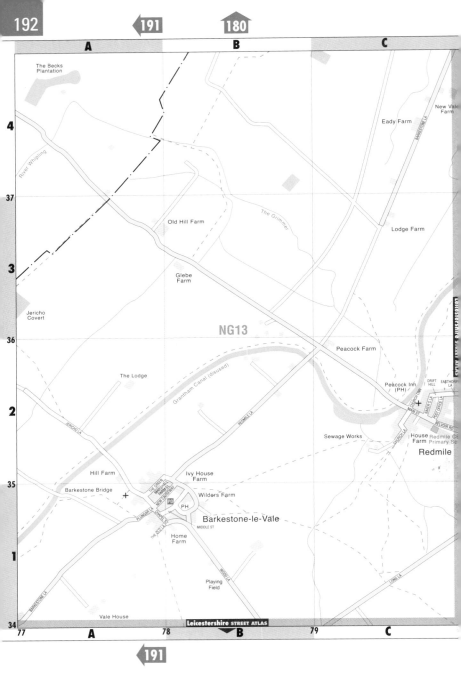

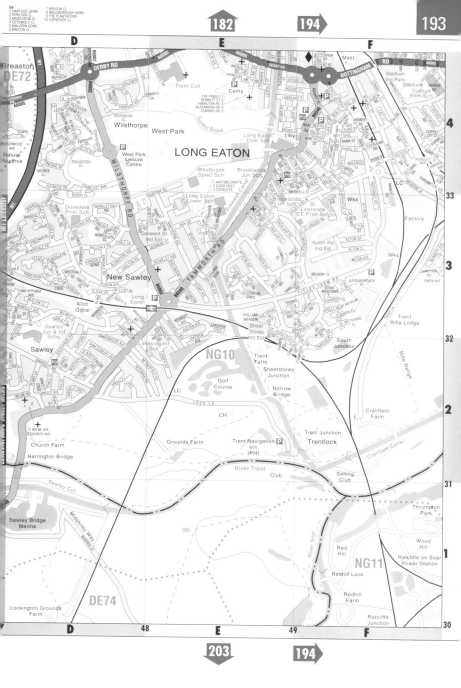

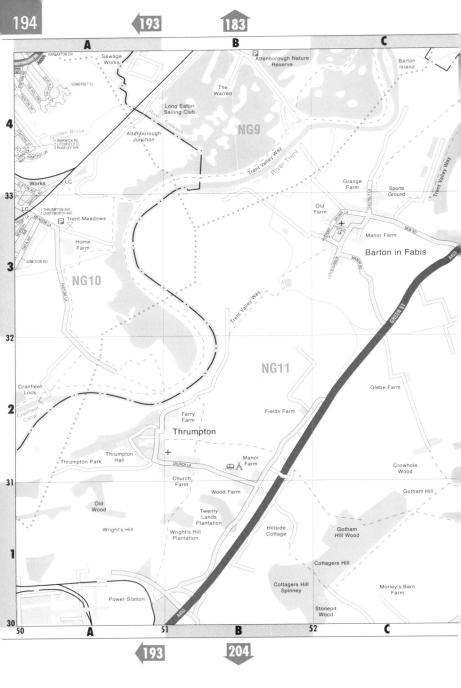

A   **B**   **C**

Attenborough Nature Reserve

Barton Island

Sewage Works

HARLAXTON DR

SOMERSET CL

The Warren

NG9

Long Eaton Sailing Club

River Erewash

Golden Brook

Attenborough Junction

1 WARWICK RD
2 LITCHFIELD CL
3 RUGELEY AVE

Trent Valley Way

River Trent

Trent Valley Way

Grange Farm

Sports Ground

4

33

Works

LC

Old Farm

Manor Farm

Barton in Fabis

LC

1 THRUMPTON AVE
2 CHATSWORTH AVE

Trent Meadows

Home Farm

JUNCTION RD

NG10

PASTURE LA

NEW RD

CHESTNUT LA

LITTLE LUNNON

MANOR RD

GREEN ST

A453

3

Trent Valley Way

NG11

32

Cranfleet Lock

Glebe Farm

Cranfleet Canal

Ferry Farm

Fields Farm

Thrumpton

Thrumpton Park

Thrumpton Hall

Manor Farm

Crowhole Wood

2

CHURCH LA

Church Farm

Wood Farm

Gotham Hill

31

Old Wood

Twenty Lands Plantation

Wright's Hill

Wright's Hill Plantation

Hillside Cottage

Gotham Hill Wood

Cottagers Hill

1

Cottagers Hill Spinney

Morley's Barn Farm

Power Station

Stonepit Wood

A453

30

50   **A**   **51**   **B**   **52**   **C**

D E F

FOX COVERT LA

Trent Valley Way

Burrows Farm

Brandshill Wood

Mill Hill

Brands Hill

Drift Lane Plantation

PORTER CL

SHERRINGTON CL 1
BLACKETTS WLK 2
DIRCA CT 3
ANGELL GREEN 4
ELIOT WLK 5
FLOREY WLK 6
TODD CT 7
SANGER GDNS 8
HARDEN CT 9

PENNARD WLK

OLDBURY CL

Whitegate Prim Sch

RIDGMONT WALK Glapton Wood

YEWDALE

PINEWOOD GDNS

WIDECOMBE LA

HALTHAM WLK

AVEBURY CL

BRAMBER GR

HOLBROOK

FARNBOROUGH RD

CHEDDAR RD

SPRING GREEN

THE GLADE

SUMMERWOOD

Blessed Robert Widmerpool RC Prim Sch

Milford Prim Sch

GLENCOYNE RD

SPRYDON WALK

Fairham Com Coll

Highbank Prim Sch

Brecks Plantation

Fairham Brook Nature Reserve

NOTTINGHAM

4

33

Barton Lodge

Heart Lees

Clifton Pasture

Fairham Brook

Depot

BARTON LA

Shepherds Barn

3

NG11

32

Raddle Barn

Barton Moor

Ruddington Moor

2

Long Spinney

31

Round Spinney

Allotment Gardens

Recreation Gound

Industrial Estate

Glebe Farm

Gotham Moor

Moor Lane

1

Gotham

Home Farm

ORCHARD ST 1
CHURCH ST 2
FOREDRIFT CL 3

Gotham Prim Sch

Cemy

Factory

Manor Farm

THE SQUARE

Water Reclamation Works

Fairholme Farm

MOOR LA

30

B D 54 E 55 F

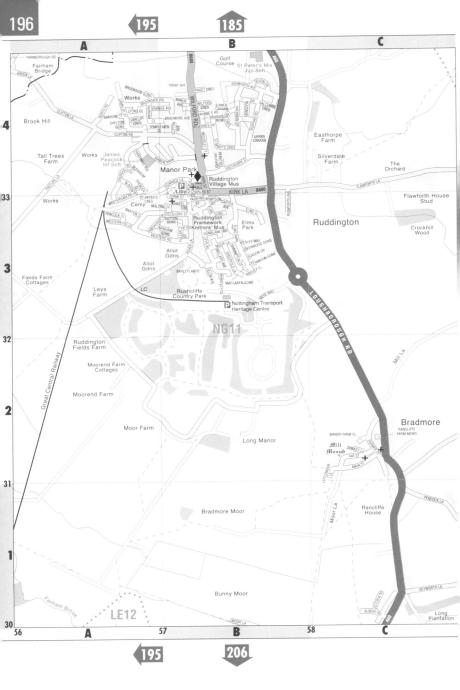

D
E
F

4

33

3

32

2

31

1

30

BENTINCK AVE

Shire
Farm

Flawford
House

Mill
Mound

Hall
Farm

YELLOWS
YD.

OLD MELTON RD

Plumtree

MELTON RD

CLIPSTON LA

THE LEYS

PH

SADDLERS CT.

CHURCH LA

MAIN RD

The
Poplars

Chestnut
Farm

NG12

STATION RD

PH

Playing
Field

Barn
Farm

Blackcliffe
Hill

BRADMORE LA

NG11

Plumtree
Park

Crossdale
Drive
Prim Sch

HILLCREST RD

RANCLIFFE AVE

DELVILLE AVE

HIGHBURY RD

ABBOT
CL.

BISHOPS
CL.

SIDMOUTH
CL.

DERDALE AVE

BEAUMONT

MELTON

CL.

CROSSDALE DR

WOLDS

FRANKLYN
GDNS

VILLA RD

WYNDELL DR

ASHLEY CRES

PARKE CL.

GREEN CL.

ROSE CL.

ASHLEY

PLATT LA

NICKER HILL

CREBER CT

LYNCOMBE
GDNS

WOLDS RISE

Sewage
Works

SPINNEY RD

MAYES RD

PLANTATION RD

INTAKE RD

Cotton's
Plantation

FAIRHAM RD

CROFT RD

THE OAK AVE

TOFT

BARNETT
CT

FEIGNIES
CT

ASHLEY
TELL

BANNOCK GDNS

CHERRY LEAS

HIGH

CHERRY GROVE

MANOR RD

Keyworth
Prim Sch

Libby

P

PARK AVE W

PARK RD

PARK AVE

ROSE AVE

WEST CL.

CHURCH DR

South Wolds
Comp Sch

Keyworth
Leisure Centre

P

FAIRWAY

BEECAR LA

Greenhays
Farm

Woodfields

Ranclifffe Wood

BUNNY LA

EAST CL.

ELM AVE

ELM CL.

WALL CL.

SELBY LA

LANE

ASH LA

Wheatcroft
Farm

Hillside
Farm

WRIGHTS
ORCHARD

HAWTHORN CL.

HOLLAND

EAST
PASTURES

THE SQUARE

PH

Keyworth

PENDOCK LA

KEYWORTH LA

COMMERCIAL RD

MAIN ST

BROOK VIEW

CEDAR DR

BARROW SLADE

PH

Holly
Farm

Long Plantation

Bunny Park

Sewage
Works

New Holme
Farm

Lings Lane
Farm

9
60
E
61
F

A

B

C

CotGRAVE RD

Glebe
Farm

Mill Lane

Hoe Hill

Smallthorne
Plantation

4

Cotgrave Forest

Grange
Plantation

Blackberry
Hill

33

Wolds La

Wolds
Farm

Avenue
Farm

Normanton-on-the-Wolds

PH

Plumtree Wolds

3

Playing
Field

Wolds
Farm

LAMING GAP LA

NG12

32

Clipston
Wolds

Normanton Wolds

British
Geological
Survey

2

MOUNT PLEASANT

MELTON RD

Hill Farm

Golf Course

31

CH

Bank
Farm

Stanton Tunnel

Willow Brook
Cty Prim Sch

Laurel
Farm

BROWNS LA

1

Manor
Farm

Business
Park

Nursery

Stanton-on-the-Wolds

Black
Plantation

The Pastures

30

62

A

63

B

64

C

D

E

F

Wolds Hill

OWTHORPE RD

A46

Taylors
Wolds

Fox
Holes

Nanny's
Plantation

Fishpond
Wood

4

Bells
Stud Farm

Owthorpe
Hill

Moat

CHURCH LA

HALME ST

Owthorpe

Fishpond
Cottage

PARK LA

33

Herrywell La

Borders
Wood

Woodman's
Cottage

Mackley's
Farm

Cotgrave
Wolds

Owthorpe
Wolds

Newfield
Farm

Mackley's
Bridge

P

3

Wolds Farm

Garston's
Hill

NG12

Wild's Bridge

32

Barn
Farm

KINOULTON LA

RING GAP LA

Devil's Elbow

2

Wynnstay
Wood

Owthorpe
Lodge

OWTHORPE LA

Lodge on the
Wolds

Kinoulton
Gorse

Vimy
Ridge

Grantham Canal (disused)

GARDNER
DR

BROOK DR GREAT

31

Roundhill
Spinney

MEADOW WAY

Woodlands

LINE CL

PINFOLD CL

Blacks
Farm

MAIN ST

BERESFORD DR

1

Kinoulton
Wolds

Ivy
Farm

Kinoulton
Prim Sch

A46

Roehoe Wood

KINOULTON LA

Needham Hill
Farm

30

D

66

E

67

F

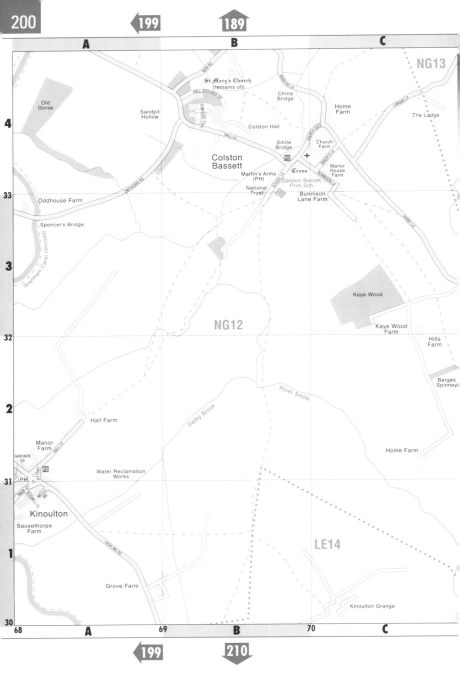

NG13

A   B   C

Bow Rd

St Mary's Church
(remains of)

HALL GROUNDS DR

WASH PIT LA

China
Bridge

Home
Farm

LANGAR LA

The Lodge

Old
Gorse

Sandpit
Hollow

Colston Hall

4

HALL LA

CHURCH GATE

Smite
Bridge

Church
Farm

HILL CLOSE RD.

PO

Colston
Bassett

Manor
House
Farm

Cross

BAKERS LA

NTHORPE RD

Martin's Arms
(PH)

Colston Basset
Prim Sch

33

SCHOOL LA

BUNNISON LA

HARBY LA

Oddhouse Farm

National
Trust

Bunnison
Lane Farm

Spencer's Bridge

Grantham Canal (disused)

Kaye Wood

3

Kaye Wood
Farm

Hills
Farm

NG12

32

Barges
Spinney

River Smite

2

Dalby Brook

Hall Farm

Home Farm

Manor
Farm

HILL LA

GARDNER
DR

PO

Water Reclamation
Works

31

PH

MAIN ST

BOSWELL CL

METS DR

Kinoulton

Sausethorpe
Farm

LE14

1

HACKLING RD

Grove Farm

Kinoulton Grange

30
68   A   69   B   70   C

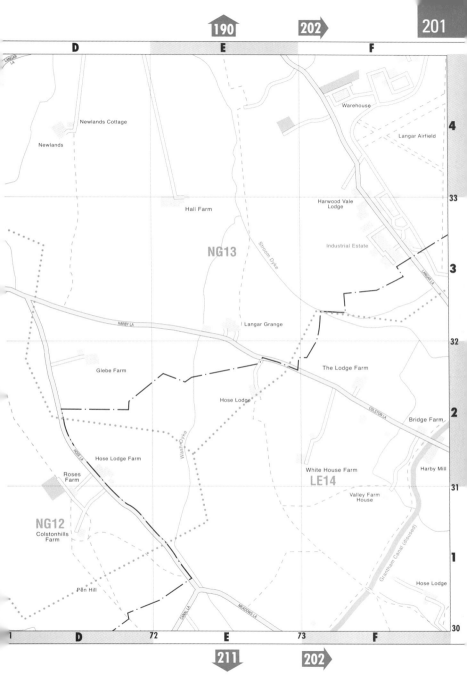

D
E
F

4

Warehouse

Langar Airfield

Newlands Cottage

Newlands

33

Hall Farm

Harwood Vale
Lodge

NG13

Stroom Dyke

Industrial Estate

3

LANGAR LA

HARBY LA

Langar Grange

32

Glebe Farm

The Lodge Farm

COLSTON LA

Hose Lodge

Warth Dyke

2

Bridge Farm

Hose Lodge Farm

White House Farm

Harby Mill

Roses
Farm

LE14

31

HOSE LA

Valley Farm
House

NG12
Colstonhills
Farm

Grantham Canal (disused)

1

Hose Lodge

Pēn Hill

DIALL LA

MEADOWS LA

30

D
E
F

1
72
73

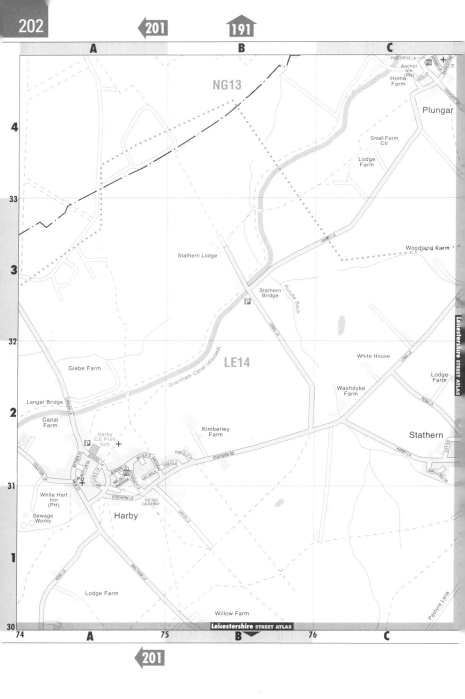

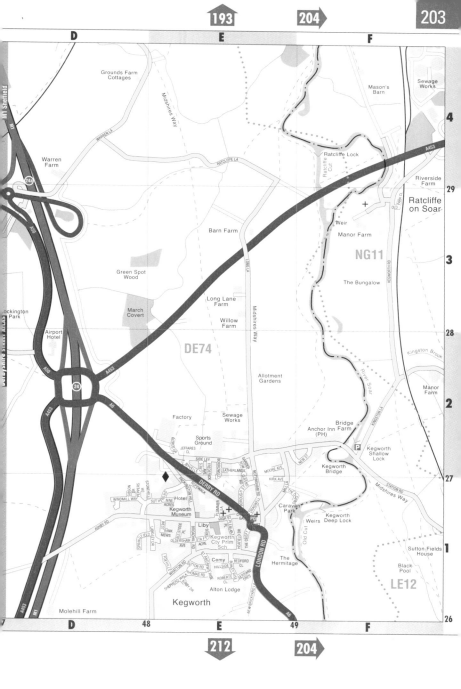

A   B   C

Power
Station

Fox Covert

Stonepit
Farm

Winking Hill

Winking Hill
Farm

Woodlands

4

Gotham
Wood

Hillside
Farm

Kingston
Spinney

The Odells

Cuckoo Bush
Farm

29

Hillside

Moor
Wood

New
Kingston

Kingston
Works

NG11

Crownend Wood

3

Whitehills
Farm

The Cottage

Kingston
Park

Kingston Fields
Farm

Lodge

KINGSTON CT

28

Kingston
Hall

Lumbry
Wood

Church
Farm

Lodge

KEGWORTH RD

THE GREEN

The
Pool

**Kingston
on Soar**

LONG
ROW

2

Station
Plantation

Woodside

Scotland
Farm

27

Scotland
Wood

DE74

LE12

Moulter Hill

Cattle
Breeding
Centre

STATION RD

Kingston Brook

1

Playing
Field

MAIN ST

Moat

MELTON LA

Midshires Way

PH

Froghole
Farm

Domleo's
Spinney

BRICKYARD LA

Sewage
Works

Univ of Nottingham
Sutton Bonington
Campus

COLLEGE RD

LANDCROFT

TROWELL LA

26

50   A   51   B   52   C

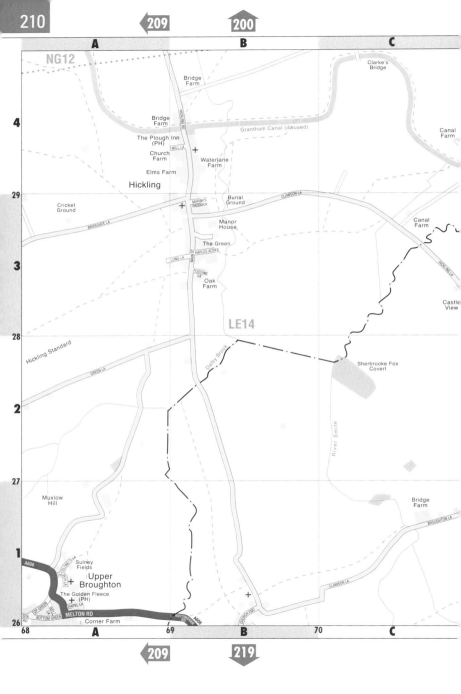

A

B

C

NG12

Clarke's
Bridge

Bridge
Farm

4

Bridge
Farm

Grantham Canal (disused)

Canal
Farm

The Plough Inn
(PH)

Church
Farm

Waterlane
Farm

Elms Farm

Hickling

29

Cricket
Ground

MARSH'S
PADDOCK

Burial
Ground

CLAWSON LA

BRIDEGATE LA

Manor
House

Canal
Farm

The Green

3

LONG LA

CHARLES ACRES

HIGH MILL LA

Castle
View

PUDDING
LA

Oak
Farm

LE14

28

Hickling Standard

Dalby Brook

Sherbrooke Fox
Covert

GREEN LA

2

River Smite

27

Muxlow
Hill

Bridge
Farm

BROUGHTON LA

1

A606

Sulney
Fields

Upper
Broughton

LYCH GATE LA

CHURCH LA

CHAPEL LA

The Golden Fleece
(PH)

CLAWSON LA

TOP GREEN

HILL

STA
RD

BOTTOM GREEN

MELTON RD

Corner Farm

CHURCH END

26

68

A

69

B

70

C

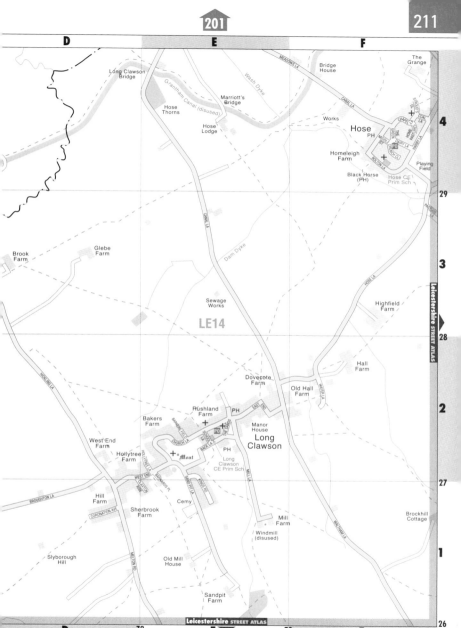

The Grange

Long Clawson Bridge

Bridge House

Grantham Canal (disused)

Wash Dyke

MEADOWS LA

CANAL LA

Marriott's Bridge

Hose Thorns

Hose Lodge

Works

Hose
PH

4

Homeleigh Farm

Black Horse (PH)

Hose CE Prim Sch

Playing Field

29

Brook Farm

Glebe Farm

Dam Dyke

CANAL LA

HOSE LA

PASTURE LA

Highfield Farm

3

Sewage Works

LE14

28

Hall Farm

Dovecote Farm

Old Hall Farm

LAST RD

WATER LA

2

Rushland Farm

PH

Bakers Farm

West End Farm

Hollytree Farm

BANKSIDE

CHURCH ST

BACK LA

Moat

Long Clawson CE Prim Sch

Manor House

PH

MILL LA

Long Clawson

WALTHAM LA

HOLT LANE LA

WEST END

BROUGHTON LA

HOLT LANE LA

CORONATION AVE

SANDPIT RD

KING'S RD

Hill Farm

Sherbrook Farm

Cemy

27

Mill Farm

Brockhill Cottage

MELTON RD

Slyborough Hill

Old Mill House

Windmill (disused)

1

Sandpit Farm

A   B   C

Springhouse Farm

DE74

Slade Spinney

PH

Slade Farm

Devil's Elbow

River Soar

Windmill Farm

His Lordships

Intensive Dairy Unit

Lodge

LONDON RD

Home Farm

Woodyard Plantation

Whatton House

Five Acre

Ash Spinney

Gallow's Wood

Gorse Covert

Manor House Farm

Marylea Farm

Lodge

Sports Ground

WEST END

Long Whatton

MILL LA

Whatton Fields Farm

Manor Farm

Long Whatton Brook

PH

Long Whatton Mill

LE12

Sewage Works

PH

HATHERN RD

Hathern Turn

Rose Hill

WHATTON RD

DERBY RD

DRY POT LA

SPRING LA

Works

WIDE LA

Piper Farm

Mitchell's Spring Farm

Oakley Wood

Oakley Grange Farm

47 A 48 B 49 C

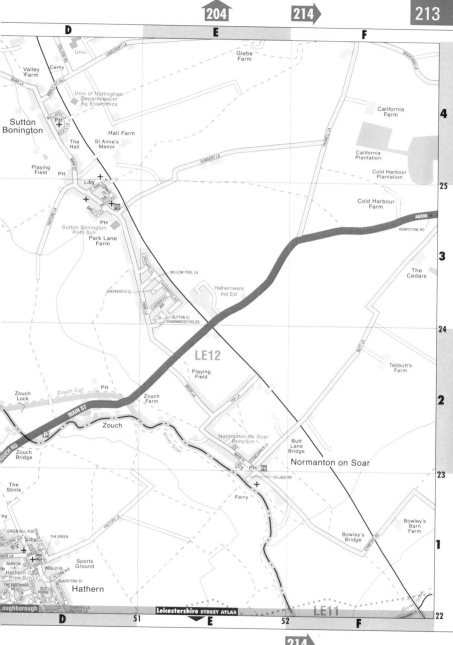

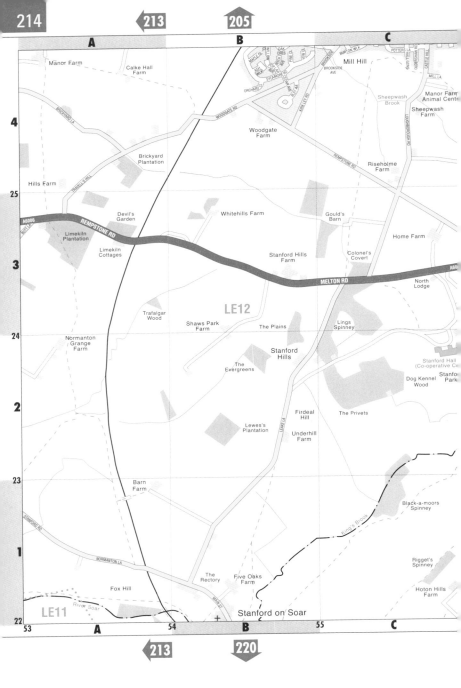

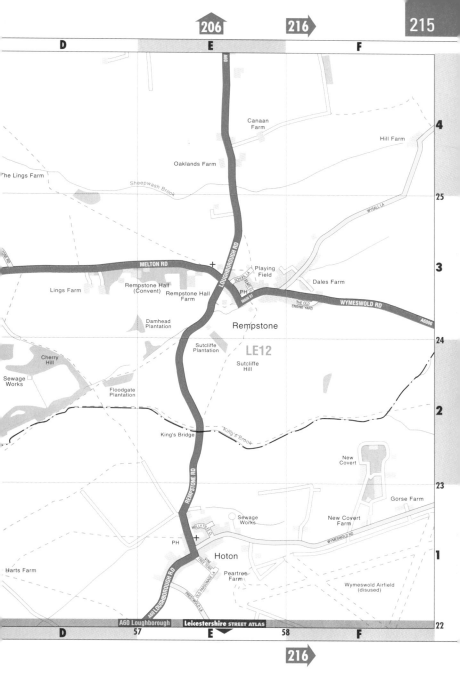

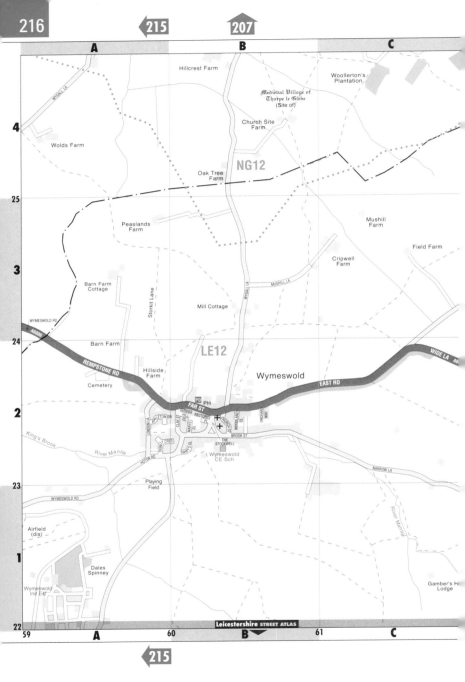

A   B   C

4

Hillcrest Farm

Woollerton's Plantation

Medieval Village of
Thorpe le Glebe
(Site of)

Church Site
Farm

Wolds Farm

NG12

Oak Tree
Farm

25

Peaslands
Farm

Mushill
Farm

Field Farm

3

Barn Farm
Cottage

Cripwell
Farm

MUSHILL LA

Storkit Lane

Mill Cottage

WYSALL LA

WYMESWOLD RD

24   A6006

Barn Farm

LE12

Hillside Farm

WIDE LA   A6

REMPSTONE RD

Wymeswold

EAST RD

Cemetery

2

FAR ST   PH

King's Brook

LONDON LA   BLETON DR

CROSS ST   HILL ST   CLAY ST   MANOR CL

RECTORY

WOODLANDS CL

ORCHARD WAY

River Mantle

HUTON RD   THORP

J CRES

SWIN CL

BROOK ST

THE
STOCKWELL

Wymeswold
CE Sch

NARROW LA

23

WYMESWOLD RD

Playing
Field

River Mantle

1

Airfield
(dis)

Dales
Spinney

Gamber's H
Lodge

Wymeswold
Ind Est

22

59   A   60   B   61   C

D
E
F

G12

Triangle
Plantation

Midshires Way

Eelpool
Field

Willoughby-on
-the-Wolds

Field Farm

Bryans Lane

A46

4

Old Hall
Farm

Willoughby
Prim Sch

Willoughby
Gorse

WEST THORPE

Green Lane

MAIN ST

MOB
LA

CHURCH LA

BRICK LA

BACK LA

PH

Broughton
Lodge

25

Midshires Way

Barrack
Cottages

OCCUPATION LA

HADES LA

3

LE14

Turnpost
Farm

Kingston Brook

LE12

24

A46

Dungehill
Farm

Eller's
Gorse

2

Hill Farm

WIDE LA

Ella's
Farm

Pasture
Lodge

23

Highthorn
Farm

NARROW LA

Common
Farm

Wymeswold
Lodge

Kingston Brook

Willoughby Fields
Farm

PADDY'S LA A6006

1

Kings
Farm

River Mantle

Wolds Farm

Wolds Farm

The Lodge

A46

A46 Leicester

22

D
63
E
64
F

210

CHURCH END

WHEADLECK LA
CHAPEL LA
Moat Farm

Nether Broughton

KING ST
BLACKSMITHS CL
BRIDGE

Manor Farm

River Smite

PH

The Grange

Sewage Works

Thompson Walk

GREAVES AVE
THE CRESCENT
DICKMAN'S LA
PRINCES CL
DUKES RD
EARLS RD

Hatton Lodge

OLD DALBY LA

NOTTINGHAM RD

A606

Broughton Lodges

Playing Field

Lodge Farm

Broughton Lodge

STATION LA

Playing Field

Old Dalby Depot

LE14

Greenhill Farm

Stonepit Spinney

Crompton's Plantation

Stonepits Farm

Marriott's Spinney

Green Hill

Friars Well Farm

Grimston Tunnel

Saxelby Lodge Farm

Marriott's Wood

Wartnaby

Tunnel Farm

Old Dalby Wood

SIX HILLS LA

Air Shafts

Tunnel Farm

Barnes Hill Plantation

Ten Acres Plantation

Friars Well

Ppg Sta

Tunnel Plantation

Midshires Way
PEGASUS

Barn Farm

Grimston Gorse

Saxelby Pastures

Grimston

Leicestershire STREET ATLAS A606 Melton Mowbray

D   E   F

69   70

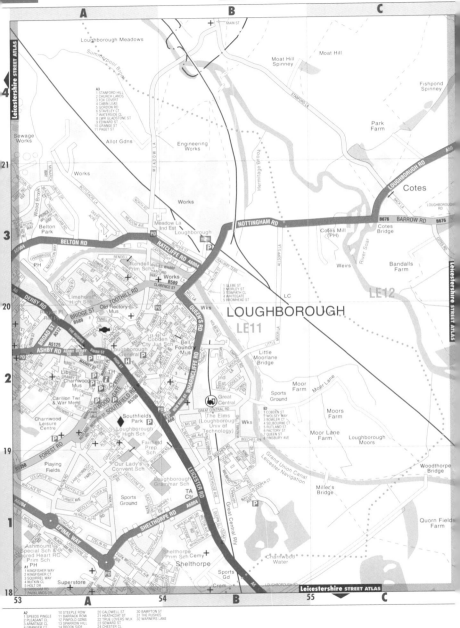

A3
1 STAMFORD HILL
2 CHURCH LANDS
3 FOX COVERT
4 CABIN LEAS
5 GORDON RD
6 STAVELEY CT
7 WATERSIDE CT
8 LWR GLADSTONE ST
9 EDWARD ST
10 GRANGE ST
11 PAGET ST

Loughborough Meadows

Summerpool Brook

MAIN ST

Moat Hill Spinney

Moat Hill

Fishpond Spinney

Sewage Works

Allot Gdns

Engineering Works

Hermitage Brook

Park Farm

Works

Belton Park

Meadow La 2nd East

NOTTINGHAM RD

Cotes

LOUGHBOROUGH RD

A60

BARROW RD

B676

Cotes Mill (PH)

Cotes Bridge

BELTON RD

RATCLIFFE RD A6004

Loughborough

LC

River Soar

Bandalls Farm

LE12

Rendell Prim School

B589

Works

Clarence St

Limehurst High Sch

DERBY RD

BRIDGE ST

FOOTHILL RD

Old Rectory Mus

QUEEN'S RD

B1
1 GLEBE ST
2 MORLEY ST
3 TOWPATH CL
4 WHITEGATE
5 BROOMHEAD ST

Wks

LOUGHBOROUGH
LE11

Little Moorlane Bridge

BROAD ST A5125

ASHBY RD

Cobden Cty Jun Sch

Bell Foundry Mus

Lib

Charnwood Mus

Carillon Twr & War Meml

WHARNCLIFFE RD

SOUTHFIELD RD

Great Central

Moor Farm

Moor Lane

Moors Farm

Sports Ground

Charnwood Leisure Centre

Southfields Park

Loughborough High Sch

The Elms (Loughborough) Univ of Technology

Wks

Moor Lane Farm

Loughborough Moors

FOREST RD

Fairfield Prep Sch

Our Lady's Convent Sch

Grand Union Canal Leicester Navigation

Woodthorpe Bridge

Playing Fields

Loughborough Grammar Sch

LEICESTER RD A6004

Miller's Bridge

B2
1 COBDEN ST
2 WOLSEY WAY
3 BOWLER CT
4 SELBOURNE CT
5 RUTLAND ST
6 FACTORY ST
7 QUEEN ST
8 FINSBURY AVE

TA Ctr

Sports Ground

Great Central Rly

EPINAL WAY

SHELTHORPE RD A6004

Quorn Fields Farm

A1
1 KINGFISHER WAY
2 KINGFISHER CT
3 SQUIRREL WAY
4 NUTON CL
5 HOLT DR
6 FARNHAM RD
7 PARKLANDS DR

Ashmount Special Sch & Sacred Heart RC Prim Sch

PH

Shelthorpe Prim Sch

Cemy

Shelthorpe

Charnwood Water

Superstore

Sports Gd

Crem

53 A 54 B 55 C

A2
1 SPEEDS PINGLE
2 PLEASANT CL
3 ARMITAGE CL
4 GRANGER CT
5 ST MARY'S CL
6 HASTINGS ST
7 RADMOOR RD
8 DEAD LA
9 RECTORY PL
10 STEEPLE ROW
11 BARRACK ROW
12 PINFOLD GDNS
13 BROOK SIDE
14 BROAD SIDE
15 GREENCLOSE LA
16 ORCHARD ST
17 GEORGE YD
18 CATTLE MARKET
19 DEVONSHIRE SQ
20 CALDWELL ST
21 HEATHCOAT ST
22 TRUE LOVERS WLK
23 SEWARD ST
24 CHESTER CL
25 BEDFORD SQ
26 BEE HIVE LA
27 PACK HORSE LA
28 GREGORY ST
29 PRINCESS ST
30 BAMPTON ST
31 THE RUSHES
32 WARNERS LANE

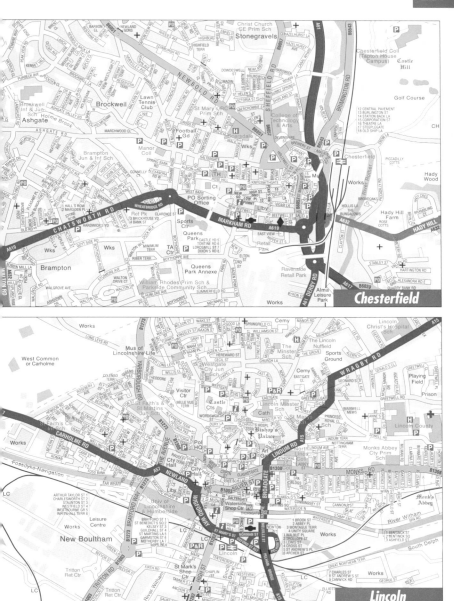

Chesterfield

Lincoln

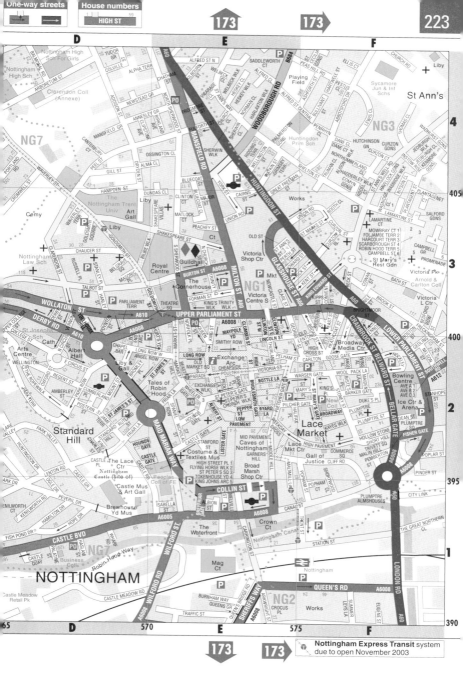

Index

Church Rd 🔲6️⃣ Beckenham BR2..........**53** C6

Place name
May be abbreviated on the map

Location number
Present when a number indicates the place's position in a crowded area of mapping

Locality, town or village
Shown when more than one place has the same name

Postcode district
District for the indexed place

Page and grid square
Page number and grid reference for the standard mapping

Public and commercial buildings are highlighted in magenta. Places of interest are highlighted in blue with a star★

Abbreviations used in the index

Acad	**Academy**	Comm	**Common**	Gd	**Ground**	L	**Leisure**	Prom	**Promenade**
App	**Approach**	Cott	**Cottage**	Gdn	**Garden**	La	**Lane**	Rd	**Road**
Arc	**Arcade**	Cres	**Crescent**	Gn	**Green**	Liby	**Library**	Recn	**Recreation**
Ave	**Avenue**	Cswy	**Causeway**	Gr	**Grove**	Mdw	**Meadow**	Ret	**Retail**
Bglw	**Bungalow**	Ct	**Court**	H	**Hall**	Meml	**Memorial**	Sh	**Shopping**
Bldg	**Building**	Ctr	**Centre**	Ho	**House**	Mkt	**Market**	Sq	**Square**
Bsns, Bus	**Business**	Ctry	**Country**	Hospl	**Hospital**	Mus	**Museum**	St	**Street**
Bvd	**Boulevard**	Cty	**County**	HQ	**Headquarters**	Orch	**Orchard**	Sta	**Station**
Cath	**Cathedral**	Dr	**Drive**	Hts	**Heights**	Pal	**Palace**	Terr	**Terrace**
Cir	**Circus**	Dro	**Drove**	Ind	**Industrial**	Par	**Parade**	TH	**Town Hall**
Cl	**Close**	Ed	**Education**	Inst	**Institute**	Pas	**Passage**	Univ	**University**
Cnr	**Corner**	Emb	**Embankment**	Int	**International**	Pk	**Park**	Wk, Wlk	**Walk**
Coll	**College**	Est	**Estate**	Intc	**Interchange**	Pl	**Place**	Wr	**Water**
Com	**Community**	Ex	**Exhibition**	Junc	**Junction**	Prec	**Precinct**	Yd	**Yard**

Index of localities, towns and villages

A

Aldercar 143 D2
Alverton 168 C1
Annesley 130 B4
Annesley Woodhouse ...129 F4
Arnold 162 A4
Askham 51 F1
Aslockton 179 D3
Astwith 85 D3
Ault Hucknall 85 F4
Austerfield 3 E1
Averham 123 F1
Awsworth 158 B2

B

Babworth 39 D3
Bagthorpe 128 C2
Balderton 140 C2
Barkestone-le-Vale 192 B1
Barnby in the Willows ..141 F3
Barnby Moor 28 B3
Barnstone 190 C2
Barton in Fabis 194 C3
Bathley 110 A2
Bawtry 10 A4
Beckingham (Lincs) 142 B4
Beckingham (Notts) 14 A1
Beeston 183 D3
Besthorpe 97 F3
Bestwood Village 146 C2
Bilsthorpe 105 F3
Bilsthorpe Moor 106 A2
Bingham 177 F2
Bircotes 9 E2
Blaxton 1 A4
Bleasby 152 A4
Blidworth 118 A2
Blyth 18 A2
Blyton 15 F4
Bole 23 F2
Bothamsall 63 F4
Bottesford 181 E2
Boughton 77 F3
Bradmore 196 C2
Breaston 193 D4
Brinsley 143 F3
Broadholme 57 D1
Brough 112 A1
Broxholme 57 F4
Budby 61 F1
Bulcote 164 A3
Bunny 206 C4
Burton Joyce 163 F2

C

Calverton 149 D4
Car Colston 166 B1
Carburton 61 F4
Carlton 162 B1
Carlton in Lindrick 25 F3
Carlton-on-Trent 96 C2
Caunton 109 D2
Caythorpe 165 D4
Church Laneham 74 A4
Church Warsop 30 C2
Claypole 156 B4
Clayworth 21 E3
Clipstone 89 F2
Coddington 126 A1
Collingham 98 A1
Colston Bassett 200 B4
Cossall 158 B1
Costock 206 B1
Cotes 220 C3
Cotgrave 187 F1
Cotham 154 C2
Cottam 43 E2
Creswell 58 B4
Cromwell 110 C4
Cropwell Bishop 189 D2
Cropwell Butler 189 D4
Cuckney 60 A2

D

Darlton 67 D4
Doddington 71 E1
Dry Doddington 156 C1
Dunham on Trent 54 B1

E

Eagle 84 B2
Eakring 92 C1
East Bridgford 165 E2
East Drayton 53 D2
East Leake 205 F1
East Markham 65 F3
East Stockwith 7 F1
East Stoke 153 E4
Eastwood 143 F2
Eaton 40 A1
Edingley 120 B2
Edwinstowe 76 A1
Egmanton 79 F3
Elkesley 50 A2
Elmton 58 A4
Elston 153 F3
Elton 179 F1
Epperstone 150 A3
Everton 11 E2

F

Farndon 139 D2
Farnsfield 119 F3
Fenton (nr Balderton) ..142 B1
Fenton (nr Saxilby) 55 E3
Finningley 1 A2
Firbeck 16 A3
Fiskerton 137 F2
Flawborough 168 B1
Fledborough 68 B3
Flintham 153 D1
Friezeland 129 D1

G

Gainsborough 24 C3
Gamston 51 D3
Girton 82 C1
Glapwell 86 B4
Gonalston 151 D2
Gotham 195 D1
Granby 191 E3
Grassthorpe 81 F2
Greasley 144 C2
Gringley on the Hill 12 C1
Grove 40 C2
Gunthorpe 164 C3

H

Halam 120 C1
Halloughton 136 A2
Harby (Leics) 202 A1
Harby (Notts) 70 C1
Hardstoft 85 D2
Harworth 8 C3
Hathern 213 D1
Haughton 63 F3
Hawksworth 167 E2
Hawton 139 F2
Hayton 30 B3
Headon 52 A4
Heanor 143 D1
Hickling 210 A4
High Markham 68 A1
Hilcote 99 E1
Hockerton 122 A3
Hodsock 26 C4
Hodthorpe 45 E3
Holbeck 59 E4
Holme 111 D2
Holme Pierrepont 175 D2
Hose 211 F4
Hoton 215 E1
Hoveringham 151 E1
Hucknall 145 F3
Huthwaite 99 F2

I

Ilkeston 157 E1
Ironville 128 A2

J

Jacksdale 128 A2

K

Kegworth 203 E1
Kelham 124 A2
Kersall 94 A1
Kettlethorpe 55 E2
Keyworth 197 F1
Kimberley 158 C4
Kingston on Soar 204 A2
Kinoulton 200 A1
Kirkby in Ashfield 115 E2
Kirklington 120 C4
Kirton 78 B3
Knapthorpe 109 D1
Kneesall 93 F3
Kneeton 152 A1

L

Lambley 163 E4
Laneham 54 A3
Langar 190 B1
Langford 111 F1
Langley Mill 143 D2
Langold 16 C2
Langwith 72 C4
Laughterton 55 D2
Laxton 79 E2
Lea 24 C1
Letwell 16 A2
Lidgett 91 D4
Linby 131 D2
Little Carlton 124 A4
Littleborough 33 F1
Long Clawson 211 E2
Long Eaton 193 E4
Long Whatton 212 B2
Loughborough 220 B2
Lound 29 E4
Low Marnham 82 A4
Lowdham 150 B1

M

Mansfield 102 B4
Mansfield Woodhouse ...88 C2
Maplebeck 108 A3
Market Warsop 57 F4
Marton 44 A4
Mattersey 20 B4
Meden Vale 74 C4
Milton 65 D4
Misson 4 A1
Misterton 6 C1
Moorgreen 144 B2
Moorhouse 80 B1
Morton (Lincs) 15 E2
Morton (Notts) 137 E2
Muston 181 F1

N

Nether Broughton 219 E4
Nether Langwith 59 D1
New Bagthorpe 129 D2
New Balderton 140 A2
New Brinsley 128 C1
New Houghton 86 C4
New Ollerton 77 E3
Newark-on-Trent 140 B4
Newington 3 E1
Newstead 130 C3
Newton (nr Bingham) ..177 D4
Newton (nr Huthwaite) ..99 D2
Newton on Trent 55 D1
Normanton
    (nr Bottesford) 181 E2
Normanton
    (nr Southwell) 121 F1
Normanton on Soar 213 F2
Normanton on Trent 81 E3
Normanton-on-
    the-Wolds 198 A3
North Clifton 68 C3
North Leverton with
    Habblesthorpe 42 B4
North Muskham 110 C1
North Scarle 83 F1
North Wheatley 31 E4
Norton 60 B3
Norwell 110 A4
Norwell Woodhouse ...95 D1
Nottingham 173 D2
Nuncargate 115 D1
Nuthall 159 E3

O

Old Clipstone 90 B3
Old Dalby 218 C2
Oldcotes 17 D3
Ollerton 77 D2
Ompton 93 D4
Orston 180 A4
Ossington 95 E3
Owthorpe 199 F4
Owthorpe 199 F4
Oxton 134 B2

P

Papplewick 131 F2
Perlethorpe 62 C2
Pinxton 113 E1
Pleasley 87 D3
Pleasleyhill 87 E2
Plumtree 197 F3
Plungar 202 C4
Pye Bridge 128 A4

R

Radcliffe on Trent 175 F2
Radmanthwaite 87 E2
Ragnall 68 A4
Rainworth 104 A1
Rampton 42 C1
Ranby 38 A3
Ranskill 19 D2
Ratcliffe on Soar 203 F3
Ravenshead 117 D1
Redmile 192 C2
Rempstone 215 E3
Retford 39 F4
Rhodesia 35 D2
Rockley 51 D1
Rolleston 138 A3
Ruddington 196 C3

S

Sandiacre 182 A3
Saundby 23 E3
Saxilby 56 C2
Saxondale 177 D2
Scaftworth 10 B2
Scarrington 178 C4
Screveton 166 C2
Scrooby 10 A1
Selston 128 C4
Selston Green 128 B4
Shelford 164 B1
Shelton 168 B3
Shipley 157 D3
Shirebrook 72 C2
Shireoaks 34 C3
Sibthorpe 167 F4
Sir James's Pk 176 C1
Skegby 100 C3
Skellingthorpe 71 F2
South Clifton 68 C1
South Leverton 42 B3
South Muskham 124 B4
South Normanton 113 D4
South Scarle 98 B3
South Wheatley 31 F4
Southwell 121 E1
Spalford 83 D4
Stainsby 85 D4
Stanford on Soar 214 B1
Stanley 82 B3
Stanton Hill 100 B3
Stanton-by-Dale 170 A1
Stanton-on-the-Wolds ..198 B1
Stapleford (Lincs) 127 F4
Stapleford (Notts) 182 C4
Stathern 202 C2
Staunton in the Vale 169 D2
Staythorpe 138 C4
Stoke Bardolph 175 F4
Strelley 171 D4
Sturton le Steeple 32 B3
Styrrup 8 B1
Sutton (nr Bottesford) ..191 F4
Sutton (nr Retford) 28 C3
Sutton Bonington 213 D4
Sutton in Ashfield 100 A1
Sutton on Trent 96 C4
Syerston 153 D2

T

Teversal 100 B4
Thorney 69 F4
Thoroton 167 F1
Thorpe 138 C1
Thorpe Salvin 34 A3
Thrumpton 194 B2
Thurgarton 151 E4
Tibshelf 99 D3
Tickhill 8 A4
Tithby 189 E3
Tollerton 186 B1
Torksey 44 A1
Torworth 19 D1
Treswell 42 B2
Trowell 170 B3
Tuxford 66 A1

U

Underwood 129 D1
Upper Broughton 210 A1
Upper Langwith 72 B4
Upper Saxondale 176 C1
Upton (nr Retford) 52 A3
Upton (nr Southwell) ..122 C1

W

Walesby 64 A1
Walkeringham 13 F3
Walkerith 14 B3
Wallingwells 25 E3
Warsop Vale 73 E2
Watnall 159 D4
Wellow 77 F1
West Bridgford 185 E3
West Drayton 51 D1
West Hallam 157 D1
West Leake 205 D1
West Markham 65 D3
West Stockwith 7 E1
Weston 81 D2
Westwood 128 B2
Westwoodside 2 C3
Whaley 58 B2
Whaley Thorns 59 D1
Whatton 179 D2
Whitwell 45 D3
Widmerpool 208 A3
Willoughby-on-
    the-Wolds 217 E4
Winkburn 108 A1
Winthorpe 125 E3
Woodbeck 53 D4
Woodborough 149 E2
Woodsetts 25 D1
Worksop 35 E3
Wroot 2 A4
Wymeswold 216 B2
Wysall 207 E2

Z

Zouch 213 D2

1

1st Ave NG7 173 D4

2

2nd Ave NG7 173 D4

3

3rd Ave NG7 173 D4

4

4th Ave NG7 173 D4

A

A Rd NG9 184 B3
Aaron Cl NG11 185 D4
Abba Cl NG16 158 C4
Abbey Bridge NG7 172 C1
Abbey CE Jun Sch S80 35 F1
Abbey Cir NG2 186 A4
Abbey Cl
Aslockton NG13 178 C3
Hucknall NG15 145 F4
Abbey Ct Beeston NG9 183 F4
Mansfield NG18 102 C4
Nottingham NG7 222 B2
Abbey Dr NG9 183 F4
Abbey Gates Prim Sch NG15 117 D1
Abbey Gr NG3 173 F4
Abbey La NG13 178 C3
Abbey Prim Sch NG18 102 C4
Abbey Rd Beeston NG9 183 F4
Bingham NG13 178 A2
Blidworth NG21 118 A3
Eastwood NG16 144 A1
Edwinstowe NG21 91 E4
Kirkby in A NG17 115 E3
Mansfield NG18 102 C4
Mattersey DN10 20 B4
Newstead NG15 130 C3
West Bridgford NG2 186 A4
Abbey Rd Prim Sch NG2 186 A3
Abbey St Ilkeston DE7 157 F1
Nottingham NG7 172 C1
Worksop S80 35 F1
Abbeydale Dr NG18 102 B2
Abbeyfield Rd NG7 184 C4
Abbot Cl NG12 197 F2
Abbot St NG16 158 B2
Abbots Cl NG5 161 E3
Abbots Dr NG15 145 F3
Abbots Rd NG15 145 F3
Abbots Wlk NG15 145 F3
Abbotsbury Cl NG5 146 C1
Abbotsford Dr NG3 223 F4
Abbotsford Mews DE7 157 E2
Abbott Lea NG19 101 E4
Abbott St NG10 193 E3
Abbotts Cres NG22 119 F4
Abbotts Croft NG19 87 F1
Abbotts Way NG24 125 D1
Abbotts Way NG8 172 B2
Abel Collins Homes NG8 171 F1
Abercarn Cl NG6 160 A4
Aberconway St NG21 118 A3
Aberdeen St 9 NG3 173 F3
Aberford Ave NG8 172 B4
Abingdon Dr NG11 196 B4
Abingdon Gdns
Arnold NG5 162 A3
Beeston NG9 183 E2
Abingdon Rd NG2 186 A4
Abingdon Sq NG8 160 A1
Abington Ave NG17 100 C3
Ablard Gdns 6 NG9 183 E1
Acacia Ave
Annesley Woodhouse NG17 130 A4
Gainsborough DN21 15 E1
Acacia Cl NG15 146 A3
Acacia Cres NG4 162 C1
Acacia Ct NG19 88 C1
Acacia Gdns NG16 158 C4
Acacia Rd NG24 140 B3
Acacia Wlk NG9 183 F3
Academy Cl NG6 160 C2
Acaster Cl NG9 184 A2
Acer Cl NG16 113 E2
Ackford Dr S80 35 E2
Acland St DN21 15 E1
Acle Gdns NG6 146 A1
Acorn Ave NG16 158 A4
Acorn Bank NG2 185 D2
Acorn Bsns Pk 11 NG18 102 A3
Acorn Cl NG24 140 B3
Acorn Dr NG4 163 D1
Acorn Pk NG7 184 C4
Acorn Ridge NG20 72 B3
Acorn Way NG18 103 D2
Acourt St NG7 222 B4
Acre Edge Rd NG22 78 C1
Acre The NG17 115 D2
Acreage La NG20 72 C1
Acton Ave
Long Eaton NG10 193 F3
Nottingham NG6 160 B2
Acton Cl NG10 193 F3
Acton Gr NG10 193 F3
Acton Rd Arnold NG5 161 F4
Long Eaton NG10 193 F3
Acton Rd Ind Est NG10 193 F3
Acton St NG10 193 F3
Adam St DE7 170 A3
Adams Ct DE7 157 F2
Adams Hill
Keyworth NG12 197 F2
Nottingham NG7 172 B1
Adams Way DN21 44 B4
Adamsway NG18 103 D2
Adbolton Ave NG4 162 C1
Adbolton Gr NG2 174 A1
Adbolton La NG12 174 C1
Adderley Cl NG5 161 D3
Addington Ct NG12 176 A2
Addington Rd NG7 222 B4
Addison Dr NG15 145 F4
Addison Rd NG4 174 A4
Addison St
Nottingham NG1 223 D4
Tibshelf DE55 99 D4
Addison Villas NG16 143 F1
Adel Dr NG4 162 C1
Adelaide Cl
Gainsborough DN21 24 C3
Stapleford NG9 170 C1
Adelaide Gr NG5 160 C4
Adenburgh Dr NG9 183 E1
Adrian Cl NG9 182 C1
Adrians Cl NG18 102 C3
Aegir Cl DN21 24 C3
Aeneas Ct 12 NG5 173 D4
Aerial Way NG15 145 F3
Agnes Villas NG3 161 F1
Aiber Cres NG5 160 C3
Aidan Gdns NG5 147 D1
Ainsdale Cres NG8 160 A2
Ainsdale Gn DN22 39 E2
Ainsley Rd NG8 172 B3
Ainsworth Dr NG2 173 D1
Aintree Cl NG16 158 C4
Aira Cl NG2 186 B3
Airedale S81 36 A4
Airedale Ave DN11 8 A4
Airedale Cl NG10 193 D3
Airedale Ct NG9 183 D2
Airedale Wlk NG8 171 E2
Aisby Wlk DN21 24 C4
Aitchison Ave NG15 145 F4
Alandale NG22 105 F3
Alandale Ave NG20 72 C3
Alandene Ave NG16 159 D4
Albany Cl Arnold NG5 161 F4
Hucknall NG15 145 E3
Mansfield Woodhouse NG19 88 B1
Albany Ct NG9 170 C1
Albany Dr NG19 88 B1
Albany Inf Sch NG9 170 C1
Albany Jun & Inf Schs NG9 182 C4
Albany Pl NG19 88 B1
Albany Rd NG7 173 D4
Albany St
Gainsborough DN21 15 E1
Ilkeston DE7 170 A3
Albemarle Rd NG5 161 E2
Albert Ave
Balderton NG24 140 B2
Carlton NG4 174 A4
Nottingham NG8 172 B4
Nuthall NG16 159 E3
Stapleford NG9 182 B4
Westwood NG16 128 A2
Albert Ball Cl NG5 160 C4
Albert Gr NG7 222 B3
Albert Hall* NG1 223 D2
Albert Pl LE11 220 A2
Albert Prom LE11 220 B2
Albert Rd Beeston NG9 184 A4
Bunny NG11 196 C1
Long Eaton NG10 193 E4
Nottingham, Alexander Park NG3 173 E4
Nottingham, Old Lenton NG7 222 A1
Retford DN22 39 F3
Sandiacre NG10 182 A3
West Bridgford NG2 185 F4
Albert Sq NG17 100 C1
Albert St
Bottesford NG13 181 D2
Carlton NG4 162 C1
Eastwood NG16 143 F2
Hucknall NG15 146 A4
Loughborough LE11 220 A2
Mansfield NG18 102 A3
Mansfield Woodhouse NG19 88 B2
Market Warsop NG20 74 A3
Newark-on-T NG24 139 F4
Nottingham NG1 223 E2
Radcliffe on T NG12 175 F2
South Normanton DE55 113 D3
Stanton Hill NG17 100 B3
Stapleford NG9 182 B4
Worksop S80 35 F2
Alberta Ave NG16 129 D4
Alberta Terr NG7 173 D4
Albine Rd NG20 72 C3
Albion Cl S80 35 F2
Albion House (Univ of Nottingham) NG9 183 F4
Albion Rd
Long Eaton NG10 193 F4
Sutton in A NG17 100 C1
Albion Rise NG5 147 F1
Albion St Beeston NG9 183 F4
Ilkeston DE7 157 F1
Mansfield NG19 87 F1
Newark-on-T NG24 139 F4
Nottingham NG1 223 E1
Albion Terr DN10 7 D1
Albury Dr NG8 160 A1
Albury Sq NG7 222 C2
Alcester St NG7 184 C4
Alcock Ave NG18 102 C4
Aldene Ct NG9 183 E3
Aldene Way NG14 149 E2
Alder Cl Mansfield NG19 88 C1
New Balderton NG24 140 B3
Shirebrook NG20 72 B3
Worksop S80 35 F1
Alder Ct NG19 101 E3
Alder Gdns NG6 160 A4
Alder Gr
Mansfield Woodhouse NG19 88 A3
New Ollerton NG22 77 E3
Alder Way
Keyworth NG12 198 A1
Shirebrook NG20 72 B2
Sutton in A NG17 100 B2
Aldercar Inf Sch NG16 143 D2
Aldercar La NG16 143 D3
Aldercar Sch NG16 143 D2
Alderman Pounder Inf Sch NG9 183 D3
Alderman White Lower Sch NG9 183 F4
Aldermens Cl NG2 173 E1
Alderney St NG7 222 B1
Alderson Cl DN11 8 A4
Alderson Dr DN11 8 A4
Alderson Rd S80 35 F1
Alderton Rd NG5 161 E3
Aldgate Cl NG6 160 A4
Aldreds La DE75 143 D1
Aldridge Cl NG9 182 C1
Aldrin Cl NG6 159 F3
Aldworth Cl NG5 161 E3
Aldwych Cl
Nottingham NG5 147 D1
Nuthall NG16 159 E1
Alec Rose Gr DN21 24 C4
Alexander Ave
Newark-on-T NG24 125 D2
Selston NG16 128 B4
Alexander Cl NG15 131 D1
Alexander Rd
Farnsfield NG22 119 F3
Nottingham NG7 222 C2
Alexander St NG16 143 F1
Alexander Terr NG16 113 E1
Alexandra Ave
Mansfield NG18 102 A2
Mansfield Woodhouse NG19 88 A3
Sutton in A NG17 100 C2
Alexandra Cres NG9 184 A3
Alexandra Rd
Bircotes DN11 9 D2
Long Eaton NG10 193 E4
Alexandra St
Kirkby in A NG17 115 D3
Market Warsop NG20 74 A3
Nottingham NG5 173 D4
Stapleford NG9 182 B3
Alexandra Terr NG17 100 B3
Alford Cl NG9 184 A3
Alford Rd NG2 186 A3
Alfred Ave NG3 162 A1
Alfred Cl NG3 223 E4
Alfred Ct 16 NG18 102 A4
Alfred St
Gainsborough DN21 15 E1
Kirkby in A NG17 115 D2
Loughborough LE11 220 A3
Pinxton NG16 113 E2
Sutton in A NG17 100 C2
Alfred St Central NG3 223 E4
Alfred St N NG3 223 E4
Alfred St S NG3 173 F3
Alfreton Rd
Huthwaite NG17 113 F4
Newton DE55 99 D2
Nottingham NG7 222 B4
Pinxton NG16 113 E2
Selston, Selston Green DE55, NG16 128 B3
Selston, Underwood NG16 129 D2
South Normanton DE55 113 D3
Sutton in A NG17 100 B1
Alison Ave NG15 131 E1
Alison Wlk NG3 223 F4
All Hallows CE Prim Sch NG4 162 C1
All Hallows Cl DN22 39 F2
All Hallows Dr NG4 162 C1
All Hallows St DN22 39 F2
All Saints Anglican/Methodist Prim Sch NG23 153 E3
All Saints CE Inf Sch NG17 99 F1
All Saints RC Comp Sch NG19 101 F4
All Saints St NG7 222 C4
All Saints Terr NG7 222 C4
Allcroft St NG19 88 B2
Allen Cl NG23 156 B4
Allen Dr NG18 102 C3
Allen Field Ct NG7 222 B1
Allen St Hucknall NG15 146 A4
Worksop S80 35 F1
Allenby Rd NG25 136 B4
Allendale Ave
Beeston NG9 183 E1
Nottingham NG8 160 A1
Allendale Rd NG21 118 A4
Allendale Way NG19 88 C1
Allens Gn Ave NG16 128 C3
Allens Wlk NG5 147 F1
Allesford La NG22 120 A2
Alliance St NG24 125 D1
Allington Ave NG7 222 B1
Allington Dr NG19 101 E4
Allison Ave DN22 40 A2
Allison Gdns NG9 183 E2
Allsopp Dr S81 35 F3
Allsopps La LE11 220 B3
Allwood Dr NG4 174 C4
Allwood Gdns NG15 146 A3
Alma Cl Carlton NG4 163 D1
Nottingham NG1 223 E4
Alma Hill NG16 158 C4
Alma Rd
Nottingham NG3 173 F3
Retford DN22 40 A4
Selston NG16 129 D3
Alma St NG7 173 D4
Almond Ave NG20 72 C3
Almond Cl
Hucknall NG15 146 A3
Kimberley NG16 158 C4
Saxilby LN1 57 D2
Almond Gr
Farndon NG24 139 D3
8 Kirkby in A NG17 114 C3
Worksop S80 35 F1
Almond Rise NG19 88 C1
Almond Wlk NG4 163 D2
Alnwick Cl NG6 160 B3
Alpha Terr NG1 223 D4
Alpine Cres NG4 174 B4
Alpine Ct S80 35 E1
Alpine St NG6 160 C1
Alport Pl NG18 103 D4
Althea Ct 1 NG7 161 D1
Althorpe St NG7 222 C3
Alton Ave NG11 185 D2
Alton Cl NG11 185 E2
Alum Ct NG5 160 C4
Alvenor St DE7 157 F1
Alverstone Rd NG3 161 E1
Alvey Rd NG24 140 C2
Alwood Gr NG11 184 B1
Alwyn Rd NG8 159 F1
Amanda Ave S81 25 F3
Amanda Rd DN11 8 C2
Amber Cl NG21 104 B1
Amber Dr NG16 143 D1
Amber Hill NG5 161 D4
Ambergate Rd NG8 172 A4
Amberley St NG1 223 D2
Ambleside
New Ollerton NG22 77 E3
West Bridgford NG2 186 B4
Ambleside Dr NG16 143 E2
Ambleside Grange S81 35 F4
Ambleside Jun Sch NG8 160 A1
Ambleside Rd NG8 160 A1
Ambleside Way NG4 175 D4
Amcott Ave DN10 14 A4
Amcott Way DN22 39 F4
Amen Cnr NG23 109 D3
American Adventure Theme Pk The* DE75 157 D3
Amersham Rise NG8 160 A1
Amesbury Circ NG8 160 A2
Amethyst Cl NG21 104 B1
Amhurst Rise S81 35 E4
Amos La NG23 98 B2
Ampthill Rise NG5 161 D2
Anastasia Cl DN21 15 E2
Ancaster Gdns NG8 172 A2
Anchor Cl NG8 160 A1
Anchor Rd NG16 143 E1
Anders Dr NG6 159 F3
Anderson Cl NG24 140 A2
Anderson Cres NG9 183 F4
Anderson Ct 6 NG5 161 D4
Anderson Rd DN21 24 C1
Andover Cl 3 NG8 172 A3
Andover Rd
Mansfield NG19 101 E4
Nottingham NG5 160 C3
Andrew Ave
Ilkeston DE7 170 A4
Nottingham NG3 162 A1
Andrew Dr NG21 118 A2
Andrews Dr NG16 143 D2
Anfield Cl NG9 183 D1
Anford Cl NG6 160 A3
Angel Alley NG1 223 F2
Angel Row NG1 223 E2
Angel Row Gall* NG1 223 D2
Angel Yd LE11 220 A2
Angela Ave NG17 115 D1
Angela Cl NG5 147 F1
Angell Gn NG11 195 E4
Anglia Way NG18 103 D2
Angrave Cl NG3 173 F4
Angus Cl Arnold NG5 148 A1
Kimberley NG16 159 D3
Anmer Cl 25 NG2 173 D1
Annan Ct NG8 172 A4
Annes Cl NG3 162 A1
Annesley Cutting NG15 130 B4
Annesley Gr NG1 223 D4
Annesley La NG16 129 D3
Annesley Prim Sch NG15 130 A4
Annesley Rd
Hucknall NG15 145 F4
West Bridgford NG2 185 F4
Annesley Way NG19 101 E3
Annie Holgate Cty Jun & Inf Schs The NG15 145 F3
Annies Wharf LE11 220 B3
Anslow Ave
Beeston NG9 184 A4
Sutton in A NG17 100 C3
Anson Wlk DE7 157 F2
Anstee Rd NG10 193 E3
Anstey Rise NG3 173 F3
Anston Ave S81 35 F3
Anthony Bek Prim Sch NG19 86 C3
Antill St NG9 182 B3
Apley Cl DN21 24 C4
Apollo Dr NG6 159 F3
Appin Rd NG19 101 E3
Apple Tree Cl NG12 186 A2
Apple Tree La NG4 162 C1
Apple Wlk NG4 174 A4
Appleby Cl NG24 140 B4
Appleby Ct S81 35 F4
Appleby Rd NG19 86 C3
Appledore Ave NG8 171 F1
Appledorne Way NG5 147 F1
Appleton Dr LE12 216 A2
Appleton Gate NG24 125 D1
Appleton Rd
Beeston NG9 184 A2
Blidworth NG21 118 A3
Appleton St NG20 74 A2
Appletree Cl NG25 121 F1
Applewood Cl S81 35 E4
Applewood Gr NG5 161 E2
Arboretum St NG1 223 D4
Arbrook Dr NG8 172 B3
Arbutus Cl NG11 184 B1
Arcade The NG24 139 F4
Arcadia Ave NG20 72 C3
Arch Hill NG5 147 F2
Archbishop Cranmer CE Prim Sch NG13 178 C3
Archdale Rd NG5 161 E3
Archer Cres NG8 171 F3
Archer Rd NG9 182 C3
Archer St DE7 157 F2
Archers Dr NG22 106 A3
Archway Rd NG21 90 B4
Arden Cl Beeston NG9 184 A4
Hucknall NG15 146 B3
Arden Gr NG13 177 E3
Ardleigh Cl NG5 146 B1
Ardmore Cl NG2 173 F2
Ardsley Cl DE75 143 D1
Argosy Cl DN10 9 F4
Argyle Cl NG20 73 F2
Argyle Ct NG7 222 B3
Argyle St
Langley Mill NG16 143 E2
Mansfield NG18 102 B3
Nottingham NG7 222 B3
Ariel Cl NG6 160 C3
Arkers Cl NG6 160 B2
Arklow Cl NG8 160 A1
Arkwright Prim Sch NG2 173 E1
Arkwright St
Gainsborough DN21 15 E1
Nottingham NG2 173 E1
Arkwright Wlk NG2 173 E1
Arleston Dr NG8 171 E2
Arlington Ave NG19 88 C2
Arlington Cl NG15 146 A2
Arlington Dr NG3 161 E1
Arlington Way DN22 39 F4
Armadale Cl NG5 162 B4
Armfield Rd NG5 162 B3
Armitage Cl 3 LE11 220 A2
Armitage Dr NG10 194 A4
Armstrong Rd
Mansfield NG19 101 E4
Nottingham NG6 159 F3
Retford DN22 39 F4
Arncliff Cl NG8 171 E2
Arndale Rd NG5 161 E3
Arne Ct 12 NG2 173 E1
Arnesby Rd NG7 222 A1
Arno Ave 8 NG7 173 D4
Arno Vale Gdns NG5 161 F3
Arno Vale Jun Sch NG5 161 F3
Arno Vale Rd NG5 161 F3
Arnold & Carlton Coll of F Ed
Carlton NG4 162 B2
Nottingham NG3 223 F3
Arnold Ave
Long Eaton NG10 193 D2
Retford DN22 40 A2
Southwell NG25 121 F1
Arnold Cres NG10 193 D2
Arnold Hill Comp Sch NG5 162 A3

Arnold La NG3 ......162 B2
Arnold Rd NG5 ......161 D3
Arnos Gr NG8 ......159 E2
Arnot Hill Rd NG5 ......161 F3
Arnside NG9 ......182 C3
Arnside Cl NG5 ......161 D3
Arnside Rd NG5 ......161 D3
Arran Cl NG9 ......170 C1
Arran Sq NG19 ......101 E3
Arthur Ave
 Nottingham NG7 ......222 B2
 Stapleford NG9 ......182 C4
Arthur Cres NG4 ......174 B4
Arthur Gn Ave NG17 ......114 C2
Arthur Mee Ctr (Coll of F Ed)
 The NG9 ......182 B4
Arthur Mee Rd NG9 ......182 C3
Arthur Short Cl S80 ......45 D3
Arthur St Carlton NG4 ......175 D3
 Mansfield NG18 ......102 B3
 Nottingham NG7 ......222 B2
 Pinxton NG16 ......113 E2
Artic Way NG16 ......158 B4
Arum Croft DN22 ......39 E2
Arun Dale NG19 ......88 B1
Arundel Cl
 Gainsborough DN21 ......15 E1
 Sandiacre NG10 ......182 A2
Arundel Dr
 Beeston NG9 ......171 D1
 Carlton in L S81 ......25 F3
 Mansfield NG19 ......101 F4
 Ranskill DN22 ......19 D3
Arundel St NG7 ......222 C3
Arundel Way DN22 ......39 E4
Arundel Wlk NG11 ......9 D3
Ascot Ave NG16 ......158 C4
Ascot Cl NG17 ......115 E2
Ascot Dr Arnold NG5 ......161 E4
 Hucknall NG15 ......145 E3
 Mansfield NG18 ......102 C4
Ascot Pk Est NG10 ......182 B4
Ascot Rd NG8 ......172 B4
Ascott Gdns NG2 ......185 D3
Ash Cl Bingham NG13 ......178 A2
 Burton Joyce NG14 ......163 F2
 Hucknall NG15 ......145 E3
 Pinxton NG16 ......113 E1
 Worksop S80 ......35 F1
Ash Cres
 Kirkby in A NG17 ......114 B3
 Nuthall NG16 ......159 D3
Ash Ct NG4 ......174 C4
Ash Gr Brinsley NG16 ......143 E4
 Gainsborough DN21 ......15 E1
 Hathern LE12 ......213 D1
 Keyworth NG12 ......198 A2
 Long Eaton NG10 ......193 E3
 Sandiacre NG10 ......182 A4
 Selston NG16 ......128 C4
 Shirebrook NG20 ......72 B3
 Stapleford NG9 ......182 B4
 Sutton in A NG17 ......100 B4
 Woodborough NG14 ......149 E2
Ash Holt Dr S81 ......35 F4
Ash La LE12 ......206 B2
Ash Lea Cl NG12 ......187 F1
Ash Lea Specl Sch
 NG12 ......187 F1
Ash Mount Rd NG16 ......143 D2
Ash Rd NG24 ......139 F2
Ash St DE7 ......157 F2
Ash Tree Ave
 Bawtry DN10 ......9 F4
 Mansfield Woodhouse
 NG19 ......88 B3
Ash Tree Cl NG25 ......136 B4
Ash Tree Sq NG9 ......183 D4
Ash Vale Rd NG22 ......64 A1
Ash Villas 8 NG7 ......161 D1
Ash Wlk LE12 ......214 B4
Ashbourne Cl NG9 ......171 D1
Ashbourne Ct NG6 ......159 F3
Ashbourne Rd NG16 ......129 E1
Ashbourne St
 Nottingham NG7 ......222 C3
 Shirebrook NG20 ......72 C2
Ashburnham Ave NG7 ......222 B2
Ashby Ave NG19 ......88 B3

Ashfield Rd
 Huthwaite NG17 ......100 A2
 Nottingham NG2 ......173 F2
Ashfield St NG17 ......101 D3
Ashford Ct DN22 ......39 E2
Ashford Dr NG15 ......117 D2
Ashford Pl DE7 ......157 F3
Ashford Rise
 Nottingham NG8 ......171 E1
 Sutton in A NG17 ......100 B2
Ashforth Ave DE75 ......143 D1
Ashforth St NG3 ......223 F4
Ashgate NG17 ......146 A3
Ashington Dr NG5 ......148 A1
Ashland Rd NG17 ......100 B2
Ashland Rd W NG17 ......100 A2
Ashlands Cl NG17 ......100 A2
Ashlea DN10 ......6 C1
Ashleigh Way NG18 ......89 D1
Ashley Cl NG9 ......183 E3
Ashley Cres NG12 ......197 F2
Ashley Ct S81 ......35 F3
Ashley La NG22 ......41 F1
Ashley Rd
 Keyworth NG12 ......197 F2
 Worksop S81 ......35 F3
Ashley St 18 NG3 ......173 F3
Ashley Terr S80 ......35 F2
Ashling St NG2 ......173 E1
Ashmore Ave NG17 ......100 B1
Ashmount Specl Sch
 LE11 ......220 A1
Ashness Cl NG2 ......186 B3
Ashover Cl
 Nottingham NG3 ......173 F4
 Ravenshead NG15 ......117 D2
Ashridge Way NG2 ......186 B2
Ashton Ave NG5 ......147 F1
Ashton Cl NG21 ......101 D3
Ashvale Rd NG12 ......173 D1
Ashwater Dr NG3 ......162 B3
Ashwell Ave NG19 ......88 C3
Ashwell Gdns NG7 ......172 C4
Ashwell St NG4 ......174 C3
Ashwick Cl NG11 ......185 D3
Ashwood Ave NG17 ......115 E3
Ashwood Cl NG19 ......88 C3
Ashwood Rd S80 ......35 D1
Ashworth Ave NG11 ......196 B4
Ashworth Cl
 Newark-on-T NG24 ......140 B4
 Nottingham NG3 ......174 B3
Ashworth Cres
 North Leverton w H DN22 ......32 B1
 Nottingham NG3 ......162 A1
Ashworth Dr NG19 ......88 C2
Askeby Dr NG8 ......159 E1
Askew La NG20 ......74 A2
Askham La DN22 ......52 A3
Askham Rd NG22 ......51 F1
Aslockton Dr NG8 ......160 B1
Aslockton Sta NG13 ......179 D3
Aspen Cl
 Bingham NG13 ......178 A2
 Laughterton LN1 ......55 D2
 Tuxford NG22 ......64 A1
 Walesby NG22 ......64 A1
Aspen Ct
 Gainsborough DN21 ......15 F1
 Mansfield NG19 ......88 C1
 Tuxford NG22 ......66 A1
Aspen Rd NG6 ......159 F4
Asper St NG4 ......174 C2
Aspinall Ct 8 NG8 ......172 B3
Aspley La NG8 ......172 B4
Aspley Pk Dr NG8 ......172 A4
Aspley Pl NG7 ......222 B4
Aspley Wood Sch
 NG8 ......172 A4
Asquith Mews NG5 ......102 C3
Asquith Prim Sch
 NG18 ......102 C3
Asquith St
 Gainsborough DN21 ......15 D1
 Mansfield NG18 ......102 C3
Assarts Rd NG16 ......159 F1
Astcote Cl DE75 ......143 D1
Aster Rd NG3 ......173 F4
Astle Ct NG5 ......162 B3
Astley Cl NG17 ......130 A4
Astley Dr NG3 ......161 F1
Aston Ave NG9 ......172 A1
Aston Ct DE7 ......157 F1
Aston Dr NG6 ......146 B1
Aston Gn NG9 ......182 C4
Astral Gdns NG15 ......145 E2
Astwith La S44, S45 ......85 D3
Astwood Cl NG8 ......171 F4
Athelstan Rd S80 ......35 F1
Atherfield Gdns NG16 ......143 F2
Atherton Rd DE7 ......157 E2
Atherton Rise NG8 ......160 A2
Athorpe Gr NG6 ......160 C2
Atkin La NG18 ......102 A2
Attenborough La NG9 ......183 E2
Attenborough Nature
 Reserve* NG9 ......183 F1
Attenborough Prep Sch
 NG9 ......183 E1
Attenborough Sta
 NG9 ......183 E1
Attercliffe Terr 12 NG2 ......173 E1

Attewell Rd NG16 ......158 A3
Attlee Ave NG19 ......89 D1
Aubrey Ave 8 NG2 ......173 F2
Aubrey Rd NG5 ......161 D1
Auckland Cl NG7 ......222 A3
Auckland Rd
 Hucknall NG15 ......145 E3
 Retford DN22 ......39 E4
Audley Cl DE7 ......157 E2
Audley Dr NG9 ......171 F1
Audon Ave NG9 ......183 F3
Audrey Cres NG17 ......131 D4
Augustine Gdns NG5 ......147 D1
Ault Hucknall La S44 ......86 A4
Aumberry Gap LE11 ......220 A2
Aurillac Way DN22 ......29 E1
Austen Ave
 Long Eaton NG10 ......193 E3
 Nottingham NG7 ......173 D4
Austin Cl NG18 ......102 C4
Austin St
 Nottingham NG6 ......160 B4
 Shirebrook NG20 ......73 D2
Austins Dr NG10 ......182 A2
Austrey Ave NG9 ......184 A4
Avalon Cl NG6 ......160 C3
Ave A NG1 ......223 F2
Ave B NG1 ......223 F2
Ave C NG1 ......223 F2
Ave D NG1 ......173 F2
Ave E 10 NG1 ......173 F3
Avebury Cl NG11 ......195 E4
Avenue Cl NG5 ......160 C4
Avenue Rd DN22 ......29 F3
Avenue The
 Calverton NG14 ......148 C4
 Gainsborough DN21 ......15 F1
 Gunthorpe NG14 ......164 C3
 Newark-on-T NG24 ......140 A4
 Sutton in A NG17 ......100 C1
Averham Cl NG19 ......101 E3
Averton Sq NG8 ......172 B2
Avocet Cl NG13 ......177 F4
Avocet Cl NG13 ......178 A2
Avocet Gr S81 ......35 E3
Avocet Wharf 22 NG7 ......172 C1
Avon Ave NG15 ......145 F2
Avon Cl NG17 ......129 F4
Avon Gdns NG2 ......185 F4
Avon Pl NG9 ......184 A4
Avon Rd Carlton NG4 ......162 C1
 Nottingham NG3 ......174 A3
Avon Rise DN22 ......40 A4
Avon Vale Rd LE11 ......220 B1
Avon Way
 Mansfield NG18 ......103 D3
 Worksop S81 ......35 F4
Avonbridge Cl NG5 ......148 B1
Avondale
 Cotgrave NG12 ......188 A2
 Mansfield NG18 ......102 C4
Avondale Cl NG10 ......193 D3
Avondale Rd NG4 ......174 B3
Avonlea Cl DE7 ......170 A3
Awsworth Inf Sch
 NG16 ......158 B2
Awsworth Jun Sch
 NG16 ......158 B3
Awsworth La NG16 ......158 B3
Awsworth Rd DE7 ......157 F1
Axford Cl NG4 ......162 C2
Aylesham Ave NG5 ......161 F3
Aylestone Dr NG8 ......172 A4
Ayr St NG7 ......222 C4
Ayscough Ave NG16 ......159 F2
Ayton Cl NG2 ......173 D1
Ayton Gdns NG9 ......183 E1
Azalea Cl NG16 ......158 B4
Azimghur Rd NG13 ......179 D2

B

B Rd NG9 ......184 B3
Babbacombe Cl NG5 ......161 D3
Babbacombe Way
 NG15 ......145 E3
Babbington Cres NG4 ......162 C1
Babbington La NG16 ......158 C2
Babbington St DE55 ......99 D3
Babbington Bsns Coll
 NG7 ......223 D1
Babington Dr NG9 ......183 E3
Babworth Cres DN22 ......39 E3
Babworth Rd DN22 ......39 D3
Back La Claypole NG23 ......156 B3
 Cotes LE12 ......220 C3
 Cropwell Butler NG12 ......189 D3
 Eakring NG22 ......106 C4
 East Markham NG22 ......66 A4
 Halam NG22 ......120 C1
 Huthwaite NG17 ......99 F2
 Keyworth NG12 ......197 F3
 Kirkby in A NG17 ......114 C4
 Long Clawson LE14 ......211 E2
 Misson DN10 ......4 A1
 Morton NG25 ......137 E2
 Ollerton NG22 ......77 D2
 Ranskill DN22 ......19 D2
 Sutton in A NG17 ......100 C1
 Thorpe Salvin S80 ......34 A3
 Willoughby-on-t-W LE12 ......217 E3
Back St
 Barnby in t W NG24 ......142 A3
 East Stockwith DN21 ......7 F1

Back St continued
 South Clifton NG23 ......68 C1
Back Terr DN22 ......39 F4
Bacon Cl NG16 ......158 A4
Bacon St DN21 ......24 B3
Bacton Ave NG6 ......160 A4
Bacton Gdns 2 NG6 ......160 A4
Baden Powell Rd NG3 ......174 A2
Bader NG11 ......185 D4
Bader Rise NG10 ......20 A4
Bader View DN10 ......20 A4
Badger Cl NG15 ......145 E3
Badger La NG19 ......103 D4
Badger Way NG19 ......103 D4
Badgers Chase DN22 ......29 F1
Baggaley Cres NG3 ......88 A1
Bagnall Ave NG5 ......161 E4
Bagnall Rd NG6 ......160 A4
Bagshaw St NG19 ......87 D2
Bagthorpe Cl NG5 ......161 D2
Bagthorpe Prim Sch
 NG16 ......129 C2
Baildon Cl NG8 ......172 B2
Bailey Brook Cres
 NG16 ......143 D2
Bailey Brook Dr NG16 ......143 D2
Bailey Brook Ind Est
 NG16 ......143 D1
Bailey Brook Wlk
 NG16 ......143 D1
Bailey Cl NG5 ......161 E4
Bailey Ct NG19 ......101 F4
Bailey Gr Rd NG16 ......143 E1
Bailey Grove Rd NG16 ......143 E1
Bailey La NG12 ......175 F1
Bailey Rd NG12 ......139 F3
Bailey St Carlton NG3 ......175 D4
 Nottingham NG6 ......160 C1
 Stapleford NG9 ......182 B3
Bainbridge Rd
 Loughborough LE11 ......220 B1
 Market Warsop NG20 ......74 A2
Bainbridge Terr NG17 ......100 B3
Bainbridge The NG14 ......149 D4
Baines Ave NG24 ......140 B2
Baines Rd DN21 ......24 C4
Bainton Gr NG7 ......184 C1
Baker Ave NG5 ......148 A1
Baker Brook Ind Pk
 NG15 ......146 B3
Baker La NG20 ......60 A1
Baker Rd
 Eastwood NG16 ......144 B1
 Mansfield Woodhouse
 NG19 ......88 B3
Baker St Hucknall NG15 ......146 A4
 22 Ilkeston DE7 ......157 F1
 Nottingham NG1 ......173 D2
Bakerdale Rd NG3 ......174 A3
Bakers Cl NG7 ......222 A4
Bakers Hollow NG12 ......187 F2
Bakers La
 Colston Bassett NG12 ......200 C4
 Redmile NG13 ......192 C2
Bakewell Ave NG4 ......162 C1
Bakewell Cl NG24 ......140 B2
Bakewell Dr NG5 ......160 C4
Bakewell Rd NG10 ......193 F3
Bala Dr NG5 ......161 D4
Balderton Cl NG19 ......101 F4
Balderton Gate NG24 ......140 A4
Balderton La NG24 ......141 D4
Baldwin Cl NG19 ......89 D1
Baldwin Ct NG7 ......222 B3
Baldwin St
 Eastwood NG16 ......144 B1
 Nottingham NG7 ......222 C3
Balfour Cl
 Kirkby in A NG17 ......115 E2
Balfour Gdns 18 NG2 ......173 D1
Ball Hill DE55 ......113 D3
Ball St NG3 ......173 F4
Ballantrae Cl NG5 ......148 C1
Ballater Cl NG17 ......87 F1
Ballerat Cres NG5 ......160 C4
Balloon Houses NG6 ......171 D2
Balloon Wood Ind Est
 NG8 ......171 D2
Balls La NG17 ......115 E1
Balmoral Ave NG2 ......185 F4
Balmoral Cl
 ... in L S81 ......25 F3
 Mansfield Woodhouse
 NG19 ......88 C3
 Sandiacre NG10 ......182 A2
Balmoral Cres NG8 ......171 E3
Balmoral Ct DN11 ......9 D3
Balmoral Dr
 Beeston NG9 ......171 E1
 Mansfield NG19 ......87 F1
Balmoral Gr NG15 ......146 A4
Balmoral Rd
 Bingham NG13 ......177 E2
 Carlton NG4 ......174 C3
 Nottingham NG1 ......223 D4
Bamburgh Cl 10 NG17 ......115 E1
Bamford Dr NG19 ......103 D3
Bamford St DE55 ......99 D2
Bamkin Cl NG15 ......146 A3
Bampton St 33 LE11 ......220 A2
Banbury Ave NG9 ......182 C2
Banbury Mount 5 NG5 ......161 E1
Banchory Cl NG19 ......87 F1
Bancroft La NG18 ......101 F4
Bancroft Rd NG24 ......140 A3

Bancroft St NG6 ......160 B4
Banes Rd NG13 ......178 A2
Bangor Wlk 8 NG3 ......173 E4
Bank Ave NG17 ......100 C1
Bank Cl Creswell S80 ......58 B4
 Shirebrook NG20 ......72 C2
Bank End Rd DN10 ......1 B2
Bank Hill NG14 ......149 D2
Bank Pl NG1 ......223 E2
Bank Side DN22 ......39 F2
Bank St
 Langley Mill NG16 ......143 E2
 Long Eaton NG10 ......193 F4
 ... NG4 ......160 A4
Bank Yd 2 NG9 ......171 E1
Banks Ave NG17 ......114 C3
Banks Cl NG5 ......162 A3
Banks Cres NG13 ......177 F2
Banks Paddock NG13 ......177 F2
Banks Rd NG9 ......182 C1
Banks Rd Inf Sch NG9 ......182 C1
Banks The NG13 ......177 F2
Bankwood Cl NG8 ......160 A1
Bannerman Rd
 Kirkby in A NG17 ......114 C3
 Nottingham NG6 ......160 B3
Baptist La NG23 ......111 F4
Bar Gate NG24 ......124 C1
Bar La NG6 ......160 B1
Bar La Ind Pk NG6 ......160 B1
Bar Rd Beckingham DN10 ......23 E4
 ... NG10 ......23 E4
Bar Rd N SN10 ......23 E4
Bar Rd S SN10 ......23 E4
Barbara Sq NG15 ......130 C1
Barber Cl DE7 ......157 F2
Barber St NG16 ......144 A1
Barbers Wood Cl
 NG15 ......117 D1
Barbrook Cl NG8 ......172 A3
Barbury Dr NG11 ......195 E4
Barclay Ct DE7 ......157 E2
Barden Rd NG3 ......162 A2
Bardfield Gdns NG5 ......146 B1
Bardney Dr NG6 ......160 A4
Bardsey Gdns NG3 ......161 D4
Barent Cl NG5 ......160 C3
Barent Wlk NG5 ......160 C3
Barker Ave
 Sutton in A NG17 ......100 B4
 Westwood NG16 ......128 A2
Barker Ave E NG10 ......182 A3
Barker Ave N NG10 ......182 A3
Barker Gate
 Hucknall NG15 ......145 F4
 Ilkeston DE7 ......157 F1
 Nottingham NG1 ......223 F2
Barker Hades Rd S81 ......16 C1
Barker La NG9 ......150 C1
Barker St NG17 ......99 F2
Barkers Field LE14 ......211 E2
Barkers La NG9 ......183 F2
Barkestone La
 Barkestone-le-V NG13 ......192 A1
 Bottesford NG13 ......181 D1
Barkla Cl NG11 ......195 E4
Barkston Cl NG24 ......140 A4
Barley Croft
 South Normanton DE55 ......113 D2
 West Bridgford NG2 ......185 E2
Barley Dale Dr NG9 ......170 B1
Barleylands NG11 ......196 B3
Barling Dr DE7 ......157 E1
Barlock Rd NG6 ......160 C2
Barlow Dr N NG16 ......158 A2
Barlow Dr S NG16 ......158 A2
Barn Cl Cotgrave NG12 ......187 F1
 Mansfield NG18 ......102 C3
 Worksop S81 ......36 A4
Barn Croft NG9 ......183 D3
Barnards Pl LE14 ......211 E2
Barnby Gate NG24 ......140 A4
Barnby La NG23 ......156 C4
Barnby Rd NG24 ......140 B3
Barnby Rd Prim Sch
 NG24 ......140 A4
Barnby Wlk NG5 ......161 E2
Barndale Cl NG2 ......185 E2
Barnes Cres NG17 ......114 C4
Barnes Ct DN22 ......29 E1
Barnes Rd NG5 ......160 C4
Barnet Rd NG3 ......174 A4
Barnett Ct NG12 ......197 F2
Barnfield NG11 ......185 D2
Barnfield Cl LE12 ......212 A2
Barnfield Rd NG23 ......98 A1
Barnsley Terr 10 NG2 ......173 E1
Barnston Rd NG2 ......174 A3
Barnstone La NG13 ......191 D3
Barnstone Rd NG13 ......190 B1
Barnum Cl NG8 ......171 F3
Barons Cl NG4 ......162 C1
Barra Mews 20 NG2 ......173 D1
Barrack La NG7 ......222 B2
Barrack Row 11 LE11 ......220 A2
Barratt Cl Beeston NG9 ......183 E1
 Cropwell Bishop NG12 ......189 D2
Barratt Cres NG9 ......183 E1
Barratt La NG9 ......183 E1
Barrhead Cl NG5 ......146 C1
Barringer Rd NG17 ......114 C4
Barrington Cl NG12 ......189 E2
Barrique Rd NG7 ......172 C1
Barrow Rd LE12 ......220 C3

Barrow Slade NG12 ....197 F1
Barrow St LE11 ....220 A2
Barrowhill Wlk NG18 ...103 D3
Barrows Hill La NG16 ..128 B3
Barry St NG6 ....160 A4
Barrydale Ave NG9 .....183 F3
Bars Hill LE12 ....206 B1
Bartlow Rd NG8 ....171 E4
Barton Cl
  Mansfield Woodhouse
  NG19 ....89 D1
  Ruddington NG11 ......196 A3
Barton La
  Barton in F NG11 ......195 D3
  Beeston NG9 ....183 E1
  Nottingham NG11 ......184 B1
Barton Rd NG10 ....194 A3
Barton St NG9 ....184 A3
Bartons Cl NG16 ....144 B1
Barwell Dr NG8 ....159 E1
Basa Cres NG5 ....160 B2
Basford Hall Coll NG6 ..160 B2
Basford Hall Coll Annexe
  NG7 ....222 B4
Basford Hall Coll F Ed
  Annexe NG7 ....222 B4
Basford Rd NG6 ....160 B1
Baskin La NG9 ....183 E2
Baslow Ave NG4 ....162 C1
Baslow Cl NG10 ....193 D3
Baslow Dr NG9 ....172 A1
Baslow Way NG18 .....103 D3
Bassetlaw District General
  Hospl S81 ....36 A3
Bassett Cl NG16 ....158 C4
Bassett Rd NG16 ......158 C4
Bassett The NG20 ......72 B3
Bassingfield La 186 C4
Bastion St NG7 ....222 A3
Bateman Gdns 20 NG2 .172 C4
Bateman Rd LE12 .....205 F1
Batemans Yd NG17 ...114 B2
Bath La Mansfield NG18 .102 B4
  Market Warsop NG19 ...73 E1
Bath St Ilkeston DE7 ..157 F1
  Mansfield NG18 ....102 A3
  Nottingham NG1 ......223 F3
  Sutton in A NG17 .....100 C2
Bathley La
  Little Carlton NG23 ...124 A4
  South Muskham NG3 ..110 A1
Bathley St NG2 ....173 E1
Baths La NG15 ....146 A4
Bathurst Dr NG8 ......172 A3
Bathurst Terr NG20 .....58 C1
Bathwood Dr
  Mansfield NG17, NG18 ..101 F3
  Sutton in A NG17,
  NG18 ....101 D1
Batley La NG19 ....86 C2
Baulk La Beeston NG9 .183 D3
  Harworth DN11 ....8 C3
  Torworth DN22 ....19 D1
  Worksop S81 ....35 F3
Baulk The
  Clarborough DN22 .....40 C4
  Worksop S81 ....35 F3
Baulker La
  Blidworth NG21 ....118 C2
  Clipstone NG21 ....90 A2
  Farnsfield NG22 ....119 D2
Baums La NG18 ....102 B3
Bawtry Cl DN11 ....8 D2
Bawtry Rd Bawtry DN10 .10 B4
  Blyth S81 ....18 A3
  Everton DN10 ....11 D2
  Harworth DN11 ....9 D3
  Misson DN10 ....4 A2
  Tickhill DN11 ....8 C4
Bawtry Wlk NG3 ....173 F3
Baxter Hill NG19 ....86 A2
Baxter St LE11 ....220 A2
Bayard Ct NG8 ....172 B3
Bayard St DN21 ....15 E1
Bayliss Rd NG4 ....162 B2
Bayswater Rd NG16 ..158 C4
Baythorn Rd NG8 .....171 E3
Beacon Dr
  Kirkby in A NG17 ......115 C3
  Loughborough LE11 ..220 A1
Beacon Hill Dr NG15 ..145 C3
Beacon Hill Rd
  Gringley on t H DN10 ..13 D1
  Newark-on-T NG24 ....140 B4
Beacon Hill Rise NG3 ..173 F3
Beacon Hts NG24 ....140 B4
Beacon Rd
  Beeston NG9 ....184 A3
  Loughborough LE11 ..220 A1
Beacon View NG13 ....181 D2
Beacon Way NG24 ....140 B4
Beaconsfield Dr NG24 ..125 F1
Beaconsfield St
  Long Eaton NG10 .....193 E4
  Nottingham NG7 ......172 C4
Bean Ave S80 ....36 A2
Bean Cl NG6 ....159 F3
Beanford La
  Calverton NG14 ....133 F2
  Oxton NG25 ....134 A2
Beardall St
  Hucknall NG15 ....146 A3
  🔟 Mansfield NG18 ....102 A4
Beardall St Prim Sch
  NG15 ....146 A3

Beardsalls Row DN22 ...39 F4
Beardsley Gdns NG2 ..173 D1
Beardsley Rd NG21 ....76 B1
Beardsmore Gr NG15 .130 C1
Beast Mkt Hill
  Newark-on-T NG24 ....124 C1
  Nottingham NG1 ......223 E2
Beatty Wlk DE7 ....157 F2
Beauclerk Dr NG5 ....160 C4
Beaufit La NG16 ....113 F1
Beaufort Ct NG11 .....185 E2
Beaufort Dr NG9 ......183 E3
Beaufort Gdns DN10 ...9 F4
Beaufort St DN21 ......15 E2
Beaufort Way S81 .....35 F4
Beaulieu Gdns NG2 ...185 E3
Beauly Dr NG19 ......101 E3
Beaumaris Dr
  Beeston NG9 ....183 D2
  Carlton NG4 ....163 D1
Beaumond Cross
  NG24 ....124 C1
Beaumont Ave NG18 ..102 C3
Beaumont Cl
  Keyworth NG12 ....197 F2
  Stapleford NG9 ....170 C1
Beaumont Ct LE11 ....220 A3
Beaumont Gdns NG2 ..185 E2
Beaumont Rd LE11 ....220 A1
Beaumont Rise S80 ...35 E2
Beaumont St
  Gainsborough DN21 ...24 B4
  Nottingham NG2 ......173 F2
Beaumont Wlk NG24 ..125 D1
Beauvale NG16 ....144 B1
Beauvale Cres NG15 ..145 F3
Beauvale Dr DE7 ......157 F3
Beauvale Rd
  Annesley Woodhouse
  NG17 ....114 F4
  Hucknall NG15 ....145 F3
  Nottingham NG2 .....173 E1
Beauvale Rise NG16 ..144 B1
Beaver Pl S80 ....35 F2
Beazley Ave NG18 ....101 F4
Beck Ave NG14 ....148 C4
Beck Cres
  Blidworth NG21 ......118 A2
  Mansfield NG19 .....101 F4
Beck La Clayworth DN22 .21 F2
  Farnsfield NG22 ......119 F3
  Sutton in A NG17,
  NG19 ....101 D3
Beck St Carlton NG4 ..174 C4
  Nottingham NG1 ......223 F3
  Thurgarton NG14 ....151 E4
Beckenham Rd NG2 ..222 B4
Becket RC Comp Sch
  NG11 ....185 D3
Becket Sch The NG2 ..185 E4
Beckett Ave
  Carlton NG4 ....25 F4
  Gainsborough DN21 ...15 F1
  Mansfield NG19 ......87 F1
Beckett Ct NG4 ....162 B2
Beckford Rd 41 NG2 ..173 E2
Beckhampton Rd NG5 .161 D4
Beckingham Ct NG19 .101 F4
Beckingham Pri Sch
  DN10 ....14 A1
Beckingham Rd DN10 ..14 A1
Beckingthorpe Dr
  NG13 ....181 D2
Beckland Hill NG22 ....65 F3
Beckley Rd NG8 ......159 F1
Beckon Mdw DN10 ....23 E4
Beckside
  Lowdham NG14 ....150 C1
  West Bridgford NG2 .186 B3
Bedale S81 ....36 A4
Bedale Ct NG9 ....183 D2
Bedale Rd NG5 ....161 E3
Bedarra Gr NG2 ......222 A2
Bede House La NG24 .140 A4
Bede Ling NG2 ....185 E3
Bedford Ave NG18 ...102 C4
Bedford Ct DE74 .....203 E1
Bedford Ct Bawtry DN10 .9 F4
  Stapleford NG9 ......170 C1
Bedford Gr NG6 ......160 B3
Bedford Row NG1 ....223 F3
Bedford Sq 42 LE11 ..220 A2
Bedford St LE11 ......220 A2
Bedlington Gdns NG3 .161 F1
Bee Hive La 48 LE11 ..220 A2
Beech Ave
  Beeston NG9 ....184 A3
  Bingham NG13 ....178 A2
  Carlton NG4 ....174 C3
  East Leake LE12 ......214 B4
  Gainsborough DN21 ...15 F1
  Hucknall NG15 ....146 A4
  Huthwaite NG17 .....100 A2
  Keyworth NG12 ......198 A1
  Kirkby in A NG17 ....114 C3
  Long Eaton NG10 ...182 C1
  🔟 Mansfield NG18 ..102 A4
  New Ollerton NG22 ...77 E2
  Nottingham, Hyson Green
  NG7 ....173 D4
  Nottingham, Mapperley
  NG3 ....162 A2
  Nuttall NG16 ....159 D3
  Pinxton NG16 ....113 F2
  Ravenshead NG15 ..116 C2
  Sandiacre NG10 ......182 A4

Beech Ave continued
  Tickhill DN11 ....8 A4
  Worksop S81 ....35 F3
Beech Cl
  Gringley on t H DN10 ..12 C1
  Nottingham NG6 .....160 B2
  Radcliffe on T NG12 .175 F1
  West Bridgford NG2 .186 A2
Beech Cres S44 ....86 A4
Beech Ct
  Nottingham NG3 .....162 A2
  Selston NG16 ....129 D2
Beech Gr
  Blidworth NG21 ......118 B3
  Carlton in L S81 ....25 F4
  South Normanton DE55 ..113 D3
  Sutton in A NG17 ....87 F1
Beech Hill Cres NG19 ..87 F1
Beech Hill Dr NG19 ....87 F1
Beech Hill Specl Sch
  NG19 ....87 F1
Beech Rd Harworth DN11 ..9 D3
  Selston NG16 ....129 D2
Beech St NG17 ....100 B4
Beech Tree Ave NG18 ..88 A3
Beech Wlk DN22 ....50 A2
Beecham Ave NG3 ...173 F4
Beechcroft S81 ....36 A3
Beechdale Ave NG17 ..100 C2
Beechdale Cres NG17 .100 C2
Beechdale Rd
  Mansfield Woodhouse
  NG19 ....89 D1
  Nottingham NG8 ....172 A4
Beechdale La DN10 ...14 A1
Beeches Rd LE11 ....220 B1
Beeches The
  Carlton NG3 ....174 A4
  Sutton in A NG17 ....100 B4
  Tuxford NG22 ....65 F1
Beechways DN22 ......39 E2
Beechwood Cl
  Mansfield Woodhouse
  NG19 ....89 D1
  Sutton in A NG17 ....101 D3
Beechwood Cres DN22 ..37 F3
Beechwood Ct NG17 .101 D3
Beechwood Dr DN22 .38 B3
Beechwood Gr NG17 .101 D3
Beechwood Rd
  Arnold NG5 ....162 A4
  🔟 Kirkby in A NG17 .114 C4
Beehive La LN6 ....84 C1
Beehive St DN22 ....39 F3
Beeley Ave NG17 ....100 C1
Beeley Cl NG18 ....103 D3
Beeston Cl NG6 ......146 C2
Beeston Ct NG6 ......160 B3
Beeston Fields Dr
  NG9 ....144 C1
Beeston Fields Jun & Inf
  Schs NG9 ....183 E3
Beeston Fields Prim Sch
  NG9 ....183 F4
Beeston La NG9 ......184 A4
Beeston Rd
  Newark-on-T NG24 ...140 A4
  Nottingham NG7 ....172 B1
Beeston Sta NG9 .....184 A3
Beethan Ct NG13 ....177 F2
Beggarlee Pk NG16 ..144 A2
Behay Gdns NG3 .....138 B4
Beighton Ct NG18 ...103 D3
Beighton St NG17 ....100 C2
Belconnen Rd NG5 ..161 D3
Belfmoor Cl S80 ....45 D3
Belford Cl NG6 ....159 F4
Belfry Cl 1 NG17 ....101 D4
Belfry Way NG2 ....186 B2
Belgrave Ct NG9 ....9 F4
Belgrave Mews NG11 .185 E2
Belgrave Rd NG6 .....160 A4
Belgrave Sq NG1 .....223 D3
Bell Foundry Mus*
  LE11 ....220 B2
Bell La Collingham NG23 ..111 F4
  Nottingham NG11 ....185 D4
  Weston NG23 ....81 D3
Bell St NG4 ....174 B4
Bellamy Rd NG18 ....103 D1
Bellar Gate NG1 .....223 F2
Belle Vue La NG21 ...118 A3
Belle-Isle Rd NG15 ..146 A4
Belleville Dr NG5 ....161 D4
Bellevue Ct NG3 .....173 F3
Bellmore Gdns NG8 ..171 E3
Bells La NG8 ....160 A4
Bellsfield Cl S80 ....45 D3
Belmond Cl NG24 ...139 F3
Belmont Ave NG6 ...160 B4
Belmont Cl
  Beeston NG9 ....183 D2
  Hucknall NG15 ....146 A2
  Mansfield Woodhouse
  NG19 ....89 D1
Belmont Rd NG17 ...115 D1
Belper Ave NG4 .....162 B1
Belper Cres NG4 ....162 B1
Belper Rd NG7 ......172 C4
Belper St NG18 ......102 B4
Belper Way NG18 ...102 B4
Belsay Rd NG5 ......161 D4
Belsford Ct NG16 ...159 D4
Belt Rd The DN21 ...15 F2
Belton Cl NG10 .....182 A2
Belton Dr NG2 ......185 D4

Belton Rd LE11 ......220 A3
Belton Rd W Extension
  LE11 ....220 A3
Belton St 20 NG7 ....172 C4
Belvedere Ave 28 NG7 .172 C4
Belvedere St NG18 ..102 A3
Belvoir Ave NG13 ....181 D1
Belvoir Cl
  Aslockton NG13 ......178 C2
  Long Eaton NG10 ...193 F3
Belvoir Cres
  Langar NG13 ....190 B1
  Newark-on-T NG24 ..140 A3
Belvoir High Sch
  NG13 ....181 D1
Belvoir Hill NG2 .....173 F2
Belvoir Pl NG24 ......140 B2
Belvoir Rd
  Balderton NG24 .....140 B2
  Bottesford NG13 ....181 D1
  Carlton NG4 ....175 D4
  Redmile NG13 ....192 C2
  West Bridgford NG2 .174 A1
Belvoir St
  Hucknall NG15 ....145 F4
  Nottingham NG3 .....161 F1
Belvoir Terr 1 NG7 ...15 D2
Belward St NG1 ......223 F2
Belwood Cl NG7 ......184 C1
Bembridge S81 ....36 A3
Bembridge Ct NG9 ..183 D4
Bembridge Dr NG5 ..161 D3
Ben Mayo Ct NG7 ...222 B4
Ben St NG7 ....222 B4
Bendigo La NG2 .....174 A2
Benedict Ct 3 NG5 ..147 D1
Benet Dr NG22 ......106 A3
Benington Dr NG8 ..171 E2
Benjamin Adlard Cty Prim
  Sch D21 ....24 B3
Benner Ave NG17 ...170 A3
Bennerley Ave NG7 ..157 F2
Bennerley Ct NG6 ...159 F4
Bennerley Fields Sch
  DE7 ....157 F2
Bennerley Rd NG6 ..159 F4
Bennerley Sch DE7 .157 F2
Bennett Rd NG3 ....102 C3
Bennett Rd NG3 ....162 A2
Bennett St
  Long Eaton NG10 ...182 B1
  Mansfield NG3 ....161 F1
  Sandiacre NG10 ....182 A3
  Sutton in A NG17 ...100 C2
Bentinck Ct NG15 ...145 F3
Bennington Wlk NG8 ..88 C2
Bentick St NG18 ....102 B4
Bentinck Ave NG12 .186 B1
Bentinck Cl NG20 ....74 A2
Bentinck Dr DE7 ....157 F3
Beresford Dr
  Long Eaton NG10 ...193 D3
  Mansfield Woodhouse
  NG19 ....88 B3
Beresford St
  Mansfield NG18 .....102 B3
  Nottingham NG7 ....222 A3
Berkeley Ave
  Long Eaton NG10 ...193 D3
  Nottingham NG3 ....173 E4
Berkeley Cres NG12 .176 B2
Bernard Ave
  Hucknall NG15 ....131 D1
  Mansfield Woodhouse
  NG19 ....88 A3
Bernard Rd NG19 ...101 F4
Bernard St NG5 .....161 E3
Bernisdale Cl NG5 ..146 C1
Berridge Int Sch NG7 .172 C4
Berridge Jun Sch
  NG7 ....172 C4
Berridge Rd NG7 ....172 C4
Berridge Rd W NG7 .173 D4
Berriedale Cl NG5 ..162 B4
Berristow Grange
  NG17 ....100 B1
Berristow La DE55 ..113 E4
Berry Ave NG17 ......114 C3
Berry Hill Cl NG18 ..102 B2
Berry Hill Gdns NG18 .102 C2
Berry Hill Gr NG4 ...162 C1
Berry Hill La NG18 ..102 B2
Berry Hill Mews NG18 .102 B2
Berry Hill Prim Sch
  NG18 ....102 C2
Berry Hill Rd NG18 ..102 B2
Berry Pk Lea NG18 ..102 B2
Berwick Ave NG19 ..101 E4
Berwick Cl NG5 ......161 E3
Berwin Cl NG10 .....182 A1
Beryldene Ave NG16 .159 D4

Bescar La NG22 ....77 D1
Bescoby St DN22 ......39 F4
Bescar Ave NG4 .....162 C1
Besecar Cl NG4 ......162 C1
Bessell La NG9 ......182 B3
Bessingham Dr NG11 .185 E2
Besthorpe Ct NG19 ..101 F4
Besthorpe Prim Sch
  NG23 ....97 F3
Besthorpe Rd
  Collingham NG23 ......98 A1
  North Scarle LN6 .....83 E1
Bestwick Ave DE75 ..143 D1
Bestwood Ave NG5 .161 F4
Bestwood Cl NG5 ...161 F4
Bestwood Ctry Pk*
  NG6 ....146 C2
Bestwood Lodge Dr
  NG5 ....161 E4
Bestwood Pk Dr NG5 .161 D4
Bestwood Pk Dr W
  NG5 ....146 C1
Bestwood Pk View
  NG5 ....147 F1
Bestwood Rd
  Hucknall NG15 ....146 B3
  Nottingham NG6 ....146 B1
  Pinxton NG16 ....113 F1
Bestwood Terr NG6 .160 B4
Bethel Gdns NG15 ..145 E3
Bethel Terr S80 ....34 C3
Bethnal Wlk 12 NG6 .160 A4
Betony Cl NG13 ......177 C2
Betula Cl NG11 ......184 B1
Beulah Rd NG17 .....115 D2
Bevan Cl NG21 ....118 A4
Bevel St NG7 ....172 C4
Bevercotes Rd NG22 ..65 E2
Beverley Cl
  Nottingham NG8 ....171 D2
  Rainworth NG21 .....104 B1
Beverley Dr
  Coddington NG24 ...125 F1
  Kimberley NG16 .....158 C4
  Kirkby in A NG17 ...115 E2
  Mansfield NG18 .....102 B1
Beverley Gdns NG4 .162 C1
Beverley Rd NG8 ....171 D2
Beverley Sq NG3 ....173 F3
Beverley Wlk S81 .....25 F4
Beverleys Ave NG3 ..178 C2
Bewcastle Rd NG5 ..147 D1
Bewick Dr NG3 ....174 B3
Bexhill Ct NG8 ......171 F1
Bexwell Cl NG11 ....195 F4
Biant Cl NG8 ....160 A2
Bidford Rd NG8 ......159 F1
Bidwell Cres NG11 .195 D1
Big Barn La NG18 ...102 C3
Big La NG20 ....30 B2
Big Wood Comp Sch
  NG5 ....147 D1
Biggart Cl 2 NG9 ...183 E1
Biggin St LE11 ....220 A2
Bigsby Rd DN22 ....30 A1
Biko Sq 50 NG2 .....172 C4
Bilberry Wlk NG3 ...173 F4
Bilbie Wlk NG1 ......223 D3
Bilborough Coll NG8 .171 E4
Bilborough Rd NG8 .171 E3
Bilby Gdns 60 NG3 ..160 C2
Billesdon Dr NG5 ...160 C2
Billingsley Ave NG16 .113 E2
Bilsthorpe Rd NG22 ..92 B1
Bilton Cl NG24 ....140 B1
Bingham Ave NG17 .101 D3
Bingham Ind Pk NG13 .177 F3
Bingham Rd
  Cotgrave NG12 ......187 E2
  Langar NG13 ....190 A2
  Mansfield NG18 .....103 D2
  Nottingham NG5 ....161 E1
  Radcliffe on T NG12 ..176 A2
Bingham Sta NG13 ..177 F3
Bingley Cl 41 NG8 ..172 A4
Birch Ave Beeston NG9 .184 A2
  Carlton NG4 ....174 B4
  Farnsfield NG22 .....119 F4
  Ilkeston DE7 ....170 A4
  Nuthall NG16 ....159 D3
  Ravenshead NG15 ..104 B1
Birch Cl Nuthall NG16 ..159 D3
  Rampton DN22 ....42 C1
  Ravenshead NG15 ..117 D1
Birch Croft Dr NG19 ..89 D1
Birch Ct NG22 ....65 F1
Birch Gr
  Gainsborough DN21 ...15 E1
  Mansfield NG18 .....103 D2
  Shirebrook NG20 .....72 B3
Birch Lea Arnold NG5 .161 E4
  East Leake LE12 ....205 E3
Birch Pas NG7 ....222 C3
Birch Rd Hoathorpe S80 .45 B3
  New Balderton NG24 ..140 B3
  New Ollerton NG22 ...77 E2
Birch Rise NG14 ....149 E3
Birch St NG20 ....73 F3
Birch Tree Cl NG17 ..119 C2
Birch Tree Cres NG17 .114 C2
Birchdale Ave NG15 .146 A3
Birchen Holme DE55 .113 D2
Birchenhall Ct NG24 .139 D2
Birches The NG3 .....117 D2
Birchfield Dr S80 .....35 D1
Birchfield Rd NG5 ..148 A1
Birchlands NG19 .....88 C1
Birchover Pl DE7 ....157 F3

Birchover Rd NG8 ....171 E3
Birchwood Ave
  Breaston NG10 ....193 D4
  Long Eaton NG10 ....193 E3
Birchwood Cl
  Ravenshead NG15 ....117 D1
  South Normanton DE55 ..113 D2
  Southwell NG25 ....121 E1
  Sutton in A NG17 ....100 C3
Birchwood Dr
  Ravenshead NG15 ....117 D1
  Sutton in A NG17 ....100 B4
Birchwood Rd NG8 ....171 E2
Bircotes & Harworth Com
  Sch The DN11 ....9 E3
Bird Cl NG8 ....102 B2
Birdcroft La DN10 ....14 A3
Birding St NG19 ....88 A1
Birds La NG17 ....114 C1
Birdsall Ave NG19 ....171 F2
Birkdale S81 ....36 A3
  Mansfield Woodhouse
  NG19 ....88 B2
Birkdale Ave NG22 ....77 E3
Birkdale Cl
  Ilkeston DE7 ....157 E1
  West Bridgford NG12 ....186 A3
Birkdale Gr 5 NG17 .....114 C3
Birkdale Gr DN22 ....39 E2
Birkdale Way NG5 ....160 C4
Birkin Ave
  Beeston NG9 ....183 D1
  Nottingham NG7 ....172 C4
  Radcliffe on T NG12 ....176 A2
  Ruddington NG11 ....196 B4
Birkland Ave
  Mansfield Woodhouse
  NG19 ....88 B2
  Market Warsop NG20 ....74 A2
  Nottingham, Mapperley
  NG3 ....162 A2
  Nottingham, St Anns
  NG1 ....223 E4
Birkland Dr NG21 ....76 A1
Birkland St NG18 ....102 B4
Birklands Ave
  New Ollerton NG22 ....77 E3
  Worksop S80 ....36 B1
Birklands Cl NG20 ....74 A3
Birklands Prim Sch
  NG20 ....74 A2
Birks Cl S80 ....45 E3
Birks Rd NG19 ....101 E4
Birley St NG9 ....182 B3
Birling Cl NG6 ....159 F4
Birrel St DN21 ....15 D1
Birrell Rd NG7 ....173 D4
Bisham Dr NG2 ....186 A4
Bishop Alexander Prim Sch
  NG24 ....125 D2
Bishop Alexandra Ct
  NG24 ....139 F4
Bishop St
  Eastwood NG16 ....143 F1
  Loughborough LE11 ......220 B2
  Mansfield NG18 ....102 A3
  Sutton in A NG17 ....100 C2
Bishopdale S81 ....36 B4
Bishopdale Cl NG10 .....193 D3
Bishopdale Dr NG16 ....159 D4
Bishopfield La DN22 .....19 D3
Bishops Cl NG12 ....197 F2
Bishops Dr NG25 ....136 C4
Bishops Hill NG21 ....103 F1
Bishops Rd NG13 ....177 E3
Bishops Way NG15 ......146 A4
Bishops Wlk NG20 ....74 A3
Bispham Dr NG9 ....182 C1
Bispham Dr Jun Sch
  NG9 ....182 C2
Black La LN6 ....177 F1
Black Scotch La NG18 ..102 C2
Blackacre NG14 ....163 F3
Blackburn Pl DE7 ....157 F2
Blackcliff Field Cl S80 ...45 D3
Blacketts Wlk NG11 .....195 E4
Blackfriars Cl NG8 ......159 E2
Blackham Rd LE11 ....220 A1
Blackhill Dr NG4 ....174 C4
Blackrod Cl NG9 ....183 D1
Blacksmith Cl NG17 .....187 F2
Blacksmith La
  Kelham NG23 ....124 A2
  Torworth DN22 ....19 D1
Blacksmiths Cl LE14 ....219 E4
Blacksmiths La LN6 ....83 E1
Blackstone La NG2 .....173 E1
Blackstope La DN22 ......40 A4
Blackthorn Cl NG13 .....178 A2
Blackthorn Way NG17 ..100 B4
Blackthorn Dr NG24 ....140 A3
Blackthorne Dr
  Lowdham NG14 ....150 B1
  Nottingham NG6 ....160 A2
Blackwell Rd NG17 ....99 F2
Bladon Cl NG3 ....161 F1
Bladon Rd NG11 ....196 A4
Blair Ct 11 NG2 ....173 E1
Blair Gr NG10 ....182 A2
Blaise Cl NG11 ....195 F4
Blake Cl NG5 ....148 C2
Blake Cres NG18 ....102 C4
Blake Ct NG10 ....193 D3
Blake Rd
  Stapleford NG9 ....182 C3
  West Bridgford NG2 .....186 A4
Blake St Ilkeston DE7 ...157 F1
  Mansfield Woodhouse
  NG19 ....88 A1

Blakeney Ct NG19 ....88 C2
Blakeney Dr NG18 ......102 B2
Blakeney Rd NG12 .....176 A2
Blakeney Wlk NG5 ......161 F3
Bland La NG14 ....150 A3
Blandford Ave NG10 ...193 D3
Blandford Dr NG22 ......39 E2
Blandford Gdns NG22 ..185 E3
Blandford Rd NG9 ......183 D2
Blankney Cl LN1 ....57 D2
Blankney St NG5 ....160 C2
Blantyre Ave NG5 ......146 C1
Blatherwick Rd NG24 ..140 B4
Blatherwicks Yd NG5 ..161 F4
Bleaberry Cl NG2 ......186 B3
Bleachers Yd NG7 ......160 C1
Bleak Hill Way NG18 ...101 F2
Bleasby CE Prim Sch
  NG14 ....151 E4
Bleasby Cres NG17 ....101 D1
Bleasby Rd NG14 ....151 E4
Bleasby St NG2 ....173 F2
Bleasby Sta NG14 ......151 F4
Bleasdale Cl NG4 ......163 D1
Blencathra Cl NG2 .....186 B3
Blenheim Ave
  Lowdham NG14 ....150 C1
  Nottingham NG3 ....162 B1
Blenheim Cl
  Mansfield NG19 ....88 B1
  Ruddington NG11 ......196 A4
Blenheim Dr NG9 ......183 E3
Blenheim Gdns NG13 ..165 E1
Blenheim Ind Est NG6 .159 F4
Blenheim La NG6,
  NG15 ....145 F1
Blenheim Pl NG17 ....99 F2
Blenheim Rise
  Bawtry DN10 ....9 F3
  Worksop S81 ....35 F4
Blenheim St NG16 ......182 A2
Blidworth Ind Pk
  NG21 ....118 A3
Blidworth La
  Blidworth NG21 ....133 E4
  Mansfield NG21 ....103 E1
  Rainworth NG21 ....117 F4
Blidworth Rd
  Farnsfield NG22 ....119 F3
  Kirkby in A NG15 ....115 F2
Blidworth Waye NG15 ..131 F4
Blind La NG25 ....134 B2
Bloomgrove Rd DE7 ...157 F1
Bloomsbury Dr NG16 ..159 F2
Bloomsbury Mews
  NG12 ....176 C2
Bloomsgrove Ind Est
  NG7 ....222 B3
Bloomsgrove St NG7 ..222 B3
Blue Bell Hill Inf Sch
  NG3 ....173 F3
Blue Bell Hill Jun Sch
  NG3 ....173 F3
Blue Bell Hill Rd NG3 .173 F3
Blue Bell Yd NG22 ......65 F2
Bluebell Bank NG13 ...177 E2
Bluebell Cl
  Hucknall NG15 ....145 E1
  Selston NG16 ....128 C1
  Shirebrook NG20 ....72 B2
  Stanton Hill NG17 ......100 A3
Bluebell Gr 15 NG17 ...114 C3
Bluebell Wood Way
  NG17 ....100 B1
Bluebells The NG17 ....101 D1
Bluecoat Cl NG1 ....223 E3
Bluecoat St NG1 ....223 E4
Blundell Cl NG3 ....173 F4
Blyth Cl NG19 ....87 E1
Blyth Gdns NG3 ....161 F1
Blyth Gr S81 ....36 A3
Blyth Rd
  Blyth, Bilby S81, DN22 ..27 F3
  Blyth, Nornay S81 ....18 A4
  Elkesley S80 ....48 C2
  Harworth DN11 ....8 C2
  New Ollerton NG22 ......77 D3
  Oldcotes S81 ....16 C1
  Ranskill DN22 ....19 D2
  Walesby NG22 ....63 D2
  Worksop, Kilton S81 ......36 A3
  Worksop, Perlethorpe
  S80, NG22 ....48 C2
Blyth St NG3 ....161 F1
Blyton Rd DN21 ....15 E2
Blyton Wlk NG5 ....161 D4
Boar La NG24 ....139 F4
Boat La Aldercar NG16 .143 D4
  Bleasby NG14 ....152 B4
  Hoveringham NG14 .....151 F1
Boatmans Cl DE7 ......157 F1
Bobbers Mill Bridge
  NG7 ....172 B4
Bobbers Mill Rd NG7 ..172 C4
Boden Dr NG16 ....159 E3
Boden St NG7 ....222 B3
Bodmin Ave NG15 .....145 E3
Bodmin Cl NG18 ....103 D1
Bodmin Dr NG8 ....160 B1
Body Rd NG9 ....183 D1
Bohem Rd NG10 ....182 B2
Bold Cl NG6 ....160 A4
Bolero Cl NG8 ....171 F3
Bolham La DN22 ....29 F1

Bolingey Way NG15 ....145 E3
Bollards La LE12 ....213 D4
Bolsover St
  Hucknall NG15 ....146 A4
  Mansfield NG18 ....102 B3
Bolton Ave NG9 ....183 E2
Bolton Cl NG2 ....186 A4
Bolton Terr NG12 ......175 F2
Bond Cl LE11 ....220 B1
Bond St Arnold NG5 ...161 F4
  Nottingham NG2 ....173 F2
Bonemill La
  Clarborough DN22 ......30 B1
  Worksop S81 ....35 E3
Bonetti Cl NG5 ....162 B3
Boniface Gdns 4 NG5 .147 D1
Bonington Art Gall*
  NG1 ....223 D3
Bonington Dr NG5 .....161 F4
Bonington Rd
  Mansfield NG19 ....101 F3
  Nottingham NG3 ....162 A1
Bonner La NG14 ....149 D3
Bonners Rd NG16 .....158 B2
Bonnington Cl NG6 ....160 A3
Bonnington Cres NG5 .161 E2
Bonnington Jun & Inf Sch
  NG6 ....160 A3
Bonny Mead NG12 ....187 F1
Bonsal Ct NG18 ....103 D3
Bonsall St NG10 ....193 F4
Bonser Cl NG4 ....174 C4
Bonser Cres NG17 ......99 F1
Bonser Gdns NG17 ....100 B1
Booth Ave NG19 ....87 D3
Booth Cl NG3 ....223 F3
Booth St NG19 ....88 A2
Boots Yd NG17 ....99 F2
Borders Ave NG17 .....114 C4
Borlace Cres NG9 .....182 C3
Borman Cl NG6 ....159 F3
Borough Rd DE74 .....203 E1
Borrow Bread La
  NG14 ....152 A4
Borrowdale Cl NG2 ...186 B3
Borrowdale Dr NG10 ..193 D3
Borrowell DE74 ....203 E2
Boscombe Rd S81 ......35 E4
Boscowan Ct DE7 .....157 F2
Bosden Cl NG8 ....171 E3
Bosley Sq NG9 ....184 A4
Bostocks La NG10 ....182 A2
Boston St NG1 ....223 F3
Boswell Cl
  Kinoulton NG12 ....200 A1
  Mansfield NG18 ....102 B2
Bosworth Dr NG16 ....144 A2
Bosworth Prim Sch
  NG2 ....173 D1
Bosworth St NG19 ....101 E4
Bosworth Way NG10 ..193 F3
Bosworth Wlk 26 NG2 .173 D1
Botany Ave
  Mansfield NG18 ....101 F3
  Nottingham NG3 ....173 F4
Botany Cl NG11 ....185 E1
Botany Dr DE7 ....157 F3
Bothe Cl NG10 ....193 E3
Bottesford CE Prim Sch
  NG13 ....181 D1
Bottesford Sta NG13 ..181 E2
Bottle La NG1 ....223 E2
Bottleacre La LE11 ....220 A3
Bottom Gn LE14 ....210 A1
Bottom Row NG24 .....140 A4
Boughton Cl NG17 ....100 C3
Boughton Rd S80 ......35 D3
Bould St NG19 ....87 E4
Boulevard Ind Pk NG7 .184 B4
Boundary Cl NG20 ......72 C3
Boundary Cres
  Beeston NG9 ....171 F1
  Bildworth NG21 ....118 A3
Boundary Ct NG24 ....139 F4
Boundary La NG16 ....143 E2
Boundary Rd
  Beeston NG9 ....183 F4
  Newark-on-T NG24 .....139 F4
  West Bridgford NG2 ...185 F2
Boundary Row S80 ......35 F1
Boundary Wlk NG20 ....58 C1
Bourne Ave
  Kirkby in A NG17 ....115 D2
  Selston NG16 ....129 D4
Bourne Cl NG9 ....171 E1
Bourne Dr NG15 ....117 D1
Bourne Mews NG4 .....175 D3
Bourne St NG4 ....175 D3
Bournmoor Ave NG7 ..184 C1
Bovill St NG7 ....222 B4
Bovington Ct NG20 .....29 F1
Bow St NG19 ....88 C2
Bowbridge Gdns
  NG13 ....181 D2
Bowbridge Jun Sch
  NG24 ....139 F3
Bowbridge La
  Bottesford NG13 ....180 C2
  New Balderton NG24 ..140 A2
Bowbridge Prim Sch
  NG24 ....140 A3
Bowbridge Rd NG24 ..140 A3
Bowden Dr NG9 ....184 A3

Bowers Ave 13 NG3 ...173 E4
Bowes Well Rd DE7 ...157 F1
Bowland Cl NG3 ....174 A4
Bowland Rd NG13 .....177 E2
Bowler Ct 8 LE11 .....220 B2
Bowling Gn Rd DN21 ..15 D1
Bowling St NG18 ......102 B3
Bowlwell Ave NG5 ....160 C4
Bowne St NG17 ....100 C2
Bowness Ave NG6 ....160 B1
Bowness Cl NG2 ......186 B4
Bowscale Cl NG2 .....186 B4
Box Cres NG17 ....114 C3
Boxley Dr NG2 ....185 E2
Boxwell Ctry Pk*
  NG1 ....159 F2
Boy La NG21 ....76 A1
Boyce Gdns NG3 ......161 F1
Boycroft Ave NG3 ....173 F4
Boyd Cl NG5 ....148 A1
Boyer St LE11 ....220 B2
Boyers Orch LE14 ....202 A2
Boynton Dr NG3 ....161 F1
Bracadale Rd NG5 ....146 C1
Bracebridge S80 ....36 A2
Bracebridge Ave NG8 ..36 A2
Bracebridge Ct S80 ....36 A2
Bracebridge Dr NG8 ..171 E4
Bracey Rise NG2 ......185 F2
Bracken Ave NG22 ....77 F3
Bracken Cl
  Carlton NG4 ....162 B1
  Gainsborough DN21 .....15 D2
  4 Kirkby in A NG17 ...114 C3
  Long Eaton NG10 ......182 A1
  Market Warsop NG20 ...74 B2
Bracken Ct NG18 .....159 F1
Bracken Hill NG18 ....103 D3
Bracken Hill La DN9 .....4 A3
Bracken Hill Specl Sch
  NG17 ....115 E3
Bracken La DN22 ....40 A3
Bracken La Prim Sch
  DN22 ....40 A3
Bracken Rd NG10 .....182 A1
Bracken Way DN11 ......8 C2
Brackendale Ave NG5 .161 F4
Brackendale Dr NG22 ..64 A1
Brackenfield Ave NG19 .88 C2
Brackenfield Dr NG16 ..158 A4
Brackenfield Rise
  NG15 ....117 D2
Brackenfield Specl Sch
  NG15 ....182 A1
Brackenhurst Coll
  NG25 ....136 B3
Brackenhurst La
  NG25 ....136 B3
Brackenwood Cl NG19 ..89 D1
Brackhills Cl NG19 ......88 C1
Bracknell Cres NG8 ..160 B1
Brackner La NG22 ....106 A2
Bracton Dr NG3 ....173 F3
Bradbourne Ave NG11 .185 D3
Bradbury St NG2 ......174 A2
Bradbury-Midway Ind Est
  NG7 ....184 B4
Bradden Ave NG9 .....170 C1
Bradder Way NG18 ...102 A3
Braddock Cl NG7 .....222 A2
Bradfield Rd NG8 ......159 F1
Bradforth Ave NG18 ..103 D4
Bradgate Cl NG10 ....182 A2
Bradgate Rd 2 NG7 ..173 D4
Bradley St NG10 ......193 E4
Bradley Wlk NG11 ....195 F4
Bradley Wlk NG14 ....151 C1
Bradman Gdns NG5 ..162 A3
Bradmore Ave NG11 ..196 B4
Bradmore Ct NG18 ...103 D2
Bradmore La NG12 ....197 E3
Bradmore Rise NG5 ..161 E2
Bradshaw St NG10 ...193 D3
Bradwell Cl NG16 .....158 B4
Bradwell Dr NG5 ......161 D4
Braefell Cl NG2 ....186 B3
Braemar Ave NG16 ...143 F1
Braemar Dr NG4 ......163 D1
Braemar Rd
  Clipstone NG19 ....89 F2
  Nottingham NG6 ....160 A4
Brailsford Cl NG18 ....103 D3
Brailsford Rd 1 NG7 ..172 C1
Brailsford Way NG9 ..183 E1
Brailwood Cl NG22 ...106 A3
Brailwood Rd NG22 ..106 A3
Brake La NG22 ....77 F4
Brake Rd NG22 ....63 F1
Brake View NG22 ....77 F3
Bramber Gr NG11 .....195 F4
Bramble Cl
  Beeston NG9 ....183 E1
  Long Eaton NG10 ......182 A1
  New Ollerton NG22 .....77 E3
  Nottingham NG6 ....159 E4
  Shirebrook NG20 ....72 C3
Bramble Croft NG17 ..100 B1
Bramble Ct NG4 ....162 C1
Bramble Dr NG3 ......174 A4
Bramble Gdns NG8 ...172 A4
Bramble La NG18 .....103 D2
Bramble Rd DN22 ......40 A2
Bramble Way DN11 .....8 C2
Brambles The NG22 ..64 A1
Brambleway NG12 ....188 A1
Brambling NG19 ....102 C4

Bramblings The S81 ....35 E4
Bramcote Ave NG9 ...183 E3
Bramcote CE Sch
  NG9 ....183 D4
Bramcote Ct NG18 ...103 D2
Bramcote Dr
  Beeston NG9 ....183 E4
  Nottingham NG8 ....171 E2
  Retford DN23 ....39 E3
Bramcote Dr W NG9 ..183 E4
Bramcote Hills Comp Sch
  NG9 ....171 D1
Bramcote Hills Prim Sch
  NG9 ....171 D1
Bramcote L Ctr NG9 ..171 D1
Bramcote La
  Beeston NG9 ....183 E3
  Nottingham NG8 ....171 E2
Bramcote Lorne Sch
  DN22 ....51 D3
Bramcote Pk Comp Sch
  NG9 ....171 D1
Bramcote Rd NG9 ....183 F4
Bramcote St NG7 .....222 A3
Bramcote Wlk NG7 ...222 A3
Bramerton Rd NG8 ...171 E3
Bramhall Rd NG8 .....171 E3
Bramley Cl
  East Leake LE12 ......205 F1
  Gunthorpe NG14 ....165 D3
  Southwell NG25 ....136 C4
Bramley Cres
  Gainsborough DN21 ...15 F1
  Kimberley NG16 ....158 C3
  Sutton in A NG17 ......100 C2
Bramley Rd NG8 ......159 F1
Bramley Wlk NG19 ...101 E4
Brammersack Cl
  NG19 ....124 A4
Brampton Ave DE75 ..143 D1
Brampton Ct NG2 .....186 B4
Brampton Dr NG9 ....182 C3
Brancaster Cl NG6 ...160 A2
Brancliffe La S81 ....34 C4
Brand La NG17 ....100 B3
Brand St NG2 ....173 F1
Brandish Cres NG11 ..184 B1
Brandon Cl NG24 .....140 C2
Brandreth Ave
  Nottingham NG3 ....173 F4
  Sutton in A NG17 ......100 B3
Brandreth Dr NG16 ...144 B4
Brankleene Cl NG16 ..158 C4
Branksome Wlk 3 NG2 .173 E1
Bransdale S81 ....36 A4
Bransdale Cl NG10 ...193 D3
Bransdale Rd NG11 ..184 B1
Branston Ave NG22 ..119 F3
Branston Cl NG24 .....125 E3
Branston Gdns NG2 ..185 E2
Branston Wlk NG5 ....161 E2
Brantford Ave NG7 ...184 C1
Brantingham Gdns DN10 .3 D1
Brassington Cl NG16 .158 C2
Brassington Ct NG19 ..88 C3
Brauston Ct NG15 ....145 E3
Brayton Cres NG6 ....160 B3
Breach Rd DE75 ......157 D4
Breadsall Ct DE7 .....157 F2
Breamer Rd NG23 ....112 A4
Brechin S81 ....36 A3
Brechin Cl NG5 ....148 A1
Brechin Ct NG19 ....88 B3
Breck Bank NG22 ......77 E3
Breck Bank Cres NG22 .77 E3
Breck Hill Rd NG3 ....161 F2
Breck La DN10 ....20 A4
Breckbank NG19 ....88 C1
Brecks La Easton NG23 .154 A1
  Stapleford LN6 ....127 F4
Brecks Rd DN22 ....39 E2
Breckswood Dr NG11 .195 F4
Brecon Cl
  4 Long Eaton NG10 ..193 D4
  Nottingham NG8 ....160 A2
  Rainworth NG21 ......104 B1
Bredon Cl 7 NG10 ...193 D4
Bredon St NG10 ......182 B1
Bredon Ct NG9 ....183 D4
Brendon Dr
  Kimberley NG16 ......158 C4
  Nottingham NG8 ......172 A3
Brendon Gdns NG8 ..172 A3
Brendon Gr NG13 ....177 E3
Brendon Rd NG8 .....172 A3
Brendon Way NG10 ..182 A1
Brentcliffe Ave NG3 ..174 A4
Brentnall Cl NG18 ....103 D3
Brett Cl NG15 ....145 F3
Bretton Rd NG15 .....117 D2
Brewers Wharf NG24 ..124 C2
Brewery La
  Everton DN10 ....11 E2
  Retford DN22 ....39 F3
Brewery St NG16 .....158 C3
Brewhouse Yd Mus-The Mus
  of Nottingham Life*
  NG1 ....223 D1
Brewsters Cl NG13 ...177 F2
Brewsters Rd NG3 ....173 F4
Brewsters Way DN22 ..29 E1
Brewsters Wlk DN10 ..10 A4
Briar Ave NG10 ....182 A2

Briar Cl Beeston NG9 .....171 F1
Hucknall NG15 ....145 F3
Keyworth NG12 ....197 F2
Rainworth NG21 ....64 D1
Stanton Hill NG17 ....100 B3
Worksop S80 ....35 E1
Briar Ct Harworth DN11 ...8 C2
New Ollerton NG22 ......77 E3
Worksop S80 ....173 D1
Briar Gate
Cotgrave NG12 ....188 A1
Long Eaton NG10 ....103 D2
Briar La NG18 ....143 F2
Briar Lea Retford DN22 ..39 E2
Worksop S80 ....35 E1
Briar Rd
Eastwood NG16 ....158 A4
Worksop S80 ....77 E3
Briarbank Ave NG3 .....174 A4
Briarbank Wlk NG3 .....174 A4
Briars The DN10 ....4 B2
Briarwood Ave NG3 .....174 A4
Briarwood Cl NG18 ......89 D1
Briarwood St NG3 ......161 F2
Briber Hill S81 ....18 A1
Briber Rd S81 ....18 A1
Brick Kiln La NG18 ....101 E4
Brick Yd Rd DN22 ....50 B3
Brickcliffe Rd LE12 .....205 F1
Brickenell Rd NG14 .....148 C3
Brickenhole La DN10 .....13 E3
Brickings Way NG22 .....32 B3
Brickley Cres LE12 .....205 F1
Brickyard NG15 ....146 B3
Brickyard Dr NG15 .....146 B3
Brickyard La
East Bridgford NG13 ....165 E1
East Leake LE12 ....214 A4
Farnsfield NG22 ....120 A3
Misson DN10 ....4 B2
Radcliffe on T NG12 ....176 A2
South Normanton DE55 ..113 D3
Sutton Bonington LE12 ..213 F4
Walkeringham DN10 .....13 E3
Bride Church La DN11 ...8 A4
Bridegate La LE14 .....209 F3
Bridge Ave NG9 ....183 F3
Bridge Cl S80 ....45 F2
Bridge Ct NG15 ....146 A3
Bridge End Ave NG16 ...128 C4
Bridge Farm La NG7 ....184 C1
Bridge Gn Wlk ⑤ NG8 .159 F1
Bridge Pl Saxilby LN1 ...57 D2
Worksop S80 ....35 F2
Bridge Rd
Gainsborough DN21 .....24 B4
Nottingham NG8 ....171 E3
Bridge St
Gainsborough DN21 .....24 B4
Ilkeston DE7 ....157 F2
Langley Mill NG16 .....143 E2
Long Eaton NG10 ....182 B1
Loughborough LE11 .....220 A2
Mansfield NG18 ....102 B4
Newark-on-T NG24 .....139 F4
Sandiacre NG10 ....182 A3
Saxilby LN1 ....57 D2
Worksop S80 ....35 F1
Bridgegate 39 F4
Bridgend Cl NG9 ......182 B3
Bridgeway Ct NG2 .....173 E1
Bridgeway Ctr NG2 ....173 E1
Bridgford Rd
Kneeton NG13 ....166 A4
West Bridgford NG2 ....185 E4
Bridgford St NG18 .....102 C3
Bridgnorth Dr NG7 ....184 B1
Bridgnorth Way NG9 ...182 C2
Bridle Cl NG17 ....100 A3
Bridle Rd Beeston NG9 .183 D4
Burton Joyce NG14 .....163 F3
Bridle Ways NG13 .....165 E1
Bridlesmith Gate NG1 ..223 E2
Bridleway The NG19 ....88 C1
Bridlington St NG7 ....172 C4
Bridport Ave ⑥ NG8 ..172 B3
Brielen Rd NG12 ......176 A2
Brierfield Ave NG11 ...185 D2
Brierley Gn NG4 ......175 D4
Brierly Cotts NG17 ....100 C2
Brierly Rd NG17 ......100 B3
Brigg Inf Sch DE55 ....113 D3
Bright Sq NG19 ....87 E1
Bright St
Gainsborough DN21 .....24 B4
Ilkeston DE7 ....157 F2
Nottingham NG7 ....222 A3
South Normanton DE55 .113 D3
Brightmoor St NG1 ....223 F3
Brimington Cl NG19 ....88 C2
Brindley Rd NG8 ......171 E3
Brinkhill Cres NG11 ...184 C2
Brinkhill Prim Sch
NG11 ....184 C2
Brinkley Hill NG25 ....137 D3
Brinsley Cl NG16 .....160 A1
Brinsley Hill NG16 ....128 B1
Brinsley Prim Sch
NG16 ....143 E4
Brisbane Cl NG19 ......88 B3
Brisbane Ct NG24 .....140 B2
Brisbane Dr
Nottingham NG5 ....160 C4
Stapleford NG9 ....170 C1

Bristol Rd DE7 ....157 F1
Britannia Ave NG6 .....160 C3
Britannia Rd NG10 ....182 B1
Britannia Terr DN21 ...24 B4
British Fields NG22 ....65 E2
British Horological Inst*
NG23 ....122 C1
Brittania La NG24 .....139 F4
Britten Gdns NG3 .....173 F3
Brixham Rd NG15 .....145 E3
Brixton Rd NG7 ....222 A3
Brixworth Way DN22 ...40 A4
Broad Cl NG14 ....149 E2
Broad Eadow Rd NG6 .159 F4
Broad Fen La NG23 ...156 A4
Broad Gate NG22 ......66 C4
Broad Gores DN22 .....30 B2
Broad La Brinsley NG16 .143 F4
Hodthorpe S80 ....45 E3
South Leverton DN22 ...43 D3
Broad Marsh Sh Ctr
NG1 ....223 E2
Broad Meer NG12 .....187 F2
Broad Oak Cl NG3 ....173 F4
Broad Oak Dr
Brinsley NG16 ....143 F4
Stapleford NG9 ....182 B3
Broad Pl S80 ....45 E3
Broad St
Long Eaton NG10 .....193 E4
Loughborough LE11 ....220 A2
Nottingham NG1 ....223 F3
Broad Valley Dr NG6 ..146 C2
Broad Wlk NG6 ....160 B2
Broadfields NG14 .....148 C4
Broadgate NG9 ....184 A4
Broadgate Ave NG9 ...184 A4
Broadgate La
Beeston NG9 ....184 A4
Kelham NG23 ....123 F3
Broadhill Rd DE74 ....203 E1
Broadholme Rd LN1 ....52 C2
Broadhurst Ave NG6 ..146 B1
Broadings La DN22 ....54 A3
Broadlands
Sandiacre NG10 ......182 A3
South Normanton DE55 .113 D3
Broadleigh Cl NG11 ..185 E2
Broadleigh Ct DN22 ...39 E2
Broadmead NG14 .....163 F3
Broadoak Pk NG17 ...114 C1
Broadstairs Rd NG9 ..182 C1
Broadstone Cl NG2 ...185 E3
Broadway Carlton NG3 .174 A4
Ilkeston DE7 ....157 F2
Nottingham NG1 ......223 F2
Broadway E NG4 .....174 B3
Broadway Media Ctr*
NG1 ....223 F2
Broadway The NG18 ..102 B4
Broadwood Cl NG4 ...184 A4
Broadwood Rd NG5 ..161 D4
Brockdale Gdns NG12 .197 F2
Brockenhurst Rd
NG19 ....88 C2
Brockhall Rise DE75 ..143 D1
Brockhole Cl NG2 ....186 B3
Brockhurst Gdns NG3 .173 F3
Brocklehurst Dr NG21 .91 E4
Brocklesby Cl DN21 ...24 C4
Brocklewood Jun & Inf Schs
NG8 ....171 E4
Brockley Rd NG2 .....186 A4
Brockton Ave NG24 ...139 D3
Brockwell The DE55 ..113 D2
Brockwood Cres NG17 .197 F2
Bromfield Cl NG3 .....174 B4
Bromhead St LE11 ....220 B2
Bromley Ave NG24 ...140 A3
Bromley Cl NG6 ......160 A3
Bromley Pl NG1 ......223 D2
Bromley Rd NG2 .....185 F3
Brompton Cl NG5 .....147 D1
Brompton Way NG11 .185 E2
Bronte Cl NG10 ......193 D4
Bronte St NG24 ......222 C4
Brook Ave NG5 ......162 A4
Brook Cl
Eastwood NG16 ......144 B1
Long Eaton NG10 .....193 F3
Nottingham NG6 .....160 A3
Brook Cotts DE7 .....157 F2
Brook Ct NG16 ......143 D1
Brook Dr NG7 ....199 F1
Brook Gdns NG5 ....162 A4
Brook La NG2 ....186 B4
Brook Rd NG9 ......183 F4
Brook Side ⑭ LE11 ..220 A2
Brook St
Hucknall NG15 ......146 A4
Nottingham NG1 .....223 F3
Sutton in A NG17 ....100 C1
Tibshelf DE55 ....99 D3
Wymeswold LE12 ....216 B2
Brook Terr S80 ....35 F1
Brook Vale Rd NG16 ..143 E1
Brook View Ct NG12 ..197 F1
Brook View Dr NG12 ..197 F1
Brookdale Ct NG5 ....161 E3
Brookdale Rd NG17 ..101 D2
Brooke Cl
Balderton NG24 ......140 B3
Worksop S81 ....36 B2
Brooke St Ilkeston DE7 .170 A3
Sandiacre NG10 .....182 A3
Brookfield Ave
Hucknall NG15 ......146 A3

Brookfield Ave continued
Sutton in A NG17 ....100 B2
Brookfield Cres NG20 .72 C3
Brookfield Ct ⑳ NG2 .173 E1
Brookfield Dr NG14 ..151 E2
Brookfield Gdns NG5 .162 A4
Brookfield Prim Sch
NG20 ....72 C3
Brookfield Rd DE75 ..143 D1
Brookfield St NG2 ...173 E1
Brookfields Way LE12 .205 F1
Brookhill Ave NG16 ..113 E2
Brookhill Cres NG8 ..171 F2
Brookhill Dr NG8 ....171 F2
Brookhill Ind Est
NG16 ....113 E1
Brookhill La NG16 ...113 F3
Brookhill Leys Inf Sch
NG16 ....144 A1
Brookhill Leys Jun Sch
NG16 ....144 A1
Brookhill Leys Rd
NG16 ....143 F1
Brookhill Rd NG16 ..113 E1
Brookhill St NG9 ....182 B3
Brookland Ave NG18 .101 F4
Brookland Cl NG14 ..165 D3
Brookland Dr NG9 ...183 E3
Brooklands NG12 ....208 B2
Brooklands Cl NG23 ..98 A1
Brooklands Cres NG4 .163 D1
Brooklands Dr NG4 ..163 D1
Brooklands Inf Sch
NG4 ....193 E4
Brooklands Jun Sch
NG4 ....193 E4
Brooklands Rd NG3 ..163 F3
Brooklyn Ave NG3 ...163 F3
Brooklyn Cl NG6 .....160 B3
Brooklyn Rd NG6 ....160 B3
Brooks Cl NG13 .....165 E2
Brooksby La NG11 ...184 C2
Brooksby Prim Sch
NG11 ....184 C2
Brookside
East Leake LE12 .....214 C4
Eastwood NG16 .....143 F2
Hucknall NG15 ......146 A3
Lowdham NG14 .....150 B1
Brookside Ave
East Leake LE12 ....205 F1
Mansfield Woodhouse
NG19 ....88 B3
Nottingham NG8 ....171 E1
Brookside Cl NG10 ..193 D4
Brookside Gdns NG11 .196 A4
Brookside Prim Sch
NG11 ....205 F1
Brookside Rd NG11 ..196 A4
Brookside Way NG17 ..99 F1
Brookside Wlk DN11 ...9 D2
Brookthorpe Way
NG11 ....185 D2
Brookvale Cl NG18 ..103 D3
Brookwood Cres NG4 .174 B4
Broom Cl
Calverton NG14 .....148 C4
Carlton in L S81 ....25 E1
Tickhill DN11 ....8 A4
Broom Rd NG4 ......148 C4
Broom Wlk NG4 .....174 A4
Broome Acre DE55 ..113 E2
Broome Cl NG24 ....140 A3
Broomfield Cl NG10 .182 A3
Broomfield La
Farnsfield NG22 .....119 F3
Mattersey DN10 ......19 F4
Broomhill Ave
Ilkeston DE7 ....170 A3
Worksop S81 ....35 F4
Broomhill Jun Sch
NG19 ....101 F4
Broomhill La NG19 ..101 F4
Broomhill Pk View
NG15 ....146 B3
Broomhill Rd
Hucknall NG15 .....146 A3
Kimberley NG16 ....159 D3
Nottingham NG6 ...160 B3
Broomston La DN9 ....2 C1
Brora Rd NG6 ....160 B4
Brotts La NG23 ....81 F3
Brotts Rd NG23 ......81 F3
Brough La
Brough NG23 ....112 A2
Elkesley DN22 ....50 A2
Broughton Ave NG19 .87 E1
Broughton Cl DE7 ..157 E1
Broughton Dr NG8 ..172 B2
Broughton Gdns
NG22 ....140 C2
Broughton Ind Est
NG22 ....78 A3
Broughton La LE14 ..211 D1
Broughton Rd LN6 ..127 F4
Broughton St NG9 ..183 F4
Broughton Way NG22 .78 A2
Brown Ave NG19 .....88 A2
Brown Cres NG17 ..101 D2
Brown La
Barton in F NG11 ...194 C3
Thorney NG23 ....70 A3
Brown Md Rd NG7 ..172 C4
Brown St
Mansfield NG19 ....101 F4
Nottingham NG7 ....172 C4
Brownes Rd NG13 ..178 A3

Brownhill Cl NG12 ..189 D2
Browning Cl
Arnold NG5 ....161 E4
Worksop S81 ....36 A3
Browning Rd NG24 ..140 C3
Browning St ⑤ NG18 .102 A4
Brownlow Cl NG23 ..153 E4
Brownlow Dr NG5 ..146 C1
Brownlow Rd NG17 ..87 D3
Brownlows Hill NG24 .126 A1
Browns Croft NG6 ..160 B2
Browns Flats NG16 ..158 C3
Browns La NG13 ....165 E2
Browns Lane
Loughborough LE11 ..220 A2
Stanton-on-t-W NG12 .198 B1
Browns Rd NG10 ...193 F4
Broxholme La LN1 ....57 E3
Broxtowe Ave NG16 .160 A2
Broxtowe Cl
Kimberley NG16 ....158 B3
Nottingham NG6 ...160 B1
Broxtowe Coll NG9 .183 F3
Broxtowe Dr
Hucknall NG15 .....131 D1
Mansfield NG18 ....102 B3
Broxtowe Hall Cl NG8 .160 A2
Broxtowe La NG8 ..160 A1
Broxtowe St ⑤ NG5 ..161 E1
Bruce Cl NG2 ....173 E1
Bruce Dr NG2 ......185 E4
Brunel Ave NG16 ...144 A2
Brunel Cl DN11 ....8 C1
Brunel Dr NG24 ....125 E1
Brunel Gate
The DE55 ....113 D2
Brunner Ave NG20 ...72 C2
Brunswick Dr NG9 ..182 C3
Brunts NG18 ....102 B4
Brunts Comp Sch NG19 .88 B1
Brunts La NG13 ....165 E1
Brunts St NG18 ....102 B3
Brushfield St NG7 ..172 C4
Brussels Terr ① DE7 .157 F1
Brusty Pl NG14 ....163 F3
Bryans Cl La DN10 ...11 D2
Brynsmoor Rd NG16 .143 F4
Buckfast Way NG2 ..186 A4
Buckingham Ave
NG15 ....146 A4
Buckingham Cl
⑧ Kirkby in A NG17 ...114 C3
Mansfield Woodhouse
NG19 ....88 C3
Buckingham Ct NG10 .182 A2
Buckingham Dr NG12 .176 C2
Buckingham Rd
Arnold NG5 ....161 F3
Sandiacre NG10 .....182 A2
Buckingham Rise S81 .35 F4
Buckingham Way
NG16 ....159 D4
Buckland Dr NG14 ..149 E2
Buckler Dr NG14 ...148 C4
Bucklow Cl NG8 ....160 B1
Bucks La LE12 ....213 D4
Budby Ave NG18 ...102 C3
Budby Cres NG20 ...74 C4
Budby Rd NG20 .....60 A2
Budge Rise NG15 ..146 A4
Bulcote Dr NG14 ...163 E2
Bulcote Rd NG11 ..184 C2
Bulgrave Mews NG2 .185 E2
Bulham La NG23 .....81 F1
Bull Cl Rd NG7 .....184 C4
Bull Yd Southwell NG25 .121 F1
Worksop S80 ....35 F1
Bullace Ct NG19 .....88 C1
Bullace Rd NG3 ....173 F4
Buller Cl NG23 ....98 A1
Buller St DE7 ....170 A3
Buller Terr ⑤ NG5 ..161 E2
Bullfinch Rd NG6 ..160 B3
Bullins Cl NG5 .....147 E1
Bullivant Ave S80 ...58 B4
Bullivant St NG3 ..223 F4
Bullock Cl NG6 ....140 A3
Bullpit Rd NG24 ...140 C3
Bulpit La LN6 ....98 C3
Bulstode Pl DE74 ..203 E1
Bulwell Bsns Ctr NG6 .160 A4
Bulwell High Rd NG6 .160 A4
Bulwell La NG6 ....160 B2
Bulwell St Marys CE Prim
Sch NG6 ....160 B4
Bulwell St NG19 ...160 B3
Bulwer Rd
Kirkby in A NG17 ..114 C3
Nottingham NG7 ...222 B3
Bunbury St NG2 ...173 E1
Bungalow La NG12 .106 A3
Bunnison La NG12 .200 C4
Bunny CE Prim Sch
NG11 ....206 C4
Bunny Hill LE12.
Bunny La
East Leake NG11 ...205 F3
Keyworth NG12 ....197 F1
Bunting St ⑤ NG7 ..172 C1
Buntings La NG4 ..174 B4
Bunyan Gn Rd NG16 .128 B4
Burbage Ct NG18 ..103 D3
Burden Cres NG20 ..53 D4
Burden La Harby LE14 .202 A2
Shelford NG12 ......164 B1
Burder St LE11 .....220 B3
Burfield Ave LE11 ..220 A3

Burford Prim Sch
NG5 ....161 E3
Burford Rd NG7 ...172 C4
Burford St NG5 ....161 E3
Burgage NG25 .....121 F1
Burgage La NG25 ..121 F1
Burgass Rd NG3 ..174 A4
Burge Cl NG2 .....173 E1
Burgh Hall Cl NG9 .183 E1
Burhill NG12 ....188 A1
Burke St NG7 .....222 C3
Burleigh Cl NG4 ..174 C4
Burleigh Rd
Loughborough LE11 .220 A2
West Bridgford NG2 .186 A3
Burleigh Sq NG9 ..183 E2
Burleigh St ② DE7 .157 F1
Burley Rise DE74 ..203 E1
Burlington Ave
Nottingham NG5 ..161 D2
Shirebrook NG20 ...72 C3
Burlington Dr NG19 .87 F1
Burlington Rd
Carlton NG4 ....174 C4
Nottingham NG5 ..161 E2
Burma Rd NG21 ..118 A3
Burmaston Rd NG18 .103 D3
Burn St NG17 .....101 D2
Burnaby St NG6 ..160 B2
Burnaston Ct NG19 .88 C2
Burnbank Cl NG2 ..186 B3
Burnbreck Gdns NG8 .171 F2
Burndale Wlk NG5 .160 C4
Burneham Cl NG13 .165 E1
Burnham Ave NG9 .183 F2
Burnham Ct NG18 .102 B2
Burnham St NG5 ..161 E1
Burnham Way NG2 .223 E1
Burnmoor La NG22 ..80 A4
Burnor Pool NG14 .148 C4
Burns Ave
Mansfield Woodhouse
NG19 ....88 B1
Nottingham NG7 ..222 C4
Burns La NG20 ......74 A3
Burns Rd S81 ....36 A2
Burns St
Gainsborough DN21 ..15 D1
Mansfield NG18 ...102 A4
Nottingham NG7 ..222 C4
Burns The NG20 ....74 A3
Burnside Cl ② NG17 .114 C4
Burnside Dr
Beeston NG9 ....171 E1
Mansfield NG19 ....87 F1
Burnside Gn NG8 ..171 E3
Burnside Gr NG12 .186 B1
Burnside Rd
Nottingham NG8 ..171 E3
West Bridgford NG2 .185 F3
Burnt Oak Cl NG16 .159 E2
Burnt Oaks Cl NG19 .88 B2
Burntleys Rd DN22 .50 A2
Burntstump Ctry Pk*
NG5 ....132 B1
Burntstump Hill NG5 .132 B1
Burnwood Ave NG18 .103 D4
Burnwood Dr NG8 ..171 E3
Burr La ② DE7 .....157 F1
Burrow Wlk NG17 .114 C3
Burrows Ave NG9 ..171 F1
Burrows Cres NG9 .171 F1
Burrows Ct NG3 ...223 F3
Burrows The LE12 .205 F1
Burtness Rd NG7 ..184 C1
Burton Ave NG4 ...174 C1
Burton Cl Carlton NG4 .175 D4
Harby LE14 ....202 A2
Burton Dr NG9 ....183 E2
Burton Cl
Gainsborough DN21 ..24 B4
Loughborough LE11 .220 A1
Nottingham NG1 ..223 E3
Burton Wlk LE12 ..214 C4
Burwell Ct NG19 ...88 C2
Burwell St NG7 ...222 B4
Bush Cl NG5 ....160 C4
Bushmead Mews ④ S80 .35 F1
Bushy Cl NG10 ....193 D3
Buskeyfield La NG20 .59 F2
Bute Ave NG7 .....222 B2
Butler Ave NG12 ..176 A2
Butler Cl NG12 ....189 D3
Butlers Hill Inf Sch
NG15 ....146 B3
Butt Hill S80 ....45 D3
Butt La
East Bridgford NG13 .165 F1
Mansfield Woodhouse
NG19 ....88 B1
Normanton on S LE12 .213 F2
Butt Rd NG13 .....178 A2
Butt St NG10 ......182 A2
Butten Mew DN10 ...3 E1
Buttercup NG24 ...140 B3

Butterhall Cl S80 .....45 D3
Buttermead Cl NG9 .....170 B1
Buttermere Cl
  Long Eaton NG10 .....182 A1
  West Bridgford NG2 .....186 B3
Buttermere Cl 1 NG5 .....161 E1
Butterton Dr NG9 .....183 E4
Butterton Cl DE7 .....170 A4
Buttery La NG17 .....100 C4
Butts Cl DE7 .....170 A2
Buxton Dr NG4 .....162 C1
Buxton Ct DE7 .....157 E1
Buxton Rd NG10 .....87 E1
Byard La NG1 .....223 E2
Bycroft Rd DN21 .....15 E2
Bye Pass Rd NG14 .....164 C3
Bye Path Rd DN22 .....39 F4
Byfield Cl NG7 .....222 B4
Byford Cl NG5 .....161 F1
Byley Rd NG8 .....171 D3
By-Pass Rd NG9 .....183 E2
Byrne Ct NG5 .....162 A3
Byron Ave
  Kirkby in A NG17 .....115 D4
  Long Eaton NG10 .....182 A2
  Mansfield Woodhouse NG19 .....88 B1
  Sutton in A NG17 .....101 D2
Byron Cl Darlton NG22 .....67 D4
  Newark-on-T NG24 .....140 A3
Byron Cres
  Awsworth NG16 .....158 B2
  Ravenshead NG16 .....116 C2
Byron Ct
  Balderton NG24 .....140 C2
  7 Nottingham NG2 .....173 F2
  Stapleford NG9 .....170 C1
Byron Est NG5 .....162 A4
Byron Gdns NG25 .....121 F1
Byron Gr NG5 .....161 E2
Byron Rd
  Annesley NG15 .....130 B3
  West Bridgford NG2 .....185 F4
Byron St Arnold NG5 .....161 E3
  Bidworth NG21 .....118 A3
  Hucknall NG15 .....146 A3
  Ilkeston DE7 .....157 F1
  Mansfield NG18 .....102 A4
  Newstead NG15 .....113 A4
  Shirebrook NG20 .....72 C2
Byron Way S81 .....36 A2
Bythorn Cl NG11 .....101 D3

C

C Rd NG9 .....184 B3
Cabin Leas 4 LE11 .....220 A3
Cad La NG13 .....81 F4
Caddaw Ave NG15 .....146 A3
Cadlan Cl NG5 .....161 D4
Cadlan Ct 6 NG5 .....161 D4
Caenby Cl DN21 .....24 C4
Caernarvon Pl NG9 .....183 D2
Caincross Rd NG8 .....171 E4
Cairngorm Dr NG5 .....147 D1
Cairns Cl NG5 .....161 D3
Cairns St NG7 .....223 E3
Cairnsmore Cl NG10 .....182 A1
Cairo St NG7 .....160 C1
Caister Rd NG11 .....195 F4
Caithness Ct 16 NG5 .....161 D4
Calcroft Cl NG8 .....160 B1
Caldbeck Cl NG2 .....186 B4
Caldbeck Ct NG9 .....183 D2
Caldbeck Wlk 33 NG5 .....161 D4
Calder Wlk 22 NG6 .....160 A4
Calderdale NG8 .....171 D2
Calderdale Dr NG10 .....193 D3
Calderhall Gdns 2 NG5 .....161 E4
Caldon Gn NG6 .....146 B1
Caldwell St 8 LE11 .....220 A3
Caledon Rd NG5 .....161 D2
Caledonian Rd DE72 .....40 A3
Calf Croft S80 .....45 D3
California Rd NG24 .....139 D2
Calke Ave NG17 .....99 F1
Calladine La NG17 .....114 B4
Callaway Cl NG8 .....171 F3
Calstock Rd NG5 .....161 E4
Calveley Rd NG8 .....171 F4
Calver Cl NG8 .....172 B2
Calver St NG19 .....88 C2
Calverton Ave NG4 .....162 A1
Calverton Cl NG9 .....183 D2
Calverton Dr NG18 .....103 D2
Calverton Dr NG6 .....159 E1
Calverton Folk Mus* NG14 .....148 C4
Calverton Rd
  Arnold NG5 .....148 A1
  Bidworth NG21 .....118 A1
Cambell Gdns NG5 .....148 B1
Camberley Cl NG16 .....160 A4
Camberley Rd NG6 .....160 A4
Camborne Cl DN22 .....29 F1
Camborne Cres DN22 .....29 F1
Camborne Dr NG8 .....160 B1
Cambourne Gdns NG15 .....116 C1
Cambrai Terr S80 .....35 F2
Cambria Mews NG3 .....173 E4
Cambria Rd NG19 .....87 E2
Cambridge Cl NG21 .....118 A4
Cambridge Cres NG9 .....170 B1
Cambridge Rd
  Harworth DN11 .....8 C2

Cambridge Rd continued
  Nottingham NG8 .....172 A2
  Rainworth NG21 .....118 A4
  West Bridgford NG2 .....186 A3
Cambridge St
  Carlton NG4 .....174 C4
  Loughborough LE11 .....220 A3
  Mansfield NG16 .....102 A2
Camdale Cl NG9 .....183 D3
Camden Cl NG2 .....173 F2
Camelia Ave NG11 .....184 B1
Camelot Ave NG5 .....161 D2
Camelot Cres NG11 .....196 A4
Camelot St NG11 .....196 A4
Cameo Cl NG4 .....174 C3
Cameron St NG5 .....161 E1
Camerons The NG19 .....101 E3
Camomile Cl NG5 .....160 C4
Camomile Gdns 15 NG7 .....172 C4
Campbell Cl S81 .....35 F4
Campbell Dr NG4 .....174 B4
Campbell Gr NG3 .....223 F3
Campbell St
  Gainsborough DN21 .....15 D1
  Langley Mill NG16 .....143 D2
  Nottingham NG3 .....223 F3
Campden Gn NG7 .....184 C1
Campion Cl NG20 .....72 B2
Campion St NG5 .....161 F4
Campion Way NG13 .....177 F2
Camrose Cl NG8 .....171 E4
Canal La Harby NG13 .....202 B3
  Hose LE14 .....211 F4
  Long Clawson LE14 .....211 E3
  West Stockwith DN10 .....7 F1
Canal Rd S80 .....35 F2
Canal Side NG9 .....184 A2
Canal St Ilkeston DE7 .....158 A1
  Long Eaton NG10 .....182 B1
  Nottingham NG1 .....223 E1
  Retford DN22 .....39 F3
  Sandiacre NG10 .....182 B3
Canal Terr S80 .....36 A2
Canberra Cl NG9 .....170 C1
Canberra Gdns NG22 .....185 E2
Canberra Rd NG24 .....125 F1
Candle Mdw NG2 .....173 D1
Candleby Cl NG12 .....187 F2
Candleby Ct NG12 .....187 F2
Candleby La NG12 .....187 F2
Candlemass Cl NG19 .....88 B1
Canning Circ NG7 .....222 C3
Cannock Way NG10 .....194 A4
Cannon Cl NG24 .....125 F1
Cannon Sq DN22 .....39 F4
Cannon St NG5 .....161 E2
Canon Cl DE7 .....157 F3
Canonbie Cl NG5 .....148 A1
Canons Cl NG25 .....121 F1
Cantabury Ave NG7 .....172 C4
Cantelupe Rd DE7 .....170 A4
Canterbury Cl
  Mansfield Woodhouse NG19 .....88 B3
  Nuthall NG16 .....159 E2
  Worksop S81 .....36 A4
Canterbury Rd NG8 .....172 B3
Canterbury Wlk S81 .....25 F4
Cantley Ave NG4 .....162 C1
Cantrell Prim Sch NG6 .....160 B4
Cantrell Rd NG6 .....160 B4
Canver Cl NG8 .....171 E3
Canwick Cl NG8 .....171 E3
Capenwray Gdns 3 NG5 .....161 E4
Capes The NG13 .....178 C2
Capitol Ct 11 NG8 .....172 A3
Caporn Cl NG6 .....160 B3
Capps Pl NG22 .....66 A1
Capt Ball Meml Homes NG7 .....222 A1
Car La NG13 .....166 B1
Carburton Ave NG20 .....74 B4
Carburton Way NG17 .....115 E3
Cardale Rd
  Nottingham NG3 .....174 A3
  Radmanthwaite NG19 .....87 E2
Cardiff St 10 NG3 .....173 F3
Cardinal Cl NG3 .....173 F3
Cardinal Hinsley Cl NG24 .....139 E2
Carding Cl NG22 .....120 A3
Cardington Cl NG5 .....146 C1
Cardle Cl NG19 .....89 D1
Cardwell St NG7 .....172 C4
Carew Rd NG7 .....184 C1
Carey Rd NG6 .....160 B4
Carisbrook Ave NG18 .....103 D4
Carisbrooke Ave
  Beeston NG9 .....184 A4
  Carlton NG4 .....163 D1
  Nottingham NG3 .....161 F1
Carisbrooke Cl NG17 .....115 E3
Carisbrooke Dr NG3 .....161 F1
Carlile Rd NG4 .....174 C4
Carlin St NG6 .....160 A4
Carling Ave S80 .....35 E2
Carlingford Rd NG15 .....146 A4
Carlisle Ave NG6 .....160 B4
Carlisle St DN21 .....15 E1
Carlswark Gdns 4 NG5 .....146 C1
Carlton Ave S81 .....35 F3

Carlton Bsns & Tech Ctr NG4 .....174 C4
Carlton Central Inf Sch NG4 .....174 B4
Carlton Central Jun Sch NG4 .....174 B4
Carlton Cl
  Clipstone NG19 .....89 E2
  Heanor DE75 .....143 D2
  Newark-on-T NG24 .....139 F3
  Worksop S81 .....35 F4
Carlton Cres LE12 .....205 F1
Carlton Digby Sch NG3 .....162 B2
Carlton Dr NG10 .....9 F3
Carlton Ferry La NG23 .....97 E1
Carlton Fold 38 NG2 .....173 F2
Carlton Hall La S81 .....25 F3
Carlton Hill NG4 .....174 C4
Carlton Hill Nature Reserve* NG5 .....148 A2
Carlton La
  Broxholme LN1 .....57 F4
  Sutton on T NG23 .....97 D3
Carlton Mews NG4 .....174 C4
Carlton Phoenix Ind Est S80 .....36 A2
Carlton Pk Inf Sch S81 .....25 F3
Carlton Rd
  Long Eaton NG10 .....193 D3
  Newark-on-T NG24 .....140 A3
  Nottingham NG3 .....173 F3
  Worksop S80, S81 .....35 F3
Carlton Sq NG4 .....174 C4
Carlton St
  Mansfield Woodhouse NG19 .....88 B1
  Nottingham NG1 .....223 F2
  Carlton Sta NG4 .....174 C4
Carlton-Vale Cl NG4 .....162 B1
Carlton-le-Willows Comp Sch NG4 .....163 D1
Carlyle Rd NG2 .....185 F4
Carman Cl NG16 .....159 D4
Carmel Gdns NG5 .....161 F4
Carnaby Cl NG12 .....176 C2
Carnarvon Cl NG13 .....177 F3
Carnarvon Dr NG14 .....164 A3
Carnarvon Gr
  Carlton, Gedling NG4 .....162 C1
  Carlton, Thorneywood NG4 .....174 B4
  Sutton in A NG17 .....100 C3
Carnarvon Pl NG13 .....177 E2
Carnarvon Prim Sch NG13 .....178 A2
Carnarvon Rd
  Huthwaite NG17 .....99 F1
  West Bridgford NG2 .....185 F3
Carnarvon St
  Carlton NG4 .....175 D3
  Teversal NG17 .....100 A4
Carnforth Cl NG9 .....182 B3
Carnforth Ct 16 NG5 .....161 E4
Carnoustie S81 .....36 A3
Carnoustie Ct 7 NG17 .....114 C4
Carnwood Rd NG5 .....161 D3
Carolgate DN22 .....39 F3
Caroline Cl NG15 .....117 D2
Caroline Ct DE7 .....170 A3
Caroline Wlk NG3 .....173 E4
Carpenter Ave NG19 .....87 E1
Carpenters Cl NG12 .....189 D3
Carr Cl DE55 .....113 E4
Carr Farm Rd NG17 .....114 C1
Carr Hill Cl NG17 .....114 C1
Carr Hill Prim Sch DN22 .....29 F1
Carr La Blyton DN21 .....15 E4
  Doddington LN6 .....71 D2
  East Stockwith DN21 .....7 F1
  Gainsborough DN21 .....24 B3
  Market Warsop NG20 .....74 A2
  Misterton DN10 .....6 C1
  South Normanton DE55 .....113 D4
Carr Rd Bingham NG13 .....178 A3
  Gringley on t H DN10 .....12 B3
  Retford DN22 .....39 F3
Carr View DN10 .....11 E2
Carradale Cl NG5 .....162 B4
Carradale Ave NG10 .....182 C1
Carrfield Cl NG17 .....100 B2
Carrgate La NG23 .....153 F3
Carrington Ct NG5 .....161 E1
Carrington La NG14 .....149 D4
Carrington Prim Sch NG5 .....161 D1
Carrington St NG1 .....223 E1
Carroll Gdns NG2 .....173 E1
Carsic Inf Sch NG17 .....100 B2
Carsic Jun Sch NG17 .....100 B2
Carsic La NG17 .....100 C2
Carsic Rd NG17 .....100 B2
Carside Ave NG5 .....160 C4
Carsington Ct NG19 .....88 C2
Carson Rd DN21 .....15 E1
Carswell Cl NG24 .....139 F3
Cartbridge NG12 .....187 F1
Carter Ave
  Radcliffe on T NG12 .....176 A2
  Ruddington NG11 .....196 B3
Carter Gate NG24 .....139 F4
Carter La
  Mansfield NG18 .....102 C3
  Shirebrook NG20 .....72 C2
  Warsop Vale NG19 .....73 E2
Carter La E DE55 .....113 E3

Carter La W
  Shirebrook NG20 .....72 B2
  South Normanton DE55 .....113 E3
Carter Rd NG9 .....183 D2
Carters Wood Dr NG16 .....159 F2
Cartwright Cl NG22 .....54 A1
Cartwright St
  Loughborough LE11 .....220 B3
  Shireoaks S81 .....34 C4
Carver Cl NG21 .....76 A4
Carver St NG7 .....172 C4
Carvers Hollow NG22 .....120 A1
Carwood Rd NG9 .....171 E1
Caskgate St DN21 .....24 B4
Casper Ct NG5 .....161 D4
Castellan Rise NG5 .....161 E4
Casterton Rd NG5 .....161 D4
Castle Brewery Ct NG24 .....139 F3
Castle Bridge Rd NG2 .....173 D1
Castle Bvd NG7 .....222 C1
Castle Cl
  Bottesford NG13 .....181 E1
  Calverton NG14 .....148 C4
Castle Farm La S80 .....46 B3
Castle Gate
  Newark-on-T NG24 .....139 F4
  Nottingham NG1 .....223 E2
  Tickhill DN11 .....8 A4
Castle Gdns NG7 .....222 B1
Castle Gr NG7 .....223 D1
Castle Hill LE12 .....205 F1
Castle Hill NG17 .....114 C3
Castle Hills Sch (Arts College) NG6 .....15 E1
Castle Marina Pk NG2 .....173 D1
Castle Marina Rd NG2 .....173 D1
Castle Mdw Rd NG2 .....223 D1
Castle Mdw Ret Pk NG2 .....222 C1
Castle Mews
  Eastwood NG16 .....144 A1
  18 Mansfield NG18 .....102 A4
  Mansfield Woodhouse NG19 .....88 A2
  Worksop S80 .....35 F1
Castle View
  Aldercar NG16 .....143 D2
  West Bridgford NG2 .....185 E3
Castle View Rd NG13 .....181 E1
Castlebridge NG22 .....173 D1
Castledine St LE11 .....220 A1
Castledine St Extension LE11 .....220 A1
Castlefields NG2 .....173 E1
Castlerigg Cl NG2 .....186 B3
Castleton Ave
  Arnold NG5 .....161 F3
  Carlton NG4 .....162 C1
  Ilkeston DE7 .....157 F3
Castleton Cl
  Hucknall NG15 .....145 E3
  Mansfield Woodhouse NG19 .....88 B2
  8 Nottingham NG2 .....173 D1
  Ravenshead NG15 .....117 D2
Castleton Ct NG6 .....159 F3
Caterham Cl NG8 .....171 E4
Catfoot La NG4 .....162 C4
Catherine Ave NG18 .....88 B2
Catherine Cl
  24 Kirkby in A NG17 .....114 C4
  Nottingham NG6 .....160 A4
Catkin Dr NG16 .....158 B4
Catkin Way NG24 .....140 A2
Catlow Wlk 4 NG5 .....161 E4
Caton Cl NG17 .....100 B2
Cator Cl NG4 .....162 B2
Cator La NG9 .....183 E3
Cator La N NG9 .....183 E3
Cator Rd NG19 .....87 E2
Catriona Cres NG5 .....148 A1
Catterley Hill Rd NG3 .....173 F4
Cattle Mkt 8 LE11 .....220 A2
Cattle Mkt Rd NG2 .....173 E1
Cattle Rd DN10 .....6 B1
Cattle Rd NG6 .....160 A4
Caudwell Cl NG25 .....121 F1
Caudwell Dr NG18 .....102 B2
Cauldwell Rd NG17 .....101 F1
Caulton St NG7 .....222 B4
Caunton Ave NG3 .....161 F1
Caunton Cl
  Mansfield NG18 .....101 F3
  Meden Vale NG20 .....74 B4
Caunton Rd
  Bathley NG23 .....109 F2
  Hockerton NG25 .....122 A3
Caunts Cres NG17 .....100 B2
Causeway DN21 .....24 C2
Causeway La
  Gamston DN22 .....51 D4
  Morton NG25 .....137 E2
Causeway Mews 19 NG2 .....173 D1
Cavan Ct 10 NG2 .....173 E1
Cavell Cl NG11 .....184 B1

Cavell Cl
  Woodbeck DN22 .....53 D4
Cavell Ct NG7 .....172 B1
Cavendish Ave
  Carlton NG4 .....162 B1
  Edwinstowe NG21 .....75 F1
  Newark-on-T NG24 .....140 A3
  Nottingham NG5 .....161 E2
  Sutton in A NG17 .....100 C2
Cavendish Cl
  Bawtry DN10 .....9 F3
  Hucknall NG15 .....146 B3
Cavendish Cres
  Annesley Woodhouse NG17 .....130 A3
  Carlton NG4 .....162 B1
  Stapleford NG9 .....170 B1
Cavendish Cres N NG7 .....222 C2
Cavendish Cres S NG7 .....222 C1
Cavendish Dr
  Carlton NG4 .....174 C4
  Lea DN21 .....24 C1
Cavendish Pl NG9 .....183 F3
Cavendish Rd
  Carlton NG4 .....162 B1
  Ilkeston DE7 .....170 A3
  Long Eaton NG10 .....182 B1
  Retford DN22 .....40 A2
  Worksop S80 .....47 D4
Cavendish Rd E NG7 .....222 C2
Cavendish Rd W NG7 .....222 C2
Cavendish St
  Arnold NG5 .....161 F4
  Langwith NG20 .....72 C4
  Mansfield NG18 .....102 B3
  Mansfield Woodhouse NG19 .....88 A2
  Nottingham NG7 .....184 C4
  Sutton in A NG17 .....101 D2
Cavendish Vale NG5 .....161 E2
Caves La DN10 .....13 E3
Caves of Nottingham* NG1 .....223 E2
Cawdron Wlk NG5 .....184 C1
Cawston Gdns 4 NG6 .....160 A4
Cawthorne Cl NG23 .....98 A1
Cawthorne Way NG18 .....102 C4
Caxmere Dr NG8 .....171 F3
Caxton Cl NG4 .....175 D4
Caythorpe Cres NG5 .....161 E2
Caythorpe Ct NG13 .....88 C2
Caythorpe Rd NG14 .....150 C1
Caythorpe Rise NG5 .....161 E2
Cecil Cl S80 .....35 D2
Cecil St
  Gainsborough DN21 .....15 E1
  Nottingham NG7 .....222 B1
Cedar Ave
  Beeston NG9 .....184 A4
  East Leake LE12 .....214 B4
  Kirkby in A NG17 .....114 C2
  Long Eaton NG10 .....193 E3
  Mansfield Woodhouse NG19 .....88 B3
  Newark-on-T NG24 .....125 F2
  Nuthall NG16 .....159 F2
Cedar Cl Carlton in L S81 .....25 F4
  Gainsborough DN21 .....15 D2
  Sandiacre NG10 .....182 A4
  Sutton in A NG17 .....100 B4
Cedar Ct NG9 .....184 A4
Cedar Dr
  Keyworth NG12 .....197 F3
  Selston NG16 .....128 C4
Cedar Gr Arnold NG5 .....162 A4
  Hucknall NG15 .....146 A3
  Nottingham NG8 .....171 F2
  South Normanton DE55 .....113 D2
Cedar La NG22 .....77 E3
Cedar Rd Beeston NG9 .....183 F3
  Loughborough LE11 .....220 B1
  Nottingham NG7 .....173 D4
Cedar St NG18 .....102 B3
Cedar Tree Rd
  Elkesley DN22 .....50 A2
  Nottingham NG5 .....147 D1
Cedarland Cres NG16 .....159 F2
Cedars The NG5 .....161 E2
Celandine Cl NG5 .....160 C4
Celandine Gdns NG13 .....177 E2
Celia Dr NG4 .....174 B4
Cemetery Rd
  Stapleford NG9 .....182 C4
  Worksop S80 .....36 A1
Centenary Ct NG24 .....140 B2
Central Ave
  Arnold NG5 .....161 F4
  Beeston NG9 .....183 F4
  Beeston, Chilwell NG9 .....183 E3
  Blidworth NG21 .....118 A3
  Creswell S80 .....58 B4
  Hucknall NG15 .....146 A3
  Kirkby in A NG17 .....115 D2
  Mansfield NG18 .....102 B3
  Nottingham, Mapperley NG3 .....162 A2
  Nottingham, New Basford NG7, NG5 .....161 D1
  Sandiacre NG10 .....182 A3
  South Normanton DE55 .....113 D3
  Stapleford NG9 .....182 C4
  Walesby NG22 .....64 A1
  West Bridgford NG2 .....185 F4

Central Ave continued
Worksop S80 . . . . .35 F2
Central Ave S NG5 . . . . . . .161 F4
Central Cl NG20 . . . . .72 C2
Central Ct NG7 . . . . .172 C1
Central Dr Bawtry DN10 . . .10 A4
Clipstone NG21 . . . . .89 F1
Elston NG23 . . . . .153 F2
Shirebrook NG20 . . . . .72 C2
Central St
5 Nottingham NG3 . . . . . .173 F3
Sutton in A NG17 . . . . .101 D2
Central Wlk NG15 . . . . .146 A4
Centre Way NG21 . . . . . . .175 F2
Centurion Way NG11 . . . . .185 D4
Century Ave NG18 . . . . . . .101 F3
Century Rd DN22 . . . . .39 F3
Century St NG24 . . . . .140 A4
Cernan Ct NG6 . . . . .159 F3
Cerne Cl NG7 . . . . .184 C1
Chaceley Way NG11 . . . . .185 D2
Chad Gdns NG5 . . . . .147 D1
Chadborn Ave NG11 . . . . .195 D1
Chadburn Rd NG18 . . . . . .102 C4
Chaddesden The NG3 . . . .173 E4
Chadwick Rd NG7 . . . . . . .172 C4
Chadwick Way DN22 . . . . . .53 D4
Chaffinch Cl NG18 . . . . . . .102 C4
Chaffinch Mews S81 . . . . . .35 E4
Chain Bridge Rd DN22 . . . .29 E4
Chain La
Newark-on-T NG24 . . . . .139 F4
Nottingham NG7 . . . . .172 C1
Chainbridge Cl LE11 . . . . .220 A3
Chainbridge La DN22 . . . . .29 E4
Chalfield Cl NG11 . . . . . . .184 B1
Chalfont Dr NG8 . . . . .172 B3
Chalons Cl DE7 . . . . .157 F1
Chamberlain Cl NG11 . . . .184 B1
Chambers Ave DE7 . . . . . .170 A4
Champion Ave DE7 . . . . . .157 E2
Champion Cres NG19 . . . .101 F4
Chancery Cl NG17 . . . . . . .101 D3
Chancery Ct NG11 . . . . . . .185 D3
Chancery La DN22 . . . . . . .39 E4
Chancery The NG9 . . . . . .183 E4
Chandos Ave NG4 . . . . . . .175 D4
Chandos Ct NG22 . . . . .65 F2
Chandos St
Carlton NG4 . . . . .175 D4
Nottingham NG3 . . . . .173 E4
Chantrey Cl NG9 . . . . .183 E2
Chantrey Rd NG2 . . . . .185 F4
Chantry Cl
Kimberley NG16 . . . . .159 D3
Long Eaton NG10 . . . . .193 D2
Newark-on-T NG24 . . . . .139 F3
Chantry Tne NG18 . . . . . . .102 C3
Chantry Wlk NG22 . . . . . . .65 F2
Chapel Bar NG1 . . . . .223 D2
Chapel Cl DE7 . . . . .157 F2
Chapel Garth NG13 . . . . . .179 F3
Chapel Gate S81 . . . . .26 A3
Chapel La Arnold NG5 . . . .161 F4
Aslockton NG13 . . . . .179 D3
Bathley NG23 . . . . .110 A2
Bingham NG13 . . . . .177 F3
Caunton NG23 . . . . .109 D3
Claypole NG23 . . . . .156 B4
Coddington NG24 . . . . .126 A1
Costock LE12 . . . . .206 B1
Cotgrave NG12 . . . . .187 F2
Epperstone NG14 . . . . .150 A3
Everton DN10 . . . . .9 F4
Farndon NG24 . . . . .138 C2
Farnsfield NG22 . . . . .119 F3
Granby NG13 . . . . .191 D3
Hose LE14 . . . . .211 F4
Lambley NG4 . . . . .163 D4
Laxton NG22 . . . . .79 E1
Misterton DN10 . . . . .6 C1
Morton DN21 . . . . .15 D2
Nether Broughton LE14 . . . . .219 E4
North Scarle LN6 . . . . .83 E2
Old Dalby LE14 . . . . .218 C2
Oxton NG25 . . . . .134 B2
Ravenshead NG15 . . . . .117 D1
Scrooby DN10 . . . . .10 A1
Upper Broughton LE14 . . . . .210 A1
Walesby NG22 . . . . .64 A1
Willoughby-on-t-W LE12 . . . .217 E4
Winthorpe NG24 . . . . .125 E3
Chapel Mews Ct NG9 . . . .183 D4
Chapel Pl NG16 . . . . .158 C3
Chapel Rd NG16 . . . . .128 C3
Chapel St
Annesley Woodhouse
NG17 . . . . .115 D1
Barkestone-le-V NG13 . . . . .192 A1
Beckingham LN5 . . . . .142 B4
Beeston NG9 . . . . .183 D4
Bottesford NG13 . . . . .143 F1
Eastwood NG16 . . . . .157 D4
Heanor DE75 . . . . .157 D4
Hucknall NG15 . . . . .146 A4
17 Ilkeston DE7 . . . . .157 F1
Kimberley NG16 . . . . .158 C3
Kirkby in A NG17 . . . . .114 C3
Long Eaton NG10 . . . . .193 F4
New Houghton NG19 . . . . . . .87 D4
Orston NG13 . . . . .179 F4
Ruddington NG11 . . . . .196 B3
Selston NG16 . . . . .129 D4

Chapel St continued
Whaley Thorns NG20 . . . . . . .59 D2
Chapel Staith DN21 . . . . . .24 B4
Chapel Wlk S80 . . . . .35 F1
Chapelgate NG24 . . . . .39 F4
Chapman Ct NG8 . . . . .172 A4
Chapman St LE11 . . . . . . .220 B2
Chappel Gdns NG22 . . . . .106 A2
Chapter Dr NG16 . . . . .159 D3
Chard St NG7 . . . . .160 C1
Charlbury Ct NG9 . . . . .171 D2
Charlbury Rd NG8 . . . . . . .172 A3
Charlecote Dr NG8 . . . . . .171 E2
Charlecote Pk Dr NG2 . . . .185 E2
Charles Ave
Beeston NG9 . . . . .172 A1
Beeston, Chilwell NG9 . . . . . .183 E2
Eastwood NG16 . . . . .144 A1
Sandiacre NG10 . . . . .182 A3
Stapleford NG9 . . . . .182 C4
Charles Bains Prim Sch
DN21 . . . . .24 C4
Charles Cl Carlton NG4 . . .162 C1
Ilkeston DE7 . . . . .170 A3
Charles Pk NG6 . . . . .160 A3
Charles St Arnold NG5 . . . .161 F4
Gainsborough DN21 . . . . .15 E1
Hucknall NG15 . . . . .146 A4
Long Eaton NG10 . . . . .193 E3
Loughborough LE11 . . . . . . .220 A3
Mansfield NG19 . . . . .88 A1
Mansfield Woodhouse
NG19 . . . . .88 B2
Newark-on-T NG24 . . . . .140 A4
Ruddington NG11 . . . . .196 B4
Sutton in A NG17 . . . . .101 D2
Charlesworth Ave
NG7 . . . . .172 C4
Charlesworth Ct NG19 . . . .88 C2
Charlock Cl NG5 . . . . .160 C4
Charlock Gdns NG13 . . . . .177 E2
Charlotte Cl
Arnold NG5 . . . . .147 F1
Kirton NG22 . . . . .78 A3
Newark-on-T NG24 . . . . .140 A4
Charlotte Gr NG9 . . . . .171 F1
Charlotte Inf Sch DE7 . . . .157 F1
Charlton Ave NG10 . . . . . .182 C1
Charlton Gr NG9 . . . . .183 F3
Charlton Rd S81 . . . . .26 A1
Charnock Ave NG8 . . . . . .172 B2
Charnwood Ave
Beeston NG9 . . . . .183 F3
Keyworth NG12 . . . . .197 F1
Long Eaton NG10 . . . . .193 D2
Sandiacre NG10 . . . . .182 A2
Sutton Bonington LE12 . . . . .213 E3
Charnwood Cres S81 . . . . .99 D2
Charnwood Fields
LE12 . . . . .213 E3
Charnwood Gr
Bingham NG13 . . . . .177 E2
Hucknall NG15 . . . . .145 F4
Mansfield NG18 . . . . .103 D4
Mansfield Woodhouse
NG19 . . . . .88 A3
West Bridgford NG2 . . . . . . .185 F4
Charnwood La NG5 . . . . . .162 A3
Charnwood Mus*
LE11 . . . . .220 A2
Charnwood Rd LE11 . . . . .220 A1
Charnwood St NG17 . . . . .100 B1
Charnwood Way NG14 . . .149 E2
Charter Pl NG22 . . . . .66 A2
Charters Cl 8 NG17 . . . . .114 C4
Chartwell Ave NG11 . . . . .196 A4
Chartwell Gr NG3 . . . . . . .162 B3
Chartwell Rd NG17 . . . . . .115 E3
Chase Pk NG22 . . . . .174 A2
Chatham Ct NG24 . . . . . . .139 F4
Chatham St
Nottingham NG1 . . . . .223 E4
Southwell NG25 . . . . .121 F1
Chatsworth Ave
Beeston NG9 . . . . .183 E1
Carlton NG4 . . . . .162 C1
Long Eaton NG10 . . . . .194 A3
Nottingham NG7 . . . . .160 C1
Radcliffe on T NG12 . . . . . . .176 A2
Selston NG16 . . . . .129 D4
Shirebrook NG20 . . . . .72 C3
Southwell NG25 . . . . .121 E1
Chatsworth Cl
Mansfield NG18 . . . . .102 C1
Ravenshead NG15 . . . . .117 D2
Sandiacre NG10 . . . . .182 A2
Sutton in A NG17 . . . . .100 C3
Chatsworth Ct
Harworth DN11 . . . . .9 D3
Hucknall NG15 . . . . .146 A3
Chatsworth Dr
Mansfield NG18 . . . . .146 A3
Mansfield NG18 . . . . .102 C1
Chatsworth Rd
Creswell S80 . . . . .58 B4
Newark-on-T NG24 . . . . .140 A3
West Bridgford NG2 . . . . . . .186 A4
Worksop S81 . . . . .35 F4
Chatsworth St
Sutton in A NG17 . . . . .101 D2
Chaucer Cres NG17 . . . . .101 D2
Chaucer Rd NG24 . . . . . . .140 C2
Chaucer St
Ilkeston DE7 . . . . .157 F1
Mansfield NG18 . . . . .102 A4
Nottingham NG1 . . . . .223 D3
Chaworth Ave NG16 . . . . .145 D1

Chaworth Rd
Bingham NG13 . . . . .177 E2
Carlton NG4 . . . . .174 C3
West Bridgford NG2 . . . . . . .185 F3
Chaworth St NG21 . . . . . . .118 A3
Cheadle Cl
Nottingham, Bulborough

NG19 . . . . .171 E4
Nottingham, Porteshester
NG3 . . . . .162 A1
Cheapside
Nottingham NG1 . . . . .223 E2
Worksop S80 . . . . .36 A1
Cheddar Cl NG21 . . . . .104 B1
Cheddar Rd NG11 . . . . . . .195 F4
Chedington Ave NG3 . . . . .162 B3
Chediston Vale NG5 . . . . .161 D4
Chedworth Cl 10 NG3 . . . .173 F3
Chelmorton Cl NG19 . . . . . .88 C2
Chelmsford Rd NG7 . . . . . .160 C1
Chelmsford Terr NG7 . . . .160 C1
Chelsea Cl NG16 . . . . .159 F2
Chelsea St NG7 . . . . .160 C1
Cheltenham Cl NG9 . . . . . .182 C1
Cheltenham Ct NG18 . . . . .102 C4
Cheltenham St NG6 . . . . . .160 C2
Chennel Nook NG12 . . . . .188 A1
Chepstow Rd NG11 . . . . . .195 F4
Chepstow Wlk NG18 . . . . .102 C4
Chequers La NG22 . . . . . . .54 A1
Cherhill Cl NG11 . . . . .195 E4
Cheriton Cl NG19 . . . . .87 F1
Cheriton Dr
Ravenshead NG15 . . . . .117 D1
Shipley DE7 . . . . .157 E2
Chermside Cl NG15 . . . . . .117 D1
Chernside NG15 . . . . .117 D2
Cherry Ave
Hucknall NG15 . . . . .146 A3
Kirkby in A NG17 . . . . .114 B4
Cherry Cl Arnold NG5 . . . .161 F4
Nottingham NG5 . . . . .147 D1
Cherry Gr
Mansfield NG18 . . . . .101 F3
Market Warsop NG20 . . . . . . .74 B2
Nottingham NG12 . . . . .197 F2
Cherry Holt
Newark-on-T NG24 . . . . .139 F3
Retford DN22 . . . . .40 A2
Cherry La NG18 . . . . .102 A2
Cherry Orch NG12 . . . . . . .187 F2
Cherry Orch Mount
NG5 . . . . .161 D4
Cherry St NG13 . . . . .177 F2
Cherry Tree Ave S81 . . . . .34 C4
Cherry Tree Cl
Brinsley NG16 . . . . .143 F4
Mansfield Woodhouse

NG19 . . . . .88 A2
Radcliffe on T NG12 . . . . . . .175 F1
Cherry Tree La NG12 . . . . .186 A2
Cherry Tree Rd DN21 . . . . .15 F1
Cherry Tree Wlk DN22 . . . .39 E4
Cherry Wood Dr NG8 . . . . .172 A4
Cherryholt Cl NG13 . . . . . .165 E2
Cherryholt La NG13 . . . . . .165 E2
Cherrywood Gdns

NG3 . . . . .174 A4
Chertsey Cl NG3 . . . . .161 F1
Cherwell Ct NG6 . . . . .159 F3
Chesham Dr
Beeston NG9 . . . . .171 D1
Nottingham NG5 . . . . .161 D1
Cheshire Way NG16 . . . . . .128 B2
Chesil Ave 5 NG8 . . . . . . .172 B3
Chesil Cotts 6 NG8 . . . . . .172 B3
Chesil Way NG8 . . . . .172 B3
Chess Burrow NG19 . . . . . .88 B1
Chester Cl 24 LE11 . . . . . .220 A2
Chester Gn NG9 . . . . .182 C1
Chester Rd NG3 . . . . .174 A3
Chester St NG19 . . . . .87 F1
Chesterfield Ave
Bingham NG13 . . . . .177 F3
Carlton NG4 . . . . .162 B1
Long Eaton NG10 . . . . .193 F4
Chesterfield Ct NG4 . . . . .162 B2
Chesterfield Dr
Burton Joyce NG14 . . . . .164 A3
Retford DN22 . . . . .40 A4
Chesterfield Rd
Hardstoft DE55 . . . . .85 D1
Huthwaite NG17 . . . . .99 F2
New Houghton NG19 . . . . . . .86 C4
Pleasley NG19 . . . . .87 D3
Chesterfield Rd N

NG19 . . . . .87 E2
Chesterfield Rd S

NG18 . . . . .102 A4
Chesterfield St NG4 . . . . . .174 B4
Chesterman Cl NG16 . . . . .158 A2
Chesterton Dr S81 . . . . . . .36 A3
Chestnut Ave
Beeston NG9 . . . . .183 F4
Bingham NG13 . . . . .177 F2
Gainsborough DN21 . . . . .15 E1
Kirkby in A NG17 . . . . .114 C2
Newark-on-T NG24 . . . . .125 D2
Nottingham NG3 . . . . .162 A1
Retford DN22 . . . . .39 F2
Chestnut Cl
Bottesford NG13 . . . . .181 E2
New Ollerton NG22 . . . . .77 E3
Ravenshead NG18 . . . . .116 C4
Worksop S80 . . . . .35 F1
Chestnut Copse NG24 . . . .140 A3

Chestnut Dr Bawtry DN10 . . .9 F4
Mansfield NG18 . . . . .102 C1
New Ollerton NG22 . . . . .77 E3
Nuthall NG16 . . . . .159 D3
Selston NG16 . . . . .128 C4
Shirebrook NG20 . . . . .72 B2
South Normanton DE55 . . . .113 D2
Chestnut Gdns NG17 . . . . .100 B1
Chestnut Gr
Arnold NG5 . . . . .162 A4
Burton Joyce NG14 . . . . .163 F2
Carlton NG4 . . . . .162 C1
Farndon NG24 . . . . .138 C2
Hucknall NG15 . . . . .146 A2
Kirkby in A NG17 . . . . .114 C3
Mansfield Woodhouse

NG19 . . . . .88 A3
Nottingham NG3 . . . . .173 E4
Radcliffe on T NG12 . . . . . . .175 F2
Sandiacre NG10 . . . . .182 A4
West Bridgford NG2 . . . . . . .185 E4
Chestnut Hill NG18 . . . . . .102 C1
Chestnut La NG13 . . . . . . .194 C3
Chestnut Mews NG18 . . . .102 C1
Chestnut Rd
Langley Mill NG16 . . . . .143 D3
Nottingham NG3 . . . . .162 A1
Chestnut St LE11 . . . . .220 A2
Chestnut Way NG17 . . . . . .66 A1
Chestnuts The
Carlton NG4 . . . . .163 D1
Long Eaton NG10 . . . . .193 D4
Nottingham NG3 . . . . .161 F1
Radcliffe on T NG12 . . . . . . .175 F2
Chettles Ind Est NG8 . . . . .172 B3
Chetwin Rd NG8 . . . . .171 E3
Chetwynd Rd
Beeston, Chilwell NG9 . . . . . .183 E2
Beeston, Toton NG9 . . . . . . .183 D1
Chetwynd Rd Prim Sch

NG9 . . . . .183 D1
Chewerton Ct 12 NG3 . . . .173 E4
Chevin Gdns 12 NG5 . . . . .147 D1
Cheviot Cl NG5 . . . . .147 D1
Cheviot Ct S81 . . . . .25 F4
Cheviot Dr NG6 . . . . .159 F4
Cheviot Rd NG10 . . . . .182 A1
Chewton Ave NG16 . . . . . .144 A1
Chewton Cl NG22 . . . . .105 E3
Chewton St NG16 . . . . .144 A1
Cheyne Dr NG22 . . . . .106 A2
Cheyne Wlk Bawtry DN10 . . . .9 F4
Retford DN22 . . . . .39 E2
Cheyny Cl NG2 . . . . .173 E1
Chichester Cl
Ilkeston DE7 . . . . .170 A4
Mansfield NG18 . . . . .101 E3
Nottingham NG5 . . . . .160 C4
Chichester Dr NG12 . . . . . .187 F2
Chichester Wlk S81 . . . . . .25 F4
Chidlow Rd NG8 . . . . .171 E4
Chigwell Cl NG16 . . . . .159 F2
Childrens Highway

NG24 . . . . .140 C1
Chillon Way NG15 . . . . . . .145 E3
Chiltern Cl NG5 . . . . .147 D1
Chiltern Gdns NG10 . . . . . .182 A1
Chiltern Way
Carlton in L S81 . . . . .25 F4
Nottingham NG5 . . . . .161 D4
Chilton Cres NG19 . . . . . . .88 B3
Chilton Dr NG16 . . . . .159 D4
Chilvers Cl NG5 . . . . .161 D4
Chilwell Comp Sch

NG9 . . . . .183 E2
Chilwell Cl NG6 . . . . .160 B4
Chilwell La NG9 . . . . .183 E3
Chilwell Olympia NG9 . . . .183 E2
Chilwell Rd NG9 . . . . .183 F3
Chilwell Ret Pk NG9 . . . . .183 D1
Chilwell St NG7 . . . . .222 B1
Chimes Mdw NG25 . . . . . .136 C4
Chine Gdns NG2 . . . . .185 E3
Chine The DE55 . . . . .113 D2
Chingford Rd NG8 . . . . . . .171 F4
Chiomere DN22 . . . . .39 E2
Chippendale St NG7 . . . . .222 B1
Chippenham Rd NG5 . . . . .161 E4
Chirnside NG19 . . . . .101 E3
Chisbury Gn NG11 . . . . . . .195 E4
Chisholm Way NG5 . . . . . .161 D3
Chisworth Ct NG19 . . . . . . .88 C2
Christ Church CE Inf Sch

NG24 . . . . .139 F4
Christ the King RC Comp Sch

NG5 . . . . .162 A4
Christchurch Rd NG15 . . . .145 E2
Christina Ave NG6 . . . . . . .160 B2
Christina Cres NG6 . . . . . .160 B2
Christine Cl NG15 . . . . . . .131 E1
Christopher Cl NG8 . . . . . .171 F3
Christopher Cres

NG24 . . . . .140 B2
Chrysalis Way NG16 . . . . .143 E2
Church Ave Arnold NG5 . . .161 F4
Long Eaton NG10 . . . . .193 D2
Nottingham NG7 . . . . .222 B1
Sutton in A NG17 . . . . .100 B1
Church Cl Arnold NG5 . . . .161 F4
Bingham NG13 . . . . .177 F3
East Leake LE12 . . . . .205 F2
Hose LE14 . . . . .211 F4
North Wheatley DN22 . . . . . . .31 F4
Nottingham NG3 . . . . .223 F4
Radcliffe on T NG12 . . . . . . .175 F2
Trowell NG9 . . . . .170 B2
Church Cnr NG13 . . . . .192 C2

Church Cres
Arnold NG5 . . . . .161 F4
Beeston NG9 . . . . .183 D2
Church Croft NG2 . . . . .185 F4
Church Dr Arnold NG5 . . . .161 F4
Hucknall NG15 . . . . .146 A4
Ilkeston DE7 . . . . .157 E2
Keyworth NG12 . . . . .197 F2
Misterton DN10 . . . . .6 C1
Nottingham NG5 . . . . .161 D1
Ravenshead NG15 . . . . .117 D1
Sandiacre NG10 . . . . .182 A4
Shirebrook NG20 . . . . .72 C2
West Bridgford NG2 . . . . . . .185 F4
Church Dr E NG5 . . . . .161 D1
Church Dr Prim Sch

NG5 . . . . .161 F4
Church End LE14 . . . . .210 B3
Church Farm Gdns

NG22 . . . . .93 F2
Church Field Cl S81 . . . . . .26 A3
Church Gate
Colston Bassett NG12 . . . . .200 C4
Cotgrave NG12 . . . . .198 B4
Kegworth DE74 . . . . .203 E1
Loughborough LE11 . . . . . . .220 A2
Church Gr NG7 . . . . .222 A1
Church Hill
Bilsthorpe NG22 . . . . .106 A3
Keyworth NG12 . . . . .197 F4
Kimberley NG16 . . . . .158 C3
Kirkby in A NG17 . . . . .114 B2
Mansfield Woodhouse

NG19 . . . . .88 B2
Newton DE55 . . . . .99 F3
North Wheatley DN22 . . . . . . .31 F4
Sutton in A NG17 . . . . .100 C1
Church Hill Ave NG19 . . . . .88 B2
Church La Arnold NG5 . . . .147 F1
Averham NG23 . . . . .123 F1
Balderton NG24 . . . . .140 C2
Barton in F NG11 . . . . .194 C3
Beeston NG9 . . . . .183 E1
Besthorpe NG23 . . . . .98 A3
Bingham NG13 . . . . .177 F3
Bothamsall DN22 . . . . .63 F4
Bottesford NG13 . . . . .181 D2
Boughton NG22 . . . . .77 F3
Brinsley NG16 . . . . .143 F4
Car Colston NG13 . . . . .166 B2
Carlton in L S81 . . . . .25 F2
Clarborough DN22 . . . . .30 C2
Clayworth DN22 . . . . .21 E3
Collingham NG23 . . . . .98 A1
Cossall NG16 . . . . .158 B1
Costock LE12 . . . . .206 B1
Cotgrave NG12 . . . . .110 C4
Cromwell NG23 . . . . .110 A4
Eagle LN6 . . . . .84 B2
Eakring NG22 . . . . .92 C1
East Drayton DN22 . . . . .53 D2
East Stoke NG23 . . . . .138 A1
Edingley NG22 . . . . .150 A3
Gamston DN22 . . . . .50 C2
Halam NG22 . . . . .120 C1
Harworth DN11 . . . . .8 C2
Hayton DN22 . . . . .30 B3
Hucknall NG15 . . . . .131 D1
Letwell S81 . . . . .16 A1
Long Clawson LE14 . . . . . . .211 E2
Lowdham NG14 . . . . .150 B1
Mansfield NG18 . . . . .102 B3
Maplebeck NG22 . . . . .108 A3
Misterton DN10 . . . . .6 C1
Morton NG25 . . . . .137 E2
North Clifton NG23 . . . . .68 B2
North Scarle LN6 . . . . .83 E1
Nottingham NG6 . . . . .160 B4
Old Dalby LE14 . . . . .218 C2
Owthorpe NG12 . . . . .199 F4
Pleasley NG19 . . . . .87 D4
Plumtree NG12 . . . . .197 F4
Plungar NG13 . . . . .191 F1
Redmile NG13 . . . . .192 C2
Retford DN22 . . . . .39 F2
Saxilby LN1 . . . . .56 C3
Screveton NG13 . . . . .166 C2
Scrooby DN10 . . . . .10 A1
Selston, Selston Green

NG16 . . . . .128 B4
Selston, Underwood

NG16 . . . . .129 D2
Sibthorpe NG23 . . . . .167 F4
South Muskham NG23 . . . . .124 C4
Stapleford NG9 . . . . .182 B4
Sutton in A NG17 . . . . .100 C1
Thrumpton NG11 . . . . .194 B2
Tibshelf DE55 . . . . .99 D3
Tickhill DN11 . . . . .8 A4
Upper Broughton LE14 . . . . .210 A1
Upton NG23 . . . . .122 C1
West Drayton DN22 . . . . .50 C1
Widmerpool NG12 . . . . .208 A3
Willoughby-on-t-W LE12 . . . .217 E4
Church Lands 3 LE11 . . . .220 A3
Church Mdw NG14 . . . . . . .148 C4
Church Mead NG17 . . . . . . .99 F2
Church Mews
Nottingham NG2 . . . . .173 E1
Sutton in A NG17 . . . . .100 C1
Church Rd
Bestwood Village NG6 . . . . .146 C2
Bircotes DN11 . . . . .9 E2
Burton Joyce NG14 . . . . .163 F2
Church Warsop NG20 . . . . . . .74 A3
Clipstone NG21 . . . . .89 F2
Greasley NG16 . . . . .144 C2
Harby NG23 . . . . .70 B1

Church Rd continued
Nottingham NG3 . . . . .223 F4
Saxilby LN1 . . . . .57 D2
Church Side
Farnsfield NG22 . . . . .119 F3
Huthwaite NG17 . . . . .99 F2
Mansfield NG18 . . . . .102 B3
Church Sq NG7 . . . . .222 B1
Church St Arnold NG5 . . . .161 F4
Bawtry DN10 . . . . .10 A3
Beckingham DN10 . . . . .14 A1
Beeston NG9 . . . . .183 F3
Beeston, Bramcote
NG9 . . . . .183 D4
Bilsthorpe NG22 . . . . .105 E3
Bingham NG13 . . . . .177 F2
Bottesford NG13 . . . . .181 D1
Bunny NG11 . . . . .206 C4
Carlton NG4 . . . . .174 C4
Collingham NG23 . . . . .111 F4
Cropwell Bishop NG12 . . . .189 D2
East Markham NG22 . . . . . .66 A3
Eastwood NG16 . . . . .143 F1
Edwinstowe NG21 . . . . .76 A1
Everton DN10 . . . . .11 E2
Farndon NG24 . . . . .138 C2
Gainsborough DN21 . . . . . .15 E1
Gotham NG11 . . . . .195 D1
Granby NG13 . . . . .191 D3
Hathern LE12 . . . . .213 D1
Ilkeston DE7 . . . . .157 F2
Kirkby in A NG17 . . . . .114 B3
Lambley NG4 . . . . .163 E4
Langold S81 . . . . .16 C1
Mansfield NG18 . . . . .102 A4
Mansfield Woodhouse
NG19 . . . . .88 B2
Market Warsop NG20 . . . . .74 A3
Misterton DN10 . . . . .6 C1
Newark-on-T NG24 . . . . . .139 F4
North Wheatley DN22 . . . . .31 F4
Nottingham NG7 . . . . .222 A1
Nottingham, Old Basford
NG6 . . . . .160 C1
Ollerton NG22 . . . . .77 D2
Orston NG13 . . . . .180 A4
Pleasleyhill NG19 . . . . .87 D2
Ruddington NG11 . . . . .196 B4
Sandiacre NG10 . . . . .182 A4
Shelford NG12 . . . . .164 B1
South Leverton DN22 . . . . .42 B4
South Normanton DE55 . . .113 D3
Southwell NG25 . . . . .136 C4
Stapleford NG9 . . . . .182 B4
Sturton le S DN22 . . . . .32 B2
Sutton in A NG17 . . . . .100 C1
Sutton on T NG23 . . . . .97 D4
Whaley Thorns NG20 . . . . .59 D1
Whatton NG13 . . . . .179 D2
Wymeswold LE12 . . . . .216 B2
Church St E NG16 . . . . . .113 E2
Church St W NG16 . . . . . .113 E2
Church Vale Prim Sch
NG20 . . . . .74 A4
Church View
Balderton NG24 . . . . .140 B2
Beckingham DN10 . . . . .14 A1
Bottesford NG13 . . . . .181 D2
Carlton NG4 . . . . .162 C1
Glapwell S44 . . . . .86 A4
New Houghton NG19 . . . . .86 C4
Ollerton NG22 . . . . .77 D2
Scrooby DN10 . . . . .10 A1
Stanton Hill NG17 . . . . .100 B3
Church View Cl NG15 . . .147 D1
Church Way DN22 . . . . . . .29 D3
Church Wlk
Bawtry DN10 . . . . .10 A4
Brinsley NG16 . . . . .143 F4
Carlton NG4 . . . . .162 C1
Eastwood NG16 . . . . .143 F1
Harworth DN11 . . . . .8 C2
Stapleford NG9 . . . . .182 C4
Upton NG23 . . . . .138 A2
Weston NG23 . . . . .81 D3
Whatton NG13 . . . . .179 D2
Worksop S80 . . . . .35 F2
Churchdale Ave NG9 . . . .170 C1
Churchfield Ct NG5 . . . . .147 D1
Churchfield Dr NG21 . . . .103 F1
Churchfield La NG7 . . . . .222 A4
Churchfield Terr NG7 . . . .160 C1
Churchgate DN22 . . . . . . .39 F4
Churchill Cl NG5 . . . . .161 F4
Churchill Dr
Newark-on-T NG24 . . . . . .139 F3
Ruddington NG11 . . . . .196 A4
Churchill Gdns NG18 . . . .88 B2
Churchill Pk NG4 . . . . . . .174 C3
Churchill Way DN21 . . . . .24 C2
Churchmoor Ct NG5 . . . . .147 F1
Churchmoor La NG5 . . . . .147 F1
Churchside Gdns NG7 . . .172 C4
Churnet Cl NG11 . . . . .184 C2
Chuter Ede Prim Sch
NG24 . . . . .140 C2
Cinder La NG22 . . . . .77 D1
Cinderhill Gr NG4 . . . . . . .162 C1
Cinderhill Rd NG6 . . . . . .160 A3
Cinderhill Wlk NG6 . . . . . .160 A3
Circle The NG19 . . . . .88 A2
Citadel St NG7 . . . . .172 A4
Citrus Gr DE74 . . . . .203 E2
**City Gd (Nottingham Forest
FC) The** NG2 . . . . .173 F1
City Hospl NG5 . . . . .161 D2
City Link NG1, NG2 . . . . .173 F2

City Rd Beeston NG9 . . . . .184 A3
Nottingham NG7 . . . . .172 B1
Stathern LE14 . . . . .202 C2
City The NG9 . . . . .184 A3
Clandon Dr NG5 . . . . .161 D1
Clanfield Rd NG8 . . . . . . .171 F4
Clapham St NG7 . . . . .222 A3
Clapton La NG7 . . . . .184 C1
Clara Mount Rd DE75 . . .143 D1
Clarborough Cty Inf Sch
DN22 . . . . .30 B2
Clarborough Cty Prim Sch
DN22 . . . . .30 C2
Clarborough Dr NG5 . . . . .162 A3
Clarborough Hill DN22 . .30 C2
Clare Cl NG6 . . . . .160 C2
Clare Hill NG21 . . . . .118 A2
Clare Rd NG17 . . . . .114 C4
Clare St NG1 . . . . .223 E3
Clare Valley NG7 . . . . . . .223 D2
Clarehaven NG9 . . . . .182 C3
Claremont Ave
Beeston NG9 . . . . .183 E4
Hucknall NG15 . . . . .146 A3
Claremont Dr NG11 . . . . .185 E2
Claremont Prim Sch
NG5 . . . . .161 D1
Claremont Rd
Gainsborough DN21 . . . . . .24 C3
Nottingham NG5 . . . . .161 D1
Claremount Cl NG19 . . . . .88 C2
Clarence Rd
Beeston NG9 . . . . .183 E2
Long Eaton NG10 . . . . .193 E3
Worksop S80 . . . . .35 F2
Clarence St
Loughborough LE11 . . . . . .220 B3
Mansfield NG18 . . . . .102 A3
Nottingham NG3 . . . . .173 F3
Pleasleyhill NG19 . . . . .87 D2
Clarendon Coll (Annexe)
NG1 . . . . .223 D4
**Clarendon Coll (Hamilton
Annexe)** NG5 . . . . .173 D4
**Clarendon Coll (Sherwood
Annexe)** NG5 . . . . .173 D4
Clarendon Coll Berridge Ctr
NG7 . . . . .173 D4
Clarendon Ct [11] NG5 . . .173 D4
Clarendon Dr S81 . . . . . . .35 E3
Clarendon Pk NG5 . . . . . .173 D4
Clarendon Rd NG19 . . . . .101 F4
Clarendon St NG1 . . . . . . .223 D3
Clarewood Gr NG11 . . . . .195 F4
Clarges St NG6 . . . . .160 B3
Clark La NG22 . . . . .119 E1
Clarke Ave Arnold NG5 . . .161 F4
Newark-on-T NG24 . . . . . .139 F3
Clarke Cl NG12 . . . . .189 D2
Clarke Dr NG10 . . . . .193 D2
Clarke Rd NG2 . . . . .173 F3
Clarkes La NG24 . . . . .125 D1
Clarkson Dr NG9 . . . . .184 A3
Claters Cl DN22 . . . . .40 A4
Claude St NG7 . . . . .172 C1
Clawson La
Hickling LE14 . . . . .210 B3
Nether Broughton LE14 . . .210 C1
Claxton Rise LE14 . . . . . .211 E1
Clay Ave NG3 . . . . .162 A4
Clay La NG24 . . . . .140 B4
Clay St LE12 . . . . .216 B2
Clay St NG10 . . . . .193 F4
Clayfield Cl NG6 . . . . .160 A3
Claygate NG3 . . . . .174 A4
Claylands Ave NG20 . . . . .35 E3
Claylands Cl S81 . . . . .35 E3
Claylands La S81 . . . . .35 E3
Claypit La NG25 . . . . .137 D2
Claypole CE Prim Sch
NG23 . . . . .156 C4
Claypole La NG23 . . . . . . .156 C1
Claypole Rd [37] NG7 . . . .172 C4
Claythorne Dr DN21 . . . . .24 C4
Clayton Cl NG24 . . . . .140 A3
Clayton Ct NG7 . . . . .222 B3
Claytons Dr [18] NG7 . . . .172 C4
Claytons Wharf [8] NG7 . .172 C1
Clayworth Comm DN22 . .21 F2
Clayworth Ct NG18 . . . . . .103 D2
Clayworth Rd DN10 . . . . . .12 C1
Clegg Hill Dr NG17 . . . . . .99 F2
Clement Ave NG24 . . . . . .140 C2
Clensey La NG23 . . . . .156 C1
Clerkson St [4] NG18 . . . .102 B4
Clerksons Alley [10]
NG18 . . . . .102 A4
Clether Rd NG8 . . . . .171 E3
Cleve Ave NG9 . . . . .182 C2
Cleveland Ave NG10 . . . . .182 C1
Cleveland Cl
Carlton in L S81 . . . . .25 F4
Nottingham NG7 . . . . .222 A3
Cleveland Sq NG24 . . . . . .139 F3
Cleveland St DN21 . . . . . . .24 B4
Cleveleys Rd NG9 . . . . . . .182 C2
Cleve Way NG11 . . . . .184 C2
Cliff Ave NG15 . . . . .158 C4
Cliff Cres NG12 . . . . .175 F2
Cliff Dr NG12 . . . . .176 A3
Cliff Gate NG22 . . . . .65 E4
Cliff La NG17 . . . . .115 E2
Cliff Nook DE55 . . . . .113 D2
Cliff Nook La NG24 . . . . . .125 D1
Cliff Rd Carlton NG4 . . . . .174 B4
Nottingham NG1 . . . . .223 F2
Radcliffe on T NG12 . . . . . .175 F2

Cliff St NG18 . . . . .102 B4
Cliff The NG6 . . . . .160 A2
Cliff Way NG12 . . . . .175 F2
Cliffe Hill Ave NG9 . . . . . .182 B4
Cliffgrove Ave NG9 . . . . .183 E3
Cliffhill La NG13 . . . . .179 F2
Cliffmere Wlk NG11 . . . . .184 B1
Clifford Ave NG9 . . . . .183 F4
Clifford Cl
Keyworth NG12 . . . . .197 F2
Long Eaton NG10 . . . . .193 D2
Clifford Ct NG7 . . . . .222 B3
Clifford St
Long Eaton NG10 . . . . .193 F4
Mansfield NG18 . . . . .102 A2
Nottingham NG7 . . . . .222 B3
Clifton Ave
Long Eaton NG10 . . . . .194 A4
Ruddington NG11 . . . . .196 B4
Clifton Bvd NG7 . . . . .184 C4
Clifton Cres
Beeston NG9 . . . . .183 F2
Newark-on-T NG24 . . . . . .125 E2
Clifton Dr Carlton NG4 . . .162 C1
Mansfield NG18 . . . . .102 C2
Clifton La
Nottingham NG11 . . . . .184 C2
Ruddington NG11 . . . . .196 A4
Clifton Pl [6] NG18 . . . . . .102 A4
Clifton Rd NG11 . . . . .196 A4
Clifton St NG9 . . . . .184 A3
Clifton Terr NG7 . . . . .222 C1
Clifton Way DN22 . . . . . . .39 E4
Clinthill La S80 . . . . .45 D4
Clinton Ave
Brinsley NG16 . . . . .143 E3
Nottingham NG5 . . . . .173 D4
Clinton Ct NG1 . . . . .223 E4
Clinton Gdns La NG22 . . .65 F1
Clinton St Arnold NG5 . . .161 F4
Beeston NG9 . . . . .183 F4
Newark-on-T NG24 . . . . . .139 F4
Worksop S80 . . . . .36 A1
Clinton St E NG1 . . . . .223 E3
Clinton St W NG1 . . . . . . .223 E3
Clinton Terr DN21 . . . . . . .24 B4
Clipston La NG12 . . . . . . .197 F4
Clipstone Ave
Mansfield NG18 . . . . .102 B4
Nottingham NG3 . . . . .223 D4
Nottingham, Mapperley
NG3 . . . . .162 A2
Sutton in A NG17 . . . . .101 D2
Clipstone Cl NG8 . . . . . . .159 E1
Clipstone Dr NG19 . . . . . . .89 E2
Clipstone Rd E NG19 . . . .89 E2
Clipstone Rd W NG19 . . . .89 E2
Clive Cres NG16 . . . . .159 D3
Cliveden Gn NG11 . . . . . . .184 B1
Cloister St NG7 . . . . .172 C1
Cloisters The NG9 . . . . . . .184 A4
Close Quarters NG9 . . . . .183 E4
Close The
Averham NG23 . . . . .123 F1
Beeston NG9 . . . . .183 E2
Mansfield NG21 . . . . .103 F1
Newark-on-T NG24 . . . . . .140 A4
Nottingham NG5 . . . . .161 E2
Shirebrook NG20 . . . . .72 C3
Upton NG23 . . . . .122 C2
Closes Side La NG13 . . . .165 F2
Cloud Ave NG9 . . . . .182 C4
Clouds Hill NG11 . . . . . . .195 F4
Cloudside Ct NG10 . . . . . .182 A4
Cloudside Jun Sch
NG10 . . . . .182 A4
Cloudside Rd NG10 . . . . .182 A4
Clough Ct NG8 . . . . .172 A4
Clouster's La NG14 . . . . . . .150 C1
Clover Rise NG16 . . . . . . .158 A4
Clover St NG17 . . . . .115 D3
Cloverdale NG12 . . . . .188 A1
Cloverfields NG14 . . . . . . .149 D2
Cloverlands NG11 . . . . . . .185 D2
Cloverlands Dr NG16 . . . .159 D4
Club Ct NG24 . . . . .140 B2
Cludd Ave NG24 . . . . .140 C4
Clumber Ave
Beeston NG9 . . . . .183 E3
Brinsley NG16 . . . . .128 C1
Carlton NG4 . . . . .175 D4
Edwinstowe NG21 . . . . .75 F2
Mansfield NG21 . . . . .103 F1
Newark-on-T NG24 . . . . . .140 A3
Nottingham, Hyson Green
NG5 . . . . .173 D4
Nottingham, Mapperley
NG3 . . . . .162 A2
Clumber Dr
Radcliffe on T NG12 . . . . . .176 A3
Clumber Pk Cctry Pk* . . .
Clumber Pl S80 . . . . .35 F2
Clumber Rd
West Bridgford NG2 . . . . . .185 F4
Worksop S80 . . . . .47 D3
Clumber Rd E NG7 . . . . . .222 C2

Clumber Rd W NG7 . . . . .222 C2
Clumber St
Hucknall NG15 . . . . .146 B3
Kirkby in A NG17 . . . . .115 E3
Long Eaton NG10 . . . . .193 E4
Mansfield NG18 . . . . .102 A4
Market Warsop NG20 . . . . .74 A2
Nottingham NG1 . . . . .223 E3
Retford DN22 . . . . .39 F3
Sutton in A NG17 . . . . .100 B1
Clumber Way NG22 . . . . .106 A3
Retford DN22 . . . . .39 F3
Clun Cl NG19 . . . . .88 B1
Clyro Pl DN22 . . . . .28 C3
Coach Dr NG16 . . . . .143 F2
Coach Gap La NG13 . . . . .190 B1
Coach Rd NG20 . . . . .74 B1
Coachmans Croft [9]
NG8 . . . . .172 A3
Coal La LE14 . . . . .211 F4
Coal Yd La NG23 . . . . .82 C4
Coalfields Cl NG17 . . . . . .100 B1
Coalpit La DN22 . . . . .49 F2
Coates Ave NG15 . . . . . . .130 C1
Coates Rd DN22 . . . . .43 E4
Coatsby Rd NG16 . . . . . . .158 C4
Cobden Cty Jun Sch
LE11 . . . . .220 A2
Cobden Pl NG19 . . . . .87 F1
Cobden St
Gainsborough DN21 . . . . . .24 B4
Kirkby in A NG17 . . . . .115 D2
Long Eaton NG10 . . . . .193 F4
Nottingham NG7 . . . . .173 D4
Coburn St NG17 . . . . .100 C1
Cobwell Rd DN22 . . . . .39 F3
Cochrane Terr NG17 . . . . .100 B3
Cock Hill La DN10 . . . . . . .10 A3
Cockayne Cl NG10 . . . . . .182 A2
Cocker Beck NG4 . . . . . . .163 E4
Cockerhouse Rd NG16 . . .143 F2
Cocking Hill NG22 . . . . . . .78 B2
Cocking La DN22 . . . . .42 B1
Cockington Rd NG8 . . . . . .171 E3
Cockeys NG10 . . . . .193 E4
Cockshut La NG20 . . . . . . .59 D2
Coddington CE Prim Sch
NG24 . . . . .126 A1
Coddington La LN6 . . . . . .127 D3
Coddington Rd NG24 . . . .126 A1
Codnorgton Gdns [5]
NG5 . . . . .161 E4
Cogenhoe Wlk NG5 . . . . .147 F1
Coggins La NG20 . . . . .74 B3
Coghill Ct NG25 . . . . .136 C4
Coging Cl NG24 . . . . .140 C4
Cogley La NG13 . . . . .178 A2
Cohen Cl NG5 . . . . .162 A3
Cokefield Ave NG16 . . . . .159 F2
Col Frank Seely Comp Sch
NG14 . . . . .148 C4
Colbeck St S80 . . . . .35 F2
Colborn St NG3 . . . . .173 F4
Colby Cl NG19 . . . . .89 D1
Coleby Ave NG7 . . . . .222 A1
Coleby Rd NG8 . . . . .159 F1
Coledale NG2 . . . . .186 B3
Coleman Ave NG24 . . . . . .140 A2
Coleridge Cres NG5 . . . . .161 E4
Coleridge Rd
Balderton NG24 . . . . .140 C3
Worksop S80 . . . . .36 A3
Coleridge St NG7 . . . . . . .222 B4
Colesbourne Rd NG7 . . . .184 C1
Colgrove Rd LE11 . . . . . . .220 A1
Colin Broughton Ct
NG6 . . . . .160 B4
Colindale Gdns NG16 . . . .159 F2
Colinwood Ave NG5 . . . . .146 C1
College Dr
Nottingham NG11 . . . . .184 B1
Nottingham NG11 . . . . .184 C2
College House Jun Sch
NG9 . . . . .183 F3
College La
East Markham NG22 . . . . . .66 A4
Worksop S80 . . . . .36 A1
College St
East Bridgford NG13 . . . . .165 E2
Long Eaton NG10 . . . . .182 B1
Nottingham NG1 . . . . .223 D2
Colley La NG23 . . . . .81 D2
Colleymoor Leys La
NG11 . . . . .184 C1
Collier Ave NG19 . . . . .88 A3
Colliers Way NG6 . . . . . . .160 A2
Colliery Cl NG2 . . . . .173 D1
Colliery Rd DN11 . . . . .9 D2
Collin Ave NG10 . . . . .182 A4
Collin Cl NG5 . . . . .161 E2
Collin St Beeston NG9 . . .183 F3
Nottingham NG1 . . . . .223 E1
Collingham Rd
Collingham LN6 . . . . .98 C1
Mansfield NG19 . . . . .87 E1
Collingham Sta NG23 . . . .112 A4
Collington St NG9 . . . . . . .183 F3
Collington Way NG2 . . . . .185 E3
Collingwood Cl NG11 . . . .184 C2
Collingwood Rd NG10 . . .194 A4
Collins Ave
South Normanton DE55 . . .113 D4
Sutton in A NG17 . . . . .114 C4

Collins Cl NG6 . . . . .159 F3
Collins Wlk DN22 . . . . .39 F4
Collis Cl NG24 . . . . .140 B4
Collison St NG7 . . . . .222 B4
Colly Gate NG16 . . . . .159 D3
Collyer Rd NG14 . . . . .148 B4
Collygate Rd NG2 . . . . . . .173 E1
Colne Ct NG19 . . . . .88 B1
Colonels La LE14 . . . . . . .210 A1
Colonsay Cl NG9 . . . . .170 B2
Colsterdale S81 . . . . .36 A4
Colston Basset Prim Sch
NG12 . . . . .200 B4
Colston Cres NG2 . . . . . . .185 E2
Colston Gate NG12 . . . . . .188 A2
Colston La LE14 . . . . .201 F2
Colston Rd
Cropwell Bishop NG12 . . . .189 D1
Mansfield NG18 . . . . .103 D2
Nottingham NG6 . . . . .160 B4
Colton St DN10 . . . . .6 C1
Columbia Ave
Mansfield NG18 . . . . .102 C3
Sutton in A NG17 . . . . .100 B1
Columbia Cl NG16 . . . . . .129 D4
Columbia St NG17 . . . . . .100 A1
Colville St NG1 . . . . .173 D4
Colville Terr
Gainsborough DN21 . . . . . .24 B4
Nottingham NG1 . . . . .173 D4
Colville Villas [14] NG1 . .173 D4
Colwick Bsns Pk NG4 . . .174 C3
Colwick Cl NG19 . . . . .87 F1
Colwick Ctry Pk* . . . .
. . . . .174 B2
Colwick Ind Est NG4 . . . .174 C4
Colwick Loop Rd NG4 . . .175 D4
Colwick Manor Farm
NG4 . . . . .174 C3
Colwick Pk Cl NG4 . . . . . .174 C3
Colwick Rd
Nottingham NG2 . . . . .174 A2
West Bridgford NG2 . . . . . .173 F1
Comery Ave NG3 . . . . .174 A3
Comfrey Cl NG5 . . . . .160 C4
Commerce Sq NG1 . . . . . .223 F2
Commercial Ave NG9 . . . .183 F3
Commercial Gate
NG18 . . . . .102 A3
Commercial Rd
Keyworth NG12 . . . . .197 F1
[11] Nottingham NG6 . . . .160 A4
Commercial St [5] NG18 . .102 A3
Commodore Gdns
NG5 . . . . .160 B1
Common La
Beeston NG9 . . . . .183 D3
Blyth S81 . . . . .18 A2
Hucknall NG15 . . . . .145 E3
Mansfield Woodhouse
NG19 . . . . .88 A2
Ranskill DN22 . . . . .19 E2
Shirebrook NG20 . . . . .72 B2
Sturton le S DN22 . . . . .32 B2
Tickhill DN11 . . . . .8 A4
Watnall NG16 . . . . .159 D4
Common Rd
Hathwaite NG17 . . . . .99 F1
Retford DN22 . . . . .39 F4
Thorpe Salvin S80 . . . . .34 A3
South Side NG16 . . . . .128 C4
Common The
Hucknall NG15 . . . . .145 E3
South Normanton DE55 . . .113 D3
Commons Cl NG16 . . . . . .158 A4
Compton Acres NG2 . . . . .185 D3
Compton Acres Sh Ctr
NG2 . . . . .185 E2
Compton Rd NG5 . . . . .161 D2
Compton St NG20 . . . . . . .72 C4
Comyn Gdns NG3 . . . . . . .223 F4
Conduit Cl NG2 . . . . .173 E1
Coneries The LE11 . . . . . .220 A2
Conery Gdns NG13 . . . . . .179 D2
Conery La NG13 . . . . .178 C1
Coneygrey Spinney
NG12 . . . . .152 C1
Conifer Cres NG11 . . . . . .195 F4
Conifer Wlk NG3 . . . . .174 A4
Coningsby Cl DN21 . . . . . .24 C4
Coningsby Gdns E
NG5 . . . . .161 F2
Coningsby Rd NG5 . . . . . .161 F3
Coningswath Rd NG4 . . . .162 B1
Conisborough Ave NG4 . .163 D1
Coniston Ave NG6 . . . . . . .160 B1
Coniston Cl
Mansfield Woodhouse
NG19 . . . . .88 C2
West Bridgford NG2 . . . . . .186 B4
Coniston Rd
Beeston NG9 . . . . .183 E4
Hucknall NG15 . . . . .145 E4
Kirkby in A NG17 . . . . .115 E3
Long Eaton NG10 . . . . .182 A1
Worksop S81 . . . . .35 F4
Connaught Rd NG16 . . . . .159 D3
Connelly Ct NG5 . . . . .162 B3
Connery Mews NG9 . . . . .183 D1
Connery The NG15 . . . . . .146 A4
Conrad Cl S80 . . . . .36 A2

Constance St NG7 . . . . . . 161 D1
Convent St NG1 . . . . 223 F3
Conway Ave NG4 . . . . 175 D4
Conway Cl
  Mansfield NG19 . . . . 101 E4
  Nottingham NG3 . . . . 173 E4
Conway Cres NG4 . . . . . . 175 D4
Conway Dr S81 . . . . 25 F3
Conway Gdns
  Arnold NG5 . . . . 161 F3
  Retford DN22 . . . . 39 D4
Conway Rd
  Carlton NG4 . . . . 175 D4
  Hucknall NG15 . . . . 145 E2
Conway St NG10 . . . . 193 F4
Conway Wlk ⑨ NG3 . . . 173 E4
Cook Dr DE7 . . . . 170 A3
Cooks La
  Fiskerton NG23 . . . . 137 E1
  Southwell NG25 . . . . 136 A4
Cookson Ave NG4 . . . . . . 162 B1
Cookson St NG17 . . . . . . 114 C3
Coombe Cl NG8 . . . . 172 B2
Coombe Rd NG16 . . . . . . 144 A2
Cooper Cl Arnold NG5 . . 162 B3
  Cropwell Bishop NG12 . . 189 D2
  Nottingham NG6 . . . . 159 F3
Cooper Cl LE11 . . . . 220 B1
Cooper St NG4 . . . . 175 D3
Co-Operative Ave
  NG15 . . . . 146 A4
Co-Operative St
  Long Eaton NG10 . . . . . . 193 F3
  Stanton Hill NG17 . . . . . 100 B3
Coopers Gn NG8 . . . . . . 171 F1
Coopers Rise NG21 . . . . . 104 A1
Coopers Yd NG24 . . . . . . 139 F4
Cope St NG7 . . . . 222 B4
Copeland Ave
  ① Kirkby in A NG17 . . . . 114 C3
  Stapleford NG9 . . . . 182 C4
Copeland Gr NG13 . . . . . . 177 E3
Copeland Rd
  Hucknall NG15 . . . . 146 B4
  Kirkby in A NG17 . . . . . . 114 C3
Copenhagen Ct NG3 . . . . 161 E1
Copper Hill NG23 . . . . 81 F2
Coppice Cl NG15 . . . . . . 145 F3
Coppice Croft NG17 . . . . 100 B1
Coppice Dr NG16 . . . . . . 143 E2
Coppice Farm Prim Sch
  NG5 . . . . 162 A4
Coppice Gr NG3 . . . . 161 F1
Coppice Rd
  Arnold NG5 . . . . 162 A4
  Clipstone NG19 . . . . 89 E2
  Worksop S81 . . . . 35 F4
Coppice The
  Barnby Moor DN22 . . . . . . 28 B3
  Shirebrook NG20 . . . . 72 B2
Coppice Way DE55 . . . . . 113 D2
Coppice Way S81 . . . . 25 F2
Copplestone Dr NG3 . . . 162 B3
Copse Cl
  Burton Joyce NG14 . . . . . 163 F3
  Ravenshead NG15 . . . . . 116 B2
Copse The
  Beeston NG9 . . . . 183 E3
  Farndon NG24 . . . . 139 D2
  Hucknall NG15 . . . . 146 B3
  Ilkeston DE7 . . . . 157 E3
  Stanton Hill NG17 . . . . . 100 B3
Copseside Cl ⑩ NG10 . . 193 D4
Copsewood DE55 . . . . . . 113 D2
Copsey Croft Ct
  Long Eaton NG10 . . . . . . 193 F4
  Long Eaton NG10 . . . . . . 193 F4
Corben Gdns NG6 . . . . . . 159 F4
Corby Rd NG3 . . . . 161 F1
Cordy La NG16 . . . . 143 F4
Corene Ave NG17 . . . . . . 100 C1
Coriander Dr NG6 . . . . . . 160 B2
Corinth Rd NG7 . . . . 184 C1
Corkhill La NG22 . . . . 121 E3
Corn Cl Cotgrave NG12 . . 187 F1
  Sutton in A NG17 . . . . . . 100 C1
Corncrake Ave NG6 . . . . 160 B2
Corncrake Dr NG5 . . . . . 162 B4
Cornell Dr NG5 . . . . 162 B4
Corner The NG14 . . . . . . 150 B1
Cornfield Ave DE55 . . . . . 113 D2
Cornfield Rd NG16 . . . . . 158 C4
Cornhill Rd NG4 . . . . 174 A4
Cornley Rd DN10 . . . . 6 B2
Cornwall Ave
  Beeston NG9 . . . . 184 B3
  Mansfield NG18 . . . . 102 C3
Cornwall Cl NG16 . . . . . . 128 B2
Cornwall Rd NG22 . . . . 77 D2
Cornwall Rd
  Arnold NG5 . . . . 161 E4
  Retford DN22 . . . . 30 A1
  Shireoaks S81 . . . . 34 C4
Cornwallis Cl NG10 . . . . . 193 E3
Coronation Ave
  Long Clawson LE14 . . . . 211 D3
  Misson DN10 . . . . 4 A2
  New Houghton NG19 . . . . 86 C4
  Nottingham NG11 . . . . . . 185 D4
  Sandiacre NG10 . . . . 182 A4
Coronation Dr
  Mansfield NG19 . . . . 103 D4
  Shirebrook NG20 . . . . 72 C1
  South Normanton DE55 . . 113 D3

Coronation Rd
  Arnold NG5 . . . . 161 F2
  Bestwood Village NG6 . . 146 C2
  Cossall NG16 . . . . 158 A1
  Hucknall NG15 . . . . 145 F4
  Nuthall NG16 . . . . 159 E3
Coronation St
  Mansfield NG18 . . . . 102 B3
  New Balderton NG24 . . . 140 A3
  Retford DN22 . . . . 39 F3
  Sutton in A NG17 . . . . . . 100 C1
  Whitwell S80 . . . . 45 D3
Coronation Wlk NG4 . . . 163 D1
Corporation Oaks
  NG3 . . . . 173 E4
Corporation Rd DE7 . . . . 170 A3
Corporation St ⑧ NG18 . 102 A4
Corringham Rd DN21 . . . . 15 F1
Corsham Gdns NG3 . . . . 174 A4
Cosby Rd ㉒ NG2 . . . . . . 173 F2
Cosgrove Ave NG17 . . . . 101 D3
Cossall Ind Est NG16 . . . 158 A1
Cossall Rd NG9 . . . . 170 B3
Costhorpe Ind Est S81 . . 16 C1
Costhorpe Villas S81 . . . . 16 C1
Costock Ave NG5 . . . . . . 161 D2
Costock CE Prim Sch
  LE12 . . . . 206 B1
Costock Rd
  East Leake LE12 . . . . . . 206 A1
  Wysall NG12 . . . . 207 E1
Costume & Textile Mus*
  NG1 . . . . 223 E2
Cotes Rd LE12 . . . . 220 C3
Cotgrave Ave NG4 . . . . . . 162 C1
Cotgrave CE Prim Sch
  NG12 . . . . 187 F2
Cotgrave Cl NG8 . . . . 159 F1
Cotgrave Cntry Pk*
  NG12 . . . . 188 A3
Cotgrave Inf Sch
  NG12 . . . . 187 F2
Cotgrave La NG12 . . . . . . 187 D1
Cotgrave Rd
  Cotgrave NG12 . . . . 187 D1
  Mansfield NG19 . . . . 87 F1
Cotmanhay Inf & Jun Sch
  DE7 . . . . 157 F3
Cotmanhay Rd DE7 . . . . . 157 F2
Coton Cl
  Mansfield Woodhouse
  NG19 . . . . 88 C2
  Nottingham NG11 . . . . . 185 D2
Cotswold Cl ④ NG10 . . . 193 D4
Cotswold Ct
  Beeston NG9 . . . . 171 E1
  Carlton in L S81 . . . . 25 F4
Cotswold Gr NG18 . . . . . 103 D3
Cotswold Rd NG8 . . . . . . 159 F1
Cottage Ave NG13 . . . . . . 178 C2
Cottage Cl
  Balderton NG24 . . . . 140 B1
  Bidworth NG21 . . . . 117 F2
  Ilkeston DE7 . . . . 157 E2
Cottage La
  Gamston NG13 . . . . 111 F3
  Market Warsop NG20 . . . . 74 B1
  North Clifton NG23 . . . . . 69 D2
Cottage Mdw NG4 . . . . . . 174 C2
Cottage Pasture La
  NG14 . . . . 164 C4
Cottage Terr NG1 . . . . . . 222 C3
Cottam Dr NG5 . . . . 161 D4
Cottam Gdns NG5 . . . . . 161 D4
Cottam Gr NG19 . . . . 101 E3
Cottam Rd DN22 . . . . 42 C4
Cottans Cl NG25 . . . . 136 C4
Cottesmore Rd NG7 . . . . 222 B2
Cotton Mill La NG22 . . . . 120 A3
Coulby Cl NG23 . . . . 156 B2
Coultons Ave NG17 . . . . . 100 B2
Coultons Cl NG17 . . . . . . 100 B2
County Bsns Pk NG2 . . . 173 F1
County Cl NG9 . . . . 184 A4
County Rd Carlton NG4 . . 162 B2
  Nottingham NG2 . . . . . . 173 F1
Court Cres NG8 . . . . 171 F2
Court Gdns NG19 . . . . . . 185 D2
Court St ㊸ NG7 . . . . 172 C4
Court Yd NG9 . . . . 183 D4
Courtenay Gdns NG3 . . . 173 E4
Court-Field Rd NG17 . . . 101 D3
Courtlett Way NG6 . . . . . 160 A3
Courtney Cl NG8 . . . . 171 F3
Cove Rd DN9 . . . . 2 C3
Covedale Rd NG5 . . . . . . 161 E3
Covent Gdns NG12 . . . . . 176 C2
Coventry Cl NG6 . . . . 160 B3
Coventry Dr S81 . . . . 36 A3
Coventry La NG9 . . . . 171 D3
Coventry Rd
  Beeston NG9 . . . . 184 A4
  Nottingham NG6 . . . . . . 160 A3
Coverdale S81 . . . . 36 A4
Covert Cl
  Burton Joyce NG14 . . . . . 163 F3
  Hucknall NG15 . . . . 146 B3
  Keyworth NG12 . . . . 197 F2
Covert Rd NG2 . . . . 186 A3
Cow La Beeston NG9 . . . . 183 E3
  Newark-on-T NG24 . . . . 124 C1
Cow Pasture La NG17 . . 114 A3
Cowan St NG1 . . . . 223 F3
Cowdray Cl LE11 . . . . . . 220 A1
Cowdrey Gdns NG5 . . . . 162 A3
Cowlairs NG5 . . . . 160 C4
Cowley St NG6 . . . . 160 C2
Cowpasture La NG17 . . . 100 C1

Cowper Cl S81 . . . . 36 A3
Cowper Rd Arnold NG5 . . 161 F2
  Eastwood NG16 . . . . 158 A4
Cowper Cres NG17 . . . . . 100 C2
Cox Dr NG13 . . . . 180 C2
Coxmoor Cl NG2 . . . . 186 B2
Coxmoor Ct ㉔ NG5 . . . . 147 D1
Coxmoor Prim Sch
  NG17 . . . . 115 D3
Coxmoor Rd NG17,
  NG5 . . . . 115 F4
Coxs Hill DN1 . . . . 15 E1
Coxs La NG19 . . . . 88 A3
Crab La NG23 . . . . 110 C1
Crab Nook La NG22 . . . . 119 F3
Crabtree Field NG2 . . . . . 174 B2
Crabtree La
  Beckingham DN10 . . . . . . 23 D4
  High Marnham NG23 . . . . 67 F1
Crabtree Rd NG6 . . . . 160 A3
Craddock St LE11 . . . . . . 220 A2
Crafts Way NG25 . . . . . . 121 F1
Cragdale Rd NG5 . . . . . . 161 E3
Cragg La DE55 . . . . 99 D1
Cragmoor Rd NG14 . . . . 163 F2
Crago Rd S80 . . . . 45 D1
Craig Moray NG12 . . . . . 176 A2
Craig St NG10 . . . . 193 F4
Craigs Gn NG19 . . . . 101 E4
Craigston Rd S81 . . . . 25 F3
Crammond Cl ⑨ NG2 . . 173 D1
Crampton Cl NG17 . . . . . 100 A2
Crampton Cres NG5 . . . . 161 E4
Crampton Rd NG18 . . . . . 102 C4
Cranworth Dr ⑪ NG5 . . 161 E2
Cranberry Cl NG2 . . . . . . 185 D3
Cranborne Cl NG19 . . . . 101 E4
Cranbourne Cl NG9 . . . . 170 B1
Cranbourne Gr NG15 . . . 145 F4
Cranbrook Cl NG19 . . . . . 88 B3
Cranbrook St NG1 . . . . . 223 F3
Cranfleet Way NG10 . . . . 193 D4
Cranford Gdns NG2 . . . . 185 E2
Cranleigh Dr NG14 . . . . . 150 B1
Cranmer Ave NG13 . . . . . 178 C2
Cranmer Gr
  ㉒ Nottingham NG3 . . . 173 E4
  Radmanthwaite NG19 . . . 87 E2
Cranmer Rd NG24 . . . . . . 139 F3
Cranmer St
  Ilkeston DE7 . . . . 157 F1
  Long Eaton NG10 . . . . . . 182 B1
  Nottingham NG3 . . . . . . 173 E4
Cranmore Cl NG5 . . . . . . 148 A1
Cranshaw Cl LE12 . . . . . 212 B2
Cransley Ave NG8 . . . . . . 171 E1
Cranston Ave NG5 . . . . . 147 F1
Cranston Rd NG9 . . . . . . 171 E1
Cranswick Cl NG19 . . . . . 89 D1
Cranthorne Dr NG3 . . . . 174 B3
Crantock Gdns NG12 . . . 197 F2
Cranwell Cl NG6 . . . . 159 F3
Cranwell Rd NG8 . . . . . . 159 E1
Craster Dr Arnold NG5 . . 148 A1
  Newark-on-T NG24 . . . . 125 E1
Craster St NG17 . . . . 100 C1
Crathie Rd S81 . . . . 25 F3
Craven Rd NG7 . . . . 172 C4
Crawford Ave NG9 . . . . . 182 B3
Crawford Cl NG8 . . . . . . 171 F3
Crawford Rise NG5 . . . . 162 B4
Crees La NG24 . . . . 139 D3
Crescent Ave NG4 . . . . . 162 C1
Crescent Prim Sch
  NG19 . . . . 87 E1
Crescent Rd NG16 . . . . . 128 B3
Crescent The
  Arnold NG5 . . . . 161 F2
  Beckingham DN10 . . . . . . 14 A1
  Beeston, Chilwell NG9 . . 183 E2
  Beeston, Toton NG9 . . . . 183 D1
  Bilsthorpe NG22 . . . . 105 F3
  Bircotes DN11 . . . . 9 F2
  Bidworth NG21 . . . . 118 A3
  East Leake LE12 . . . . 205 F1
  Eastwood NG16 . . . . 144 A1
  Lea DN21 . . . . 24 C1
  Mansfield NG18 . . . . 102 B3
  Newark-on-T NG24 . . . . 140 A3
  Nottingham NG3 . . . . . . 173 E4
  Old Dalby LE14 . . . . 219 D3
  Radcliffe on T NG12 . . . . 176 A2
  Retford DN22 . . . . 53 E3
  Shirebrook NG20 . . . . 72 C3
  Stapleford NG9 . . . . 170 C1
  Sutton in A NG17 . . . . . . 100 B4
Cresswell Rd
  Beeston NG9 . . . . 183 D3
  Worksop S80 . . . . 35 F2
Cresswell St S80 . . . . 35 F2
Cresta Gdns NG3 . . . . . . 161 E1
Creswell Crags Visitor Ctr*
  S80 . . . . 59 D3
Creswell Ct NG19 . . . . 88 C2
Creswell Rd NG20 . . . . . . 60 A2
Crew La NG25 . . . . 137 D4
Crew La Ind Est NG25 . . 137 D4
Crew Rd NG23 . . . . 98 A1
Crewe Cl
  Bilsworth NG23 . . . . 118 A3
  Nottingham NG7 . . . . . . 222 B4
Crewe Rd DN11 . . . . 9 D2
Cribb Cl NG11 . . . . 185 D4
Crich Vale
  Newton DE55 . . . . 99 D2
  Nottingham NG5 . . . . . . 161 E1
Cricket Cl NG17 . . . . 129 F4
Cricket Field La DN22 . . . 39 F4

Cricketers Ct NG2 . . . . . 173 F1
Criftin Rd NG14 . . . . 164 A2
Crink La NG25 . . . . 136 C3
Cripps Hill NG7 . . . . 172 B1
Critchley St DE7 . . . . 157 F1
Crocus Flatts NG4 . . . . . 158 C3
Crocus Pl NG2 . . . . 173 E1
Crocus St
  Kirkby in A NG17 . . . . . . 115 D2
  Nottingham NG2 . . . . . . 173 E1
Croft Ave
  Hucknall NG15 . . . . 146 A3
  Mansfield NG18 . . . . 102 B1
Croft Cl Pineton NG16 . . 113 E2
  Rolleston NG23 . . . . 138 A3
Croft Cres NG16 . . . . 158 B3
Croft Ct NG17 . . . . 99 F2
Croft Dr DN11 . . . . 8 A4
Croft Farm Cl
  Everton DN10 . . . . 11 E2
  Rolleston NG23 . . . . 138 A3
Croft Gdns LE14 . . . . . . 218 C2
Croft Prim Sch NG17 . . . 100 C1
Croft Rd Arnold NG5 . . . . 161 F4
  Keyworth NG12 . . . . 197 F2
  West Bridgford NG2 . . . . 186 A2
  Bottle Rise NG13 . . . . . . 165 E2
Croft The
  Beckingham DN10 . . . . . . 23 E4
  Kegworth DE74 . . . . 203 E1
  Newark-on-T NG24 . . . . 140 A4
  Retford DN22 . . . . 39 F4
  South Normanton DE55 . 113 D3
  Stanton Hill NG17 . . . . . 100 B3
Croft Way DN10 . . . . 11 E2
Croft Wlk S80 . . . . 45 D3
Crofton Cl
  Beeston NG9 . . . . 183 E2
  ⑤ Nottingham NG8 . . . 172 A3
Crofton Rd NG9 . . . . 183 E1
Crofts The NG13 . . . . 177 F2
Cromarty Cl NG19 . . . . . 101 E3
Cromarty Ct ⑨ NG2 . . . 173 D1
Cromdale Cl NG5 . . . . . . 148 B1
Cromer Cl NG18 . . . . 102 B2
Cromer Rd NG3 . . . . 173 F4
Cromford Ave
  Carlton NG4 . . . . 174 B4
  Mansfield NG18 . . . . 102 A2
Cromford Cl
  Aldercar NG16 . . . . 143 D2
  Long Eaton NG10 . . . . . . 193 D3
Cromford Rd
  Annesley Woodhouse
  NG17 . . . . 115 D1
  Langley Mill NG16 . . . . . 143 D2
  West Bridgford NG2 . . . . 185 F3
Cromford St DN21 . . . . . . 15 E1
Crompton Ct
  New Houghton NG19 . . . . 86 C4
  Teversal NG17 . . . . 100 A4
Crompton View Prim Sch
  NG22 . . . . 105 F4
Cromwell Ave DE7 . . . . . 170 A3
Cromwell Cres NG4 . . . . 163 D4
Cromwell Dr LE12 . . . . . . 205 F1
Cromwell Rd
  Aslockton NG13 . . . . 178 C2
  Beeston NG9 . . . . 183 F3
  Newark-on-T NG24 . . . . 140 A4
Cromwell St
  Carlton NG4 . . . . 174 C4
  Eastwood NG16 . . . . 158 B4
  Gainsborough DN21 . . . . 24 B3
  Mansfield NG18 . . . . 102 B3
  Nottingham NG7 . . . . . . 222 C3
Cromwell Way DN21 . . . . 24 C2
Crookdole La NG14 . . . . 148 C4
Crooked Billet St DN21 . 15 D2
Crookes Ave NG19 . . . . . 87 D3
Crooks Ave NG19 . . . . . . 88 B2
Croome Cl LE11 . . . . 220 B1
Cropston Cl NG2 . . . . 185 F2
Cropton Cres NG8 . . . . . 172 A3
Cropton Gr NG13 . . . . . . 177 E2
Cropwell Bishop Prim Sch
  NG12 . . . . 189 D2
Cropwell Bishop Rd
  NG12 . . . . 189 D2
Cropwell Butler Rd
  NG12 . . . . 189 D2
Cropwell Cl NG18 . . . . . . 102 B4
Cropwell Gdns NG12 . . . 176 A1
Cropwell Gn NG3 . . . . . . 173 F3
Cropwell Rd
  Langar NG13 . . . . 176 A1
  Radcliffe on T NG12 . . . 176 A1
Crosby Cl NG19 . . . . 89 D1
Crosby Rd NG2 . . . . 185 F4
Cross Dr
  Kirkby in A NG17 . . . . . . 115 D4
  Ramworth NG21 . . . . . . 104 A1
Cross Hill DN10 . . . . 12 C1
Cross Hill Cl LE12 . . . . . 216 B2
Cross La Austerfield DN10 . 3 E3
  Balderton NG24 . . . . 140 B1
  Bidworth NG21 . . . . 117 E3
  Callingham NG23 . . . . . 112 B4
  East Bridgford NG13 . . . 165 E2
  Elkesley DN22 . . . . 49 F2
  Elston NG23 . . . . 154 A2
  Farndon NG24 . . . . 138 C2
  Gringley on t H DN10 . . . . 5 D1

Cross La continued
  Harby NG23 . . . . 70 B1
  Huthwaite NG17 . . . . . . 100 A1
  Stanton Hill NG17 . . . . . 100 B3
Cross St Arnold NG5 . . . . 161 F4
  Barnby in t W NG24 . . . . 141 F3
  Beeston NG9 . . . . 183 F4
  Bilsthorpe NG22 . . . . . . 105 F3
  Carlton, Netherfield
  NG4 . . . . 175 D4
  Carlton, Thorneywood
  NG4 . . . . 174 B4
  Eastwood NG16 . . . . 24 B4
  Gainsborough DN21 . . . . 24 B4
  Hathern LE12 . . . . 213 D1
  Langold S81 . . . . 16 C2
  Long Eaton NG10 . . . . . . 193 F4
  Loughborough LE11 . . . . 220 B3
  Mansfield Woodhouse
  NG19 . . . . 88 A1
  Morton DN21 . . . . 15 D2
  Newark-on-T NG24 . . . . 140 A4
  Retford DN22 . . . . 40 A3
  Sandiacre NG10 . . . . . . 182 B3
  Sturton le S DN22 . . . . . . 32 B3
Cross The
  Carlton in L S81 . . . . 26 A3
  Cotgrave NG12 . . . . 187 F2
Crossdale Dr NG12 . . . . . 197 F2
Crossdale Dr Prim Sch
  NG12 . . . . 197 F2
Crossdale Wlk NG5 . . . . 160 C4
Crossfield Dr NG5 . . . . . 161 D4
Crossgate Rd NG22 . . . . 173 D1
Crosshill NG12 . . . . 188 A2
Crosslands Mdw NG4 . . 174 C2
Crossley Ave NG17 . . . . 100 A2
Crossley Hill La S81 . . . . 26 B2
Crossley St NG5 . . . . 161 D1
Crossman St NG5 . . . . . . 161 E1
Crossways
  East Markham NG22 . . . . 66 A4
  Retford DN22 . . . . 39 F4
Crossways Dr NG13 . . . . 165 E2
Crow Ct NG13 . . . . 178 A2
Crow Hill Ct NG18 . . . . . . 87 D3
Crow Hill Ct NG18 . . . . . 102 A4
Crow Hill Dr NG18 . . . . . 102 A4
Crow Hill La NG19 . . . . . . 88 A1
Crow Hill Rd NG4 . . . . . . 174 C4
Crow La NG23, NG24 . . . 124 B4
Crow Pk Ave NG23 . . . . . . 81 F1
Crow Pk Dr NG14 . . . . . . 163 F2
Crowborough Ave
  NG8 . . . . 171 F1
Crowcroft Way NG10 . . . 182 A3
Crowley Cl NG8 . . . . 171 E3
Crown Ave NG19 . . . . . . 103 D4
Crown Cl
  Collingham NG23 . . . . 98 A1
  Long Eaton NG10 . . . . . . 193 D4
  Rainworth NG21 . . . . . . 118 A4
Crown Ct DN22 . . . . 32 B3
Crown Farm Way
  NG19 . . . . 103 D4
Crown St
  Mansfield NG18 . . . . 102 C3
  Newark-on-T NG24 . . . . 139 F4
  Worksop S80 . . . . 35 F2
Crowthorne Cl NG5 . . . . 146 C1
Crowthorne Gdns
  NG5 . . . . 146 C1
Crowtrees Dr NG17 . . . . 100 B1
Croxall Cl NG11 . . . . 184 C2
Croxley Gdns NG16 . . . . 159 E2
Croxton Ct NG19 . . . . 88 C2
Croydon Rd NG7 . . . . . . 222 A3
Crummock Cl NG9 . . . . . 183 E4
Cuckney CE Prim Sch
  NG20 . . . . 60 A1
Cuckney Hill NG20 . . . . . . 74 A4
Cuckoo Holt S81 . . . . 35 E4
Cuillin Cl NG10 . . . . 182 A1
Cul-de-sac NG22 . . . . . . 105 F3
Cullen Cl NG24 . . . . 124 C1
Cullens Ct NG5 . . . . 161 E1
Cullin Cl NG5 . . . . 146 C1
Cumberland Ave
  Beeston NG9 . . . . 183 E3
  Market Warsop NG20 . . . . 74 A3
Cumberland Cl
  Bircotes DN11 . . . . 9 E2
  Carlton in L S81 . . . . 25 F4
  Westwood NG16 . . . . . . 128 B2
Cumberland Dr NG19 . . . 101 E4
Cumberland Pl NG1 . . . . 223 D2
Cumberlands Mid Sch
  NG19 . . . . 101 E4
Cumbria Rd S81 . . . . 36 A3
Cundy Hill NG25 . . . . 136 A3
Cunningham Cl DN10 . . . 19 F4
Cupar Cl NG20 . . . . 74 B3
Curie Cl NG7 . . . . 172 C1
Curlew Cl NG3 . . . . 174 B3
Curlew Wharf ㊶ NG7 . . 172 C2
Currie Rd NG24 . . . . 125 D1
Cursley Way NG9 . . . . . . 183 E1
Curtis Cl NG23 . . . . 98 A1
Curtis St NG15 . . . . 146 A3
Curzon Ave NG4 . . . . 174 B4
Curzon Cl NG21 . . . . 118 A4
Curzon Ct NG3 . . . . 223 F4
Curzon Dr S81 . . . . 25 F3
Curzon Gdns NG3 . . . . . 223 F4
Curzon Pl NG3 . . . . 223 F4
Curzon St Carlton NG4 . . 175 D4
  Gainsborough DN21 . . . . 15 E1
  Gotham NG11 . . . . 195 D1

Curzon St continued
Long Eaton NG10 ....182 A1
Loughborough LE11 .....220 A2
Nottingham NG3 ....223 F3
Cusworth Way S80 ....35 E2
Cuttings Ave NG17 ....114 A4
Cuxton Cl NG8 ....159 E1
Cycle Rd NG2 ....222 A2
Cypress Ct NG15 ....145 E3
Cyprus Ave NG9 ....183 F4
Cyprus Dr NG9 ....183 F4
Cyprus Rd NG3 ....161 C1
Cyril Ave Beeston NG9 ...183 F4
Nottingham NG3 ....172 B4
Stapleford NG9 ....182 B4
Cyril Rd NG2 ....186 A4

D
D H Lawrence Birthplace
Mus* NG16 ....143 F2
Dabek Rise NG17 ....115 D1
Dabell Ave NG6 ....159 F4
Dadley Rd S81 ....25 F4
Dadsley Rd DN11 ....8 A4
Dagfa House Sch NG9 .....184 A3
Dagmar Gr
Beeston NG9 ....184 A3
Nottingham NG3 ....161 E1
Dahlia Ave DE55 ....113 D4
Dairy La LE14 ....211 F4
Daisy Cl NG12 ....187 F1
Daisy Farm Rd NG16 ....158 A4
Daisy Rd NG3 ....162 A1
Dakeyne St NG3 ....173 F3
Dalbeattie Cl NG5 ....162 B4
Dalby Sq NG8 ....172 B2
Dale Ave Carlton NG4 .....174 B4
Long Eaton NG10 ....182 B1
Newton DE55 ....99 D4
Nottingham NG3 ....162 A1
Dale Cl Hucknall NG15 ....145 E3
Langwith NG20 ....72 C4
Retford DN22 ....39 F2
Sutton in A NG17 ....101 D3
West Bridgford NG2 ....186 A4
Whaley Thorns NG20 ....58 C1
Dale Cres NG24 ....140 C1
Dale Farm Ave NG3 ....174 A3
Dale Gr NG2 ....173 F2
Dale La Ault Hucknall S44 ...86 B4
Beeston NG9 ....183 F3
Blidworth NG21 ....118 A3
Dale Rd Carlton NG4 ....174 B4
Keyworth NG12 ....197 F2
Kimberley NG16 ....158 C3
Market Warsop NG20 ....74 B3
Dale St Mansfield NG19 ....88 A1
Nottingham NG2 ....173 F2
Dale View S81 ....36 A4
Dale View Rd NG3 ....174 A4
Dalebrook Cres NG15 ......145 E3
Dalehead Rd NG11 ....184 B1
Dalemoor Gdns NG8 ....172 A4
Dales Ave NG17 ....100 C3
Dales La DN10 ....4 C2
Daleside NG12 ....187 F1
Daleside Rd NG2 ....174 A2
Daleside Rd E NG2,
NG3 ....174 B2
Dalestorth Ave NG19 ....87 E1
Dalestorth Cl NG17 ....101 D3
Dalestorth Gdns
NG17 ....101 D3
Dalestorth Prim Sch
NG17 ....101 D3
Dalestorth St NG17 ....101 D3
Daleswood Cres DE55 .....113 D2
Dallas St NG18 ....102 A3
Dallas York Rd NG9 ....184 A3
Dalley Cl NG9 ....182 C4
Dalton Cl NG9 ....182 C3
Daltons Cl NG16 ....144 B1
Dam Rd DN11 ....8 A3
Dame Flogan St NG18 ....102 A3
Dame La DN10 ....4 A1
Damson Wlk NG3 ....174 A4
Danbury Mount NG5 ....161 E1
Dane Cl NG3 ....223 F4
Dane Ct NG3 ....223 F4
Danes Cl NG5 ....161 E4
Danes Rd DN21 ....15 F1
Danesfield Rd S80 ....35 F1
Daneshill Lakes Nature
Reserve* D22 ....19 E1
Daneshill Rd DN22 ....20 A4
Daneswood Jun Sch
NG17 ....100 C4
Danethorpe La NG24 ......124 C2
Danethorpe Vale NG5 ....161 E2
Daniel Cres NG18 ....101 F4
Daniels Way NG15 ....114 C2
Danners Hill NG17 ....131 F3
Darfield Ct DN11 ....8 A4
Darfield Dr DE75 ....143 D1
Dark La
Askerton NG13 ....179 D2
Barnby in V W NG24 ....142 A3
Bingham NG13 ....178 A2
West Leake LE12 ....204 C1
Darkey La NG9 ....182 C3
Darley Ave
Beeston NG9 ....182 C2
Carlton NG4 ....175 D4
Kirkby in A NG17 ....115 E3

Darley Ave continued
Nottingham NG7 ....172 C4
Darley Dr NG10 ....193 D3
Darley Rd NG7 ....172 C4
Darley Sq DE7 ....157 F3
Darleydale Cl NG18 ....102 B2
Darlton Dr NG5 ....162 A4
Darlton Rd
East Drayton DN22 ....53 D1
Tuxford NG22 ....66 B2
Darlton St NG19 ....101 E3
Darnal Cl NG5 ....160 C4
Darnhall Cres NG8 ....171 E4
Daron Gdns [52] NG5 ......161 D4
Darrel Rd DN22 ....39 F3
Darricott Cl NG21 ....118 A4
Darvel Dr NG8 ....172 A3
Darwin Cl Elston NG23 ...153 F3
Mansfield NG18 ....102 B2
Nottingham NG5 ....160 C4
Darwin Dr DN22 ....42 A1
Darwin Rd NG10 ....193 D3
Darwin St NG21 ....24 B3
Daubeney Ave LN1 ....57 D2
Davey Rd NG18 ....102 A4
David Gr NG9 ....171 E1
David La NG6 ....160 B2
David St NG17 ....115 D4
Davids La NG14 ....165 D3
Davidson Cl NG5 ....162 B4
Davidson St [58] NG2 ......173 F3
Davies Ave NG17 ....100 C2
Davies Cl NG17 ....100 C2
Davies Rd NG2 ....186 A4
Davis Cl NG21 ....90 A2
Davis Rd NG9 ....183 D2
Davy Cl NG15 ....131 D1
Dawber St S81 ....35 E4
Dawgates La NG19 ....86 C1
Dawlish Cl NG15 ....145 E3
Dawlish Ct NG16 ....143 E2
Dawlish Dr NG5 ....161 D3
Dawn Cl NG15 ....131 E1
Dawn House Sch
NG21 ....103 F2
Dawn View NG9 ....170 B1
Dawns La NG13 ....179 D3
Dawson Cl NG16 ....144 A1
Day St NG20 ....74 A2
Daybell Cl NG13 ....181 D2
Daybill Cl NG25 ....137 E2
Daybrook Ave [4] NG5 ....161 E2
Daybrook St NG5 ....161 E2
Dayncourt Comp Sch
NG12 ....176 A2
DAyncourt Wlk NG12 ......120 A3
De Ferrers Cl NG17 ....205 F1
De Lacy Ct NG22 ....77 D2
De Morgan Cl NG16 ....129 D1
De Vere Gdns NG5 ....162 A3
Deabill St NG4 ....175 D3
Dead La Cossall NG16 ....158 B1
[51] Loughborough LE11 ....220 A2
Deadwong La NG23 ....153 F1
Deakins Pl NG7 ....222 A3
Deal Gdns NG6 ....159 F4
Dean Ave NG3 ....162 A2
Dean Cl
Mansfield NG18 ....102 B2
Nottingham NG8 ....171 E3
Dean Hole CE Sch
NG23 ....109 D3
Dean Rd NG5 ....161 F3
Dean St
Langley Mill NG16 ....143 E2
Nottingham NG1 ....223 F2
Deane Cl NG23 ....98 A1
Deans Cl NG23 ....109 D3
Deans Cl DN10 ....6 C1
Deans Croft NG9 ....171 D1
Deanscourt NG12 ....188 A2
Deansgate NG19 ....87 D3
Death La DN22 ....21 E3
Debdale Gate NG19 ....88 A1
Debdale Hill LE14 ....218 C2
Debdale La
Keyworth NG12 ....197 F2
Mansfield NG19 ....88 A1
Debdhill Rd DN10 ....6 C1
Deben Down NG19 ....88 A4
Deddington La NG9 ....171 E1
Deep Furrow Ave NG4 ....174 B4
Deeps La S45 ....85 D2
Deepdale Ave NG9 ....182 B3
Deepdale Cl NG2 ....186 B4
Deepdale Gdns NG17 .....100 C2
Deepdale Pk NG17 ....100 C2
Deepdale Rd
Long Eaton NG10 ....193 D3
Mansfield NG19 ....88 C1
Nottingham NG8 ....171 E2
Deepdale St NG17 ....100 C2
Deepdene Cl NG8 ....160 A1
Deepdene Way NG8 ....160 A1
Deeps La DN10 ....6 A4
Deer Pk DE7 ....171 F2
Deer Pk Dr Arnold NG5 ..147 E1
Nottingham NG5 ....161 E4
Deerleap Dr NG5 ....161 E4
Deers Acre LE11 ....220 A3
Deetleton Cl NG16 ....129 D4
Delamere Cl NG16 ....129 D4
Delamere Dr NG18 ....102 B2
Delia Ave NG16 ....131 E1
Dell Lea NG18 ....103 D3
Dell The NG17 ....129 F4
Dell Way NG11 ....184 C1

Dellwood Cl NG4 ....162 B1
Delta St NG7 ....160 C1
Delville Ave NG14 ....197 F2
Denacre Ave NG10 ....182 C1
Denbigh Cl NG21 ....104 B1
Denbigh Ct NG23 ....98 A1
Denbury Rd NG15 ....117 D1
Denby Dr NG18 ....102 B1
Denby Dr DN22 ....53 D4
Dene Cl DN10 ....20 A4
Dene The S80 ....35 E1
Denehurst Ave NG8 ....160 B1
Denewood Ave NG8 ....171 E1
Denewood Cres NG8 ....171 F4
Denholme Rd NG8 ....171 D2
Denison Ave NG22 ....40 A2
Denison St
Beeston NG9 ....183 F4
Nottingham NG7 ....222 B4
Denman St NG22 ....39 E4
Denman St Central
NG7 ....222 B3
Denman St E NG7 ....222 B3
Denman St W NG7 ....222 B3
Denmark Gr [1] NG3 ....173 E4
Dennett Cl NG3 ....173 F3
Dennis Ave NG9 ....183 F4
Dennis St Carlton NG4 ....175 D4
Worksop S80 ....35 F3
Dennor Dr NG19 ....88 C3
Denstone Rd NG3 ....173 F3
Dentdale Dr NG8 ....171 D2
Denton Ave NG10 ....182 A3
Denton Cl
Balderton NG24 ....140 B2
Nottingham NG5 ....88 C1
Denton Dr NG2 ....186 A4
Denton Gn NG8 ....159 F1
Denver Ct NG9 ....170 C1
Deptford Cres NG6 ....160 B3
Derby Rd NG7 ....222 B3
Derby Rd
Annesley Woodhouse
NG15, NG17 ....130 A4
Beeston NG9 ....171 E1
Eastwood NG16 ....143 E2
Hathern LE12 ....212 C1
Kegworth DE74 ....203 E1
Kirkby in A NG17 ....115 E2
Langley Mill NG16 ....143 E2
Long Eaton NG10 ....193 D4
Loughborough LE11 ....220 A3
Mansfield NG17, NG18 ....116 A4
Nottingham NG7 ....222 B2
Sandiacre NG10 ....182 A3
Derby Rd Ind Est
Sandiacre NG10 ....182 A3
Stapleford NG10 ....182 A3
Derby St Arnold NG5 ......161 E4
Beeston NG9 ....183 F4
Mansfield NG18 ....102 B3
Nottingham NG1 ....223 D3
Derbyshire Ave NG9 ....170 B2
Derbyshire Cres NG8 ......172 A4
Derbyshire Dr NG16 ....128 B2
Derbyshire La NG15 ....146 A4
Dereham Dr NG5 ....162 A3
Derry Dr NG5 ....147 F1
Derry Hill Rd NG5 ....147 F1
Derry La NG13 ....179 D3
Derrymount Specl Sch
NG5 ....147 F1
Derwent Ave
Ilkeston DE7 ....157 E1
Mansfield NG18 ....103 D3
Derwent Cl
Beeston NG9 ....183 F2
Mansfield NG18 ....103 D3
Market Warsop NG20 ....74 B3
Rainworth NG21 ....118 A4
West Bridgford NG2 ....186 B4
Worksop S81 ....35 F3
Derwent Cres NG5 ....162 A3
Derwent Ct
Balderton NG24 ....140 B2
Nottingham NG7 ....222 C4
Derwent Dr
Annesley Woodhouse
NG17 ....130 A4
Hucknall NG15 ....146 A2
Selston NG16 ....129 D4
Derwent St Ind Est
NG10 ....193 E3
Derwent Terr [5] NG5 .....161 E1
Derwent Way NG24 ....125 D1
Desborough Rd NG16 .....128 B4
Desford Cl NG5 ....161 D2
Devitt Dr NG15 ....131 E1
Devon Cir NG5 ....147 E1
Devon Dr
Eastwood NG16 ....144 A1
Nottingham NG5 ....161 E2
Devon Dr
Mansfield NG19 ....101 F4
Nottingham NG5 ....161 E1
Ruddington NG11 ....196 B4
Devon Rd NG24 ....139 F3
Devon St Ilkeston DE7 ....170 A3
Nottingham NG3 ....173 F3
Devonshire Ave
Beeston NG9 ....183 F3
Long Eaton NG10 ....194 A4
Devonshire Cl
Huthwaite NG17 ....100 A1
Ilkeston DE7 ....157 F3

Devonshire Cres NG5 .....161 E1
Devonshire Dr
Eastwood NG16 ....143 F1
Langwith NG20 ....72 C4
Ollerton NG22 ....77 D2
Stapleford NG9 ....170 B1
Devonshire La LE11 ....220 A2
Devonshire Prom
NG7 ....222 A1
Devonshire Rd
Harworth DN11 ....8 C2
Nottingham NG5 ....161 D1
Retford DN22 ....39 E3
West Bridgford NG2 ....186 B3
Devonshire Sq [1] LE11 ..220 A2
Devonshire St
New Houghton NG19 ....87 D4
Worksop S80 ....35 F1
Dewberry La NG12 ....176 A1
Dial The NG12 ....187 F1
Diamond Ave
Kirkby in A NG17 ....115 E2
Rainworth NG21 ....104 B1
Dickens Ct NG16 ....144 B2
Dickens Rd S81 ....36 A2
Dickenson Terr DN21 ....24 B4
Dickenson Way NG23 ......110 C2
Dickmans La LE14 ....202 A2
Dicks La NG16 ....144 B1
Dickson Dr NG11 ....196 B3
Didcot Dr NG8 ....148 B1
Digby Ave NG3 ....162 B2
Digby Cl NG14 ....148 C3
Digby Hall Dr NG4 ....162 B2
Digby St Cossall DE7 ......158 A1
Kimberley NG16 ....158 B4
Dingley Cl NG19 ....88 C3
Dirca Cl NG11 ....195 E4
Disworth Gr [22] NG2 .....173 E1
Distillery St NG11 ....196 B3
Division Rd NG20 ....72 C2
Dixie St NG16 ....128 A2
Django Cty Tech Coll
NG7 ....161 D1
Dobbin Cl NG12 ....189 D2
Dock Rd S80 ....35 F2
Dockholm Rd NG10 ....182 B2
Doddington Hall* IN6 ....71 D1
Doddington La
Claypole NG23 ....156 A1
Dry Doddington NG23 .....156 A1
Dodford Cl DE75 ....143 D1
Dog & Ducks La DN21 ......15 D2
Dog La DN10 ....10 A1
Doghill La NG23 ....153 D1
Dogwood Ave NG6 ....160 A4
Doles La
Kirkby in A NG17 ....114 B3
Whitwell S80 ....45 D4
Dolphin Ct NG5 ....161 D4
Dominie Cross Rd
DN22 ....39 F3
Donbas Cl NG6 ....160 A2
Doncaster Ave NG10 ....182 A3
Doncaster Gr NG10 ....182 C1
Doncaster Rd
Bawtry DN10 ....10 A4
Carlton in L S81 ....25 F4
Langold S81 ....16 C2
Tickhill DN11 ....8 A4
Westwoodside DN9 ....2 C2
Doncaster Terr [10] NG2 .173 E1
Donington Rd NG7 ....184 C1
Donkey La NG11 ....196 C2
Donner Cres DE7 ....157 F3
Dooland Dr NG3 ....161 F1
Dorchester Cl NG18 ....102 B1
Dorchester Dr NG18 ....102 B1
Dorchester Gdns NG2 ....185 F2
Dorchester Rd
Annesley Woodhouse
NG17 ....115 D1
Harworth DN11 ....9 D3
Kimberley NG16 ....158 C4
Doreen Dr NG17 ....101 D2
Dorewood Ct NG24 ....140 C2
Doris Rd DE7 ....170 A4
Dorket Cl NG5 ....148 A1
Dorket Dr NG8 ....172 B2
Dorking Rd NG7 ....222 B4
Dormy Cl Beeston NG9 ...183 E4
Mansfield Woodhouse
NG19 ....88 C3
Sandiacre NG10 ....182 A3
Dorothy Dr NG19 ....88 C1
Dorset Dr DN11 ....9 D3
Dorset Gdns NG2 ....185 E3
Dorset St NG8 ....172 B3
Dorset Way NG18 ....103 D2
Dorterry Cres DE7 ....170 A3
Dorton Ave DN21 ....24 C4
Douglas Ave
Awsworth NG16 ....158 B3
Carlton NG4 ....174 C3
Douglas Cl NG12 ....175 F1
Douglas Cres NG4 ....174 C3

Douglas Ct NG15 ....183 D1
Douglas Prim Sch
NG7 ....222 B3
Douglas Rd
Bingham NG13 ....178 A3
Long Eaton NG10 ....182 A1
Nottingham NG7
NG19 ....89 D1
Nottingham NG7 ....222 B3
Sutton in A NG17 ....100 B1
Douro Dr NG5 ....148 A1
Dove Cl Bingham NG13 ...177 F2
Ollerton NG22 ....77 D2
Worksop S81 ....35 F4
Dove Croft NG22 ....77 D2
Dove Dr NG16 ....129 D4
Dove La NG10 ....193 E4
Dove St NG6 ....160 C4
Dovecoat St LE12 ....213 D1
Dovecote Cl NG23 ....165 E2
Dovecote Dr NG8 ....171 F2
Dovecote La NG9 ....184 A3
Dovecote Rd NG16 ....131 E1
Dovedale Ave
Long Eaton NG10 ....193 D3
Nottingham NG3 ....100 B1
Dovedale Cir DE7 ....157 F3
Dovedale Cl
Edwinstowe NG21 ....76 A1
Mansfield NG18 ....102 B2
Dovedale Ct NG10 ....193 D3
Dovedale Prim Sch
NG10 ....193 D3
Dovedale Rd
Nottingham NG3 ....174 B3
West Bridgford NG2 ....186 B4
Dovenby Rd NG7 ....184 C1
Dover Beck Cl
Calverton NG14 ....149 D4
Ravenshead NG15 ....116 C1
Dover Beck Dr NG14 ....149 E2
Dover Bottom DN22 ....50 B2
Doveridge Ave NG4 ....175 D4
Doveridge Ct NG15 ....117 D2
Doveridge Rd NG4 ....175 D4
Doveys Orch NG14 ....148 B4
Downes Cl NG6 ....160 A4
Downham Cl NG5 ....162 A3
Downham Gdns NG15 .....117 D1
Downing Cl NG6 ....160 A4
Downing Gdns [6] NG6 ...160 A4
Downing St
Nottingham NG6 ....160 A4
South Normanton DE55 ...113 D3
Sutton in A NG17 ....100 C2
Downs The NG11 ....185 D2
Dowson St NG3 ....173 F3
Doyne Ct [2] NG2 ....173 E1
Dragon St NG13 ....191 D3
Dragwell DE74 ....203 E1
Drake Rd NG4 ....175 D3
Drake St DN21 ....24 B3
Drakemyre Cl NG5 ....148 A1
Draycott Cl DE7 ....157 F2
Draycott Rd NG10 ....193 D2
Drayton Ave NG19 ....87 E1
Drayton St [3] NG5 ....161 E1
Drift Hill NG13 ....192 C2
Drift The
Hucknall NG15 ....131 D1
Nottingham NG11 ....184 C2
Drinsey Nook La NG23 ......70 B4
Drive The Beeston NG9 ...183 F2
Clipstone NG21 ....90 A2
Gainsborough DN21 ....24 C4
Winthorpe NG24 ....125 D2
Drive The Pk La DN21 ....30 A1
Dronfield Pl DE7 ....157 F3
Dronley Dr NG20 ....74 B4
Drove La NG24 ....124 C3
Drovers Ct DN21 ....24 C3
Droversdale Rd DN11 ....9 E2
Drummond Ave NG4 ....175 D4
Drummond Dr NG16 ....159 F2
Drummond Rd DE7 ....157 F1
Drury La DN11 ....8 A4
Dry Pot La LE12 ....212 A1
Dryden Ave NG24 ....140 C3
Dryden Ct NG9 ....170 C1
Dryden Dale S81 ....36 A2
Dryden St NG1 ....223 D4
Drysdale Cl NG3 ....160 A3
Duchess Gdns [9] NG6 ...160 A4
Duchess St Creswell S80 ..58 C4
Nottingham NG6 ....160 A4
Whitwell S80 ....45 D3
Ducie La DN22 ....23 F2
Dudley Ct NG9 ....183 D4
Duesbury The DE55 ....113 D2
Duffield Cl NG10 ....193 D2
Duffield Ct NG5 ....160 C4
Duke Cl NG6 ....160 A3
Duke Cres NG16 ....144 B1
Duke Pl S80 ....35 F2
Duke St Arnold NG5 ....161 F4
Hucknall NG15 ....146 A4
Huthwaite NG17 ....100 A3
Ilkeston DE7 ....157 F2
Loughborough LE11 ....220 A3
Nottingham NG7 ....222 B3
Retford DN22 ....39 F3
South Normanton DE55 ...113 D3
Sutton in A NG17 ....100 C1

Duke St
Whitwell S80 ....45 D3
Duke William Mount
NG7 ....222 C2
Dukeries Cl S81 ....35 E3
Dukeries Com Coll The
NG22 ....77 E3
Dukeries Cres S80 ....36 B1
Dukeries Ind Est The
S81 ....35 E3
Dukeries Way S81 ....35 E3
Dukes Cl NG11 ....101 E1
Dukes Dr S44 ....86 A4
Dukes Pl DE7 ....157 F2
Dukes Pl NG1 ....223 F2
Dukes Rd LE14 ....219 D3
Dukes Terr DN10 ....10 A4
Dukes Wood Nature
Reserve * NG22 ....107 D3
Dulverton Vale NG8 ....160 A2
Dulwich Rd NG7 ....222 A3
Dumb Hall La S80 ....34 A2
Dumbles The
Lambley NG4 ....163 D4
Sutton in A NG17 ....100 B1
Dunbar Cl DN21 ....15 F1
Dunbar Dr NG19 ....101 E3
Dunblane Rd NG11 ....196 B3
Duncan Ave NG15 ....117 D1
Duncombe Cl NG3 ....173 F4
Duncroft Ave NG4 ....162 C1
Dundas Cl NG1 ....223 E3
Dundee Dr NG19 ....88 A3
Dunelm Cl NG17 ....100 B2
Dunelm Dr NG14 ....149 D4
Dungannon Rd NG11 ....195 F4
Dunham CE Prim Sch
NG22 ....54 A1
Dunham Cl
Newton on T LN1 ....55 D1
Southwell NG25 ....136 B4
Dunham Rd
Laneham DN22 ....54 A3
Newton on T DN22, LN1 ....54 C1
Dunholme Ave NG24 ....139 F4
Dunholme Cl
Gainsborough DN21 ....24 C4
Nottingham NG6 ....160 A4
Dunholme Rd DN21 ....24 C4
Dunkery Rd NG11 ....195 F4
Dunkirk Prim Sch
NG7 ....172 C1
Dunkirk Rd 4 NG7 ....172 C1
Dunlin Wharf 2 NG2 ....173 D1
Dunlop Ave NG7 ....222 A2
Dunn Brigg NG19 ....88 B1
Dunnett Rd NG19 ....101 F3
Dunoon Cl NG5 ....146 C1
Dunoon Rd NG19 ....101 F3
Dunsby Cl NG7 ....184 C1
Dunsford Dr NG3 ....162 B3
Dunsil Dr NG11 ....185 D4
Dunsil Rd
Eastwood NG16 ....144 A2
Pinxton NG16 ....113 E1
Dunsmore Cl NG9 ....184 A2
Dunstall Wlk DN21 ....24 C4
Dunstan Cres S80 ....35 F1
Dunstan St NG4 ....175 D4
Dunster Rd
Eastwood NG16 ....144 A1
Gainsborough DN21 ....15 F1
West Bridgford NG2 ....186 A3
Dunston Cl NG10 ....193 F4
Dunvegan Dr NG5 ....146 C1
Dunwoody Cl NG18 ....102 C4
Durham House Heritage Ctr
NG16 ....143 F2
Durham Ave NG2 ....173 F2
Durham Cl
Mansfield Woodhouse
NG19 ....88 B2
10 Nottingham NG2 ....173 F2
Worksop S81 ....36 A4
Durham Cres NG6 ....160 B3
Durham Gr DN22 ....30 A1
Durham St 3 DE7 ....157 F1
Duriston Cl NG2 ....185 D3
Durnford St NG7 ....160 C1
Dursley Cl NG6 ....160 A3
Dyce Cl NG6 ....159 F4
Dykes End NG23 ....112 A4
Dylan Thomas Rd
NG5 ....161 E4
Dyscarr Cl S81 ....16 B3
Dyscarr Prim Sch S81 ....16 B2

E

Eagle Cl Arnold NG5 ....162 A4
Beeston NG9 ....183 E4
Eagle Cl NG6 ....160 B4
Eagle Cty Prim Sch
LN6 ....84 B2
Eagle Moor LN6 ....84 C2
Eagle Pl DN22 ....39 F4
Eagle Rd Eagle LN6 ....84 A2
North Scarle LN6 ....83 F2
Eakring Cl NG18 ....102 C4
Eakring Rd
Bilsthorpe NG22 ....105 F4
Kneesall NG22 ....93 F3
Mansfield NG18, NG21,
NG22 ....103 E4

Eakring Rd continued
Wellow NG22 ....92 B4
Ealing Ave NG6 ....160 B2
Eardley Rd NG5 ....160 C3
Earl Cres NG4 ....162 C2
Earl Dr NG16 ....144 B1
Earl Howe Cres NG13 ....190 B1
Earles Ct DN22 ....29 E1
Earls Cl NG8 ....171 E3
Earls Rd LE14 ....219 D3
Earlsfield Dr NG5 ....146 C1
Earlswood Dr NG12 ....186 A2
Earp Ave NG24 ....140 A4
Easedale Cl NG10 ....186 B4
Easegill Ct NG5 ....160 C2
East Acres NG12 ....187 F2
East Cir St NG1 ....223 D2
East Cl NG12 ....197 F1
East Cres NG9 ....184 A3
East Dr NG7 ....172 B1
East End LE14 ....211 E2
East Gr Bingham NG13 ....177 F2
Nottingham NG7 ....173 D4
East Markham Prim Sch
NG22 ....65 F4
East Moor NG12 ....188 A1
East Rd LE12 ....216 C2
East St Bingham NG13 ....177 F2
Bole DN22 ....23 F2
Gotham NG11 ....195 D1
Harworth DN11 ....9 D3
Heanor DE75 ....157 D4
Long Eaton NG10 ....193 F4
Nottingham NG1 ....223 F3
Retford DN22 ....39 F3
Sutton in A NG17 ....101 D2
East View Bawtry DN10 ....10 A4
East Markham NG22 ....65 F3
Shirebrook NG20 ....72 C3
West Bridgford NG2 ....185 E3
East Wlk DN22 ....39 E4
Eastcliffe Ave NG4 ....162 B2
Eastcote Ave NG9 ....171 D1
Eastcroft LN1 ....57 D3
Eastcroft La NG22 ....52 A1
Eastdale Rd NG3 ....174 A3
Eastern Ave DN21 ....15 F1
Eastern Ct NG24 ....140 A4
Eastern Dr NG24 ....140 C1
Eastern Terr La NG24 ....140 A4
Eastfield
North Muskham NG23 ....110 C1
North Wheatley DN22 ....31 F4
Eastfield Cl NG21 ....89 F1
Eastfield Cres NG5 ....136 B4
Eastfield Dr DE55 ....113 D3
Eastfield Side NG17 ....101 D2
Eastgate
Normanton on T NG23 ....81 F4
Worksop S80 ....35 F2
Eastglade Prim Sch
NG5 ....161 D3
Eastglade Rd NG5 ....161 D3
Eastham Cl NG3 ....173 F3
Eastham Rd NG5 ....162 B3
Easthorne Croft NG12 ....174 B3
Easthorpe NG25 ....136 C4
Easthorpe La NG13 ....192 C2
Easthorpe Rd NG13 ....161 E1
Easthorpe St NG11 ....196 B4
Easthorpe View NG13 ....181 E1
Eastland Terr NG24 ....74 C4
Eastlands Jun Sch
NG20 ....74 A3
Eastlands La NG20 ....74 A3
Eastleigh Dr NG19 ....88 A3
Eastmoor Dr NG4 ....174 C4
Eastwell St NG15 ....146 A4
Eastwood NG12 ....188 A1
Eastwood Ave NG20 ....72 C4
Eastwood Cl NG15 ....145 F2
Eastwood Comp Sch
NG16 ....143 F2
Eastwood Cl S81 ....35 F4
Eastwood Day Hospl
NG24 ....140 A3
Eastwood Jun & Inf Sch
NG16 ....143 F1
Eastwood La DN10 ....4 B2
Eastwood Rd
Kimberley NG16 ....158 C3
Radcliffe on T NG12 ....176 A2
Eastwood St NG6 ....160 B3
Easy Par S80 ....45 D3
Eather Ave NG19 ....88 B2
Eaton Ave NG5 ....162 A4
Eaton Cl Beeston NG9 ....184 A3
Farnsfield NG22 ....119 F3
Eaton Ct NG18 ....103 D2
Eaton Grange Dr
NG10 ....193 D4
Eaton Pl NG21 ....118 A4
Eaton St NG3 ....161 F1
Eaton Terr NG3 ....161 F1
Eatons Rd NG9 ....182 B3
Ebenezer St
Ilkeston DE7 ....157 F2
Langley Mill NG16 ....143 D2
Ebers Gr NG3 ....173 E4
Ebers Rd NG3 ....173 E4
Ebony Wlk NG3 ....174 A4
Ebury Rd NG5 ....161 D1
Eckington Terr 15 NG2 ....173 E1
Eckington Wlk NG18 ....103 D3
Eclipse Yd 12 NG18 ....102 A4
Ecton Cl NG5 ....146 C1
Edale Cl Hucknall NG15 ....145 E3
Long Eaton NG10 ....193 D3

Edale Cl continued
Mansfield NG18 ....103 D2
Edale Cl NG17 ....100 B2
Edale Rd
Mansfield NG18 ....103 D3
Nottingham NG2 ....174 A3
Edale Rise NG9 ....182 C2
Edale Sq DE7 ....157 F3
Eddery View NG18 ....102 C4
Eddington Cl NG12 ....188 A1
Eddison Cl S81 ....36 A4
Eddison Pk Ave S81 ....35 F4
Eddleston Dr NG7 ....184 C1
Edelin Rd LE11 ....220 A1
Eden Cl NG5 ....162 A2
Eden Cl DN22 ....39 F2
Eden Low NG19 ....88 C2
Edenbridge Ct NG8 ....171 E1
Edenhall Gdns NG7 ....184 C1
Edern Cl NG5 ....161 D4
Edern Gdns 51 NG5 ....161 D4
Edgar Ave NG18 ....102 B4
Edgbaston Gdns 1 NG8 ....172 B4
Edgcote Way NG5 ....161 D3
Edge Hill Ct NG10 ....193 E2
Edge Way NG8 ....159 E1
Edgehill Dr NG24 ....140 C4
Edgehill Gr NG19 ....88 B1
Edgehill Prep Sch
NG22 ....120 B2
Edgewood Dr NG15 ....145 E3
Edgewood Prim Sch
NG15 ....145 E2
Edgewood Rd NG16 ....158 C3
Edginton St NG3 ....173 F4
Edgware Rd NG6 ....160 B4
Edinbane Cl NG5 ....146 C1
Edinboro Row NG16 ....158 A3
Edingdon Dr NG13 ....177 E3
Edinburgh Rd S80 ....45 D2
Edinburgh Wlk S80 ....47 D2
Edingale Ct NG9 ....171 D2
Edingley Ave
Mansfield NG19 ....101 E4
Nottingham NG5 ....161 E2
Edingley Hill NG22 ....120 B2
Edingley Sq NG5 ....161 D2
Edison St NG17 ....114 C1
Edlington Dr NG8 ....171 E2
Edmond Gr NG15 ....146 B4
Edmonds Cl NG5 ....147 D1
Edmonton Ct NG2 ....185 E3
Edmonton Rd NG21 ....89 F1
Edna G Olds Prim Sch
NG7 ....222 B1
Ednaston Rd NG7 ....172 B1
Edwald Rd NG12 ....186 A2
Edwaltram Ave NG2 ....186 A4
Edwalton Cl NG12 ....186 A2
Edwalton Ct
Mansfield NG18 ....103 D2
Nottingham NG6 ....160 C3
Edwalton Lodge Cl
NG12 ....186 B2
Edward Ave
Newark-on-T NG24 ....139 F4
Nottingham NG8 ....172 B4
Sutton in A NG17 ....100 C2
Westwood NG16 ....128 A2
Edward Cl NG15 ....145 E2
Edward Rd
Eastwood NG16 ....144 A1
Gainsborough DN21 ....15 E1
Long Eaton NG10 ....193 E4
Nuthall NG16 ....159 E3
West Bridgford NG2 ....185 F4
Edward St
Aldercar NG16 ....143 D2
Kirkby in A NG17 ....115 D3
9 Loughborough LE11 ....220 A3
Market Warsop NG20 ....74 A3
Stapleford NG9 ....182 B4
Worksop S80 ....35 F2
Edwards Cl S80 ....35 E2
Edwards La NG5 ....161 E3
Edwin St Arnold NG5 ....161 E3
Sutton in A NG17 ....100 C2
Edwinstowe Dr
Nottingham NG5 ....161 D2
Selston NG16 ....129 D4
Eel La NG22 ....79 E1
Eel Pool Rd DN10 ....11 F1
Eelwood Rd NG15 ....145 E2
Egerton Cl NG18 ....103 D4
Egerton Dr NG9 ....170 B1
Egerton Rd NG2 ....185 F4
Egerton St NG3 ....173 E4
Egerton Wlk 7 NG3 ....173 E4
Egham Cl NG21 ....104 B1
Egling Croft NG4 ....174 C2
Egmanton Rd
Mansfield NG18 ....103 D2
Meden Vale NG20 ....74 B4
Tuxford NG22 ....65 F1
Egmanton Rd 8 NG22 ....73 C1
Egret Rd NG7 ....160 C1
Eider Cl NG20 ....72 B2

Elder St
Kirkby in A NG17 ....114 C3
Sutton in A NG17 ....100 C3
Eldon Rd NG9 ....183 E1
Eldon St
Newark-on-T NG24 ....139 F4
Tuxford NG22 ....65 F2
Eleanor Ave DE7 ....170 A3
Eleanor Cres NG9 ....182 C4
Electric Ave NG11 ....185 D4
Eley Cl DE7 ....157 E1
Elford Rise NG3 ....173 F3
Elgar Dr NG10 ....193 D3
Elgar Gdns NG3 ....173 F4
Eliot Cl NG10 ....193 D3
Eliot Wlk NG11 ....195 E4
Elizabeth Cl
Gainsborough DN21 ....15 E2
Nottingham NG16 ....145 F3
Elizabeth Ct DE7 ....157 E1
Elizabeth Gr NG4 ....162 C1
Elizabeth Rd NG24 ....139 F3
Elizabethan H Comp Sch
(Lower Sch Site)
DN22 ....39 E4
Elizabethan H Comp Sch
(Upper Sch Site)
DN22 ....39 F3
Elkesley Prim Sch
DN22 ....50 A2
Elkesley Rd NG20 ....74 C4
Ella Bank Rd DE75 ....143 D1
Ella Rd NG2 ....173 F1
Ellastone Ave NG5 ....161 E4
Ellerby Ave NG7 ....184 C1
Ellerslie Cl NG24 ....125 D3
Ellerslie Gr NG10 ....182 A3
Ellesmere Bsns Pk
NG5 ....161 D1
Ellesmere Cl NG5 ....162 A4
Ellesmere Dr NG9 ....170 B3
Ellesmere Rd
Mansfield NG18 ....102 C4
West Bridgford NG2 ....185 F2
Ellington Rd NG5 ....148 A1
Elliott Durham Comp Sch
NG3 ....161 F1
Elliott St NG7 ....222 C3
Ellis Ave NG15 ....146 A3
Ellis Cl NG10 ....193 E2
Ellis Cl NG3 ....223 F4
Ellis Gr NG9 ....183 F3
Ellis Guilford Comp Sch
NG6 ....160 B1
Ellis St NG17 ....115 D3
Ellsworth Rise NG5 ....160 C3
Ellwood Cres NG8 ....172 A3
Elm Ave Beeston, Attenborough
NG9 ....183 E1
Beeston, Chilwell NG9 ....183 F3
Bingham NG13 ....178 A2
Carlton NG4 ....174 C4
East Leake LE12 ....205 F2
Hucknall NG15 ....145 F3
Keyworth NG12 ....197 F1
Long Eaton NG10 ....193 E4
Newark-on-T NG24 ....140 A3
Nottingham NG3 ....173 E4
Nuthall NG16 ....159 D3
Sandiacre NG10 ....182 A4
Elm Bank NG3 ....173 E4
Elm Bank Dr NG3 ....173 E4
Elm Cl Keyworth NG12 ....197 F1
Newark-on-T NG24 ....140 A3
Nottingham NG3 ....173 E4
Pinxton NG16 ....57 D2
Saxilby LN1 ....57 D2
Elm Dr NG4 ....174 C4
Elm Gr Arnold NG5 ....148 A1
Church Warsop NG20 ....74 A3
Elm Tree Ave
Mansfield Woodhouse
NG19 ....88 A2
Shirebrook NG20 ....72 B2
West Bridgford NG2 ....185 E4
Elm Tree Cl S80 ....35 F3
Elm Tree Dr DN10 ....9 F4
Elm Tree Pl DN22 ....50 A2
Elm Tree Rd NG17 ....114 C3
Elm Tree Rise NG22 ....93 F3
Elm Tree St NG18 ....102 B4
Elm Wlk DN22 ....40 A3
Elma La NG20 ....59 E3
Elmbridge NG5 ....161 D4
Elmcroft NG25 ....134 A2
Elmdale Gdns NG8 ....172 A4
Elmhurst Ave
Nottingham NG3 ....162 B1
South Normanton DE55 ....113 D2
Elmhurst Cl NG15 ....115 E3
Elmhurst Dr NG17 ....100 A2
Elmhurst Rd NG19 ....88 C1
Elmore Cl NG7 ....222 B4
Elmores Mdw NG14 ....152 A4
**Elms (Loughborough Univ of
Technology) The**
LE11 ....220 B2
Elms Cl
Rempstone LE12 ....215 E3
Ruddington NG11 ....196 B3
Elms Gdns NG11 ....196 B3
Elms Gr LE11 ....220 B2
Elms Pk NG11 ....196 B3
Elms Prim Sch The
NG3 ....173 E4
Elms Rd S80 ....35 F2
Elms The Carlton NG4 ....174 C3

Elms The continued
Watnall NG16 ....158 C4
Elmsfield Ave DE75 ....143 D1
Elmsham Ave NG5 ....146 C1
Elmsmere Dr S81 ....17 D3
Elmsthorpe Ave NG7 ....222 A2
Elmswood Gdns NG5 ....161 E2
Elmton Cl S80 ....58 B4
Elmton Rd S80 ....58 B4
Elmtree Ave NG16 ....128 C4
Elmtree Cl S81 ....34 C4
Elmtree Rd NG14 ....148 B4
Elmwood Cl DN22 ....30 A1
Elnor St NG16 ....143 E2
Elsham Wlk DN21 ....24 C4
Elson St NG7 ....172 C4
Elston Cl NG19 ....87 E1
Elston Gdns NG11 ....184 C2
Elston Hall NG23 ....153 E2
Elston La NG23 ....153 E3
Elswick Cl NG5 ....161 D4
Elswick Dr NG9 ....184 B2
Elterwater Dr NG2 ....186 B3
Eltham Cl NG8 ....159 F2
Eltham Dr NG8 ....160 A1
Eltham Rd NG2 ....186 A4
Elton & Orston Sta
NG13 ....180 A3
Elton Cl
Balderton NG24 ....140 B2
Mansfield NG18 ....103 D3
Stapleford NG9 ....182 B4
Elton Rd
Mansfield NG18 ....102 C3
10 Nottingham NG5 ....161 D1
Elton Rd N NG5 ....161 D1
Elvaston Cl NG18 ....103 D3
Elvaston Dr NG10 ....193 D2
Elvaston Rd NG8 ....172 A3
Elveden Dr DE7 ....157 E2
Ely Cl
Mansfield Woodhouse
NG19 ....88 B2
Worksop S80 ....36 A1
Emerald Cl NG19 ....87 F1
Emerald Gr NG17 ....115 E2
Emerys Rd NG4 ....175 D4
Emma Bates Way
NG21 ....118 A3
Emmanuel Ave
Nottingham, Porchester
NG3 ....162 A1
Nottingham, Rise Park
NG5 ....147 D1
Emneth Cl NG3 ....173 F4
Empingham Cl NG9 ....183 D1
Empire St NG18 ....102 B3
Empress Cl LE11 ....220 B2
Empress Rd LE11 ....220 B2
Emsworth Ave DN22 ....29 F1
Emsworth Cl DE7 ....157 E2
Ena Ave NG2 ....173 F3
Enderby Cres
Gainsborough DN21 ....24 C4
Mansfield NG18 ....102 C3
Enderby Gdns NG5 ....147 F1
Enderby Sq NG9 ....183 F4
Endsleigh Gdns
Beeston NG9 ....183 F4
West Bridgford NG12 ....186 A2
Enfield St NG9 ....183 F4
Engine La NG16 ....144 A2
England Cres DE75 ....143 D1
English Martyrs RC Prim Sch
NG10 ....182 A1
Ennerdale Cl NG2 ....186 B4
Ennerdale Rd
Long Eaton NG10 ....182 A1
Nottingham NG5 ....161 E3
Ennismore Mews
NG11 ....185 E1
Enright Cl NG24 ....139 F3
Enthorpe St 8 NG8 ....172 A3
Epinal Way LE11 ....220 A1
Epperstone By-pass
NG14 ....150 A2
Epperstone Ct NG18 ....103 D1
Epperstone Rd
Lowdham NG14 ....150 B1
Oxton NG25 ....134 A1
West Bridgford NG2 ....185 F4
Epping Way NG19 ....103 D4
Epsom Rd NG9 ....182 C2
Epsom St NG18 ....102 C3
Erdington Way NG9 ....182 C2
Erewash Ct DE7 ....157 E1
Erewash Dr DE7 ....157 E1
Erewash Gdns NG5 ....161 D4
Erewash Gr NG9 ....182 C1
Erewash Rd NG16 ....113 F1
Erewash Sq DE7 ....170 A3
Erewash St
Kirkby in A NG17 ....115 D3
Long Eaton NG10 ....193 F4
Pye Bridge DE55 ....128 A3
Eric Ave NG15 ....130 C1
Erica Dr DE55 ....113 D4
Erith Cl NG8 ....159 E1
Ernehale Jun & Inf Schs
NG5 ....162 A3
Erskine Rd 1 NG5 ....161 D1
Esher Gr NG3 ....161 E1
Eskdale Cl NG10 ....193 D3
Eskdale Ct NG2 ....186 B4
Eskdale Dr
Beeston NG9 ....183 D3
Nottingham NG8 ....172 A4
Worksop S81 ....35 F4

Eskdale Jun Sch NG9	183 D3
Eskhouse Cl NG2	186 B2
Essex Dr DN11	9 E2
Essex Rd DN11	9 E2
Essex St 4 DE7	157 F1
Estwic Ave NG16	143 F2
Ethel Ave	
Hucknall NG15	131 E1
Nottingham NG3	162 A1
Ethel Rd NG2	185 F4
Ethel Wainwright Prim Sch NG19	101 F4
Ethelbert Ave NG17	115 E1
Etheldene NG12	188 A2
Etherington St DN21	24 B4
Eton Cl NG24	139 F3
Eton Gr NG8	172 A2
Eton Rd NG2	185 F3
Eucalyptus Ave NG11	184 B1
Eugene Gdns NG2	173 E1
Eugene St NG2	223 F1
Europa Way NG2	185 E2
Evelyn St NG2	100 B2
Evans Rd NG6	160 B2
Evedon Wlk NG11	147 D1
Evelyn St Beeston NG9	184 A4
11 Nottingham NG2	173 F2
Eversley Wlk NG5	161 D4
Everton City Prim Sch DN10	11 D2
Everton Sluice La DN10	11 E2
Everton St NG19	87 F1
Evesham Ct NG9	183 D1
Evesham Mews 7 S80	35 F1
Ewart Rd NG7	173 D4
Ewe Lamb Cl NG9	170 C1
Ewe Lamb La NG9	170 C1
Ewell Rd NG8	171 F3
Exbourne Rd NG8	159 F1
Exbury Gdns NG2	185 D2
Exchange Rd NG2	185 F4
Exchange Row 12 NG18	102 A4
Exchange St NG22	39 F4
Exchange Wlk NG1	223 E2
Exe Fold NG19	88 B1
Exeter Cl Carlton NG4	162 C1
East Leake LE12	205 E1
Exeter Rd	
Nottingham NG7	173 D4
West Bridgford NG2	185 F3
Export Dr NG17	113 F4
Exton Rd NG5	161 D2
Eyam Cl Beeston NG9	171 E1
Eyam Rd NG18	103 D3
Eyre St NG2	173 F2
Eyres Gdns DE7	157 F1
Eyres La NG11	205 D4

F

Fabis Dr NG11	184 C1
Fackley Rd NG17	100 B3
Fackley Way NG17	100 B3
Factory La	
Beeston NG9	183 F4
Ilkeston DE7	157 F1
Factory St 6 LE11	220 B2
Factory Yd NG2	101 D2
Failsworth Cl NG11	184 C2
Fair Lea Cl NG10	193 E3
Fair Vale NG23	110 A4
Fair View NG19	89 D1
Fairbank Cres NG5	161 E1
Fairburn Cl NG8	171 E2
Faircroft Ave NG10	182 A3
Fairdale Dr NG16	144 A1
Fairfax Cl	
Gainsborough DN21	24 C3
Nottingham NG7	160 C1
Fairfield DN22	39 F2
Fairfield Ave	
Radcliffe on Trent NG24	139 D3
Hilcote DE55	99 E1
New Balderton NG24	140 B3
Fairfield Cl	
Nether Langwith NG20	59 D2
Nottingham NG11	185 D3
Fairfield Cres NG10	193 D2
Fairfield Dr	
Mansfield NG18	103 D4
Ravenshead NG15	116 B2
Fairfield Prep Sch LE11	220 A2
Fairfield Prim Sch NG9	182 B3
Fairfield Rd NG17	101 D2
Fairfield St NG13	177 F2
Fairham Ave NG11	195 D1
Fairham Cl NG11	196 A4
Fairham Com Coll NG11	195 F4
Fairham Dr NG8	172 B2
Fairham Rd NG12	197 E2
Fairhaven NG17	115 D2
Fairholme Cl NG21	89 F1
Fairholme Dr NG19	87 F1
Fairisle Cl NG11	185 D1
Fairland Cres NG2	185 F2
Fairlawn Pl NG5	161 E1
Fairlawns NG18	103 D4
Fair Lea Ave NG19	101 E3
Fairlight Way NG5	161 D4
Fairmaid Gr NG7	184 C1
Fairmead Cl NG3	174 A4
Fairnley Rd NG8	171 E4
Fairview Ave NG16	128 C1

Fairview Ct NG11	185 E1
Fairview Rd NG5	161 F2
Fairway Keyworth NG12	198 A1
Newark-on-T NG24	139 E3
Retford DN22	39 E2
Fairway Ave DN11	15 D2
Fairway Cres NG13	177 D4
Fairway Dr	
Beeston NG9	183 E3
Nottingham NG6	160 B4
Fairway The NG4	162 C2
Fairways Dr NG17	114 C2
Fairways The NG19	88 B3
Fairweather Cl NG22	77 F3
Fal Paddock NG19	88 B1
Falcon Cl Eagle LN6	84 B2
Nottingham NG7	222 A2
Falcon Ct DE7	157 E1
Falcon Gr NG7	161 D1
Falcon St	
Loughborough LE11	220 B3
6 Nottingham NG7	161 D1
Falconers Wlk 8 NG5	161 E4
Falconwood Gdns NG11	184 B1
Fallow Cl	
Nottingham NG7	184 C1
Retford DN22	29 F1
Fallow Ct S81	36 A4
Falston Rd NG8	172 A4
Falstone Ave NG24	140 A3
Far Back La NG22	119 F3
Far Croft Ave NG17	100 B2
Far Holme La NG23	97 D4
Far La LE12	213 E2
Far New Cl NG10	182 A3
Far Pasture Cl NG12	197 F1
Far Rd NG22	67 E2
Far Rye NG8	171 F3
Far St Bradmore NG11	196 C2
Wymeswold LE12	216 B2
Faraday Ave NG22	66 A2
Faraday Ct NG7	170 C1
Faraday Rd	
Mansfield NG18	102 C3
Nottingham NG7	222 A2
Farfield Ave NG9	183 F4
Farfield Gr NG9	183 F4
Farfield Rd DE7	170 A4
Farleys La NG15	146 A4
Farm Ave NG15	145 E2
Farm Cl	
East Bridgford NG13	165 E2
Ilkeston DE7	170 A4
Long Eaton NG10	193 F3
Nottingham NG7	184 C1
Farm Croft Rd NG19	88 B3
Farm Gr S81	36 A4
Farm La NG2	65 F4
Farm Rd Arnold NG5	162 A4
Beeston NG9	183 E1
Farm View NG22	39 F2
Farm View Rd NG17	115 E3
Farmer St NG11	196 C2
Farmhouse Cl NG13	181 E2
Farmilo Cres NG19	87 E1
Farmilo Prim Sch NG19	87 E2
Farmway NG19	88 B1
Farnborough Comp Sch NG11	185 D1
Farnborough Rd NG11	185 D1
Farndale S81	36 A4
Farndale Cl	
Long Eaton NG10	193 D3
Sutton in A NG17	100 C3
Farndale Dr NG8	171 D2
Farndale Rd NG17	100 C3
Farndon Dr NG9	182 C2
Farndon Gn NG8	172 B2
Farndon Gr S81	35 E4
Farndon Rd	
Newark-on-T NG24, NG23	139 E3
Sutton in A NG17	101 E1
Farndon Way NG19	101 F4
Farnes Ct S81	36 A3
Farnham Rd 6 LE11	220 A1
Farnsfield Ave NG14	164 A3
Farnsfield Ct NG18	103 D2
Farnsfield Endowed CE Prim Sch NG22	119 F3
Farnsfield Rd	
Blisthorpe NG22	105 F3
Blidworth NG21	106 A2
Farnsworth Ave NG21	103 F1
Farnsworth Cl NG16	145 D1
Farr Way NG21	118 A2
Farrar Cl NG24	125 D1
Farrendale Cl NG19	88 B1
Farrier Croft DE7	157 E2
Farriers Gn NG11	184 B1
Farringdon Cl NG8	159 E2
Farthing Ct NG10	193 D4
Farthingate NG25	136 C4
Farthingate Cl NG25	136 C4
Farthings The LE12	213 D1
Farwells Cl NG6	160 B2
Faulconbridge Cl NG6	160 A3
Fawcett St DN21	15 E1
Fearn Chase NG4	174 C4
Fearn Cl DE72	193 D4
Fearnleigh Dr NG6	160 B1
Fearon Cl NG4	164 C3
Featherbed La S80	34 C1
Featherston Ave S80	36 A1

Featherstone Cl	
Carlton NG4	162 B2
Mansfield NG18	101 E2
Feignes Ct NG12	197 F2
Felen Cl NG5	161 D4
Fell Croft NG24	139 D3
Fell Side NG5	162 A3
Fell Wilson St NG20	74 B2
Fellbarrow Cl NG2	186 B4
Felley Ave NG17	114 C1
Felley Mill La N NG16	129 E1
Felley Priory Gdn* NG16	129 E4
Fellows Rd NG9	183 F4
Fellows Yd NG12	197 F4
Fellside Cl NG2	186 B3
Felly Cl NG15	145 F3
Felly Mill La S NG16	129 D1
Felstead Ct NG9	171 E1
Felton Ave NG19	88 B3
Felton Cl NG9	183 D3
Felton Rd NG2	173 E1
Fen La Balderton NG24	141 D2
Balderton NG23	155 E2
Fenchurch Cl NG5	147 D1
Fenimore Ct NG12	176 A2
Fennel St LE11	220 A2
Fenroth Cl NG6	159 F4
Fenton Cl NG24	125 D1
Fenton Dr NG6	146 B1
Fenton Rd	
Fenton NG23	142 B1
Nottingham NG6	160 C2
Fenwick Cl NG8	159 F1
Fenwick Rd NG8	159 F1
Fenwick St NG20	74 A2
Ferguson Ave NG19	88 A2
Ferguson Cl 1 NG9	183 E1
Fern Ave NG14	161 D1
Fern Bank Ave NG12	186 A4
Fern Cl Beeston NG9	183 E4
Bilsthorpe NG22	106 A3
Ravenshead NG15	117 D1
Shirebrook NG20	72 C2
Fern Cres NG16	143 E2
Fern Lea Ave NG12	187 F1
Fern Rd NG12	189 D2
Fern St NG17	100 B2
Ferndale Cl	
Beeston NG9	183 F1
New Ollerton NG22	77 F3
Ferndale Gr NG3	174 A3
Ferndale Rd NG3	174 A3
Ferndene Dr NG10	193 D4
Ferngill Cl 17 NG2	173 D1
Fernleigh Ave NG3	162 A1
Fernleigh Rise NG19	88 B1
Fernwood Cl NG19	89 D1
Fernwood Comp Sch NG8	171 E2
Fernwood Cres NG8	171 E2
Fernwood Dr NG12	175 F2
Fernwood Inf Sch (Russell Annexe) NG8	171 F2
Fernwood Jun & Inf Sch NG8	171 E2
Ferny Hollow Cl NG5	160 C4
Ferous Cl NG11	195 F4
Ferrers Wlk NG3	173 F3
Ferriby Terr 20 NG2	173 E1
Ferry Farm Ctry Pk* NG14	151 F1
Ferry La Everton DN10	11 E2
North Muskham NG23	110 C1
Festival Ave DN11	9 D2
Festival Dr LE11	220 A1
Festus Cl NG3	223 F4
Festus St Carlton NG4	175 D4
Kirkby in A NG17	115 D2
Field Ave NG15	145 E2
Field Cl Beeston NG9	183 D2
Carlton NG4	162 C1
Mansfield Woodhouse NG19	88 B3
Worksop S81	36 A4
Field Dr	
Balderton NG24	140 C1
Shirebrook NG20	72 C1
Field End Cl LE12	205 E1
Field House Cl NG8	171 E3
Field La	
Ault Hucknall NG, S44	86 B3
Beeston NG9	183 D2
Blidworth NG21	117 F2
Cropwell Bishop NG12	189 D2
Morton DN21	15 D2
Woodborough NG14	149 E3
Field Mill (Mansfield Town FC) NG18	102 A3
Field The DE75	157 D3
Field View	
South Normanton DE55	113 D4
Sutton in A NG17	100 B1
Fielden Ave NG19	87 E1
Fieldfare Dr S81	35 E4
Fields Ave NG11	196 B3
Fields Dr NG13	178 C3
Fields Farm Rd NG10	193 F3
Fieldway NG11	185 D2
Fiennes Cres NG7	222 C1
Fifth Ave Beeston NG9	184 B3
Clipstone NG21	89 F2
Edwinstowe NG21	75 F1
Mansfield NG19	103 D4
Fiftyeights Rd DN10	1 B2
Filey St NG6	160 B4

Finch Cl NG7	184 C4
Finchley Cl NG11	184 B1
Findern Ct NG18	103 D3
Findern Gn NG3	174 A3
Fingal Cl NG7	184 C1
Fingle St DN22	32 B1
Fingleton S81	36 A3
Finkell St DN10	12 C2
Finley Way DE55	113 D2
Finningley Rd NG18	103 D3
Finsbury Ave	
8 Loughborough LE11	220 B2
Nottingham NG2	173 F2
Finsbury Pk Cl NG2	185 E3
Finsbury Rd	
Beeston NG9	171 E2
Nottingham NG5	147 D1
Fir Cl Nottingham NG6	159 F4
Shirebrook NG20	72 B3
Fir Dale NG12	188 A2
Fir Tree Cl NG19	89 E1
Fir View NG22	77 E3
Firbank Ct NG9	183 D3
Firbeck Ave NG18	102 C3
Firbeck Cres S81	16 C2
Firbeck Prim Sch NG8	171 D2
Fircroft Ave NG8	171 F4
Fircroft Dr NG15	145 E3
Firecrest Way NG6	160 B2
Firemans Row NG17	100 C1
Firs Ave NG9	183 F4
Firs Rd NG12	186 A2
Firs St NG10	193 D2
Firs The 8 NG5	161 E2
Firsby Rd NG8	159 F1
First Ave Beeston NG9	184 B3
Carlton, Colwick NG4	174 C3
Carlton, Gedling NG4	162 C1
Carlton, Thorneywood NG4	174 B4
Clipstone NG21	90 A2
Edwinstowe NG21	76 A1
Mansfield NG21	103 F1
Mansfield Woodhouse NG19	89 D1
Nottingham NG6	160 A4
First Holme La NG23	97 E3
Firth Cl NG5	148 B1
Firth Dr NG9	183 E1
Firth Rd DN22	39 E4
Firth Way NG6	146 A1
Fish Pond Dr NG7	223 D1
Fisher Ave NG5	161 F3
Fisher Cl	
Collingham NG23	98 A1
East Leake LE12	205 F1
Fisher Ct DE7	157 F2
Fisher Gate NG1	223 F2
Fisher La	
Bingham NG13	177 F2
Mansfield NG18	102 B3
Fisher St 17 NG7	172 C4
Fishers St NG17	115 D1
Fishpool Rd NG21	117 E2
Fiskerton Ct NG18	103 D2
Fiskerton Rd	
Rolleston NG23	138 A3
Southwell NG25	137 D3
Fiskerton Sta NG25	137 F2
Fitzherbert St NG20	74 B2
Five Acres NG11	185 D2
Five Fields Cl DN22	40 A2
Five Fields La DN22	40 A2
Flagholme NG12	187 F1
Flamingo Ct 11 NG2	173 D1
Flamstead Ave NG4	163 D4
Flamstead Rd DE7	157 F1
Flamsteed Rd NG8	159 E1
Flash La NG22	93 D4
Flat La S81	16 A3
Flatts La	
Calverton NG14	133 F1
Westwood NG16	128 B2
Flatts The NG9	183 E1
Flawforth Ave NG11	196 B3
Flawforth La NG11	196 C4
Flaxendale NG12	188 A1
Flaxton Way NG5	160 C4
Fleam Rd NG11	184 C2
Fleeman Gr NG2	174 A1
Fleet Cl NG7	172 B3
Fleetway S81	35 F4
Fleetway Cl NG16	144 A1
Fleetwith Cl NG2	186 B3
Fleming Ave	
Bottesford NG13	181 E2
Tollerton NG22	66 A2
Fleming Cl NG16	159 D4
Fleming Dr	
Carlton NG4	174 B4
Newark-on-T NG24	125 D2
Woodbeck DN22	53 D3
Fleming Gdns NG11	184 B1
Fletcher Ct NG22	119 F4
Fletcher Gate NG1	223 E2
Fletcher Rd NG9	184 A4
Fletcher St NG10	182 C2
Fletcher Terr NG3	161 F1
Fletcher Way NG19	103 D4
Flewitt Gdns NG3	173 F3
Flint Ave NG5	88 C1
Flintham Dr NG5	161 E2
Flintham La NG23	166 C3
Flintham Mus* NG23	153 D1

Flintham Prim Sch NG23	153 D1
Flixton Rd NG16	158 C4
Flood Rd The DN21	24 A4
Floral Villas NG23	96 C2
Florence Ave NG10	182 C1
Florence Boot Cl NG9	184 A4
Florence Cres NG4	175 D4
Florence Ct DE7	157 F1
Florence Gr NG3	174 A4
Florence Rd	
Carlton NG4	175 D4
Nottingham NG3	162 A1
West Bridgford NG2	186 A4
Florence St NG15	146 A3
Florence Terr DN21	24 B4
Florey Ct NG7	172 C1
Florey Wlk NG11	195 E4
Florin Gdns NG10	193 D3
Floss La DN22	43 E2
Flowers Cl NG5	162 A3
Flying Horse Wlk NG1	223 E2
Foljambe Terr NG3	223 F3
Folkton Gdns NG3	161 F1
Folly Hall La LE12	212 B1
Folly La Besthorpe NG23	98 A4
Stapleford LN6	112 C3
Folly Nook La DN22	19 D3
Fonton Hall Dr NG17	114 A4
Forbes Cl NG10	193 F3
Ford La NG23	109 D3
Ford St NG7	161 D1
Ford St N NG7	161 D1
Fordbridge La DE55	113 D4
Fordham Gn NG11	195 E4
Foredrift Cl NG11	195 D1
Forest Ave NG18	102 B3
Forest Cl	
Annesley Woodhouse NG17	130 A4
Cotgrave NG12	187 F2
Rainworth NG21	104 B1
Selston NG16	129 D4
Forest Ct	
Mansfield NG18	103 D4
Nottingham NG7	222 C3
Forest Fields Prim Sch NG7	173 D4
Forest Gdns NG15	130 A4
Forest Glade Prim Sch NG21	101 D2
Forest Gr NG7	222 C4
Forest Hill NG18	102 B3
Forest Hill Rd S81	36 A4
Forest La	
Papplewick NG15	131 F2
Walesby NG22	63 F2
Worksop S80	36 B1
Forest Link NG22	105 F3
Forest Rd	
Annesley Woodhouse NG17	130 A4
Bingham NG13	177 E2
Blidworth NG21	118 A3
Calverton NG14	148 B4
Clipstone NG21	89 F2
Loughborough LE11	220 A2
Mansfield NG18	102 B3
Market Warsop NG20	74 B1
New Ollerton NG22	77 E2
Oxton NG25	134 A3
Sutton in A NG17	101 D3
Forest Rd E NG1	173 D4
Forest Rd W NG7	222 C4
Forest Rise NG20	74 B1
Forest Sch NG17	173 D4
Forest St	
Annesley Woodhouse NG17	130 A4
Kirkby in A NG17	115 D2
Sutton in A NG17	100 C1
Forest Town Prim Sch NG19	89 D1
Forest View	
New Ollerton NG22	77 D2
Retford DN22	39 E2
Forest View Dr NG15	145 F4
Forest View Jun Sch NG22	77 D2
Forester Cl NG9	183 E2
Forester Gr NG4	174 B4
Forester Rd NG3	174 A4
Forester St NG4	175 D4
Forewood La DN22	42 A2
Forge Ave NG14	148 C4
Forge Cl	
South Muskham NG23	124 C4
Sutton on T NG23	96 C4
Forge Hill NG9	183 E2
Forge Mill Gr NG15	146 B3
Forge The NG7	170 A3
Forman St NG1	223 E3
Forrests Yd S80	35 F1
Forster Ave NG24	139 F3
Forster St	
Gainsborough DN21	15 E1
Kirkby in A NG17	114 C3
Nottingham NG7	222 A3
Forsythia Gdns NG7	172 C1
Fosbrooke Dr NG10	193 E3
Fossdyke Gdns LN1	57 D2
Fosse Gr LN1	57 D2
Fosse Rd NG24, NG23	139 D2
Fosse Wlk NG12	188 A1
Fossetts Ave NG16	128 C4

Foster Ave NG9 . . . . .183 F3
Foster Rd NG23 . . . . .98 A1
Foster St NG18 . . . . .102 B3
Fosters Dr NG5 . . . . .161 E2
Fosters La NG13 . . . . .177 F2
Foston Cl NG21 . . . . .103 D3
Fothergill Cl **3** NG3 . . . .173 E4
Foundry Cl NG24 . . . . . . .124 C1
Fountain Dale Ct **16**
NG3 . . . . .173 E4
Fountain Hill DN10 . . . . . .13 E4
Fountain Hill Rd DN10 . .13 E4
Fountaindale Specl Sch
NG18 . . . . .116 B3
Fountains Cl
Kirkby in A NG17 . . . . . .115 E3
West Bridgford NG2 . . . .186 A3
Fourth Ave
Beeston NG9 . . . . .184 B3
Carlton NG4 . . . . .174 B4
Clipstone NG21 . . . . .89 F2
Edwinstowe NG21 . . . . . .76 A1
Mansfield NG19 . . . . . . .103 D4
Rainworth NG21 . . . . . . .103 F1
Fowler St NG3 . . . . .173 E4
Fox Cl NG10 . . . . .193 E3
Fox Covert
Carlton NG4 . . . . .174 C4
3 Loughborough LE11 . .220 A3
Fox Covert Cl NG17 . . . .100 B1
Fox Covert La
Misterton DN10 . . . . . . .14 A4
Nottingham NG11 . . . . . .185 D4
Fox Covert Way NG19 . .103 D4
Fox Gr NG5 . . . . .160 C2
Fox Gr Ct NG6 . . . . .160 C2
Fox Hill NG17 . . . . .187 F1
Fox Mdw NG15 . . . . .145 F3
Fox Rd Nottingham NG2 . .173 F1
Whitwell S80 . . . . .45 D3
Fox St
Annesley Woodhouse
NG17 . . . . .130 A4
Sutton in A NG17 . . . . . .100 C2
Foxby Hill DN21 . . . . .24 C3
Foxby La DN21 . . . . .24 C3
Foxearth Ave NG11 . . . . .185 D1
Foxes Cl NG7 . . . . .222 C1
Foxglove Cl
New Balderton NG24 . . . .140 B2
Worksop S80 . . . . .36 A1
Foxglove Rd NG16 . . . . . .158 A4
Foxgloves The NG13 . . . .177 E2
Foxhall Rd NG7 . . . . .173 D4
Foxhill Cl NG17 . . . . .100 A2
Foxhill Ct NG4 . . . . .174 C4
Foxhill Rd
Burton Joyce NG14 . . . . .163 F3
Carlton NG4 . . . . .174 B4
Foxhill Rd Central
NG4 . . . . .174 B4
Foxhill Rd E NG4 . . . . . . .174 B4
Foxhill Rd W NG4 . . . . . .174 A4
Foxhills DE74 . . . . .203 E1
Foxhollies Gr NG5 . . . . . .161 D2
Foxton Cl NG6 . . . . .159 F4
Foxwood Cl S81 . . . . .25 E1
Foxwood Foundation Specl
Sch NG9 . . . . .171 D1
Foxwood Gr NG14 . . . . . .148 C4
Foxwood La NG14 . . . . . .149 D3
Fradley Cl NG6 . . . . .146 B1
Frampton Rd NG8 . . . . . .172 A4
Frances Gr NG15 . . . . . . .131 D1
Frances St NG16 . . . . 128 B1
Francis Chichester Wlk
DN21 . . . . .24 C4
Francis Gr NG6 . . . . .160 C2
Francis Rd NG4 . . . . .174 C4
Francis St
Mansfield NG18 . . . . . . .102 C4
Nottingham NG7 . . . . . .222 C4
Francklin Rd NG14 . . . . . .150 B1
Franderground Dr
NG17 . . . . .114 C3
Frank Ave NG18 . . . . .101 F3
Franklin Cl NG5 . . . . .161 E4
Franklin Dr NG12 . . . . . . .186 B1
Franklin Rd NG16 . . . . . .128 A2
Franklyn Gdns
Keyworth NG12 . . . . . . .197 F2
Nottingham NG8 . . . . . .172 B3
Fraser Cres NG4 . . . . . . .162 A1
Fraser Rd Carlton NG4 . .162 A1
Nottingham NG2 . . . . . .173 E1
Fraser Sq NG4 . . . . .162 A1
Fraser St NG15 . . . . .130 B3
Frearson Farm Ct
NG16 . . . . .143 F1
Freckingham St NG1 . . . .223 F2
Freda Ave NG4 . . . . .162 B1
Freda Cl NG4 . . . . .162 B2
Frederick Ave
Carlton NG4 . . . . .174 A4
Ilkeston DE7 . . . . .170 A3
Kegworth DE74 . . . . . . .203 E2
Kirkby in A NG17 . . . . . .114 C4
Frederick Gent Sch
DE55 . . . . .113 D3
Frederick Harrison Inf Sch
NG9 . . . . .182 C4
Frederick Rd NG9 . . . . . .182 B4
Frederick St
Long Eaton NG10 . . . . . .193 F4
Loughborough LE11 . . . .220 A2

Frederick St continued
Mansfield NG18 . . . . . . .102 B3
Retford DN22 . . . . .39 F3
Sutton in A NG17 . . . . . .100 B1
Worksop S80 . . . . .35 F2
Freeby Ave NG19 . . . . . . .88 B3
Freehold St LE11 . . . . . . .220 B2
Freeland Cl NG9 . . . . . . .182 C2
Freemans La DN22 . . . . . .32 B3
Freemans Rd NG4 . . . . . .175 D4
Freemans Terr NG4 . . . . .175 D4
Freemantle Wlk NG5 . . . .160 C4
Freeston Dr NG6 . . . . . . .159 F4
Freeth St NG2 . . . . .173 F1
Freeth St **5** NG2 . . . . . .173 F1
Fremount Dr NG8 . . . . . .172 A4
French St DE7 . . . . .170 A3
French Terr NG20 . . . . . . .59 D1
Fretwell St **3** NG7 . . . . .172 C4
Friar La
Market Warsop NG20 . . . .74 B1
Nottingham NG1 . . . . . .223 D2
Friar St
Long Eaton NG10 . . . . . .193 E4
12 Nottingham NG7 . .172 C1
Friar Wlk NG13 . . . . .177 E4
Friars Cl NG16 . . . . .129 D4
Friars Cres NG24 . . . . . . .139 F3
Friars Ct NG7 . . . . .222 C1
Friary Cl **14** NG7 . . . . . .172 C1
Friary Gdns NG24 . . . . . .139 F3
Friary Rd **2** NG24 . . . . .140 A4
Friary The NG7 . . . . .172 C1
Friday La NG4 . . . . .162 C1
Friend La NG21 . . . . .76 A1
Frinton Rd NG8 . . . . .159 F1
Frisby Ave NG10 . . . . . . .193 F3
Fritchley Ct NG18 . . . . . .103 D3
Frith Gr NG19 . . . . .101 F4
Frithwood La S80 . . . . . . .58 B4
Frobisher Gdns NG5 . . . .161 E3
Frog La NG13 . . . . .202 C4
Frogmore St NG1 . . . . . .223 E4
Front St
Barnby in t W NG24 . . . .141 F3
East Stockwith DN21 . . . .7 E1
Morton DN21 . . . . .15 D2
South Clifton NG23 . . . . .68 C1
Frost Ave NG16 . . . . .143 D2
Fryar Rd NG16 . . . . .143 F2
Fulford Ave DN22 . . . . . . .39 E4
Fulforth St NG1 . . . . .223 E4
Fuller Cl NG18 . . . . .102 A2
Fuller St NG11 . . . . .196 B3
Fullwood Ave **11** DE7 . .157 F1
Fullwood Cl NG9 . . . . . . .183 E2
Fullwood St **16** DE7 . . .157 F1
Fulmar Way NG18 . . . . . . .35 E4
Fulwood Cres NG8 . . . . . .160 A1
Fulwood Dr NG10 . . . . . .193 D4
Fulwood Rd N
Huthwaite NG17 . . . . . . .99 F1
Sutton in A NG17 . . . . . .114 A4
Fulwood Rd S NG17 . . . .114 A4
Fulwood Rise NG17 . . . . .114 A4
Furlong Ave NG5 . . . . . . .161 F4
Furlong Cl NG9 . . . . .182 B4
Furlong St NG5 . . . . .161 F4
Furnace Rd DE7 . . . . . . .170 A3
Furness Cl NG2 . . . . .186 A4
Furness Rd NG6 . . . . . . .160 B2
Furnival St S80 . . . . .36 A1
Furze Gdns NG3 . . . . . . .173 E4
Furze The NG22 . . . . .78 B3
Furzebrook Rd NG4 . . . . .162 C1
Fylde Cl NG9 . . . . .182 C1
Fylingdale Way NG8 . . . .171 E2

G

Gables Farm Dr LE12 . . . .206 B1
Gables Lea LE12 . . . . . . .213 D3
Gabor Cl NG11 . . . . .195 E4
Gabrielle Cl NG6 . . . . . . .160 B2
Gadd St NG7 . . . . .222 B4
Gaddick View NG22 . . . . . .79 F3
Gadsby Cl DE7 . . . . .170 A2
Gainas Ave DN21 . . . . . . .15 E1
Gainsborough Central Sta
DN21 . . . . .24 B4
Gainsborough Cl
Kinoulton NG12 . . . . . . .199 F1
Long Eaton NG10 . . . . . .193 F3
Stapleford NG9 . . . . . . .182 C3
Gainsborough Dr
NG24 . . . . .125 D2
Gainsborough Rd
Bawtry DN10 . . . . .10 A3
Everton DN10 . . . . .11 E1
Girton NG23 . . . . .82 C1
Gainsborough in t P DN10 .12 B1
Lea DN21 . . . . .24 C1
North Wheatley DN22 . . .22 C1
Saundby DN22 . . . . .23 E3
Saxilby LN1 . . . . .56 C1
Sturton le S DN22 . . . . .32 B3
Winthorpe NG24 . . . . . .125 E3
Gainsford Cl NG5 . . . . . .160 C3
Gainsford Cres NG5 . . . .160 C3
Gaitskell Cres NG21 . . . . .76 B1
Gaitskell Way NG24 . . . . .140 C2
Gala Way NG5 . . . . .160 C3
Gale Cl NG9 . . . . .184 A3
Galen Ave DN21 . . . . .42 A1
Galen Ct **6** NG7 . . . . . .172 C1
Galena Dr NG3 . . . . .174 A4

Galleries of Justice*
NG1 . . . . .223 F2
Galley Hill Rd NG25 . . . . .122 A1
Gallows Inn Cl DE7 . . . . .170 A3
Galway Ave DN11 . . . . . . .9 E3
Galway Cres DN22 . . . . . .39 E4
Galway Dr DN11 . . . . .9 E3
Galway Rd Arnold NG5 . .161 F4
Bircotes DN11 . . . . .9 E3
Nottingham NG7 . . . . . .222 B1
Gamage Cl NG24 . . . . . . .140 C2
Gamble St NG7 . . . . .222 C3
Gamston CE Prim Sch
DN22 . . . . .50 C3
Gamston Cres NG5 . . . . .161 E2
Gamston Lings Bar Rd
NG2 . . . . .186 B2
Gamston Rd NG18 . . . . . .103 D2
Ganton Cl DN11 . . . . .8 A4
Ganton Cl NG3 . . . . .161 F1
Garden Ave
Carlton NG4 . . . . .174 B4
New Houghton NG19 . . . .86 C4
Ranmworth NG21 . . . . . .104 A1
Shirebrook NG20 . . . . . . .72 C2
Garden City NG4 . . . . . . .174 C4
Garden La NG17 . . . . . . .101 D2
Garden Rd
Bingham NG13 . . . . .177 E2
Eastwood NG16 . . . . . . .144 A2
Hucknall NG15 . . . . .145 F4
5 Mansfield NG18 . . . .102 A3
Garden Row DE74 . . . . . .203 E2
Garden St NG7 . . . . .222 B3
Gardendale Ave NG11 . . .184 B1
Gardenia Cres NG3 . . . . .162 A1
Gardenia Gr NG3 . . . . . . .162 A1
Gardens Ct NG2 . . . . . . .186 A4
Gardiner Terr NG17 . . . . .100 B3
Gardinia Cl NG9 . . . . .183 D1
Gardner Dr NG12 . . . . . . .199 F2
Garfield Cl NG9 . . . . .170 C1
Garfield Rd NG7 . . . . .222 B3
Garforth Cl NG8 . . . . . . .160 A4
Garibaldi Comp Sch
NG16 . . . . .89 E1
Garibaldi Cl NG16 . . . . . .89 E1
Garner St NG3 . . . . .173 F3
Garnet Ct NG3 . . . . .174 A4
Garner St NG4 . . . . .174 C4
Garnon St NG18 . . . . . . .101 F3
Garratt Ave NG18 . . . . . .102 B4
Garrett Gr NG11 . . . . . . .184 B1
Garsdale Cl NG2 . . . . . . .186 B4
Garsdale Dr NG11 . . . . . .185 D2
Garside St S80 . . . . .36 A2
Garth Ave NG17 . . . . . . .114 C4
Garth Rd NG18 . . . . .102 A4
Garton Cl Beeston NG9 . .183 D3
Nottingham NG6 . . . . . .160 A3
Garton Rd LE11 . . . . .220 A2
Garwick Cl NG19 . . . . . . .89 D1
Gas St NG10 . . . . .182 B3
Gas Wlk LE14 . . . . .202 A2
Gatcombe Cl NG12 . . . . .176 A2
Gatcombe Gr NG10 . . . . .182 A2
Gateford Ave S81 . . . . . . .35 E3
Gateford Cl
Beeston NG9 . . . . .171 E1
Worksop S81 . . . . .35 E4
Gateford Dr S81 . . . . .35 E3
Gateford Gdns S81 . . . . .35 E3
Gateford Glade S81 . . . . .35 E3
Gateford Ind Est S81 . . . .35 D3
Gateford Pk Prim Sch
S81 . . . . .35 F4
Gateford Rd S81, S80 . . .35 E3
Gateford Rise S81 . . . . . .35 E4
Gateside Rd NG2 . . . . . . .173 D1
Gatling St NG7 . . . . .222 A3
Gattlys La NG22 . . . . .77 D2
Gaul St NG6 . . . . .160 A4
Gauntley Ct **1** NG7 . . . .172 C4
Gauntley St NG7 . . . . . . .172 C4
Gautries Cl NG5 . . . . . . .161 D4
Gawthorne St NG7 . . . . . .161 D1
Gayhurst Gn NG6 . . . . . . 160 C3
Gayhurst Rd NG6 . . . . . . 160 C3
Gaynor Cl NG8 . . . . .172 A3
Gayrigg Ct NG9 . . . . .183 D2
Gayton Cl NG8 . . . . .171 E4
Gaywood Cl NG11 . . . . . .195 F4
Gedling Comp Sch
NG4 . . . . .162 C2
Gedling Gr NG7 . . . . .222 C4
Gedling Rd Arnold NG5 . .162 A3
Carlton NG4 . . . . .174 C4
Gedling St
Mansfield NG18 . . . . . . .102 A3
Nottingham NG1 . . . . . .223 F2
Gedling Gr NG3 . . . . .173 F4
Gedling Rd NG5 . . . . .161 F4
Gell Rd NG9 . . . . .183 D2
George Ave
Beeston NG9 . . . . .183 F3
Long Eaton NG10 . . . . . .182 C1
George Dere Cl NG22 . . . .77 E3
George Rd Carlton NG4 . .174 C4
West Bridgford NG2 . . . .185 F4
George Spencer Foundation
Sch & Tech Coll NG9 . .182 C3
George St Arnold NG5 . . .161 F3
Gainsborough DN21 . . . .15 D1
Hucknall NG15 . . . . .146 A4
Langley Mill NG16 . . . . .143 D2
Mansfield NG19 . . . . . . .101 F4

George St continued
Mansfield Woodhouse
NG19 . . . . .88 B2
Mansfield Woodhouse,
Forest Town NG19 . . . . .89 D1
Market Warsop NG20 . . . .74 A2
Market Warsop, Spion Cop
NG20 . . . . .73 F1
Newark-on-T NG24 . . . . .125 D1
Nottingham NG1 . . . . . .223 E3
Pinxton NG16 . . . . .113 E2
Retford DN22 . . . . .39 F3
Sutton in A NG17 . . . . . .100 A2
Whaley Thorns NG20 . . . .59 D1
Worksop S80 . . . . .35 F2
George Yd **17** LE11 . . . .220 A2
Georges La NG14 . . . . . . .148 B3
Georgia Dr NG5 . . . . .147 F1
Georgina Rd NG9 . . . . . . .183 F3
Gerrard Cl NG5 . . . . .147 D1
Gerrard Cres DE74 . . . . .203 E1
Gertrude Rd NG2 . . . . . . .174 A1
Gervase Gdns NG11 . . . .184 B1
Ghest Villas S81 . . . . .16 C1
Ghost House La NG9 . . . .183 D2
Gibb St NG10 . . . . .193 F4
Gibbet Hill La DN10 . . . . . .9 F2
Gibbons Ave NG9 . . . . . . .182 B3
Gibbons Rd NG18 . . . . . .101 F3
Gibbons St NG7 . . . . .172 C1
Gibdyke DN10 . . . . .4 B2
Gibson Cres NG24 . . . . . .140 B2
Gibson Rd NG7 . . . . .173 D4
Gibsons La LE14 . . . . . . .218 B1
Gifford Gdns NG2 . . . . . .173 D1
Gilbert Ave
Gotham NG11 . . . . .195 D1
Tuxford NG22 . . . . .66 A2
Gilbert Gdns NG3 . . . . . .174 A3
Gilbert Rd DN11 . . . . .9 D2
Gilcroft St
Mansfield NG18 . . . . . . .102 B3
Sutton in A NG17 . . . . . .100 C3
Gilead St NG6 . . . . .160 A4
Giles Ave NG2 . . . . .185 E3
Gill Gn Wlk DN22 . . . . . . .30 B2
Gill St Nottingham NG1 . .223 D4
Selston NG16 . . . . .129 D3
Sutton in A NG17 . . . . . .100 B1
Gillercomb Cl NG2 . . . . . .186 B3
Gilles The NG19 . . . . .101 F3
Gilliver La NG12 . . . . .187 E1
Gillot St DE75 . . . . .157 D4
Gillotts Cl NG13 . . . . .177 F3
Gilpet Ave NG3 . . . . .173 F4
Gilstrap Cl NG24 . . . . . . .140 B4
Gilstrap Mus* NG24 . . . .124 C1
Gilt Hill NG16 . . . . .158 B4
Giltbrook Cres NG16 . . . .158 B4
Gilthill Prim Sch
NG16 . . . . .158 B4
Giltway NG16 . . . . .158 B4
Gimson Cl DE7 . . . . .157 E2
Gin Cl Way NG16 . . . . . . .158 B3
Gipsy La NG14 . . . . .152 A4
Girton Cl NG18 . . . . .103 D1
Girton La LN6 . . . . .83 D1
Girton Rd NG6 . . . . .161 D2
Gisburn Cl NG11 . . . . . . .185 D2
Gisburn Gr NG19 . . . . . . .103 D4
Glade Ave NG8 . . . . .172 B3
Glade Hill Prim Sch
NG5 . . . . .161 E4
Glade The NG11 . . . . . . .195 F4
Gladehill Rd NG5 . . . . . . .161 E4
Gladstone Ave
Gotham NG11 . . . . .195 D1
Loughborough LE11 . . . .220 A3
Gladstone Dr NG16 . . . . .143 F4
Gladstone Rd NG24 . . . . .139 F3
Gladstone St
Beeston NG9 . . . . .183 F3
Carlton NG4 . . . . .174 B4
Gainsborough DN21 . . . .15 E1
Hathern LE12 . . . . .213 D1
Kirkby in A NG17 . . . . . .115 D3
Langley Mill NG16 . . . . .143 E2
Long Eaton NG10 . . . . . .193 E3
Loughborough LE11 . . . .220 A3
Mansfield NG18 . . . . . . .102 B4
Mansfield Woodhouse
NG19 . . . . .88 B1
Nottingham NG7 . . . . . .173 D4
South Normanton DE55 . .113 D3
Worksop S80 . . . . .35 F2
Gladstone Terr
3 Kirkby in A NG17 . .114 C3
Mansfield Woodhouse
NG19 . . . . .88 B1
Gladys St NG7 . . . . .161 D1
Glaisdale S81 . . . . .36 A4
Glaisdale Dr E NG8 . . . . .171 E3
Glaisdale Dr W NG8 . . . . .171 E3
Glaisdale Parkway
NG8 . . . . .171 E3
Glaisdale Pk Ind Est
NG8 . . . . .171 E3
Glamis Rd
Carlton in L S81 . . . . . . .25 F3
Nottingham NG5 . . . . . .161 D1
Glannis Sq NG20 . . . . . . .74 B3
Glanton Way NG5 . . . . . .148 A1
Glapton Rd NG11 . . . . . . .184 B1
Glaramara Cl **16** NG2 . .173 D1
Glasby Cl NG22 . . . . .77 D2
Glasshouse St NG1 . . . . .223 E3

Glastonbury Cl NG19 . . . .88 B2
Glaven Cl NG19 . . . . .88 B1
Glebe Ave
Market Warsop NG20 . . . .74 B2
Pinxton NG16 . . . . .113 E2
Glebe Cl
North Wheatley DN22 . . . .31 F4
South Normanton DE55 . .113 D3
Worksop S80 . . . . .35 E2
Glebe Cres DE7 . . . . .170 A4
Glebe Dr NG14 . . . . .163 E2
Glebe Farm Cl NG12 . . . .185 E2
Glebe Farm View NG6 . . .162 C2
Glebe Junc Sch DE55 . . .113 D3
Glebe Pk NG24 . . . . .140 B3
Glebe Rd Carlton NG4 . . .162 B1
Nuthall NG16 . . . . .159 E3
West Bridgford NG2 . . . .185 F4
Glebe St
Annesley Woodhouse
NG17 . . . . .129 F4
Beeston NG9 . . . . .183 F3
Hucknall NG15 . . . . .146 A4
Loughborough LE11 . . . .220 B3
Glebe The
Awsworth NG16 . . . . . . .158 A2
Retford DN22 . . . . .39 E4
Glebe View NG18 . . . . . . .102 C4
Glen Ave NG16 . . . . .144 A1
Glen Cl DE55 . . . . .99 D2
Glen Eagles Way DN22 . .39 E2
Glen Helen NG4 . . . . .174 C3
Glen Moor Cl NG17 . . . . .89 D1
Glen Parva Ave NG5 . . . .147 F1
Glen Rd NG14 . . . . .163 F3
Glen St NG17 . . . . .100 C2
Glen The NG7 . . . . .184 C1
Glenbrook NG12 . . . . . . .188 A2
Glenbrook Cres NG8 . . . .172 A4
Glenbrook Prim Sch
NG8 . . . . .171 F4
Glencairn Dr NG8 . . . . . .172 A4
Glencoe Rd NG11 . . . . . .185 D1
Glencoyne Rd NG11 . . . .195 F4
Glendale Cl NG4 . . . . . . .162 B1
Glendale Ct NG9 . . . . . . .183 F2
Glendale Gdns NG5 . . . . .161 F4
Glendoe Gr NG13 . . . . . .177 E2
Glendon Dr
Hucknall NG15 . . . . .146 A3
Nottingham NG5 . . . . . .161 D2
Gleneagles Cl NG12 . . . .186 B2
Gleneagles Dr
Arnold NG5 . . . . .148 A1
Kirkby in A NG17 . . . . . .114 C4
Glenfield Ave NG16 . . . . .158 B4
Glenfield Rd NG10 . . . . . .193 E3
Glenlivet Gdns NG7 . . . . .184 C1
Glenloch Dr NG11 . . . . . .195 F4
Glenmore Rd NG2 . . . . . .186 A3
Glenorchy Cres NG5 . . . .160 C4
Glenridding Cl NG2 . . . . .186 B3
Glensford Gdns NG5 . . . .146 C1
Glenside Arnold NG5 . . . .162 A3
Glenside Rd NG9 . . . . . . .171 E1
Glenstone Ct **22** NG7 . .172 C4
Glenthorn Cl S81 . . . . . . .34 C4
Glentworth Rd NG7 . . . . .222 A4
Glenwood Ave NG8 . . . . .171 E2
Glinis Rd NG5 . . . . .160 C4
Glossop Ave NG18 . . . . . .103 D3
Gloucester Ave
Beeston NG9 . . . . .183 F3
Nottingham NG7 . . . . . .222 A2
Nuthall NG16 . . . . .159 F2
Sandiacre NG10 . . . . . . .182 A2
Gloucester Rd S81 . . . . . .36 A4
Glover Ave NG8 . . . . .171 E2
Glover Cl DN22 . . . . .42 B3
Glovers La NG24 . . . . . . .140 B2
Goatchurch Ct **3** NG5 . .147 D1
Goathland Cl **12** NG5 . .161 D4
Godber Rd NG15 . . . . . . .145 F3
Godfrey St NG4 . . . . .175 D3
Godfreys Ct S80 . . . . .35 F2
Godkin Dr NG16 . . . . . . .143 D2
Goldcrest Cl NG13 . . . . . .178 A2
Goldcrest Rd NG6 . . . . . .160 A2
Goldenholme La DN22 . . .43 D1
Goldfinch Cl NG18 . . . . . .102 C4
Goldhill Rd NG18 . . . . . . .171 E4
Goldsmith Rd
Balderton NG24 . . . . . . .140 B3
Sutton in A NG17 . . . . . .36 A3
Goldsmith Sq NG1 . . . . . .223 D3
Goldsmith St
Mansfield NG18 . . . . . . .102 A4
Nottingham NG1 . . . . . .223 D3
Goldswong Terr NG3 . . . .173 E4
Goldthorpe Ave S81 . . . . .16 C2
Goldthorpe Cl S81 . . . . . .16 C2
Golf Club Rd DE7 . . . . . .170 A1
Golf Course Rd NG12 . . . .198 A1
Golf Rd NG12 . . . . .176 A2
Gomersall Cl DN22 . . . . . .40 A3
Gonalston La
Epperstone NG14 . . . . . .150 B2
Hoveringham NG14 . . . . .151 E1
Good Shepherd Cath Prim
Sch NG5 . . . . .162 A3
Goodacre St NG18 . . . . . .102 B4
Goodall Cres NG15 . . . . .146 B4
Goodall St **3** NG7 . . . . .172 C4
Goodhand Cres NG18 . . .101 F3
Goodliffe St **16** NG7 . . .172 C4

Goodman CI NG16 ....158 B4
Goodwin CI
  Newark-on-T NG24 ....140 B4
  Sandiacre NG10 ....182 A3
Goodwin Dr NG12 ....119 F4
Goodwin Dr NG16 ....158 C3
Goodwin St NG7 ....222 C4
Goodwood Ave NG5 ......161 F4
Goodwood Dr NG18 ......182 C1
Goodwood Rd NG8 ....171 E2
Goodwood Way NG18 ....102 C4
Goose Gate
  Cotgrave NG12 ....187 F2
  Nottingham NG1 ....223 F2
Goosedale La NG6 ....147 D4
Goosemoor La 39 F2
Gopher Rd NG24 ....139 F3
Gordon Ave NG18 ....102 C3
Gordon Brae NG18 ....102 B2
Gordon CI Beeston NG9 .183 E1
  Farnsfield NG22 ....119 F3
  Worksop S80 ....36 A2
Gordon Cres DE55 ....113 D2
Gordon Rd
  Burton Joyce NG14 ......164 A3
  5 Loughborough LE11 ...220 A3
  Nottingham NG3 ....173 F3
  West Bridgford NG2 .....185 F4
Gordon Rise NG3 ....161 F1
Gordon Sq NG2 ....185 F4
Gordon St
  Gainsborough DN21 ....24 B3
  Ilkeston DE7 ....158 A1
  Nottingham NG6 ....160 B2
Gordondale Rd NG19 .....88 A1
Gorman Ct NG5 ....162 A4
Gorse Ave NG18 ....103 D3
Gorse CI
  Calverton NG14 ....148 B4
  Eastwood NG16 ....158 A4
  Long Eaton NG10 ....182 A1
Gorse Ct NG6 ....160 C3
Gorse Hill NG15 ....117 D1
Gorse Rd
  Keyworth NG12 ....197 E2
  Newark-on-T NG24 ....139 F3
Gorselands Ave NG8 .....36 B1
Gorseway NG21 ....90 A2
Gorsey Rd NG3 ....173 E4
Gorsy La NG25 ....137 E1
Gosforth Ct NG2 ....173 E1
Goshawk Rd DE7 ....170 A2
Gotham La NG11 ....206 B4
Gotham Prim Sch
  NG11 ....195 D1
Gotham Rd
  East Leake LE12 ....205 F2
  Kingston-on-S NG11 .....204 B3
Gothic CI NG6 ....160 C2
Goverton Hill NG14 ......136 C1
Goverton Sq NG6 ....160 B2
Gowan Cl 7 NG9 ....183 E1
Goyden Cl NG5 ....161 D4
Grace Ave NG9 ....184 A3
Grace Dr NG8 ....172 B4
Gracefield La NG23 .....81 F4
Grafton Ave NG5 ....161 F3
Grafton Cl NG17 ....101 D3
Grafton Ct NG7 ....222 C3
Grafton St S80 ....35 F1
Graham Cl NG24 ....140 A2
Graham St NG7 ....222 B3
Grainger Ave
  Annesley Woodhouse
  NG17 ....115 D1
  West Bridgford NG2 .....185 F2
Grainger Terr NG15 .....146 A3
Grampian Dr NG5 ....161 D4
Grampian Way NG10 ....193 D4
Granary Cl DN21 ....15 D2
Granary Ct S81 ....26 A3
Granby Ave
  Mansfield NG18 ....102 A4
  Newark-on-T NG24 ......140 A3
Granby Ct NG13 ....177 E2
Granby Dr
  Balderton NG24 ....140 B2
  Bottesford NG13 ....181 D1
Granby Hill NG13 ....191 D3
Granby Jun Sch DE7 ....157 F2
Granby La
  Plungar NG13 ....191 F1
  Whatton NG13 ....178 A1
Granby St Ilkeston DE7 .157 F1
  Loughborough LE11 .....220 A2
Grandfield Ave NG12 ...175 F2
Grandfield Cres NG12 ..175 F2
Grange Ave Bawtry DN10 .9 F4
  Beeston NG9 ....183 E3
  Mansfield NG18 ....101 F3
  Misterton DN10 ....14 A4
  Newark-on-T NG24 ......139 F2
  Ollerton NG22 ....77 D2
  Ruddington NG11 ....196 B4
Grange Cl
  Harworth DN11 ....9 D3
  Long Eaton NG10 ....193 F4
  Misterton DN10 ....14 A4
Grange Cres NG4 ....162 C2
Grange Ct
  Kirkby in A NG17 ....115 E3
  West Bridgford NG2 ....185 E1
Grange Dr
  Harworth DN11 ....9 D3
  Long Eaton NG10 ....193 F4
  Misterton DN10 ....14 A4

Grange Farm Cl NG9 ...183 D1
Grange La NG24 ....155 D2
Grange Pk
  Cropwell Butler NG12 ..189 D4
  Gainsborough DN21 ......15 D3
  West Bridgford NG2 ....186 B3
Grange Prim Sch
  NG10 ....193 F4
Grange Rd Arnold NG5 .161 F2
  Blidworth NG21 ....118 A3
  Hucknall NG15 ....193 F4
  Nottingham NG6 ....160 B2
  Retford DN22 ....39 F2
  West Bridgford NG2 ....186 A2
Grange The
  North Muskham NG23 ...110 C2
  Retford DN22 ....39 F2
  South Normanton DE55 .113 D2
Grange View
  Eastwood NG16 ....143 F2
  Harworth DN11 ....9 D3
Grange View Rd NG4 ...163 D1
Grange Wlk DN10 ....7 D1
Grangelea Gdns NG9 ...183 E4
Granger Ct 4 LE11 .....220 A2
Grangewood Ct NG8 ...171 E2
Grangewood Rd
  16 Kirkby in A NG17 ...114 C4
  Nottingham NG8 ....171 E2
Grannis Dr NG8 ....172 A4
Grant St NG7 ....222 B3
Grantham Cl NG16 .....158 B4
Grantham Rd
  Bingham NG13 ....178 B2
  Bottesford NG13 ....181 E1
  Radcliffe on T NG4 .....175 F1
Grantleigh Cl NG8 .....171 F3
Granton Ave NG11 .....195 F4
Granton Rise NG19 ....101 E3
Granville Ave NG10 ....182 B1
Granville Cres NG12 ...175 F1
Granville Ct 2 NG3 ....173 F3
Granville Gr 2 NG3 ....173 F3
Granville St LE11 ......220 A2
Grasmere Cl
  Gainsborough DN21 .....15 F1
  Hucknall NG15 ....145 F4
Grasmere Rd
  Beeston NG9 ....183 E4
  Long Eaton NG10 ......182 A1
  Worksop S81 ....35 F4
Grasmere St NG10 ....182 A3
Grass Ct DE7 ....157 F2
Grassingdale Cl NG4 ..162 B1
Grassington Rd NG8 ..172 B4
Grassmere NG12 ......188 A2
Grassthorpe Rd NG23 .81 F1
Grassy La NG9 ....184 A3
Gratton Ct 14 NG17 ..114 C4
Gravel Pit La DN22 ....79 E4
Gravel Pit La DN22 ....50 C1
Gravelholes La DN10 ..6 C1
Gravelly Hollow NG14 .133 D1
Gravelly La NG25 ......137 F2
Graveney Gdns NG5 ..162 B3
Graves Moor La S81 ..18 C1
Gray Fallow DE55 ....113 D2
Gray La NG22 ....120 C1
Gray St LE11 ....220 A1
Graylands Rd NG8 ....171 F3
Grays Dr NG15 ....132 A3
Graystones Cl NG2 ...186 B3
Grazingfield NG11 ....185 D3
Greasley Ave NG16 ...144 B1
Greasley Beauvale DH
  Lawrence Inf Sch
  NG16 ....144 A1
Greasley Beauvale Jun Sch
  NG16 ....144 B1
Greasley Cl NG18 ....103 D2
Greasley St NG6 .....160 A4
Great Central Rd
  Loughborough LE11 ..220 A2
  Mansfield NG18 ......102 B3
Great Central Rly*
  LE11 ....220 B1
Great Central Sta
  LE11 ....220 B2
Great Freeman St
  NG3 ....223 E4
Great Hoggett Dr
  NG9 ....183 D3
Great La NG22 ....65 F4
Great N Rd
  Balderton NG23, NG24 .155 F3
  Barnby Moor DN22 .....28 B3
  Carlton-on-T NG23 ....96 C3
  Eaton DN22 ....40 A1
  Gamston DN22 ....51 D2
  North Muskham NG23 ..110 A4
  Ranskill DN22 ....19 D2
  Scrooby DN10 ....10 A1
  South Muskham NG23,
  NG24 ....124 B3
  West Markham NG22 ....65 E3
  Weston NG23 ....81 E2
Great Northern Cl The
  NG2 ....223 F1
Great Northern Rd
  NG4 ....143 E1
Great Northern Way
  NG4 ....175 D4
Greaves Ave LE14 .....134 B3
Greaves CI Arnold NG5 .162 A3
  Newark-on-T NG24 .....140 B4
  Nottingham NG8 ....159 E1
Greaves La NG22 .....120 A2

Grebe Cl NG24 ....140 B3
Greek Sk NG7 ....222 C3
Green Acre
  Nottingham NG8 ....171 D3
  West Bridgford NG12 ..186 A2
Green Ave NG4 ....175 D4
Green Bank NG21 ......118 B4
Green Cl
  Blidworth NG21 ....118 A2
  Hucknall NG15 ....146 B3
  Keyworth NG12 ....197 F2
  Newton DE55 ....99 D2
Green Cres NG16 ....128 C3
Green Farm Rd NG16 ..128 B3
Green Hill LE12 ....213 D1
Green Hill Rise LE12 ...213 D1
Green Inf Sch The
  DE55 ....113 D3
Green La Babworth DN22 .38 C3
  Bathley NG23 ....110 A1
  Collingham NG23 ......112 A4
  Darlton NG22 ....67 E2
  Dry Doddington NG23 ..156 C1
  Eagle LN6 ....84 C2
  Granby NG13 ....191 D3
  Harby LE14 ....202 B1
  Hodthorpe S80 ....45 E3
  Ilkeston DE7 ....170 A4
  Lambley NG4 ....149 D1
  Laxton NG22 ....79 E1
  Laxton, Moorhouse
  NG23 ....80 A1
  Lea DN21 ....24 C2
  Mansfield NG18 ....102 B2
  Mansfield, Moorhaigh
  NG19 ....87 D1
  Nottingham NG7 ....174 B3
  Pleasley S44 ....86 B4
  Ranskill DN10 ....18 C4
  South Leverton DN22 ..42 B3
  Upper Broughton LE14 .210 A2
  Walesby NG22 ....64 A1
Green Leys NG2 ....185 E2
Green Mile La DN22 ...38 C4
Green Platt NG12 .....187 F2
Green Rd DN10 ....13 D1
Green St
  Barton in F NG11 ......195 D4
  Nottingham NG2 ....173 E1
Green The
  Barkestone-le-V NG13 .192 A1
  Beeston NG9 ....183 F2
  Bilsthorpe NG22 ....105 F4
  Carlton in L S81 ....26 A3
  Coddington NG24 ......126 A1
  Collingham NG23 ......111 F4
  East Leake LE12 ......205 F1
  Elston NG23 ....153 E2
  Gainsborough DN21 ...24 C4
  Glapwell S44 ....86 A4
  Hardstoft S45 ....85 D2
  Harworth DN11 ....8 C2
  Hathern LE12 ....213 D1
  Hose LE14 ....211 F4
  Hulthwaite NG17 ....99 F1
  Kingston-on-S LE12 ...204 A2
  Kirklington NG22 ......120 C4
  Long Whatton LE12 ...212 B2
  Lowdham NG14 ....149 F1
  Mansfield Woodhouse
  NG19 ....88 A3
  Orston NG13 ....179 F4
  Radcliffe on T NG12 ...175 F2
Green Wlk NG13 ......178 C2
Greencare
  Burton Joyce NG14 ...163 F3
  Mansfield NG18 ....102 C3
  Stanton Hill NG17 ....100 B3
Greenacre Ave DE75 .143 D2
Greenacre Rd S81 ....36 A3
Greenacres NG17 ....115 D1
Greenacres Cl NG16 .144 B1
Greenacres Dr DE55 .113 D3
Greenbank Dr NG17 .100 C3
Greenburn Cl NG2 ...186 B3
Greenclose La LE11 ..220 A2
Greencroft NG11 ....184 C2
Greencroft Prim Sch
  NG11 ....184 C2
Greendale Ave NG21 .76 A2
Greendale Cl
  Market Warsop NG20 ...74 A2
  Stanton Hill NG17 ....100 B3
Greendale Gdns NG8 .172 A4
Greendale Rd
  Arnold NG5 ....161 F3
  Nottingham NG3 ......174 B3
Greenfield Cl
  Edwinstowe NG21 .....91 D4
  Mansfield Woodhouse
  NG19 ....89 D1
Greenfield Gr NG4 ...174 B4
Greenfield St NG7 ...172 B1
Greenfields NG16 ....143 D2
Greenfields Cres NG22 .77 E2
Greenfields Dr NG12 .187 F1
Greenfinch Dale S81 ..35 E4
Greenfinch Cl NG16 ..159 F2
Greengage Rd NG2 ...53 D2
Greengates Ave NG3 .161 F2
Greenhill Cres NG4 ..174 C3
Greenhill La NG17 ....129 F4
Greenhill Rd NG4 .....174 C3

Greenhill Rise NG4 ....174 C4
Greenhills Ave NG16 ..144 A2
Greenhills Rd NG16 ...144 A2
Greenholme Cl NG17 ..115 D2
Greenholme Pk NG19 ..88 C3
Greenholme Sch NG7 .222 A1
Greenland Cres NG9 ..183 E2
Greenland Rd NG11 ...100 C4
Greens Ct DE7 ....157 E1
Greens Farm La NG4 ..163 D1
Greens La NG16 ....159 D3
Greens Mill & Science Ctr*
  NG3 ....173 F4
Greensfields NG17 ....101 D3
Greenside Ave DN22 ..42 C1
Greenside Cl NG10 ...193 F4
Greensquare Rd NG16 .158 A3
Greenvale NG22 ....120 A3
Greenview Cl NG19 ....89 E1
Greenway
  Carlton in L S81 ....26 A3
  Clipstone NG19 ....89 E2
  Newark-on-T NG24 ....139 F3
  Retford DN22 ....39 E2
Greenway Cl NG12 ....175 F2
Greenway The NG10 ..182 A3
Greenwich Ave NG6 ..160 B2
Greenwich Pk Cl NG2 .185 E3
Greenwood Ave
  Edwinstowe NG21 .....76 A1
  Harworth DN11 ....8 C3
  Hucknall NG15 ....145 F4
  Huthwaite NG17 ......99 F1
  Ilkeston DE7 ....170 A4
Mansfield Woodhouse
  NG19 ....88 A2
  Nottingham NG3 ......174 B3
Greenwood Cl
  Carlton in L S81 ......25 E1
  Farnsfield NG22 ......120 A3
  Worksop S81 ....35 E4
Greenwood Cotts
  NG18 ....102 C4
Greenwood Cres
  Boughton NG22 ....77 F3
  Carlton NG4 ....174 C3
Greenwood Dale Comp Sch
  NG3 ....174 A2
Greenwood Dr NG17 ..114 C3
Greenwood Gdns
  NG11 ....196 B3
Greenwood Inf Sch
  NG3 ....174 A3
Greenwood Jun Sch
  NG3 ....174 A3
Greenwood Prim Sch
  NG17 ....114 C3
Greenwood Rd NG3 ..174 B3
Greenwood Vale
  NG15 ....145 F4
Greer La S44 ....86 B4
Greet La NG22 ....120 C4
Greetwell Cl NG8 .....171 D2
Gregory Ave
  Aldercar NG16 ....143 D2
  Nottingham, New Lenton
  NG7 ....222 B1
  Nottingham, Portchester
  NG3 ....162 A1
Gregory Bvd NG7 .....173 D4
Gregory Cl NG9 ....182 C4
Gregory Cres DN11 ..8 C2
Gregory Ct
  Beeston NG9 ....183 D2
  Nottingham NG7 .....222 A1
Gregory Gdns NG22 ..119 F3
Gregory St
  23 Loughborough LE11 .220 A2
  Nottingham NG7 .....172 C1
Gregson Gdns NG9 ...183 D1
Gregson Rd NG9 .....183 D1
Grendon Way NG17 ..101 D3
Grenville Dr
  Ilkeston DE7 ....157 F2
  Stapleford NG9 ......182 C4
Grenville Rd NG9 ....184 A2
Grenville Rise NG5 ..147 F1
Gresham Cl
  Newark-on-T NG24 ...140 C4
  West Bridgford NG2 .185 E4
Gresham Gdns
  Arnold NG5 ....162 A3
  West Bridgford NG2 .185 E4
Gresley Dr NG2 ....173 F2
Gresley Rd
  23 Ilkeston DE7 .....157 F1
  Retford DN22 ....39 E3
Gressy Rd NG7 ....184 C1
Gretton Cl NG3 ......159 B3
Gretton Rd NG3 .....162 A2
Grey St Eastwood NG16 .144 A1
  Gainsborough DN21 ...15 D1
  Newark-on-T NG24 ...140 A3
Greyfriar Gate NG1 ..223 E1
Greys Rd NG5 ....161 F2
Greystoke Dr NG8 ...171 E4
Greystones Rd DN21 .15 D2
Greythorn Dr NG2 ...185 E2
Greythorn Prim Sch
  NG2 ....185 E3
Gricenson Cl NG22 ..77 D1
Grierson Ave NG5 ...161 D4
Griffs Hollow NG4 ...174 C4
Grimesmoor Rd NG14 .149 D4
Grimsby Terr NG3 ...223 E4
Grimston Rd NG7 ....222 A4
Grindon Cres NG6 ...146 B1

Gringley Rd
  Clayworth DN22 ....21 F3
  Misterton DN10 ....6 C1
  Walkeringham DN10 ....13 F2
Grinsbrook NG24 ......222 A2
Gripps Comm NG12 ...187 F1
Grisedale Ct NG9 .....183 D2
Gritley Mews NG2 ....173 D1
Grives La NG17 ....115 D1
Grizedale Cl NG19 ....103 D4
Grizedale Gr NG13 ...177 D2
Grosvenor Ave
  Long Eaton NG10 .....193 D2
  Nottingham NG3 ......161 E1
  Sutton in A NG17 ....100 B1
Grosvenor Ct NG12 ..176 C2
Grosvenor Rd
  Bircotes DN11 ....9 D2
  Eastwood NG16 ......143 F1
  New Balderton NG24 ..140 A2
Grosvenor Sch NG2 ..186 A2
Grouville Dr NG5 .....162 A3
Grove Ave Beeston NG9 .183 F3
  Mansfield NG18 ......102 C4
Grove Ct NG14 ....163 F3
Grove Coach Rd DN22 .40 A2
Grove Comp Sch The
  NG24 ....140 B3
Grove La DN22 ....40 A3
Grove Mews NG16 ...143 F1
Grove Pk DN10 ....6 C1
Grove Rd
  Church Warsop NG20 .74 A3
  Grove DN22 ....41 E3
  Nottingham NG7 .....222 B1
  Retford DN22 ....40 B2
  Sutton in A NG17 ....101 D2
Grove Sports Ctr
  NG24 ....140 B3
Grove St Beeston NG9 .184 A3
  6 Mansfield NG18 ....102 A3
  Mansfield Woodhouse
  NG19 ....88 A2
  New Balderton NG24 ..140 B3
  Retford DN22 ....39 F4
Grove The
  Beckingham DN10 ....14 A1
  Calverton NG14 ......149 D4
  Newton on T LN1 .....55 D1
  Nottingham NG2 .....222 B4
  Nottingham, Carrington
  NG5 ....161 D1
Grove Way NG18 .....88 A2
Grove Wood Rd DN10 ..6 C1
Grove Wood Terr DN10 ..6 C1
Grover Ave NG3 .....162 A2
Groveside Cres NG11 .184 B2
Grovewiew Rd NG24 ..140 B3
Grundy Ave NG16 ....128 B4
Grundy Nook S80 ....45 D3
Grundy St NG7 ......172 C4
Guildford Ave NG19 .88 B3
Guildhall St NG24 ...140 A4
Guinea Cl NG10 .....193 D4
Gunn Cl NG6 ....160 A4
Gunnersbury Way
  NG8 ....159 F2
Gunthorpe CE Prim Sch
  NG14 ....165 D3
Gunthorpe Cl NG18 .101 D2
Gunthorpe Dr NG5 ..161 E2
Gunthorpe Rd
  Carlton NG4 ....162 B2
  Lowdham NG14 ......164 C4
  West Stockwith DN9 .7 F4
Gutersloh Ct NG9 ...182 C4
Guy Cl NG9 ....182 C3
Gwenbrook Ave NG9 .183 F3
Gwenbrook Rd NG9 .183 E3
Gwndy Gdns 23 NG5 .161 D4
Gypsum Way NG11 ..205 D4

Habblesthorpe Cl DN22 ..32 C1
Habblesthorpe Rd
  DN22 ....32 C1
Hackers Cl DN10 ....165 E2
Hackworth Cl NG16 ..144 B4
Hadbury Rd NG5 ....160 C2
Hadden Ct NG8 ......171 E3
Hadden Pk High Sch
  NG8 ....171 F4
Hadderley Wlk NG3 ..223 F4
Haddon Cl Carlton NG4 .162 B1
  Hucknall NG15 ......146 A3
  Selston NG16 ....129 D3
Haddon Cres NG9 ...183 E1
Haddon Dr NG24 ....140 B2
Haddon Nurseries
  DE7 ....157 F2
Haddon Pl NG20 ....72 B3
Haddon Prim Sch
  NG4 ....162 B1
Haddon Rd
  Mansfield NG18 .....102 A4
  Ravenshead NG15 ..117 D2
  Retford DN22 ....40 A2
  West Bridgford NG2 .185 F3
Haddon St Ilkeston DE7 .157 F2
  Nottingham NG5 .....161 D1
  Sutton in A NG17 ...100 C2
Tibshelf DE55 ....99 D3

Haddon Way NG12 ....176 A2
Hades La LE12 ....217 E3
Hadfield Wlk NG18 ....103 D3
Hadleigh Cl NG9 ....182 C1
Hadley St DE7 ....170 A3
Hadrian Gdns NG5 ....147 D1
Hadstock Ct NG10 ....182 A2
Hagg La Bawtry DN10 ......10 C4
  Egmanton NG22 ....80 A3
  Epperstone NG14 ....150 A3
Haggonfields Prim Sch
  S80 ....35 D2
Hagley Cl NG3 ....174 A3
Haileybury Cres NG2 ......185 F3
Haileybury Rd NG2 ....185 F3
Hainton Cl DN22 ....24 C4
Haise Ct NG6 ....159 F3
Halam CE Prim Sch
  NG22 ....120 C1
Halam Cl NG16 ....101 E4
Halam Hill NG22 ....121 D1
Halberton Dr NG2 ....185 E2
Haldane St DN21 ....15 D1
Hales Cl NG12 ....187 F2
Haley Cl NG16 ....158 B3
Halfmoon Dr NG17 ....115 D2
Halifax Cl NG3 ....159 E1
Halifax Dr S81 ....35 F4
Halifax Pl NG1 ....223 E2
Halina Barn La NG21 ......101 E4
Hall Cl
  Radcliffe on T NG12 ....175 F2
  Rainworth NG21 ....118 A4
Hall Cl The NG12 ....66 A4
Hall Croft NG9 ....183 F3
Hall Dr Beeston NG9 ......183 E3
  Clayworth DN22 ....21 E3
  Cropwell Bishop NG12 ..195 D1
  Gotham NG11 ....171 F2
  Nottingham NG8 ....182 A3
  Sandiacre NG10 ....182 A3
Hall Gdns Beeston NG9 ....183 F3
  East Leake LE12 ....214 C4
Hall Grounds NG12 ....200 B4
Hall Grounds Dr NG12 .....200 B4
Hall La Brinsley NG16 .....143 E4
  Colston Bassett NG12 ...203 E2
  East Markham NG22 ......66 A4
  Kinoulton NG12 ....200 A2
  Newton DE55 ....99 D2
Hall Rd NG16 ....143 E2
Hall St Mansfield NG18 ...102 C3
  Nottingham NG5 ....161 D2
  Sutton in A NG17 ....100 C3
Hall View DN10 ....20 A4
Hall View Dr NG8 ....182 C3
Hallam Fields Rd DE7 .....170 A2
Hallam Rd
  Beeston NG9 ....183 F3
  Nottingham NG3 ....162 A1
Hallams La NG9 ....161 F4
Hallams La NG9 ....183 E3
Hallamway NG18 ....88 B1
Hallcroft Ave DN22 ....39 E4
Hallcroft Ind Est DN22 ....29 E1
Hallcroft Inf Sch DN22 ....29 E1
Hallcroft Rd DN22 ....29 E1
Hallfield Rd DE55 ....99 D2
Hallfields NG12 ....186 A2
Halliday Cl S80 ....35 E2
Halliday Cl S80 ....35 E2
Halliday Ave NG2 ....74 A4
Halliwell Cl NG24 ....125 D2
Halloughton Rd NG25 .....136 B4
Hallowell Dr NG8 ....171 F2
Halls Brook LE12 ....205 F1
Halls La NG16 ....158 A4
Halls Rd DN10 ....13 D2
Halls Rd NG9 ....182 B3
Hallum Ct DE7 ....157 F2
Halstead Cl
  Beeston NG9 ....183 E2
  Nottingham NG8 ....160 A2
Haltham Gn **2** DN21 ....24 C4
Haltham Wlk NG11 ....195 E4
Hamble Cl NG19 ....88 B2
Hambledon Dr NG8 ....172 A3
Hambleton Cl NG10 ....182 A1
Hambleton Cl S81 ....25 F4
Hambling Cl NG6 ....160 A4
Hamilton Cl
  Arnold NG5 ....148 B1
  Beeston NG9 ....182 C1
Hamilton Dr
  Market Warsop NG20 .....74 A2
  Nottingham NG2 ....223 D1
  Radcliffe on T NG12 ....175 F2
Hamilton Gdns **18** NG5 .161 D1
Hamilton Rd
  Long Eaton NG10 ....182 B3
  Nottingham NG5 ....173 D4
  Sutton in A NG17 ....101 E1
Hamilton St
  Mansfield NG18 ....102 C3
  Worksop S81 ....35 F3
Hamlet La DE55 ....113 D3
Hamlet The DE55 ....113 D3
Hammersmith Cl
  Nuthall NG16 ....159 F2
  Radcliffe on T NG12 ....176 B1
Hammerwater Dr NG20 ....74 A2
Hammond Gr NG17 ....115 D1
Hampden Gr NG9 ....183 F3
Hampden St
  Eastwood NG16 ....158 B4
  Kirkby in A NG17 ....114 C3

Hampden St continued
  Nottingham NG1 ....223 D3
Hampshire Cl S81 ....36 A4
Hampshire Dr NG10 ......182 A2
Hampstead Rd NG3 ....161 F1
Hampton Cl NG9 ....182 C2
Hampton Rd NG2 ....185 F3
Hanbury Ct NG18 ....103 D3
Handel House Sch
  DN21 ....15 E1
Handel St NG3 ....173 F3
Handley Arc **17** NG1 ..102 A4
Handley Ct NG24 ....124 C1
Hands Rd DE7 ....143 D1
Hands Wlk NG13 ....181 D1
Hanford Way LE11 ....220 A3
Hangar Hill S80 ....45 D3
Hankin Ave NG16 ....129 D1
Hankin St NG15 ....146 B3
Hanley Ave NG9 ....183 D4
Hanley St NG1 ....223 D3
Hannah Cres NG11 ....185 D4
Hannah Pk Wood Nature
  Reserve* S80 ....47 D4
Hannams Yd DN22 ....39 E4
Hanover Ct NG8 ....171 E3
Hanslope Cres NG8 ......171 E4
Hanson Cres NG15 ....146 A4
Hanstubbin Rd NG16 .....128 C3
Hanworth Gdns NG5 .....161 E4
Harberton Cl NG5 ....147 F1
Harby Ave
  Mansfield Woodhouse
  NG19 ....88 B3
  Sutton in A NG17 ....101 E1
Harby CE Prim Sch
  NG23 ....202 A2
Harby Cl NG24 ....140 B2
Harby Dr NG8 ....172 B2
Harby La
  Colston Bassett NG12 ..200 C3
  Hose LE14 ....211 F4
  Plungar LE14 ....202 C3
Harby Rd NG13 ....190 B1
Harcourt Cres NG16 ......159 F2
Harcourt Pl DN22 ....40 A2
Harcourt Rd NG7 ....173 D4
Harcourt St
  Beeston NG9 ....183 F3
  Kirkby in A NG17 ....115 D3
  Mansfield NG18 ....102 B3
  Newark-on-T NG24 .....124 C1
Harcourt Terr NG3 ....223 F3
Harden Ct NG11 ....195 E4
Hardie Ave DE55 ....113 D3
Hardigate Rd NG12 ......189 D4
Hardstaff Cl
  Annesley Woodhouse
  NG17 ....114 C1
  Retford DN22 ....29 E1
Hardstaff Rd NG3 ....174 A2
Hardwick Ave
  Mansfield NG21 ....103 F1
  Newark-on-T NG24 .....139 F4
  Shireброok NG20 ....72 C2
  Sutton in A NG17 ......101 D3
Hardwick Cl NG17 ....101 D3
Hardwick Cres S80 ....36 A1
Hardwick Ct DN11 ....9 D3
Hardwick Dr
  Ollerton NG22 ....77 D2
  Selston NG16 ....129 D4
Hardwick Gr
  Nottingham NG7 ....222 B2
  West Bridgford NG2 ....173 F1
Hardwick Hall* S44 ......85 E2
Hardwick Hall Ctry Pk*
  S44 ....85 E3
Hardwick La NG17 ....100 C1
Hardwick Old Hall (NT)*
  S44 ....85 E2
Hardwick Pk Nature Wlk*
  S44 ....85 E2
Hardwick Rd
  1 Nottingham, Carrington
  NG5 ....161 E2
  Nottingham, The Park
  NG7 ....222 C1
Hardwick Rd E S80 ......36 A1
Hardwick Rd W S80 .....36 A1
Hardwick St
  Langwith NG20 ....72 C4
  Mansfield NG18 ....102 B4
  Shirebrook NG20 ......73 D2
  Sutton in A NG17 ......100 C1
  Tibshelf DE55 ....99 D4
Hardwick View NG17 ....101 D3
Hardwicke Rd NG9 ....183 E2
Hardwood Cl NG6 ....159 F4
Hardy Barn DE75 ....157 D4
Hardy Cl
  Kimberley NG16 ....158 C4
  Long Eaton NG10 ......193 E3
Hardy Pl NG18 ....101 F4
Hardy St
  Kimberley NG16 ....158 C4
  Nottingham NG7 ....222 C4
  Worksop S80 ....35 F1
Hardys Cl NG12 ....189 D2
Hardys Dr NG4 ....162 C1
Harefield LE12 ....205 F2
Hareholme St NG18 ......102 A4

Harewood Ct
  Harworth DN11 ....9 D3
  Sandiacre NG10 ....182 A2
Harewood Dr DN10 ......10 A4
Harewood Rd S81 ....35 F4
Hargon La NG24 ....125 E3
Harkstead Rd NG5 ......147 D1
Harlaxton Dr
  Long Eaton NG10 ......194 A4
  Nottingham NG7 ....222 B2
Harlaxton Wlk NG3 .....223 E4
Harlech Cl DE7 ....157 E2
Harlech Rise NG9 ....183 D2
Harlequin Cl NG12 ......176 A2
Harlequin Ct NG16 ......143 E2
Harles Acres LE14 ....210 B3
Harley Gall The* S80 .....45 F1
Harley St NG7 ....222 B1
Harlow Ave NG18 ......100 B2
Harlow Cl
  Mansfield Woodhouse
  NG19 ....88 B3
  Sutton in A NG17 ......100 C3
Harlow Gr NG4 ....162 C1
Harlow St NG21 ....118 A3
Harmston Rise NG5 .....160 C2
Harold Ave NG16 ....143 D2
Harold St NG2 ....173 F2
Harpenden Sq NG8 .....160 A2
Harpole Wlk NG5 ....147 F1
Harrier Gr NG15 ....145 F2
Harriett St NG9 ....182 B4
Harrimans La NG7 ......184 C4
Harrington Cl NG4 ......163 D1
Harrington Dr NG7 .....222 B2
Harrington Jun Sch
  NG10 ....182 A1
Harrington St
  Long Eaton NG10 ......193 D3
  Mansfield NG18 ....88 A4
  Worksop S80 ....35 E1
Harris Cl NG8 ....171 F3
Harris Rd NG9 ....183 E3
Harrison Cl NG13 ....177 E2
Harrison Dr S81 ....16 C2
Harrison Rd
  Mansfield NG18 ....101 F3
  Stapleford NG9 ....182 B4
  Stenson Way NG25 ....121 F1
Harrogate Rd NG3 ......174 B3
Harrogate St NG4 ....174 C4
Harrop White Rd
  NG18 ....101 F4
Harrow Cl
  Gainsborough DN21 .....15 F1
  Rainworth NG21 ....118 A4
Harrow Dr DE7 ....170 A2
Harrow Gdns NG8 ....172 B2
Harrow La NG22 ....77 F3
Harrow Rd
  Hucknall NG15 ....145 E3
  Nottingham NG8 ....172 A2
  West Bridgford NG2 ...185 F3
Harrowby Rd NG7 ......222 B2
Harry Carlton Comp Sch
  LE12 ....205 F1
Harstoft Ave S81 ....35 F3
Hart Ave NG10 ....182 A3
Hart St NG7 ....222 B1
Hartcroft Rd NG5 ......161 D3
Hartford Cl **22** NG2 .173 E1
Hartill Dr NG19 ....101 E3
Hartington Ave
  Carlton NG4 ....162 B1
  Hucknall NG15 ....145 E3
Hartington Ct NG18 ....103 D3
Hartington Dr
  Selston NG16 ....129 D4
  Sutton in A NG17 ....101 D2
Hartington Pl DE7 ......157 F3
Hartington Rd NG5 ......161 E2
Hartington St NG20 ....72 C4
Hartland Comp Sch
  S80 ....46 C4
Hartland Rd S80 ....35 F1
Hartley Cl NG7 ....222 B4
Hartley Dr NG9 ....184 A3
Hartley Rd
  Kirkby in A NG17 ......114 C3
  Nottingham NG7 ....222 B4
Hartside Cl NG11 ......184 B4
Hartside Cl NG2 ....186 B4
Hartside Gdns **11** NG10 193 D4
Hartwell St NG3 ....223 F4
Hartwood Dr NG9 ......170 B1
Harvest Cl
  Bingham NG13 ....177 E2
  Carlton in L S81 ....25 F4
  Nottingham NG5 ......160 C4
  Worksop S80 ....35 F1
Harvey Ave NG24 ......125 F1
Harvey Cl NG11 ....196 B3
Harvey Croft NG9 ......170 B2
Harvey Ct **7** NG7 ...172 C1
Harvey Hadden Sports Ctr
  NG8 ....171 F4
Harvey Rd
  Mansfield NG18 ....102 C3
  Nottingham, Bilborough
  NG8 ....171 F4
  Nottingham, Dunkirk
  NG7 ....172 C1
Harveys Field NG25 .....136 C4
Harwell La DN10 ....11 D2
Harwell Sluice La
  DN10 ....11 D3
Harwich Cl NG6 ....160 A4
Harwill Cres NG8 ......160 A1

Harwood Cl
  Arnold NG5 ....162 A4
  Sutton in A NG17 ......101 D2
Harworth Ave NG21 ....101 D2
Harworth Ave S81 ....18 A3
Harworth CE Prim Sch
  DN11 ....8 C2
Harworth Cl NG19 ......101 E3
Haslam St NG7 ....223 D1
Haslehurst Gdns NG5 ...35 F1
Haslemere Gdns
  NG15 ....116 C1
Haslemere Rd
  Long Eaton NG10 ......193 D4
  Nottingham NG8 ....172 B4
Hassock La N DE75 .....157 E4
Hassock La S DE75 .....157 E3
Hassocks La NG9 ......184 A4
Hassop Wlk NG3 ....103 D3
Hastings St
  Carlton NG4 ....174 B4
  5 Loughborough LE11 220 A2
Haswell Rd NG6 ....160 A3
Hatchets La NG24 ......125 D2
Hatfield Ave
  Meden Vale NG20 ......74 C4
  Sandiacre NG10 ....182 A2
Hatfield Cl NG21 ....104 A1
Hatfield Dr NG2 ....185 E2
Hatfield Rd NG3 ....161 E1
Hatfield St DN22 ....40 A3
Hather Cl DN22 ....51 D3
Hatherleigh Cl NG3 ....162 B3
Hathern CE Prim Sch
  LE12 ....213 D1
Hathern Cl NG10 ....193 E3
Hathern Gn NG9 ....184 A4
Hathern Rd LE12 ....212 B1
Hathernware Ind Est
  LE12 ....213 E3
Hathersage Rise
  NG15 ....117 D2
Hathersage Way
  NG17 ....100 C2
Hathersage Wlk NG18 ..103 D3
Hatley Cl **28** NG2 ....173 D1
Hatton Cl NG5 ....147 D1
Hatton Crofts NG10 ....193 E3
Hatton Ct NG18 ....103 D3
Hatton Gdns
  Newark-on-T NG24 ....140 A4
  Nuthall NG8 ....159 F2
Haughgate Hill DN22 ..22 A1
Havelock Gdns NG3 ....223 F4
Havelock St NG20 ....72 C4
Haven Cl Clipstone NG21 .89 F2
  Sutton in A NG17 ......100 B2
  West Bridgford NG2 ...185 E3
Haven Hill S81 ....16 B3
Havenden Gdns **3** NG5 172 C4
Havenwood Rise
  NG11 ....195 E4
Haverhill Cres NG5 ....146 B1
Haversage Ave NG10 ..193 D3
Haversham Cl NG6 .....160 B1
Hawarden Terr **30** NG7 172 C4
Hawbush Rd NG21 .....81 D3
Hawk Ridge Gdns **7**
  NG5 ....173 F3
Hawkesworth Ave
  NG19 ....89 D1
Hawkhill Cl NG22 ....77 D2
Hawkhurst Dr NG8 ....171 E1
Hawking La S44 ....85 D4
Hawkins Ct DE7 ....157 F2
Hawkshead Cl NG2 ....186 B3
Hawksley Gdns NG11 ..184 B1
Hawksley Rd **32** NG7 172 C4
Hawkswood Cl NG9 ....183 D2
Hawksworth Ave NG5 ..161 E2
Hawksworth Rd
  Hawksworth NG13 ....167 D2
  Scarrington NG13 .....178 C4
  Syerston NG23 ....153 D2
  West Bridgford NG2 ...173 F1
Hawksworth St
  Gainsborough DN21 ....24 B4
  10 Nottingham NG3 ..173 F3
Hawley Cl LE12 ....205 F1
Hawson Way S81 ....35 E4
Hawthorn Ave
  Gainsborough DN21 ....15 E1
  Glapwell S44 ....86 A4
  Hucknall NG15 ....145 F4
  Stapleford NG9 ....182 B3
Hawthorn Cl
  Beckingham DN10 .....23 D4
  Keyworth NG12 ....197 F1
  New Ollerton NG22 .....77 E3
  2 Nottingham NG2 ..173 D1
  Old Dalby LE14 ....218 C2
  West Bridgford NG2 ...186 A2
Hawthorn Cres
  Arnold NG5 ....148 A1
  Kirkby in A NG17 ......115 D3
Hawthorn Dr NG22 ....119 E1
Hawthorn Gr DN21 .....15 E1
Hawthorn Prim Sch
  NG2 ....146 C2
Hawthorn Way S81 ....25 F4
Hawthorne Ave
  Hathern LE12 ....213 D1
  Long Eaton NG10 .....193 E3
  Shirebrook NG20 ......72 B2
  Tibshelf DE55 ....99 D4
Hawthorne Cl
  Stanton Hill NG17 .....100 A3
  Woodborough NG14 ...149 E2

Hawthorne Cres NG24 ..139 D2
Hawthorne Gr NG9 ....184 A3
Hawthorne Rd NG16 ...113 E2
Hawthorne Rise NG16 ..158 A2
Hawthorne Way NG21 ..91 E4
Hawthorns The
  Market Warsop NG20 ..74 A2
  Walesby NG22 ....64 A1
Hawton Cl
  Gainsborough DN21 ....15 F1
  Mansfield NG19 ....87 F1
Hawton Cres NG8 ......172 B2
Hawton La NG24 ....140 A2
Hawton Rd NG24 ......139 F3
Hawton Spinney NG8 ..172 B2
Hawtonville Jun Sch
  NG24 ....139 F3
Haxey Gate Rd DN10 ...6 C3
Haxey Rd DN10 ....6 C2
Haycroft Cl NG19 ......88 C3
Haycroft Way NG13 ...165 E1
Hayden La NG15 ....131 D1
Haydn Ave NG5 ....161 D1
Haydn Prim Sch NG5 ..161 E1
Haydn Rd NG5 ....161 D1
Haydock Cl NG16 ......158 C4
Hayes Cl NG16 ....113 E2
Hayes Rd NG12 ....197 F2
Hayles Cl NG5 ....161 D3
Hayling Cl DE7 ....157 E2
Hayling Dr NG8 ....160 B1
Haynes Ave NG9 ......170 B3
Haynes Cl
  Nottingham NG11 .....184 C2
  Tuxford NG22 ....66 A2
Hays Cl DE7 ....157 F1
Hayside Ave NG24 .....140 A2
Hayward Ave LE11 .....220 B1
Haywood Ave NG21 ...118 A3
Haywood Comp Sch
  NG5 ....161 E3
Haywood Ct **2** NG2 ..173 F2
Haywood La NG23 .....81 D3
Haywood Oaks La
  NG21 ....118 B2
Haywood Rd NG3 ......162 A2
Haywood St NG2 ......173 F2
Hayworth Rd NG10 ....182 A3
Hazel Bank NG18 ....102 C4
Hazel Cl NG13 ....178 A2
Hazel Cres NG20 ....72 B2
Hazel Dr Gr Hucknall NG15 146 A4
  Kirkby in A NG17 .....115 E3
Hazel Hill Cres NG5 ...161 D4
Hazel Mdws NG15 .....146 A3
Hazel St
  Nottingham NG6 ......160 A4
  Sutton in A NG17 .....100 B4
Hazel Way NG15 ....131 D1
Hazelbank Ave NG3 ...161 F1
Hazelby Rd S80 ....58 C4
Hazelford Way NG15 ..130 C4
Hazelhurst Gdns **10**
  NG6 ....160 A4
Hazelmere Gr NG7 ....222 A2
Hazelwood NG12 ......188 A2
Hazelwood Cl
  Eastwood NG16 ....144 A1
  Mansfield Woodhouse
  NG19 ....89 D1
Hazelwood Dr NG15 ...145 D3
Hazelwood La DN22 ...41 F1
Hazelwood Rd NG7 ....172 C4
Headingley Gdns **3**
  NG8 ....172 B4
Headland Ave DN22 ...50 A2
Headstead Bank DN22 .43 E3
Heafield Dr NG14 ....79 E3
Healdswood Inf Sch
  NG17 ....100 A3
Healdswood St NG17 ..100 B3
Healey Cl
  Collingham NG23 ......112 A4
  Nottingham NG23 .....173 E1
Heanor Rd DE7 ....157 E2
Heanor Wlk NG18 .....103 D3
Heapham Cres DN21 ...24 C4
Heapham Rd **8** DN21 .24 C4
Heapham Rd Cty Inf Sch
  DN21 ....24 C4
Heard Cres NG9 ......183 F4
Heath Ave NG18 ....103 D4
Heath Gdns DE72 .....193 D4
Heath The NG16 ....158 A4
Heathcoat St
  12 Loughborough LE11 220 A2
  Nottingham NG1 ......223 F3
Heathcote Pl NG17 ....101 D1
Heather Cl
  Eastwood NG16 ....144 B1
  22 Kirkby in A NG17 ..114 C3
  Mansfield NG18 ......102 A3
  Nottingham NG3 ......173 F3
  South Normanton DE55 .113 D2
  Tickhill DN11 ....8 A4
Heather Croft NG2 ....185 E2
Heather Cl DE75 ......143 D1
Heather La NG15 .....146 A4
Heather Rd NG4 ....162 B1
Heather Rise NG9 ....171 F1
Heather Way NG18 ...103 D3
Heatherley Dr
  Mansfield NG19 ....88 C3

Heatherley Dr continued
Nottingham NG6 ....160 C2
Heatherley Prim Sch
NG19 ....88 C1
Heathers The NG22 ....77 F3
Heathervale NG2 ....185 D3
Heathfield Ave DE7 ....170 A4
Heathfield Ct **12** NG17 ....114 C4
Heathfield Gdns
Retford DN22 ....39 F4
Tibshelf DE55 ....99 D4
Heathfield Gr NG9 ....183 E2
Heathfield Prim Sch
NG5 ....160 C2
Heathing Gdns NG5 ....147 D1
Heathland Cl NG18 ....103 D3
Heathrington Gdns **9**
NG5 ....147 D1
Heaton Cl
Newark-on-T NG24 ....140 B4
Nottingham NG3 ....161 F1
Heaton St DN21 ....24 B4
Heavenside LE12 ....205 F2
Heavytrees Ave NG15 ....117 D1
Hecadeck La LE14 ....219 E4
Heckdyke La DN10 ....7 F3
Heckington Dr NG8 ....172 A3
Heddington Gdns **7**
NG5 ....161 E4
Heddon Bar NG5 ....88 C2
Hedgerow Cl NG17 ....100 B1
Hedges Dr DE7 ....170 A3
Hedley St NG7 ....173 D4
Hedley Villas **5** NG7 ....161 D1
Helen Cl NG9 ....183 E3
Helenship La DN22 ....54 A4
Hellebore Cl NG5 ....160 C4
Helm Cl NG6 ....159 F4
Helmsdale Cl
Arnold NG5 ....148 A1
Mansfield NG19 ....101 F3
Helmsdale Gdns NG5 ....146 C1
Helmsley Rd NG21 ....103 F2
Helston Dr NG8 ....159 F1
Helvellyn Cl **7** NG2 ....173 E1
Helvellyn Way NG10 ....182 A1
Hemingway Cl
Carlton NG4 ....174 B4
Eastwood NG16 ....144 B1
Hemlock Ave
Long Eaton NG10 ....182 B1
Stapleford NG9 ....182 C3
Hemlock Gdns NG6 ....159 F3
Hemmingfield Cl S81 ....35 F4
Hemmingfield Cres
S81 ....35 F4
Hemmingfield Rd S81 ....36 A4
Hemmingfield Way
S81 ....36 A4
Hemplands La NG23 ....96 C4
Hemplands The NG23 ....98 A1
Hempshill Hall Prim Sch
NG6 ....159 F3
Hempshill La NG6 ....160 A4
Hemsby Gdns **6** NG6 ....160 A4
Hemscott Cl NG6 ....159 F4
Hemsley Dr NG16 ....143 E2
Hemswell Cl NG3 ....174 A3
Hendon Rise NG3 ....173 F4
Hendre Gdns **2** NG5 ....161 D4
Henley Cl NG4 ....175 D4
Henley Ct DN21 ....15 E1
Henley Gdns NG3 ....170 C1
Henley Rise NG5 ....161 D2
Henning Gdns **1** NG5 ....161 D4
Henning La NG17 ....100 A1
Hennymoor Cl S80 ....45 D3
Hennymoor La S80 ....45 E1
Henrietta St NG6 ....160 B3
Henry Ave NG19 ....88 A3
Henry Ct NG2 ....173 E1
Henry Mellish Comp Sch
NG6 ....160 B3
Henry Rd Beeston NG9 ....184 A3
Nottingham NG7 ....222 A1
West Bridgford NG2 ....185 F4
Henry St Arnold NG5 ....147 F1
Hucknall NG15 ....146 A3
6 Nottingham NG2 ....173 F2
Sutton in A NG17 ....100 C1
Henry Whipple Jun & Inf
Schs NG5 ....160 C3
Henshaw Pl DE7 ....157 F2
Henson Cl NG12 ....176 C2
Henson La NG12 ....176 C4
Hensons Sq NG9 ....183 D4
Henton Rd NG21 ....76 B1
Hepple Dr NG6 ....159 F4
Herald Cl NG9 ....184 A4
Herbert Rd
Annesley Woodhouse
NG17 ....115 D1
Nottingham NG5 ....161 D1
Herbert St
Loughborough LE11 ....220 A3
Mansfield NG18 ....102 A3
Hereford Ave
Mansfield Woodhouse
NG19 ....88 B3
Ollerton NG22 ....77 D2
Hereford Cl S81 ....36 A3
Hereford Rd
Arnold NG5 ....161 F3
Carlton NG4 ....162 C1
Nottingham NG3 ....174 A3

Hereford Rd continued
Ravenshead NG15 ....117 D2
Herewood Cl NG20 ....72 C2
Hermes Ct DN10 ....9 F2
Hermitage Ave NG18 ....101 F3
Hermitage La NG18 ....101 F2
Hermitage Sq **20** NG2 ....173 F2
Hermitage Way NG18 ....101 F2
Hermitage Wlk NG7 ....222 C1
Hermon St NG7 ....222 C3
Herne St NG17 ....101 D2
Heron Dr NG7 ....222 A2
Heron Glade S81 ....35 E4
Heron Way NG24 ....140 B3
Heron Wharf **8** NG7 ....172 C1
Herons Ct NG12 ....186 B2
Herrick Rd LE11 ....220 A1
Herril Ings DN11 ....8 A4
Herriot Dr DN11 ....9 D2
Herrods View NG17 ....100 B3
Hervey Gn NG7 ....184 C1
Heskey Cl NG3 ....223 E4
Heskey Wlk NG3 ....223 E4
Heslington Ave NG8 ....172 C4
Heslop Ct S80 ....35 E2
Hethbeth Ct **5** NG2 ....173 F1
Hethersett Gdns **5**
NG5 ....160 A4
Hetley Rd NG9 ....183 F4
Hetts La NG20 ....74 A3
Hetts La Inf Sch NG20 ....74 A3
Hewett St NG20 ....73 E3
Hewsons La NG23 ....112 A3
Hexham Ave DE7 ....170 A2
Hexham Cl
Mansfield NG18 ....102 C3
West Bridgford NG2 ....186 A3
Hexham Gdns **1** NG5 ....147 D1
Hey St NG10 ....193 E2
Heyes The NG15 ....117 D1
Heyford Ct DE75 ....143 D1
Heymann Prim Sch
NG2 ....185 E2
Heyward St NG18 ....102 B4
Heywood Cl NG25 ....121 F1
Heywood St NG18 ....102 B4
Hibbert Cres NG17 ....101 D2
Hibbert Rd NG18 ....102 B4
Hickings La NG9 ....182 C4
Hickling Ct NG18 ....102 B4
Hickling La LE14 ....211 D2
Hickling Rd
Kinoulton NG12 ....200 A1
Nottingham NG3 ....162 A1
Hickling Way NG12 ....188 A1
Hickman Cres DN21 ....15 E2
Hickman Ct DN21 ....24 B4
Hickman St DN21 ....24 B4
Hickory Cl **21** NG17 ....114 C4
Hickton Dr NG9 ....183 D1
Hide Hill View NG12 ....186 B1
High Church St NG7 ....161 D1
High Cl NG17 ....115 D1
High Comm La
Austerfield DN10 ....3 D3
Tickhill DN11 ....9 D4
High Cres NG17 ....115 D1
High Cross NG14 ....136 C1
High Cross St NG1 ....223 F3
High Field La DN10 ....3 D2
High Grounds Rd S80 ....35 E2
High Grounds Way S80 ....35 D2
High Hazles Cl NG4 ....162 C2
High Hazles Dr NG17 ....100 A1
High Hoe Ct S80 ....36 A2
High Hoe Dr S80 ....36 A2
High Hoe Rd S80 ....36 A2
High Holborn DE7 ....157 F2
High Leys Rd NG15 ....148 C4
High La E DE7 ....157 D1
High Leys Dr NG15 ....116 B2
High Leys Rd NG15 ....145 F3
High Mdw Bawtry DN10 ....9 F4
Hathern LE12 ....213 D1
Tollerton NG12 ....186 B1
High Oakham Dr
NG18 ....102 A2
High Oakham Hill
NG18 ....102 A2
High Oakham Prim Sch
NG18 ....102 A2
High Oakham Rd
NG18 ....102 A2
High Pavement
Nottingham NG1 ....223 F2
Sutton in A NG17 ....100 C1
High Pavement Sixth Form
Coll NG5 ....160 C3
High Pk Cotts NG16 ....144 B3
High Rd Beeston NG9 ....184 A4
Beeston, Chilwell NG9 ....183 E2
Beeston, Toton NG9 ....183 D1
Carlton in L S81 ....25 E4
High Ridge NG19 ....88 C1
High Spania NG16 ....158 C4
High St Arnold NG5 ....161 F4
Bawtry DN10 ....10 A4
Beckingham DN10 ....23 D4
Blyth S81 ....18 A1
Bottesford NG13 ....181 B3
Brinsley NG16 ....128 B1
Collingham NG23 ....112 A4
Eagle LN6 ....84 B2
East Markham NG22 ....65 F4
Edwinstowe NG21 ....76 A1
Elkesley DN22 ....50 A2
Everton DN10 ....11 E2

High St continued
Gainsborough DN21 ....24 B4
Girton NG23 ....82 C1
Gringley on t H DN10 ....12 C1
Harby NG23 ....70 C1
Hucknall NG15 ....146 A4
Huthwaite NG17 ....100 A3
Kegworth DE74 ....203 E1
Kimberley NG16 ....158 C3
Long Eaton NG10 ....193 F4
Loughborough LE11 ....220 A2
7 Mansfield NG18 ....102 A3
Mansfield Woodhouse
NG19 ....88 B2
Market Warsop NG20 ....74 A2
Marton DN21 ....44 B4
Misson DN10 ....4 B1
Misterton DN10 ....6 C1
Newton on T LN1 ....55 D1
North Scarle LN6 ....83 E1
Nottingham NG1 ....223 E2
Orston NG13 ....179 F4
Pleasleyhill NG19 ....87 D3
Retford DN22 ....39 F2
Ruddington NG11 ....196 B4
Saxilby LN1 ....57 D2
South Leverton DN22 ....42 B3
South Normanton DE55 ....113 D3
Stanton Hill NG17 ....100 B3
Stapleford NG9 ....182 C4
Staunton in t V NG13 ....169 D2
Sutton in A NG17 ....100 C1
Sutton on T NG23 ....96 C4
Tibshelf DE55 ....99 D4
Walkeringham DN10 ....13 F3
High St Ave NG5 ....161 F4
High St Pl NG1 ....223 E2
High Tor NG17 ....100 C4
High View Ave NG12 ....198 A2
High View Rd DE55 ....113 E4
Highbank Dr NG11 ....195 E4
Highbank Prim Sch
NG11 ....195 E4
Highbury Ave NG6 ....160 B3
Highbury Cl NG8 ....159 F2
Highbury Hospl NG6 ....160 B3
Highbury Rd
Keyworth NG12 ....197 F2
Nottingham NG6 ....160 B3
Highbury Wlk NG6 ....160 B3
Highclere Dr NG4 ....174 C4
Highcliffe Ave NG20 ....72 B2
Highcliffe Rd NG3 ....174 A2
Highcroft NG3 ....161 F2
Highcroft Cl NG10 ....193 F3
Highcroft Dr NG8 ....171 D3
Highcross Ct NG7 ....222 B4
Highcross Hill NG25,
NG14 ....136 B2
Highfield DN22 ....29 E1
Highfield Ave
Kirkby in A NG17 ....114 C3
Mansfield NG19 ....88 A1
Shirebrook NG20 ....72 B3
Highfield Cl
Gainsborough DN21 ....15 F1
Mansfield NG19 ....88 A1
Ravenshead NG15 ....117 D1
Highfield Ct NG9 ....183 F3
Highfield Dr
Bilsthorpe NG22 ....105 F2
Carlton NG4 ....174 A4
Nuthall NG16 ....159 F2
South Normanton DE55 ....113 D3
Stapleford LN6 ....127 D2
Highfield Gr
Carlton in L S81 ....26 A3
West Bridgford NG2 ....185 F4
Highfield La S80 ....36 B1
Highfield Prim Sch
Cotgrave NG12 ....187 F2
Long Eaton NG10 ....182 B1
Highfield Rd
Bawtry DN10 ....10 A4
Beeston NG9 ....183 D2
Clipstone NG21 ....90 A2
Keyworth NG12 ....197 F2
Nottingham NG7 ....172 B1
Nuthall NG16 ....159 F2
Saxilby LN1 ....57 D2
Sutton in A NG17 ....100 B3
West Bridgford NG2 ....185 F4
Highfield St NG10 ....182 B2
Highfield Terr **8** NG18 ....102 A3
Highfield Villas S81 ....25 F4
Highfield Way NG18 ....102 A3
Highfields Dr NG22 ....106 A2
Highfields Sch NG24 ....140 B3
Highfields Science Pk
NG7 ....172 B1
Highgate Cl NG4 ....162 B1
Highgate Dr DE7 ....157 E2
Highgate La NG13 ....202 C4
Highgrove Ave NG9 ....183 E3
Highgrove Gdns NG12 ....186 A2
Highland Cl NG19 ....88 B2
Highland Gr S81 ....36 A3
Highland Rd NG18 ....102 C1
Highurst St NG7 ....222 C3
Highwood Ave NG8 ....171 F4
Highwood Player Jun & Inf
Schs NG8 ....171 F4
Highway Gr NG11 ....184 B1
Hilary Cl NG8 ....171 E2
Hilcot Dr NG8 ....160 B1
Hilcote La DE55 ....99 D1
Hilcote St DE55 ....113 D3
Hill Cl Eastwood NG16 ....144 B1

Hill Cl continued
West Bridgford NG2 ....186 A3
Hill Cres
Gainsborough DN21 ....15 F1
Sutton in A NG17 ....101 D2
Hill Crest NG20 ....72 B2
Hill Crest Gr NG5 ....161 D2
Hill Dr NG13 ....177 E3
Hill Farm Cl NG12 ....186 B1
Hill Farm Ct NG12 ....186 A1
Hill Fields DE55 ....113 D2
Hill Rd Beeston NG9 ....183 D1
Bestwood Village NG6 ....146 C2
Gotham NG11 ....205 D4
Harworth DN11 ....8 C2
Orston NG13 ....180 A3
Hill Rise NG20 ....170 B2
Hill Side NG7 ....172 B2
Hill St Pleasleyhill NG19 ....87 D3
Retford DN22 ....39 F2
Worksop S80 ....35 F1
Hill Syke NG14 ....150 A1
Hill The NG17 ....114 C3
Hill Top NG13 ....180 A3
Hill Top Ave NG20 ....72 C2
Hill Top Ct DN11 ....9 D2
Hill Top View NG17 ....100 B1
Hill View Rd
Beeston NG9 ....183 D1
Kirkby in A NG17 ....115 E3
Hill Vue Gdns NG24 ....140 A4
Hill Vue Gdns NG24 ....140 A4
Hillary Way NG24 ....140 C2
Hillbeck Cres NG8 ....171 E2
Hillcrest NG25 ....136 B4
Hillcrest Ave DE55 ....113 D2
Hillcrest Cl NG16 ....159 D4
Hillcrest Dr NG15 ....145 E3
Hillcrest Gdns NG14 ....163 F3
Hillcrest Mews DN22 ....40 A4
Hillcrest Rd NG12 ....197 F2
Hillcrest View NG4 ....162 A1
Hillfield Gdns NG5 ....146 C1
Hillfield Rd NG9 ....170 C1
Hillgrove Gdns **14** NG5 ....161 D4
Hilliers Ct NG5 ....160 C4
Hillington Rise NG5 ....161 E4
Hillmoor St NG19 ....87 E2
Hillocks Prim Sch
NG17 ....101 D2
Hillsborough Ave
NG17 ....114 B4
Hillsborough Way
NG17 ....114 B4
Hillsford Cl NG8 ....172 A3
Hillside
Beckingham LN5 ....142 B4
Kegworth DE74 ....203 E1
Langley Mill NG16 ....143 D2
Long Eaton NG10 ....193 E4
Southwell NG25 ....136 B4
Hillside Gr NG10 ....182 A3
Hillside Rd
Beeston, Bramcote
NG9 ....183 E4
Beeston, Chilwell NG9 ....183 D2
Blidworth NG21 ....118 A2
Radcliffe on T NG12 ....176 A2
Hillside Wlk NG21 ....118 A2
Hillsway NG20 ....72 B2
Hillway Cres NG18 ....102 A2
Hilltop Cl LN6 ....84 B2
Hilltop Rd NG16 ....113 E2
Hillview Ave NG3 ....161 E1
Hillview Cres DN22 ....30 C2
Hillview Ct NG19 ....88 B2
Hillview Rd
Beeston NG9 ....183 E2
Carlton NG4 ....162 A1
Retford DN22 ....39 F2
Hillwood Cl S80 ....35 D1
Hilton Cres NG2 ....186 A3
Hilton Ct NG2 ....186 A3
Hilton Rd NG3 ....162 A2
Hinchin Brook NG7 ....222 A2
Hind St DN22 ....40 A3
Hindlow Ct NG18 ....103 D3
Hine Ave NG24 ....140 C4
Hinsley Cl NG5 ....162 A4
Hirst Cres NG8 ....171 F2
Hirst Rd DN22 ....40 A4
Hives La LN6 ....83 E2
Hoare Rd NG9 ....183 E1
Hobart Cl NG2 ....173 E1
Hobart Dr NG9 ....170 C1
Hobhouse Rd NG19 ....87 E1
Hobsic Cl NG16 ....143 E4
Hobsic La NG16 ....128 C4
Hobsons Acre NG14 ....165 D3
Hockerton Hts NG23 ....122 A3
Hockerton Rd NG25,
NG23 ....122 C1
Hockerwood NG11 ....184 C2
Hockerwood La NG23 ....122 B1
Hockley NG1 ....223 F2
Hockley Pl NG17 ....114 C2
Hodgkin Cl NG11 ....184 B1
Hodgkinson Rd NG17 ....115 D2

Hodgkinson St NG4 ....175 D3
Hodmire La S44 ....85 E4
Hodsock La S81 ....26 A4
Hodsock Priory Gdns*
S81 ....26 C4
Hodthorpe Prim Sch
S80 ....45 E3
Hoe La NG12 ....189 D3
Hoe Nook NG12 ....189 D3
Hoe View Rd NG12 ....189 D2
Hoefield Cres NG6 ....160 A3
Hoewood Rd NG6 ....160 A4
Hogan Gdns NG5 ....147 D1
Hogarth Cl NG9 ....182 C3
Hogarth Prim Sch
NG3 ....174 A4
Hogarth St NG3 ....173 F3
Hogg La NG12 ....175 F2
Hoggetts Cl NG9 ....183 D3
Hoggs Field NG16 ....143 F1
Holbeck La S80 ....59 E4
Holbeck Rd
Hucknall NG15 ....131 D1
Nottingham NG8 ....172 B3
Holborn Ave NG2 ....174 A1
Holborn Cl LE11 ....220 B2
Holborn Ave NG2 ....173 F2
Holborn Cl NG16 ....159 E2
Holborn Pl NG6 ....160 B4
Holbrook Cl NG19 ....87 D3
Holbrook Ct
Mansfield NG18 ....103 D3
Nottingham NG11 ....195 F4
Holbrook St DE75 ....143 D1
Holby Cl NG5 ....160 C4
Holcombe Cl NG8 ....160 A1
Holdale Rd NG3 ....174 A3
Holden Cres
Newark-on-T NG24 ....139 F3
Nuthall NG16 ....159 E3
Holden Gdns NG9 ....182 C3
Holden Rd NG9 ....183 F4
Holden St
Mansfield NG18 ....102 A3
Nottingham NG7 ....222 C3
Holdenby Cl DN22 ....40 A4
Holderness Cl DN11 ....9 D2
Holding S81 ....36 A3
Holds La DN22 ....19 D1
Holgate NG11 ....184 B1
Holgate Comp Sch The
NG15 ....145 F3
Holgate Rd NG2 ....173 E1
Holgate Wlk NG15 ....145 F3
Holkham Ave NG9 ....183 E3
Holkham Cl
Arnold NG5 ....162 A3
Shipley DE7 ....157 E2
Holland Cl NG11 ....195 D1
Holland Cres NG16 ....129 D4
Holland Mdw NG10 ....193 E3
Holland St NG7 ....222 C4
Holles Cl NG22 ....77 F3
Holles St S81 ....35 F1
Hollies Ave NG24 ....125 D2
Hollies Cres NG2 ....222 C1
Hollies Dr NG12 ....186 A2
Hollies The
Eastwood NG16 ....143 F1
Ranworth NG21 ....104 A1
Ravenshead NG16 ....116 C1
Sandiacre NG10 ....182 A3
Hollington Rd NG8 ....172 A3
Hollington Way NG18 ....103 D4
Hollingwood La NG14 ....133 E1
Hollingworth Ave
NG10 ....182 A2
Hollins The NG14 ....149 D4
Hollinwell Ave NG8 ....172 B3
Hollinwell Cl **9** NG17 ....114 C4
Hollinwell Ct NG12 ....186 A2
Hollis Mdw LE12 ....205 F2
Hollis St NG7 ....161 D1
Hollow Stone NG1 ....223 F2
Holloway Cl NG13 ....165 E2
Hollowdyke La NG24 ....140 C1
Hollowgate La NG23 ....68 A1
Hollows The
Long Eaton NG10 ....194 A4
Maplebeck NG22 ....108 A4
Nottingham NG11 ....185 D2
Thurgarton NG14 ....151 E4
Holly Ave Carlton NG4 ....174 B4
Nottingham, Wilford
NG11 ....185 D4
Holly Bush Cl 50 A2
Holly Cl Bingham NG13 ....178 A2
Hucknall NG15 ....146 A3
Holly Ct Beeston NG9 ....183 E4
Harworth DN11 ....8 C2
Mansfield NG19 ....88 C1
Retford DN22 ....39 F3
Rolleston NG23 ....138 A3
Holly Dr NG19 ....89 D1
Holly Farm Ct NG16 ....144 B1
Holly Gdns NG3 ....173 F4
Holly Gr NG17 ....114 C3
Holly Hill Prim Sch
NG16 ....129 D4
Holly Hill Rd NG16 ....129 D3
Holly La NG9 ....183 F3
Holly Prim Sch NG19 ....89 D1
Holly Rd
Mansfield Woodhouse
NG19 ....89 D1

Holly Rd continued
Retford DN22 .... 39 F3
Watnall NG16 .... 159 D4
Holly Rise NG22 .... 77 E3
Hollybrook Gr NG16 ... 159 D4
Hollycroft NG2 .... 186 A2
Hollydale Rd NG3 ..... 174 A3
Hollydene Cl NG15 .... 145 E3
Hollydene Cres NG6 .. 160 A2
Hollygate Ind Pk
NG12 .... 188 A2
Hollygate La NG12 .... 188 A3
Hollygirt Sch NG3 ..... 173 E4
Hollyhouse Dr DE55 .. 113 D3
Hollythorpe Pl NG15 . 145 E3
Hollytree La LE12 ..... 215 E1
Hollytree La LE14 ..... 211 F1
Hollywell Prim Sch
NG16 .... 158 C4
Holme Ave LE12 .... 205 F2
Holme Cl Ilkeston DE7 . 157 E1
Woodborough NG14 ... 149 E2
Holme Gr NG2 .... 174 A1
Holme La
Egmanton NG22 .... 79 F3
Halam NG22 .... 120 C2
Langford NG23 .... 111 F2
Normanton on T NG23 . 82 A4
Radcliffe on T NG12 ... 175 E2
Rockley DN22 .... 51 E1
Winthorpe NG24 ...... 125 E4
Holme Pierrepont CE Prim
Sch NG12 .... 187 D4
Holme Pierrepont Ctry Pk***
NG12 .... 174 C2
Holme Pierrepont Hall***
NG12 .... 175 D2
Holme Rd
Bingham NG13 .... 178 A2
West Bridgford NG2 ... 174 A1
Holme St NG2 .... 173 F1
Holme The NG5 .... 136 A4
Holme Way S81 .... 25 E1
Holme Wlk DN11 .... 15 F1
Holmecroft Ave NG17 . 100 C3
Holmefield NG24 ...... 139 D2
Holmefield Cres DE7 .. 170 A4
Holmefield Rd S80 ..... 45 D3
Holmefield Wlk NG18 . 103 D3
Holmes Cl NG15 .... 143 D2
Holmes Rd DN22 .... 39 F4
Holmesfield Dr DE75 .. 157 D4
Holmewood Cres NG5 . 161 D3
Holmewood Dr NG16 . 158 A4
Holmfield Cl S81 .... 36 A3
Holmfield Rd NG9 ..... 183 E2
Holmhurst Cl S81 ...... 35 F3
Holmsfield NG12 ...... 197 F1
Holmwood Rd NG21 ... 104 B1
Holocaust Ctr The***
NG22 .... 78 C2
Holroyd Ave NG2 ...... 173 F2
Holt Dr 5 LE11 .... 220 A1
Holt Gr NG14 .... 148 C4
Holt The NG2 .... 139 E3
Holwood Ct NG6 ...... 160 A3
Holy Cross RC Prim Sch
NG15 .... 131 D1
Holy Family RC Prim Sch
S80 .... 47 D4
Holy Trinity Inf Sch
NG25 .... 136 B4
Holy Trinity RC Prim Sch
NG24 .... 139 F4
Holyoake Rd NG3 ..... 162 B2
Holyrood Ct NG9 ..... 171 E1
Holywell Rd DE7 ...... 157 E2
Home Cl NG5 .... 161 E4
Home Croft The NG9 . 183 D4
Home Farm Cl NG11 . 195 D1
Home Fm Ct NG16 ... 128 B3
Home Mdws DN11 ..... 8 A3
Home Pastures LE14 . 211 F4
Homecroft Dr NG16 .. 128 C4
Homefarm La NG23 ... 70 A3
Homefield Ave NG5 ... 148 A1
Homefield Croft DN10 . 10 A1
Homefield Rd NG8 ... 172 B4
Homelands The NG17 . 100 C1
Homestead NG16 .... 143 D2
Homesteads The NG20 . 74 A2
Homewood Dr NG17 .. 114 C4
Honeycroft Cl DE55 .. 113 D2
Honeyknab La NG25 .. 134 B3
Honeys La NG23 ...... 139 D1
Honeysuckle Cl
New Balderton NG24 .. 140 B2
4 Nottingham NG8 .... 159 F1
Honeysuckle Gr
Bingham NG13 .... 177 E2
Nottingham NG6 ...... 160 A2
Honeywood Dr NG3 ... 174 A4
Honeywood Wlk NG3 . 174 A4
Honing Dr NG25 ...... 136 B4
Honingham Cl NG5 ... 162 A3
Honingham Rd DE7 ... 157 D2
Honister Cl
Mansfield NG18 .... 102 B2
Nottingham NG11 ..... 195 E4
West Bridgford NG2 ... 186 B4
Honister Ct NG18 ..... 102 B2
Honiton Cl NG9 .... 183 D1
Honiton Rd NG8 ...... 159 F1
Hood St NG5 .... 161 E1
Hooley Cl NG10 .... 193 D3

Hooley Pl 10 NG5 ..... 161 E2
Hooley St NG16 .... 128 C3
Hoopers Wlk 6 NG2 . 173 E1
Hooton Rd NG4 .... 174 B4
Hooton St NG3 .... 173 F3
Hope Cl NG2 .... 173 D1
Hope Dr NG7 .... 223 D1
Hope St Beeston NG9 . 183 F4
Nottingham NG1 ...... 102 B3
Hopedale Cl NG7 ...... 222 A3
Hopewell Cl NG12 .... 176 A2
Hopewell Wlk DE7 .... 157 F3
Hopkin La NG25 .... 121 E1
Hopkins Ct NG16 ..... 143 F2
Hopyard La
Egmanton NG22 .... 79 F4
Normanton on T NG23 . 82 A3
Horace Ave NG9 .... 182 C3
Hornbeam Cl DE7 .... 170 A4
Hornbeam Gdns NG6 . 159 F4
Hornbuckle Ct NG7 ... 222 B3
Hornchurch Rd NG8 .. 171 E4
Hornsby Wlk NG5 ..... 160 C4
Horridge St DE7 ...... 157 F2
Horsecroft Cl DE7 .... 157 E1
Horsendale Ave NG16 . 159 F2
Horsendale Prim Sch
NG16 .... 159 F2
Horsewells St DN10 ... 12 C1
Horsham Dr NG5 ...... 160 C4
Horsley Cres NG16 ... 143 D2
Hosse CE Prim Sch
LE14 .... 211 F4
Hose La
Colston Bassett LE14 .. 201 D2
Harby LE14 .... 202 A1
Hose LE14 .... 211 F3
Hoselett Field Rd
NG10 .... 193 F3
Hosiery St NG17 ...... 115 D3
Hospital Rd DN22 ..... 39 F4
Hoten Rd 5 NG2 ...... 173 F2
Hoton Rd LE12 .... 216 A2
Hotspur Cl NG6 .... 160 C3
Hotspur Rd DN21 ..... 15 E1
Houfton Rd NG18 ..... 102 C4
Hougham Rd NG23 ... 156 C1
Houghton Ave DE7 ... 157 E2
Houghton Cl NG16 ... 159 F2
Houldsworth Rise
NG5 .... 147 F1
Hound Rd NG2 .... 185 F4
Hounds Gate NG1 .... 223 D2
Hounsfield Cl NG4 ... 174 C4
Hounsfield Way NG23 . 96 C4
Houseman Gdns NG2 . 173 E1
Houston Cl NG5 ...... 146 C1
Hove Rd NG5 .... 160 C3
Hoveringham Rd
NG14 .... 165 E4
Howard Cl NG10 ...... 182 C1
Howard Rd Bircotes DN11 . 9 E2
Mansfield NG19 .... 101 F4
Howard St
Loughborough LE11 ... 220 A3
Nottingham NG1 ...... 223 E3
Sutton in A NG17 ..... 100 C2
Worksop S80 .... 36 A1
Howbeck Gdns NG24 . 140 B2
Howbeck La DN22 .... 30 C2
Howbeck Rd NG5 ..... 162 A4
Howden Rd NG6 ...... 146 B1
Howe Rd LE11 .... 220 A1
Howell-Jones Rd
NG9 .... 183 D2
Howells Cl NG5 .... 161 E4
Howes Ct NG24 ...... 140 A4
Howick Dr NG6 .... 159 F4
Howitt St Heanor DE75 . 143 D1
Long Eaton NG10 ..... 193 F4
Howitts Rd NG13 ..... 181 D1
Hoylake Cl NG19 ..... 88 C6
Hoylake Cres NG8 .... 171 E4
Hoyland Ave NG7 ..... 172 C1
Hubert St NG7 .... 222 B4
Huckerby Rd DE7 .... 157 E1
Hucklow Ct NG18 .... 103 D3
Hucknall Cl NG8 ...... 159 E1
Hucknall Coll NG15 .. 146 A4
Hucknall Cres NG4 ... 162 C1
Hucknall Ind Est NG15 . 145 F2
Hucknall Ind Pk NG15 . 145 F2
Hucknall Rd
Newstead NG15 .... 130 B3
Nottingham NG5 ...... 160 C3
Hucknall Sta NG15 ... 146 B4
Huddlestones Wharf
NG14 .... 139 F4
Hudson St
Loughborough LE11 ... 220 B2
Nottingham NG3 ...... 173 F3
Huffons Dr DE75 ...... 157 D4
Huftons St DE75 ...... 157 D4
Hugessen Ave NG15 .. 146 B4
Hugget Gdns 4 NG5 . 161 D4
Humber Cl NG2 ...... 173 E1
Humber La NG23 ..... 153 D4
Humber Rd
Beeston NG9 .... 184 A4
Long Eaton NG10 ..... 182 B1
Humber Rd S NG9 ... 184 A4
Humber St Retford DN22 . 40 A3
Worksop S80 .... 35 F2
Humberston Rd NG8 . 171 E2
Hume St LE11 .... 220 A1
Humphrey Cl LE11 ... 220 A1
Humphries Gdns S80 . 35 F1
Hundred Acre La S81 . 26 B2

Hundred Acres La
NG24 .... 140 B1
Hundreds La DN10 ..... 5 D2
Hungary La LE12 ...... 213 E4
Hungerhill Rd NG3 ... 173 E4
Hungerton St NG7 .... 222 B1
Hunston Cl NG8 ...... 172 A4
Hunter Rd NG5 .... 162 B3
Hunters Cl NG11 ..... 114 C3
Hunters Ct NG17 ..... 114 C3
Hunters Dr DN10 ...... 12 C1
Huntingdon Dr NG7 .. 223 D2
Huntingdon Prim Sch
NG3 .... 223 F4
Huntingdon St NG1 .. 223 E3
Huntingdon Way NG9 . 182 C1
Huntingdon Wlk NG10 . 182 A3
Huntly Cl
Mansfield NG19 .... 101 E3
Nottingham NG7 ...... 184 C1
Hunts Hill NG16 ...... 144 A4
Huntsman Pl DN22 .... 19 D1
Hurcomb St NG3 ..... 173 F4
Hurst Cl NG21 .... 103 F1
Hurts Croft NG9 ...... 183 E2
Hurts Yd NG1 .... 223 E2
Huss La NG10 .... 193 F4
Hutchinson Gn NG3 .. 223 F4
Hutchinson Rd NG4 . 140 C4
Huthwaite La DE55 .... 99 E1
Huthwaite Rd NG17 .. 100 B1
Hutton Cl NG9 .... 171 E1
Hutton St NG2 .... 173 F2
Huxley Cl NG8 .... 171 E4
Hyde Cl NG11 .... 184 C2
Hyde Pk Cl NG2 ...... 185 E3
Hyson Cl 4 NG7 ..... 172 C4
Hyson Gn St Marys Cath
Prim Sch NG7 ...... 172 C4
Hyson St 13 NG7 .... 172 C4

I

Ian Gr NG4 .... 174 C4
IBTE Mus of
Telecommunications*
S81 .... 35 F1
Idle Bank DN9 .... 2 C3
Idle Ct DN10 .... 10 A4
Idle View DN22 .... 29 F1
Idlewells Sh Ctr NG17 . 100 C1
Ilam Sq DE7 .... 157 F3
Ilford Cl DE7 .... 157 E2
Ilion St NG19 .... 87 F1
Ilkeston Com Hospl
DE7 .... 157 E2
Ilkeston Rd
Sandiacre NG10 .... 182 B4
Stapleford NG9 .... 170 C1
Trowell NG9 .... 170 B3
Imperial Ave
Beeston NG9 .... 183 F3
Carlton NG4 .... 162 C1
Imperial Rd
Beeston NG9 .... 183 F3
Nottingham NG6 ...... 160 B3
Inchwood Cl NG8 .... 159 D1
Incinerator Rd NG2 .. 173 F1
Independent St NG7 . 222 B4
Industrial Mus & Art Gall*
NG8 .... 172 A2
Infield La Cuckney NG20 . 60 A3
North Leverton w H DN22 . 32 C1
Weston NG23 .... 81 D2
Ingham Gr NG7 ...... 222 A1
Ingham Rd Bawtry DN10 . 9 F4
Long Eaton NG10 ..... 182 B1
Ingleborough Gdns 8
NG10 .... 193 D4
Ingleby Cl
Cotgrave NG12 .... 187 F1
4 Nottingham NG8 .. 171 D2
Ingleby Medieval Village of*
LN1 .... 57 C4
Inglefield Rd DE7 .... 170 A3
Inglemere Cl S81 ..... 36 A3
Inglewood Cl NG24 .. 140 B1
Inglewood Rd NG7 ... 184 C1
Ingram La NG23 ...... 82 A2
Ingram Rd NG6 ...... 160 B3
Ingram Terr NG6 ..... 160 B3
Ings Rd DN10 .... 12 C3
Inham Cir NG9 .... 183 E3
Inham Cl NG9 .... 183 D3
Inham Fields NG14 .. 165 D3
Inham Rd NG9 .... 183 D3
Inholms Gdns NG23 . 152 C1
Inholms Rd NG23 .... 152 C1
Inkerman Rd NG16 .. 128 C3
Inkerman St NG16 ... 128 C2
Innes Rd NG4 .... 174 B4
Institute St NG17 .... 100 B3
Instow Rise NG3 ..... 223 F4
Intake Ave NG18 ..... 101 F3
Intake Farm Prim Sch
NG19 .... 101 F4
Intake Rd
Clipstone NG21 .... 90 A2
Keyworth NG12 ...... 197 E2
Iona Cl DN21 .... 15 F1
Iona Dr NG9 .... 170 B1
Iona Gdns NG5 ...... 147 D1
Ipswich Cir NG3 ..... 174 A3
Ireland Ave NG9 ..... 184 A3
Ireland Cl NG9 .... 184 A3
Iremonger Rd NG2 ... 173 E1
Irene Terr NG7 .... 160 C1

Ireton Gr NG9 .... 183 E1
Ireton St Beeston NG9 . 183 F3
Nottingham NG7 ...... 222 C3
Irving Cl NG22 .... 120 A3
Irwin Dr NG6 .... 160 A3
Isaacs La NG9 .... 182 B4
Isabella St NG7 ...... 223 E1
Islay Cl Arnold NG5 ... 147 F1
Stapleford NG9 .... 170 B2
Ivatt Cl DN10 .... 10 A4
Ivatt Dr NG2 .... 173 F2
Iveagh Cl NG20 .... 74 B3
Ives Cl NG2 .... 185 E2
Ivies The NG24 .... 139 E3
Ivy Cl NG16 .... 144 C1
Ivy Gr Carlton NG4 ... 174 B4
Kirkby in A NG17 ...... 114 C3
Nottingham NG7 ...... 173 D4
Ivy La NG16 .... 143 F1
Ivy Lodge La S81 ..... 16 A2
Ivy Row NG13 .... 179 D2

J

Jacklin Gdns NG5 .... 147 D1
Jacksdale Prim Sch
NG16 .... 128 A2
Jackson Ave NG10 ... 182 A3
Jackson Terr NG20 ... 74 C4
James Murray Mews
NG18 .... 102 B4
James Peacock Inf Sch
NG11 .... 196 A4
James St
Annesley Woodhouse
NG17 .... 115 D1
Arnold NG5 .... 161 F4
Kimberley NG16 ...... 158 C3
Worksop S81 .... 35 F2
James William Turner Ave
NG17 .... 100 C1
Japan Rd NG18 .... 101 D1
Japonica Dr NG6 ..... 160 A2
Jardine S81 .... 36 A3
Jardines The NG9 .... 171 E1
Jarrow Gdns NG5 .... 146 C1
Jarvis Ave NG3 .... 174 A3
Jasmin Cl NG20 ...... 72 B3
Jasmine Cl
Beeston NG9 .... 171 E1
5 Nottingham, Broxtowe
NG8 .... 159 F1
Nottingham, Glapton
NG11 .... 184 B1
Jasmine Dr DE55 ..... 99 D4
Jasmine Rd NG5 ..... 160 C2
Jasper Cl NG12 ...... 175 F1
Jay Gr Carlton NG4 ... 163 D1
Nottingham NG8 ..... 171 F3
Jays Cl NG13 .... 181 D1
Jedburgh Cl NG3 ..... 223 F4
Jedburgh Wlk NG3 .. 223 F4
Jeffares Cl DE74 ..... 203 E2
Jellicoe St NG20 ...... 59 D1
Jenford St NG18 ..... 101 F3
Jenkins Ave NG19 ... 101 E4
Jenned Rd NG5 ...... 148 A1
Jenner St 8 NG5 ..... 161 D1
Jenness Ave NG5 .... 146 C1
Jennison St
Mansfield NG19 ...... 88 A1
Nottingham NG6 ..... 160 B4
Jenny Becketts La
NG18 .... 102 C2
Jenny Burton Way
NG15 .... 146 B3
Jephson Rd NG17 ... 114 C4
Jericho La NG13 ..... 192 A2
Jericho Rd NG24 .... 140 B1
Jermyn Dr NG5 ...... 147 D1
Jersey Gdns NG3 .... 173 F3
Jersey St NG3 .... 139 F3
Jerusalem LN6 .... 71 F1
Jervis Ct DE7 .... 157 F2
Jesmond Rd NG6 .... 160 B3
Jesse Boot Prim Sch
NG3 .... 174 A3
Jesse Gray Sch NG2 . 185 F3
Jessop Cl NG24 ...... 125 E1
Jessop Way NG24 ... 125 E1
Jessops La NG4 ...... 162 C1
Job La DN10 .... 20 A4
Jobs La LN6 .... 84 C1
Jockey La DN22 ...... 50 A3
John Barrow Cl NG21 . 118 B4
John Blow Prim Sch
NG23 .... 112 A4
John Carroll Ct 2 NG3 . 173 F3
John Clifford Prim Sch
NG9 .... 184 A3
John Coupland Hospl
DN21 .... 15 D2
John Davies Prim Sch
NG17 .... 99 F2
John Hunt Inf Sch
NG24 .... 140 B2
John Hunt Jun Sch
NG24 .... 140 B2
John King Inf Sch
NG16 .... 113 E2
John King Workshop Mus*
NG16 .... 113 E2
John Pope Way NG24 . 125 D2
John St Ilkeston DE7 .. 157 F1
Nottingham NG7 ...... 160 C1
Sutton in A NG17 ..... 100 C2

John St continued
Worksop S80 .... 35 F2
John T Rice Inf Sch
NG5 .... 89 F2
Johns Rd NG12 ...... 176 A2
Johnson Ave NG15 .. 146 A3
Johnson Dr NG18 ... 102 B2
Johnson Rd NG7 .... 222 A2
Joseph Whitaker Sch
NG21 .... 117 F4
Joyce Ave
Beeston NG9 .... 182 C2
Nottingham NG5 ..... 161 E3
Joyce Cl NG5 .... 161 E2
Jubilee Cl DN10 .... 4 A2
Jubilee Dr LE11 ...... 220 A3
Jubilee Rd Arnold NG5 . 161 F3
Retford DN22 .... 39 E3
Sutton in A NG17 ..... 100 B2
Jubilee St
Kimberley NG16 ...... 158 C4
Newark-on-T NG24 ... 140 A4
8 Nottingham NG2 .. 173 F2
Jubilee Way N NG18 . 103 E3
Jubilee Way S NG18 . 103 D2
Judges St LE11 ...... 220 B2
Judson Ave NG9 ..... 182 C3
Julian Cl DE7 .... 170 A3
Julian La NG12 ...... 164 B1
Julian Rd NG2 .... 174 A1
Julie Ave DE75 ...... 143 D1
Jumelles Dr NG14 ... 148 B4
Junction Rd
Long Eaton NG10 ..... 194 A3
Sutton in A NG17 ..... 101 D1
Juniper Cl NG11 ..... 184 B1
Juniper Cl NG16 ..... 158 B4
Juniper Gdns NG13 . 178 A2

K

Kansington Ct 5 NG5 . 161 E2
Kappler Cl NG4 ...... 175 D4
Karen Rise NG5 ...... 148 A1
Katherine Dr NG9 ... 182 C2
Kaye Rd NG19 .... 101 E4
Kayes Wlk NG1 ...... 223 F2
Keats Ave NG17 ..... 100 A2
Keats Cl Arnold NG5 . 161 F4
Long Eaton NG10 ..... 193 D3
Nuthall NG16 .... 159 D3
Keats Cres S81 .... 36 A2
Keats Dr NG15 ...... 145 E3
Keats Rd NG24 ...... 140 B3
Kedleston Cl
Beeston NG9 .... 183 E3
Long Eaton NG10 ..... 193 D3
Kedleston Dr DE7 ... 157 E2
Kedleston Rd S81 .... 35 F3
Kedlestone Cl NG17 .. 99 F1
Keel Dr NG13 .... 181 D1
Keeling Cl NG16 .... 144 A1
Keep The LE12 ...... 205 F1
Keepers Cl NG6 ..... 146 C2
Kegworth Cty Prim Sch
DE74 .... 203 E1
Kegworth La DE74 ... 212 B3
Kegworth Mus* DE74 . 203 E1
Kegworth Rd
Gotham NG11 .... 195 D1
Kingston-on-S NG11 . 204 C4
Ratcliffe on S NG11 .. 203 F3
Keighton Hill NG7 ... 172 B1
Keilder Dr NG13 ..... 177 E2
Kelfield Cl NG6 ...... 160 C3
Kelham Gn NG3 ..... 173 F3
Kelham La NG24 ..... 124 B2
Kelham Rd
Mansfield NG19 ...... 101 F4
Newark-on-T NG24 ... 124 C1
Kelham Way NG16 ... 143 F2
Keller Ct DN22 .... 53 D4
Kelling Cl NG5 .... 161 D3
Kelly Wlk NG2 .... 185 D4
Kelsey Cl NG9 .... 183 F2
Kelso Gdns NG2 .... 173 D1
Kelstedge Dr NG18 .. 103 D3
Kelstern Cl
Mansfield NG18 ...... 103 D4
Nottingham NG8 ..... 160 B2
Kelvedon Gdns NG3 . 173 F3
Kelvin Cl NG9 .... 182 B3
Kelvin Rd
Clipstone NG19 .... 89 E2
Nottingham NG3 ..... 174 A4
Kemmel Rd NG6 ..... 160 B3
Kempsey Cl NG5 ..... 160 C4
Kempson St NG11 ... 196 B3
Kempton Cl NG16 ... 158 C4
Kempton Dr NG5 .... 148 A1
Kempton Rd NG18 .. 102 C4
Kendal Cl
Annesley Woodhouse
NG17 .... 130 A4
Hucknall NG15 .... 145 F4
Worksop S81 .... 35 F4
Kendal Ct NG2 .... 186 A4
Kendal Dr NG9 ...... 183 E4
Kendal Rd NG12 .... 189 D2
Kendale Ct NG3 ..... 161 F1
Kenia Cl NG4 .... 174 B4
Kenilworth Ave NG17 . 101 D2
Kenilworth Ct
Saxilby LN1 .... 57 D2
Worksop S80 .... 36 A1
Kenilworth Dr
Beeston NG9 .... 184 A4

Kenilworth Ct *continued*
Nottingham NG7 223 D1
Kenilworth Dr S81 25 F3
Kenilworth Rd
Beeston NG9 184 A4
Nottingham NG7 223 D1
Kenley Cl S81 35 E4
Kenmare Cres DN21 24 C3
Kenmore Cl NG19 101 F3
Kenmore Gdns NG3 223 F4
Kennack Cl DE55 113 E3
Kennedy Ave
Long Eaton NG10 193 E3
Mansfield Woodhouse NG19 88 B2
Kennedy Cl NG5 161 F4
Kennedy Ct
Walesby NG22 64 A1
Worksop S81 36 A2
Kennedy Dr NG9 170 C1
Kennedy Rise NG22 64 A1
Kennedy Wlk NG24 140 C2
Kennel Dr DN22 28 B3
Kennel La LN6 71 E1
Kennet Paddock NG19 88 B2
Kenneth Rd NG5 147 F1
Kennington Rd NG8 172 B3
Kenrick Rd NG3 162 A1
Kenrick St NG4 175 D4
Kensington Cl
Beeston NG9 183 D1
Mansfield Woodhouse NG19 88 C3
Sutton in A NG17 100 C1
Kensington Ct NG5 161 E2
Kensington Gdns
Carlton NG4 174 C4
Ilkeston DE7 170 A4
Kensington Jun Sch DE7 170 A4
Kensington Pk Cl NG2 185 E3
Kensington Rd NG10 182 A2
Kenslow Ave 38 NG7 172 C4
Kent Ave Beeston NG9 183 F2
Westwood NG16 128 A2
Kent Cl S81 36 A3
Kent Rd
Eastwood NG16 158 B4
Nottingham NG3 162 A2
Kent St NG1 223 F3
Kentmere Cl NG2 186 B4
Kenton Ave NG16 159 E2
Kenton Ct 26 NG2 173 E1
Kentwood Rd NG2 173 F2
Kenyon Rd NG7 172 B2
Keppel Ct DE7 157 F2
Kersall Ct NG6 160 B3
Kersall Dr NG6 160 B3
Kersall Gdns NG15 146 A4
Kestral Dr NG13 177 F2
Kestral Rd NG18 101 F2
Kestrel Cl NG4 162 A1
Kestrel Mews S81 35 E4
Kestrel Rise LN6 84 B1
Keswick Cl
Beeston NG9 183 E4
West Bridgford NG2 186 B4
Keswick Ct
Long Eaton NG10 182 A1
3 Nottingham NG2 173 F2
Keswick Rd S81 35 F4
Keswick St NG2 173 F2
Ketlock Hill La DN22 32 B1
Kett St NG6 160 A3
Kettlethorpe Rd LN1 55 E3
Keverne Cl NG8 160 B1
Kevin Rd NG8 171 E1
Kew Cl NG11 185 E2
Kew Cres DE75 143 D1
Kew Gdns
New Balderton NG24 140 A2
Nuthall NG8 159 F2
Kexby Wlk DN21 24 C4
Key St NG3 173 F3
Keyes Cl DN10 19 F4
Keyes Ct DN10 19 F4
Keyes Rise DN10 19 F4
Keys Cl NG6 160 A4
Keyworth Cl NG19 101 F4
Keyworth Dr NG19 89 E1
Keyworth Prim Sch NG12 197 F2
Keyworth Rd
Carlton NG4 162 B2
Widmerpool NG12 208 B3
Wysall NG12 207 E3
Kibworth Cl NG5 160 C2
Kid La S81 16 A3
Kiddier Ave NG5 162 A4
Kighill La NG15 132 A4
Kilbourn St NG3 223 E4
Kilbourne Rd NG5 148 A1
Kilburn Cl NG9 171 D1
Kilby Ave NG3 174 A3
Kildare Rd NG3 173 F4
Kildonan Cl NG8 159 E1
Killerton Gn NG11 195 F4
Killerton Pk Dr NG11 185 D2
Killisick Jun Sch NG5 148 A1
Killisick Rd NG5 162 A4
Kilnbrook Ave NG5 148 A1
Kilnwood Cl NG3 174 A4
Kilsby Rd NG7 184 C1
Kilton Cl S81 36 A2
Kilton Cres S81 36 A2
Kilton Glade S81 36 A2
Kilton Hill S81 36 A3
Kilton Rd S80 36 A2
Kilton Terr S80 36 A2
Kilton Terr Ind Est S80 36 A2
Kilverston Rd NG10 182 A3
Kilverton Cl NG8 172 B2
Kilvington Rd NG5 162 A4
Kimber Cl NG8 171 E3
Kimberley Cl NG16 158 C3
Kimberley Comp Sch NG16 159 D3
Kimberley Prim Sch NG16 159 D3
Kimberley Rd
Nottingham NG2 174 A2
Nuthall NG16 159 E3
Kimbolton Ave NG7 222 B2
Kindlewood Dr NG9 183 D1
King Charles St NG1 223 D2
King Edward Ave NG18 102 A2
King Edward Gdns NG10 182 A3
King Edward Prim Sch NG18 102 B3
King Edward Rd LE11 220 B2
King Edward St
Hucknall NG15 146 A3
Nottingham NG1 223 F3
Sandiacre NG10 182 A3
Shirebrook NG20 72 C2
King Edward VI Comp Sch (Lower) DN22 40 A3
King Edwards Terr DN22 39 F3
King Edwin Prim Sch NG21 75 F1
King George Ave LE11 220 B1
King George Rd LE11 220 B1
King George V Ave NG18 102 C3
King Johns Arc NG1 223 E2
King Johns Rd NG21 90 A2
King Rd NG20 74 A2
King St Beeston NG9 184 A3
Eastwood NG16 143 F1
Gainsborough DN21 24 B4
Hodthorpe S80 45 E3
Huthwaite NG17 100 A2
Ilkeston DE7 157 F1
Kirkby in A NG17 115 D2
Long Eaton NG10 193 E4
Loughborough LE11 220 B2
Mansfield NG18 102 B4
Mansfield Woodhouse NG19 88 B1
Nether Broughton LE14 219 E4
Newark-on-T NG24 139 F4
Nottingham NG1 223 E3
Pinxton NG16 113 E2
South Normanton DE55 113 D3
Southwell NG25 121 F1
Sutton in A NG17 100 C1
Tibshelf DE55 99 D4
Warsop Vale NG20 73 E3
Worksop S80 35 F1
King St E DN21 24 B4
Kingerby Cl DN21 24 C4
Kingfield Cl NG21 118 A4
Kingfisher Cl
New Balderton NG24 140 B3
Nottingham NG6 160 B2
Kingfisher Ct
Beeston NG9 184 A3
2 Loughborough LE11 220 A1
Kingfisher Way 1 LE11 220 A1
Kingfisher Wharf 20 NG7 172 C1
Kingfisher Wlk S81 35 E4
Kingfishers Ct NG2 186 B2
Kinglake Pl NG2 173 E1
Kingrove Ave NG9 183 E3
Kings Ave NG4 162 C1
Kings Ct NG25 121 F1
Kings Dr NG16 143 F4
Kings Lodge Dr NG18 101 F2
Kings Mdw Rd NG2 173 D1
Kings Mill Ctr Hospl NG17 101 E3
Kings Mill La NG18 101 E2
Kings Mill Rd E NG17, NG19 114 C4
Kings Mill Way NG18 101 F2
Kings Moor NG5 160 C4
Kings Pl NG1 223 F2
Kings Rd LE14 211 E1
Kings Rd NG24 124 C1
Kings Rd NG10 182 A3
Kings Sch The NG2 173 E1
Kings Stand NG18 102 C2
Kings Way S80 45 E3
Kings Wlk NG18 102 C2
Kings Wlk NG1 223 E3
Kings Wood Cl DN10 10 A4
Kingsbridge Ave NG3 162 B3
Kingsbridge Way NG9 183 E3
Kingsbury Dr NG8 172 A4
Kingsdale S81 36 A4
Kingsdale Cl NG10 193 D3
Kingsdown Mount NG8 171 F1
Kingsford Ave NG7 222 A4
Kingshaugh Ancient Mon & Royal Manor* NG22 66 C4
Kingsley Ave NG19 88 B3
Kingsley Cl NG19 88 B2
Kingsley Cres NG10 193 D2
Kingsley Ct NG19 88 B3
Kingsley Dr NG4 175 D4
Kingsley Rd NG2 174 A2
Kingsley St NG17 115 D2
Kingsmead DN22 39 E2
Kingsmead Ave NG9 170 B1
Kingsmeadow NG21 118 B4
Kingsnorth Cl NG24 140 A4
Kingsthorpe Cl
Mansfield NG19 88 C1
Nottingham NG3 161 F1
Kingston Ave DE7 170 A2
Kingston Cl S80 47 E4
Kingston Ct
Kingston-on-S NG11 204 B3
14 Nottingham NG2 173 F2
Kingston Dr
Cotgrave NG12 187 F1
Ollerton NG22 77 D2
Kingston Jun Sch S81 25 F3
Kingston La DE74 203 F2
Kingston Rd
Carlton in L S81 25 F3
Mansfield NG18 102 B4
West Bridgford NG2 185 F3
Worksop S80 47 E4
Kingsway Ilkeston DE7 170 A3
Kirkby in A NG17 115 D2
Mansfield Woodhouse NG19 89 D1
New Balderton NG24 140 B2
Radcliffe on T NG12 175 F1
Worksop S81 36 A2
Kingsway Ave NG22 77 E3
Kingsway Gdns NG15 145 F2
Kingsway Prim Sch NG17 115 D2
Kingsway Rd NG15 145 F2
Kingswell Rd NG5 161 F3
Kingswood Cl
Firbeck S81 16 A3
West Bridgford NG2 185 E3
Kingswood Dr NG17 114 C3
Kingswood Rd NG8 172 A3
Kinlet Rd NG5 161 D3
Kinoulton La
Kinoulton NG12 209 D4
Kinoulton, Owthorpe NG12 199 F2
Kinoulton Prim Sch NG12 199 F1
Kinoulton Rd NG12 188 C1
Kinsdale Wlk NG11 184 C2
Kipling Cl
Nottingham NG11 195 E4
Worksop S81 36 A3
Kipling St 6 NG18 102 A4
Kipps St NG1 223 F3
Kirby Cl
Blidworth NG21 118 A2
Eastwood NG16 144 A2
Kirby Dr DE74 203 E1
Kirby Rd NG16 144 A2
Kirk Ave DE74 203 E1
Kirk Cl NG9 183 E2
Kirk Dr NG22 77 F3
Kirk Gate NG24 124 C1
Kirk Hill NG13 165 D1
Kirk La NG11 196 B4
Kirk Ley Rd LE12 214 B4
Kirk Rd NG3 162 A1
Kirk White Ct NG2 173 E1
Kirkbride Ct NG9 183 D2
Kirkby Cl NG25 121 F1
Kirkby Coll NG17 115 D2
Kirkby Folly Rd NG17 101 D1
Kirkby Gdns NG2 173 E1
Kirkby House Dr NG17 114 C3
Kirkby La NG16 114 A2
Kirkby Mill View NG17 114 C3
Kirkby Rd
Ravenshead NG15 116 B2
Sutton in A NG17 100 C1
Kirkby Woodhouse Prim Sch NG17 114 C1
Kirkby-in-Ashfield Sta NG17 115 D3
Kirkdale Cl NG8 171 D2
Kirkdale Gdns NG10 193 D3
Kirkdale Rd
Long Eaton NG10 193 D3
Nottingham NG3 174 A3
Kirke Cl NG22 66 A4
Kirke St DN22 39 F4
Kirkewhite Ave NG10 193 E4
Kirkfell Cl NG2 186 B3
Kirkham Dr NG9 182 C1
Kirkhill NG13 177 F3
Kirkland Ave NG18 101 F3
Kirkland Cl NG17 115 D4
Kirkland Dr NG9 183 E1
Kirkley Gdns NG5 162 A4
Kirklington Cty Prim Sch NG22 120 C4
Kirklington Rd
Bilsthorpe NG22 105 E1
Eakring NG22 106 C4
Rainworth NG21, NG22 104 B1
Southwell NG25 121 E1
Kirkpatrick Dr S81 35 E4
Kirks Bldgs NG4 174 B4
Kirkstead Cl NG16 113 E2
Kirkstead Gdns 28 NG7 172 C4
Kirkstead Jun Sch NG16 113 E2
Kirkstead Rd NG16 113 E2
Kirkstead St 27 NG7 172 C4
Kirkstone Ct NG10 182 A1
Kirkstone Dr NG2 186 B4
Kirtle Cl NG8 172 A4
Kirtley Dr NG2 173 D1
Kirton Ave NG10 193 E4
Kirton Cl
Balderton NG24 140 B2
Mansfield NG19 101 E4
Meden Vale NG20 74 C4
Kirton Ct NG22 78 A3
Kirton Pk NG22 78 B3
Kirton Rd NG22 79 E3
Kitchener Dr NG18 102 B3
Kitchener Gdns S81 35 F4
Kitchener Terr NG20 59 D1
Kitson Ave NG16 128 B2
Kittiwake Mews NG7 222 A2
Kiwi Cl NG15 145 E3
Knapp Ave NG16 143 F1
Knaton Rd S81 25 F4
Kneesall CE Prim Sch NG22 93 F3
Kneesall Cl NG20 74 B4
Kneesall Gr NG15 146 A4
Kneeton Cl
Carlton NG4 162 B2
Nottingham NG5 161 E2
Kneeton Rd NG13 165 F3
Kneeton Vale NG5 161 E2
Knight St NG4 175 D3
Knighton Ave NG7 222 A4
Knighton Rd NG5 161 E3
Knights Cl NG5 160 C4
Knights Cl NG13 166 C2
Knights Cl NG2 185 E2
Knights Ct NG24 140 A4
Knightsbridge Dr
Nuthall NG8 159 F2
West Bridgford NG2 185 E2
Knightsbridge Gdns NG15 130 C1
Knipton Cl NG24 140 B2
Knole Rd NG8 171 F3
Knoll Ave NG15 145 E3
Knoll The
Mansfield NG18 101 F3
Shirebrook NG20 72 B2
Knott End S81 16 C2
Knotts Ct NG24 140 B2
Knowle Hill NG16 159 D3
Knowle La NG16 159 D3
Knowle Pk NG16 159 D3
Knowles Wlk 10 NG5 161 E4
Krebs Cl NG11 184 B1
Kyle View NG5 147 D1
Kyme St NG7 222 B3
Kynance Cl DE55 113 E3
Kynance Gdns NG11 185 D3

L

Labray Rd NG14 148 C4
Laburnium Cl NG24 140 B3
Laburnum Ave
Gainsborough DN21 15 E1
Keyworth NG12 198 A1
Kirkby in A NG17 114 B2
Shirebrook NG20 72 C3
Laburnum Cl
Hathern LE12 213 D1
Sandiacre NG10 182 A4
South Normanton DE55 113 D4
Worksop S80 35 E1
Laburnum Gr
Beeston NG9 184 A3
Hucknall NG15 146 A3
Mansfield Woodhouse NG19 88 A2
Laburnum Rd S81 16 C2
Laburnum St NG3 173 E4
Lace Ctr The* NG1 223 D2
Lace Mkt Ctr The* NG1 223 E2
Lace Rd NG9 183 F4
Lace St NG7 172 B1
Laceby Ct NG19 88 C2
Lacey Ave NG15 146 A3
Lacey Cl DE7 157 E2
Lacey Fields Rd DE75 143 D1
Lacey Gn NG24 140 C2
Ladbrooke Cres NG6 160 B2
Lady Bay Ave NG2 173 F1
Lady Bay Bridge NG2 173 F1
Lady Bay Prim Sch NG2 174 A1
Lady Bay Rd NG2 174 A1
Lady Well La DN22 52 A4
Lady Wlk S81 35 E4
Ladybank Rise NG5 162 B4
Ladybridge Cl NG9 183 F2
Ladybrook La NG18 101 F4
Ladybrook Pl NG19 101 F4
Ladybrook Prim Sch NG19 101 E4
Ladycroft Ave NG15 146 A4
Ladycross Inf Sch NG10 182 A3
Ladylea Cl S80 35 D1
Ladylea Rd NG10 193 D2
Ladysmith Rd NG2 174 A2
Ladysmock Gdns NG2 173 E1
Ladywood La NG23 80 C3
Lake Ave NG19 101 F4
Lake Farm Rd NG21 103 F1
Lake St NG7 222 B4
Lake View Dr NG17 129 F3
Lake View Prim Sch NG21 103 F1
Lakeland Ave NG15 146 B3
Lakeside Arts Ctr* NG7 172 B1
Lakeside Ave NG10 193 E3
Lakeside Cres NG10 193 E3
Lakeside Inf Sch NG10 193 E3
Lamartine Ct NG3 223 F3
Lamartine St NG3 223 F3
Lamb Cl NG24 139 E4
Lamb Cl Dr NG16 144 A2
Lamb La S81 16 B3
Lambcroft Rd NG16 113 E2
Lambert Ct NG9 184 A4
Lambert Gdns NG8 172 B4
Lambert St NG7 172 C4
Lambeth Rd NG5 147 D1
Lambie Cl NG8 172 B3
Lambley Ave
Mansfield NG18 102 C3
Nottingham NG3 162 A2
Lambley Bridle Rd NG14 163 E3
Lambley La
Burton Joyce NG14 163 F3
Carlton NG4 162 C2
Lambley Prim Sch NG4 163 D4
Lambley Rd NG14 150 A1
Lambourne Cres NG14 150 C1
Lambourne Dr NG8 172 A3
Lambourne Gdns NG5 162 A3
Lambton Cl DE7 157 F2
Lamcote Gdns NG12 175 F2
Lamcote Gr NG2 173 E1
Lamcote Mews NG4 175 F2
Lamcote St NG2 173 E1
Laming Gap La NG12 198 C3
Lamins La NG5 147 E2
Lammas Cl NG17 100 C1
Lammas Gdns
East Bridgford NG13 165 E2
Nottingham NG2 173 E1
Lammas La NG13 165 E2
Lammas Rd NG17 100 C1
Lammas Sch The NG17 100 C1
Lamond Cl NG19 101 F3
Lamorna Gr NG11 185 D3
Lamp Wood Cl NG14 148 C4
Lamplands NG12 187 F2
Lanark Cl NG8 172 B2
Lancaster Ave
Sandiacre NG10 182 A2
Stapleford NG9 182 C4
Lancaster Cl DN11 8 A4
Lancaster Dr DN10 9 F4
Lancaster Rd
Bestwood Village NG6 146 C2
Gringley on t H DN10 22 A4
Hucknall NG15 145 E2
Nottingham NG3 174 A4
Lancaster Way NG8 159 E1
Lancaster Wlk S81 35 F4
Lancastrian Way S81 36 A3
Lancelot Dr NG16 145 D1
Lancelyn Gdns NG2 185 F2
Lancster Cres DN11 8 A4
Landa Gr NG22 66 A2
Landcroft Cres NG5 161 D3
Landcroft La LE12 204 B1
Landmere Cl DE7 157 E2
Landmere Gdns NG3 161 F1
Landmere La
West Bridgford NG11 185 E2
West Bridgford NG11, NG12 185 F1
Landsdown Gr NG10 182 C1
Landsdowne Ct DN22 39 E2
Landsdowne Rd NG5 160 C2
Landseer Cl
Nottingham NG7 222 A4
Southwell NG25 136 B4
Landseer Rd NG25 136 B4
Lane End NG17 115 D3
Lane The
Awsworth NG16 158 B2
Cotham NG23 154 C2
Laneham Ave NG5 162 A4
Laneham Rd NG22 54 A1
Laneham St DN22 43 D1
Lanercost Mews 3 S80 35 F1
Lanesborough Ct LE11 220 A1
Laneside Ave NG9 182 C1
Laneward Cl DE7 157 E2
Langar CE Prim Sch NG13 190 B1
Langar Cl NG5 161 E2
Langar La
Colston Bassett NG12 200 C4
Harby LE14 202 A2
Langar Pl NG19 103 D4
Langar Rd NG13 177 F2
Langdale Cl NG24 139 F2
Langdale Dr
Long Eaton NG10 193 D3
Tickhill DN11 8 A4
Langdale Gr NG13 177 D2
Langdale Rd
Nottingham NG3 174 B3
Worksop S81 35 F4
Langdon Cl NG10 182 A1
Langdown Cl NG6 160 A4
Langford La NG23 111 D2

Langford Rd
Arnold NG5 . . . . 162 A4
Mansfield NG19 . . . . 101 E3
Langford St NG17 . . . . 100 C2
Langham Ave NG3 . . . . 174 A3
Langham Dr NG14 . . . . 163 F3
Langham Pl NG18 . . . . 101 F4
Langley Ave
Arnold NG5 . . . . 161 F3
Ilkeston DE7 . . . . 157 E3
Langley Cl NG19 . . . . 87 F1
Langley Dr DE74 . . . . 203 E1
Langley Mill CE Inf Sch . . . 143 D1
NG16
Langley Mill CE Jun Sch . . . 143 D2
NG16
Langley Mill Sta NG16 . . . 143 D2
Langley Pk NG16 . . . . 143 D2
Langley St S80 . . . . 35 F1
Langold Ctry Pk* S81 . . . . . 16 C1
Langstrath Dr NG2 . . . . 186 B2
Langstrath Rd NG2 . . . . 184 C1
Langton Ave NG17 . . . . 114 B3
Langton Cl NG3 . . . . 174 C3
Langton Hollow NG16 . . . . 128 B3
Langton Rd NG17 . . . . 100 C1
Langtree Gdns NG13 . . . . . 177 F3
Langtry Gr NG7 . . . . 161 D1
Langwell Dr NG19 . . . . 89 E1
Langworth Bassett Prim Sch . . . 72 C4
NG20
Langwith Dr NG20 . . . . 58 C1
Langwith Maltings 72 C4
NG20
Langwith Rd
Cuckney NG20 . . . . 60 A1
Shirebrook NG20 . . . . 72 C3
Langwith-Whaley Thorns Sta . . . 58 C1
NG20
Lansbury Ave NG22 . . . . 77 E3
Lansbury Dr
Bilsthorpe NG22 . . . . 105 F4
South Normanton DE55 . . . . . 113 D3
Lansbury Gdns NG18 . . . . . 102 C4
Lansbury Rd
Bilsthorpe NG22 . . . . 105 F4
Edwinstowe NG21 . . . . 76 A1
New Balderton NG24 . . . . 140 B2
Sutton in A NG17 . . . . 100 C1
Lansdall Ave DN21 . . . . 24 C2
Lansdown Cl NG9 . . . . 183 D2
Lansdowne Ave NG18 . . . . 102 B1
Lansdowne Dr
Loughborough LE11 . . . . 220 A1
West Bridgford NG2 . . . . 185 E2
Lansic La NG14 . . . . 151 F1
Lansing Cl NG11 . . . . 195 F4
Lantern La LE12 . . . . 205 F1
Lantern La Prim Sch 205 F1
LE12
Lanthwaite Cl NG7 . . . . 184 C1
Lanthwaite Rd NG7 . . . . . . 184 C1
Lapford Cl NG3 . . . . 162 B3
Larch Ave
Mansfield Woodhouse 88 A3
NG19
Shirebrook NG20 . . . . 72 B2
Larch Cl Bingham NG13 . . . 178 A4
Hucknall NG15 . . . . 146 A3
Nottingham NG5 . . . . 161 E4
Larch Cres
Beeston NG9 . . . . 183 E4
Eastwood NG16 . . . . 143 F1
Larch Ct DN21 . . . . 15 F1
Larch Dr NG10 . . . . 182 A4
Larch Gdns NG6 . . . . 160 A4
Larch Way NG9 . . . . 198 A1
Larchdale Cl DE55 . . . . 113 D2
Larchdene Ave NG17 . . . . . 171 E2
Largs Cl NG5 . . . . 146 C1
Lark Cl NG9 . . . . 183 D3
Lark Spinney S81 . . . . 35 E3
Larkdale St NG7 . . . . 222 C4
Larkfield Ave NG17 . . . . . . 114 C1
Larkfield Rd NG16 . . . . 159 D3
Larkfields Jun & Inf Schs . . . 159 D3
NG16
Larkhall Pl NG19 . . . . 101 F3
Larklands Ave DE7 . . . . 170 A4
Larklands Inf Sch DE7 . . . . 170 A4
Larkspur Ave NG5 . . . . 147 F1
Larkspur Cl
Mansfield NG19 . . . . 88 B1
South Normanton DE55 . . . . . 113 D3
Larpit Gn S80 . . . . 45 D3
Larwood S81 . . . . 36 A3
Larwood Cres NG17 . . . . . . 114 C1
Larwood Gr NG5 . . . . 161 E2
Lascelles Ave NG4 . . . . 162 B1
Latham St NG6 . . . . 160 A4
Lathkill Ave DE7 . . . . 157 F3
Lathkill Cl NG6 . . . . 160 A4
Lathkill Dr NG16 . . . . 128 C4
Lathkilldale Cres 193 D3
NG10
Latimer Cl NG6 . . . . 160 B3
Latimer Dr NG9 . . . . 171 D2
Laughton Ave NG2 . . . . 185 E2
Laughton Cres NG15 . . . . . 145 F2
Laughton Rd DN21 . . . . 15 E4
Launceston Cres 185 D2
NG11

Launder St
Nottingham NG2 . . . . 173 E1
Orston NG13 . . . . 179 F4
Launds Ave NG16 . . . . 128 B4
Laurel Ave
Church Warsop NG20 . . . . 74 A4
Keyworth NG12 . . . . 197 F1
Mansfield NG18 . . . . 102 B3
Mansfield Woodhouse 89 D1
NG19
Misterton DN10 . . . . 6 C2
Laurel Cl
Gainsborough DN21 . . . . 15 F1
Shirebrook NG20 . . . . 72 B3
Wysall NG12 . . . . 207 E2
Laurel Cres
Long Eaton NG10 . . . . 193 E3
Nuthall NG16 . . . . 159 D3
Laurel Gr
Kirkby in A NG17 . . . . 115 E3
South Normanton DE55 . . . . . 113 D2
Laurel Rd NG4 . . . . 174 B4
Laurie Ave NG7 . . . . 173 D4
Laurie Cl ⁴ NG7 . . . . 173 D4
Lauriston Dr NG6 . . . . 160 B2
Lavender Cl
🛈 Nottingham NG8 . . . . 159 F1
Tibshelf DE55 . . . . 99 C4
Lavender Cres NG4 . . . . 162 B1
Lavender Gdns DE75 . . . . . 143 D1
Lavender Gr NG9 . . . . 184 A3
Lavender Wlk NG3 . . . . 173 E4
Lavenham Mews 🛈 S80 . . . 35 F1
Laver Cl NG5 . . . . 162 A4
Laverick Rd NG16 . . . . 128 A2
Lawdon Rd NG5 . . . . 148 A1
Lawley Ave NG9 . . . . 172 A1
Lawn Ave NG17 . . . . 100 C1
Lawn La Old Dalby LE14 . . . 218 C1
Sutton in A NG17 . . . . 100 C1
Lawn Mill Rd NG16 . . . . . . 158 C4
Lawn Rd Carlton in L S81 . . 25 F4
Sutton in A NG17 . . . . 101 D2
Lawns Rd NG17 . . . . 129 F4
Lawns The
Collingham NG23 . . . . 98 A1
Whatton NG13 . . . . 179 D2
Lawnwood Ave DN22 . . . . . 50 A2
Lawnwood La DN22 . . . . . . 50 A2
Lawrence Ave
Awsworth NG16 . . . . 158 B2
Carlton NG4 . . . . 174 C3
Eastwood NG16 . . . . 143 F1
Kirkby in A NG17 . . . . 114 C3
Mansfield Woodhouse 88 A2
NG19
Lawrence Cl NG12 . . . . 187 F2
Lawrence Cres NG17 . . . . . 100 C2
Lawrence Dr NG16 . . . . 143 E4
Lawrence Pk NG16 . . . . 129 D2
Lawrence Pl NG24 . . . . 125 D1
Lawrence St
Long Eaton NG10 . . . . 193 E4
Newark-on-T NG24 . . . . 125 D1
Sandiacre NG10 . . . . 182 A4
Stapleford NG9 . . . . 182 B3
Lawrence Way 🛈 NG2 . . . 173 D1
Lawson Ave NG10 . . . . 193 F4
Lawson Cl DN22 . . . . 50 C1
Lawson Sq S81 . . . . 18 A1
Lawson St NG7 . . . . 222 C4
Laxton Dr NG6 . . . . 146 B1
Laxton Ave
Nottingham NG6 . . . . 160 B3
Sutton in A NG17 . . . . 101 E1
Laxton Dr
Hucknall NG15 . . . . 145 F3
Meden Vale NG20 . . . . 74 B4
Laxton Heritage Mus* 79 E2
NG22
Laxton Rd NG22 . . . . 79 E2
Laxton Visitors Ctr* 79 E2
NG22
Laycock Ave DN10 . . . . 12 C1
Layton Ave NG18 . . . . 102 A4
Layton Burroughs 🛈 102 A4
NG18
Le Brun Sq S81 . . . . 25 F4
Le Page Ct NG8 . . . . 172 A4
Lea Cl NG15 . . . . 117 D1
Lea Ct S80 . . . . 35 E1
Lea La NG16 . . . . 128 C3
Lea Rd
Gainsborough DN21 . . . . 24 C3
Market Warsop NG20 . . . . 74 B2
Ravenshead NG15 . . . . 117 D1
Lea Rd Sta DN22 . . . . 24 B3
Lea Rd W DN21 . . . . 24 B3
Lea Vale DE55 . . . . 113 D2
Leabrook Cl NG11 . . . . 184 B2
Leabrook Gdns NG15 . . . . . 146 B4
Leabrooks Ave
Mansfield Woodhouse 88 B3
NG19
Sutton in A NG17 . . . . 101 E1
Leach Cl NG22 . . . . 54 B1
Leachcroft Hill NG25 . . . . . 136 A4
Leacroft Rd NG8 . . . . 172 B4
Lead Hill S80 . . . . 35 F1
Leadale Ave NG15 . . . . 146 B4
Leadale Cres NG19 . . . . 88 C3
Leaf Cl NG15 . . . . 131 D1
Leafe Cl NG9 . . . . 183 E1
Leafield DN22 . . . . 39 F3
Leafield Gn NG7 . . . . 184 C1
Leahurst Gdns NG2 . . . . . . 186 A3
Leahurst Rd NG2 . . . . 186 A3
Leake La LE12 . . . . 214 B2

Leake Rd Costock LE12 . . . . 206 A1
Gotham NG11 . . . . 195 D3
Leam Glen NG19 . . . . 88 B1
Leamington Dr
Beeston NG9 . . . . 183 E2
South Normanton DE55 . . . . . 113 D3
Sutton in A NG17 . . . . 114 C4
Leamington Hall 100 C1
NG17
Leamington Prim Sch 114 C4
NG17
Leander Cl NG11 . . . . 185 D3
Leas Ave NG19 . . . . 87 D3
Leas Pk Jun Sch NG19 . . . . . 88 B2
Leas Rd NG19 . . . . 88 B2
Leas The NG14 . . . . 164 A3
Leatherlands DE74 . . . . 203 E2
Leaway The NG20 . . . . 72 B2
Lechlade Rd NG5 . . . . 161 D3
Ledbury Vale NG8 . . . . 172 A4
Lee Cres DE7 . . . . 170 A4
Lee La DE75 . . . . 143 D1
Lee Rd
Burton Joyce NG14 . . . . 164 A3
Calverton NG14 . . . . 148 B4
Leech Ct NG16 . . . . 158 A4
Leeds Rd S81 . . . . 34 C4
Leeks Rd NG25 . . . . 121 F1
Leeming Cl NG20 . . . . 74 B3
Leeming La NG19,
NG19 . . . . 88 C4
Leeming La N NG19 . . . . 88 C3
Leeming La S NG19 . . . . 88 B1
Leeming Pk NG19 . . . . 88 B2
Leeming St NG18 . . . . 102 A4
Leen Cl
Bestwood Village NG6 . . . . . . 146 C2
Hucknall NG15 . . . . 146 B4
Leen Ct NG22 . . . . 79 A2
Leen Dr Hucknall NG15 . . . . 131 D1
Nottingham NG6 . . . . 146 B1
Leen Gate NG7 . . . . 172 C1
Leen Mills La NG15 . . . . 131 D1
Leen Mills Prim Sch 146 A4
NG15
Leen Pl NG7 . . . . 222 A3
Leen Valley Dr NG20 . . . . . . 72 C2
Leen Valley Way 146 B3
NG15
Lees Ave NG19 . . . . 101 E4
Lees Barn Rd NG12 . . . . 175 E1
Lees Hill St NG2 . . . . 173 F2
Lees La DE55 . . . . 113 D3
Lees Rd NG3 . . . . 162 A1
Leeway Cl NG21 . . . . 103 F1
Leeway Rd
Mansfield NG21 . . . . 103 F1
Southwell NG25 . . . . 121 E1
Legion Dr NG17 . . . . 100 B3
Leicester Rd LE11 . . . . 220 B1
Leicester St NG10 . . . . 193 F3
Leigh Cl NG2 . . . . 185 E3
Leigh Rd NG9 . . . . 182 C2
Leighton St NG3 . . . . 173 F3
Leiston Gdns NG5 . . . . 161 D4
Leivers Ave NG5 . . . . 161 F4
Leivers Cl LE12 . . . . 205 F1
Lema Cl NG6 . . . . 160 B4
Lemont Rd NG19 . . . . 89 D1
Lemynton St LE11 . . . . 220 A2
Lendrum Ct NG14 . . . . 163 F2
Lennox St NG1 . . . . 223 F3
Lenton Ave
Nottingham NG7 . . . . 222 C1
Tollerton NG12 . . . . 186 B1
Lenton Bvd NG7 . . . . 222 B2
Lenton Cir NG12 . . . . 186 B1
Lenton Ct NG7 . . . . 222 B2
Lenton Hall Dr NG7 . . . . . . 172 B1
Lenton Ind Est E NG7 . . . . 184 C4
Lenton Ind Est W NG7 . . . . 184 C4
Lenton La NG7 . . . . 184 C3
Lenton Manor NG7 . . . . 222 A1
Lenton Rd NG7 . . . . 223 D2
Lenton Sch NG7 . . . . 222 B1
Lenton St NG10 . . . . 182 B4
Leonard Ave NG5 . . . . 161 D1
Leonard Cheshire Cl 143 D1
DE75
Leonard St NG6 . . . . 160 B3
Leopold St
Long Eaton NG10 . . . . 193 E4
Loughborough LE11 . . . . 220 A3
Sutton in A NG17 . . . . 100 C1
Leroy Wallace Ave 222 B4
NG7
Lerwick Cl NG11 . . . . 185 D1
Leslie Ave Beeston NG9 . . . 183 F3
Kimberley NG16 . . . . 158 C4
Leslie Cl 🛈 Nottingham NG7 . . 173 D4
Leslie Gr NG14 . . . . 148 C4
Leslie Rd NG7 . . . . 173 D4
Letchworth Cres NG9 . . . . . 183 E2
Letcombe Rd NG11 . . . . 184 C2
Letwell Ave S81 . . . . 16 A1
Levellers Way NG24 . . . . . . 140 C4
Levels La Blaxton DN9 . . . . . 1 A4
Misson DN10 . . . . 4 C4
Levens Cl NG2 . . . . 186 B3
Leverton Gn NG7 . . . . 184 C1
Leverton Rd
Mansfield NG19 . . . . 101 F4
Retford DN22 . . . . 40 B4
Sutton S DN22 . . . . 32 B2
Leverton Wlk NG5 . . . . 162 A4
Levick Ct 🛈 NG2 . . . . 173 E1
Lewcote La DE7 . . . . 157 D1
Lewindon Ct NG5 . . . . 161 F2

Lewis Cl NG3 . . . . 223 F4
Lewis St DN21 . . . . 24 B4
Lexington Cl NG22 . . . . 65 F1
Lexington Gdns
Nottingham NG5 . . . . 161 E2
Tuxford NG22 . . . . 65 F1
Ley Croft NG19 . . . . 88 B3
Ley La East Drayton DN22 . . 53 E2
Retford DN22 . . . . 40 B4
Mansfield Woodhouse 88 B2
NG19
Ley St NG4 . . . . 175 D3
Leybourne Dr NG5 . . . . 160 C3
Leyland Cl NG9 . . . . 182 C1
Leys La DN10 . . . . 12 C1
Leys Rd NG11 . . . . 196 B3
Leys The
Lowdham NG14 . . . . 150 B1
Normanton-on-t-W
NG12 . . . . 197 F4
Nottingham NG11 . . . . 184 B1
Leyton Ave NG17 . . . . 101 D3
Leyton Cres NG9 . . . . 184 A3
Liber Cl NG18 . . . . 102 C4
Library Rd NG7 . . . . 172 B1
Lichfield Ave NG18 . . . . . . 102 B1
Lichfield Cl
Beeston NG9 . . . . 182 C2
Mansfield NG18 . . . . 102 B1
Worksop S81 . . . . 36 A4
Lichfield La NG18 . . . . 102 B2
Lichfield Rd NG2 . . . . 174 A2
Lichfield Wlk S81 . . . . 25 F4
Liddell Gr NG8 . . . . 171 F2
Liddington St NG7 . . . . 160 C1
Lidget La DN22 . . . . 40 A4
Lifton Ave DN22 . . . . 29 F1
Lightfoot Cl NG24 . . . . 140 C4
Lilac Ave NG4 . . . . 174 B4
Lilac Cl Keyworth NG12 . . . 198 A1
Newark-on-T NG24 . . . . 139 F2
🛈 Nottingham NG8 . . . . 159 F1
Lilac Cres NG9 . . . . 184 A3
Lilac Gr Bawtry DN10 . . . . 9 F4
Beeston NG9 . . . . 184 A3
Carlton in L S81 . . . . 25 F4
Clipstone NG19 . . . . 89 E1
Glapwell S44 . . . . 86 A4
Market Warsop NG20 . . . . 73 F4
Shirebrook NG20 . . . . 72 C3
South Normanton DE55 . . . . . 113 D2
Lilac Mews DE7 . . . . 157 E2
Lilac Rd NG15 . . . . 146 A3
Lilburne Cl NG24 . . . . 140 C4
Lillee Ct S81 . . . . 36 A3
Lilleker Rise NG5 . . . . 147 F1
Lillington Rd NG6 . . . . 160 A4
Lily Ave NG4 . . . . 175 D4
Lily Gr NG9 . . . . 184 A3
Limb Cres NG17 . . . . 100 C1
Lime Ave Firbeck S81 . . . . . . 16 A3
Huthwaite NG17 . . . . 100 A3
Langley Mill NG16 . . . . 143 E1
Loughborough LE11 . . . . 220 B2
Sutton in A NG17 . . . . 100 C2
Lime Cl Nuthall NG16 . . . . . 159 D3
Radcliffe on T NG12 . . . . 175 F2
Lime Cres NG20 . . . . 73 F4
Lime Gr
Bottesford NG13 . . . . 181 D1
Long Eaton NG10 . . . . 193 E4
Mansfield Woodhouse . . . .
NG19 . . . . 89 E1
Newark-on-T NG24 . . . . 139 F4
Retford DN22 . . . . 39 E4
Sandiacre NG10 . . . . 182 A3
South Normanton DE55 . . . . . 113 D3
Stapleford NG9 . . . . 182 B3
Lime Gr Ave NG9 . . . . 183 F3
Lime Kiln Pl NG18 . . . . 102 A3
Lime La NG5 . . . . 147 F2
Lime St
Kirkby in A NG17 . . . . 115 D3
Nottingham NG6 . . . . 160 A4
Sutton in A NG17 . . . . 101 D2
Lime Terr NG10 . . . . 193 E4
Lime Tree Ave
Carlton in L S81 . . . . 25 F4
Gainsborough DN21 . . . . 15 E1
Glapwell S44 . . . . 86 A4
Kirkby in A NG17 . . . . 114 C3
Mansfield Woodhouse . . . .
NG19 . . . . 88 A3
Nottingham NG8 . . . . 160 B2
Retford DN22 . . . . 39 E4
Sutton in A NG17 . . . . 100 C2
Lime Tree Cl
Collingham NG23 . . . . 112 A4
New Ollerton NG22 . . . . 77 E3
Lime Tree Cres DN10 . . . . 9 F4
Lime Tree Ct NG9 . . . . 172 A1
Lime Tree Dr NG18 . . . . 116 C4
Lime Tree Gdns NG14 . . . . 150 C1
Lime Tree Pl
Mansfield NG18 . . . . 102 B3
Rainworth NG21 . . . . 104 A1
Lime Tree Rd
Elkesley DN22 . . . . 50 A2
Hucknall NG15 . . . . 146 A2
New Ollerton NG22 . . . . 77 E3
Limehurst Ave LE11 . . . . . . 220 B3
Limehurst High Sch (Annexe) . . . . .
LE11 . . . . 220 A3
Limehurst High Sch . . . .
LE11 . . . . 220 A3
Limekiln Ct NG6 . . . . 160 A4
Limes Ave NG20 . . . . 59 D1
Limes Cres NG20 . . . . 72 B3

Limes Ct NG17 . . . . 101 E1
Limes The DN10 . . . . 14 A1
Limestone Terr NG19 . . . . . . 88 A2
Limetree Ave S80 . . . . 48 B3
Limetree Cl NG12 . . . . 197 F1
Limmen Gdns NG3 . . . . 173 F3
Limpenny St NG7 . . . . 222 C4
Linby Ave
Hucknall NG15 . . . . 146 A4
Mansfield NG19 . . . . 101 E3
Linby Cl Carlton NG4 . . . . . . 162 C1
Nottingham NG5 . . . . 147 D2
Linby Cum Papplewick CE . . . .
Prim Sch NG15 . . . . 131 D2
Linby Dr NG8 . . . . 159 E1
Linby Gr NG15 . . . . 146 A4
Linby La NG15 . . . . 131 E2
Linby Rd NG15 . . . . 146 A4
Linby Wlk NG15 . . . . 146 A4
Lincoln Ave NG10 . . . . 182 A2
Lincoln Cir NG7 . . . . 222 C2
Lincoln Cl
Stapleford NG9 . . . . 170 C1
Tibshelf DE55 . . . . 99 D3
Lincoln Ct NG8 . . . . 171 F4
Lincoln Dr NG19 . . . . 88 B2
Lincoln Gr NG12 . . . . 175 F2
Lincoln Rd
East Markham NG22 . . . . 66 A4
Fenton LN1 . . . . 55 E3
Newark-on-T NG24 . . . . 125 D2
Saxilby LN1 . . . . 57 E2
Tuxford NG22 . . . . 66 A2
Lincoln Rd Bridge 125 D1
NG24
Lincoln St
Gainsborough DN21 . . . . 15 E1
Newark-on-T NG24 . . . . 125 D1
Nottingham NG1 . . . . 223 E2
Nottingham, Old Basford
NG6 . . . . 160 C2
Tibshelf DE55 . . . . 99 D3
Worksop S80 . . . . 36 A1
Lincoln View S80 . . . . 36 A1
Lind Cl NG21 . . . . 103 F1
Lindale Cl NG2 . . . . 186 B3
Lindale Rd NG8 . . . . 159 F1
Linden Ave
New Balderton NG24 . . . . 140 A3
Nottingham NG11 . . . . 184 B1
Tuxford NG22 . . . . 66 A1
Linden Gr Beeston NG9 . . . 184 A3
Carlton NG4 . . . . 163 D1
Kirkby in A NG17 . . . . 114 B3
Sandiacre NG10 . . . . 182 A4
Shirebrook NG20 . . . . 72 C2
Stapleford NG9 . . . . 182 C3
Linden Rd
Loughborough LE11 . . . . 220 A3
Mansfield NG18 . . . . 102 C4
Linden St
Mansfield NG19 . . . . 88 A1
Nottingham NG3 . . . . 173 E4
Shirebrook NG20 . . . . 72 C2
Linden Terr DN21 . . . . 24 B4
Lindfield Cl NG8 . . . . 160 A1
Lindfield Rd NG8 . . . . 159 F1
Lindholme Way NG17 . . . . 100 C3
Lindhurst La NG18 . . . . 102 C2
Lindisfarine Gdns 🛈 . . . .
NG5 . . . . 147 D1
Lindley St
Eastwood NG16 . . . . 144 A2
Mansfield NG18 . . . . 102 A4
Selston NG16 . . . . 128 B3
Lindley Terr 🛈 NG7 . . . . . . 172 C4
Lindleys Ct NG17 . . . . 115 D2
Lindleys La NG17 . . . . 115 D3
Lindrick DN11 . . . . 8 A3
Lindrick Cl
Carlton in L S81 . . . . 25 F4
Mansfield Woodhouse . . . .
NG19 . . . . 88 B3
West Bridgford NG2 . . . . 186 B2
Worksop S81 . . . . 36 A3
Lindrick Ct DN22 . . . . 39 E1
Lindrick La DN11 . . . . 8 A3
Lindrick Rd NG17 . . . . 114 C4
Lindsay Ave
Annesley Woodhouse
NG17 . . . . 115 D1
Newark-on-T NG24 . . . . 139 F2
Lindsay Cl NG18 . . . . 102 A3
Lindsey Dr NG18 . . . . 103 D2
Lindsey Rd DN11 . . . . 9 D3
Lindum Gr 🛈 NG2 . . . . 173 F2
Lindum Mews NG24 . . . . . . 140 A4
Lindum Rd NG6 . . . . 160 B2
Lindum St 🛈 NG24 . . . . . . 140 A4
Lindwall Ct S81 . . . . 36 A3
Lindy Cl NG12 . . . . 199 F1
Linecroft La DN10 . . . . 14 B4
Linette Cl NG5 . . . . 161 D2
Linford NG9 . . . . 171 D2
Ling Beeches DN22 . . . . 39 E2
Ling Cres NG11 . . . . 196 B4
Ling Rd LE11 . . . . 220 A1
Lingdale Cl LE11 . . . . 220 A1
Lingfield Cl NG18 . . . . 102 C3
Lingfield Ct NG8 . . . . 171 E2
Lingford NG12 . . . . 188 A2
Lingford St NG15 . . . . 146 A3
Lingforest Cl NG18 . . . . 103 D3
Lingforest Rd NG18 . . . . . . 103 D3
Lings Bar House Hospl . . . .
NG2 . . . . 186 B3
Lings La NG12 . . . . 207 F4
Lings View NG20 . . . . 74 B2

Lingwood Gr NG18 ...103 D4
Lingwood La NG14 ...149 D2
Linkin Rd NG9 ...183 E3
Linkmel Cl NG2 ...173 D1
Linkmel Rd NG16 ...143 E2
Linkmell Cl NG2 ...186 B3
Links The NG18 ...103 D3
Linksfield Ct NG11 ...185 E1
Linley Cl NG23 ...112 A4
Linnell St NG3 ...173 F3
Linnets Dr NG18 ...102 C4
Linnets The S81 ...35 E4
Linsdale Cl NG8 ...171 D3
Linsdale Gdns NG4 ...162 B2
Lintin Ave NG21 ...75 F1
Linton Cl
Farndon NG24 ...139 D3
Mansfield NG18 ...103 D3
Linton Dr NG22 ...77 F3
Linton Rise NG3 ...174 A3
Linwood Cl DN21 ...24 C4
Linwood Cres
Eastwood NG16 ...144 A1
Ravenshead NG15 ...116 C2
Linwood Ct NG19 ...88 C2
Lion Cl NG8 ...160 B1
Liquorice La S81 ...26 A2
Lisle St LE11 ...220 A3
Lismore Cl NG7 ...222 A3
Lismore Ct NG19 ...101 E3
Lissington Rd DN21 ...24 C4
Lister Ct 8 NG7 ...172 C1
Lister Gate NG1 ...223 E2
Lister Rd NG7 ...172 C1
Listowel Cres NG11 ...195 F4
Litchen Cl DE7 ...157 F1
Litchfield Cl NG10 ...194 A4
Litchfield Rise NG5 ...147 F1
Little Acre NG19 ...88 C3
Little Barn Ct NG18 ...102 C3
Little Barn Gdns NG18 ...102 C3
Little Barn La NG18 ...102 C3
Little Belt The DN21 ...15 E2
Little Breck DE55 ...113 D2
Little Carter La NG18 ...102 C4
Little Debdale La NG19 ...87 F1
Little Hallam La DE7 ...170 A3
Little Hayes NG2 ...185 E2
Little Hollies NG19 ...89 D1
Little John Ave NG20 ...74 B1
Little John Cl NG22 ...77 E3
Little John Dr NG21 ...104 A1
Little John Wlk 14 NG3 ...173 E4
Little La Blyth S81 ...18 A2
Calverton NG14 ...148 B4
Collingham NG23 ...111 F4
Edingley NG22 ...120 B2
Gringley on t H DN10 ...12 C1
Huthwaite NG17 ...99 F1
Kimberley NG16 ...158 C3
Pleasleyhill NG19 ...87 D3
Shirebrook NG20 ...72 B2
Thorpe Salvin S80 ...34 A3
Tollerton NG12 ...186 C2
Little Lunnon NG11 ...194 C3
Little Mdw NG12 ...188 A1
Little Moor La LE11 ...220 B2
Little Oak Ave NG17 ...130 A4
Little Oak Dr NG17 ...129 F4
Little Oakwood Dr
NG5 ...146 B1
Little Ox NG4 ...174 C2
Little Ricket La NG15 ...116 B2
Little Tennis St NG2 ...174 A2
Little Tennis St S NG2 ...174 A1
Little Top La DN22 ...20 B1
Little Wlk DN21 ...7 E1
Littleborough Rd DN22 ...33 D2
Littlegreen Rd NG5 ...161 F3
Littlemoor La NG11 ...196 C2
Littleover Ave NG18 ...103 D3
Littlewood Gdns NG8 ...171 E3
Littlewood La NG19 ...88 A3
Littleworth NG18 ...102 B3
Litton Ave NG17 ...101 D3
Litton Cl Arnold NG5 ...161 F2
Ilkeston DE7 ...157 F2
Ravenshead NG15 ...117 D2
Litton Rd NG19 ...88 C2
Littondale S81 ...36 A4
Liverpool St NG3 ...173 F3
Livingstone St NG15 ...130 C3
Llanberis Gr NG8 ...160 B1
Lloyd St NG5 ...161 E1
Loach Ct NG8 ...172 B3
Lobelia Cl NG3 ...173 E4
Lock La
Long Eaton NG10 ...193 E2
Sandiacre NG10 ...182 B2
Lockerbie St NG4 ...174 C3
Locksley La NG11 ...184 C2
Lockwood Cl
Beeston NG9 ...184 B2
16 Nottingham NG5 ...147 D1
Lockwood Dr DN22 ...39 E2
Lodge Cl Arnold NG5 ...147 F1
Nottingham NG8 ...172 B4
Lodge Farm La NG5 ...147 F1
Lodge La Elston NG23 ...153 E3
Kirkby in A NG17 ...115 E2
Screveton NG13 ...166 B3
Tuxford NG22 ...66 A1
Lodge Rd
Eastwood NG16 ...158 A4
Long Eaton NG10 ...193 E3
Lodgefield La NG14 ...151 F1
Lodgewood Cl NG6 ...160 A3
Lodore Cl NG2 ...186 B3
Lodore Rd S81 ...35 F4
Logan St NG6 ...160 B3
Lois Ave NG7 ...222 B1
Lombard Cl NG7 ...222 B2
Lombard St
Newark-on-T NG24 ...139 F4
Orston NG13 ...180 A3
Lonan Cl NG19 ...89 D1
London La
Willoughby-on-t-W LE12 ...217 E4
Wymeswold LE12 ...216 A2
London Rd
Kegworth DE74 ...203 E1
Newark-on-T NG24 ...140 B3
Nottingham NG2 ...173 E1
Retford DN22 ...40 A2
Long Acre NG15 ...145 E4
Long Brecks La S81 ...18 B1
Long Clawson CE Prim Sch
LE14 ...211 E2
Long Eaton Com Sch
NG10 ...193 E4
Long Eaton Lower Sch
NG10 ...193 E3
Long Eaton Sta NG10 ...193 D3
Long Hill Rise NG15 ...145 F3
Long La
Barkestone-le-V NG13 ...192 C1
Barnby in t W NG24 ...141 F4
Beeston NG9 ...183 F2
Carlton in L S81 ...25 F3
East Drayton DN22 ...53 E2
Farndon NG24 ...139 D3
Hickling LE14 ...210 B3
Kegworth DE74 ...203 E3
Shipley DE75 ...157 E3
Shirebrook NG20 ...72 C2
Stathern LE14 ...202 C2
Watnall NG16 ...145 D1
Long Mdw
Farnsfield NG22 ...120 A3
Mansfield Woodhouse
NG19 ...88 B3
Long Mdw Hill NG14 ...150 A1
Long Mdws DN10 ...11 D2
Long Row
Kingston-on-S LE12 ...204 A2
Newark-on-T NG24 ...140 A4
Nottingham NG1 ...223 E2
Long Row W NG1 ...223 E2
Long Stoop Way
NG19 ...103 D4
Longacre NG5 ...161 F2
Longbeck Ave NG3 ...162 A1
Longcliff Cl LE14 ...218 C2
Longcliff Hill LE14 ...218 C2
Longcroft View S80 ...45 D3
Longdale NG19 ...88 C1
Longdale Ave NG15 ...117 D1
Longdale Craft Ctr & Mus*
NG15 ...132 B3
Longdale La
Calverton NG21 ...133 D3
Ravenshead NG15 ...132 B4
Longdale Rd NG5 ...161 E3
Longden Cl NG9 ...170 C1
Longden St 11 NG3 ...173 F3
Longden Terr
Market Warsop NG20 ...74 A2
Stanton Hill NG17 ...100 B3
Longfellow Dr
Balderton NG24 ...140 B3
Worksop S81 ...36 A2
Longfellows Cl NG5 ...161 D4
Longfield La DE7 ...170 A3
Longford Cres NG6 ...146 B1
Longford Wlk NG18 ...103 D3
Longhedge La
Bottesford NG13 ...180 C2
Flawborough NG13,
NG23 ...168 A1
Orston NG13 ...180 C4
Pleasley NG19 ...86 C3
Sibthorpe NG13 ...167 F3
Longhill Rise NG17 ...114 C1
Longholme Rd DN22 ...40 A4
Longhurst S81 ...36 A3
Longhurst View S80 ...45 D3
Longland La NG22 ...119 E2
Longlands Cl NG9 ...184 A2
Longlands Dr NG2 ...186 B3
Longlands Rd NG9 ...184 A2
Longleat Cres NG9 ...183 E3
Longmead Cl NG5 ...161 E3
Longmead Dr
Fiskerton NG25 ...137 F2
Nottingham NG5 ...161 E3
Longmoor Ave NG14 ...164 C4
Longmoor Gdns NG10 ...182 A1
Longmoor La
Long Eaton NG10 ...182 A1
Scarrington NG13 ...179 D4
Longmoor Prim Sch
NG10 ...182 B2
Longmoor Rd NG10 ...182 A1
Longnor Wlk NG18 ...103 D3
Longore Sq NG8 ...172 B2
Longridge Rd NG5 ...161 F3
Longshaw Rd NG18 ...103 D3
Longster La NG20 ...73 E2
Longstone Way NG19 ...101 E3
Longue Dr NG14 ...148 B4
Longwall Ave NG2 ...173 D1
Longwest Croft NG14 ...148 B4
Longwood Ct NG5 ...160 C4
Longwood Inf Sch
NG16 ...113 E1
Longwood Rd NG16 ...113 F1
Lonscale Cl NG2 ...186 B4
Lonsdale Dr NG9 ...182 C1
Lonsdale Rd NG7 ...222 A4
Lord Haddon Rd DE7 ...157 F1
Lord Nelson St NG2 ...173 F2
Lord St
Gainsborough DN21 ...24 B4
Mansfield NG18 ...102 A3
Nottingham NG2 ...173 F2
Lordship La NG13 ...180 A3
Lorimer Ave NG4 ...162 C1
Lorne Cl 10 NG3 ...173 E4
Lorne Gr NG12 ...175 F2
Lorne House Sch DN22 ...40 A3
Lorne Wlk 11 NG3 ...173 E4
Lortas Rd NG5 ...160 C1
Loscoe Gdns 9 NG5 ...161 D1
Loscoe Mount Rd
NG5 ...161 E1
Loscoe Rd NG5 ...161 E1
Lothian Rd NG12 ...186 B1
Lothmore Ct 7 NG2 ...173 D1
Lotus Cl NG3 ...173 F4
Loughbon NG13 ...180 A4
Loughborough Ave
NG2 ...173 F2
Loughborough Carillon Twr
& War Meml* LE11 ...220 A2
Loughborough Endowed
Schs LE11 ...220 A2
Loughborough General Hospl
LE11 ...220 A2
Loughborough Gram Sch
LE11 ...220 B1
Loughborough High Sch
LE11 ...220 A1
Loughborough Rd
Bradmore NG11 ...196 C3
Bunny NG11 ...206 C4
East Leake LE12 ...214 C4
Hathern LE12 ...213 D1
Hoton LE12 ...215 E1
Loughborough LE11 ...220 B1
Rempstone LE12 ...215 E3
West Bridgford NG12 ...185 F3
Loughborough Shelthorpe
Prim Sch LE11 ...220 B1
Loughborough Sta
LE11 ...220 B3
Loughborough Univ Sch of
Art & Design LE11 ...220 A2
Loughborough Rd LE12 ...220 C3
Loughrigg Cl 18 NG2 ...173 D1
Louis Ave NG9 ...183 F4
Louise Ave NG4 ...175 D4
Lound House Cl NG17 ...100 C3
Lound House Rd
NG17 ...100 C3
Lound Low Rd DN22 ...29 E4
Louwil Ave NG19 ...88 C3
Love La DN21 ...15 E1
Loveden Cl NG24 ...140 B2
Lovell Cl NG6 ...159 F3
Lovers La NG24 ...125 D1
Lovers La Prim Sch
NG24 ...125 D1
Low Field La DN10 ...3 E1
Low Holland La DN22 ...32 C2
Low Moor Rd NG17 ...115 D3
Low Pavement NG1 ...223 E2
Low Rd Besthorpe NG23 ...97 F3
Scrooby DN10 ...10 A1
Sutton in A NG17 ...100 C4
Low St Beckingham DN10 ...14 B1
Carlton in L S81 ...26 A3
Collingham NG23 ...111 F4
East Drayton DN22 ...53 D2
East Markham NG22 ...66 A3
Elston NG23 ...153 E3
Gringley on t H DN10 ...12 C1
Harby NG23 ...70 B1
North Wheatley DN22 ...31 E4
Sutton in A NG17 ...100 C1
Torworth DN22 ...19 D1
Low Wood La LN6 ...98 C4
Low Wood Rd NG6 ...159 F3
Lowater St NG4 ...174 A4
Lowcroft NG5 ...161 F2
Lowdam Rd NG14 ...150 A3
Lowdham CE Prim Sch
NG14 ...150 B1
Lowdham La NG14 ...149 F2
Lowdham Rd
Carlton NG4 ...162 B2
Gunthorpe NG14 ...164 C4
Lowdham St 14 NG3 ...173 F3
Lowdham Sta NG14 ...164 C4
Lower Bagthorpe
NG16 ...128 C2
Lower Beauvale NG16 ...144 A2
Lower Bloomsgrove Rd
DE7 ...157 F1
Lower Brook St NG10 ...193 F4
Lower Cambridge St
LE11 ...220 A3
Lower Canaan NG11 ...196 B4
Lower Chapel St 18 DE7 ...157 F1
Lower Clara Mount Rd
DE75 ...143 D1
Lower Ct NG9 ...184 A4
Lower Dunstead Rd
NG16 ...143 D2
Lower Eldon St 12 NG2 ...173 F2
Lower Gladstone St 8
LE11 ...220 A3
Lower Granby St DE7 ...157 F1
Lower Kirklington Rd
NG25 ...121 E1
Lower Maples DE75 ...157 D4
Lower Middleton St
DE7 ...158 A1
Lower Oakham Way
NG18 ...101 F2
Lower Orch St NG9 ...182 B4
Lower Parliament St
NG1 ...223 F2
Lower Pasture La DN22 ...31 F4
Lower Pk St NG9 ...182 B3
Lower Rd NG9 ...184 A4
Lower Regent St NG9 ...184 A3
Lowes Wong NG25 ...136 B4
Lowes Wong Anglican
Methodist Jun & Inf Sch
NG25 ...121 E1
Loweswater Ct NG2 ...186 B4
Lowfield DN22 ...29 E1
Lowfield La NG24 ...140 B1
Lowlands Dr NG12 ...197 F2
Lowmoor Rd Ind Est
NG17 ...115 D4
Lows La DE7 ...170 A1
Lowther Sq S81 ...25 F4
Lowther Way LE11 ...220 A1
Lowtown Cl S80 ...36 A1
Lowtown St S80 ...36 A1
Lowtown View S80 ...36 A1
Loxley Dr NG18 ...103 D2
Lucerne Cl NG11 ...185 D3
Lucknow Ave NG3 ...161 E1
Lucknow Ct NG3 ...173 E4
Lucknow Dr
Mansfield NG17, NG18 ...101 F3
Nottingham NG3 ...161 E1
Sutton in A NG17,
NG18 ...101 D2
Lucknow Rd NG3 ...173 E4
Ludborough Wlk NG19 ...88 C2
Ludford Cres DN21 ...24 C4
Ludford Rd NG6 ...160 B4
Ludgate Cl NG5 ...147 D1
Ludgate Dr NG13 ...165 E1
Ludham Ave NG6 ...160 A4
Ludlam Ave NG16 ...158 A4
Ludlow Cl NG9 ...171 E1
Ludlow Hill Rd NG2 ...185 F3
Lulworth Cl NG2 ...185 E3
Lulworth Ct NG16 ...158 C4
Lumley Dr DN11 ...8 A4
Lune Cl NG9 ...183 F2
Lune Mdw NG19 ...88 C2
Lunn La NG23 ...111 F4
Lupin Cl NG3 ...173 E4
Luther Ave NG17 ...100 C1
Luther Cl NG3 ...173 F4
Luton Cl NG8 ...160 B1
Lutterell Ct NG2 ...185 E3
Lutterell Way NG2 ...186 B3
Lybster Mews 12 NG2 ...173 D1
Lydia Gdns NG16 ...143 F1
Lydney Pk NG2 ...185 E3
Lyle Cl NG16 ...158 C4
Lyme Pk NG2 ...185 D3
Lymington Gdns NG3 ...174 A3
Lymington Rd NG19 ...101 E3
Lymn Ave NG4 ...162 C1
Lyncombe Ct DN22 ...39 E2
Lyncombe Gdns NG12 ...197 F2
Lyncroft Prim Sch
NG16 ...144 A2
Lynd Cl NG16 ...129 D4
Lyndale Rd NG9 ...183 D4
Lynden Ave NG10 ...193 E3
Lyndhurst Ave NG21 ...118 A3
Lyndhurst Gdns NG2 ...185 E2
Lyndhurst Rd NG2 ...173 F2
Lynds Cl NG21 ...76 A1
Lyngs The NG13 ...165 E1
Lynmouth Cres NG7 ...172 C4
Lynmouth Dr DE7 ...157 E2
Lynncroft NG16 ...144 A2
Lynnes Cl NG21 ...118 A2
Lynstead Dr NG15 ...145 E3
Lynton Gdns NG5 ...162 A4
Lynton Rd NG9 ...183 E3
Lyons Cl NG11 ...196 A4
Lytham Dr NG12 ...186 B2
Lytham Gdns NG5 ...147 D1
Lytham Rd NG17 ...114 C4
Lythe Cl NG11 ...185 D3
Lytton Cl NG3 ...173 F3

M

Mabel Ave NG17 ...101 D1
Mabel Gr NG2 ...186 A4
Mabel St NG2 ...173 E1
Mable St S80 ...35 D2
Macaulay Cl
Balderton NG24 ...140 B3
Worksop S81 ...36 B2
Macaulay Dr NG24 ...140 B3
Macaulay Gr NG16 ...159 D3
Machin Gr S81 ...35 E4
Machins La NG12 ...186 A2
Mackinley Ave NG9 ...170 C1
Mackleys La NG23 ...110 C1
Mackworth Ct NG18 ...103 D3
Maclaren Gdns NG11 ...196 B3
Maclean Rd NG4 ...174 B4
Macmillan Cl NG3 ...161 F1
Madison Dr DN10 ...9 F3
Madryn Wlk 23 NG5 ...161 D4
Mafeking St NG2 ...174 A2
Mag La NG20 ...58 B3
Magdala Rd NG3 ...173 E4
Magdalen Dr NG13 ...165 E2
Magdalene View
NG24 ...140 A4
Magdalene Way NG15 ...146 A4
Magna Cl NG14 ...150 C1
Magnolia Cl 3 NG8 ...159 F1
Magnolia Ct NG9 ...171 E1
Magnolia Gr NG15 ...146 A2
Magnus CE Comp Sch The
NG24 ...140 A3
Magnus Rd NG5 ...161 E2
Magnus St NG24 ...140 A4
Magpie Cl S81 ...35 E4
Magpie La DN22 ...32 C1
Magson St NG3 ...173 F3
Maid Marian Ave
NG16 ...129 D4
Maid Marian Way
NG1 ...223 E2
Maid Marion Ave
NG22 ...106 A2
Maid Marion Way NG22 ...77 E3
Maid Marrion Dr NG21 ...76 B1
Maida La NG22 ...77 D2
Maiden La NG1 ...223 F2
Maidens Dale NG5 ...161 E4
Maidstone Dr NG8 ...171 E1
Main Ave NG19 ...103 D4
Main La NG12 ...164 B1
Main Rd
Annesley Woodhouse
NG17 ...114 C1
Barnstone NG13 ...190 C2
Beeston NG9 ...184 B3
Boughton NG22 ...77 F3
Carlton NG4 ...163 D1
Cotgrave NG12 ...187 F2
Kelham NG23 ...124 A2
Nether Langwith NG20 ...59 D1
Nottingham NG11 ...185 D4
Old Dalby LE14 ...218 C2
Plumtree NG12 ...197 F4
Pye Bridge DE55 ...128 A3
Radcliffe on T NG12 ...175 F2
Radcliffe on T, Shelford
NG12 ...176 B4
Ravenshead NG15 ...117 D2
Selston NG16 ...128 C1
Upton NG23 ...122 C1
Watnall NG16 ...159 D4
Westwood NG16 ...128 A2
Main St
Annesley Woodhouse
NG17 ...129 F4
Aslockton NG13 ...179 D3
Awsworth NG16 ...158 B3
Balderton NG24 ...140 C2
Bathley NG23 ...110 A2
Bleasby NG14 ...152 A4
Blidworth NG21 ...117 F2
Bothamsall DN22 ...63 F4
Bradmore NG11 ...196 C2
Brinsley NG16 ...128 B1
Bunny NG11 ...206 C4
Burton Joyce NG14 ...163 F2
Calverton NG14 ...148 B4
Caunton NG23 ...109 D3
Clarborough DN22 ...30 B3
Coddington NG24 ...126 A1
Costock LE12 ...206 B1
Cromwell NG23 ...110 C4
Cropwell Butler NG12 ...189 D4
Doddington LN6 ...71 E1
Dry Doddington NG23 ...156 C1
Eakring NG22 ...92 C1
East Bridgford NG13 ...165 E1
East Leake LE12 ...205 F1
Eastwood NG16 ...143 F1
Eastwood, Beauvale
NG16 ...144 B1
Edingley NG22 ...120 B2
Egmanton NG22 ...79 F3
Farndon NG24 ...139 D2
Farnsfield NG22 ...119 F3
Fenton NG23 ...142 B1
Fiskerton NG25 ...137 F2
Flintham NG13 ...167 D4
Granby NG13 ...191 E2
Gunthorpe NG14 ...165 D3
Harby LE14 ...202 A2
Harworth DN11 ...8 C2
Hickling LE14 ...210 B3
Hoveringham NG14 ...151 E1
Huthwaite NG17 ...99 F2
Keyworth NG12 ...197 F1
Kimberley NG16 ...158 C3
Kinoulton NG12 ...199 F1
Kirton NG22 ...78 A3
Lambley NG4 ...163 E4
Laneham DN22 ...54 A3
Langar NG13 ...190 B1
Laxton NG22 ...79 E2
Linby NG15 ...131 D2
Long Eaton NG10 ...193 F4
Long Whatton LE12 ...212 A2
Lowdham NG14 ...150 B1
Mattersey DN10 ...20 A4
Morton NG25 ...137 E2
Newton DE55 ...99 D2
Normanton on S LE12 ...213 E2
North Leverton w H DN22 ...32 B1
North Muskham NG23 ...110 C1
Nottingham NG6 ...160 B4
Oldcotes S81 ...16 C3
Ollerton NG22 ...77 D2

Main St continued
Ossington NG23 . . . . .95 E3
Oxton NG25 . . . . .134 A2
Papplewick NG15 . . . . .131 F3
Redmile NG13 . . . . .192 C2
Scarrington NG13 . . . . .178 C4
Shirebrook NG20 . . . . .72 B2
Sibthorpe NG23 . . . . .167 F4
South Muskham NG23 . . . . .124 B4
South Normanton DE55 . . . . .113 D3
Stanford on S LE12 . . . . .214 B1
Strelley NG16 . . . . .159 D1
Sutton Bonington LE12 . . . . .213 D4
Sutton on T NG23 . . . . .96 C4
Torksey LN1 . . . . .44 A1
Walesby NG22 . . . . .64 A1
West Bridgford NG2 . . . . .186 B4
West Leake LE12 . . . . .204 C1
West Stockwith DN10 . . . . .7 F1
Weston NG23 . . . . .81 D2
Whaley Thorns S44 . . . . .59 D1
Whatton NG13 . . . . .179 D2
Willoughby-on-t-W LE12 . . . . .217 E4
Woodborough NG14 . . . . .149 E2
Wysall NG12 . . . . .207 D2
Zouch LE12 . . . . .213 D2
Mainside Cres NG16 . . . . .129 D1
Maitland Ave NG5 . . . . .161 F2
Maitland Rd NG5 . . . . .161 F2
Major St NG1 . . . . .223 F3
Making It* NG18 . . . . .102 B3
Malbon Cl NG3 . . . . .173 F4
Malcolm Cl NG3 . . . . .173 E4
Malden Cl NG9 . . . . .183 E2
Malham Cl NG10 . . . . .9 F4
Malin Hill NG1 . . . . .223 F2
Malkin Ave NG12 . . . . .176 A2
Mallam Rd NG22 . . . . .77 E3
Mallard Cl
Bingham NG13 . . . . .178 A2
Nottingham NG6 . . . . .160 C2
Shirebrook NG20 . . . . .72 C2
Mallard Ct NG9 . . . . .184 A3
Mallard Gn NG24 . . . . .140 A3
Mallard Rd NG4 . . . . .175 D3
Mallards The S81 . . . . .35 E4
Mallatratt Pl NG19 . . . . .88 A3
Mallow Way NG13 . . . . .177 E2
Malmesbury Rd NG3 . . . . .162 A2
Malpas Ave DN21 . . . . .15 E1
Malt Cotts NG17 . . . . .160 C1
Malt St NG11 . . . . .195 D1
Maltby Cl NG8 . . . . .160 A1
Maltby Rd
Mansfield NG18 . . . . .102 C3
Nottingham NG3 . . . . .162 A2
Oldcotes S81 . . . . .16 C3
Malthouse Cl NG16 . . . . .143 F1
Malthouse Rd
Ilkeston DE7 . . . . .170 A2
Whitwell S80 . . . . .45 D3
Malting Cl NG11 . . . . .196 B3
Maltings The Blyth S81 . . . . .18 A2
Cropwell Bishop NG12 . . . . .189 D2
Maltings Ct NG22 . . . . .77 E1
Maltkiln La NG24 . . . . .124 C1
Maltkiln Rd LN1 . . . . .55 E3
Maltkins The DN22 . . . . .42 B4
Maltmill La NG1 . . . . .223 E2
Malton Rd NG5 . . . . .160 C1
Maltsters The NG24 . . . . .139 E3
Malvern Cl NG3 . . . . .161 F1
Malvern Cres NG2 . . . . .185 E3
Malvern Rd
Nottingham NG3 . . . . .161 F1
West Bridgford NG2 . . . . .185 F3
Manby Ct NG20 . . . . .74 B4
Manchester St NG10 . . . . .193 E3
Mandalay St NG6 . . . . .160 B2
Mandeen Gr NG18 . . . . .103 D2
Manesty Cres NG11 . . . . .195 F4
Mangham La DN11 . . . . .8 A4
Manifold Dr NG16 . . . . .129 D4
Manifold Rd NG23 . . . . .173 E1
Manitoba Way NG16 . . . . .128 C4
Manly Cl NG5 . . . . .160 C4
Mann St NG 16 NG7 . . . . .172 C4
Manners Ave DE7 . . . . .157 E1
Manners Ind Est DE7 . . . . .157 F1
Manners Rd
Balderton NG24 . . . . .140 B2
Ilkeston DE7 . . . . .157 F1
Newark-on-T NG24 . . . . .124 C1
Manners St DE7 . . . . .170 A3
Manners Sutton Prim Sch
NG23 . . . . .123 F1
Manning Comp Sch
NG8 . . . . .172 A4
Manning St NG3 . . . . .173 E4
Manning View DE7 . . . . .157 F1
Mannion Cres NG10 . . . . .193 D3
Manns Leys NG12 . . . . .187 F1
Manor Ave
Beeston NG9 . . . . .183 F3
17 Nottingham NG2 . . . . .173 F2
Stapleford NG9 . . . . .182 B4
Manor Ct Bleasby NG14 . . . . . . .152 A4
BOughton NG22 . . . . .77 F2
Costock LE12 . . . . .206 B1
Eagle LN6 . . . . .84 B2
Gamston DN22 . . . . .50 C3
Long Whatton LE12 . . . . .212 A2
Misson DN10 . . . . .4 B2
Newton DE55 . . . . .99 D2

Manor Cl continued
Southwell NG25 . . . . .121 F1
Walesby NG22 . . . . .64 A1
West Bridgford NG12 . . . . .186 A2
Worksop S80 . . . . .35 E1
Manor Comp Sch NG16 . . . . . . .88 B3
Manor Cres
Carlton NG4 . . . . .174 C4
Kirkby in A NG17 . . . . .115 D2
Manor Croft NG6 . . . . .160 C2
Manor Ct Beeston NG9 . . . . .183 D4
Carlton NG4 . . . . .174 C4
Church Warsop NG20 . . . . .74 B3
Manor Dr NG25 . . . . .137 E2
Manor Farm Animal Ctr*
LE12 . . . . .214 C4
Manor Farm Cl
Bradmore NG11 . . . . .196 C2
Rolleston NG23 . . . . .138 A3
Manor Farm La NG7 . . . . .184 C1
Manor Farm Mdw
LE12 . . . . .205 F1
Manor Farm Rise NG23 . . . . .32 B1
Manor Gn Wlk NG4 . . . . .174 C4
Manor Gr S80 . . . . .35 E1
Manor House Cl NG14 . . . . .150 B1
Manor House Ct NG17 . . . . .114 B2
Manor House Dr
North Muskham NG23 . . . . .110 C2
Wysall NG12 . . . . .207 E2
Manor House La NG23 . . . . .156 B1
Manor House Rd
NG10 . . . . .193 F3
Manor La
Broadholme LN6 . . . . .71 D4
Shelford NG12 . . . . .164 B1
Whatton NG13 . . . . .179 D1
Manor Pk NG11 . . . . .196 B4
Manor Pk Inf Sch
NG14 . . . . .148 C4
Manor Rd
Barton in F NG11 . . . . .194 C3
Bingham NG13 . . . . .177 F2
Bottesford NG13 . . . . .181 E1
Calverton NG14 . . . . .148 C4
Carlton NG4 . . . . .174 C4
Caunton NG23 . . . . .109 D2
Church Warsop NG20 . . . . .74 B3
Collingham NG23 . . . . .112 A4
East Leake LE12 . . . . .205 F2
Eastwood NG16 . . . . .143 F1
Ilkeston DE7 . . . . .157 F1
Keyworth NG12 . . . . .197 F2
Mansfield Woodhouse
NG19 . . . . .88 A2
Morton DN21 . . . . .15 D2
Saxilby LN1 . . . . .57 D2
Scrooby DN10 . . . . .10 A1
Sutton in A NG17 . . . . .100 C4
Manor Rise NG16 . . . . .165 E2
Manor St
Nottingham NG2 . . . . .173 F2
Sutton in A NG17 . . . . .100 C4
Manorwood Rd NG12 . . . . .187 F1
Manse Ave S80 . . . . .58 B4
Manse Cl S80 . . . . .58 B4
Mansell Cl NG16 . . . . .144 A1
Mansfield Com Hospl
NG18 . . . . .102 A3
Mansfield Ct NE NG5 . . . . .173 D4
Mansfield Gr NG1 . . . . .223 D4
Mansfield La
Calverton NG14 . . . . .148 C4
Sutton in A NG17 . . . . .101 D3
Mansfield Mus & Art Gall*
NG18 . . . . .102 B4
Mansfield Rd
Annesley NG15 . . . . .130 A3
Arnold NG5, NG15 . . . . .147 E3
Babworth DN22 . . . . .38 B2
Bilsthorpe NG22 . . . . .105 F2
Blidworth NG21 . . . . .118 A3
Brinsley NG16 . . . . .143 F2
Clipstone NG21 . . . . .90 A3
Cuckney NG20 . . . . .60 A2
Eastwood NG16 . . . . .143 F2
Edingley NG22 . . . . .120 B3
Edwinstowe NG21 . . . . .75 F1
Farnsfield NG22 . . . . .119 E4
Glapwell S44 . . . . .86 B4
Heanor DE75 . . . . .143 D1
Mansfield Woodhouse
NG19 . . . . .88 B1
Market Warsop NG20 . . . . .73 F1
Nottingham NG5 . . . . .161 E2
Ollerton NG22 . . . . .76 C2
Ravenshead NG15 . . . . .116 C1
Selston NG16 . . . . .128 C4
Selston, Friezeland
NG16 . . . . .129 E2
South Normanton DE55 . . . . .113 E3
Sutton in A, Skegby
NG17 . . . . .100 C3
Sutton in A, Sutton Forest Side
NG17 . . . . .101 D2
Tibshelf DE55 . . . . .99 D4
Worksop S80 . . . . .46 A4
Mansfield St NG5 . . . . .161 E1
Mansfield Town Sta
NG18 . . . . .102 A3
Mansfield Woodhouse Sta
NG19 . . . . .88 A2
Manston Way S81 . . . . .35 E4
Manthorpe Cres NG5 . . . . .161 F2
Manthorpe House
NG24 . . . . .140 C2
Manthorpe Way NG24 . . . . .140 C2
Manton Cl NG21 . . . . .118 A4

Manton Cres
Beeston NG9 . . . . .184 A4
Worksop S80 . . . . .36 A1
Manton Dale S80 . . . . .36 B1
Manton Prim Sch S80 . . . . .36 B1
Manton Villas S80 . . . . .36 B1
Manton Wood Enterprise
Zone S81 . . . . .36 C1
Manvers Cres NG21 . . . . .75 F1
Manvers Ct
Market Warsop NG20 . . . . .73 D2
2 Nottingham NG2 . . . . .173 F2
Manvers Gr NG12 . . . . .175 F2
Manvers Jun Sch
NG21 . . . . .187 F2
Manvers Rd
Retford DN22 . . . . .39 E3
West Bridgford NG2 . . . . .185 F3
Manvers St
Carlton NG4 . . . . .175 D3
Mansfield NG18 . . . . .102 A4
Mansfield Woodhouse
NG19 . . . . .88 A2
Market Warsop NG20 . . . . .74 A2
Nottingham NG2 . . . . .173 F2
Shirebrook NG20 . . . . .73 D2
Worksop S80 . . . . .35 F2
Manvers View NG22 . . . . .77 F3
Manville Cl
Beeston NG9 . . . . .171 D2
Nottingham NG8 . . . . .172 B3
Maori Ave NG15 . . . . .145 E3
Maple Ave
Beeston NG9 . . . . .184 A3
Sandiacre NG10 . . . . .182 A4
Maple Cl
East Leake LE12 . . . . .214 B4
Gainsborough DN21 . . . . .15 D2
Keyworth NG12 . . . . .198 A1
Mansfield NG19 . . . . .88 C1
Radcliffe on T NG12 . . . . .175 F1
Tuxford NG22 . . . . .66 A1
Maple Cres NG17 . . . . .114 C3
Maple Dr Carlton NG4 . . . . .163 D1
Elkesley DN22 . . . . .50 A2
Hucknall NG15 . . . . .145 F3
Nuthall NG16 . . . . .159 E3
Ravenshead NG15 . . . . .116 B4
South Normanton DE55 . . . . .113 D2
Worksop S80 . . . . .36 A4
Maple Gr Bawtry DN10 . . . . .9 F4
Glapwell S44 . . . . .86 A4
Newark-on-T NG24 . . . . .139 F2
Maplebeck Ave NG20 . . . . .74 B4
Maplebeck Cl
Arnold NG5 . . . . .162 A4
Beeston NG9 . . . . .183 F4
Kirkby in A NG17 . . . . .115 D3
Long Eaton NG10 . . . . .182 C1
Mansfield NG19 . . . . .87 F1
Maplebeck St
Gainsborough DN21 . . . . .24 B4
2 Nottingham NG2 . . . . .172 C1
Marldon Cl NG8 . . . . .171 E3
Marle Pit Hill LE12 . . . . .213 D4
Marlock Cl NG25 . . . . .137 F2
Marlow Ave NG6 . . . . .160 C1
Marlow Rd DN21 . . . . .15 F1
Marlow Dr NG24 . . . . .140 B2
Marlowe Gdns S81 . . . . .36 A2
Marlpool Inf Sch
DE75 . . . . .157 D4
Marlpool Jun Sch
DE75 . . . . .143 D1
Marlwood NG12 . . . . .188 A1
Marmion Rd NG3 . . . . .174 A3
Marnham Dr NG3 . . . . .161 F1
Marnham Rd NG22 . . . . .66 B1
Marple Sq NG3 . . . . .173 E4
Marquis Ave NG4 . . . . .163 E1
Marquis Ave NG24 . . . . .140 B2
Marquis Gdns DN22 . . . . .40 A2
Marquis Rd LE14 . . . . .219 D3
Marris La NG21 . . . . .117 F2
Marriott Ave
Beeston NG9 . . . . .183 D3
Mansfield NG18 . . . . .101 F4
Marriott Cl NG9 . . . . .183 D3
Marriott St 2 NG8 . . . . .172 B3
Marsh La
Farndon NG24 . . . . .139 D3
Misterton DN10 . . . . .7 D1
North Leverton w H DN22 . . . . .33 E1
North Wheatley DN22 . . . . .31 F4
Saundby DN22 . . . . .23 E3
Marsh Rd DN10 . . . . .14 B3
Marshall Ave NG17 . . . . .115 E2
Marshall Dr NG9 . . . . .140 C2
Marshall Dr NG9 . . . . .183 D4
Marshall Farm Cl
NG13 . . . . .192 A1
Marshall Hill Dr NG3 . . . . .162 A1
Marshall Rd
Cropwell Bishop NG12 . . . . .189 D2
Nottingham NG3 . . . . .162 A1
Marshall St
Heanor DE75 . . . . .143 D1
Nottingham NG5 . . . . .161 E1
Marshall Terr NG17 . . . . .100 B3
Marshs Paddock LE14 . . . . .210 B3
Marston Ave NG20 . . . . .74 B4
Marston Cl NG24 . . . . .140 B2
Marston Moor Rd
NG24 . . . . .125 D2
Marston Rd NG3 . . . . .174 A4
Martin Cl NG6 . . . . .160 A4
Martin Ct NG6 . . . . .160 A4
Martin La DN10 . . . . .4 A3
Martindale Cl NG2 . . . . .186 B4
Martinmass Cl NG7 . . . . .222 A1
Martins Hill NG4 . . . . .174 C4

Market Pl continued
Gainsborough DN21 . . . . .24 B4
Hucknall NG15 . . . . .146 A4
Huthwaite NG17 . . . . .99 F2
Kegworth DE74 . . . . .203 E1
Long Eaton NG10 . . . . .193 F4
Loughborough LE11 . . . . .220 A2
24 Mansfield NG18 . . . . .102 A4
Mansfield Woodhouse
NG19 . . . . .88 B2
Nottingham NG6 . . . . .160 A4
Ollerton NG22 . . . . .77 D2
Retford DN22 . . . . .39 F4
South Normanton DE55 . . . . .113 D3
Southwell NG25 . . . . .136 C4
Stanton Hill NG17 . . . . .100 C1
Tickhill DN11 . . . . .8 A4
Tuxford NG22 . . . . .65 F2
Worksop S80 . . . . .35 F1
Market Pl The NG5 . . . . .161 F4
Market Side 22 NG6 . . . . .160 A4
Market St
Bingham NG13 . . . . .177 F2
Bottesford NG13 . . . . .181 D1
Gainsborough DN21 . . . . .24 B4
Huthwaite NG17 . . . . .99 F2
Loughborough LE11 . . . . .220 A2
27 Mansfield NG18 . . . . .102 A4
Nottingham NG1 . . . . .223 E2
Shirebrook NG20 . . . . .72 C2
South Normanton DE55 . . . . .113 D3
Sutton in A NG17 . . . . .100 C1
Worksop S80 . . . . .35 F2
Markham Ave NG24 . . . . .125 D2
Markham Ct NG22 . . . . .77 D2
Markham Cres NG5 . . . . .161 E2
Markham Pl NG19 . . . . .101 E4
Markham Rd
Beeston NG9 . . . . .171 E1
Langold S81 . . . . .16 C2
Tuxford NG22 . . . . .65 F2
Markham St NG15 . . . . .130 B3
Markhams The NG20 . . . . .77 D2
Markland La NG20 . . . . .58 A4
Marklew Cl NG21 . . . . .118 A3
Markwick Cl NG24 . . . . .140 B4
Marl Rd NG12 . . . . .176 A2
Marlborough Cl
Newark-on-T NG24 . . . . .139 E3
Worksop S81 . . . . .35 E4
Marlborough Ct NG24 . . . . .139 E3
Marlborough Rd
Arnold NG5 . . . . .161 F3
Beeston NG9 . . . . .183 F4
Kirkby in A NG17 . . . . .115 D3
Long Eaton NG10 . . . . .182 C1
Mansfield NG19 . . . . .87 F1
Marlborough St
Gainsborough DN21 . . . . .24 B4
2 Nottingham NG2 . . . . .172 C1

Martlet Way S80 . . . . .47 D4
Marton Cty Prim Sch
DN21 . . . . .44 B4
Marton Rd
Beeston NG9 . . . . .183 E2
Newark-on-T NG24 . . . . .140 A3
Nottingham NG6 . . . . .146 B1
Martyn Ave NG17 . . . . .100 C1
Marvin Rd NG9 . . . . .183 F3
Marwood Cres NG4 . . . . .162 B1
Marwood Rd NG4 . . . . .162 B1
Mary Rd NG16 . . . . .144 A1
Mary St
Kirkby in A NG17 . . . . .115 D3
Rhodesia S80 . . . . .35 D2
Whaley Thorns NG20 . . . . .59 D1
Maryfield Cl NG22 . . . . .29 F1
Maryland Ct NG9 . . . . .170 C1
Marys Cl LE12 . . . . .216 B2
Masefield Cres NG24 . . . . .140 B2
Masefield Pl S81 . . . . .36 A2
Mason Rd DE7 . . . . .157 E1
Mason St NG17 . . . . .101 D2
Masonic Pl NG1 . . . . .223 D3
Massey Cl NG14 . . . . .163 F2
Massey Gdns 3 NG3 . . . . .173 F3
Massey St NG24 . . . . .140 A4
Masson Ct 4 NG5 . . . . .147 D1
Mather Rd NG24 . . . . .124 C1
Matlock Ave NG18 . . . . .102 A3
Matlock Cl NG10 . . . . .182 C1
Matlock St NG4 . . . . .174 C4
Mattersey Ct NG19 . . . . .88 C1
Mattersey Cty Prim Sch
DN10 . . . . .20 A4
Mattersey Priory*
DN10 . . . . .20 C4
Mattersey Rd
Everton DN10 . . . . .11 E1
Lound DN22 . . . . .20 C2
Ranskill DN22 . . . . .19 E3
Sutton DN22 . . . . .29 D4
Matthew Holland Comp Sch
NG16 . . . . .128 C4
Matthews Ct NG9 . . . . .170 C1
Mattingly Rd NG6 . . . . .160 A3
Mattley Ave NG17 . . . . .115 D1
Maud St NG7 . . . . .161 D1
Maun Ave
Kirkby in A NG17 . . . . .115 D4
Nottingham NG7 . . . . .172 B3
Maun Cl
Mansfield NG18 . . . . .101 F2
Retford DN22 . . . . .39 F3
Maun Cres NG22 . . . . .77 E3
Maun Gn NG24 . . . . .125 D1
Maun Inf Sch NG22 . . . . .77 D3
Maun Valley Ind Pk
NG17 . . . . .101 E1
Maun Way
Mansfield NG18 . . . . .101 F2
Wellow NG22 . . . . .78 A2
Maundale Ave NG17 . . . . .101 D2
Maunleigh NG19 . . . . .88 C1
Maunside NG18 . . . . .101 F2
Maunside Ave NG17 . . . . .101 D1
Maurice Dr NG3 . . . . .161 F2
Mavis Ave NG15 . . . . .131 D1
Mawkin La NG16 . . . . .113 F3
Maws La NG16 . . . . .158 C4
Maxtoke Rd NG7 . . . . .222 E1
Maxwell Cl NG7 . . . . .222 B1
May Ave NG8 . . . . .171 F2
May Ct 8 NG5 . . . . .161 D1
May Fair Pl NG22 . . . . .66 A1
May Hill NG25 . . . . .136 B4
May Lodge Dr NG22 . . . . .91 F3
May St DE7 . . . . .157 F2
Maycroft Gdns NG3 . . . . .174 A4
Maydene Cl NG11 . . . . .184 B1
Mayes Rise NG6 . . . . .146 C2
Mayfair NG12 . . . . .176 B2
Mayfair Ave NG18 . . . . .102 B3
Mayfair Cl DN11 . . . . .8 C2
Mayfair Ct NG17 . . . . .160 C1
Mayfair Gdns NG5 . . . . .160 C3
Mayfield Ave
Burton Joyce NG14 . . . . .163 F3
Gainsborough DN21 . . . . .15 D2
Mayfield Cl NG18 . . . . .103 D3
Mayfield Ct NG2 . . . . .173 E1
Mayfield Dr
Loughborough LE11 . . . . .220 A1
Stapleford NG9 . . . . .170 C1
Mayfield Gr NG10 . . . . .182 C1
Mayfield Rd NG17 . . . . .115 D3
Mayfield Terr NG20 . . . . .74 A2
Mayflower Ave DN10 . . . . .10 A1
Mayflower Cl
Bawtry DN10 . . . . .10 A4
Gainsborough DN21 . . . . .24 C2
West Bridgford NG2 . . . . .186 A4
Mayflower Jun & Inf Sch
DN10 . . . . .10 A4
Mayflower Rd NG16 . . . . .158 A4
Mayflower Way NG16 . . . . .88 A2
Mayo Rd NG5 . . . . .161 D1
Maypole Cl NG11 . . . . .184 C2
Maypole Ct NG22 . . . . .92 C4
Maypole Yd NG1 . . . . .223 E3
Mays Ave NG4 . . . . .174 B3
Mays Cl NG4 . . . . .174 B3

Mays La LN1 ....57 E2
Maythorn Cl NG11 ......185 E2
Maythorn Gr NG21 ....76 A2
Maythorne Cl NG24 ....140 B3
Maythorne Wlk 🔟 NG5 ..161 E4
Mcintosh Rd NG4 ....162 B2
Mead Way NG24 ....140 B2
Meade Dr S81 ....36 A4
Meadow Ave
Loughborough LE11 ......220 A3
Mansfield NG18 ....102 B3
Meadow Bank
Mansfield Woodhouse
NG19 ....88 C3
South Normanton DE55 ..113 D4
Meadow Cl
Aslockton NG13 ....179 D3
Eastwood NG16 ....143 F2
Farnsfield NG22 ....120 A3
Hucknall NG15 ....145 E3
🔁 Kirkby in A NG17 ......114 C3
North Muskham NG23 ...110 C1
Nottingham NG2 ....173 F1
Retford DN22 ....29 F1
Worksop S81 ....99 D4
Meadow Cotts
Carlton NG4 ....174 C4
Mansfield Woodhouse
NG19 ....88 B2
Meadow Ct
Nottingham NG2 ....173 F1
South Normanton DE55 ..113 D2
Meadow Dr
Keyworth NG12 ....198 A2
Misterton DN10 ....6 C1
Sutton in A NG17 ....100 B2
Tickhill DN11 ....8 B4
Worksop S80 ....35 E1
Meadow End
Gotham NG11 ....195 D1
Radcliffe on T NG12 .....176 B2
Meadow Farm View
NG17 ....114 C3
Meadow Gdns NG9 ..183 F2
Meadow Gr
Bilsthorpe NG22 ....106 A2
Newton DE55 ....99 D2
Nottingham NG2 ....173 F1
Meadow La (Notts Cty FC)
NG2 ....173 F1
Meadow La
Beeston NG9 ....183 F2
Bothamsall DN22 ....63 F4
Burton Joyce NG14 ......163 F2
Girton NG23 ....82 C2
Long Eaton NG10 ....193 F4
Loughborough LE11 ......220 A4
North Scarle LN6 ....83 F1
Nottingham NG2 ....173 F2
South Normanton DE55 ..113 D4
Weston NG23 ....81 D2
Meadow La Ind Est
LE11 ....220 A3
Meadow La Inf Sch
NG9 ....183 F2
Meadow Pl NG20 ....74 A2
Meadow Rd
Awsworth NG16 ....158 B3
Beeston NG9 ....184 A2
Blidworth NG21 ....118 A3
Carlton NG4 ....174 C4
New Balderton NG24 ....140 B2
Worksop S80 ....35 E1
Meadow Rise
Nottingham NG6 ....159 F3
Saxilby LN1 ....57 E2
Meadow St DE7 ....157 F1
Meadow The DN22 .....39 F4
Meadow View NG25 ..121 F1
Meadow Way
Harworth DN11 ....8 C3
Hucknall NG15 ....199 F1
Meadowbank Day Hospl
NG2 ....173 D1
Meadowbank Way
NG16 ....143 E2
Meadows La LE14 .....201 E1
Meadows Prim Sch
NG2 ....173 E1
Meadows The
Beckingham DN10 ....23 D4
Farndon NG24 ....139 D3
South Wheatley DN22 ...31 F4
Woodborough NG14 ....149 D2
Meadows Way NG2 ...173 E1
Meadowsweet Hill
NG13 ....177 E2
Meadowvale Cres
NG7 ....184 C1
Medawar Cl NG11 ....184 B1
Meden Ave
Market Warsop NG20 .....74 B3
New Houghton NG19 .....86 C4
Meden Bank
Bothamsall DN22 ....63 F4
Pleasleyhill NG19 ....87 D3
Stanton Hill NG17 ....100 B3
Meden Cl
Nottingham NG11 ....184 C2
Pleasleyhill NG19 ....87 D3
Meden Comp Sch
NG20 ....74 A3
Meden Cres NG17 ....100 B2
Meden Gdns NG7 .....172 B4
Meden Glen NG20 ......74 B3
Meden Rd
Mansfield Woodhouse
NG19 ....88 B2

Meden Rd continued
Wellow NG22 ....78 A2
Meden Sq NG19 ....87 D3
Meden Way DN22 ....39 F3
Medina Dr NG12 ....186 C1
Medway DN22 ....29 E1
Medway Ct NG9 ....222 A3
Meeks Rd NG5 ....162 A4
Meer Rd NG9 ....183 D3
Meering Ave NG24 ....125 D2
Meering Cl NG23 ....98 A1
Meerings The NG23 ....81 F1
Meeting House Cl
LE12 ....205 F1
Meetinghouse La DN22 ..42 A3
Melbourne Ct
Mansfield NG18 ....103 D3
Nottingham NG8 ....160 B1
Melbourne Gr DN11 .....8 C2
Melbourne Rd
Nottingham NG8 ....160 B1
Stapleford NG9 ....170 C1
West Bridgford NG2 ....174 A1
Melbourne St
Mansfield Woodhouse
NG19 ....88 B3
Selston NG16 ....129 D3
Melbury Prim Sch
NG8 ....171 E4
Melbury Rd
Nottingham, Bilborough
NG8 ....171 E4
Nottingham, Woodthorpe
NG3 ....162 A2
Meldreth Rd NG8 .....171 F4
Meldrum Cres NG24 ..139 F3
Melford Hall Dr NG2 ..185 E2
Melford Rd NG8 ....171 E4
Melksham Rd NG5 ....161 E4
Mellbreak Cl NG2 .....186 B4
Mellers Prim Sch NG7 ..222 B4
Mellish Rd S81 ....16 C1
Mellors Rd Arnold NG5 ..147 F1
Mansfield NG19 ....101 E4
West Bridgford NG2 ....185 F3
Melrose Ave
Beeston NG9 ....184 A3
Mansfield NG18 ....102 B3
🔁 Nottingham NG5 ....161 E2
Melrose Gdns NG2 ...185 E2
Melrose Rd DN21 ....15 E1
Melrose St NG5 ....161 E2
Melrose Wlk 🔢 NG5 ...35 E1
Melton Cl NG10 ....182 A3
Melton Gdns NG12 ....186 A2
Melton Gr NG2 ....185 F4
Melton La LE12 ....204 B1
Melton Rd
East Leake LE12 ....214 C3
Long Clawson LE14 .....211 D1
Plumtree NG12 ....197 F4
Rempstone LE12 ....215 E3
Stanton-on-t-W NG12 ...198 B2
Tollerton NG12 ....197 F4
Upper Broughton LE14 ..210 A1
West Bridgford NG12 ...186 A2
Widmerpool NG12,
LE12 ....209 E2
Melton Way NG18 ....101 F2
Melville Cl 🔢 NG3 ....173 E4
Melville Gdns NG3 ....173 F3
Melville St NG1 ....223 E1
Melvyn Dr NG13 ......177 F2
Memorial Ave S80 ....35 F1
Mendip Cl NG10 ....182 A1
Mendip Ct
Carlton in S81 ....25 E4
Nottingham NG5 ....160 C4
Mensing Ave NG12 ...187 F2
Mercer Rd DN21 ....15 D1
Merchant St
Nottingham NG6 ....160 A4
Shirebrook NG20 ....73 D2
Mercia Ave NG12 ......189 D2
Mercia Cl S81 ....36 A4
Mercia Rd NG24 ....139 F3
Mercury Cl NG6 ....160 C3
Mere Ave NG14 ....148 C4
Mere Cl NG14 ....148 C4
Mere Way NG11 ....196 B3
Meredith Cl NG2 ......173 D1
Meredith Ct NG9 ......170 C1
Meregill Cl NG5 ....146 C1
Merevale Ave NG11 ..184 C2
Merevale Cl NG14 ....150 C1
Meriac Cl NG5 ....160 C4
Meriden Ave NG9 .....184 A4
Meridian Cl DE7 ....157 F2
Meridian Ct NG5 ......161 D1
Merlin Cl NG11 ....184 C1
Merlin Dr NG15 ....145 F2
Merlin Way DE7 ....170 A2
Merrick Dr S81 ....36 B2
Merryvale Dr NG19 ..101 E3
Merryweather Cl
Edwinstowe NG21 ....91 E4
Southwell NG25 ....121 F1
Mersey St NG6 ....160 A4
Merton Ave DN22 ......29 F1
Merton Cl NG5 ....148 A1
Merton Ct NG9 ....170 C1
Metcalf Cl NG22 ......105 F4
Metcalf Rd NG16 .....144 A2
Metcalfe Cl NG25 ....136 C4
Methuen St NG18 .....102 C3
Metro Ave DE55 ....99 D2
Mettham St NG7 ......222 B1

Mews La NG14 ....148 C4
Mews The S81 ....18 A2
Meynell Gr 🔲 NG7 ....160 C1
Meynell Rd NG10 .....193 E3
Meyrick Rd NG24 .....125 D1
Miall Ct NG7 ....222 A3
Michael House-Rudolf
Steiner Sch DE75 .....157 D3
Micklebarrow Cl
NG25 ....136 B4
Mickleborough Ave
NG3 ....174 A4
Mickleborough Way
NG2 ....185 E2
Mickledale Cl NG22 ..105 F4
Mickledale La NG22 ..105 F4
Mickleden Cl 🔲 NG2 ..173 D1
Mickledon Cl 🔳 NG10 ..193 D4
Middle Ave NG4 ....174 B4
Middle Furlong Gdns 🔲
NG2 ....173 D1
Middle Furlong Mews 🔲
NG2 ....173 D1
Middle Gate NG24 ....139 F4
Middle Hill NG1 ....223 E2
Middle Holme La NG23 ..97 D4
Middle La Beeston NG9 ..183 F3
Morton NG25 ....137 E2
Nether Broughton LE14 ..219 E4
Middle Pavement
NG1 ....223 E2
Middle St
Barkestone-le-V NG13 ..192 B1
Beeston NG9 ....184 A3
Hose LE14 ....211 F4
Misson DN10 ....4 B1
Middle Wood La DN10 ...4 B3
Middlebeck Ave NG5 ..162 B4
Middlebeck Dr NG5 ...162 B4
Middlebridge Rd DN10 ..12 C2
Middlebrook Rd NG16 ..129 D2
Middledale Rd NG4 ...174 B3
Middlefell Way NG11 ..184 B1
Middlefield La DN21 ...24 C4
Middlefield Rd DN22 ..31 F4
Middlefield Sch The
DN21 ....24 C4
Middlegate Field Dr
S80 ....45 D3
Middleton Blvd NG8 ..172 B2
Middleton Cl NG16 ...159 E3
Middleton Cres NG9 ..171 F1
Middleton Ct
Mansfield NG18 ....103 D3
New Ollerton NG22 ....77 E3
Middleton Pl LE11 ....220 A1
Middleton Prim Sch
NG8 ....172 B2
Middleton Rd
Ilkeston DE7 ....170 A3
Mansfield Woodhouse
NG19 ....88 B3
Newark-on-T NG24 .....125 E2
Middleton St
Awsworth NG16 ....158 B2
Beeston NG9 ....183 F4
Cossall DE7 ....158 A1
Nottingham NG7 ....222 A3
Midfield Rd NG17 .....115 D1
Midhurst Cl NG9 ......183 D1
Midhurst Way NG7 ...184 C1
Midlame Gdns NG6 ..159 F4
Midland Ave
Carlton NG4 ....175 D4
Nottingham NG7 ....222 A1
Stapleford NG9 ....182 B3
Midland Cres NG4 ....174 C4
Midland Ct NG7 ....172 B3
Midland Gr NG4 ....175 D4
Midland Rd
Carlton NG4 ....174 C4
Eastwood NG16 ....143 F1
Sutton in A NG17 ....101 D1
Midland St NG10 .....193 F4
Midway The NG7 ......184 C4
Midworth St NG18 ...102 A3
Mikado Rd NG10 ......193 E3
Milburn Gr NG13 ......177 E2
Mildenhall Cres NG5 ..161 E4
Mile End Rd NG4 ....174 C3
Miles Yd LE11 ....220 A2
Milford Ave NG10 ....182 A2
Milford Cl NG6 ....160 A4
Milford Cres NG19 ...101 E4
Milford Ct NG5 ....161 E3
Milford Dr
Ilkeston DE7 ....157 E2
Nottingham NG3 ....174 B4
Milford Prim Sch
NG11 ....195 F4
Mill Baulk Rd DN10 ...14 A3
Mill Cl Hathwaite NG17 ..100 A2
North Leverton w DN22 ..32 B1
Sutton on S NG23 ....96 C4
Mill Cl The NG8 ....160 C2
Mill Cres Arnold NG5 ..161 F4
Whitwell S80 ....45 D3
Mill Croft NG17 ....100 C1
Mill Field Cl
Burton Joyce NG14 ......163 F2
Harby NG23 ....70 B1
Mill Gate
East Bridgford NG13 ....165 E2
Newark-on-T NG24 .....139 F4
Mill Gdns S80 ....35 E1
Mill Gn NG24 ....140 A4
Mill Heyes NG13 ......165 E2
Mill Hill DN10 ....12 B1

Mill Hill Rd NG13 .....177 E2
Mill Holme DE55 ......113 D2
Mill La
Annesley Woodhouse
NG17 ....114 C1
Arnold NG5 ....161 F4
Caunton NG23 ....109 D3
Cossall NG16 ....158 B1
Cotgrave NG12 ....187 F2
Eagle LN6 ....84 C2
East Leake LE12 ....214 C4
Edwinstowe NG21 ....91 E4
Hickling LE14 ....210 B4
Hathwaite NG17 ....100 A1
Kegworth DE74 ....203 E1
Lambley NG4 ....163 D4
Long Clawson LE14 .....211 E2
Long Whatton LE12 .....212 B2
Loughborough LE11 .....220 B3
Morton DN21 ....15 E3
Newark-on-T NG24 .....139 F4
Normanton on T NG23 ...81 E4
North Clifton NG23 ......68 C3
North Leverton w H DN22 ..42 A4
North Muskham NG23 ..110 C1
Orston NG13 ....180 A4
Pinxton NG16 ....113 E1
Rockley DN22 ....51 D1
Sandiacre NG10 ....182 B3
Saxilby LN1 ....57 D2
Scarrington NG13 ....178 C4
Scrooby DN10 ....10 A2
South Leverton DN22 ...42 B4
Stainsby S44 ....85 E4
Upton NG23 ....137 F4
Walesby NG22 ....63 F1
Walkeringham DN10 .....13 F2
Whitwell S80 ....45 D3
Woodnesborough-W LE12 ..217 E4
Mill Lakes Ctry Pk*
NG5 ....146 B2
Mill Mdw View S81 ...18 A2
Mill Pk NG25 ....121 F1
Mill Rd Eastwood NG16 ..144 A2
Elston NG23 ....153 F2
Heanor DE75 ....157 D4
Stapleford NG9 ....182 B4
Mill St Ilkeston DE7 ...157 F1
Mansfield NG18 ....102 B3
Nottingham NG6 ....160 B2
Retford DN22 ....39 F3
Sutton in A NG17 ....100 C1
Worksop S80 ....35 D3
Mill Vlk S80 ....45 D3
Mill Yd Beeston NG9 ..183 F3
Hucknall NG15 ....146 A4
Millbank S80 ....45 D2
Millbank DE75 ....157 D4
Millbank Cl DE7 ....157 E2
Millbaulk La NG22 .....93 F4
Millbeck Ave NG8 ....171 E2
Millbeck Cl NG2 ....186 B3
Milldale Cl NG11 ......184 B1
Milldale Ct NG18 .....103 D3
Milldale Rd
Farnsfield NG22 ....120 A3
Long Eaton NG10 ....193 D3
Milldale Wlk NG17 ...100 B2
Millennium Way E
NG6 ....160 A2
Millennium Way W
NG6 ....160 A2
Miller Hives Cl NG12 ..187 F2
Millers Bridge NG12 ..187 F1
Millers Cl Retford DN22 ..39 F3
Shelford NG12 ....164 B1
Millers Ct NG7 ....222 A4
Millers La LE12 ....206 B1
Millers Way DN22 ......39 E4
Millersdale Ave
Ilkeston DE7 ....157 F3
Mansfield NG18 ....101 F2
Millfield Ave LN1 ....57 D2
Millfield Cl
Ilkeston DE7 ....157 E2
Retford DN22 ....39 F2
Millfield Rd
Ilkeston DE7 ....170 A4
Kimberley NG16 ....158 C4
South Leverton DN22 ...42 A3
Millgate NG24 ....139 F4
Millgate Mus* NG24 ..139 F4
Millicent Gr NG2 ......185 F4
Millicent Rd NG2 .....185 F4
Millingham Ave NG16 ..159 D2
Millman Way DN22 ....29 E1
Mills Dr NG24 ....139 D3
Millview Cl 🔁 NG2 ...173 F2
Millview Ct 🔳 NG2 ...173 F2
Milnay NG19 ....88 B1
Milne Ave DN11 ....9 E2
Milne Dr DN11 ....9 E2
Milne Rd DN11 ....9 E2
Milner Rd
Long Eaton NG10 ....193 E4
Nottingham NG5 ....161 E1
Milner St
Newark-on-T NG24 .....140 A4
Sutton in A NG17 ....101 D3
Milnercroft DN22 ....29 E1
Milnercroft Gn DN22 ..29 E1
Milnhay Rd NG16 .....143 E1
Milton Ave DE7 ....157 E2
Milton Cl NG17 ....101 D2
Milton Cres
Beeston NG9 ....183 E1
Ravenshead NG15 ....117 D1

Milton Ct NG5 ....162 A4
Milton Dr
Ravenshead NG15 ....117 D1
Worksop S81 ....36 A2
Milton Rd
Gainsborough DN21 ......15 F1
Ilkeston DE7 ....157 F2
West Markham NG22 .....65 D3
Milton Rise NG15 .....145 E3
Milton St Ilkeston DE7 ..157 F2
Kirkby in A NG17 ....115 D3
Long Eaton NG10 ....193 F4
Mansfield NG18 ....102 A4
New Balderton NG24 ...140 B3
Nottingham NG1 ....223 E3
Milton Wlk S81 ....36 A2
Milverton Rd NG5 .....161 E4
Mimosa Cl NG11 ......184 B1
Minerva St NG6 ....160 A4
Minster CE Comp Sch
NG25 ....136 C4
Minster Cl
Hucknall NG15 ....146 A4
Kirkby in A NG17 ....114 C3
Minster Gdns NG16 ..144 A1
Minster Rd DN10 ....6 C1
Minster Sch The
NG25 ....136 B4
Mint Cl NG10 ....193 D4
Minver Cres NG8 ......160 A1
Mirberry Mews NG7 ..222 A1
Mire La DN22 ....28 C3
Misk Hollows NG15 ..145 F4
Misk View NG16 ....144 A1
Mission St NG3 ....161 F1
Mission Sch South Clifton DN10 ..4 A2
Misterton Cres NG15 ..116 C1
Misterton Ct NG19 .....88 A1
Misterton Prim Sch
DN10 ....13 F4
Mitchel Ave NG24 ....125 F1
Mitchell Ave NG16 ...143 D2
Mitchell Cl
Nottingham NG6 ....160 A3
Worksop S81 ....36 A3
Mitchell St NG10 ......193 F4
Mitchell Terr DE7 ......170 A3
Mob La S81 ....217 E4
Model Village S80 ......58 C4
Model Village Prim Sch
NG20 ....72 C2
Moffat Cl NG3 ....173 F4
Moira St LE11 ....220 A2
Mollington Sq NG6 ...160 A2
Mona Rd NG2 ....174 A3
Mona St NG9 ....184 A3
Monarch Way LE11 ...220 A3
Monckton Rd
Bircotes DN11 ....9 E2
Retford DN22 ....39 E4
Monks Cl DE7 ....170 A4
Monks La NG11 ....195 D1
Monks Mdw LE12 .....205 F1
Monks Way S81 ....34 C4
Monksway NG11 ....185 D2
Monkton Cl DE7 ....157 E2
Monkton Dr
Nottingham NG8 ....171 F4
Southwell NG25 ....121 F1
Monkwood Cl NG23 ...98 A1
Monmouth Cl NG8 ...171 D2
Monmouth Rd S81 .....36 A3
Monroe Wlk 🔲 NG5 ...161 D4
Monsaldale Cl NG10 ..193 D3
Monsall Ave DE7 ....157 F3
Monsall St NG7 ....160 C1
Monsell Dr NG5 ....147 F1
Montague Rd NG15 ..146 A4
Montague St
Beeston NG9 ....183 F4
Mansfield NG18 ....102 C3
Nottingham NG6 ....160 B4
Montfort Cres NG5 ...161 E2
Montfort St NG7 ......222 C3
Montgomery Cl 🔟 NG9 ..183 E1
Montgomery Rd NG24 ..140 A3
Montgomery St NG7 ..222 C4
Montpelier Rd NG7 ...172 C1
Montrose S81 ....36 A3
Montrose Ct NG9 .....170 C1
Montrose Sq NG19 .....88 A3
Monty Mdw S81 ....35 E4
Monyash Cl DE7 ....157 F2
Moor Bridge NG6 ......146 B1
Moor Farm Inn La
NG9 ....171 D1
Moor La
Aslockton NG13 ....178 B3
Beeston NG9 ....171 D2
Besthorpe NG23 ....98 B3
Bingham NG13 ....177 E3
Blyth S81 ....18 B1
Bunny NG11 ....206 B4
Calverton NG14 ....149 E3
Dry Doddington DN23 ..169 F3
Elston NG23 ....153 E4
Gotham NG11 ....205 E4
Kelham NG23 ....123 F1
Loughborough LE11 ....220 B2
Mansfield NG18 ....101 F3
Morton NG25 ....137 E2
Normanton on S LE12 ..213 D2
North Clifton NG23 ......68 C3
Ruddington NG11 ....196 B3
South Clifton NG23 ....69 E2
Stathern NG13 ....202 C3

Moor La continued
Syerston NG23 ....153 E2
Upper Langwith S44 ....72 A4
Moor La Fst Sch NG18 ....101 F3
Moor Rd
Bestwood Village NG6 ...146 C3
Brinsley NG16 ....143 F4
Calverton NG14 ....149 D4
Collingham NG23 ....98 A1
Nottingham NG8 ....159 E1
Moor St Carlton NG4 ...175 D4
Mansfield NG18 ....102 A3
Moor The NG4 ....143 E4
Moor Top Rd NG11 ....8 C3
Moorbridge Cotts
NG6 ....146 B1
Moorbridge Ct NG13 ......177 F3
Moorbridge La NG10 ......170 B1
Moorbridge Rd NG13 .....177 F3
Moorbridge Rd E
NG13 ....177 F3
Moore Ave DE74 ....203 E2
Moore Cl
Claypole NG23 ....156 C4
East Leake LE12 ....205 F1
West Bridgford NG2 ......174 A1
Moore Gate NG9 ....184 A3
Moores Ave NG10 ....182 B4
Moorfield Cres NG10 .....182 A3
Moorfield Ct NG6 ....170 C1
Moorfield La NG20 ....58 C2
Moorfield Pl NG20 ....74 B3
Moorfields Ave NG16 ....143 F2
Moorgate Ave NG19 ......86 C4
Moorgate Pk DN22 ....39 F2
Moorgate St NG7 ....222 C3
Moorgreen NG16 ....144 B2
Moorgreen Dr NG8 ....159 E1
Moorhaigh La NG19 ......87 D2
Moorhouse Rd
Egmanton NG22 ....80 B2
Nottingham NG8 ....171 F3
Moorings The **19** NG7 ...172 C1
Moorland Ave
Stapleford NG9 ....182 B3
Walkeringham DN10 ....13 F3
Moorland Cl
Sutton in A NG17 ....101 D3
Walkeringham DN10 ....13 F3
Moorland Way NG18 .....103 D3
Moorland Wlk DN10 ....13 F3
Moorlands Cl NG10 ......182 A1
Moorshorn Dr NG8 ....171 E2
Moray Ct NG16 ....158 C4
Moray Sq NG19 ....101 E3
Morden Cl NG8 ....171 E4
Morden Rd NG16 ....158 B4
Moreland Ct
Carlton NG4 ....174 B4
37 Nottingham NG2 ......173 F2
Moreland Pl **38** NG2 .....173 F2
Moreland St NG2 ....173 F2
Morello Ave NG4 ....174 C4
Moreton Rd NG11 ....195 F4
Morgan Mews NG7 ......184 C1
Morgans Cl NG24 ....126 A1
Morkinshire Cres
NG12 ....187 F2
Morkinshire La NG12 ....187 F2
Morley Ave
Nottingham NG3 ....161 F1
Retford DN22 ....29 E1
Morley Cl NG18 ....103 D3
Morley Ct **5** NG2 ....173 F2
Morley Dr DE7 ....157 E2
Morley Rd NG3 ....162 A1
Morley St Arnold NG5 ...162 A1
Gainsborough DN21 ....24 B4
Kirkby in A NG17 ....115 F3
Loughborough LE11 ......220 B3
Stanton Hill NG17 ....100 B3
Sutton in A NG17 ....100 C1
Morleys Cl NG10 ....150 C1
Mornington Cl NG10 .....182 B3
Mornington Cres NG8 ...159 E2
Mornington Prim Sch
NG16 ....159 E2
Morrell Bank NG5 ....160 C3
Morris Ave NG9 ....183 D1
Morris Cl LE12 ....220 B2
Morris Rd NG8 ....159 E1
Morris St NG4 ....175 D4
Morton Cl
Mansfield NG18 ....103 D3
Morton DN21 ....15 D2
Radcliffe on T NG12 .....176 B2
Morton Gdns NG12 ......176 B2
Morton Hall Gdns *
DN22 ....35 F4
Morton Rd DN21 ....15 E2
Morton St NG19 ....87 F1
Morton Terr DN21 ....15 E1
Morton Trentside Cty Prim
Sch DN21 ....15 D2
Morval Rd NG8 ....171 F4
Morven Ave
Hucknall NG15 ....146 A3
Mansfield Woodhouse
NG19 ....88 A1
Sutton in A NG17 ....100 C1
Morven Pk Prim Sch
NG17 ....115 D3

Morven Rd NG17 ....115 D3
Morven St S80 ....58 C4
Morven Terr NG20 ....74 A2
Mosborough Rd NG17 ...100 A1
Moseley Rd NG15 ....130 B4
Moses View S81 ....34 C4
Mosgrove Cl S81 ....35 E4
Mosley St
Hucknall NG15 ....146 A3
Nottingham NG7 ....172 C4
Moss Cl Arnold NG5 .....147 E1
East Bridgford NG13 ....165 E2
Moss Dr NG9 ....183 D4
Moss Rd NG15 ....145 F4
Moss Rise NG3 ....162 A1
Moss Side NG11 ....185 D2
Mosscroft Ave NG11 ....184 B1
Mossdale S81 ....36 A4
Mossdale Rd
Mansfield NG18 ....102 C4
Nottingham NG5 ....161 E3
Mosswood Cres NG5 ...161 D4
Mottram Rd NG9 ....183 E3
Moulton Cres NG24 ....140 B2
Mount Ave S81 ....35 F3
Mount CP Prim Sch
NG24 ....125 D1
Mount Cl DN11 ....8 C3
Mount Cres
Market Warsop NG20 .....74 B2
South Normanton DE55 ..113 D2
Mount Ct NG24 ....140 B2
Mount Hooton Rd
NG7 ....222 C4
Mount La NG24 ....140 A4
Mount Milner NG18 ....102 B3
Mount Pleasant
Carlton NG4 ....174 C4
Ilkeston DE7 ....157 F2
Keyworth NG12 ....198 A2
Lowdham NG14 ....150 B1
2 Mansfield NG18 ......102 A4
Nottingham NG6 ....160 B4
Radcliffe on T NG12 ....175 F2
Retford DN22 ....39 F4
Sutton in A NG17 ....100 C2
Mount St
Nottingham, New Basford
NG7 ....160 C1
Nottingham, Standard Hill
NG1 ....223 D2
Mount The NG5 ....182 C4
Mount The Arnold NG5 ..147 E1
Bestwood Village NG6 ..146 C2
Clipstone NG19 ....89 E2
Nottingham, Brotxewe
NG8 ....159 F1
3
Stapleford NG9 ....182 B2
Mount View Cl NG18 ...102 B3
Mountbatten Ct DE7 ....157 F2
Mountbatten Gr NG4 ...162 C1
Mountbatten Way
NG9 ....183 E1
Mountfield Ave NG10 ...182 A2
Mountfield Dr NG5 ......161 D4
Mountsorrel Dr NG2 ....186 A3
Mowbray Ct NG3 ....223 F3
Mowbray Gdns NG2 ....185 F3
Mowbray Rise NG5 .....161 F3
Mowbray Str NG21 ......15 E1
Moyra Dr NG5 ....161 E4
Mozart Ct NG7 ....222 A3
Mr Straws House (NT) *
.........................36 A3
Muir Ave NG12 ....197 E4
Muirfield NG5 ....160 C4
Muirfield Cl **3** NG17 ..114 C4
Muirfield Rd NG5 ....147 D1
Muirfield Way NG18 .....88 C3
Mulberry Cl NG13 ......177 F3
Mulberry Gdns **3** NG6 ..160 A4
Mulberry Gr NG15 .....146 A2
Mumby Cl NG24 ....125 D1
Mundella Rd NG2 ....173 E1
Mundy St DE7 ....157 F2
Munford Circ NG6 ......160 A2
Munks Ave NG15 ....145 F4
Murby Cres NG6 ....160 A4
Murden Way NG9 ......184 A3
Muriel Rd NG9 ....183 F4
Muriel St NG6 ....160 A4
Muschamp Terr NG20 ...74 A2
Mushill La LE12 ....219 F3
Muskham Ave DE7 ......157 F2
Muskham Ct NG19 ....88 A1
Muskham La NG23 ......110 B1
Muskham Prim Sch
NG23 ....110 C1
Muskham St NG2 ....173 E1
Musters Cres NG2 ......185 F3
Musters Croft NG4 .....174 C2
Musters Rd
Bingham NG13 ....177 E2
Langar NG13 ....190 B1
Newstead NG15 ....130 B3
Ruddington NG11 ....196 B3
West Bridgford NG2 ....185 F3
Musters St NG20 ....73 D2
Musters Wlk **13** NG6 ..160 A4
Muston La NG13 ....181 E1
Mutton La DN10 ....23 D4

Muttonshire Hill DN22 ...50 C3
Mynd The NG19 ....88 C2
Myrtle Ave
Long Eaton NG10 ....193 E3
7 Nottingham NG7 ......173 D4
Stapleford NG9 ....182 C3
Myrtle Cl NG20 ....72 B3
Myrtle Gr NG9 ....184 A4
Myrtle Rd NG4 ....174 B4
Myrtle St DN22 ....39 E3
Myrtus Cl NG11 ....184 B1

N

Nabbs La NG15 ....145 F3
Naburn Ct **5** NG8 ......172 B4
Nairn Cl Arnold NG5 ...148 A1
Farnsfield NG22 ....119 F3
Nairn Mews NG4 ....174 C4
Nan Sampson Bank DN9 ..1 B4
Nansen St NG6 ....160 B3
Naomi Cres NG6 ....146 B1
Naomi Ct NG6 ....146 B1
Narrow La Bawtry DN10 ...10 A4
Greasley NG16 ....145 D2
Hathern LE12 ....213 D1
Wymeswold LE12 ....217 D1
Naseby Cl NG5 ....160 C2
Naseby Dr NG10 ....193 E2
Naseby Rd NG24 ....140 C4
Nash Cl S81 ....36 B2
Nathaniel Rd NG10 ....193 F3
Nathans La NG12 ....187 D4
National CE Jun & Inf Sch
The NG15 ....146 A4
National Sch The
NG15 ....130 C1
National Water Sports Ctr
NG12 ....174 C2
Natural History Mus
(Wollaton Hall) *
NG8 ....172 A2
Naturescape Wild Flower
Farm * NG13 ....190 C1
Navenby Wlk NG7 ......184 C1
Navigation Way LE11 ..220 A3
Navigation Yd NG24 ....139 F4
Naworth Cl NG6 ....160 C3
Naylor Ave
Gotham NG11 ....195 D1
Loughborough LE11 ....220 B1
Neal Ct NG16 ....143 D2
Neale St NG10 ....193 F4
Near Mdw NG10 ....193 F3
Nearsby Dr NG2 ....186 A3
Needham Rd NG5 ......162 A4
Needham St NG13 .....177 F2
Needwood Ave NG9 ...170 B1
Neeps Croft NG14 .....150 A3
Negus Ct NG4 ....163 D3
Neighwood Cl NG9 ....182 C1
Nell Gwyn Cres NG5 ..147 E1
Nelper Cres DE7 ....170 A3
Nelson La NG23 ....110 C1
Nelson Rd Arnold NG5 ..147 F4
Beeston NG9 ....184 A2
New Balderton NG24 ...140 A2
Nottingham NG6 ....160 B4
Nelson St
Gainsborough DN21 ....15 E1
Ilkeston DE7 ....157 F2
Long Eaton NG10 ......193 E3
Nottingham NG1 ....223 F2
2 Retford DN22 ....39 F3
South Normanton DE55 ..113 D3
Sutton in A NG17 ....100 C1
New Terr Pleasley NG19 ..86 C3
Sandiacre NG10 ....182 A3
New Tythe St NG10 ....193 F4
New Vale Rd NG4 ....174 A4
Nevall Dr Beeston NG9 ..183 E1
Everton DN10 ....11 D1

New Cl Blidworth NG21 ...118 A3

New Cl continued
Kirkby in A NG17 ....115 D3
New Coll Nottingham
NG5 ....173 D4
New Cotts NG20 ....59 F2
New Cross St NG17 ...100 C2
New Cswy NG13 ....192 B1
New Derby Rd NG16 ..143 E1
New Eaton Rd NG9 ....182 C3
New England Way
NG19 ....87 E2
New Fall St NG17 ....99 F2
New Farm La NG16 ...159 E3
New Hill
Farnsfield NG22 ....119 F3
Walesby NG22 ....64 A1
New Holles Ct S80 ......35 F1
New Inn Wlk DN22 ......39 F3
New King St LE11 .....220 B2
New La Aslockton NG13 ..178 C3
Blidworth NG21 ....117 F3
Girton NG23 ....83 D2
Hilcote DE55 ....99 E1
Stanton Hill NG17 .....100 B3
New Linden St NG20 ....73 D2
New Line Rd NG17 ....114 C3
New Mill La NG19 ....88 C2
New Pl DN22 ....40 A4
New Rd
Barton in F NG11 ....194 C3
Bilsthorpe NG22 ....105 F3
Blidworth NG21 ....118 A3
Colston Bassett NG12 ..189 E1
Firbeck S81 ....16 A3
Greasley NG16 ....144 C3
Hawksworth NG13 .....167 E2
Morton NG25 ....137 E3
Nottingham NG7 ....159 D4
Radcliffe on T NG12 ...175 F2
Stapleford NG9 ....170 B1
Staunton in t V NG13 ..169 E2
Tickhill DN11 ....8 A4
Treswell DN22 ....42 B2
New Rose Prim Sch
NG19 ....101 E4
New Row Carlton NG4 ..174 B4
Westwood NG16 ....128 A3
New St
Gainsborough DN21 ....15 E1
Hilcote DE55 ....113 E4
Huthwaite NG17 ....99 F2
Kegworth DE74 ....203 F2
Kirkby in A NG17 ......115 D2
Long Eaton NG10 ......193 F4
Newark-on-T NG24 ....140 A4
Newton NG25 ....99 D2
22 Nottingham NG5 ...161 D1
Retford DN22 ....39 F3
South Normanton DE55 ..113 D3
Sutton in A NG17 ....101 D1
Tuxford NG22 ....65 E2
Wellow NG22 ....77 E1
Newark St **4** NG2 .....173 F2
Newark Hosp NG24 ...140 A3
Newark Mus & Tudor Hall *
NG24 ....140 A4
Newark Orch Sch
NG24 ....125 D1
Newark Rd
Barnby in t W NG24 ...141 E3
Caunton NG23 ....109 D2
Coddington NG24 .....125 F1
Collingham LN6 ....112 C2
Eakring NG22 ....92 C1
Kirklington NG22 ......120 C4
Laughterton LN1 ....55 D4
Ollerton NG22 ....77 D2
Southwell NG25 ....136 C4
Stapleford LN6 ....127 E4
Sutton in A NG17 ......101 E1
Tuxford NG22 ....65 E2
Wellow NG22 ....77 E1
Newark Tech Coll the Grange
Ctr NG24 ....126 A2
Newark Town Treasures *
NG24 ....139 F4
Newark Way NG18 ...103 D1
Newbarn Cl NG20 ......72 B1
Newberry Cl NG12 ....189 D2
Newbery Ave NG10 ..193 F3
Newbery Cl NG21 .....76 A1
Newbold Way NG13 ..199 F1
Newbound La NG17 ....86 B1
Newbridge Cl DE7 ...170 A3
Newbury Cl NG3 ......162 A3
Newbury Ct **5** NG5 ..173 D4
Newbury Dr NG16 ....159 E2
Newbury Mews **5** S80 ...35 F1
Newbury Rd
Balderton NG24 ....140 C4

Newbury Rd continued
Newark-on-T NG24 ....125 F1
Newcastle Ave
Beeston NG9 ....183 F3
Carlton NG4 ....162 C1
Newark NG24 ....140 A3
Worksop S80 ....35 F1
Newcastle Cir NG7 ...222 C2
Newcastle Dr NG7 ...222 C2
Newcastle Farm Dr
NG8 ....160 B1
Newcastle St
Huthwaite NG17 ....100 A3
4 Mansfield NG18 ....102 A4
Mansfield Woodhouse
NG19 ....88 A2
Market Warsop NG20 ...74 A2
Nottingham NG1 ....223 E3
Nottingham, Bulwell
NG6 ....160 B4
Tuxford NG22 ....65 F1
Worksop S80 ....35 F1
Newcombe Dr NG5 ...162 B4
Newdigate Rd NG16 ...159 D4
Newdigate St
Ilkeston DE7 ....170 A3
Kimberley NG16 ....159 D3
Nottingham NG7 ....222 C3
Newdigate Villas * NG7 ..222 C3
Newfield La NG23 .....167 E3
Newfield Rd NG5 ......161 D2
Newgate Cl NG4 ....174 C4
Newgate Ct NG7 .....222 B2
Newgate La NG18 ....102 B4
Newgate Prim Sch
NG18 ....102 B4
Newgate St
Bingham NG13 ....177 F3
Worksop S80 ....35 F1
Newhall Gr NG2 ....173 F1
Newham La NG22 .....120 B1
Newham Cl DE75 ....143 E1
Newhaven Ave NG19 ..88 A2
Newholm Dr NG11 ...185 D2
Newings La DN22 .....42 C4
Newington Rd DN10 ...10 B4
Newland Cl
Beeston NG9 ....183 D1
Nottingham NG8 ......172 B3
Newlands
Gainsborough DN21 ....15 F1
Retford DN22 ....29 D3
Newlands Ave NG22 ..77 F3
Newlands Cl NG2 ....186 B2
Newlands Cres DE55 ..99 F3
Newlands Dr
Carlton NG4 ....162 C1
Clipstone NG19 ....89 E1
NG19 ....89 F2
Newlands Rd
Clipstone NG19 ....89 E1
Mansfield NG19 ....103 D4
Newlyn Dr
Nottingham NG8 ....172 B4
South Normanton DE55 ..113 E3
Newlyn Gdns NG8 ....172 B4
Newman Rd NG14 ....148 C4
Newmanleys Rd NG16 ..157 F4
Newmanleys Rd S
NG16 ....157 F3
Newmarket Rd NG6 ..160 A3
Newmarket St NG18 ..102 C3
Newmarket Way NG9 ..182 C1
Newnham Rd NG24 ...125 D1
Newport Cres NG19 ...87 F1
Newport Dr NG8 ......160 A1
Newquay Ave **1** NG7 ..160 C1
Newstead Abbey *
NG15 ....131 E4
Newstead Ave
Newark-on-T NG24 ....125 D1
Nottingham NG3 ......162 B1
Radcliffe on T NG12 ..176 A2
Newstead Cl
Kirkby in A NG17 ......115 E3
Selston NG16 ....129 D4
Newstead Dr NG2 ....186 A4
Newstead Gr
Bingham NG13 ....177 E2
Nottingham NG1 ......223 D4
Newstead Ind Est
NG5 ....162 A4
Newstead Prim Sch
NG15 ....130 B3
Newstead Rd
Long Eaton NG10 .....182 B2
Newstead NG15 ....130 B4
Newstead Rd S DE7 ..157 E2
Newstead St
Mansfield NG18 ....101 E4
6 Nottingham NG5 ...161 E2
Newstead Sta NG15 ..130 B4
Newstead Terr NG15 ..146 A4
Newstead Way S81 ...159 E1
Newthorpe Comm
NG16 ....144 A3
Newthorpe St NG2 ...173 E1
Newton Ave
Bingham NG13 ....177 E2
Radcliffe on T NG12 ..176 A2
Newton Cl Arnold NG5 ..162 A3
11 Gainsborough DN21 ..24 C4
Lowdham NG14 ....150 C1
Worksop S81 ....35 E4
Newton Dr
Stapleford NG9 ....182 C3
West Bridgford NG2 ..185 E2

Newton Gdns NG13 ....177 E3
Newton on Trent CE Prim
 Sch LN1 ....55 D1
Newton Prim Sch DE55 ...99 D2
Newton Rd
 Carlton NG4 ....162 C2
 Newton DE55 ....99 D2
Newton St
 Beeston NG9 ....183 F3
 Mansfield NG18 ....102 B3
 Newark-on-T NG24 ....140 A4
 Nottingham NG7 ....172 C1
 Retford DN22 ....39 F2
Newtondale Ave NG19 ....88 C1
Newtondale Cl NG8 ....160 B1
Newtons La NG16 ....158 A2
Newtonwood La DE55 ......99 D3
Nicholas Pl NG22 ....66 A2
Nicholas Rd NG9 ....171 E1
Nicholson St NG24 ....140 A4
Nicholsons Row NG20 .....72 C2
Nicker Hill NG12 ....198 A2
Nicklaus Ct 5 NG5 ....161 D4
Nidderdale NG8 ....171 E2
Nidderdale Cl NG8 ....171 E2
Nightingale Ave
 Hathern LE12 ....213 D1
 Pleasley NG19 ....87 D2
Nightingale Cl
 Balderton NG24 ....140 C2
 Nuthall NG16 ....159 E3
Nightingale Cres
 NG16 ....129 D3
Nightingale Dr NG19 ....87 F1
Nightingale St S81 ....35 E4
Nightingale Way
 Bingham NG13 ....178 A2
 Woodbeck DN22 ....53 D4
Nile St NG1 ....223 F3
Nilsson Rd NG9 ....183 D2
Nine Acres Gdns NG6 ....159 F4
Nine Acres DE74 ....203 E1
Nine Scores La DN9 ....1 C4
Ninth Ave NG19 ....89 D3
Nixon Rise NG15 ....145 E3
Noble La NG13 ....179 D3
Noburn Cres NG6 ....160 C2
Noel St
 Gainsborough DN21 ....15 E1
 Kimberley NG16 ....159 D3
 Mansfield NG18 ....102 A4
 Nottingham NG7 ....172 C4
Nook The Beeston NG9 ...184 A4
 Beeston, Chilwell NG9 ...183 F2
 Calverton NG14 ....148 C4
 East Leake LE12 ....205 F1
 Halam NG22 ....131 F2
 Shirebrook NG20 ....72 B2
Nookin NG22 ....66 A3
Norbett Cl NG9 ....183 D2
Norbett Ct NG5 ....148 A1
Norbett Rd NG5 ....148 A1
Norbreck Cl NG8 ....160 A2
Norbridge Prim Sch
 S81 ....35 F3
Norbury Dr NG18 ....102 C2
Norbury Way NG10 ....182 A3
Nordean Rd NG5 ....162 A3
Norfolk Ave
 Beeston NG9 ....183 D1
 Bircotes DN11 ....9 E2
Norfolk Cl
 Hucknall NG15 ....145 E3
 Market Warsop NG20 ......74 A2
Norfolk Ct NG19 ....88 C3
Norfolk Dr Bircotes DN11 ...9 E2
 Mansfield NG18 ....102 A4
Norfolk Gr DN11 ....9 E2
Norfolk Pl Arnold NG5 ....162 A3
 Nottingham NG1 ....223 E3
Norfolk Rd Bircotes DN11 ...9 E2
 Long Eaton NG10 ....182 C1
Norfolk St S80 ....35 F1
Norfolk Wlk NG10 ....182 A3
Norland Cl NG3 ....173 F4
Norman Ave
 Newark-on-T NG24 ....125 D2
 Sutton in A NG17 ....101 D1
Norman Cl
 Beeston NG9 ....183 D3
 Nottingham NG3 ....223 E4
Norman Cres DE7 ....157 F2
Norman Dr
 Eastwood NG16 ....144 A1
 Hucknall NG15 ....145 F2
Norman Rd NG3 ....174 A4
Norman St
 Carlton NG4 ....175 D3
 Ilkeston DE7 ....157 F2
 Kimberley NG16 ....158 C4
Normanby Rd NG8 ....171 E2
Normanton Cl NG21 ....75 F2
Normanton Dr NG18 ......102 C4
Normanton La
 Bottesford NG13 ....181 D3
 Keyworth NG12 ....197 F2
 Stanford on S LE12 ......214 A1
Normanton on Soar Prim Sch
 LE12 ....213 E2
Normanton Rd NG25 .....121 F1
Nornay Cl S81 ....18 A2
North Ave Bawtry DN10 ...10 A4
 Rainworth NG21 ....104 A1
 Sandiacre NG10 ....182 A3
North Border Inf Sch
 DN12 ....9 D2
North Border Jun Sch
 DN11 ....9 D2

North Carr Rd DN10 ....7 E2
North Church St NG1 ....223 E3
North Cir St NG1 ....223 D2
North Clifton Prim Sch
 ....68 C2
North Cres
 Bottesford NG13 ....181 D1
 Clipstone NG21 ....90 A2
North Cty Prim Sch
 ....15 D1
North Cres
 Balderton NG24 ....140 C1
 Beeston NG9 ....183 F3
 Bilsthorpe NG22 ....105 F4
North End NG24 ....138 C3
North Gate
 Newark-on-T NG24 ....125 D1
 Nottingham NG7 ....160 C1
 Tickhill DN11 ....8 A4
North Gate Pl NG7 ....160 C1
North Gn
 East Drayton DN22 ....53 D2
North Hill Ave NG15 ......145 F4
North Hill Cres NG15 .....145 F4
North Leverton CE Prim Sch
 DN22 ....32 B1
North Leys Rd DN22 ....43 E4
North Lincolnshire Coll
 DN21 ....15 E1
North Marsh Rd DN21 ....15 E1
North Moor Dr DN10 ......13 F3
North Moor Rd DN10 .....13 F3
North Nottinghamshire Coll
 ....35 F3
North Par DN21 ....24 C4
North Pk NG10 ....102 C2
North Rd
 Long Eaton NG10 ....193 E3
 Loughborough LE11 ......220 A3
 Nottingham NG7 ....222 C2
 Retford DN22 ....29 D1
 West Bridgford NG2 ......185 F4
North Scarle Cty Prim Sch
 LN6 ....83 E1
North Scarle Rd NG23 ....98 C4
North Sherwood St
 NG1 ....223 E4
North St Beeston NG9 ...183 F3
 Eastwood NG16 ....144 B1
 Gainsborough DN21 ....15 E1
 Huthwaite NG17 ....100 A2
 3 Ilkeston DE7 ....157 F1
 Kimberley NG16 ....159 D3
 Kirkby in A NG17 ....115 D1
 Langley Mill NG16 ....143 D2
 Morton DN21 ....15 D2
 4 Nottingham NG2 ....173 F2
 Pinxton NG16 ....113 E2
 South Normanton DE55 ...113 D3
 Sturton le S DN22 ....32 B3
 Sutton in A NG17 ....100 C2
 Warsop Vale NG20 ....73 E2
 Whaley Thorns NG20 .....59 D1
North Warren Rd DN21 ...15 D1
North Way S81 ....25 F4
North Wheatley CE Prim Sch
 DN22 ....31 F4
North Wlk 39 E4
Northall Ave NG6 ....160 B3
Northampton St 4 NG3 ..173 F3
Northcliffe Ave NG3 ......162 A1
Northcote St NG10 ....193 F4
Northcote Way NG6 ......160 B3
Northcroft LN1 ....57 D3
Northdale Rd NG3 ....174 A4
Northdown Dr NG9 ....183 E2
Northdown Rd NG8 ....172 B3
Northern Ct NG6 ....160 B2
Northern Dr NG9 ....170 B2
Northern Rd NG24 ....125 D1
Northern View NG17 .....100 C2
Northfield Ave
 Ilkeston DE7 ....157 F1
 Long Eaton NG10 ....193 D2
 Mansfield Woodhouse
 NG19 ....88 A2
 Radcliffe on T NG12 .....176 B2
Northfield Cres NG9 ......183 D2
Northfield Dr DN18 ....102 C3
Northfield La
 Mansfield Woodhouse
 NG19 ....88 A3
 Treswell DN22 ....42 A2
Northfield Pk NG19 ....88 A3
Northfield Prim Sch
 NG19 ....88 A3
Northfield Rd
 Beeston NG9 ....183 D2
 North Leverton w H DN22 ...33 E1
Northfield Way NG19 ......39 E4
Northfields NG10 ....193 D2
Northfields Cl NG17 ......100 C2
Northfields Way LE12 ....205 F2
Northgate
 NG7 ....160 C1
Northgate St 6 DE7 .....157 F1
Northgate Sta DN21 ......15 E1
Northolme DN21 ....15 E1
Northolme Ave NG6 ......160 B4
Northolt Dr NG8 ....159 F2
Northrowe NG17 ....129 F4
Northside La DN22 ....32 C1
Northside Wlk NG3 ....147 F1
Northumberland Ave
 S81 ....25 F4

Northumberland Cl
 NG3 ....223 F4
Northumbria Cl S81 ....36 A3
Northumbria Dr DN22 .....39 E3
Northwood Ave NG2 .....185 E3
Northwood Cl 36 A3
Northwood Cres NG5 ....161 E3
Northwood Rd NG5 ....161 E3
Northwood St NG9 ....182 B4
Norton La NG20 ....60 A2
Norton Rd LN6 ....127 F4
Norton St NG7 ....222 B3
Norwell CE Prim Sch
 ....110 A4
Norwell Ct NG19 ....88 A1
Norwell La
 Brough NG23 ....112 B1
 Cromwell NG23 ....110 B4
 Norwell NG23 ....109 E3
Norwich Cl NG19 ....88 B3
Norwich Gdns NG6 ....146 A1
Norwood Cl NG17 ....100 A2
Norwood Gdns NG25 ....121 F1
Norwood Rd NG7 ....222 A3
Nostell Mews 6 S80 .....35 F1
Notintone St NG2 ....173 F2
Nottingham Airport
 NG12 ....186 C3
Nottingham Bluecoat Sch
 NG8 ....172 B4
Nottingham Castle (site of)*
 NG7 ....223 D2
Nottingham Cath*
 NG1 ....223 D2
Nottingham High Sch
 NG7 ....223 D4
Nottingham Ice Ctr & Arena
 NG1 ....223 F2
Nottingham La LE14 ......218 B3
Nottingham Nuffield Hospl
 The NG5 ....161 F3
Nottingham Rd
 Arnold NG5 ....161 F3
 Beeston NG9 ....183 D1
 Bingham NG13 ....177 E2
 Bottesford NG13 ....180 C1
 Burton Joyce NG14 ....163 E2
 Costock LE12 ....206 B1
 Cropwell Bishop NG12 ..188 C2
 Eastwood NG16 ....144 A1
 Gotham NG11 ....158 B4
 Gunthorpe NG14 ....164 A4
 Hucknall NG15 ....146 B2
 Ilkeston DE7 ....170 A3
 Kegworth DE74 ....203 E1
 Keyworth NG12 ....197 F2
 Kimberley NG16 ....159 D3
 Kirkby in A NG17 ....115 D1
 Long Eaton NG10 ....193 F4
 Loughborough LE11 ......220 B3
 Mansfield NG18 ....102 B2
 Nether Broughton LE14 ..219 F4
 Nottingham, New Basford
 NG7 ....160 C1
 Nottingham NG7 ....160 C2
 Oxton NG25 ....134 A1
 Radcliffe on T NG12 .....175 E1
 Ravenshead NG15 ....116 C2
 Selston NG16 ....129 D3
 Southwell NG25 ....136 B3
 Stapleford NG9 ....182 C4
 Thurgarton NG14 ....151 E3
 Trowell NG9 ....170 C3
 Woodborough NG14 .....148 C1
Nottingham Rd E
 NG16 ....144 A1
Nottingham S & Wilford Ind
 Est NG2 ....185 D2
Nottingham Sta NG2 .....223 F1
Nottingham Transport Her
 Ctr* NG11 ....196 B3
Nottingham Trent Univ The
 Nottingham NG11 ....184 B2
 Nottingham NG1 ....223 D3
Nuart Rd NG9 ....183 F4
Nugent Gdn NG3 ....173 F3
Nugent 6 NG3 ....173 F3
Nuncar Ct NG17 ....115 D1
Nuncargate Rd NG17 .....114 C1
Nunn Brook Rd NG17 .....99 F1
Nunn Brook Rise NG17 ...99 F1
Nunn Cl NG17 ....99 F1
Nurseries The NG16 .....144 A1
Nursery Ave
 Beeston NG9 ....183 E4
 Farndon NG24 ....139 D3
 Sutton in A NG17 ....100 B1
Nursery Cl
 Hucknall NG15 ....146 A2
 Radcliffe on T NG12 .....176 A2
 Saxilby LN1 ....57 D2
Nursery Dr
 Carlton NG4 ....174 B4
 Nottingham NG3 ....162 B1
Nursery End NG25 ....136 C3
Nursery Gdns DE55 ......113 C2
Nursery La
 Nottingham NG6 ....160 C2
 Sutton in T NG23 ....96 C4
Nursery Rd Arnold NG5 .162 A3
 Bingham NG13 ....178 A3
 Radcliffe on T NG12 .....176 A2
Nursery St NG18 ....102 B4
Nursury Gdns NG14 ......150 B1

Nuthall Gdns NG8 ....172 B4
Nuthall Rd NG8 ....160 B1
Nuthatch Cres S81 ....25 E1
Nutkin Cl 4 LE11 ....220 A1

O

Oak Acres NG9 ....183 D3
Oak Ave Aldercar NG16 .143 D3
 Bingham NG13 ....177 E2
 Blidworth NG21 ....118 A2
 Farndon NG24 ....139 D2
 Mansfield NG18 ....102 B4
 New Ollerton NG22 ....77 E2
 Radcliffe on T NG12 .....175 F2
 Rainworth NG21 ....104 B1
 Sandiacre NG10 ....182 A4
 Shirebrook NG20 ....72 B2
Oak Bank Cl NG18 ....102 A4
Oak Cl Pinxton NG16 ....113 E2
 Worksop S80 ....35 F1
Oak Cres LE12 ....214 B4
Oak Dr Eastwood NG16 .143 F3
 New Balderton NG24 .....140 B2
 Nuthall NG16 ....159 D3
Oak Flatt NG9 ....183 D3
Oak Gr NG15 ....146 A2
Oak Lodge Dr NG16 .....158 C4
Oak Rise NG22 ....75 D3
Oak St Kirkby in A NG17 .115 D3
 Nottingham NG5 ....161 D1
 Sutton in A NG17 ....100 B4
Oak Tree Ave
 Edwinstowe NG21 ....76 A1
 Glapwell S44 ....86 A4
 Radcliffe on T NG12 .....175 F2
Oak Tree Bsns Pk
 NG18 ....103 D2
Oak Tree Cl
 Hucknall NG15 ....145 E2
 Mansfield NG18 ....102 C4
 West Bridgford NG2 ......186 A4
Oak Tree Dr NG4 ....163 D1
Oak Tree La NG18 ....103 D3
Oak Tree La Prim Sch
 NG18 ....103 D3
Oak Tree Rd Bawtry DN10 ...9 F4
 Sutton in A NG17 ....101 D2
Oak Tree Rise S81 ....101 D2
Oak View Rise NG18 .....116 B4
Oakdale Dr NG9 ....183 E2
Oakdale Pupil Referral Unit
 ....87 F1
Oakdale Rd
 Arnold NG5 ....162 A4
 Carlton NG3 ....174 B3
 South Normanton DE55 .113 D2
Oakenhall Ave NG15 .....146 B4
Oakfield LN1 ....57 D2
Oakfield Ave
 Market Warsop NG20 ......74 A2
 Sutton in A NG17 ....114 C4
Oakfield Cl
 Mansfield NG18 ....102 C1
 Nottingham NG8 ....171 E2
Oakfield Dr NG10 ....182 A2
Oakfield La NG20 ....74 A1
Oakfield Rd
 Hucknall NG15 ....146 A3
 Nottingham NG8 ....171 E2
 Stapleford NG9 ....182 B4
Oakfields Rd NG2 ....174 A1
Oakford Cl NG8 ....160 A1
Oakham Bsns Pk
 NG18 ....101 F2
Oakham Cl
 Mansfield NG18 ....102 A1
 Nottingham NG5 ....160 C4
Oakham Rd NG11 ....185 E1
Oakham Way DE7 ....157 F2
Oakhampton Cres
 NG3 ....162 B3
Oakholme Ave S81 ....35 F3
Oakholme Rise S81 ....35 F3
Oakington Cl NG5 ....161 D3
Oakland Ave
 Huthwaite NG17 ....99 F1
 Long Eaton NG10 ....193 E3
Oakland Cl NG11 ....195 D3
Oakland Gr NG14 ....148 C4
Oakland Rd NG18 ....102 B3
Oakland St 8 NG17 ......172 C4
Oakland Terr NG10 ....193 E3
Oaklands DE7 ....170 B3
Oaklands Ave DE75 ......143 D1
Oaklands Cl DN11 ....8 B1
Oaklands La DN22 ....40 A3
Oaklands The DE55 ......113 D2
Oakleaf Cres NG17 ....100 B1
Oakleigh Ave
 Mansfield Woodhouse
 NG19 ....88 C2
 Nottingham NG3 ....162 B1
Oakleigh St NG6 ....160 B2
Oakley Dr LE12 ....212 B1
Oakley Mews NG6 ....159 F3
Oakleys Rd NG10 ....193 F4
Oakleys Rd W NG10 .....193 F4
Oakmead Ave NG8 ....171 F4
Oakmere Cl NG2 ....186 B2
Oakridge Cl NG19 ....88 C2
Oaks Ave S80 ....58 B4
Oaks Cl NG23 ....98 D3
Oaks Ind Est LE11 ....220 A3
Oaks La Oxton NG25 .....133 F4
 Walkeringham DN10 ....13 F2

Oaktree Ave NG21 ....15 F1
Oaktree Dr NG22 ....106 A2
Oaktree Rd DE55 ....99 E1

New - Old 249

Oakwood Dr
 Nottingham NG8 ....172 B4
 Ravenshead NG15 ....117 D1
Oakwood Gr NG21 ....91 E4
Oakwood Mews S80 ....35 E2
Oakwood Rd NG18 ....103 D2
Oardale Rd NG18 ....101 F4
Oatfield La NG12 ....176 B3
Oban Rd NG9 ....183 E3
Occupation La
 Kirkby in A NG17 ....114 C3
 Rolleston NG25 ....137 F3
 Willoughby-on-t-W LE12 .217 F3
Occupation Rd
 Hucknall NG15 ....146 A3
 New Houghton NG19 ......86 C4
 Nottingham NG6 ....160 A3
Ockbrook Ct DE7 ....157 F2
Ockerby St NG6 ....160 B3
Oddicroft La NG17 ....101 D1
Odesa Dr NG6 ....160 A2
Ogdon Ct NG3 ....173 F3
Ogle Dr NG7 ....223 D1
Ogle St NG15 ....146 A4
Old Basford Prim Sch
 NG6 ....160 B2
Old Bell La NG23 ....96 C2
Old Blyth Rd DN22 ....38 A3
Old Brickyard NG3 ....174 A4
Old Chapel Cl NG17 .....114 C3
Old Chapel La
 Elston NG23 ....153 F3
 Selston NG16 ....129 D2
Old Church St 8 NG7 ...172 C1
Old Coach Rd
 Nottingham NG8 ....171 F3
 Worksop S80 ....47 F4
Old Ctyd The DN21 ....44 B4
Old Dalby CE Sch
 LE14 ....218 C2
Old Dalby La LE14 ....219 E3
Old Derby Rd NG16 ......143 E2
Old Dr NG9 ....183 E4
Old Engine Yd The
 LE12 ....215 F3
Old Epperstone Rd
 NG14 ....150 A2
Old Farm Rd NG5 ....160 C4
Old Forge Cl LE12 ....213 D1
Old Forge La NG13 ....191 E3
Old Forge Rd DN10 ....6 C1
Old Grantham Rd
 NG13 ....179 D2
Old Great N Rd NG23 ....96 C4
Old Hall Cl
 Calverton NG14 ....148 C4
 Farndon NG24 ....138 C2
 Market Warsop NG20 ......74 B3
Old Hall Dr
 Nottingham NG3 ....161 E1
 Widmerpool NG12 ....208 B3
Old Hall Gdns NG24 .....125 F1
Old Hall La
 East Markham NG22 ......65 F4
 Norwell NG23 ....110 A4
Old Hall The* DN21 ....15 E1
Old La The NG17 ....185 E1
Old La The NG14 ....192 A4
Old Lenton Cl NG12 .....189 D2
Old Lenton St NG1 ....223 F2
Old London Rd
 Babworth DN22 ....49 F4
 Barnby Moor DN22 ....28 B2
 West Drayton DN22 ....50 C1
Old Main Rd
 Bulcote NG14 ....164 A3
 Costock LE12 ....206 B1
Old Manor Cl NG14 ......149 E2
Old Manor Rd NG19 ......88 B2
Old Melton Rd NG12 .....197 F4
Old Mill Cl
 Beeston NG9 ....183 D1
 Bestwood Village NG6 ..146 B2
 Nottingham NG7 ....222 B3
Old Mill Cres NG24 ......140 A4
Old Mill Ct NG13 ....177 F3
Old Mill La
 Cuckney NG20 ....60 A2
 Mansfield NG19 ....88 C1
Old Mkt Pl
 Mansfield NG18 ....102 A4
 South Normanton DE55 .113 D3
 Old Mkt Sq NG1 ....223 E2
Old Newark Rd NG18 ...102 C1
Old Parsonage La
 LE12 ....215 E1
Old Pk Cl NG11 ....203 F3
Old Pk The NG12 ....187 F2
Old Post Office St
 DN10 ....11 E2
Old Rd NG17 ....100 C3
Old Rectory Cl LE12 .....205 F1
Old Rectory Mus*
 LE11 ....220 A2
Old Rufford Rd
 Bilsthorpe NG22 ....105 E2
 Calverton NG14 ....133 E4
 Edwinstowe NG22 ....91 E2
 Farnsfield NG22 ....119 D3
 Ollerton NG22 ....77 D2
Old Sch Cl NG11 ....195 F4

Old Sch House Cl
Old Sch La NG16 .... 189 D4
Old Sch La NG16 .... 87 D3
Old Showfields DN21 .... 15 E1
Old Sookholme La
  NG20 .... 74 A2
Old St NG1 .... 223 E3
Old Sta Yd NG13 .... 181 E2
Old Storth La DE55 .... 113 D2
Old Terr NG19 .... 86 C2
Old Tollerton Rd NG12 ..... 186 B4
Old Trent Rd DN10 .... 14 C1
Old Way LE12 .... 213 D1
Oldacres NG14 .... 149 E2
Oldbury Cl NG11 .... 195 E4
Oldershaw Ave DE74 .... 203 E1
Oldershaw Rd LE12 .... 205 F1
Oldknow St NG7 .... 172 C4
Oldoak Rd NG11 .... 185 D1
Olga Rd NG3 .... 173 F3
Olive Ave
  Long Eaton NG10 .... 182 C1
  Shirebrook NG20 .... 72 B3
Olive Ct NG17 .... 100 C2
Olive Gr
  Burton Joyce NG14 ...... 163 F3
  Mansfield NG19 .... 103 D4
Oliver Cl Heanor DE75 .... 143 D1
  Nottingham NG7 .... 222 C4
Oliver Ct NG24 .... 140 A3
Oliver Quibell Cty Inf Sch
  NG24 .... 140 A3
Oliver Rd LE11 .... 220 A1
Oliver St NG7 .... 222 C4
Ollerton Jun & Inf Schs
  NG22 .... 77 E3
Ollerton Rd Arnold NG5 ... 147 F3
  Calverton NG14 .... 132 C1
  Edwinstowe NG21 .... 76 B2
  Farnsfield NG22 .... 119 D1
  Gamston DN22 .... 50 C3
  Kelham NG23 .... 124 A3
  Kirton NG22 .... 78 C4
  Ollerton NG22 .... 77 D2
  Retford DN22 .... 39 F2
  South Muskham NG23 ..... 124 A4
  Tuxford NG22 .... 65 E1
  Worksop S80 .... 47 D2
Ollerton Water Mill*
  NG22 .... 77 D2
Olton Ave NG9 .... 183 F4
Olympus Ct NG15 .... 145 E2
Omberley Ave NG17 .... 101 D3
Onchan Ave NG4 .... 174 C3
Ontario Dr NG16 .... 129 D4
Opal Cl NG21 .... 104 B1
Orange Cl NG20 .... 72 C3
Orange Croft DN11 .... 8 A4
Orange Gdns NG2 .... 173 E1
Orby Cl NG3 .... 173 F3
Orby Wlk NG3 .... 173 F3
Orchard Ave
  Bingham NG13 .... 177 E2
  Carlton NG4 .... 174 C4
  North Leverton w H DN22 .. 42 B4
Orchard Bsns Pk
  Ilkeston DE7 .... 157 E1
  Sandiacre NG10 .... 182 B3
Orchard Cl
  Barnstone NG13 .... 190 C2
  Bleasby NG14 .... 152 A4
  Burton Joyce NG14 ...... 163 F3
  East Bridgford NG13 .... 165 E2
  East Leake LE12 .... 214 B4
  Gunthorpe NG14 .... 165 D3
  Mansfield NG18 .... 102 B1
  Morton DN21 .... 15 D3
  North Leverton w H DN22 .. 42 B4
  Radcliffe on T NG12 .... 175 F2
  Rampton DN22 .... 43 D1
  Shirebrook NG20 .... 72 C3
  South Muskham NG23 ..... 124 C4
  Southwell NG25 .... 121 E1
  Sutton Bonington LE12 .. 213 E3
  Tollerton NG12 .... 186 B1
Orchard Cres
  Beeston NG9 .... 183 E3
  Glapwell S44 .... 86 A4
  Tuxford NG22 .... 65 F1
Orchard Ct
  Carlton NG4 .... 174 C4
  Gelding NG4 .... 162 B1
  Hucknall NG15 .... 146 A3
  Langley Mill NG16 ...... 143 D2
  Nottingham NG8 .... 172 C4
Orchard Dr NG14 .... 149 D2
Orchard Gr Arnold NG5 .... 161 E3
Orchard La LN1 .... 57 D2
Orchard Leigh DN22 .... 39 E2
Orchard Rd NG17 .... 114 C3
Orchard Rise NG4 .... 162 A1
Orchard Specl Sch
  NG24 .... 140 B3
Orchard St
  Eastwood NG16 .... 144 A1
  Gotham NG11 .... 195 D1
  Hucknall NG15 .... 146 A3
  Kimberley NG16 .... 158 C3
  Langley Mill NG16 ..... 143 D2
  Long Eaton NG10 .... 193 F4
  Loughborough LE11 ..... 220 A2
  Mansfield NG18 .... 88 A1
  Stapleford NG9 .... 182 B4

Orchard The
  Elston NG23 .... 153 F2
  Sutton in A NG17 ...... 101 D2
Orchard View NG19 .... 88 A2
Orchard Way
  Balderton NG24 .... 140 B2
  Sandiacre NG10 .... 182 A2
  Sutton in A NG17 ...... 114 B4
  Wymeswold LE12 .... 216 B2
Orchard Wlk NG17 .... 114 C3
Orchards The
  Carlton NG4 .... 163 D1
  Lowdham NG14 .... 164 C4
  Oxton NG25 .... 134 B2
  Westwood NG16 .... 128 A2
Orchid Cl
  17 Kirkby in A NG17 .. 114 C4
  New Balderton NG24 .... 140 A3
  West Bridgford NG11 ... 185 E2
Orchid Dr
  Farndon NG24 .... 139 D3
  Sutton in A NG17 ...... 101 D1
Orchid Way NG20 .... 72 B2
Ordsall Hall Comp Sch
  DN22 .... 39 E3
Ordsall Jun Schs DN22 .... 39 E2
Ordsall Pk Cl DN22 .... 39 E3
Ordsall Pk Dr DN22 .... 39 E3
Ordsall Pk Rd DN22 .... 39 E3
Ordsall Rd DN22 .... 39 E3
Ordsall Village Inf Sch
  DN22 .... 39 E2
Orford Ave
  Nottingham NG11 .... 184 C2
  Radcliffe on T NG12 ... 175 F1
Orion Cl NG8 .... 171 F4
Orion Dr NG8 .... 171 F4
Orlando Dr NG4 .... 174 C4
Orlock Wlk NG5 .... 161 D3
Ormonde St NG16 .... 143 D2
Ormonde Terr
  Aldercar NG16 .... 143 D2
  Nottingham NG5 .... 161 E1
Ornsay Cl N5 .... 146 C1
Orpean Way NG9 .... 182 C2
Orston Ave Arnold NG5 .... 162 A4
Orston Dr NG8 .... 139 F3
Orston City Prim Sch
  NG13 .... 180 A4
Orston Dr NG8 .... 172 B2
Orston Gn NG8 .... 172 B2
Orston La NG13 .... 180 C2
Orston Rd E NG2 .... 173 F1
Orston Rd W NG2 .... 173 F1
Orton Ave NG9 .... 183 E3
Ortzen St NG7 .... 222 B4
Orville Rd NG5 .... 160 C3
Osberton Rd NG8 .... 39 F3
Osberton View S81 .... 36 A3
Osborne Ave **2** NG5 .... 161 E2
Osborne Cl NG10 .... 182 A2
Osborne Gr NG5 .... 161 E2
Osborne St NG7 .... 222 A3
Osbourne Cl NG16 .... 159 D4
Osbourne St NG17 .... 129 F4
Osgood Rd NG5 .... 162 B3
Osier Dr NG15 .... 130 A3
Osier Rd NG2 .... 173 E1
Osiers The
  Kegworth DE74 .... 203 E1
  Newark-on-T NG24 ...... 139 E3
Osman Cl NG2 .... 173 D1
Osmaston St
  Nottingham NG7 .... 222 B1
  Sandiacre NG10 .... 182 B3
Osprey Cl NG11 .... 184 B1
Ossington Cl
  Meden Vale NG20 .... 74 B4
  Nottingham NG1 .... 223 E4
Ossington Rd NG22 .... 93 F3
Ossington St NG7 .... 222 B4
Ossington Way NG24 ...... 124 C1
Oster Fen La NG23 .... 156 C4
Osterley Gr NG8 .... 159 E1
Otter Ave LN1 .... 57 D2
Oulton Cl NG5 .... 161 F3
Oundle Dr Ilkeston DE7 ... 170 A4
  Mansfield NG18 .... 87 E1
  Nottingham NG8 .... 172 B2
Our Lady & St Edwards Cath
  Prim Sch NG3 .... 173 F3
Our Lady of Perpetual
  Succour RC Sch NG6 ... 160 B3
Our Ladys Convent Sch
  LE11 .... 220 A1
Oursham St NG17 .... 100 C2
Ouse Bridge Dr NG4 .... 175 D4
Ousebridge Cres NG4 ...... 175 D4
Outgang La
  Mansfield Woodhouse
    NG19 .... 88 B2
  Pleasley NG19 .... 87 D3
  Treswell DN22 .... 42 C2
Outgang Rd DN22 .... 43 E2
Outram St NG17 .... 100 C2
Oval Gdns **3** NG8 ...... 172 B4
Oval The Retford DN22 .... 39 E2
  Sutton in A NG17 ...... 100 B2
Tickhill DN11 .... 8 A4
Overdale Ave NG17 .... 100 C4
Overdale Ct NG10 .... 193 D3
Overdale Rd NG6 .... 160 B2
Overend Rd S80 .... 35 F2
Overmoor View DE55 .... 99 D4
Overstone Ct NG17 .... 100 C3
Overstrand Cl NG5 .... 161 F3
Owday La S81 .... 25 E2
Owen Ave NG10 .... 194 A3

Owlston Cl NG16 .... 143 F2
Owsthorpe Cl NG5 .... 161 D4
Owston Ferry Rd DN9 ...... 7 F4
Owston Rd DN10 .... 7 F2
Owthorpe Gr NG5 .... 161 D1
Owthorpe La NG12 .... 199 F2
Owthorpe Rd
  Colston Bassett NG12 .. 200 A4
  Cotgrave NG12 .... 187 F1
Oxborough Rd NG5 .... 161 E4
Oxbow Cl NG2 .... 173 E1
Oxbury Rd NG16 .... 158 C4
Oxclose La
  Mansfield Woodhouse
    NG19 .... 88 A2
  Nottingham NG5 .... 161 E3
  Radmanthwaite NG19 .... 87 E2
Oxcroft La NG20 .... 58 A4
Oxendale Cl NG2 .... 186 B3
Oxengate NG5 .... 161 E3
Oxford Cl NG21 .... 118 A4
Oxford Dr DN11 .... 8 C3
Oxford Rd
  Carlton in L S81 .... 25 F3
  West Bridgford NG2 .... 186 A4
Oxford St Carlton NG4 .... 174 C4
  Eastwood NG16 .... 143 F1
  Kirkby in A NG17 ...... 115 D2
  Long Eaton NG10 .... 193 E4
  Loughborough LE11 ..... 220 A2
  Mansfield Woodhouse
    NG19 .... 88 B1
  Nottingham NG1 .... 223 D2
  Sutton in A NG17 ...... 100 B1
Oxpasture La NG20 .... 58 A3
Oxton Ave NG5 .... 161 E2
Oxton By-Pass NG25 ...... 134 A2
Oxton Cl
  Mansfield NG19 .... 101 F4
  Retford DN22 .... 39 F2
Oxton Hill NG25 .... 134 C2
Oxton Rd
  Calverton NG14 .... 133 E1
  Southwell NG25 .... 135 E3
Ozier Holt Carlton NG4 ... 174 C2
  Long Eaton NG10 .... 193 E3

P

Pack Horse La **27** LE11 . 220 A2
Packe St LE11 .... 220 A2
Packington Hill DE74 .... 203 E1
Packman Dr NG11 .... 196 B4
Paddock Cl
  Calverton NG14 .... 148 C4
  Edwinstowe NG21 .... 76 A2
  Nottingham NG6 .... 160 A3
  Radcliffe on T NG12 ... 175 F1
Paddock The
  Beeston NG9 .... 183 E1
  Bingham NG13 .... 177 F2
  Collingham NG23 .... 112 A4
  Gunthorpe NG14 .... 164 C3
  Kirkby in A NG17 ...... 114 C2
  Stanton Hill NG17 ..... 100 B3
  Tickhill DN11 .... 8 A4
Paddocks Cl
  Elston NG23 .... 153 F2
  Pinxton NG16 .... 113 E2
Paddocks The
  Beckingham DN10 .... 14 A1
  Bottesford NG13 .... 181 D1
  Elston NG23 .... 153 F2
  Hockerton NG25 .... 122 A3
  Long Eaton NG10 .... 20 B1
  Mansfield Woodhouse
    NG19 .... 88 C3
  Marton DN21 .... 44 B4
  Newark-on-T NG24 ...... 140 A4
  Newton on T LN1 .... 55 D1
  Sandiacre NG10 .... 182 A3
  Stapleford NG9 .... 127 F4
  Sutton Bonington LE12 . 213 D3
  West Bridgford NG12 ... 186 A2
  Worksop S81 .... 36 A3
Paddocks View NG10 ...... 193 D4
Paddys La LE14 .... 218 A1
Padge Rd NG9 .... 184 A3
Padgham Ct **11** NG5 .... 161 D4
Padley Hill NG18 .... 102 A3
Padleys La NG14 .... 163 F3
Padstow Rd NG5 .... 160 C3
Pagdin Dr DN11 .... 9 D2
Paget Cres NG11 .... 196 B4
Paget St **11** LE11 ..... 220 A3
Paignton Cl NG8 .... 160 A1
Paisley Ave NG10 .... 193 D3
Palace View NG25 .... 136 C4
Palatine St NG7 .... 223 D1
Paling Cres NG17 .... 100 C2
Palin St NG7 .... 222 B4
Palm Ct Ind Ctr NG7 ..... 160 C1
Palm St NG7 .... 160 C1
Palm Wood Ct NG6 .... 160 B3
Palmer Ave NG15 .... 146 A4
Palmer Cres NG4 .... 174 B4
Palmer Dr NG9 .... 182 B3
Palmer Rd
  Beeston NG9 .... 183 D1
  Retford DN22 .... 30 A1
Palmerston Gdns NG3 ..... 223 E4
Palmerston St
  Selston NG16 .... 128 C1

Palmerston St continued
  Westwood NG16 .... 128 B2
Palmwood Ct NG6 .... 160 B3
Paper Mill La DN11 .... 8 B2
Papplewick Grange
Papplewick La NG15 ...... 146 B4
Papplewick Ppg Sta*
  NG15 .... 132 C3
Paradise La LE14 .... 218 C2
Parfitt Dr NG22 .... 120 A3
Parish Church CE Prim Sch
  The DN21 .... 15 E1
Park Ave
  Annesley Woodhouse
    NG17 .... 130 A4
  Arnold NG5 .... 161 F3
  Awsworth NG16 .... 158 A3
  Blidworth NG21 .... 118 A3
  Burton Joyce NG14 ..... 163 F2
  Carlton NG4 .... 174 C4
  Eastwood NG16 .... 143 F2
  Hucknall NG15 .... 145 F4
  Keyworth NG12 .... 197 F2
  Kimberley NG16 .... 159 D2
  Loughborough LE11 ..... 220 A1
  Mansfield NG18 .... 102 B4
  Mansfield Woodhouse
    NG19 .... 88 B2
  Misterton DN10 .... 6 C2
  Nottingham NG3 .... 173 E4
  Shirebrook NG20 .... 72 C2
  West Bridgford NG2 .... 185 F4
  Woodborough NG14 ...... 149 D2
Park Ave E NG12 .... 197 F2
Park Ave W NG12 .... 197 E2
Park Chase NG6 .... 160 A3
Park Cl Lea DN21 .... 24 C1
  Nottingham NG3 .... 161 F1
  Pinxton NG16 .... 113 E1
Park Cres
  Eastwood NG16 .... 143 F2
  Ilkeston DE7 .... 170 A4
  Newark-on-T NG24 ...... 125 D2
  Nottingham NG8 .... 171 E2
  Retford DN22 .... 40 A4
Park Ct
  Loughborough LE11 ..... 220 A1
  Mansfield NG18 .... 102 B4
Park Dr Blyth S81 .... 18 A2
  Hucknall NG15 .... 146 A3
  Nottingham NG7 .... 222 C2
  Sandiacre NG10 .... 182 B3
Park Farm Cotts LN1 ...... 55 F1
Park Gate NG15 .... 131 D1
Park Hall Gdns NG19 ...... 88 B3
Park Hall Rd NG19 .... 88 B3
Park Hill NG16 .... 128 C2
Park Hill Dr S81 .... 16 A3
Park Hospl NG5 .... 132 B1
Park House Gates
  NG3 .... 161 E1
Park Hts NG7 .... 222 C1
Park Jun & Inf Schs The
  NG20 .... 72 C3
Park La Elkesley DN22 .... 50 B2
  Holbeck NG20 .... 59 E3
  Kirkby in A NG17 ...... 114 B3
  Lambley NG4 .... 163 F4
  Mansfield NG18 .... 102 A3
  Nottingham NG6 .... 160 C2
  Owthorpe NG12 .... 199 F4
  Pinxton NG16 .... 113 E1
  Retford DN22 .... 40 A4
  Southwell NG25 .... 136 B3
  Sutton Bonington LE12 . 213 E3
Park Mews
  Mansfield Woodhouse
    NG19 .... 88 B2
  Nottingham NG3 .... 173 E4
Park Pl S80 .... 35 F2
Park Ravine NG7 .... 222 C1
Park Rd Arnold NG5 ...... 161 F3
  Barnstone NG13 .... 190 C2
  Bawtry DN10 .... 9 F4
  Beeston, Bramcote
    NG9 .... 183 D4
  Beeston, Chilwell NG9 . 183 F3
  Bestwood Village NG6 .. 146 C2
  Calverton NG14 .... 148 C4
  Carlton NG4 .... 174 C4
  Hucknall NG15 .... 145 F4
  Ilkeston DE7 .... 170 A4
  Keyworth NG12 .... 197 F3
  Mansfield Woodhouse
    NG19 .... 88 A2
  Nottingham NG7 .... 222 B1
  Radcliffe on T NG12 ... 175 F2
  Shirebrook NG20 .... 72 C3
Park Rd E NG14 .... 149 D4
Park Rd N NG9 .... 183 F3
Park Row NG1 .... 223 D2
Park Springs Rd DN21 .... 24 C3
Park St Beeston NG9 ..... 183 F3
  Kirkby in A NG17 ...... 114 C2
  Long Eaton NG10 .... 182 B1
  Loughborough LE11 ..... 220 A2

Park The continued
  Mansfield NG18 .... 102 B4
  Mansfield NG18 .... 102 A4
  North Muskham NG23 .... 110 C2
Park Valley NG7 .... 223 D2
Park View Beeston NG9 ... 183 F3
  Nottingham NG3 .... 161 F1
Park View Way NG18 ...... 102 B4
Parkcroft Rd NG2 .... 185 F3
Parkdale Prim Sch
  NG3 .... 174 B3
Parkdale Rd NG3 .... 174 B3
Parker Cl NG5 .... 162 B4
Parker St
  Hucknall NG15 .... 146 A4
  Newark-on-T NG24 ...... 140 A4
Parkers La NG19 .... 88 B2
Parkes Cl NG24 .... 126 A1
Parkham Rd NG16 .... 158 C4
Parkin Cl NG12 .... 189 D2
Parkland Cl
  Mansfield NG18 .... 102 C1
  Nottingham NG11 .... 184 B2
Parklands Cl
  Coddington NG24 .... 125 F1
  Nottingham NG5 .... 147 D1
Parklands Dr **7** LE11 .. 220 A1
Parklands Inf Sch
  .... 182 A1
Parkside
  Huthwaite NG17 .... 100 A3
  Keyworth NG12 .... 197 F2
  Nottingham NG8 .... 171 F1
Parkside Ave NG10 .... 193 D4
Parkside Dr NG10 .... 193 D4
Parkside Gdns NG8 .... 171 F1
Parkside Rd NG21 .... 75 F1
Parkside Rise NG8 .... 171 F1
Parkstone Ave NG21 ...... 103 F1
Parkstone Cl NG2 .... 185 E3
Parkview Rd NG5 .... 161 D4
Parkway Clipstone NG19 .. 89 E2
  Newark-on-T NG24 ...... 139 F3
  Sutton in A NG17 ...... 100 A2
  Whitwell S80 .... 45 D3
Parkway Ct NG8 .... 171 E3
Parkwood Cres NG5 .... 161 F2
Parkwood Ct NG6 .... 160 C3
Parkyn Rd NG5 .... 161 F3
Parkyns St NG11 .... 196 B3
Parliament Ct NG24 ...... 139 F4
Parliament Rd NG19 ...... 101 F4
Parliament St
  Newark-on-T NG24 ...... 139 F4
  Sutton in A NG17 ...... 100 C1
Parliament Terr NG1 ..... 223 D3
Parliament Wlk NG24 ..... 139 F4
Parnell St DN21 .... 24 B4
Parnhams Cl LE14 .... 219 E4
Parr Gate NG9 .... 183 D3
Parr La NG14 .... 150 A3
Parrs The NG9 .... 184 A3
Parry Way NG5 .... 162 A4
Parsons Mdw NG4 .... 174 C2
Paschall Rd NG7 .... 115 D1
Pasteur Ct **9** NG7 ..... 172 C1
Pasture Cl Carlton NG2 .. 174 C2
  Carlton in L S81 .... 26 A4
  Stanton Hill NG17 ..... 100 B3
  Worksop S80 .... 35 E1
Pasture Farm Victorian
  Carriages Mus* NG22 .. 78 A4
Pasture La
  Hathern LE12 .... 213 D1
  Hilcote DE55 .... 99 E1
  Hose LE14 .... 211 F3
  Long Eaton NG10 .... 194 A3
  Ruddington NG11 .... 196 A4
  Sutton Bonington LE12 . 213 D3
Pasture Rd
  Gainsborough DN21 ..... 24 C4
  Stapleford NG9 .... 170 B1
Pasture View NG14 .... 165 D3
Pastures Ave NG11 .... 195 E4
Pastures The
  Bawtry DN10 .... 10 A3
  Calverton NG14 .... 148 B4
  Eastwood NG16 .... 158 A4
  Mansfield Woodhouse
    NG19 .... 88 C3
  Rampton DN22 .... 43 D1
  Tuxford NG22 .... 65 F1
Patchills The NG18 ...... 102 C4
Patchings Farm Art Ctr*
  NG14 .... 148 A4
Pateley Rd NG3 .... 162 A2
Paton Rd NG5 .... 160 C3
Patricia Dr NG5 .... 148 A1
Patrick Rd NG2 .... 185 F4
Patterdale Cl NG2 .... 186 B3
Patterdale Rd NG5 .... 161 F3
Patterson Pl NG18 .... 102 B4
Patterson Rd **32** NG7 .. 172 C4
Paul Ave NG18 .... 103 D3
Paulsons Dr NG18 .... 102 A4
Pavilion Cl
  Market Warsop NG20 .... 74 A2
  22 Nottingham NG2 .. 173 E1
Pavilion Ct NG14 .... 164 C4
Pavilion Gdns
  New Houghton NG19 ..... 86 C4
  Sutton in A NG17 ...... 101 D3
Pavilion Rd
  Ilkeston DE7 .... 157 F3
  Nottingham NG5 .... 147 D1
  West Bridgford NG2 .... 173 F3
Paxton Gdns NG3 .... 173 F3
Paxtons Ct NG24 .... 124 C1

Payne Rd NG9 ....183 D2
Peach Ave
  Selston NG16 ....128 C3
  South Normanton DE55 ....113 D4
Peache Way NG4 ....183 E4
Peachey St NG1 ....223 E3
Peacock Cl
  Gunthorpe NG14 ....165 D2
  Ruddington NG11 ....196 A3
Peacock Cres NG7 ....184 C1
Peacock Dr NG21 ....118 B4
Peacock Pl DE7 ....157 E2
Peacock Rd ❷ NG18 ....102 A3
Peafield La Prim Sch
  NG19 ....88 C2
Peak Hill Cl S81 ....95 F4
Peak The NG20 ....72 C2
Peakdale Cl NG10 ....193 D3
Peakes Croft DN10 ....10 A4
Pear Tree Cl DN22 ....30 B2
Pear Tree Ct NG6 ....160 C2
Pear Tree Dr NG20 ....72 C3
Pearce Dr NG8 ....172 A4
Pearl Ave NG17 ....115 D2
Pearl Cl NG21 ....104 B1
Pearmain Dr NG3 ....173 F4
Pearson Ave NG9 ....183 D3
Pearson Cl NG9 ....183 D3
Pearson St
  Carlton NG4 ....175 D3
  Nottingham NG7 ....160 C1
Peartree La NG17 ....160 C1
Peartree Orch NG11 ....196 B4
Peary Cl NG5 ....160 C3
Peary Hill Rd NG3 ....223 F4
Peatfield Rd NG9 ....170 B1
Peck La NG1 ....223 E2
Pecks Hill NG18 ....102 C4
Pedmore Valley NG5 ....161 D4
Peebles Rd NG4 ....139 E3
Peel Ave Retford DN22 ....40 A2
  Tuxford NG22 ....65 F1
Peel Cres NG19 ....87 E1
Peel Dr NG11 ....220 B2
Peel Rd NG19 ....101 F4
Peel St
  Langley Mill NG16 ....143 D2
  Long Eaton NG10 ....193 F4
  Nottingham NG1 ....223 D4
  South Normanton DE55 ....113 D3
  Sutton in A NG17 ....101 D2
Peets Dr NG23 ....110 C1
Pelham Ave
  Ilkeston DE7 ....157 F1
  Nottingham NG5 ....173 D4
Pelham Cres
  Beeston NG9 ....184 A4
  Nottingham NG7 ....222 B2
Pelham Cl ❶ NG5 ....173 D4
Pelham Gdns NG24 ....139 F4
Pelham Rd
  Kirkby in A NG17 ....115 D3
  Nottingham NG5 ....173 D4
  Retford DN22 ....39 E3
Pelham St
  Mansfield NG18 ....102 B4
  Newark-on-T NG24 ....139 F4
  Nottingham NG1 ....223 E2
  Sutton in A NG17 ....100 B1
  Worksop S80 ....36 A1
Pelham Way NG19 ....89 E2
Pemberton St NG1 ....223 F2
Pemberton Dr NG19 ....87 E1
Pembrey Cl NG9 ....170 B1
Pembridge Cl NG6 ....160 B1
Pembroke Cres NG24 ....125 E2
Pembroke Dr
  Carlton in S NG17 ....25 F3
  Nottingham NG3 ....161 E1
Pembroke Rd S81 ....34 C4
Pembury Rd NG8 ....171 F3
Pen Cl DE55 ....99 D2
Pen La NG12 ....208 B2
Penarth Gdns NG5 ....161 F2
Penarth Rise NG5 ....161 F2
Pendeen Cl DN11 ....15 F1
Pendennis Cl NG4 ....163 D1
Pendine Cl Arnold NG5 .....147 E1
  South Normanton DE55 ....113 E3
Pendle Cres NG3 ....161 F1
Pendock La NG12 ....197 D1
Penhale Dr NG15 ....145 E3
Penhurst Cl NG11 ....185 D2
Penllech Cl NG5 ....161 D4
Penllech Wlk ❷ NG5 ....161 D4
Penn Ave NG7 ....222 A1
Penn Cl NG12 ....202 C2
Penn Moor Cl NG10 ....206 C1
Penn St NG17 ....100 C2
Pennant Rd NG6 ....160 B1
Pennard Wlk NG11 ....195 E4
Pennhome Ave ❽ NG5 .....161 E3
Penniment La NG19 ....87 D1
Pennine Cl
  Huthwaite NG17 ....99 F2
  Long Eaton, Breaston
  NG10 ....182 A1
  Long Eaton, New Sawley
  NG10 ....193 D2
  Mansfield Woodhouse
  NG19 ....88 B2
  Newton DE55 ....99 D2
  Nottingham NG5 ....147 D1

Pennine Dr
  Kirkby in A NG17 ....114 B2
  Selston NG16 ....128 C4
Pennington Wlk DN22 ....40 A3
Penny Gn S80 ....45 D3
Pennyfields Bvd NG10 ....193 D4
Pennyfoot St NG1 ....173 F2
Penrhyn Cl NG3 ....223 F4
Penrhyn Cres NG9 ....183 D2
Penrith Ave NG12 ....186 A4
Penrith Cres NG8 ....160 B1
Penrith Pl NG19 ....101 E4
Penshore Ct NG11 ....184 B1
Penswick Gr NG24 ....125 F1
Pentland Ct NG19 ....101 E3
Pentland Dr
  Carlton in S NG17 ....25 F4
  Nottingham NG5 ....147 D1
Pentland Gdns NG10 ....182 A1
Pentrich Wlk NG18 ....103 D3
Pentwood Ave NG5 ....147 F1
Penzance Pl NG18 ....103 D4
Peoples Coll (Annexe)
  NG7 ....222 B4
Peoples Coll of Further Ed
  NG1 ....223 E1
Pepper Rd NG14 ....148 C4
Pepper St
  Nottingham NG1 ....223 E2
  Sutton in A NG17 ....101 D1
Peppercorn Gdns
  NG8 ....172 B3
Peppers Dr DE74 ....203 D1
Percival Cl NG17 ....100 C2
Percival Cres NG17 ....100 C2
Percival Rd NG5 ....161 E1
Percival St S81 ....35 F3
Percy St
  Eastwood NG16 ....144 A1
  Nottingham NG6 ....160 B2
  Sutton in A NG17 ....100 B1
Peregrine Cl NG7 ....222 A2
Peregrine Ct S81 ....35 E4
Perivale Cl NG16 ....159 E2
Perkins La LE14 ....219 D1
Perlethorpe Ave
  Carlton NG4 ....162 C1
  Mansfield NG19 ....88 A1
  ❼ Nottingham NG1 ....173 F2
Perlethorpe Cl
  Carlton NG4 ....162 C1
  Edwinstowe NG21 ....75 F2
Perlethorpe Cres NG4 ....162 C1
Perlethorpe Dr
  Carlton NG4 ....162 C1
  Hucknall NG15 ....146 A4
Perlethorpe Environmental
  Ed Ctr NG22 ....62 C1
Perry Gdns NG5 ....146 C1
Perry Gr Bingham NG13 ....177 F2
  Loughborough LE11 ....220 B1
Perry Rd NG5 ....161 D2
Perth Cl NG19 ....88 B3
Perth Dr NG9 ....170 C1
Perth St NG1 ....223 E3
Peterborough Rd NG23 ....98 A1
Peters Cl Arnold NG5 ....162 B3
  Eastwood NG16 ....144 B1
Petersfield Cl
  Mansfield NG19 ....101 E4
  Nottingham NG5 ....160 C4
Petersgate NG10 ....182 A1
Petersgate Cl NG10 ....182 A1
Petersham Mews NG7 ....222 B1
Petersham Rd NG10 ....182 A1
Petersmiths Cl NG22 ....77 E3
Petersmiths Cres NG22 ......77 E3
Petersmiths Dr NG22 ....77 E3
Petworth Ave NG9 ....182 C2
Petworth Dr NG5 ....160 C2
Peveril Cres NG10 ....193 D3
Peveril Dr Ilkeston DE7 ......157 E1
  Nottingham NG7 ....223 D1
  Sutton in A NG17 ....100 B1
  West Bridgford NG2 ....185 F2
Peveril Mews NG7 ....222 C2
Peveril Rd NG9 ....184 A4
Peveril St
  Hucknall NG15 ....146 A4
  Nottingham NG7 ....222 B4
Pheasant Hill NG19 ....88 B3
Philip Ave
  Eastwood NG16 ....144 A1
  Kirkby in A NG17 ....115 D1
  Nuthall NG16 ....159 E3
Philip Cl NG21 ....118 B4
Philip Gr NG4 ....162 C1
Philip Rd NG24 ....139 F3
Phoenix Ave NG4 ....162 C1
Phoenix Cl NG2 ....173 D1
Phoenix Ct
  Eastwood NG16 ....144 A1
  Nottingham NG7 ....184 C4
Phoenix Ctr NG6 ....160 A2
Phoenix Inf Sch NG4 ....162 C1
Phoenix St NG17 ....101 D2
Phyllis Cl NG15 ....130 C1
Phyllis Gr NG10 ....193 F4
Piccadilly NG6 ....160 B3
Pickard St NG18 ....102 C4
Pickering Ave NG16 ....143 F1
Pieris Dr NG11 ....184 C1
Pierrepont Art Gall*
  NG22 ....62 B2
Pierrepont Ave NG14 ....163 C2
Pierrepont Gamston CE Sch
  NG2 ....186 B3

Pierrepont Rd NG2 ....174 A1
Pierson St NG24 ....139 F3
Pilcher Gate NG1 ....223 E2
Pilgrim Cl Ranby DN22 ....38 C3
  Ravenshead NG15 ....116 C1
Pilgrim Ct S81 ....34 C4
Pilgrim Rise DN10 ....3 E1
Pilgrim Way S80 ....35 F1
Pilkington Rd NG3 ....162 A1
Pilkington St ❺ NG6 ....160 A4
Pillard House La
  DN21 ....24 B4
Pimlico Ave NG9 ....171 D2
Pimlico Cl NG12 ....176 C2
Pinder St NG1 ....223 F2
Pine Ave
  Langley Mill NG16 ....143 D2
  New Ollerton NG22 ....77 E2
Pine Cl East Leake LE12 ....214 B4
  Everton DN10 ....11 E2
  Kirkby in A NG17 ....114 C3
  Mansfield NG21 ....103 F1
  Mansfield Woodhouse
  NG19 ....88 B3
  Newark-on-T NG24 ....125 D2
  Shirebrook NG20 ....72 C3
Pine Hill Cl NG5 ....146 C1
Pine Tree Cl S80 ....35 F1
Pine Tree Wlk NG16 ....143 E1
Pinehurst Ave NG15 ....145 E3
Pines The
  Gainsborough DN21 ....24 C3
  Worksop S80 ....35 F1
Pines Way NG18 ....116 B4
Pineview Ct NG18 ....102 C1
Pinewood Ave
  Arnold NG5 ....148 A1
  Edwinstowe NG21 ....91 E4
Pinewood Cl
  Kirkby in A NG17 ....115 E3
  Southwell NG25 ....121 E1
Pinewood Dr NG18 ....102 C2
Pinewood Gdns NG11 ....195 E4
Pinewood Inf Sch
  NG5 ....148 A1
Pinfold NG13 ....177 F2
Pinfold Cl
  Bottesford NG13 ....181 D2
  Collingham NG23 ....98 A1
  Cotgrave NG12 ....187 F2
  Kinoulton NG12 ....199 F1
  Lound DN22 ....20 B1
  Woodborough NG14 ....149 E2
Pinfold Cres NG14 ....149 E2
Pinfold Dr S81 ....25 F4
Pinfold Gate LE11 ....220 A2
Pinfold Gdns ❷ LE11 ....220 A2
Pinfold Jetty LE11 ....220 B2
Pinfold La
  Averham NG23 ....123 F1
  Balderton NG24 ....140 B2
  Bottesford NG13 ....181 D2
  Clarborough DN22 ....40 C4
  Elston NG23 ....153 E3
  Harby LE14 ....202 B2
  Kinoulton NG12 ....199 F1
  Nottingham NG11 ....185 D3
  Shelford NG12 ....164 B1
  Stapleford NG9 ....182 C4
  Styrrup DN11 ....8 B2
Pinfold Rd LE14 ....202 B2
Pinfold Rd NG16 ....144 B1
Pinfold The DN10 ....4 A1
Pingle CI DN10 ....24 C4
Pingle Cres NG5 ....160 C4
Pingle The NG10 ....193 E4
Pingley Cl NG23 ....138 B4
Pingley La NG23 ....138 B4
Pintail Cl NG4 ....175 D3
Pinxton Ct NG18 ....103 D3
Pinxton Gn NG16 ....113 F2
Pinxton La
  Kirkby in A, Fulwood
  NG17 ....114 A4
  Kirkby in A, Tichfield Park
  NG17 ....114 B2
  South Normanton DE55 ....113 E3
Pinxton Rd NG17 ....114 B2
Piper Cl Hucknall NG15 .....131 D1
  Long Whatton LE12 ....212 B1
Piper Dr LE12 ....212 B1
Piper La S80 ....61 E4
Pippin Cl
  Mansfield NG24 ....125 D1
  Nottingham NG3 ....173 F4
Pit La DE75 ....157 D3
Pitcairn Cl NG2 ....173 E1
Pithouse La LE12 ....204 C1
Pit Hill NG14 ....58 C1
Pitt La DN10 ....12 C2
Plains Farm Cl NG3 ....162 B3
Plains Gr NG3 ....162 A2
Plains Rd NG3 ....162 A2
Plainspot Rd NG16 ....128 C1
Plane Cl NG6 ....159 F4
Plant La NG10 ....193 D2
Plantagenet Ct NG3 ....223 F3
Plantagenet St NG3 ....223 F3
Plantation Ave NG22 ....66 A4
Plantation Cl NG5 ....147 D1
Plantation Dr DN10 ....11 D1
Plantation Hill S81 ....36 A2
Plantation La DN22 ....27 D4
Plantation Rd
  East Markham NG22 ....66 A3
  Keyworth NG12 ....197 E2
  Nottingham NG5 ....171 E2
Plantation Side NG7 ....172 C4

Plantations The ❾
  NG10 ....193 D4
Plains Yd S80 ....35 F1
Platt La NG13 ....198 A3
Platt St NG16 ....113 E1
Platts The NG24 ....139 F3
Player St NG7 ....222 B4
Playworld* NG6 ....160 C2
Plaza Gdns NG6 ....160 C2
Pleasant Cl ❷ LE11 ....220 A2
Pleasant Pl DE74 ....203 E1
Pleasant Row NG7 ....172 C4
Pleasley Rd NG17 ....101 D3
Plot La NG23 ....98 C2
Plough Dr S81 ....25 F4
Plough La
  Lowdham NG14 ....150 B1
  Nottingham NG2 ....173 F2
Ploughman Ave NG14 ....149 E2
Plover Dene S81 ....35 E4
Plover Wharf ❸ NG2 ....173 D1
Plowman Ct NG9 ....182 B3
Plowright Cl ❶ NG3 ....173 E4
Plowright St ❼ NG3 ....173 E4
Plum Tree Ave NG19 ....89 D1
Plumb Rd NG15 ....145 F4
Plummer La DE74 ....203 E1
Plumptre NG16 ....143 D3
Plumptre Almshouses
  NG1 ....223 F1
Plumptre Cl LE11 ....143 F1
Plumptre Pl NG1 ....223 F2
Plumptre Sq NG1 ....223 F2
Plumptre St NG1 ....223 F2
Plumptre Way NG16 ....143 F1
Plumtree Gdns NG14 ....148 C4
Plumtree Rd
  Bircotes DN11 ....9 E3
  Cotgrave NG12 ....187 F2
Plungar Cl NG8 ....172 A3
Plungar La NG13 ....192 A1
Plungar Rd NG13 ....191 E3
Plymouth Ave NG16 ....113 F1
Poachers La DN22 ....31 E4
Pocklington Cres
  NG24 ....125 E3
Pocklington Rd NG23 ....98 A1
Podder La NG3 ....162 B3
Point The NG3 ....173 E4
Pollard Dr NG18 ....102 B4
Pollards La NG25 ....136 C4
Polly Taylors Rd NG23 ....67 F1
Polperro Way NG15 ....145 E3
Pond Hills La NG5 ....147 F1
Pond St NG17 ....115 D3
Pool Cl NG16 ....113 E1
Poole Mdw NG12 ....174 C2
Popham Ct NG1 ....223 F1
Popham St NG1 ....223 F1
Poplar Ave
  East Leake LE12 ....214 B4
  Kirkby in A NG17 ....115 E3
  Nottingham NG5 ....161 D1
  Worksop S80 ....35 E1
Poplar Cl
  Bingham NG13 ....178 A2
  Carlton NG4 ....174 B3
  Sutton in T NG23 ....96 C4
  Worksop S80 ....35 E1
Poplar Cres NG16 ....159 E3
Poplar Dr Glapwell S44 ....86 A4
  Pleasleyhill NG19 ....87 D2
Poplar Gr
  Church Warsop NG20 ....74 A3
  Mansfield Woodhouse
  NG19 ....89 E1
Poplar Rd DE55 ....113 D4
Poplar St
  Mansfield NG19 ....88 B2
  New Ollerton NG22 ....77 E2
  Nottingham NG1 ....173 F2
  Retford DN22 ....39 F3
Poplars Ave NG14 ....164 A3
Poplars Cl NG12 ....197 F2
Poplars The
  Beeston NG9 ....183 F4
  Sutton in A NG17 ....101 D2
  West Bridgford NG2 ....185 F4
  Whitwell S80 ....45 D3
Poplars Way NG18 ....116 C4
Poppy Cl NG5 ....72 B2
Poppy Gdn DE55 ....99 D4
Porchester Cl NG15 ....146 B4
Porchester Jun & Inf Sch
  NG4 ....162 A1
Porchester Rd
  Bingham NG13 ....177 E2
  Nottingham NG3 ....162 A1
Porlock Cl ❸ NG10 ....193 D2
Port Arthur Rd NG2 ....174 A2
Portage Cl NG12 ....175 F1
Porter Cl NG11 ....195 E4
Portinscale Cl NG2 ....186 B3
Portland Coll for People with
  Disabilities NG18 ....116 C3
Portland Comp Sch
  S80 ....46 C4
Portland Cres
  Mansfield Woodhouse
  NG19 ....88 B2
  Stapleford NG9 ....182 C3
Portland Cres NG17 ....161 D3
Portland Ct Mews
  NG19 ....88 B2
Portland Gdns NG15 ....145 F4
Portland Grange
  NG15 ....145 F4

Portland Hill NG7 ....172 B1
Portland Ind Est NG17 ....115 D4
Portland Mdws DN22 ....29 D3
Portland Pk Cl NG15 ....145 F4
Portland Pl Sutton DN22 ......29 D3
  Worksop S80 ....35 F2
Portland Prim Sch
  NG8 ....171 E3
Portland Rd
  Beeston NG9 ....182 C1
  Carlton NG4 ....162 B1
  Eastwood NG16 ....158 A4
  Hucknall NG15 ....146 A3
  Ilkeston DE7 ....157 F2
  Long Eaton NG10 ....193 D2
  Nottingham NG7 ....222 C2
  Retford DN22 ....39 E3
  Selston NG16 ....129 D4
  Shirebrook NG20 ....72 C2
  West Bridgford NG2 ....185 F3
  Whaley Thorns NG20 ....59 D1
Portland Row NG21 ....91 E4
Portland Sq NG17 ....100 C1
Portland St Arnold NG5 .....161 F3
  Beeston NG9 ....184 A4
  Kirkby in A NG17 ....115 D3
  Mansfield NG18 ....102 A3
  Mansfield Woodhouse
  NG19 ....88 B2
  Market Warsop NG20 ....74 A2
  New Houghton NG19 ....87 D4
  Newark-on-T NG24 ....139 F4
  Sutton in A NG17 ....100 C1
  Worksop S80 ....35 F2
Portland Terr
  Gainsborough DN21 ....24 B4
  Meden Vale NG20 ....60 C1
  Whaley Thorns NG20 ....59 D1
Portman Ct DN10 ....9 F4
Portree Dr NG5 ....146 C1
Post Office La
  Plungar NG13 ....202 C4
  Redmile NG13 ....192 C2
Post Office Rd NG17 ....115 D3
Post Office Yd NG14 ....151 E1
Postern St NG1 ....223 D2
Posts The NG22 ....189 D3
Pot Yd The NG22 ....119 F3
Potter La NG22 ....92 B4
Potter St
  Sutton in A NG17 ....101 D2
  Worksop S80 ....35 F1
Potters Cl NG5 ....161 D4
Potters Gr NG9 ....171 E1
Potters La LE12 ....214 C4
Potters Nook S81 ....34 C4
Potters Way DE7 ....170 A4
Poulter Cl NG8 ....58 C1
Poulter Ctry Pk* NG20 ....58 C2
Poulton Dr NG2 ....173 F1
Poultry NG1 ....223 E2
Powell Gdns S81 ....35 E4
Powtrell Pl DE7 ....170 A3
Poynton St NG1 ....223 D3
Poyser Cl ❷ NG7 ....161 D1
Pratt Cl NG19 ....87 E1
Prebends Cl NG24 ....138 C2
Precinct Rd NG17 ....115 D3
Precinct The NG12 ....187 F2
Premier Rd NG7 ....173 D4
Prendwick Gdns NG5 ....161 D4
Prest Ave NG20 ....74 C4
Preston Rd
  Balderton NG24 ....140 C4
  Rainworth NG21 ....118 A4
Prestwick Cl NG8 ....159 E1
Prestwold Ave
  Mansfield NG19 ....103 D4
  Mansfield Woodhouse
  NG19 ....89 D1
Prestwood Dr NG8 ....172 A4
Previn Gdns NG3 ....173 F3
Priestgate NG22 ....65 F3
Priestsic Prim Sch
  NG17 ....100 C2
Priestsic Rd NG17 ....100 C2
Primrose Ave
  Farndon NG24 ....139 D3
  Newark-on-T NG24 ....125 D2
  Selston NG16 ....128 C1
Primrose Bank NG13 ....177 E2
Primrose Cl
  ❷❸ Kirkby in A NG17 ....114 C4
  Nottingham NG3 ....173 E4
  South Normanton DE55 ....113 D4
Primrose Cres NG4 ....174 C4
Primrose Ct NG17 ....101 D1
Primrose La NG22 ....78 B3
Primrose Rise NG16 ....158 A4
Primrose St
  Carlton NG4 ....174 C4
  Gainsborough DN21 ....24 B4
  Ilkeston DE7 ....157 F2
Primrose Way
  Sutton in A NG17 ....100 B1
  Worksop S81 ....36 A3
Primula Cl NG11 ....184 B1
Prince Charles Rd S81 ....35 E3
Prince Edward Cres
  NG12 ....175 F1
Prince of Wales St
  DN22 ....39 F3

Prince St Ilkeston DE7 . . .157 F2
Long Eaton NG10 . . . . . . .193 E4
Prince William Rd
LE11 . . . . .220 A3
Prince William Way
LE11 . . . . .220 A3
Princes Rd LE14 . . . . .219 D3
Princes St NG18 . . . . .102 A3
Princes St NG24 . . . . .139 F4
Princess Ann Rd S81 . . . . .35 F3
Princess Ave
Beeston NG9 . . . . .184 A3
Mansfield NG19 . . . . .103 D4
Market Warsop NG20 . . . . .74 B2
South Normanton DE55 . . .113 D3
Princess Cl NG4 . . . . .162 C1
Princess Diana Ct
DN21 . . . . .15 E2
Princess Dr NG10 . . . . . . .182 A2
Princess St
Eastwood NG16 . . . . .143 F2
Kirkby in A NG17 . . . . . . .114 B2
Long Eaton NG10 . . . . . . .193 E4
Loughborough LE11 . . . . .220 A2
Princess Wlk DN21 . . . . . .15 F1
Prior Cl NG17 . . . . .101 D2
Prior Rd NG5 . . . . .161 E3
Prioridge NG12 . . . . .188 A1
Priors Cl NG13 . . . . .178 A3
Priors The NG14 . . . . .150 B1
Priorswell Rd S80 . . . . . . .35 F1
Priory Ave
Annesley Woodhouse
NG17 . . . . .130 A4
Ravenshead NG15 . . . . . .117 D1
Tollerton NG12 . . . . .186 B1
Priory Cir NG12 . . . . .186 B1
Priory Cl
Balderton NG24 . . . . .140 C2
Blyth S81 . . . . .18 A2
Gainsborough DN21 . . . . .24 C4
Mattersey DN10 . . . . .20 A3
Priory Cres NG4 . . . . .162 C1
Priory Ct NG4 . . . . .162 C1
Priory Ctr The S80 . . . . . .35 F2
Priory Gr NG17 . . . . .115 E3
Priory Jun Sch NG7 . . . . .172 C1
Priory La NG14 . . . . .151 E4
Priory Mews NG7 . . . . . .172 C1
Priory Pk NG7 . . . . .151 E4
Priory RC Prim Sch
NG16 . . . . .144 A3
Priory Pk
Blidworth NG21 . . . . .118 A3
Carlton NG4 . . . . .162 C1
Eastwood NG16 . . . . .143 F1
Hucknall NG15 . . . . .145 F4
Mansfield Woodhouse
NG19 . . . . .88 A2
West Bridgford NG2 . . . . .186 A4
Priory Sq NG17 . . . . .115 E3
Priory St NG7 . . . . .172 C1
Pritchard Dr NG9 . . . . . . .182 C3
Private Rd
Hucknall NG15 . . . . .161 E1
Nottingham NG5, NG3 . . .161 E1
Southwell NG25 . . . . .121 F1
Woodborough NG14 . . . . .149 E3
Private St NG24 . . . . .140 A4
Privet Ave NG17 . . . . .115 D3
Prize Cl NG11 . . . . .184 B1
Procters Dr NG3 . . . . .82 C1
Promenade NG3 . . . . .223 F3
Promenade The NG17 . . . .115 E3
Prospect Cl NG12 . . . . . . .187 F3
Prospect Ct NG17 . . . . . . .99 F1
Prospect Dr
Shirebrook NG20 . . . . . . .72 C2
Worksop S81 . . . . .35 F3
Prospect Hill Inf Sch
S81 . . . . .36 A4
Prospect Hill Jun Sch
S81 . . . . .36 A4
Prospect Pl
Nottingham NG2 . . . . .222 B1
Sutton in A NG17 . . . . . . .100 C1
Prospect Prec S81 . . . . . .36 A3
Prospect Rd
Carlton NG4 . . . . .162 A1
Heanor DE75 . . . . .157 D4
Prospect St
Mansfield NG18 . . . . .102 B3
Nottingham NG7 . . . . .222 A4
Prospect Terr
Gainsborough DN21 . . . . .24 B4
Nottingham NG7 . . . . .222 A4
Providence Pl DE7 . . . . . .157 F1
Providence Rd NG16 . . . . .128 A2
Prudhoe Ct NG2 . . . . .173 E1
Pudding La LE14 . . . . .219 D3
Pulborough Cl NG5 . . . . . .160 C2
Pullman Rd NG2 . . . . .173 F2
Pump Hollow La
NG18 . . . . .103 D4
Pump Hollow Rd
NG19 . . . . .103 D4
Pump La Fenton NG23 . . .142 C1
Wolseley NG22 . . . . .64 A1
Purbeck Cl
Long Eaton NG10 . . . . . . .193 D4
Mansfield Woodhouse
NG19 . . . . .88 B3
Purbeck Dr NG2 . . . . .185 E3
Purdy Mdw NG10 . . . . . . .193 D3

Pureland Japanese Gdn*
NG23 . . . . .68 C3
Pyatt St NG2 . . . . .173 E1
Pye Ave NG19 . . . . .101 E4
Pye Hill Rd NG16 . . . . . . .128 A2
Pygall Ave NG11 . . . . .195 D1
Pym St NG3 . . . . .173 F3
Pym Wlk NG3 . . . . .173 F3
Python Hill Jun & Inf Sch
NG21 . . . . .104 A1
Python Hill Rd NG21 . . . .104 A1

Q

Quadrangle The
Blidworth NG21 . . . . .118 A3
Newstead NG15 . . . . .130 B3
Quakefield Rd NG22 . . . . .66 A3
Quaker La
Farnsfield NG22 . . . . .119 F3
Mansfield NG18 . . . . .102 A4
Quaker Way NG18 . . . . . . .102 A4
Quantock Cl NG5 . . . . . . .147 D1
Quantock Gr NG13 . . . . . .177 E2
Quantock Rd NG10 . . . . . .182 A1
Quarries Way NG17 . . . . .114 C1
Quarry Ave NG6 . . . . .160 A3
Quarry Cl NG15 . . . . .132 A4
Quarry Dr NG17 . . . . .115 D2
Quarry Gr S81 . . . . .35 E4
Quarry Hill NG10 . . . . . . .182 A4
Quarry La Linby NG15 . . .131 D2
Mansfield NG18 . . . . .102 A3
Quarry Rd NG15 . . . . .132 A4
Quarry Yd NG17 . . . . .100 C3
Quarrydale Ave NG17 . . . .100 C3
Quarrydale Dr NG17 . . . . .100 C2
Quarrydale Rd NG17 . . . . .100 C2
Quayside Cl NG2 . . . . .173 F1
Queen Eleanor Cty Prim Sch
NG23 . . . . .70 B2
Queen Elizabeth Cres
S80 . . . . .35 D2
Queen Elizabeth High Sch
DN21 . . . . .15 E2
Queen Elizabeth Rd
NG9 . . . . .183 D2
Queen Marys Cl NG12 . . .176 B1
Queen St Arnold NG5 . . . .148 A1
Balderton NG24 . . . . .140 C2
Bottesford NG13 . . . . .181 D1
Collingham NG23 . . . . . . .98 A1
Gainsborough DN21 . . . . .24 B4
Hucknall NG15 . . . . .145 F4
Kirkby in A NG17 . . . . . . .115 D2
Langley Mill NG16 . . . . . .143 E2
Long Eaton NG10 . . . . . . .193 F4
Loughborough LE11 . . . . .220 B2
Mansfield NG18 . . . . .102 A4
Market Warsop NG20 . . . .74 A3
Newark-on-T NG24 . . . . .139 F4
Nottingham NG1 . . . . .223 E3
Pinxton NG16 . . . . .113 E2
Retford DN22 . . . . .39 E3
South Normanton DE55 . . .113 D3
Southwell NG25 . . . . .121 E1
Sutton in A NG17 . . . . . . .100 C1
Worksop S80 . . . . .35 F1
Queens Ave NG4 . . . . .162 C1
Queens Ave NG9 . . . . .170 A3
Queens Bower Rd
NG5 . . . . .161 E4
Queens Bridge Rd
NG2 . . . . .223 E1
Queens Cl S80 . . . . .45 E3
Queens Cres DN10 . . . . . .10 A4
Queens Ct
Bingham NG13 . . . . .177 E3
Clipstone NG19 . . . . .89 E2
Newark-on-T NG24 . . . . .125 D1
Queens Dr
Beeston NG9 . . . . .184 A3
Brinsley NG16 . . . . .143 F4
Nottingham NG11 . . . . . .185 D4
Sandiacre NG10 . . . . .182 A2
Queens Dr NG16 . . . . .159 E3
Queens Gr NG2 . . . . .223 E1
Queens Head Ct NG24 . . .139 F4
Queens Rd Beeston NG9 . .184 A4
Queens Rd N NG16 . . . . . .143 F1
Queens Rd S NG16 . . . . . .143 F1
Queens Rd W NG9 . . . . . .183 F2
Queens Sq NG16 . . . . .143 F1
Queens Wlk NG18 . . . . . . .102 A4
Queens Wlk
Nether Langwith NG20 . . .59 D1
Nottingham NG2 . . . . .173 D1
Queensberry St NG6 . . . . .160 C2
Queensbury Ave NG2 . . . .185 E2
Queensway
Gainsborough DN21 . . . . .24 C4

Queensway continued
Kirkby in A NG17 . . . . . . .115 D1
Mansfield Woodhouse
NG19 . . . . .89 D1
Nether Broughton LE14 . .219 E3
Saxilby LN1 . . . . .57 D2
Skellingthorpe LN6 . . . . .71 F2
Worksop S81 . . . . .35 F2
Quenemby Ave NG3 . . . . .161 F1
Quernby Rd NG3 . . . . .161 F1
Quibell Rd NG24 . . . . .140 A3
Quibells La NG24 . . . . .125 D2
Quines Hill Rd NG19 . . . . .89 D1
Quinton Cl NG11 . . . . .185 D3
Quorn Cl Beeston NG9 . . .183 F2
Loughborough LE11 . . . . .220 B1
Quorn Gr NG5 . . . . .161 D1
Quorn Rd NG5 . . . . .161 D1
Quorndon Cres NG10 . . . .193 E3

R

Rabbithill La NG23 . . . . . .83 D3
Racecourse Rd
Mansfield NG18 . . . . .102 C3
Nottingham NG2 . . . . .174 A2
Rachel Cl DN21 . . . . .15 E2
Rad Mews NG10 . . . . .193 E3
Radbourne Rd NG7 . . . . . .172 F2
Radbourne St NG19 . . . . . .88 C2
Radburn Ct NG9 . . . . .170 C1
Radcliffe Gdns NG4 . . . . .174 B4
Radcliffe Mount NG2 . . . .173 F1
Radcliffe on Trent Inf Sch
NG12 . . . . .176 A2
Radcliffe on Trent Jun Sch
NG12 . . . . .175 F1
Radcliffe Rd
Carlton NG12 . . . . .175 D1
Cropwell Butler NG12 . . . .189 D4
West Bridgford NG2 . . . . .186 B4
Radcliffe St NG2 . . . . .173 E1
Radcliffe Sta NG12 . . . . . .175 F2
Radford Bridge Rd
NG8 . . . . .172 B3
Radford Bvd NG7 . . . . . . .222 A4
Radford Cres NG4 . . . . . . .162 C1
Radford Ct NG7 . . . . .222 B3
Radford Gr La NG7 . . . . . .222 A4
Radford Prim Sch
NG7 . . . . .222 A3
Radford Rd NG7 . . . . .172 C4
Radford St
Mansfield NG18 . . . . .102 A3
Worksop S80 . . . . .36 A1
Radham Ct NG5 . . . . .161 E2
Radley Ave NG22 . . . . . . .135 E4
Radley Sq NG6 . . . . .160 B3
Radmanthwaite Rd
NG19 . . . . .87 E2
Radmoor Rd LE11 . . . . . . .220 A2
Radnor Gr NG13 . . . . .177 E2
Radnor Pl NG17 . . . . .87 E2
Radstock Rd NG3 . . . . . . .174 A4
Radway Dr NG11 . . . . .185 D3
Raeburn Dr NG9 . . . . .182 C1
Ragdale Rd NG6 . . . . .160 B4
Raglan Cl NG3 . . . . .173 E4
Raglan Ct Beeston NG9 . . .172 A1
Newark-on-T NG24 . . . . .140 A4
Raglan Dr NG4 . . . . .163 D2
Raglan Gdns NG24 . . . . . .140 A4
Raglan Rd NG16 . . . . .144 A1
Raibank Gdns NG5 . . . . . .161 F3
Railway Cotts NG5 . . . . . .161 E2
Railway Ct LN1 . . . . .57 D2
Railway Terr LE11 . . . . . . .220 B3
Raines Ave S81 . . . . .35 F3
Raines Pk Rd S81 . . . . . . .35 F4
Rainham Gdns NG11 . . . . .196 B3
Rainworth Wr Rd
NG21 . . . . .103 F1
Raithby Cl NG5 . . . . .161 D4
Raleigh Cl Ilkeston DE7 . . .157 F2
Nottingham NG11 . . . . . .184 B1
Raleigh Rd NG19 . . . . . . .101 F4
Raleigh St NG7 . . . . .222 C3
Ralf Cl NG2 . . . . .185 F2
Ramblers Cl NG4 . . . . .174 C3
Ramper Rd Letwell S81 . . .16 A2
Saundby DN22 . . . . .23 E4
Rampton Cty Prim Sch
DN22 . . . . .42 B1
Rampton Gn Rd DN22 . . . .42 C1
Rampton Hospl DN22 . . . .53 D4
Rampton La DN22 . . . . . . .42 B3
Rampton Rd
Laneham DN22 . . . . .54 A3
Rampton DN22 . . . . .42 C2
Ramsdale Ave NG14 . . . . .148 B4
Ramsdale Cres NG5 . . . . .161 E2
Ramsdale Rd NG4 . . . . . . .162 C1
Ramsden Ave S81 . . . . . . .16 C1
Ramsden Cres S81 . . . . . .25 F4
Ramsden Croft NG21 . . . .104 A1
Ramsden Prim Sch
S81 . . . . .26 A3
Ramsey Cl
Mansfield Woodhouse
NG19 . . . . .89 D1
Stapleford NG9 . . . . .170 C1
Ramsey Ct NG5 . . . . .161 D1
Ramsey Dr NG5 . . . . .162 B3
Ranby CE Prim Sch
DN22 . . . . .38 A4

Ranby House Prep Sch
DN22 . . . . .38 A4
Ranby Wlk NG3 . . . . .173 F3
Rancliffe Ave NG12 . . . . . .197 E2
Rancliffe Farm Mews
NG11 . . . . .196 C2
Randal Gdns NG7 . . . . . . .172 C4
Randall St NG7 . . . . .172 C4
Randall Cl NG24 . . . . .140 B4
Randall Way DN22 . . . . . .29 E1
Randol Cl NG18 . . . . .101 E2
Ranelagh Gr NG8 . . . . . . .172 A3
Ranmere Rd NG8 . . . . .172 A4
Ranmoor Rd NG4 . . . . . . .162 C1
Ranmore Cl NG9 . . . . .171 D1
Rannerdale Cl NG2 . . . . . .186 B4
Rannoch Dr NG19 . . . . . . .101 F3
Rannoch Rise NG5 . . . . . .147 F1
Rannock Gdns NG12 . . . . .197 F2
Ranskill Gdns NG5 . . . . . .161 D4
Ranskill Prim Sch
DN22 . . . . .19 D3
Ranskill Rd DN22 . . . . .19 F3
Ransom Dr NG3 . . . . .161 F1
Ransom Rd
Mansfield NG21 . . . . .103 E2
Nottingham NG3 . . . . .173 F4
Ransom Wood Bsns Pk
NG21 . . . . .103 E2
Ransome Cl NG24 . . . . . . .140 B4
Ransome Rd NG9 . . . . . . .183 E1
Ratcher Way NG19 . . . . . .103 D4
Ratcliffe Gate NG18 . . . . .102 B3
Ratcliffe La DE74 . . . . .203 E4
Ratcliffe Rd LE11 . . . . .220 B3
Ratcliffe St NG16 . . . . . . .143 F1
Rathgar Cl NG8 . . . . .171 E2
Rathmines Cl NG7 . . . . . . .222 A1
Rathvale Ct NG9 . . . . .183 D2
Raven Ave NG5 . . . . .161 D2
Ravencroft La DN10 . . . . .14 A1
Ravendale Rd DN21 . . . . .24 C4
Ravenhill Cl NG9 . . . . .183 D2
Ravens Ct NG5 . . . . .161 D3
Ravenscourt S81 . . . . .36 A3
Ravensdale Ave
Long Eaton NG10 . . . . . . .182 A1
Mansfield NG18 . . . . .102 A4
Ravensdale Dr NG8 . . . . . .171 E2
Ravensdale Mid Sch
NG18 . . . . .102 C4
Ravensdale Rd NG18 . . . . .102 C4
Ravensdene Ct NG3 . . . . .173 E4
Ravenshead CE Prim Sch
NG15 . . . . .117 D2
Ravenshill Cl DN22 . . . . . .19 D2
Ravensmore Rd NG5 . . . . .161 D1
Ravenswood Rd NG5 . . . . .162 A4
Ravensworth Rd NG6 . . . .160 A4
Rawson St
Nottingham NG7 . . . . .160 C1
Selston NG16 . . . . .129 D3
Raylawn St NG18 . . . . . . .103 D3
Raymede Cl NG5 . . . . .160 C3
Raymede Dr NG5 . . . . . . .160 C3
Raymond Cl NG17 . . . . . . .114 C4
Raymond Dr NG13 . . . . . .178 A2
Raymoth La S81 . . . . .35 F4
Rayneham Rd DE7 . . . . . . .157 E2
Rayner Ct NG7 . . . . .222 B3
Raynford Ave NG9 . . . . . .183 E2
Raysmith Cl NG25 . . . . . . .121 F1
Rayton Ct NG11 . . . . .9 D2
Rayton La S81 . . . . .36 B2
Rayton Spur S81 . . . . .36 A2
Read Ave NG9 . . . . .184 A3
Readman Rd NG9 . . . . . . .183 D2
Rearsby Cl NG8 . . . . .171 E3
Recreation Dr NG20 . . . . .72 C1
Recreation Rd
Annesley NG15 . . . . .130 B4
New Houghton NG19 . . . . .86 C4
Sandiacre NG10 . . . . .182 A3
Shirebrook NG20 . . . . . . .72 C2
Recreation St
Long Eaton NG10 . . . . . . .193 F4
Mansfield NG18 . . . . .102 B4
Selston NG16 . . . . .129 D3
Recreation Terr NG9 . . . . .182 B3
Recreation View NG20 . . .72 C3
Rectors Gate DN22 . . . . . .39 F4
Rectory Ave
Gainsborough DN21 . . . . .15 E1
Nottingham NG8 . . . . .171 F2
Rectory Dr The NG4 . . . . .162 C1
Rectory Gdns
Beckingham DN10 . . . . . .14 A1
Kirton NG22 . . . . .78 A3
Nottingham NG8 . . . . .171 F2
Rectory La
Bottesford NG13 . . . . .181 D2
Claypole NG23 . . . . .156 C4
Gamston DN22 . . . . .50 C3
Lea DN21 . . . . .24 C1
Rectory Pl
Barton in F NG11 . . . . . . .194 C3
Wymeswold LE12 . . . . . . .220 A2
Wymeswold LE12 . . . . . . .216 B2
Rectory Rd
Carlton NG4 . . . . .174 C3
Church Warsop NG20 . . . .74 B4
Cotgrave NG12 . . . . .187 F2
Loughborough LE11 . . . . .220 A3
Retford DN22 . . . . .39 F4
Treswell DN22 . . . . .42 A2
West Bridgford NG2 . . . . .185 F4
Rectory St LN5 . . . . .142 B4

Red Barn Cl DE55 . . . . . . .99 D2
Red Cswy The LE14 . . . . . .202 A1
Red Hill La NG22 . . . . .92 C2
Red La Brinsley NG16 . . . .128 C1
Carlton in L S81 . . . . .26 A1
Lowdham NG14 . . . . .150 B1
Red Lodge La NG13 . . . . .166 A4
Redan La DE55 . . . . .99 D2
Redbarn Way NG17 . . . . .100 B1
Redbourne Dr NG8 . . . . . .172 B3
Redbridge Dr NG16 . . . . .159 E2
Redcar Cl Carlton NG4 . . .162 C1
Mansfield NG18 . . . . .102 C3
Redcliffe Gdns NG3 . . . . .173 E4
Redcliffe Rd
Mansfield NG18 . . . . .102 B3
Nottingham NG3 . . . . .173 E4
Redcliffe St NG17 . . . . . . .101 D2
Redcroft Cl NG21 . . . . . . .75 F1
Redfield Rd NG7 . . . . .184 C4
Redfield Way NG7 . . . . . . .184 C4
Redforde Pk Ave DN22 . . .29 E1
Redforde Pk Dr DN22 . . . .29 E1
Redforde Pk Rd DN22 . . . .29 E1
Redgate Cl NG19 . . . . . . .101 F4
Redgate Specl Sch
NG19 . . . . .101 F4
Redgate St
Mansfield NG19 . . . . .101 F4
Pinxton NG16 . . . . .113 E1
Redgates Ct NG14 . . . . . .148 B4
Redhill Comp Sch
NG5 . . . . .147 F1
Redhill La DN22 . . . . .63 F4
Redhill Lodge Dr NG5 . . . .147 E1
Redhill Rd NG5 . . . . .147 F1
Redland Ave NG4 . . . . . . .174 C4
Redland Cl
Beeston NG9 . . . . .183 E2
Ilkeston DE7 . . . . .157 F2
Redland Dr NG9 . . . . .183 E2
Redland Gr NG4 . . . . .174 C4
Redlands Prim Sch S80 . . .35 E2
Redman Cl DN21 . . . . .15 F1
Redmays Dr NG14 . . . . . . .164 A3
Redmile CE Prim Sch
NG13 . . . . .192 C2
Redmile La NG13 . . . . . . .192 B2
Redmile Rd NG8 . . . . .160 B1
Redoubt St NG7 . . . . .222 A3
Redruth Cl NG8 . . . . .171 E3
Redruth Dr NG18 . . . . . . .103 D1
Redthorn Way NG23 . . . . .156 C2
Redwing Cl S81 . . . . .35 E3
Redwood NG2 . . . . .185 D3
Redwood Ave NG8 . . . . . .171 E2
Redwood Cres NG9 . . . . . .184 A3
Redwood Ct NG15 . . . . . .145 E4
Reedham Wlk NG5 . . . . . .161 D4
Reedman Rd NG10 . . . . . .193 D2
Rees Gdns NG5 . . . . .147 D1
Rees Row DN22 . . . . .42 A1
Reform St
Annesley Woodhouse
NG17 . . . . .129 F4
Sutton in A NG17 . . . . . . .100 C1
Regal Arts Ctr* S80 . . . . . .35 F2
Regatta Way NG2 . . . . . . .186 B4
Regency Ct NG9 . . . . .184 A4
Regent St Beeston NG9 . . .184 A4
Kimberley NG16 . . . . .158 C3
Kirkby in A NG17 . . . . . . .114 C2
Langley Mill NG16 . . . . . .143 D2
Long Eaton NG10 . . . . . . .193 E4
Loughborough LE11 . . . . .220 A2
Mansfield NG18 . . . . .102 A4
Nottingham, New Basford
NG7 . . . . .161 D1
Nottingham, Standard Hill
NG1 . . . . .223 D2
Stapleford NG10 . . . . .182 B3
Sutton in A NG17 . . . . . . .100 B1
Regents Cl NG25 . . . . .112 A4
Regents Pk Cl NG2 . . . . . .185 E3
Regina Cl NG12 . . . . .175 F1
Regina Cres NG15 . . . . . .116 C1
Reid Gdns NG16 . . . . .159 D4
Reigate Cl NG9 . . . . .183 F1
Reigate Dr NG9 . . . . .183 F1
Reigate Rd NG7 . . . . .160 C1
Reindeer St NG18 . . . . . . .102 C3
Rempstone Dr NG6 . . . . . .160 B3
Rempstone Rd
East Leake LE12 . . . . .214 C4
East Leake, Stanford Hills
LE12 . . . . .214 A1
Hoton LE12 . . . . .215 E1
Wymeswold LE12 . . . . . . .216 A2
Renals Way NG14 . . . . . . .148 C4
Rendell Prim Sch
LE11 . . . . .220 A3
Renfrew Ct NG9 . . . . .101 F3
Renfrew Dr NG8 . . . . .171 F2
Repton Cl NG19 . . . . .88 C2
Repton Dr DE7 . . . . .170 A4
Repton Rd
Nottingham NG6 . . . . .160 B3
West Bridgford NG2 . . . . .185 E3
Retford Gate DN22 . . . . . .41 F4
Retford Hospl DN22 . . . . .39 E4
Retford Rd
Askham DN22 . . . . .52 C2
Blyth S81 . . . . .18 A1
Boughton NG22 . . . . .77 E3
Mattersey DN10 . . . . .20 B3
North Leverton w H DN22 . .41 F4
North Wheatley DN22 . . . .31 E4
Nottingham NG5 . . . . .161 D2

Retford Rd continued
| | |
Rampton DN22 .... 42 B1
Ranby S81 .... 37 E2
South Leverton DN22 ... 42 A4
Worksop S80 .... 36 B1
Retford Sta DN22 .... 39 F3
Revelstoke Ave NG5 .... 146 B1
Revelstoke Way NG5 ... 146 C1
Revesby Gdns NG8 ..... 172 B4
Revesby Rd NG5 .... 161 F3
Revill Cl Claypole NG23 156 B4
Ilkeston DE7 .... 157 F1
Revill Cres NG9 .... 182 C4
Revill Ct 15 NG17 ... 114 C4
Reydon Dr NG8 .... 160 B1
Reynolds Dr NG8 ...... 171 F3
Rhodes Wlk NG8 ...... 101 F3
Rhyl Cres NG4 .... 162 C1
Ribblesdale S81 .... 36 A4
Ribblesdale Cl NG9 ... 183 D2
Ribblesdale Rd
Long Eaton NG10 .... 193 D3
Nottingham NG5 ..... 161 E3
Riber Cl
Annesley Woodhouse
NG17 .... 115 D1
Long Eaton NG10 .... 193 E3
Richard Bonington Prim Sch
NG5 .... 147 F1
Richard St DN22 ...... 40 A3
Richards Cl NG12 ..... 189 D2
Richardson Cl NG11 .. 184 B1
Richborough Pl NG8 .. 171 F1
Richey Cl NG5 .... 162 A4
Richmond Ave
Breaston DE72 ...... 193 D4
Calverton NG14 ..... 149 D4
Eastwood NG16 ...... 144 A1
Ilkeston DE7 .... 157 F2
Nottingham NG3 ..... 173 F4
Sandiacre NG10 ..... 182 A2
Richmond Cl NG24 .... 140 A2
Richmond Dr
Beeston NG9 .... 183 F3
Mansfield Woodhouse
NG19 .... 88 B1
Nottingham NG3 ..... 161 E1
Radcliffe on T NG12 173 F3
Richmond Gdns NG5 .. 147 F1
Richmond La DN10 .... 9 F3
Richmond Rd
Carlton in S81 ...... 25 F3
Gainsborough DN21 .. 24 C4
Kirkby in A NG17 ... 115 E3
Retford DN21 .... 30 A1
West Bridgford NG2 . 173 F1
Worksop S80 .... 36 A1
Richmond St NG18 .... 102 C3
Richmond Terr NG17 . 175 F2
Rick St NG1 .... 223 F3
Ricket La
Blidworth NG21 ..... 117 E3
Ravenshead NG15 ... 116 C2
Ricklow Ct 1 NG5 ... 161 D4
Riddell Ave S81 ...... 16 C2
Ridding La DN10 ...... 3 D2
Ridding Terr NG3 .... 223 E4
Ridge Cl NG17 .... 100 B2
Ridge Hill NG14 ..... 150 B1
Ridge La NG12 .... 176 A3
Ridgeway
Nottingham NG5 .... 161 D4
Southwell NG25 ..... 121 E1
Worksop S81 .... 36 A3
Ridgeway Cl NG22 .... 119 F3
Ridgeway La NG20 .... 74 A2
Ridgeway St NG3 ..... 173 F3
Ridgeway Terr NG20 .. 74 A2
Ridgeway The NG22 .. 120 A3
Ridgeway Wlk 17 NG5. 161 D4
Ridgewood Dr NG9 .. 183 E2
Ridgewood Gr NG15 . 117 D1
Ridgmont Wlk NG11 . 195 E4
Ridgway Cl NG2 ..... 186 B3
Riding La DN10 ...... 3 D2
Ridings The
Bulcote NG14 .... 164 A3
East Bridgford NG13 165 E2
Keyworth NG12 ..... 198 A2
Mansfield Woodhouse
NG19 .... 88 C1
Ridsdale Rd NG5 ..... 161 E3
Rifle St NG7 .... 222 A3
Rigg La NG21 .... 132 C4
Rigley Ave 8 DE7 ... 157 F1
Rigley Dr NG5 .... 160 C4
Riley Ave NG17 ...... 100 B3
Riley Cl NG17 .... 100 B2
Ring Leas NG12 ...... 188 A2
Ringrose Cl NG24 .... 140 B4
Ringstead Cl NG2 .... 185 E3
Ringstead Wlk NG5 .. 161 D4
Ringwood S81 .... 36 A4
Ringwood Ave NG18 .. 102 B2
Ringwood Cres NG8 .. 172 B3
Ringwood Rd NG13 .. 177 E2
Rio Dr NG23 .... 98 A1
Ripon Rd NG3 .... 174 A3
Rise Pk Prim Sch NG5 146 C4
Rise Pk Rd NG5 ...... 146 C1
Rise The NG5 .... 161 E2
Riseborough Wlk NG6 146 B1
Risegate NG12 .... 187 F2
Riseholme Ave NG8 .. 171 F2
Riseholme Rd DN21 .. 24 C4
Risley Ct DE7 .... 157 F2
Risley Dr NG2 .... 173 D1
Ristes Pl NG1 .... 223 F2

Ritchie Cl NG12 ...... 188 A1
Ritson Cl NG3 .... 223 F4
River Cl DN22 .... 29 F1
River La Misson DN10 .. 4 B3
Retford DN22 .... 39 F4
River Leen Comp Sch The
NG6 .... 160 B4
River Rd NG4 .... 174 C4
River View
Market Warsop NG20 . 74 A3
Nottingham NG2 ..... 173 E1
Pye Bridge DE55 ..... 128 A3
Retford DN22 .... 39 F2
Riverdale Rd NG9 .... 183 E1
Rivergreen NG11 .... 184 C2
Rivergreen Cl NG9 .. 171 E1
Rivergreen Cres NG9 171 E1
Rivermead
Cotgrave NG12 ..... 188 A2
Newark-on-T NG24 .. 139 F3
Riverside
Southwell NG25 ..... 121 F1
Whatton NG13 .... 179 D2
Riverside Cl
Bottesford NG13 ... 181 D2
Cuckney NG20 ...... 60 A2
Riverside Rd
Beeston NG9 .... 184 A2
Newark-on-T NG24 .. 139 E3
Riverside Ret Pk
NG11 .... 185 D4
Riverside Way
Mansfield Woodhouse
NG19 .... 88 B3
Nottingham NG2 ..... 173 D1
Riverside Wlk NG13 .. 181 D2
Riverview Cotts DN10 . 4 B1
Riverway Gdns NG2 .. 173 E1
Rivington Rd NG9 .... 182 C1
Road No 1 NG4 ...... 174 C3
Road No 2 NG4 ...... 174 C3
Road No 3 NG4 ...... 174 C3
Road No 4 NG4 ...... 175 E3
Road No 5 NG4 ...... 175 D3
Road No 7 NG4 ...... 174 C3
Road No 8 NG4 ...... 174 C3
Roadwood La NG23 .. 69 F4
Rob Roy Ave NG2 .... 222 B1
Robbie Burns Rd NG5. 161 E4
Robert Ave NG18 .... 101 F3
Robert Dukeson Ave
NG5 .... 225 D2
Robert Jones Jun Sch
NG21 .... 118 A3
Robert Mellors Prim Sch
NG5 .... 161 F4
Robert Miles Inf Sch
NG13 .... 177 F3
Robert Miles Jun Sch
NG13 .... 177 F3
Robert Shaw Prim Sch
NG8 .... 172 B3
Roberts Ave NG17 ... 99 F1
Roberts Cl
Dunham on T NG22 .. 54 A1
Kegworth DE74 ..... 203 E1
Sutton in A NG15 ... 145 F4
Roberts St
Ilkeston DE7 .... 170 A3
Nottingham NG2 ..... 173 F2
Roberts Yd NG9 ..... 184 A4
Robey Cl
Hucknall NG15 ..... 131 D1
Mansfield Woodhouse
NG19 .... 89 D1
Robey Dr NG16 ...... 143 E2
Robin Down Cl NG18 102 B1
Robin Down La NG18 102 B1
Robin Gr NG15 ...... 117 D1
Robin Hood Ave
Edwinstowe NG21 ... 91 E4
Market Warsop NG20 . 74 B1
Robin Hood Dr NG16 143 F1
Robin Hood Dr NG15 145 F3
Robin Hood Ind Est 5
NG3 .... 173 F3
Robin Hood Inf & Jun Sch
NG5 .... 161 D3
Robin Hood Prim Sch
NG19 .... 88 A2
Robin Hood Rd
Annesley Woodhouse
NG17 .... 130 A4
Arnold NG5 .... 147 E1
Blidworth NG21 .... 118 A3
Nottingham NG5 .... 173 F3
Robin Hood Terr
Nottingham NG3 ... 223 F3
Ravenshead NG15 ... 117 D2
Robin Hood Way NG2 173 E1
Robin Hoods Cave*
NG22 .... 63 E1
Robina Dr NG16 .... 158 B4
Robinet Rd NG9 .... 183 F3
Robinettes La NG16 . 158 B3
Robinia Ct NG2 ..... 186 A3
Robins Ct NG24 ..... 140 A4
Robins Wood Rd NG8 172 A4
Robinson Cl NG24 ... 140 A4
Robinson Dr S80 .... 35 F1
Robinson Gdns NG11 184 B1
Robinson Rd NG3 ... 162 A1
Rochdale Ct NG18 ... 103 D3
Roche Cl NG5 .... 162 B4
Rochester Ave NG4 . 175 D4
Rochester Cl
Long Eaton NG10 ... 193 D4
Worksop S81 .... 36 A4

Rochester Ct NG6 .... 159 F3
Rochester Rd NG21 .. 118 A4
Rochester Wlk NG7 .. 184 C1
Rochford Ct NG12 ... 186 B2
Rock Ct Mansfield NG18 102 B4
Rock Dr NG7 .... 222 C1
Rock Hill NG18 ...... 102 B3
Rock St Mansfield NG18 102 B3
Nottingham NG6 .... 160 A4
Rock Valley NG18 ... 102 B4
Rockford Ct NG9 .... 170 C3
Rockford Rd NG5 ... 160 C2
Rockingham Gr NG13 177 E2
Rocklands The NG20 . 72 C2
Rockley Ave
Eastwood NG16 ..... 144 A1
Radcliffe on T NG12 175 F2
Rockley Cl NG5 ..... 145 E3
Rockley Way NG20 .. 72 C2
Rockleys View NG14 150 A1
Rockwell Ct NG18 .. 102 A4
Rockwood Wlk NG15 145 F3
Rodel Ct NG3 .... 223 F4
Roden St NG3 .... 173 F3
Roderick Ave NG17 .. 115 D1
Roderick St NG6 .... 160 B2
Rodney Rd NG2 ..... 186 A3
Rodney Sch NG22 .. 121 D4
Rodney Way DE7 ... 157 F2
Rodwell Cl NG8 ..... 172 B3
Roe Hill NG14 ...... 149 E3
Roebuck Cl NG5 .... 161 D4
Roebuck Dr NG18 .. 102 A2
Roebuck Way S80 .. 48 A4
Roecliffe NG2 ...... 185 F2
Roehampton Dr NG9 170 B1
Roes La NG14 ...... 149 D4
Roewood Cl NG17 .. 114 C4
Roewood La NG22 .. 107 F1
Roger Cl NG17 ..... 100 C3
Roker Cl NG8 ...... 160 A1
Rolaine Cl NG19 ... 88 B2
Roland Ave
Nottingham NG11 .. 185 D4
Nuthall NG16 ...... 159 F2
Rolleston Cl NG15 .. 145 E3
Rolleston Cres NG16 144 C1
Rolleston Dr
Arnold NG5 .... 162 A4
Eastwood NG16 .... 158 A4
Nottingham NG7 ... 222 B1
Rolleston Sta NG25 . 137 F1
Roman Bank NG19 .. 88 B2
Roman Bank La DN10 18 C3
Roman Dr NG6 ..... 160 C2
Romans Ct NG6 .... 160 C1
Romiley Cl NG9 .... 172 A1
Romney Ave NG8 .. 171 E1
Romsey Pl NG19 ... 101 E3
Rona Cl NG19 ...... 101 F3
Rona Ct NG6 .... 160 C1
Ronald St NG7 ..... 222 B3
Rookery Gdns NG5 . 161 F4
Rookery La NG17 .. 114 A4
Rookery The
Collingham NG23 .. 98 A1
1 Mansfield NG18 .. 102 A4
Rooks La DN10 ..... 6 C1
Rookwood Cl NG9 . 183 F3
Rookwood Cres NG15 145 E3
Rooley Ave NG17 .. 100 B2
Rooley Dr NG17 ... 100 B2
Roosa Cl NG6 ..... 159 F3
Roosevelt Ave NG10 193 E3
Roosevelt Rd NG17 101 D2
Rooth St NG18 ..... 102 B1
Rope Wlk LE12 .... 205 E1
Ropery Rd DN21 ... 15 E1
Ropewalk DE7 ..... 203 E1
Ropewalk Ind Ctr DE7 158 A1
Ropewalk The
Ilkeston DE7 ...... 158 A1
Kirkby in A NG17 .. 114 C3
Newark-on-T NG24 140 A4
Southwell NG25 ... 121 F1
Ropsley Cres NG5 . 186 A4
Roscoe Ave NG5 .. 147 F1
Rose Ash La NG5 .. 161 D4
Rose Ave Ilkeston DE7 157 F1
Retford DN22 ...... 40 A2
Rose Cl NG3 .... 173 E4
Rose Cottage Dr NG17 99 F1
Rose Cotts NG14 .. 163 F3
Rose Ct NG10 ..... 182 A1
Rose Farm Dr NG23 96 C4
Rose Gr Beeston NG9 184 A3
Keyworth NG12 ... 197 F2
Rose La NG19 ..... 88 B2
Rose Lea DN22 .... 39 E2
Roseacre NG9 ..... 184 A3
Rosebank Dr NG5 . 148 A1
Rosebay Ave NG7 . 173 D4
Roseberry Gdns NG15 146 B3
Roseberry St NG17 115 E2
Rosebery Hill NG18 102 B3
Rosebery St NG6 .. 160 C2
Rosecroft Dr NG5 .. 161 E2
Rosedale S81 ...... 36 A4
Rosedale Cl NG10 .. 193 D3
Rosedale Dr NG8 .. 171 D2
Rosedale La NG14 . 150 C2
Rosedale Rd NG3 . 174 B3
Rosedale Way NG19 88 C1
Rosegarth Wlk NG6 160 B2
Rosegrove Ave NG5 147 F1

Rosehill Cl LN1 ...... 57 D2
Rosehill Sch NG3 .... 173 F3
Roseleigh Ave NG3 .. 162 A1
Rosemary Ave NG18 . 102 A4
Rosemary Cl 11 NG8 159 F1
Rosemary St NG18 .. 102 A4
Rosemont Cl NG17 .. 100 C3
Roseneath Ave NG5 . 146 C1
Rosetta Rd NG7 .... 160 C1
Rosewall Ct NG5 ... 162 A4
Roseway DN21 ..... 15 E1
Rosewood Cl
Carlton in S81 ..... 25 E1
Newark-on-T NG24 . 125 D1
South Normanton DE55 113 D4
Rosewood Cres DE75 143 D1
Rosewood Dr NG17 . 115 E3
Rosewood Gdns
Nottingham NG6 .... 159 F4
West Bridgford NG2 185 E2
Rosings Ct NG17 ... 100 C1
Roslyn Ave NG4 .... 162 C1
Ross Cl
Coddington NG24 .. 126 A1
Lowdham NG14 .... 150 C1
Ross La NG4 ...... 163 D4
Rossell Dr NG9 .... 182 C3
Rossendale DE7 ... 157 F2
Rossett Cl NG2 .... 186 B3
Rossetti Gdns S81 . 36 B2
Rossington Rd NG2 173 F3
Rosslyn Dr
Hucknall NG15 .... 146 B4
Nottingham NG8 .. 160 A1
Rosslyn Jun Sch NG8 160 A1
Rosthwaite Cl NG2 186 B3
Roston Cl NG18 .... 103 D3
Rothbury Ave NG9 . 170 B1
Rothbury Gr NG13 177 E3
Rotherham Baulk S81 34 C4
Rotherham Rd NG17 86 C4
Rothesay Ave NG7 222 B2
Rothley Ave NG3 .. 173 F3
Rothwell Cl
Gainsborough DN21 24 C4
Nottingham NG11 .. 185 D2
Roughs Wood La
NG15 .... 145 E2
Roulstone Cres LE12 205 F2
Roundhill Cl NG17 . 101 E1
Roundhill Cty Prim Sch
NG9 .... 183 F4
Roundwood Jun Sch
NG5 .... 161 E4
Roundwood Rd NG5 161 E4
Row The NG19 ..... 179 F3
Rowan Ave
Hathern LE12 ..... 213 D1
Ravenshead NG15 . 117 D1
Stapleford NG9 ... 170 C1
Rowan Cl
Calverton NG14 ... 148 B4
Kirkby in A NG17 . 114 C3
Mansfield NG19 ... 88 B1
Rowan Cres S80 ... 35 F1
Rowan Croft NG17 . 99 F2
Rowan Ct NG16 .... 159 D3
Rowan Dr
Keyworth NG12 ... 198 A1
Kirkby in A NG17 . 114 C3
Nottingham NG11 .. 185 D2
Selston NG16 ..... 128 B4
Shirebrook NG20 .. 72 C2
Rowan Gdns NG6 .. 159 F4
Rowan Way NG24 .. 140 A3
Rowan Wlk NG4 ... 174 A4
Rowe Gdns NG6 ... 160 B3
Rowland Ave NG3 . 162 A1
Rowland Mews NG3 173 F4
Rowsley Ave NG10 . 193 D3
Rowston Cl DN21 .. 15 E1
Rowthorne La S44 . 86 A4
Roxton Ct NG16 ... 158 C4
Roy Ave NG9 ...... 184 A2
Royal Ave NG10 ... 182 B1
Royal Cres S81 .... 35 F3
Royal Mews NG9 .. 183 E2
Royal Oak Ct NG21 76 A1
Royal Oak Dr NG16 129 D4
Royal Way LE11 ... 220 A3
Royce Ave NG15 .. 145 F3
Royds Cres S80 ... 35 D3
Royland Rd LE11 .. 220 A2
Royston Cl NG2 ... 173 D1
Ruby Paddocks NG16 158 C3
Ruddington Ct NG18 103 D1
Ruddington Framework
Knitters Mus* NG11 196 B3
Ruddington La NG11 185 D3
Ruddington Village Mus*
NG11 .... 196 B4
Rudge Cl NG8 ..... 171 F3
Rue De L'Yonne NG23 68 B3
Ruffles Ave NG5 .. 162 A3
Rufford Abbey* NG22 91 F3
Rufford Ave
Beeston NG9 ...... 183 D4
Bilsthorpe NG22 .. 105 F2
Carlton NG4 ...... 162 B4
Mansfield NG18 .. 102 B4
Meden Vale NG20 . 74 C4
New Ollerton NG22 . 77 E2
Newark-on-T NG24 . 139 F4
Rainworth NG21 .. 104 B1
Retford DN22 ..... 39 E2
Rufford Cl
Bilsthorpe NG22 .. 106 A2

Ret - Rut **253**

Rufford continued
Hucknall NG15 .... 146 B3
Sutton in A NG17 . 100 C3
Rufford Craft Ctr*
.... 91 F3
Rufford Ct NG21 ... 104 B1
Rufford Ctry Pk* NG22 91 F3
Rufford Dr NG19 .. 88 C2
Rufford Gr NG13 .. 177 E2
Rufford Jun & Inf Sch
NG6 .... 160 A4
Rufford La
Edwinstowe NG22 . 91 F4
Wellow NG22 ..... 92 A4
Rufford Rd
Edwinstowe NG22 . 91 E4
Long Eaton NG10 . 193 D2
Nottingham NG5 .. 161 E2
Ruddington NG11 . 196 B4
Rufford Sch The NG21 75 F1
Rufford St S80 .... 47 D4
Rufford Way NG2 . 186 A3
Rufford Wlk 14 NG6 160 A4
Rufford Wlk NG15 145 F3
Rugby Cl NG5 ..... 160 C4
Rugby Rd
Rainworth NG21 .. 118 A4
West Bridgford NG2 185 F3
Rugeley Ave NG10 194 A4
Ruislip Cl NG16 ... 158 C4
Runcie Cl NG12 ... 187 F1
Runnymede Ct NG7 222 C3
Runswick Dr
Arnold NG5 .... 161 F4
Nottingham NG8 .. 172 A3
Runton Dr NG6 ... 160 C2
Rupert Cres NG24 140 A4
Rupert Rd NG13 .. 177 E2
Rupert St DE7 .... 158 A1
Rush Leys NG10 .. 193 E3
Rushcliffe Ave
Carlton NG4 ...... 174 B4
Radcliffe on T NG12 175 F2
Rushcliffe Ctr NG6 160 A4
Rushcliffe Ctry Pk*
NG11 .... 196 B3
Rushcliffe Gr LE12 205 F2
Rushcliffe Rd NG15 145 E4
Rushcliffe Rise NG5 161 E3
Rushes The
Gotham NG11 ..... 195 D1
31 Loughborough LE12 220 A2
Mansfield Woodhouse
NG19 .... 88 B3
Rushey Cl S80 .... 36 A1
Rushford Dr NG8 . 171 E2
Rushley View NG17 100 B3
Rushmere Wlk NG5 161 F3
Rushpool Ave NG19 88 B2
Rushton Gdns NG3 173 F4
Rushworth Ave NG2 185 F4
Rushworth Cl NG3 173 F4
Rushy Cl NG8 ..... 171 E3
Ruskin Ave
Beeston NG9 ...... 183 E2
Long Eaton NG10 . 193 D3
Ruskin Cl NG5 .... 161 E4
Ruskin Rd NG19 .. 87 E1
Ruskin St DN21 ... 24 B3
Russell Ave
Harworth DN11 ... 8 C2
New Balderton NG24 140 A2
Nottingham NG8 .. 171 F2
Russell Cres NG8 . 171 F2
Russell Dr NG8 ... 171 F2
Russell Gdns 5 NG9 183 E1
Russell Rd NG7 .. 172 C4
Russell St
Long Eaton NG10 . 182 B1
Loughborough LE11 220 B2
Nottingham NG7 .. 222 C3
Sutton in A NG17 . 100 C2
Russet Ave NG4 .. 174 C4
Russet Gr DN10 .. 10 A4
Russey Cl NG14 .. 150 C1
Russley Rd NG9 .. 183 D4
Ruth Dr NG5 ..... 148 A3
Rutherford Ave NG18 102 C2
Ruthwell Gdns NG5 147 D1
Rutland NG17 .... 115 E3
Rutland Ave
Beeston NG9 ...... 183 D2
Newark-on-T NG24 140 A3
Rutland Cl NG20 .. 74 A2
Rutland Cres DN11 8 C3
Rutland Ct DE7 ... 157 E1
Rutland Dr DN11 .. 8 C3
Rutland Gr NG10 . 182 B3
Rutland House Sch
NG3 .... 173 F4
Rutland La NG13 .. 181 D1
Rutland Rd
Bingham NG13 ... 177 F3
Carlton NG4 ..... 162 B2
Retford DN22 .... 40 A2
West Bridgford NG2 186 A4
Westwood NG16 .. 128 B2
Rutland St
Ilkeston DE7 ..... 157 F1
8 Loughborough LE11 220 B2
Mansfield NG18 .. 102 B3
Nottingham NG1 .. 223 D2
Rutland Terr DE7 . 157 F1

Rydal Ave NG10 ....182 A1
Rydal Dr Beeston NG9 ..183 E4
Hucknall NG15 ....145 F4
Worksop S81 ....35 F4
Rydal Gdns NG2 ....186 A3
Rydal Gr NG4 ....161 E3
Rydale Rd NG5 ....161 E3
Ryder St NG6 ....160 B2
Rye Croft DN11 ....8 A4
Rye St NG7 ....160 C1
Ryecroft St NG9 ....182 C4
Ryedale Ave NG18 ......103 D3
Ryehill Cl NG2 ....173 E1
Ryehill St NG2 ....173 E1
Ryeholme Cl LE12 ......205 F2
Ryeland Gdns NG2 ......173 E1
Ryemere Cl NG16 ....143 F1
Rylands Cl NG9 ....184 A2
Ryton Cl S81 ....18 A1
Ryton Ct NG2 ....173 E1
Ryton Fields S81 ....18 A1
Ryton Pk Prim Sch S81 ..35 F1
Ryton Pl S80 ....35 F2
Ryton Sq NG8 ....160 A1
Ryton St S80 ....35 F2

S

Sacheverall Ave NG16 ..113 E4
Sacred Heart Cath Prim Sch
NG4 ....174 B4
Sacred Heart RC Prim Sch
LE11 ....220 A1
Saddlers Cl NG19 ....88 C1
Saddlers Yd NG12 ......197 F4
Saddleworth Ct NG2 .....173 E1
Sadler St NG19 ....101 F4
Saffron Gdns NG2 ......173 D1
St Agnes Cl NG8 ....171 E4
St Aidans Ct NG6 ....160 C2
St Albans Cl NG10 .....193 E3
St Albans Ct NG5 ......147 D1
St Albans Inf Sch NG5 ..161 E3
St Albans Mews NG6 ..160 B3
St Albans Rd
  Arnold NG5 ....161 E3
  Bestwood Village NG6 ..146 C2
  Nottingham NG6 ....160 B4
St Albans St NG5 ....161 E3
St Andrew Cl NG11 ....195 D1
St Andrew St NG18 ....102 B3
St Andrews CE Prim Sch
  NG17 ....100 C3
St Andrews Cl NG15 ...146 A4
St Andrews Ct NG3 .....161 E1
St Andrews Cres
  NG17 ....100 C3
St Andrews Rd NG6 ....160 B4
St Andrews Rd NG3 .....56 C2
St Andrews Rise
  DE74 ....203 E1
St Andrews St
  Kirkby in A NG17 ....115 D3
  Sutton in A NG17 ......100 C3
St Andrews Way DN22 ..39 F2
St Annes Cl S80 ....35 E2
St Annes Dr S80 ....35 E2
St Annes La LE12 ......213 D3
St Annes Mews S80 ....35 E2
St Annes Prim Sch S80 ..35 E1
St Annes View S80 ......35 E2
St Anns Gdns NG3 .....173 F4
St Anns Hill NG3 ....173 E4
St Anns Hill Rd NG3 ...173 E4
St Anns Hospl NG3 ....174 A4
St Anns St NG1 ....223 E3
St Anns Valley NG3 ....173 F3
St Anns Way
  Nottingham NG3 ....223 E4
  Shelton NG23 ....168 B3
St Anns Well Jun Sch
  NG3 ....173 F4
St Anns Well Rd NG3 ..173 F3
St Anthony Ct NG7 ....172 C1
St Augustines Cath Prim Sch
St Augustines Cl 3
  NG7 ....161 D1
St Augustines Jun & Inf Schs
  S81 ....36 A2
St Austell Dr NG11 ....185 D3
St Austins Ct NG4 .....174 C4
St Austins Dr NG4 .....174 C4
St Bartholomews Rd
  NG3 ....173 F4
St Botolphs Cl LN1 ......57 D3
St Catherine St NG18 ..102 B3
St Catherines Ct NG24 ..139 F4
St Catherines St NG12 ..175 F1
St Cecilia Gdns NG3 ...223 F4
St Chads Cl NG18 ......102 B2
St Chads Rd NG3 ......173 F4
St Christopher St 11
  NG2 ....173 F2
St Clares Gate NG24 ..140 A3
St Cuthbert St S80 ....35 F1
St Cuthberts Rd 17 NG3 ..173 F4
St Davids Cl S81 ....36 A3
St Edmund Campion RC Prim
  Sch NG2 ....186 A3
St Edmunds Ave NG19 ..88 B2

St Edmunds CE Prim Sch
  NG19 ....88 B2
St Edwins Dr NG21 ......76 A1
St Ervan Rd NG11 ......185 D3
St Francis Hospl NG5 ..161 D2
St Georges CE Prim Sch
  DN21 ....24 C3
St Georges Ct NG15 ...146 A4
St Georges Dr NG2 ....173 E1
St Giles Specl Sch
  DN22 ....39 E4
St Giles Way NG24 ....140 C2
St Giles Way NG12 ....189 D2
St Helens Ave NG16 ...113 E2
St Helens Cres
  Burton Joyce NG14 ....163 F2
  Trowell NG9 ....170 B2
St Helens Ct NG16 ....128 B4
St Helens Gr NG14 ....163 F2
St Helens La NG12 ....120 C1
St Helens Rd
  Retford DN22 ....40 A2
  West Bridgford NG2 ...185 E2
St Helens St NG7 ......222 C3
St James Ave DE7 .....170 A4
St James Ct NG10 .....193 D3
St James Dr NG16 .....143 E4
St James Terr NG9 ....223 D2
St James Ct NG15 .....146 A4
St Jamess
  Nottingham NG1 ....223 D2
  Stapleford NG9 ....182 B3
St Jamess Terr NG9 ...182 B3
St John St
  Mansfield NG18 ....102 A4
  Worksop S80 ....39 F4
St John the Baptist CE Prim
  Sch NG4 ....174 C3
St Johns Ave NG17 ....115 D2
St Johns CE Mid Sch
  NG18 ....102 A4
St Johns CE Prim Sch
  NG9 ....182 C4
St Johns Cl NG16 .....128 B1
St Johns Coll NG9 ....183 D4
St Johns Cres NG16 ..146 B3
St Johns Ct NG4 ......174 B4
St Johns Dr DN22 ....30 B2
St Johns Pl 9 NG18 ...102 A4
St Johns Rd
  Ilkeston DE7 ....170 A4
  Ruddington NG11 ......196 B4
  Selston NG16 ....128 C4
St Johns St NG10 .....193 E4
St Johns Terr DN21 ....24 B4
St Josephs Prim Sch
  DN22 ....39 E4
St Josephs RC Prim Sch
  Boughton NG22 ....77 F3
  Shirebrook NG20 ....72 C3
St Josephs Sch NG1 ..223 D3
St Jude Ave NG3 ......161 F1
St Judes Way NG21 ...104 A1
St Laurence Ct NG10 ..193 F3
St Lawrence Bvd
  NG12 ....175 F1
St Lawrence CE Prim Sch
  NG11 ....193 F3
St Leonards DN11 ....8 A4
St Leonards Ct NG24 ..124 C1
St Leonards Dr NG8 ...171 F2
St Leonards Way
  NG19 ....103 D4
St Leven Cl NG8 ......160 A1
St Lukes CE Prim Sch
  S81 ....34 C4
St Lukes St NG3 ......186 A3
St Lukes St 12 NG3 ..173 F3
St Lukes Way NG14 ...175 D4
St Lukes Way DN22 ....53 D4
St Margaret Clitherow RC
  Prim Sch NG5 ....161 E4
St Margaret St NG18 ..102 B3
St Margarets Ave NG8 ..172 B4
St Marks Cl S81 ....35 E4
St Marks La NG3 ......139 F4
St Marks Pl NG3 ......139 F4
St Marks St NG3 ......223 F3
St Martins Ave DN10 ...9 F4
St Martins Cl S81 ....18 A1
St Martins Cl
  Firbeck S81 ....16 A3
  Nottingham NG8 ......171 F4
St Martins Rd DN22 ....42 B4
St Martins Rd NG8 ....171 F4
St Martins Wlk S80 .....45 E3
St Mary & St Martin Prim Sch
  S81 ....18 A1
St Marys Ave LE12 ....162 C1
St Marys CE Sch NG21 ..76 A2
St Marys Cl NG15 .....147 F1
St Marys Cl NG9 ......183 E1
St Marys Cl
  Bottesford NG13 ....181 D1
  5 Loughborough LE11 ..220 A2
  Lowdham NG14 ....150 B1
St Marys Cres
  East Leake LE12 ....205 F2
  Ruddington NG11 ......196 B4
  Tickhill DN11 ....8 A4
St Marys Ct NG17 ....100 B2
St Marys Dr NG21 ......76 A1
St Marys Gate
  Nottingham NG1 ....223 F2
  Tickhill DN11 ....8 A4
St Marys Gdns NG24 ..139 F3
St Marys La NG13 ....181 D1
St Marys Mews DN11 ...8 A4
St Marys Pl NG1 ......223 F2

St Marys Prim Sch
  NG17 ....100 B2
St Marys RC Prim Sch
  LE11 ....220 A2
St Marys Rd NG13 ....177 F3
St Marys Rd
  Sutton in A NG17 ......100 B2
St Marys St NG17 ....100 B2
St Marys Wlk NG16 ...128 A2
St Matthias Rd NG3 ..173 F3
St Mawes Ave NG11 ..114 C4
St Mellion Way 3 NG17 ..114 C4
St Michaels Ave NG4 ..162 C1
St Michaels Ave NG8 ..171 E4
St Michaels Cl NG22 ..120 C1
St Michaels Dr DE55 ..113 D4
St Michaels Gn DN22 ...39 E4
St Michaels Sq NG9 ..183 D4
St Michaels St NG17 ..101 D2
St Michaels View
  ....131 D1
St Nicholas Cl NG5 ...161 F4
St Nicholas St NG1 ...223 E2
St Patricks RC Prim Sch
  Bircotes DN11 ....9 D2
  Mansfield NG18 ....103 D3
  Nottingham NG11 .....185 D4
St Patricks Rd
  Hucknall NG15 ....145 F4
  Nuthall NG16 ....159 E3
St Pauls Ave NG7 ....172 C4
St Pauls Rd
  Gainsborough DN21 ....15 D2
  Worksop S80 ....36 A3
St Pauls St 4 NG8 ....172 B3
St Pauls Terr NG7 ....172 C4
St Peters Ave NG20 ....74 A3
St Peters Ave LE12 ...213 D1
St Peters CE Prim Sch
  East Bridgford NG13 ..165 E2
  Farndon NG24 ....139 D3
  Gringley on t H DN10 ..12 C1
  Mansfield NG18 ....103 D1
St Peters Church Wlk
  NG11 ....223 E2
St Peters Cl
  East Stockwith DN21 ...7 F1
  Farndon NG24 ....138 C2
  New Ollerton NG22 .....77 D2
St Peters Cres NG11 ..196 B4
St Peters Dr NG21 ....104 A1
St Peters Gate NG1 ...223 E2
St Peters La DN22 .....21 E3
St Peters Mix Jun Sch
  NG11 ....196 B4
St Peters Sq NG1 .....223 E2
St Peters St NG7 .....222 A3
St Peters Way NG18 ..102 B3
St Philip Neri with St Bede
  Cath Prim Sch NG18 ..102 A4
St Saviours Ct DN22 ....40 A4
St Saviours Gdns NG2 ..173 E1
St Stephens Ave 25
  NG2 ....173 F2
St Stephens Rd
  Nottingham NG2 ....173 F2
  Retford DN22 ....40 A2
St Swithuns CE Prim Sch
  DN22 ....39 F4
St Teresas Cath Prim Sch
  NG8 ....172 A4
St Thomas Ave NG17 ..115 D2
St Thomas Dr NG13 ..179 D3
St Vincent Cl NG10 ...193 F3
St Wilfrids Cl NG13 ...110 C1
St Wilfrids Dr NG17 ..114 C4
St Wilfrids Prim CE Sch
  NG14 ....148 C4
St Wilfrids Sq NG14 ..148 C4
Salamander Cl NG4 ...162 B2
Salcey Dr NG9 ....170 B1
Salcombe Cir NG5 ....147 E1
Salcombe Cl NG16 ....144 B1
Salcombe Cres NG11 ..196 B4
Salcombe Dr NG5 .....147 E1
Salcombe Rd NG5 ....160 C2
Salford Gdns NG3 ....223 F3
Salisbury Ave LE12 ...205 F1
Salisbury Cl NG19 .....88 B2
Salisbury Rd
  Beeston NG9 ....184 A4
  Gainsborough DN21 ...15 E1
  Long Eaton NG10 .....193 F4
  Loughborough LE11 ..220 B2
  Nottingham NG7 ....222 A2
Sallie Bank La LN1 ....55 D2
Salmon Cl NG6 ....159 F4
Salmon La NG17 ....129 E4
Salop St NG5 ....161 E4
Salt Hill S81 ....16 A3
Salterford Rd NG14 ...148 A3
Salterford La NG14 ...148 C4
Salterford House Sch
  NG14 ....133 E3
Salterford La NG14 ...133 E3
Saltford Cl NG4 ....162 C1
Salthouse Cl NG9 .....184 A4
Salthouse La NG9 ....184 A4
Saltney Way NG11 ....185 D2
Salvin Cl NG12 ....189 D2
Sampson St NG17 ....130 A4

St Sampsons La NG19 ...87 D2
Samson Ct NG11 .....196 A4
Samuel Barlow Prim Sch
  NG21 ....90 A2
Samuel Cl NG11 ......101 F4
Samuel Way NG18 ....102 B4
Sand La Besthorpe NG23 ..97 F4
  Broadholme NG23 ......70 C4
  Spalford NG23 ....83 D4
  Torksey LN1 ....44 B1
Sand Pit La LE14 .....211 E2
Sandale Cl NG2 ....186 B3
Sandalwood Cl NG18 ..103 D2
Sandalwood Dr NG17 ..115 E3
Sandays Cl NG12 .....173 E1
Sandbeck Ct DN10 .....10 A4
Sandby Cl NG3 ....183 E3
Sanders Ave NG18 ....102 C4
Sanders Cl NG23 ....97 F4
Sandersons Bank DN9 ...2 A4
Sandfield Ave NG15 ..132 A4
Sandfield Cl NG18 ....103 D2
Sandfield La NG22 .....78 A3
Sandfield Rd
  Annesley Woodhouse
  NG17 ....129 F4
  Arnold NG5 ....161 F3
  Beeston NG9 ....182 C1
  Nottingham NG7 ....222 B2
Sandfield Way NG24 ..139 D3
Sandford Ave NG10 ..193 F4
Sandford Rd NG3 .....162 A2
Sandgate NG9 ....171 E1
Sandgate Ave NG19 ...88 B2
Sandhill Rd 11 NG3 ....88 B2
Sandhill Rd
  Farndon NG24 ....139 D3
  Selston NG16 ....129 D2
Sandhill St S80 ....35 F2
Sandhills Cl NG24 ....124 C1
Sandhills Pk NG24 ....124 C1
Sandholes The NG22 ..119 F3
Sandhurst Ave NG18 ..102 B2
Sandhurst Dr
  Beeston NG9 ....183 E1
  Ruddington NG11 .....196 A3
Sandhurst Rd NG6 ....146 B1
Sandiacre Rd NG9 ....182 B3
Sandlands S81 ....35 E4
Sandon St NG7 ....161 D1
Sandown Rd
  Beeston NG9 ....182 C1
  Mansfield NG18 ....103 D2
  Sutton in A NG17 .....101 D2
Sandpiper Cl NG13 ...177 F2
Sandpiper Way NG7 ..222 A2
Sandringham Ave
  NG2 ....185 F4
Sandringham Cres
  Nottingham NG8 ....171 E3
  Worksop S81 ....35 F3
Sandringham Ct
  Harworth DN11 ....9 D3
  Mansfield Woodhouse
  ....88 A3
Sandringham Dr
  Beeston NG9 ....171 E1
  Mansfield Woodhouse
  ....88 A3
Sandringham Pl NG15 ..146 A4
Sandringham Rd
  Mansfield Woodhouse
  ....88 C3
  20 Nottingham NG2 ..173 F2
  Retford DN22 ....29 E1
  Sandiacre NG10 ....182 A2
Sandrock Rd DN11 .....8 D2
Sands Cl NG4 ....174 C3
Sands The LE14 ....211 E2
Sandsfield La DN21 ...24 B3
Sandside NG12 ....187 F1
Sandwell Cl NG10 ....193 D3
Sandwich Cl 5 NG7 ..114 C4
Sandwood Cl DE55 ....99 D2
Sandy La Beeston NG9 ..171 E1
  Carlton NG12 ....175 D1
  Edwinstowe NG21 ......91 D4
  Gamston DN22 ....50 C2
  Hucknall NG15 ....146 A4
  Mansfield NG18 ....102 B4
  Market Warsop NG20 ..74 A3
  Oxton NG25 ....134 B2
  Ravenshead NG15 ....117 D2
  Worksop S80 ....35 E2
Sandycliffe Cl NG18 ...88 C1
Sandyford Cl NG6 ....160 B2
Sandymount DN11 ....9 D3
Sandymount E DN11 ...9 D2
Sandymount W DN11 ...9 D2
Sanger Cl NG11 ......195 E4
Sanger Gdns NG11 ...195 E4
Sankey Dr NG6 ....160 A4
Santon Cl NG19 ....89 D1
Santon La NG23 ......110 A4
Sapele Cl NG4 ....163 D1
Sapling Cl NG24 ......140 B3
Sapphire Cl NG21 ....104 B1
Sapphire Dr NG17 ....115 E2
Saracen Cl DN21 ....24 C3
Saracen La DN10 ....3 E2
Saracens Head NG24
  ....139 F4
Sargent Gdns 1 NG3 ..173 F3
Sartfield Rd NG19 ....101 E4
Saskatoon Cl NG12 ..175 F1
Saucers The NG13 ....178 C4
Saunby Cl NG5 ....162 A4
Saundby Ave NG19 ....87 E1

Saundby Rd DN22 .....23 E2
Savages Rd NG11 ....196 B4
Savages Row NG11 ..196 B4
Saversick La NG25 ...136 A4
Savile Rd NG22 ....105 F3
Savile St DN22 ....39 F3
Saville Cl NG9 ....182 C4
Saville St Arnold NG5 ..161 F3
  Sutton in A NG17 .....100 C3
Saville St NG21 ....118 A3
Saville Way NG20 ......74 A2
Saw Pit Ind Est DE55 ..99 D3
Saw Pit La DE55 ....99 D3
Sawley Dr NG18 ......103 D3
Sawley Jun & Inf Schs
  NG10 ....193 D3
Sawyers Cl NG24 ....140 A4
Saxby Dr NG18 ....103 D2
Saxelby Gdns NG6 ...160 A4
Saxilby CE Prim Sch
  LN1 ....57 D2
Saxilby Rd LN6 ....71 F4
Saxilby Sta LN1 ....57 D2
Saxon Gn NG7 ....222 A1
Saxon Way
  Cotgrave NG12 ....188 A1
  Harworth DN11 ....8 C2
Saxondale Dr
  Nottingham NG6 ....160 C3
  Radcliffe on T NG12 ..176 B2
Saxton Cl Beeston NG9 ..184 A3
  Worksop S80 ....35 E1
Scafell Way NG11 ....195 E4
Scalby Cl NG16 ....143 E1
Scalford Dr NG8 ......172 B2
Scampton Way NG24 ..24 C4
Scarborough St NG3 ..105 F3
Scarborough Rd NG23 ..223 F3
Scarbrough Cl DN11 ....8 A4
Scarcliffe Cl NG17 ...100 C2
Scarcliffe La NG20 .....72 B4
Scarcliffe St NG18 ...102 B4
Scarcliffe Terr NG20 ...59 D1
Scarf Wlk NG2 ....185 D4
Scarfell Cl NG2 ....186 B3
Scargill Ave NG16 ....144 A1
Scargill Cl NG16 .....144 A1
Scargill Wlk NG16 ...143 F2
Scarle La NG24 ....103 D1
Scarrington Ct NG18 ..103 D3
Scarrington Rd NG2 ..173 F1
Sceptre St NG5 ....161 E1
School Cl Newton DE55 ..99 D2
School Cl NG15 ....130 A4
School House La DN10 ..13 F3
School La
  Beckingham LN5 ......142 B4
  Beeston NG9 ....183 E2
  Bingham NG13 ....177 F3
  Caunton NG23 ....109 D2
  Claypole NG23 ....156 C4
  Colston Bassett NG12 ..200 B4
  Cuckney NG20 ....60 A2
  Eakring NG22 ....92 C1
  East Stoke NG23 .....153 E4
  Farndon NG24 ....139 D2
  Halam NG22 ....121 D2
  Harby LE14 ....202 A2
  Kneesall NG22 ....93 F3
  Long Clawson LE14 ..211 E2
  Mansfield Woodhouse
  NG19 ....88 B2
  North Scarle LN6 ......83 E1
  Norwell NG23 ....110 A4
  Ollerton NG22 ....77 D2
  Rempstone LE12 ......215 E3
  South Normanton DE55 ..113 D2
  Whatton NG13 ....179 D2
School Rd Langold S81 ..16 C2
  Selston NG16 ....129 D4
School St
  Kirkby in A NG17 .....115 D3
  Loughborough LE11 ..220 A2
School View NG13 ....181 D1
School Wlk
  Bawtry DN10 ....10 A4
  Bestwood Village NG6 ..146 C2
Scrimshires Rd DN22 ...32 A1
Science Rd NG7 ......172 B1
Scot La DN10 ....10 A4
Scotholme Ave 21 NG7 ..172 C4
Scotholme Prim Sch
  NG7 ....172 C4
Scotland Bank NG12 ..187 F2
Scotland Rd NG5 .....160 C2
Scotswood Rd NG19 ..88 A3
Scott Ave NG9 ....184 A3
Scott Cl Claypole NG23 ..156 B4
  Nottingham NG6 ....159 F3
  Worksop S81 ....36 B2
Scott St
  Gainsborough DN21 ...15 E1
  Whaley Thorns NG20 ..59 D1
Scotton Sq DN22 ......29 E1
Scotts Way NG17 ....115 D1
Scratta La S80 ....34 B1
Scrimshire La NG12 ..187 F2
Script Dr NG6 ....160 C2
Scrivelsby Gdns NG9 ..183 E2
Scrooby Rd Bircotes DN11 ..9 E2
  Harworth DN11 ....8 C2
Seaburn Rd NG9 .....182 C1
Seaford Ave NG8 .....172 A3
Seaford Way DE7 ....157 F3

Seaforth Sq NG19 ....101 E3
Seagrave Ave NG17 ......115 D1
Seagrave Prim Sch
  NG8 ....159 E1
Seagrave Rd NG8 ....159 E1
Seamer Rd NG16 ....158 C4
Searby Rd NG17 ....101 E1
Searwood Ave NG17 ......114 C4
Seatallen Cl NG22 ....186 B2
Seathwaite Cl NG2 ....186 B2
Seatoller Cl NG2 ....186 B3
Seaton Cres NG8 ....160 A1
Second Ave
  Beeston NG9 ....184 B3
  Carlton, Gedling NG4 ...162 C1
  Carlton, Thorneywood
    NG4 ....174 B4
  Clipstone NG21 ....90 A2
  Edwinstowe NG21 ....76 A1
  Mansfield NG21 ....103 F1
  Mansfield Woodhouse
    NG19 ....89 D1
  Nottingham NG6 ....160 A4
Sedgebrook Cl NG6 ......160 B2
Sedgebrook St NG19 .....88 C2
Sedgeley Rd NG12 ....186 B1
Sedgewood Gr NG11 ......184 C2
Sedgley Ave NG2 ....173 F3
Sedgmere DN22 ....39 E2
Sedgwick St
  Langley Mill NG16 ......143 D2
  Westwood NG16 ....128 A2
Sedley Ave NG15 ....159 E3
Seely Ave NG14 ....148 C4
Seely CE Prim Sch
  NG5 ....132 C1
Seely Jun & Inf Sch
  NG5 ....161 E2
Seely Rd NG7 ....222 C3
Sefton Ave NG9 ....182 C4
Sefton Dr NG3 ....161 E1
Selbourne Ct ⚫ LE11 ...220 B2
Selbourne St LE11 ....220 B2
Selby Cl NG9 ....182 C2
Selby La NG12 ....145 F3
Selby Rd Stirrup DN11 ..8 C1
  West Bridgford NG2 .....185 F3
Selhurst Ct NG7 ....172 C4
Selhurst St ⊠ NG7 ....172 C4
Selkirk Way ⊠ NG5 ......161 D1
Sellars Ave NG11 ....196 B3
Sellers Wood Dr NG6 ....160 A4
Sellers Wood Dr W
  NG6 ....159 F4
Sellers Wood Nature
  Reserve* NG6 ....159 F4
Selsey Cl DN22 ....29 F1
Selside Ct NG9 ....183 D2
Selston CE Inf Sch
  NG16 ....128 C3
Selston Dr NG8 ....172 B2
Selston Rd NG16 ....128 A3
Selwyn Cl NG6 ....160 C2
Selwyn St NG18 ....102 C3
Sennen Ct DN22 ....29 F1
Serlby Rd NG16 ....144 A2
Serlby Rise NG3 ....173 F3
Serpentine Cl NG12 .....176 B1
Seven Hills NG24 ....125 D2
Seven Oaks Cres NG9 ...171 E1
Seven Oaks Rd DE7 .....170 A1
Seventh Ave
  Beeston NG9 ....184 B3
  Clipstone NG21 ....89 F1
  Mansfield NG19 ....103 D4
Severals NG9 ....182 C4
Severn St NG6 ....160 A4
Seward St ⊠ LE11 ......220 A2
Seymour Dr
  Eastwood NG16 ....143 F1
  Hucknall NG15 ....145 F3
  West Bridgford NG2 ....186 A4
Seymour St NG3 ....173 F3
Shackleton Cl NG8 ......159 E1
Shacklock Cl NG5 ....147 D1
Shadwell Gr NG12 ....175 F2
Shady La NG9 ....183 E1
Shaftesbury Ave
  Burton Joyce NG14 .....164 A3
  Long Eaton NG10 ....193 D2
  Mansfield NG19 ....87 F1
  Radcliffe on T NG12 ....176 C2
  Sandiacre NG10 ....182 A3
Shaftesbury St ⚫ NG7 ...161 D1
Shaftesbury Way NG12 ..98 A1
Shakespeare Ave NG16 ..88 A2
Shakespeare Cl NG4 .....174 C3
Shakespeare Rd NG16 ..158 B3
Shakespeare St
  Gainsborough DN21 .....24 B3
  Long Eaton NG10 ....182 B1
  Loughborough LE11 .....220 A2
  New Balderton NG24 ...140 A3
  Nottingham NG1 ....223 E3
  Worksop S81 ....36 A2
Shakespeare Villas
  NG1 ....223 E3
Shaldon Cl NG5 ....146 C1
Shandwick Cl NG5 ......148 A1
Shanklin Dr NG9 ....182 B4
Shanwell Cl NG8 ....159 E1
Shardlow Way NG18 ....103 D4
Sharnford Way NG9 .....171 D2
Sharp Cl NG10 ....193 E3
Sharphill Rd NG12 ......186 A2
Sharpley Dr LE12 ....205 F2
Sharrard Cl NG16 ....129 D1
Sharrat Ct NG18 ....103 D1

Shaw Cres NG15 ....145 F2
Shaw Croft NG17 ....100 C3
Shaw Rd DN10 ....12 C2
Shaw St
  Mansfield NG18 ....102 C4
  Ruddington NG11 ......196 B3
  Worksop S80 ....35 F2
Shaw St E DE7 ....170 A3
Shaw St W DE7 ....170 A3
Sheaf Pl S81 ....35 F4
Shearing Cl NG4 ....163 D1
Shearing Hill NG4 ......163 D1
Sheepbridge La NG18 ..101 F3
Sheepfold La NG17 .....196 B3
Sheepwalk La NG15 ....116 C1
Sheepwash La
  Sutton in A NG17 ......101 D1
  Tickhill DN11 ....8 C4
Sheet Stores Ind Est
  NG10 ....193 E3
Sheffield Rd S81 ....18 A2
Shelby Cl NG22 ....222 A2
Sheldon Cl NG10 ....182 A2
Sheldrake Rd NG24 ....140 B4
Shelford Ave NG17 .....114 B3
Shelford Cl
  Beeston NG9 ....183 E2
  Radcliffe on T NG12 ..176 A2
Shelford Cres NG14 ....164 A3
Shelford Dr NG13 ......177 E2
Shelford Hill
  Mansfield NG18 ....101 F3
  Radcliffe on T NG12 ..176 B4
Shelford Rd
  Carlton NG4 ....162 B2
  Radcliffe on T NG12 ..176 A3
Shelford Rise NG3 .....174 A3
Shellburne Cl NG5 .....160 C4
Shelley Ave
  Mansfield Woodhouse
    NG19 ....88 A2
  Nottingham NG11 .....184 C2
Shelley Cl
  Balderton NG24 ....140 B2
  Hucknall NG15 ....145 E3
  Nuthall NG16 ....159 D3
Shelley Rd NG5 ....161 E4
Shelley St S80 ....36 A2
Shelthorpe Ave LE11 ..220 A1
Shelthorpe Prim Sch
  LE11 ....220 A1
Shelton Ave
  Hucknall NG15 ......146 B2
  Newark-on-T NG24 ..139 F3
Shelton Cl NG19 ......87 F1
Shelton Gdns NG11 ..196 A4
Shelton Rd NG18 ....103 D1
Shelton St NG3 ....223 F4
Shenfield Gdns NG15 .146 B1
Shepard Cl NG6 ......159 F3
Shepherd Sch NG8 ...171 F4
Shepherd Wlk DE7 ...203 E1
Shepherds Ave S81 ...35 E2
Shepherds Cl LE12 ...213 E3
Shepherds Cl NG8 ....172 A4
Shepherds La NG7 ....100 C3
Shepherds Way NG17 .101 D1
Shepherds Wood Dr
  NG8 ....172 B4
Shepshed Rd LE12 ...212 C1
Shepton Cl DE7 ......157 E2
Shepton Cres NG8 ...160 A1
Sheraton Dr NG8 ....171 F2
Sherborne Rd
  Nottingham NG8 .....160 A1
  West Bridgford NG2 .185 F3
Sherbrook Ave NG5 ..161 E3
Sherbrook Cl NG14 ..148 C4
Sherbrook Rd NG5 ...161 E3
Sherbrooke Rd NG5 .161 E3
Sherbrooke Rd NG5 .161 D1
Sheridan Cl NG24 ...140 B3
Sheridan Ct NG9 ....170 C1
Sheriffs Way NG2 ...173 E1
Sheringham Cl NG5 .161 F3
Sheringham Dr NG18 .102 B3
Sherman Dr NG9 ....183 E1
Sherriffs Lea NG9 ...182 C1
Sherrington Cl NG11 .195 E4
Sherview Ave NG18 ..103 D4
Sherwin Cl NG3 .....223 E4
Sherwin Gr NG7 ....222 A1
Sherwin Rd
  Nottingham NG7 ....222 A1
  Stapleford NG9 ....170 C1
Sherwin Wlk NG3 ...223 E4
Sherwood Ave
  Blidworth NG21 .....118 B3
  Calverton NG14 .....148 B4
  Edwinstowe NG21 ...76 A1
  Newark-on-T NG24 ..140 A4
  13 Nottingham NG5 .161 D3
  Pinxton NG16 ....113 D2
  Shirebrook NG20 ...72 C2
Sherwood Cl NG18 ...102 C4
Sherwood Cres S81 ..18 A1
Sherwood Day Hospl
Sherwood Dr
  New Ollerton NG22 ..77 E2
  Shirebrook NG20 ...72 C2
Sherwood Forest Art & Craft
  Ctr* NG21 ....76 A2
Sherwood Forest Ctry Pk*
  NG22 ....76 A2
Sherwood Forest Farm Pk*
  NG20 ....89 F4

Sherwood Gr
  Bingham NG13 ....177 E2
  Calverton NG14 ....148 C4
Sherwood Hall Comp Sch
  NG18 ....102 C4
Sherwood Hall Gdns
  NG18 ....102 C4
Sherwood Hall Rd
  NG18 ....102 C4
Sherwood Jun Sch
  NG20 ....74 A2
Sherwood Lodge Dr
  NG21 ....*
Sherwood Pines Forest Pk*
  NG21 ....90 C2
Sherwood Pl
  Annesley Woodhouse
    NG17 ....115 D1
  Clipstone NG21 ......90 A2
Sherwood Rd
  Harworth DN11 ....8 C3
  Rainworth NG21 .....104 B1
  Retford DN22 ....39 F2
  Sutton in A NG17 ...100 C1
  Worksop S80 ....35 F2
Sherwood Rise
  Annesley Woodhouse
    NG17 ....115 D1
  Eastwood NG16 .....143 F1
  Mansfield Woodhouse
    NG19 ....88 C2
  Nottingham NG7 ...173 D4
Sherwood St
  Annesley Woodhouse
    NG17 ....130 A4
  Hucknall NG15 .....146 B3
  Huthwaite NG17 ....99 F2
  Kirkby in A NG17 ...115 D3
  16 Mansfield NG18 .102 A3
  Mansfield Woodhouse
    NG19 ....88 A1
  Market Warsop NG20 .74 A2
  Newton DE55 ....99 D2
Sherwood Vale NG5 ..112 A3
Sherwood Way NG16 .129 D4
Sherwood Wlk NG15 .131 D1
Shetland Cl NG19 ....88 C1
Shilling Way NG10 ...193 D4
Shining Cliff Ct DN10 .9 F4
Shipley Ct DE7 ......157 E1
Shipley Ctry Pk*
  DE75 ....157 D3
Shipley Rd NG8 ......159 F1
Shipley Rise NG4 ...174 C4
Shipstone St
  Ilkeston DE7 ....170 A3
  18 Nottingham NG7 .172 C4
Shipstones Rd NG6 .160 B4
Shirburn Ave NG18 .102 B4
Shire La NG23,NG24 .153 E1
Shirebrook Bsns Pk
  NG20 ....72 C1
Shirebrook Com Sch
  NG20 ....72 B3
Shirebrook Sta NG20 .72 C2
Shirebrooke Cl NG6 .160 B2
Shireoaks Comm
  Shireoaks S81 ......34 C4
  Shireoaks, Gateford Common
    S81 ....35 D4
Shireoaks Ct NG18 ..103 D1
Shireoaks Rd S80 ...35 D3
Shireoaks Row S81 ..34 C4
Shireoaks Sta S81 ...34 C4
Shires The
  Mansfield Woodhouse
    NG19 ....88 C1
  Sutton in A NG17 ...100 B1
Shirland Dr NG18 ...103 D2
Shirley Dr NG5 ......162 A4
Shirley Rd NG3 .....173 E4
Shirley St NG10 ....193 D2
Shoreswood Cl 19 NG5 .161 D4
Short Hill NG1 ......223 F2
Short St
  Market Warsop NG20 .74 A2
  Sutton in A NG17 ...101 D2
Short Wheatley La
  NG23 ....*
Shortcross Ave NG3 .161 F2
Shortwood Ave NG15 .145 F3
Shortwood Cl NG1 ..223 F1
Shortwood La NG22 .93 E4
Shorwell Rd NG3 ...174 B4
Shotton Dr NG5 ....148 A1
Shoulder of Mutton Hill
  NG17 ....115 D1
Shrewsbury Rd
  Bircotes DN11 ......9 D2
  Nottingham NG2 ...174 A2
  Worksop S80 ....36 A1
Shrewsbury View DN22 .29 E1
Shrimpton Ct NG11 .196 B3
Shropshire Ave NG16 .128 B2
Sibcy La NG24 ......140 B2
Sibson Dr DE74 ....203 D1
Sibson Wlk NG5 ...147 F1
Sibthorpe St NG18 .102 A3
Siddalls Dr NG17 ...100 A2
Side La NG22 ....106 C4
Side Ley DE74 .....203 E2
Side Row NG24 ....140 A4
Sidings Rd NG17 ...115 E4
Sidings The
  Aslockton NG13 ...179 D3
  Saxilby LN1 ....57 D2
Sidlaw Rise NG5 ..147 D1
Sidmouth Cl NG12 .197 F2

Sidney Rd NG9 ....183 F4
Sidney St
  Kimberley NG16 .....158 C3
  Long Eaton NG10 ...193 E3
Sidsaph Hill DN10 ...14 A3
Sikorski Cl NG24 ....124 C1
Silbury Cl NG11 .....195 E4
Silk St NG17 ....100 C1
Silken Holme DE55 ..113 D2
Silver Birch Cl NG6 .160 A2
Silver Hill Cl NG8 ...159 E1
Silver St
  Gainsborough DN21 .24 B4
  Grassthorpe NG23 ..81 F2
  North Clifton NG23 .68 C3
  Retford DN22 ......39 E3
Silverdale NG9 ......182 C3
Silverdale Ave NG18 ..88 A2
Silverdale Cl DN22 ..29 E1
Silverdale Rd NG7 ..160 C1
Silverhill Cotts NG17 .100 A4
Silverhill La NG17 ...99 F4
Silverhow Cl NG2 ...186 B4
Silverwood Ave NG15 .117 D1
Silverwood Rd
  Beeston NG9 ....183 F3
  Bottesford NG13 ..181 D1
Silvey Ave NG25 ...121 E1
Sime St NG3 ....35 F2
Simkin Ave NG3 ...162 A1
Simon Cl NG21 ....118 A4
Simone Gdns NG7 .184 C1
Simons Ct NG9 ....171 E1
Simpson Cl NG24 ..140 C2
Simpson Rd NG19 .101 E4
Sir Edmund Hillary Prim Sch
  S81 ....36 A2
Sir John Sherbrooke Jun Sch
  NG14 ....148 C4
Siskin Ct S81 .....35 E4
Sisley Ave NG9 ...182 C3
Sitwell Cl S81 ....36 A2
Sitwell Rd S81 ...36 A2
Six Hills La LE14 .219 D1
Sixth Ave Beeston NG9 .184 B3
  Clipstone NG21 ..89 F1
  Edwinstowe NG21 .76 A1
  Mansfield NG19 ..103 D4
Skeavington's La DE7 .157 F3
Skegby La NG17,
  NG19 ....101 E3
Skegby Mount NG5 .101 F3
Skegby Rd
  Annesley Woodhouse
    NG17 ....129 F4
  Huthwaite NG17 ..100 A2
  Normanton on T NG23 .81 D2
  Sutton in A NG17 .100 C1
Skelwith Cl NG2 ..186 B3
Skerry Hill NG18 ..102 C4
Skerry La NG13 ..181 F1
Sketchley Ct ⚫ NG6 .160 A4
Sketchley St NG3 .173 F3
Skiddaw Cl NG2 ..186 B3
Skipton Cir NG3 ..174 A3
Skipton Cl DE7 ...57 D2
Skirbeck Dr LN1 ..57 D2
Skithorne Rise NG14 .164 B4
Skylark Cl NG13 ..177 F2
Skylark Dr NG6 ..160 B2
Skylark Nature Reserve*
  NG12 ....175 D2
Slack Wlk S80 ....35 F1
Slacks La NG13 ..152 A1
Slade Cl DE55 ...113 D2
Slade Rd NG9 ...183 D3
Slaidburn Ave NG11 .185 D3
Slake La NG24 ..124 C3
Slant La NG19 ..88 A2
Slant The NG20 ..72 B2
Slater St NG17 ..100 C2
Slaughter House La
  NG24 ....124 C1
Sleaford Rd
  Beckingham LN5 ..142 B4
  Coddington NG24 ..126 B1
  Newark-on-T NG24 .125 D1
Sleights La NG16 .113 E1
Sloane Ave NG11 .195 E4
Sloane Ct NG11 ..185 E2
Slowthorne Gdns 🔟
  NG16 ....111 E4
Small Farm Ctr*
  NG13 ....202 C4
Small Gate NG19 ..88 C3
Smalley Cl NG16 ..129 D1
Smalls Croft NG14 .149 E2
Smeath La DN22 ..30 B2
Smeath Rd
  Retford DN22 ....30 A2
  Selston NG16 ....129 D1
Smedley Ave DE7 .170 A4
Smedley Cl NG8 ..160 A1
Smedleys Ave NG10 .182 A3
Smeeton St DE75 .143 D1
Smite Cl NG13 ...179 D1
Smite La NG13 ...179 F4
Smith Cl NG16 ...143 D2
Smith Sq DN11 ..8 C2
Smith St
  Mansfield NG18 ..102 C3
  Newark-on-T NG24 .140 A4
Smithfield Ave NG9 .170 B2
Smiths Cl NG12 ..189 D2
Smithson Cl NG24 .140 B2
Smithson Dr NG8 ..171 F2
Smithurst Rd NG16 .158 A4

Smithy Cl NG11 .....184 B1
Smithy Cres NG5 ...161 F4
Smithy La LE12 .....212 A1
Smithy Row NG1 ...223 E2
Smithy View NG14 ..148 C4
Snaefell Ave NG19 ..89 D1
Snape La DN11 .....9 D1
Snape Nook Ct NG6 .159 F4
Snape Wood Prim Sch
  NG6 ....160 A4
Snape Wood Rd NG6 .159 F4
Snead Ct NG5 ....147 D1
Sneinton Bvd NG2 .174 A3
Sneinton Dale NG2 .174 A3
Sneinton Hermitage
  NG2 ....173 F2
Sneinton Hollows
  NG2 ....173 F2
Sneinton Rd NG2 ..173 F2
Sneinton St Stephens CE Prim
  Sch NG2 ....173 F2
Snell Cl NG17 ....81 F1
Snipe Pk Rd DN11 ..9 D2
Snowdon Cl NG5 ...147 D1
Snowdon Rd NG24 .125 D1
Soar La
  Normanton on S LE12 .213 E2
  Sutton Bonington LE12 .212 C4
Soarbank Cl NG16 ..158 C4
Sobers Gdns NG5 ..162 A3
Softwood Cl NG6 ..159 F4
Soloman Pk NG16 ..158 A1
Soloman Rd NG16 ..158 A1
Solway Cl NG9 ....183 F3
Somerby Ct NG9 ...171 D2
Somerby Rd DN21 .15 F1
Somersall St NG19 .101 F4
Somersby Rd NG5 .162 A3
Somersby Rd NG5 .162 A3
Somerset Cl NG10 .194 A4
Somerton Ave NG11 .185 D2
Sonning Ave NG6 ..160 B2
Sookholme Cl NG20 .72 C2
Sookholme La NG20 .74 A2
Sookholme La NG20 .73 F3
Sookholme Rd
  Market Warsop NG20 .73 F1
  Shirebrook NG20 ..72 C2
Sophie Rd NG7 ...222 B4
Sorrel Dr NG13 ..177 E2
Soss La DN10 ...7 D1
Sotheby Ave NG17 .101 E1
Soudan Dr NG2 ..173 D1
Sough Rd DE55 ..113 D4
Souldern Cl Bawtry DN10 .10 A4
  Radcliffe on T NG12 ..176 A2
  Rainworth NG21 ...104 A1
  Shirebrook NG20 ..72 C2
  Worksop S80 .....36 A1
South Cl
  Bottesford NG13 ..181 D1
  Clipstone NG21 ...90 A2
South Croft NG22 .51 F1
South Cty Jun Sch
  NG2 ....185 F3
South Devon Ave NG3 .162 A1
South Dr
  Balderton NG24 ..140 C1
  Bilsthorpe NG22 ..105 F4
  Nottingham NG8 ..172 A3
South E Derbyshire Coll
  DE7 ....170 A3
South End NG23 ..111 F4
South La NG23 ...81 F3
South Moor Rd DN10 .13 F2
South Nottingham Coll
  Nottingham NG11 .185 D1
  West Bridgford NG2 .185 E3
South Par Bawtry DN10 .10 A3
  Gainsborough DN21 .24 C4
  Nottingham NG1 ..223 E2
  Saxilby LN1 ......57 D2
  Worksop S81 ....36 A2
South Rd Beeston NG9 .184 A2
  Nottingham, Dunkirk
    NG7 ....172 B1
  Nottingham, The Park
    NG7 ....222 C1
  West Bridgford NG2 .185 F3
South Ridge Dr NG18 .102 B2
South Scarle La LN6 .83 E1
South Scarle Rd NG23 .98 A1
South Sherwood St
  NG1 ....223 E3
South Snape Cl NG6 .159 F4
South St Stoke DN22 .23 F1
  Eastwood, Bailey Grove
    NG16 ....143 F1
  Eastwood, Giltbrook
    NG16 ....158 B4
  Hucknall NG15 ....146 A4
  Long Eaton NG10 .193 F4
  Loughborough LE11 .220 A2
  Morton DN21 ....15 D2
  Normanton on T NG23 .81 F3
  Retford DN22 ....39 F3
  South Normanton DE55 .113 D3
South View
  Carlton NG4 .....3 E1
  Worksop S81 ....35 F3
South View Dr DN22 .30 B2
South View Rd NG4 .162 B1
South Wilford CE Prim Sch
  NG2 ....185 D4
South Wolds Comp Sch
  NG12 ....197 F2

South Yorkshire Air Mus*
S81 ....16 A4
Southampton St NG3 ....173 F3
Southbeck Rise S80 ......36 A1
Southchurch Dr NG7 ....184 C1
Southcliffe Rd NG4 ......174 B4
Southdale Dr NG4 ....174 B4
Southdale Rd NG4 ....174 B4
Southdene S81 ....36 A3
Southend Ave NG24 ......139 F4
Southern Wood S80 ......46 C4
Southey St NG7 ....222 C4
Southfall Cl DN22 ....19 D3
Southfield NG24 ....140 C2
Southfield Dr DE55 ......113 E3
Southfield Ind Site S80 ..45 D2
Southfield La S80 ....45 D2
Southfield Rd NG8 ....172 B3
Southfields NG10 ....193 F4
Southfields Ave NG16 ....113 E2
Southfields Cl NG17 .....114 C1
Southfields Rise DN22 ...42 B4
Southgate Rd NG20 ......74 B3
Southglade Jun & Inf Sch
NG5 ....161 D4
Southglade Rd NG5 ......160 C3
Southpore La DN22 ......42 B4
Southgreen Cl NG18 .....102 C1
Southgreen Hill NG18 ...102 C1
Southlands Ave DN21 ...15 D2
Southlands Dr DN21 .....15 D2
Southlands Gdns DN21 ..15 D2
Southlea Rd NG4 ....174 B4
Southmoor La LN1 ....69 D4
Southmoor Rd S80 ....36 A1
Southolme DN21 ....24 B4
Southpark Ave NG18 ....102 C1
Southport Terr 4 NG7 ...222 C4
Southside NG5 ....162 B4
Southwark Gdns NG15 ...117 D1
Southwark Inf Sch
NG6 ....160 B2
Southwark Jun Sch
NG6 ....160 C2
Southwark St NG6 ......160 C2
Southwell Cl
East Leake LE12 ....205 F1
Kirkby in A NG17 ....115 D3
Worksop S80 ....36 A1
Southwell La NG17 ......114 C3
Southwell La Ind Est
NG17 ....115 D4
Southwell Minster*
NG25 ....136 C2
Southwell Rd
Farnsfield NG22 ....120 A3
Kirklington NG22 ....120 C4
Lowdham NG14 ....150 C1
Nottingham NG1 ....223 F2
Oxton NG25 ....134 B2
Thurgarton NG14 ....151 E4
Southwell Rd E
Mansfield NG21 ....103 F1
Rainworth NG21 ....118 A4
Southwell Rd W NG18 ..102 C3
Southwell Rise NG16 ...158 A4
Southwold Dr NG8 ......172 B3
Southwolds Prim Sch
NG8 ....172 B3
Southwood Ave NG17 ...100 B2
Sovereign Gr NG10 .....193 D4
Sowter Ave NG17 ....100 C2
Spa Cl NG17 ....114 C4
Spa La NG13 ....180 A4
Spa Rd DN22 ....39 F3
Spafford Cl DN21 ....44 B4
Spalding Rd NG3 ....173 F3
Spalford La LN6 ....83 E2
Spalford Rd LN6 ....83 F4
Spalford Warren (Nature
Reserve)* NG23 ....83 D3
Spang La NG17 ....99 F2
Spaniel Row NG1 ......223 E2
Sparken Cl S80 ....46 C4
Sparken Dale S80 ......46 C4
Sparrow Cl DE7 ....170 A2
Sparrow Hill 15 LE11 ..220 A2
Sparrow La NG23 ......68 A1
Spean Ct 11 NG8 ......172 A3
Spean Dr NG8 ....172 A4
Speeds Pingle 1 LE11 .220 A2
Speedwell La NG16 ....158 C3
Speedwell Pl S80 ......35 F2
Spencer Ave
Arnold NG3 ....162 B3
Sandiacre NG10 ....182 A3
Spencer Cl NG11 .....196 A4
Spencer Cres NG9 ....182 C4
Spencer Dr NG16 .....159 E3
Spencer St NG18 .....102 A3
Sperry Cl NG16 ....128 C3
Spey Cl NG15 ....145 E2
Spicer Cl NG9 ....183 E1
Spindle Gdns NG6 ....160 A4
Spindle View NG14 ...148 C3
Spinney Cl
Cotgrave NG12 ....187 F1
Kirkby in A NG17 .....114 C3
Mansfield Woodhouse
NG19 ....88 C3
Newark-on-T NG24 ...139 F3
West Bridgford NG2 ..186 B2
Spinney Cres NG9 ....182 C1
Spinney Dr NG10 .....182 B1

Spinney Rd
Bingham NG13 ....177 E2
Keyworth NG12 ....197 F2
Long Eaton NG10 .....182 B1
Spinney Rise NG9 ....182 C2
Spinney The
Arnold NG5 ....161 F2
Bestwood Village NG6 ..146 C3
Bulcote NG14 ....164 A3
Elston NG23 ....153 E3
Mansfield NG18 ......116 B4
Shirebrook NG20 .....72 B2
Winthorpe NG24 .....125 E3
Spinney Way NG11 ...185 D2
Spinneymead DN22 ...19 D3
Spinningdale NG5 ....162 A4
Spire View NG13 .....181 D2
Spital Hill
Gainsborough DN21 ..15 F1
Retford DN22 ....39 F4
Spital La NG18 ....18 A1
Spital Terr DN21 ....15 E1
Spitalfields S81 .....18 A1
Spondon St NG5 .....161 E1
Sporton Cl DE55 ....113 D4
Sporton La DE55 ....113 D4
Spouth View S80 ....45 D3
Spray Cl NG4 ....174 C3
Spridgeon Cl NG10 ..182 A1
Spright Cl NG4 .....125 E3
Spring Cl NG16 .....159 D4
Spring Ct NG22 ....119 F4
Spring Dale Gdns
NG9 ....170 B2
Spring Dr NG24 ....140 C1
Spring Gdn Terr DE7 .157 F1
Spring Gdns
Bawtry DN10 ....10 A4
Gainsborough DN21 ..24 B4
Newark-on-T NG24 ..139 F4
Spring Gn NG11 ....195 F4
Spring Hill
Kimberley NG16 ....158 C3
Mansfield Woodhouse
NG19 ....88 A2
Southwell NG25 ....136 C4
Whitwell S80 ....45 D3
Spring La Arnold NG3 .162 C3
Balderton NG24 ....140 C1
Elmton NG20 ....58 A4
Farnsfield NG22 ...119 F1
Flintham NG13 .....166 C4
Lambley NG4 ......163 D3
Long Whatton LE12 .212 B1
Shireoaks S80 .....34 C3
Sturton le S DN22 .32 A3
Spring Mdw NG12 ..188 A2
Spring Moor NG2 ..174 B3
Spring Rd
Nottingham NG6 ....160 B4
Sutton in A NG17 ..100 C1
Spring St
Hucknall NG15 ....146 A4
Whitwell S80 ......45 D3
Spr St Prim Sch
NG15 ....146 A4
Spring Terr NG16 ..159 E3
Spring The NG10 ..193 E3
Spring Wlk S80 ....35 F1
Springdale La NG13 .165 F1
Springfield DE74 ..203 D1
Springfield Ave
Eastwood NG16 ....144 A1
Long Eaton NG10 ..193 F4
Sandiacre NG10 ...182 A2
Shirebrook NG20 ..72 C3
Springfield Cl
Cropwell Bishop NG12 .189 D2
Gainsborough DN21 ..24 C4
Mansfield NG18 ....103 D3
Springfield Ct NG9 .170 C1
Springfield Dr NG6 .159 F3
Springfield Gdn DE7 .157 F1
Springfield Prim Sch
NG6 ....146 B1
Springfield Rd
Arnold NG5 ....147 F1
Hucknall NG15 ....145 E3
Retford DN22 ....39 F4
Southwell NG25 ...121 E1
Springfield Ret Pk
NG6 ....160 B4
Springfield St NG7 .160 C1
Springfield Way NG17 .115 E3
Springfields NG2 ..185 E3
Springhead Ct NG6 .166 A1
Springhill Cl NG6 ..146 A1
Springland Farm Cotts
NG16 ....159 E3
Springs Rd DN10 ..83 F3
Springthorpe Rd DN21 .24 C4
Springwell St NG17 .99 F1
Springwood Gdns
NG5 ....161 F2
Springwood View Cl
NG17 ....100 B2
Spruce Ave NG16 ..128 B3
Spruce Ct S80 .....35 D1
Spruce Gdns NG6 ..160 A4
Spruce Gr
Hucknall NG15 ....146 A3
Kirkby in A NG17 ..115 E3
Sprydon Wlk NG11 .195 F4
Spur Cres S80 .....47 D4
Square The
Beeston NG9 ....183 F3
Bestwood Village NG6 .146 C2
Bottesford NG13 ..181 D2

Square The continued
Costock LE12 ....206 B1
Gotham NG11 ....195 D1
Keyworth NG12 .....197 F1
Nottingham NG8 ...171 F2
Radcliffe on T NG12 .176 A1
Retford DN22 ......39 F4
Squires Ave NG6 ..160 A4
Squires Cl NG12 ..189 D2
Squires Croft NG6 .90 B3
Squires La NG21 ..90 A3
Squires Way NG2 ..185 E3
Squirrel Way 3 LE11 .220 A1
Stable Cl
East Bridgford NG13 .165 E2
Worksop S81 ....36 A4
Stacey Ave NG5 ...160 C4
Stacey Rd NG5 ....87 E1
Stadium Cl S81 ...35 E3
Stadium Ind Pk NG10 .193 F4
Stafford Ave
New Balderton NG24 .140 B2
Nottingham NG6 ..160 A3
Stafford Ct NG6 ..159 F3
Stafford St
Long Eaton NG10 .193 F4
Mansfield NG19 ..101 F4
Staffords Acre DE74 .203 E1
Stagsden Cres NG8 .171 E3
Staindale Dr NG8 ..160 B1
Stainforth St NG19 .88 B1
Stainmore Gr NG13 .177 E2
Stainsborough Rd
NG15 ....145 E3
Stainsby Dr NG18 .103 D4
Stainsby Gr NG17 ..99 F1
Stamford Cl NG10 .193 F2
Stamford Ct 2 NG5 .161 D4
Stamford Rd NG2 .186 A3
Stamford St
Awsworth NG16 ...158 B2
Eastwood NG16 ...144 B1
3 Ilkeston DE7 ...157 F1
Stamper Cres NG17 .100 C3
Stanage Ct NG18 .103 D3
Stancliffe Ave NG6 .160 B4
Standard Hill NG1 .223 D2
Standhill Ave NG4 .174 A4
Standhill Inf Sch NG4 .174 A4
Standhill Rd NG4 ..174 A4
Stanesby Rise NG7 .184 C1
Stanford Gdns NG12 .197 F3
Stanford Hall (Co-Operative
Coll) LE12 ....214 C2
Stanford Hill 4 LE11 .220 A2
Stanford La NG12 .220 B4
Stanford Rd NG9 ..213 F1
Stanford St NG1 ..223 E2
Stanhome Dr NG2 .185 E2
Stanhome Sq NG2 .185 E2
Stanhope Ave NG24 .125 E2
Stanhope Cl NG22 .64 A1
Stanhope Cres
Arnold NG5 ....161 F4
Stoke Bardolph NG14 .175 F4
Stanhope Prim Sch
NG4 ....162 B2
Stanhope Rd
Arnold NG5 ....161 F4
Carlton NG4 ......162 B2
Stanhope St
Ilkeston DE7 ......170 A3
Long Eaton NG10 .193 E4
Nottingham NG1 .223 F2
Stanhope Way NG13 .177 F2
Staniland Cl 3 NG9 .183 E1
Stanley Ave 5 NG7 .173 D4
Stanley Cl NG15 ..117 D2
Stanley Dr NG9 ..171 D1
Stanley La NG17 ..85 E1
Stanley Pl NG1 ...223 D3
Stanley Rd
Mansfield NG18 ..102 A2
Mansfield Woodhouse
NG19 ....89 D1
Nottingham, Hyson Green
NG3 ....173 D4
Nottingham, Porchester
NG3 ....162 A1
West Bridgford NG2 .185 F3
Stanley St
Gainsborough DN21 .24 B3
Long Eaton NG10 ..193 F4
Loughborough LE11 .220 A1
Newark-on-T NG24 ..125 D1
Retford DN22 ......40 A2
Worksop S81 ......35 F3
Stanley Terr NG24 .140 A4
Stanmore Cl NG8 ..159 F2
Stanmore Gdns NG5 .161 F3
Stansfield St NG7 ..222 A3
Stanstead Ave
Nottingham NG5 ..146 B1
Tollerton NG12 ...186 B1
Stanstead Prim Sch
NG5 ....160 B4
Stanthorne Cl NG11 .185 D2
Stanton Cres NG17 .100 B2
Stanton Gate DE7 .170 B1
Stanton La NG12 ..198 A1
Stanton Pl
Mansfield NG18 ..102 A4
New Houghton NG19 .86 C4
Nottingham NG1 .223 D3
Stanton Rd NG10 .182 A4
Stanton St NG19 ..86 C4
Stanway Cl NG3 ..174 B3
Stanwick Cl NG8 ..171 F4
Staple La NG24 ...140 B1

Stapleford La
Beeston NG9 ....182 C2
Brough NG23 ....112 B1
Coddington NG24 ..126 B2
Stapleford Rd NG9 .170 B2
Staplehurst Dr NG5 .161 D2
Staples St NG3 ....161 F1
Starch Cl LE12 ....205 F1
Starch La NG10 ...182 B4
Starr Ave NG17 ...100 B2
Starth Wood Rd NG15 .145 E2
Statham Ct S81 ...36 A3
Stathern La LE14 .202 A1
Stathern Rd LE14 .202 B2
Stathern Wlk NG5 .161 D4
Station Ave
Carlton NG4 ....163 D1
Ranskill DN22 ....11 D3
Station Cl NG23 ..112 A4
Station Ct 10 DE7 .157 F1
Station Hill NG19 .88 A2
Station La
Edwinstowe NG21 .76 A1
Farnsfield NG22 ..119 F4
Ironville NG16 ....128 A2
Old Dalby LE14 ...218 C2
Station Rd
Mansfield NG18 ..158 B3
Barnby Moor DN22 .28 C3
Bawtry DN10 ......10 A4
Beckingham DN10 .23 E4
Beeston NG9 ......184 A2
Bingham NG13 ...151 F4
Bottesford NG13 .181 E2
Burton Joyce NG14 .163 F2
Carlton NG4 ......174 C4
Clipstone NG21 ..89 F1
Collingham NG23 .112 A4
East Leake LE12 .205 E1
Edingley NG22 ...120 C3
Fiskerton NG25,NG23 .137 F2
Harby NG23 ......70 C2
Heanor NG16 .....143 D1
Hucknall NG15 ..146 A4
Ilkeston DE7 .....157 F1
Kegworth DE74 .203 F1
Keyworth NG12 ..197 F3
Kimberley NG16 .158 C3
Kingston-on-S LE12 .204 A2
Langley Mill NG16 .143 D1
Long Eaton NG10 .193 F4
Lowdham NG14 ..150 C1
Mansfield NG18 ..102 A3
Misson DN10 .....11 D1
Newstead NG15 ..130 C3
Nottingham NG6 ..160 B3
Ollerton NG22 ...77 D2
Rainworth NG21 .118 A4
Ranskill DN22 ....11 D3
Retford DN22 ....39 F3
Rolleston NG23 ..138 A3
Sandiacre NG10 .182 B3
Scrooby DN10 ....10 B1
Selston NG16 ....113 F1
Shirebrook NG20 .72 C3
South Leverton DN22 .42 B4
Southwell NG25 .121 F1
Sutton in A NG17 .101 D1
Sutton on T NG23 .96 C4
Thurgarton NG14 .151 E3
Torksey LN1 .....44 A4
Upper Broughton LE14 .218 B4
Walkeringham DN10 .14 A3
Whitwell S80 .....45 D3
Widmerpool NG12 .208 C3
Station St
Bingham NG13 ...177 F3
Cossall DE7 ....158 A1
Kirkby in A NG17 .115 D3
Long Eaton NG10 .193 F4
Mansfield NG18 ..102 A3
Mansfield Woodhouse
NG19 ....88 A2
Misterton DN10 ..7 D1
Nottingham NG2 .223 F1
Sutton in A NG17 .100 C1
Station Terr
Hucknall NG15 ..146 A4
Radcliffe on T NG12 .175 F2
Station View NG20 .72 C2
Station Vd NG17 .100 C4
Staunton Dr NG5 .161 E2
Staunton Hall* NG13 .169 D2
Staveley Ct
Farndon NG24 ...139 D2
6 Loughborough LE11 .220 A3
Staverton Rd NG8 .171 F4
Staythorpe Rd
Averham NG23 ...123 F1
Rolleston NG23 ..138 B4
Steadfold Cl NG6 .160 A3
Steads Cl NG14 ..164 A2
Steedman Ave NG3 .162 A2
Steeles Way NG4 .163 D4
Steeple Row 16 LE11 .220 A2
Steetley La
Rhodesia S80 ....35 D2
Whitwell S80 .....34 C2
Steinbeck Rd NG4 .174 B4
Stella Ave NG12 .187 F2
Stella Gr NG12 ..197 E4
Stella St NG18 ..102 A3
Stenton Cl NG25 ..121 F1
Stepnall Hts NG22 .77 F3
Stepney Ct NG8 ..159 F1

Sterling Cl S81 ....35 F4
Sterndale Rd NG10 ..193 D3
Sternthorpe Cl NG23 .81 F1
Steven Cl NG9 .....182 C2
Stevenholme Cres
NG5 ....161 D3
Stevens Rd NG10 ..182 A3
Stevenson Cres NG17 .100 C1
Stevenson Gdns NG11 .196 B3
Stevenson Jun Sch
NG9 ....182 C4
Stevenson Rd S81 .36 A2
Stewart Cl S81 ....25 F3
Stewart Rd S81 ...25 F3
Stewarton Cl NG5 .148 A1
Stiles Rd NG5 .....162 B3
Stillwell Gdns S81 .35 F4
Stinsford Cl 6 NG5 .161 E4
Stinting La
Mansfield Woodhouse
NG19 ....88 C1
Shirebrook NG20 .72 B1
Stirling Ave
Bawtry DN10 .....10 A4
Mansfield NG19 .101 F3
Stirling Cl DN21 ..25 F1
Stirling Dr S81 ...25 F3
Stirling Gdns NG9 .183 D1
Stirling Gr
Kimberley NG16 .158 C4
Nottingham NG11 .195 F4
Stirling Rd DN22 .39 E3
Stock Well NG6 ..160 A3
Stockdale Cl NG5 .147 D1
Stockgill Cl NG2 .186 B3
Stockhill Cir NG8 .160 B1
Stockhill La NG6 .160 B2
Stocking La
Askham DN22 ....51 F2
East Leake LE12 .205 E2
Stocks Rd NG16 ..158 C4
Stockton St 8 NG6 .160 B4
Stockwell Gate 20 NG18 .102 A4
Stockwell La NG12 .189 D2
Stockwell The LE12 .216 B2
Stockwith Rd DN10 .14 A4
Stodman Mews NG24 .139 F4
Stodman St NG24 .139 F4
Stoke Ave NG2 ...139 F4
Stoke Ferry La NG12 .164 A1
Stoke La
Burton Joyce NG14 .163 F1
Stoke Bardolph NG14 .175 E4
Stokes Trad Est NG18 .101 F2
Stolle Cl NG5 .....148 B4
Stone Bridge Rd NG3 .173 F3
Stone Cres NG19 .101 E4
Stone Cross La NG18 .102 A4
Stone La DN22 ...31 E4
Stone Mdws NG10 .193 F3
Stoneacre NG5 ..161 D4
Stonebridge Ct Ind Est 15
NG3 ....173 F3
Stonebridge La NG20 .74 A2
Stonebridge Rd NG20 .74 A2
Stonechurch View
NG15 ....130 A4
Stonehaven Cl NG5 .148 A1
Stonehill Cl DN22 .203 E1
Stonehurst La LE12 .213 E2
Stoneleigh Cl NG9 .183 E3
Stoneleigh St NG7 .222 C3
Stonemasons Mews
NG17 ....115 D3
Stonepit Cl NG3 .161 F3
Stoney Bank NG14 .150 B1
Stoney Houghton Gdns
NG6 ....159 F4
Stoney La
Brinsley NG16 ...143 E3
Selston NG16 ...128 C4
Trowell NG9 .....170 A3
Stoney St Beeston NG9 .183 F4
Nottingham NG1 .223 F2
Sutton in A NG17 .101 D2
Stoneyford Rd NG17 .100 C2
Stonish Hill NG22 .92 B1
Stoppard Cl DE7 .157 E1
Storcroft Rd DN22 .40 A3
Storey Ave NG4 ..162 C1
Stormont Cl DE55 .113 D2
Stornoway Cl NG9 .184 A3
Stort Sq NG19 ...88 B1
Storth Ave NG15 .146 A3
Storth La DN55 ..113 D2
Storthfield Way DE55 .113 D2
Story Gdns NG15 .146 B3
Stotfield Rd NG8 .171 D3
Stourdale Cl NG10 .193 D3
Stow Ct NG9 .....88 C2
Stow Pk Rd DN21 .44 B4
Stowe Ave NG2 ..185 E3
Stradford St DN21 .24 B4
Straight Mile DN22 .38 B3
Strand The NG9 ..183 F1
Stranraer Cl NG9 .182 B3
Stratford Cl NG4 .174 C3
Stratford Cres DN22 .39 E3
Stratford Rd NG2 .185 F4
Strathaven Rd S81 .25 F3
Strathglen Cl NG16 .158 C4
Strathmore Cl DN11 .9 D3
Strathmore Dr S81 .25 F3

Strathmore Rd NG5 .....148 A1
Strawberry Bank NG17 ...99 F2
Strawberry Hall La
NG24 ....125 D1
Strawberry Rd NG22 ......40 A3
Strawberry Way NG19 ..103 D4
Straws La NG13 ....165 E2
Street La Rd DN22 ....42 C4
Strelley La NG8 ....171 D4
Strelley Rd NG8 ....159 F1
Strelley St NG6 ....160 A4
Strelley Edge Cl
NG10 ....182 A1
Stripe Rd DN11 ....8 B4
Stripes View NG14 ....148 C3
Strome Cl NG2 ....173 D1
Strome Ct 1 NG2 ....173 E1
Stroud Cl NG13 ....181 D2
Strouds Cl LE14 ....211 F4
Stuart Ave
Mansfield NG18 ....102 C4
New Ollerton NG22 ....77 E3
Stuart Cl NG5 ....162 A4
Stuart St
Mansfield NG18 ....102 C4
Sutton in A NG17 ....100 C1
Stubbin Wood Sch
NG20 ....72 C3
Stubbing La S80 ....35 E2
Stubbins La NG25 ....136 B3
Stubbins Wood NG20 .....72 C2
Stubbins Wood La
NG20 ....72 C3
Stubton Rd NG23 ....156 C3
Studland Cl NG19 ....88 B3
Studland Way NG2 ......185 E3
Sturgate Wlk DN21 ....24 C4
Sturgeon Ave NG11 .....184 C2
Sturton CE Prim Sch
DN22 ....122 B2
Sturton Rd Boie DN22 ....23 E1
  North Leverton w H DN22 .32 B1
  Saxilby LN1 ....57 D4
  South Wheatley DN22 ....31 F4
Sturton St NG7 ....173 D4
Styring St NG9 ....183 F3
Styrrup La DN11 ....8 A1
Styrrup Rd DN11 ....8 C2
Sudbury Ave
  Ilkeston DE7 ....170 A4
  Sandiacre NG10 ....182 A3
Sudbury Cl NG18 ....103 D3
Sudbury Dr NG17 ....99 F1
Sudbury Mews NG16 ....143 F1
Suez St NG7 ....160 C1
Suff La NG16 ....113 E2
Suffolk Ave
  Beeston NG9 ....184 B2
  Bircotes DN11 ....9 E2
  Hucknall NG15 ....145 E3
Suffolk Gr DN11 ....9 E2
Suffolk Rd DN11 ....9 E2
Sulby Cl NG19 ....89 D1
Sullivan Cl NG3 ....174 A3
Sumburgh Rd NG11 .....185 D1
Summer Hill DN21 ....15 F1
Summer Leys La NG2 ...223 F1
Summer Way NG12 ......175 F2
Summercourt Dr
NG15 ....116 C2
Summerfield Rd 11
NG17 ....114 C4
Summerfields Way
DE7 ....157 E2
Summerfields Way S
DE7 ....157 E2
Summergangs La DN21 ...24 B3
Summers Rd NG24 ......125 D1
Summerwood La
NG11 ....195 F4
Summit Cl NG17 ....115 D3
Summit Dr NG20 ....72 C2
Sunbeam St NG13 ....179 D2
Sunbourne Ct NG7 ......222 C4
Sunbury Gdns NG5 .....148 A1
Sunderland Gr NG8 .....159 E1
Sunderland Pl DN11 ....8 A4
Sunderland St NG17 ......8 A4
Sundown Adventure Land*
DN22 ....82 C2
Sundridge Pk Cl NG2 ..185 E3
Sunfield Ave S81 ....36 A2
Sunlea Cres NG9 ....182 C3
Sunninndale Dr NG12 ...186 C1
Sunninghall Dr NG12 .....39 E1
Sunningdale Cl 4
NG17 ....114 C4
Sunningdale Dr NG14 ..149 E2
Sunningdale Rd NG6 ...160 C3
Sunninghill Dr NG11 ...184 C2
Sunninghill Rise NG5 ..148 A1
Sunny Bank
  Mansfield NG18 ....102 B2
  Newton DE55 ....99 D3
  Worksop S81 ....94 B2
Sunnydale Rd NG3 ......174 A3
Sunnymede S81 ....36 A3
Sunnyside
  Farnsfield NG22 ....119 F3
  Whitwell S80 ....45 D3
  Worksop S81 ....35 F3
Sunnyside Prim Sch
NG9 ....183 D3
Sunnyside NG9 ....183 E3
Sunridge Ct NG3 ....173 E4
Sunrise Ave NG5 ....160 C3
Surbiton Sq NG8 ....160 A2
Surfleet Cl NG11 ....171 E2

Surgery La NG21 ....118 A2
Surgeys La NG5 ....148 A1
Surrey Dr NG19 ....101 F4
Susan Cl NG15 ....131 D1
Susan Dr NG6 ....160 B2
Sutherland Ave
Sutherland Dr NG2 .....186 A2
Sutherland Rd NG3 ....174 A4
Suthers Rd DE74 ....203 E1
Sutton Ave NG24 ....139 F3
Sutton Bonington Prim Sch
LE12 ....213 D3
Sutton Cl
Sutton Bonington LE12 .213 E3
  Sutton in A NG17 ....101 D3
Sutton Ct NG16 ....143 F1
Sutton Gdns NG11 ......196 B3
Sutton La Granby NG13 .191 E3
  Retford DN22 ....29 D1
Sutton Mid La NG17 ....114 C3
Sutton on Trent Prim Sch
NG23 ....97 D4
Sutton Parkway Sta
NG17 ....115 D4
Sutton Passeys Cres
NG8 ....172 A2
Sutton Rd Arnold NG5 .147 F1
  Beckingham LN5 ....142 C3
  Huthwaite NG17 ....87 F2
  Kegworth DE74 ....203 E1
  Kirkby in a NG17 ....114 C3
  Mansfield NG18 ....101 F3
  Sutton in A NG17 ....100 C3
Sutton Rd Prim Sch
NG18 ....101 F3
Sutton-cum-Lound CE Prim
Sch DN22 ....29 D3
Swabs La
  Cropwell Bishop NG12 .188 C1
  Owthorpe NG12 ....199 F4
Swains Ave NG3 ....174 A3
Swaledale S81 ....36 A4
Swaledale Cl NG8 ....160 B1
Swales Cl DN22 ....39 E4
Swallow Cl
  Mansfield NG18 ....103 D2
  Nottingham NG6 ....160 B2
Swallow Ct NG10 ....7 F1
Swallow Dr
  Bingham NG13 ....177 F2
  Claypole NG23 ....156 B4
Swallow Gdns NG4 ......142 C4
Swallow Gr S81 ....35 E4
Swallow Wlk LE12 ......213 D1
Swallows Dr LE14 ......202 C2
Swan Ct
  Sutton Bonington LE12 .213 D3
  Worksop S81 ....35 E4
Swan La NG19 ....88 A2
Swan Mdw NG14 ....174 C2
Swan St Bawtry DN10 ...10 A3
  Loughborough LE11 ....220 A2
Swann Yd NG17 ....99 F2
Swans Quay DN22 ....79 F3
Swansdowne Dr NG7 ..184 C1
Swanson Ave NG17 ....99 F2
Swanwick Ave NG20 .....72 C3
Sweeney Ct 3 NG5 ....161 D4
Sweet Leys Dr LE12 ....205 F2
Sweet Leys Rd 10 NG2 173 E1
Swenson Ave NG7 ......222 A1
Swift Cl NG16 ....143 F1
Swifts Cl LE12 ....216 B2
Swigert Cl NG6 ....159 F3
Swildon Wlk NG5 ....160 C4
Swinburne Ct NG24 ....140 B3
Swinburne St 22 NG3 .173 F3
Swinburne Way NG5 ...161 E4
Swinderby Rd
Collingham NG23 ....112 A4
Eagle LN6 ....84 B1
North Scarle LN6 ....83 F1
Swindon Cl NG16 ....158 B4
Swinecote Rd NG21 ......76 A2
Swiney Way NG9 ....183 D1
Swinfen Broun NG18 ...102 B2
Swingate NG16 ....159 D3
Swinnow Rd DN11 ....9 E2
Swinscoe Gdns NG5 ...160 C4
Swinstead Cl NG8 ....171 F3
Swinton Coppe NG21 ....77 F3
Swinton Rise NG15 .....117 D1
Swish La NG22 ....105 F4
Swithland Dr NG2 ....185 F2
Swynford Cl LN1 ....55 D2
Sycamore Ave
Glapwell S44 ....86 A4
Kirkby in a NG17 ....114 C3
Sycamore Cl
Bawtry DN10 ....9 F4
Sandiacre NG10 ....182 A4
Sycamore Ct NG9 ......184 A4
Sycamore Dr
Coddington NG24 ....126 A1
Gainsborough DN21 .....15 F1
Ilkeston DE7 ....170 A4
Sycamore Gr NG18 ....102 C3

Sycamore Inf Sch
NG3 ....223 F4
Sycamore Jun Sch
NG3 ....223 F4
Sycamore La NG14 .....152 A4
Sycamore Millennium Ctr
NG3 ....173 D4
Sycamore Pl 4 NG3 ...173 E4
Sycamore Rd
  Awsworth NG16 ....158 B3
  Carlton in L S81 ....25 F4
  East Leake LE12 ....214 B4
  Long Eaton NG10 ......193 E3
  Mansfield Woodhouse
NG19 ....88 B3
  New Ollerton NG22 ......77 F2
Sycamore Rise NG6 ....160 B1
Sycamore St NG20 ....74 A3
Sycamores The
Eastwood NG16 ....143 F1
  South Normanton DE55 .113 D3
Sydenham Ct 1 NG7 ...172 C1
Syderstone Wlk NG5 ...161 F3
Sydney Cl NG19 ....88 B3
Sydney Gr NG12 ....175 F2
Sydney Rd NG8 ....172 A2
Sydney St NG24 ....125 D1
Sydney Terr NG14 ......140 A4
Syerston Rd NG18 ......103 D1
Syke Rd NG5 ....160 C4
Sykes La
  Balderton NG24 ....140 B2
  Saxilby LN1 ....56 C3
Sylvan Cres NG17 ......101 D3
Sylvester St NG18 ......101 F3
Synge Cl NG11 ....195 E4
Sywell Cl NG17 ....100 C3

T

Taft Ave NG10 ....182 A3
Taft Leys Rd LE12 ......205 F1
Talbot Cl NG9 ....175 F2
Talbot Dr NG9 ....170 B1
Talbot Rd Bircotes DN11 ..9 D2
  Worksop S80 ....36 A1
Talbot St
  Mansfield NG18 ....102 A2
  Nottingham NG1 ....223 D3
  Pinxton NG16 ....113 E1
Tales of Robin Hood*
NG1 ....223 D2
Tall Gables NG22 ....54 B1
Tamarix Cl NG4 ....163 D1
Tambling Cl NG3 ....162 A3
Tame Cl NG11 ....184 C2
Tamworth Gr NG7 ......184 C1
Tamworth Rd NG10 ....193 E3
Tanglewood NG6 ....84 B2
Tangmere Cres NG8 ....159 F1
Tanners La LE12 ....213 D1
Tannery Wharf NG24 ..139 F4
Tanwood Rd NG9 ....183 D1
Tanyard NG22 ....79 F3
Tarbert Cl NG2 ....173 D1
Target St NG7 ....222 A3
Tathams La DE7 ....157 F1
Tatmarsh LE11 ....220 A3
Tattersall Wlk NG19 ....88 C2
Tattershall Dr
  Beeston NG9 ....184 A4
  Nottingham NG7 ....222 C2
Taunton Rd NG2 ....185 F3
Taupo Dr NG15 ....145 E3
Tavern Ave NG8 ....160 B1
Tavistock Ave NG3 .....161 E1
Tavistock Cl NG15 .....145 E3
Tavistock Dr NG3 ......161 E1
Tavistock Rd NG2 ......185 F3
Taylor Cl NG2 ....174 A2
Taylor Cres
  Stapleford NG9 ....182 C4
  Sutton in A NG17 ....100 C1
Taylor St DE7 ....157 F1
Taylors Cl NG18 ....102 C4
Taylors Croft NG14 ....149 E2
Teague Pl S80 ....35 E2
Teak Cl NG3 ....173 E4
Teal Ave NG18 ....103 D2
Teal Cl Carlton NG4 ....175 D3
  Shirebrook NG20 ....72 B2
Teal Ct NG15 ....35 E4
Teal Wharf 4 NG2 .....173 D1
Tealby Cl NG6 ....159 F4
Tealby Wlk NG19 ....88 C2
Teasels The NG13 ......177 E2
Technology Dr NG9 ....184 A3
Tedburn Dr NG18 ......103 D1
Teddys Farm Pk*
LN5 ....142 C4
Teesbrook Dr NG8 .....171 D2
Teesdale Ct NG9 ....183 D2
Teesdale Rd
  Long Eaton NG10 ......193 D3
  Nottingham NG5 ....161 D1
Teignmouth Ave
NG18 ....102 C3
Telford Dr
  Eastwood NG16 ....144 A2
  Newark-on-T NG24 ....125 D1
Temperance La NG23 ..111 F4
Templar Rd NG9 ....183 A3
Temple Cres NG16 .....159 E2
Temple Dr NG16 ....159 F3
Templemans Way
NG25 ....136 C3
Templemen Cl NG11 ..196 A4

Templeoak Dr NG8 ....171 E2
Tenbury Cres NG8 .....160 B1
Tenby Gr S80 ....36 A1
Tene Cl NG5 ....147 E1
Tennan La NG13 ....146 A1
Tennis Ct Ind Est NG2 174 A2
Tennis Dr NG7 ....222 C2
Tennis Mews NG7 .....222 C2
Tennyson Ave
Carlton NG4 ....162 C1
Mansfield Woodhouse
NG19 ....88 B1
  Sutton in A NG15 ......145 E3
Tennyson Dr
Beeston NG9 ....183 E1
Worksop S81 ....36 B2
Tennyson Rd
Arnold NG5 ....161 F2
Balderton NG24 ....140 B2
Tennyson Sq NG16 ....158 B2
Tennyson St
Gainsborough DN21 .....15 E1
Ilkeston DE7 ....157 F2
Kirkby in A NG17 ....115 D2
10 Mansfield NG18 ....102 A4
Nottingham NG7 ....222 C4
Tenter Cl
Long Eaton NG10 ......193 E3
Nottingham NG5 ....160 C4
Tenter La NG18 ....102 A3
Tenters La NG22 ....92 C1
Tenzing Wlk NG24 ....140 C2
Terrace La NG19 ....86 C3
Terrace Rd NG18 ......102 B4
Terrace St NG7 ....172 C4
Terrian Cres NG2 ......185 F4
Terry Ave NG24 ....125 D2
Terton Rd NG5 ....160 C4
Tetford Wlk NG19 ....88 C2
Tetney Wlk NG5 ....172 A3
Tettenbury Rd NG5 ....160 C2
Teversal Ave
Nottingham NG7 ....222 B2
Pleasleyhill NG19 ....87 D2
Teversal Visitor Ctr*
NG17 ....100 A4
Tevery Cl NG9 ....182 C4
Teviot Rd NG5 ....160 C3
Tewkesbury Ave NG19 ..88 B2
Tewkesbury Cl NG2 ...186 A3
Tewkesbury Dr
Kimberley NG16 ....158 C4
Nottingham NG6 ....160 C2
Tewkesbury Rd NG10 .193 F3
Thackeray Cl S81 ....36 A3
Thackerays La NG5 ....161 F3
Thackeray St NG7 .....222 B3
Thames St NG6 ....160 A4
Thane Rd NG9 ....184 B3
Thaxted Cl NG8 ....171 E3
Theaker Ave DN21 ......15 F1
Theaker La DN10 ....10 B3
Theatre Sq NG1 ....223 D3
Thelda Ave NG12 ......197 F2
Theresa Ct NG24 ......140 B2
Thetford Cl NG5 ....162 A3
Thickley Cl NG20 ....72 C2
Thievesdale Ave S81 ...36 A4
Thievesdale Cl S81 .....36 A4
Thievesdale La S81 .....36 A4
Third Ave Beeston NG9 184 B3
Carlton, Gedling NG4 ..162 C1
Carlton, Thorneywood
NG4 ....174 A4
Clipstone NG21 ....89 F2
Edwinstowe NG21 ....76 A1
Mansfield NG21 ....103 F1
Mansfield Woodhouse
NG19 ....89 D1
Nottingham NG6 ....160 A4
Thirlbeck NG12 ....188 A1
Thirlmere NG2 ....186 B3
Thirlmere Cl
Long Eaton NG10 ......182 A1
Nottingham NG3 ....173 F4
Thirlmere Rd NG10 ...182 A1
Thistle Cl NG16 ....158 A4
Thistle Bank LE12 .....205 F2
Thistle Cl NG16 ....158 A4
Thistle Gn Cl DE75 ....143 D1
Thistledown Rd NG11 .195 F4
Thomas Ave NG12 .....176 B2
Thomas Cl NG3 ....223 F4
Thomas Parkyn Cl
NG11 ....206 C4
Thomas Rd DE74 ......203 E1
Thomas St NG19 ....39 F3
Thompson Ave DN11 ....8 C2
Thompson Cl NG9 .....183 E2
Thompson Cres NG17 .100 C1
Thompson Gdns NG5 .147 D1
Thompson St NG16 ...143 D2
Thonock Dr LN1 ....56 C2
Thonock Hill DN21 ......15 E2
Thonock Rd DN21 ......15 F3
Thor Gdns NG5 ....146 C1
Thoresby Ave
Carlton NG4 ....162 B1
Edwinstowe NG21 ....76 A1
Kirkby in A NG17 ....115 E2
Newark-on-T NG24 .....140 A3
Nottingham NG2 ....173 F2
Shirebrook NG20 ....72 C2
Thoresby Cl
Harworth DN11 ....9 D3
Meden Vale NG20 ....74 B4
Radcliffe on T NG12 ...176 A3

Thoresby Cres NG17 ..100 B3
Thoresby Ct NG3 ....173 E4
Thoresby Dale NG15 ..146 A4
Thoresby Glade NG6 ..106 A3
Thoresby Rd
Beeston NG9 ....171 E1
Bingham NG13 ....177 E2
Long Eaton NG10 ......193 E3
Mansfield NG21 ....103 F1
Mansfield Woodhouse
NG19 ....88 A2
Thoresby St
3 Mansfield NG18 .....102 A4
10 Nottingham NG2 ...173 F2
Sutton in A NG17 ......101 D2
Thoresby Way NG19 ....87 F1
Thorn Ave NG19 ....87 F1
Thorn Bank DN9 ....2 B4
Thorn Dr NG16 ....158 A4
Thorn Gr NG15 ....146 A2
Thorn Tree Gdns
NG16 ....143 F2
Thornbury Dr NG19 ...101 E4
Thornbury Hill La S81 ...16 B4
Thornbury Way NG5 ..160 C4
Thorncliffe Rd NG3 ...173 E4
Thorncliffe Rise S3 ....173 E4
Thorndale Rd
Calverton NG14 ....148 C4
Nottingham NG6 ....160 B1
Thorndike Cl NG9 .....184 A2
Thorndike Way DN21 ...24 C4
Thorne Rd DN10 ....10 A4
Thorner Cl NG6 ....160 C3
Thorney Abbey Rd
NG21 ....118 A3
Thorney Ct NG18 ......103 D1
Thorney Hill NG3 ......173 F4
Thorneywood Ave
NG17 ....129 F4
Thorneywood Mount
NG3 ....173 F4
Thorneywood Rd
NG10 ....193 F4
Thornham Cres NG17 .129 F4
Thornhill Cl NG9 ....171 D1
Thornhill Dr NG22 ....77 F3
Thornhill La DN22 ....33 E1
Thornhill Rd DN11 ....8 C2
Thornley St 7 NG3 ....172 C4
Thornthwaite Cl NG2 .186 B3
Thornthwaite Ave NG5 147 F1
Thornton Cl
Mansfield NG18 ....103 D3
Nottingham NG8 ....171 F2
Thornton Dale S81 ......36 A4
Thornton Rd NG23 ....112 A4
Thornton St
Gainsborough DN21 ....24 B4
Sutton in A NG17 ......100 C1
Thorntons Cl NG12 ...188 A1
Thorold Cl NG7 ....184 C1
Thoroton Ave NG24 ...140 B2
Thoroton St NG7 ......222 C3
Thoroughfare La
NG23 ....125 E4
Thorpe Cl
Coddington NG24 ......126 A1
Newark-on-T NG24 ....139 F2
10 Nottingham NG5 ..161 D4
Stapleford NG9 ....182 B4
Thorpe Cres NG3 ......162 A1
Thorpe La Eagle LN6 ...84 C1
Shreoaks S80 ....34 B3
Thorpe Lea NG14 .....165 D3
Thorpe Leys NG10 ....193 E3
Thorpe Rd
Eastwood NG16 ....143 F2
Mansfield NG18 ....103 D1
Mattersey DN10 ....20 A4
Thorpe St Askham DN22 .52 B4
Ilkeston DE7 ....157 F2
Thorpelands Ave NG18 ..88 C1
Thrapston Ave NG5 ...147 F1
Three Leys La DN22 ....32 B2
Three Tuns Rd NG16 .144 A1
Threlkeld Cl NG2 ......186 B3
Thrumpton Ave NG10 .194 A4
Thrumpton Cl DN22 ....39 F2
Thrumpton Dr NG2 ...173 D1
Thrumpton Hall*
NG11 ....194 A2
Thrumpton La DN22 ....39 F2
Thurcaton Way DE55 ..99 D2
Thurgarton Ave 10 NG2 173 F2
Thurgarton La NG14 ..151 F2
Thurgarton St NG2 ...173 F2
Thurgarton Sta NG14 .151 E3
Thurland Rd NG1 ......223 E2
Thurlby Cl NG23 ....189 D2
Thurlby Ct NG19 ....88 C2
Thurlby La
Stanton-on-t-W NG12 .198 B1
Widmerpool NG12 .....208 B4
Thurlby Rd DN21 ....24 C4
Thurlestone Dr NG3 ..162 B3
Thurley Wlk NG18 .....103 D2
Thurloe Ct NG11 ....185 E2
Thurman Dr NG12 ....187 F2
Thurman St
Ilkeston DE7 ....170 A3
Nottingham NG7 ....222 B4
Thursby Rd NG11 ......184 C2

Thymus Wlk NG11 ....184 B1
Thyra Ct NG3 ....161 F1
Thyra Gr Beeston NG9 ...184 A3
  Nottingham NG3 ....161 F1
Tibshelf Inf Sch DE55 ......99 D4
Tibshelf Rd NG17 ....100 A4
Tibshelf Sch DE55 ....99 D4
Tickhill Estfeld Prim Sch
  DN11 ....8 A4
Tickhill Rd Bawtry DN10 ....9 F4
  Harworth DN11 ....8 C3
Tickhill St Mary CE Prim Sch
  DN11 ....8 A4
Tideswell Ct NG15 ....117 D2
Tideswell St NG18 ....102 B4
Tidworth Cl NG8 ....172 A3
Tilberthwaite Cl NG2 ....186 B3
Tilbury Rise NG8 ....160 A2
Tilford Gdns NG9 ....182 C3
Till Bridge La DN21 ....44 C4
Tiln Ct DN22 ....29 F1
Tiln La DN22 ....29 F1
Tilstock Ct NG16 ....159 D4
Timothy Rd NG17 ....79 E2
Tindale Bank Rd DN10 .....6 B4
Tinker La DN22 ....27 F2
Tinkers La NG23 ....97 F4
Tinsley Cl NG23 ....156 C3
Tinsley Rd NG16 ....143 E1
Tintagel Gn NG7 ....184 C1
Tintern Dr NG8 ....160 C1
Tip Tree Cl NG16 ....158 C4
Tippett Ct NG3 ....173 F3
Tippings La NG22 ....119 F3
Tiree Cl NG9 ....179 E1
Tishbite St ☑ NG6 ....160 A4
Tissington Ave NG20 ......74 B4
Tissington Cl ☑ NG7 ....173 D4
Tissington Rd NG7 ....173 D4
Titchfield Ave
  Mansfield Woodhouse
  NG19 ....88 B2
  Sutton in A NG17 ....100 C1
Titchfield St
  Hucknall NG15 ....146 A4
  Mansfield NG18 ....102 A4
  Market Warsop NG20 ......74 A2
Titchfield Terr NG15 .....146 A4
Tithby Ct NG18 ....103 D1
Tithby Dr NG5 ....161 E2
Tithby Rd
  Bingham NG13 ....177 F1
  Cropwell Butler NG12 ....189 E3
Tithe Barn Ct NG14 ......125 D1
Tithe Gdns ☑ NG5 ....147 E1
Tithe La NG14 ....148 C4
Tithes La DN11 ....8 A4
Tiverton Cl
  Hucknall NG15 ....145 E3
  Nottingham NG8 ....160 A1
Toad La Elston NG23 .....153 F2
  Epperstone NG14 ....150 A3
  Laxton NG22 ....79 D1
Tobias Cl NG5 ....160 C4
Todd Cl NG11 ....195 E4
Todd Ct NG11 ....195 E4
Toft Cl NG12 ....187 F1
Toft Rd NG9 ....183 D2
Tokenhouse Yd NG1 .....223 E2
Toll Bar Ave NG13 ....181 D2
Tollerton Gn NG6 ....160 B2
Tollerton Prim Sch
  NG12 ....186 C1
Tollerton Rd NG12 ....186 C3
Tollhouse Hill NG1 ....223 D3
Tolney La NG24 ....139 F4
Tom Otters La NG23 ......70 C4
Tom Wass Rd NG17 ......114 C4
Tomlinson Ave NG11 .....195 D1
Ton La NG14 ....150 B1
Tonbridge Mount
  NG8 ....171 E1
Tooley St DN21 ....24 B4
Toot Hill Comp Sch
  NG13 ....177 F2
Toothill La NG18 ....102 B4
Toothill Rd
  Loughborough LE11 .....220 A3
  ☑ Mansfield NG18 ......102 A4
Top Gn LE14 ....210 A1
Top La NG19 ....87 D1
Top Pasture La DN22 .....31 F4
Top Rd Blidworth NG21 ..118 A1
  Misson DN10 ....4 B2
  Ruddington NG11 ....196 B3
  Thorney NG23 ....84 C3
Top Row
  Newark-on-T NG24 ......140 B4
  Westwood NG16 ....128 A3
Top Sandy La NG20 ....74 B2
Top St ☑ Askham DN22 ...51 F1
  Bawtry DN10 ....10 A4
  East Drayton DN22 ....53 D2
  Elston NG23 ....153 E2
  North Wheatley DN22 ....31 E4
  Rainworth NG21 ....104 A1
Top Valley Dr NG5 ....160 C4
Top Valley Sch NG5 .....146 C1
Top Valley Way NG5 .....160 C4
Toppard La DN22 ....30 B3
Tor La NG22 ....77 D2
Torbay Cres NG5 ....161 D3
Torkard Dr NG5 ....160 C4
Torksey Ave LN1 ....56 C2
Torksey Ferry Rd DN22 ..43 E1

Torksey Mews DN22 ......39 E1
Torksey St DN22 ....43 D1
Torksey Wlk NG19 ....88 C2
Torr St DN21 ....24 B4
Torvill Dr NG8 ....171 F3
Toston Dr NG8 ....160 B2
Totland Dr NG8 ....160 B1
Totland Rd NG8 ....160 B1
Totley Cl NG6 ....146 B1
Totnes Cl NG15 ....145 E3
Totnes Rd NG3 ....174 A3
Toton Cl NG6 ....160 B3
Toton La NG9 ....182 C3
Tottle Gdns ☑ NG7 .....172 B3
Tottle Rd NG11 ....185 D4
Tow Ct NG24 ....139 D2
Tower Cres NG16 ....159 D2
Tower St NG1 ....15 E1
Towes Mount NG4 ....174 C4
Towle St NG10 ....193 D2
Towlsons Croft NG6 .....160 B2
Town End La NG23 ......167 D4
Town St Askham NG22 ....52 A2
  Beeston NG9 ....183 D4
  Claypole NG23 ....156 B4
  Clayworth DN22 ....21 E3
  Cottam DN22 ....43 E3
  Grassthorpe NG23 ....81 E2
  Hawksworth NG13 ....167 E2
  Lound DN22 ....20 B1
  Pinxton NG16 ....113 F2
  Sandiacre NG10 ....182 A3
  South Leverton DN22 .....42 B4
  Sutton DN22 ....28 C3
  Treswell DN22 ....42 A2
Town View NG16 ....158 C4
Townroe Dr NG19 ....101 E4
Townsend Ct NG5 ....147 D1
Townside Cl NG10 ......193 D2
Townside La DN22 ....82 B2
Townside Rd DN22 ......32 B1
Towpath Cl LE11 ....220 B3
Towson Ave NG16 ......143 E1
Towson Field LE12 .....205 F1
Towyn Ct ☑ NG5 ....161 D4
Tracy Cl NG9 ....171 F1
Trafalgar Cl NG7 ....222 B4
Trafalgar Ct
  Beeston NG9 ....184 A2
  Long Eaton NG10 ......193 E3
Trafalgar Sq
  Long Eaton NG10 ......193 E4
  Sutton on T NG23 ....97 D4
Traffic St NG2 ....223 E1
Trafford Gdns ☑ NG8 ..172 B4
Tranby Gdns NG8 ....171 F2
Tranker La S81 ....35 D3
Travells Hill LE12 ......214 A4
Travers Rd NG10 ....182 A1
Tree View Cl NG5 ....147 E1
Treegarth Sq NG5 ......147 D1
Trefan Gdns NG5 ....161 D4
Trelawn Cl ☑ NG5 .....161 E1
Tremayne Rd NG8 ......160 A1
Trenchard Ave NG24 ...125 F1
Trenchard Cl NG13 ....177 E4
Trenchfam Gdns
  NG14 ....163 E2
Trent Ave NG11 ....196 B4
Trent Bridge
  (Nottinghamshire Cty
  Cricket Ground) NG2 ..173 F1
Trent Bridge Prim Sch
  NG2 ....185 E4
Trent Bvd NG2 ....174 A1
Trent Coll NG10 ....179 E1
Trent Cres NG9 ....183 F2
Trent Dr NG15 ....145 E2
Trent La Besthorpe NG23 .97 F3
  Burton Joyce NG14 .....164 A2
  East Bridgford NG13 ....165 D2
  Girton NG23 ....82 C1
  Kelham NG23 ....124 A3
  Long Eaton NG10 ......193 F3
  Newark-on-T NG24 .....125 D1
  North Clifton NG23 ......68 C3
  Nottingham NG2 ....174 A2
  South Clifton NG23 ......68 B1
Trent Port Rd DN21 .....44 A4
Trent Rd Beeston NG9 ..184 A2
  Nottingham NG2 ....173 F2
  Wellow NG22 ....78 A2
Trent S Ind Pk NG2 ....174 A2
Trent St
  Gainsborough DN21 ......24 B4
  Long Eaton NG10 ......193 F4
  Nottingham NG1 ....223 F1
  Retford DN22 ....40 A3
  Worksop S80 ....35 F2
Trent Vale Rd NG9 .....184 A2
Trent Vale Sch NG9 ....184 A2
Trent Valley View
  NG3 ....162 A1
Trent View Gdns
  NG12 ....176 A3
Trent Way NG24 ....125 D1
Trent Wlk NG19 ....88 C2
Trentdale Rd NG4 ......174 B3
Trentham Dr NG8 ......172 A4
Trentham Gdns NG8 ...172 A4
Trenton Cl NG9 ....171 D1
Trenton Dr NG10 ......194 A4
Trentside NG14 ....165 D2

Trentside N NG2 ....173 F1
Trentview Ct NG2 ......173 F1
Tressall Cl DE7 ....170 A4
Treswell Ct NG18 ......103 D1
Treswell Rd
  Rampton DN22 ....42 C1
  South Leverton DN22 ....42 B3
Treswell Wood Nature
  Reserve* DN22 ....41 F2
Trevelyan Rd NG2 ......173 F1
Trevino Gdns ☑ NG5 ..147 D1
Trevone Ave NG9 ......182 C3
Trevor Rd Beeston NG9 .183 F3
  West Bridgford NG2 ....186 A3
Trevose Gdns NG5 .....161 E2
Treyford Cl NG11 ......185 D2
Triangle The DE7 ......170 A3
Tricornia Dr NG6 ......160 A2
Tring Vale NG5 ....161 D2
Trinity Ave NG7 ....222 B1
Trinity Cl DE7 ....157 F2
Trinity Cres
  East Markham NG22 .....66 A4
  Lambley NG4 ....163 F4
  Wymeswold LE12 ......216 A2
Trinity Hospl DN22 ......39 E4
Trinity Rd
  Newark-on-T NG24 .....139 F4
  Retford DN22 ....29 E1
  Southwell NG25 ....136 B4
Trinity Sch NG8 ....172 A4
Trinity Sq NG1 ....223 E3
Trinity St
  Gainsborough DN21 ......24 B4
  Loughborough LE11 ....220 B2
Trinity Wlk NG1 ....223 E3
Trinstead Way NG5 ....161 E4
Triumph Cl NG22 ......106 C4
Triumph Rd
  Eakring NG22 ....106 C4
  Nottingham NG7 ....172 B2
Trivett Sq NG1 ....223 E2
Troon Cl NG16 ....158 C4
Trough La NG16 ....158 C4
Trough Rd NG16 ....159 D4
Troutbeck NG12 ....188 A2
Troutbeck Cres NG9 ...183 E4
Trowell Ave
  Ilkeston DE7 ....170 A3
  Nottingham NG8 ....171 D3
Trowell CE Prim Sch
  NG9 ....170 B2
Trowell Cl NG18 ....103 D1
Trowell Gr
  Long Eaton NG10 ......182 B1
  Nottingham NG9 ....170 C2
Trowell La LE12 ....213 F4
Trowell Pk Dr NG9 ....170 B1
Trowell Rd
  Nottingham NG8 ....171 E3
  Stapleford NG9 ....170 B1
True Lovers Wlk ☑
  LE11 ....220 A2
Trueman Ct S81 ....36 A3
Trueman Gdns NG5 ....162 A3
Trueman St DE7 ....157 F2
Truman Cl NG3 ....223 F4
Truman Dr NG15 ......146 A3
Truman St Cossall DE7 ..158 B4
  Kimberley NG16 ....158 B4
Trumans Rd NG2 ......173 E1
Truro Cl DE7 ....205 F1
Truro Cres NG7 ....172 C4
Trusley Wlk NG19 ....88 C2
Tryst The NG9 ....125 D1
Tuckers Cl LE11 ....220 B1
Tudor Ave NG18 ......102 C4
Tudor Cl Carlton NG4 ..174 C3
  Long Eaton NG10 ......193 D2
Tudor Cres NG21 .....118 A4
Tudor Ct Arnold NG5 ..162 A3
  Hucknall NG15 ....145 E3
Tudor Dr
  Mansfield NG18 ....102 B2
  Morton DN21 ....15 D2
Tudor Gr NG1 ....223 D4
Tudor Rd NG2 ....185 F4
Tudor Sq NG2 ....185 F4
Tudor St NG17 ....100 C1
Tudsbury Terr NG17 ...101 D2
Tudwal Cl NG6 ....161 D4
Tudwal Wlk ☑ NG6 ...161 D4
Tulip Ave NG3 ....173 E4
Tulip Rd NG16 ....158 A3
Tunnel Rd
  Nottingham NG7 ......222 C2
  Retford DN22 ....39 F3
Tunstall Cres NG8 ....160 A1
Tunstall Dr NG5 ......160 C2
Tunstall Rd NG5 ......161 F2
Turnberry S81 ....36 A3
Turnberry Ave ☑ NG17 114 C4
Turnberry Cl
  Beeston NG9 ....183 E3
  Ilkeston DE7 ....157 E1
Turnberry Ct NG12 ...186 B2
Turnberry Rd NG6 ....160 B3
Turner Ave
  Langley Mill NG16 .....143 D2
  Loughborough LE11 ...220 A1
Turner Cl NG9 ....182 C3
Turner Dr
  Eastwood NG16 ....158 A4
  Worksop S81 ....35 F3
Turner St NG15 ....146 A4

Turners Croft DN22 .....42 B4
Turney St NG2 ....173 F1
Turneys Ct NG2 ....173 F1
Turnley Rd DE55 ......113 E3
Turnpike La NG9 ......184 A4
Turnstone Wharf ☑
  NG7 ....172 C1
Turpin Ave NG4 ....162 B2
Turpin Cl DN22 ....19 C2
Turton Cl NG16 ....143 D2
Turvey La NG12 ....212 B1
Turvey La LE12 ....212 B1
Tuxford Ave NG20 .....74 C4
Tuxford Comp Sch
  NG22 ....66 A2
Tuxford Ct NG18 .....103 D1
Tuxford Prim Sch NG22 .65 F1
Tuxford Rd
  Boughton NG22 ....77 F3
  East Markham NG22 ....65 F1
  Egmanton NG22 ....79 F4
  Normanton on T NG23 ..81 E3
  Walesby NG22 ....64 B1
Tuxford Windmill* ....
Tuxford Wlk NG3 .....173 F3
Twells Cl NG3 ....173 F3
Twentylands Dr LE12 ..205 E1
Twin Oaks Dr NG17 ...100 B1
Twinyards Cl NG17 ....100 B1
Twitchell The
  Beeston NG9 ....183 F2
  Newark-on-T NG24 ....139 F3
  Sutton in A NG17 ......100 B1
Two Acres S81 ....18 A1
Twycross Rd NG5 .....161 D4
Twyford Gdns NG11 ..184 C2
Twyford La DN22 ....50 B2
Tyburn Cl NG5 ....147 D1
Tylden Rd S80 ....35 D3
Tylden Way S80 ....35 D3
Tyne Gdns NG15 .....145 E2
Tynedale Cl
  Long Eaton NG10 .....193 D3
  Nottingham NG8 ......160 B1

U

Uldale Ct NG9 ....183 D2
Ullscarf Cl NG3 ....186 B3
Ullswater Cl NG2 .....162 C1
Ullswater Cres NG9 ..183 E4
Ullswater Dr NG15 ...145 E4
Ulster Rd NG3 ....162 A1
Underwood Ave DN22 ..19 C2
Underwood CE Sch
  NG16 ....128 C2
Underwood Gdns S80 ..35 C2
Union Cl NG15 ....131 D1
Union Rd NG3 ....223 F3
Union St Beeston NG9 .184 A3
  Bingham NG13 ....177 F2
  Long Eaton NG10 .....193 F4
  Loughborough LE11 ..220 A2
  Mansfield NG18 ....102 B4
  Retford DN22 ....39 F4
  Selston NG16 ....129 D4
  Sutton in A NG17 ......100 C1
Unity Rd NG17 ....115 D4
Univ of Nottingham
  Beeston NG9 ....184 A4
  Nottingham NG7 ......172 A1
Univ of Nottingham
  Department of Ag
  Economics LE12 .....213 D4
Univ of Nottingham Sutton
  Bonington Campus
  LE12 ....204 A1
University Bvd NG7 ..184 B4
Unwin Rd NG17 ......101 D2
Unwin St NG17 ......100 A2
Uplands Ct NG8 .....171 F3
Upminster Dr
  Arnold NG5 ....147 F1
  Nuthall NG16 ....159 E2
Upper Canaan St NG11 196 B4
Upper Coll St NG1 ...223 D3
Upper Dunstead Rd
  NG16 ....143 D1
Upper Eldon St NG2 .173 F2
Upper Mexborough Rd
  NG16 ....128 A3
Upper Orch St NG9 ..182 C4
Upper Parliament St
  NG1 ....223 E3
Upper Row NG22 ......54 A1
Upper Wellington St
  NG10 ....182 B1
Uppingham Cres NG3 185 E3
Uppingham Gdns NG2 173 E1
Upton Cl DE75 ....143 D1
Upton Dr NG5 ....161 E3
Upton Hill NG22 .....66 A2
Upton Mount NG19 ..87 F1
Upton Rd Askham NG22 52 A2
  Southwell NG25 ......136 B3
Upton Wlk DN21 ......24 C4
Urban Rd NG17 ......115 D3
Urnstone Cres NG8 ..160 A1
Utile Gdns ☑ NG6 ...160 A4

V

Vale Ave NG20 ....74 A2
Vale Cl Aslockton NG13 179 D2
  Eastwood NG16 ......144 A1

Vale Cl continued
  Mansfield NG18 ....102 C2
Vale Cres N NG8 ......172 B3
Vale Cres S NG8 ......172 B3
Vale Dr NG20 ....74 A2
Vale Gdns NG4 ....174 B3
Vale Rd Carlton NG4 .174 C3
  Mansfield Woodhouse
  ....88 A2
Vale The DE7 ....157 F2
Valentine Ave NG16 .128 C4
Valeside Gdns NG4 ..174 B3
Valetta Rd NG5 ....162 A4
Valiant Rd NG4 ......125 F1
Valiance St NG19 .....88 A2
Valley App NG22 .....105 F4
Valley Comp Sch S81 ..35 F3
Valley Dr NG16 ......144 A1
Valley Farm Ct ☑ NG5 161 D4
Valley Gdns NG2 .....186 B3
Valley La NG23 ......169 E3
Valley Prospect NG24 139 E3
Valley Rd Beeston NG9 183 D3
  Bilsthorpe NG22 .....105 F4
  Carlton NG4 ....162 A1
  Kimberley NG16 ......158 B4
  Nottingham NG5 ......161 E1
  Radcliffe on T NG12 ..176 A3
  Shirebrook NG20 ......72 C3
  West Bridgford NG2 ..186 A3
  Worksop S81 ....35 F3
Valley View NG24 ...126 A1
Valmont Ave NG18 ..103 D3
Valmont Rd
  Beeston NG9 ....183 D4
  Nottingham NG5 .....161 D2
Vancouver Ave NG12 175 F1
Vanessa Dr DN21 .....15 E2
Vanguard Rd NG10 ..193 E3
Varden Ave NG9 .....172 A1
Varney Rd NG11 ....184 C2
Vaughan Ave
  Bottesford NG13 .....181 E1
  Hucknall NG15 ....131 E1
Vaughan Pl NG20 .....72 C3
Vaughan Rd NG9 ....183 D2
Vedonis Pk NG15 ....146 A3
Vellus Ct NG17 ......101 D1
Ventnor Rise NG5 ...160 C2
Venus Cl NG6 ....160 A4
Vera Cres NG21 .....118 A4
Verbena Cl ☑ NG3 ..173 E4
Verder Gr NG5 ......160 C4
Vere Ave NG17 ....100 C3
Vere St NG6 ....160 A4
Verne Cl NG4 ....174 B4
Verney St NG19 ......86 C4
Verney Way NG19 ....86 C4
Vernon Ave
  Beeston NG9 ....183 F3
  Carlton NG4 ....162 C1
  Newark-on-T NG24 ..140 A4
  Nottingham, Old Basford
  NG6 ....160 C2
  Nottingham, Wilford
  NG11 ....185 D2
  Ravenshead NG15 ....116 C1
  Retford DN22 ....40 A2
Vernon Cres NG15 ..117 D1
Vernon Ct Nuthall NG16 159 F2
  Shirebrook NG20 ......73 D2
Vernon Dr NG16 .....159 F2
Vernon Pk Dr NG6 ..160 C2
Vernon Pk Trad Est
  NG5 ....160 C2
Vernon Rd
  Kirkby in A NG17 ....114 C3
  Nottingham NG6 .....160 C2
Vernon St Ilkeston DE7 157 F2
  Newark-on-T NG24 ..140 A4
  Nottingham NG1 .....223 D3
  Shirebrook NG20 ......73 D2
Verona Ave NG4 .....174 C3
Verona Cres NG18 ..103 D2
Veronica Dr
  Carlton NG4 ....162 B1
  Eastwood NG16 ......144 A1
Veronica Wlk NG11 ..184 B1
Veronne Dr NG17 ...101 D3
Vesper Ct NG18 ....102 C4
Vessey Cl NG24 ....140 B2
Vessey Rd S81 ....35 F4
Vexation La NG22 ....77 E4
Vicar La Misson DN10 ..4 B2
  Tibshelf DE55 ....99 D3
Vicar Water Ctry Pk*
  ....91 F4
Vicar Way NG18 ....103 D4
Vicarage Ave
  Ilkeston DE7 ....157 E2
  North Leverton w H DN22 42 B4
Vicarage Cl
  Collingham NG23 ......98 A1
  North Leverton w H DN22 42 B4
  Nottingham, Old Basford
  NG5 ....160 C2
  Nottingham, St Anns
  NG3 ....223 E4
  Shirebrook NG20 ......72 C2
Vicarage Ct NG17 ...107 D3
Vicarage Dr
  Burton Joyce NG14 ..163 F2
  Clarborough DN22 ....30 B3
Vicarage Gn NG12 ..186 A2
Vicarage La
  Beckingham DN10 .....14 B1
  Farnsfield NG22 ......119 F3
  Kneeton NG13 ....151 F1

Vicarage La continued
North Muskham NG23 ....110 B2
Radcliffe on T NG12 ....175 F2
Ruddington NG11 ....196 B4
Vicarage Rd NG25 ....136 B4
Vicarage St
Ilkeston DE7 ....183 F3
Ilkeston DE7 ....157 E2
Vicarage Way NG17 ....129 F4
Vicars Cl NG21 ....89 F1
Vicars La NG21 ....43 D1
Vicars Wlk S80 ....35 F1
Vickers St
Market Warsop NG20 ....74 A2
Nottingham NG3 ....173 F4
Vickers Way NG22 ....105 F4
Victor Cres NG10 ....182 B2
Victor Terr ➏ NG5 ....161 E1
Victoria Ave
Lowdham NG14 ....150 C1
➋ Nottingham NG2 ....173 F2
Sandiacre DE7 ....23 C3
Victoria Cres NG5 ....161 E1
Victoria Ct
Ilkeston DE7 ....157 F1
Mansfield NG18 ....102 A3
Victoria Emb NG2 ....185 E4
Victoria Gdns
Newark-on-T NG24 ....140 A4
Watnall NG16 ....145 D1
Victoria St NG15 ....131 D1
Victoria Pk NG4 ....175 D3
Victoria Pk Way NG17 ....175 D3
Victoria Rd
Bingham NG13 ....178 A3
Bunny NG11 ....196 C1
Carlton NG4 ....175 D3
Kirkby in A NG17 ....114 C3
Nottingham NG5 ....161 D2
Pinxton NG16 ....113 E2
Retford DN22 ....39 F3
Sandiacre NG10 ....182 A3
Selston NG16 ....129 D4
West Bridgford NG2 ....185 F4
Victoria Sh Ctr NG1 ......223 E3
Victoria Sq S80 ....35 F2
Victoria St Carlton NG4 ..162 C1
Hucknall NG15 ....146 A4
Ilkeston DE7 ....157 F2
Kimberley NG16 ....159 D3
Langley Mill NG16 ....143 E2
Long Eaton NG10 ....193 D3
Loughborough LE11 ....220 A2
Market Warsop NG20 ....74 A3
Newark-on-T NG24 ....139 F4
Nottingham NG1 ....223 E2
Radcliffe on T NG12 ....175 F2
Selston NG16 ....129 D4
Shirebrook NG20 ....72 C2
South Normanton DE55 ......113 D3
Stanton Hill NG17 ....100 B3
Stapleford NG9 ....182 B4
Sutton in A NG17 ....100 C1
Victoria Terr DE55 ....99 D4
Victory Cl
Long Eaton NG10 ....193 E3
Mansfield Woodhouse
  NG19 ....89 D1
Victory Dr NG19 ....88 C1
Victory Rd NG4 ....184 A2
Villa Rd Keyworth NG12 ...197 F2
Nottingham NG3 ....173 E4
Villa St NG9 ....183 F4
Village Cl
Farndon NG24 ....139 D3
West Bridgford NG2 ....186 A2
Village Farm Cl LE12 ....204 C1
Village Rd
Normanton on S LE12 ....213 E1
Nottingham NG11 ....184 B1
Village St
Owthorpe NG12 ....199 F4
West Bridgford NG2 ....186 A2
Villas The NG20 ....59 D2
Villiers Rd Arnold NG5 ...161 E2
Mansfield NG18 ....102 C4
West Bridgford NG2 ....186 A3
Vincent Ave NG9 ....183 F3
Vincent Gdns ➊ NG7 .....172 C4
Vine Cl NG13 ....181 D1
Vine Farm Cl NG12 ....187 F2
Vine Rd DN11 ....8 B4
Vine Terr NG17 ....146 A4
Vine Tree Terr LE12 ......215 E1
Vine Way NG4 ....140 A4
Vines Cross NG8 ....171 F1
Violet Ave NG16 ....144 A1
Violet Cl
Nottingham NG6 ....160 B2
Shirebrook NG20 ....72 B2
Violet Hill NG18 ....103 D4
Violet Rd Carlton NG4 ....162 B1
West Bridgford NG2 ....186 A4
Vista The NG9 ....182 C3
Vivian Ave NG5 ....173 D4
Voce Ct S81 ....36 A3
Vulcan Cl NG6 ....160 C2
Vulcan Pl S80 ....35 F2
Vyse Dr NG10 ....193 E3

W

Waddington Dr NG2 ....185 E2
Wade Ave DE7 ....170 A4
Wade Cl NG18 ....102 B2
Wades Ave NG7 ....161 F1
Wadham Rd NG5 ....161 F3
Wadhurst Gdns NG3 ......223 F4
Wadhurst Gr NG8 ....171 E1
Wadnal La NG23 ....80 C2
Wadsworth Rd NG9 ....182 C4
Wagstaff La NG16 ....128 B3
Wain Ct S81 ....36 A4
Waingrove NG11 ....185 D2
Wainwright Ave NG19 ....101 E4
Wakefield Ave NG12 ......176 A2
Wakefield Croft DE7 .....157 E2
Wakeling Cl NG25 ....136 C4
Walbrook Cl NG8 ....160 A2
Walcot Gn NG11 ....184 B1
Walcote Dr NG2 ....185 E2
Waldeck Rd NG5 ....161 D1
Waldemar Gr NG9 ....184 A3
Waldron Cl ➋ NG2 ....173 E1
Walesby CE Prim Sch
  NG22 ....64 A1
Walesby Dr NG18 ....103 D2
Walesby La NG22 ....115 E3
Walesby La NG27 ....115 F3
Walford Cl NG13 ....181 D1
Walgrave Wlk ➌ NG5 .....161 D4
Walk Mill Dr NG15 ....131 D1
Walk The DN21 ....24 C4
Walkden St NG18 ....102 A4
Walker Cl NG2 ....140 A4
Walker Gr NG9 ....182 C3
Walker Sq NG5 ....160 C2
Walker St
Eastwood NG16 ....144 A2
Nottingham NG2 ....173 F2
Walkeringham Prim Sch
  DN10 ....13 F3
Walkeringham Rd
Beckingham DN10 ....14 A1
Gringley on t H DN10 ....13 D2
Walkerith Rd
Morton DN21 ....15 D3
Walkerith DN10 ....14 B4
Walkers Cl
Bingham NG13 ....177 F2
Mansfield Woodhouse
  NG19 ....89 D1
Walkers Yd NG12 ....175 F3
Walks of Life Heritage Ctr*
  NG22 ....
Wall St DN21 ....24 B4
Wallace Ave NG4 ....174 C4
Wallace Rd LE11 ....220 A1
Wallace St NG11 ....195 D1
Wallan St NG7 ....222 A4
Wallet St NG4 ....175 D4
Wallett Ave NG9 ....183 F4
Wallingbrook Rise S80 ....35 D1
Wallingwells La S81 ....25 D3
Wallis Rd NG18 ....102 B4
Wallis St NG6 ....160 C2
Walnut Ave
Shreoaks S81 ....34 C4
Tickhill DN11 ....8 A4
Walnut Cl
Aslockton NG13 ....178 C3
Ilkeston DE7 ....170 A4
Walnut Dr
Beeston NG9 ....183 D4
Calverton NG14 ....148 C4
Walnut Gr
East Bridgford NG13 ....165 E3
Radcliffe on T NG12 ....175 F2
Walnut Paddock LE14 ....202 A2
Walnut Rd NG13 ....181 D1
Walnut Tree Cres NG19 ...89 E1
Walnut Tree Gdns
  NG6 ....159 F4
Walnut Tree La NG15 .....165 E1
Walsham Cl NG9 ....183 E1
Walsingham Rd NG5 ....162 A3
Walter DAyncourt Prim Sch
  NG22 ....119 F3
Walter Halls Prim Sch
  NG3 ....161 F1
Walter St NG7 ....222 C4
Walters Cl NG23 ....139 D3
Walters Cres NG16 ....128 B3
Waltham Cl
Balderton NG24 ....140 B2
West Bridgford NG2 ....186 A3
Waltham La
Harby LE14 ....202 A1
Long Clawson LE14 ....211 F1
Waltham Rd NG15 ....117 D1
Walton Ave NG3 ....173 F3
Walton Cl NG19 ....103 D4
Walton Cres NG4 ....174 C4
Walton Dr
Keyworth NG12 ....197 F2
Sutton in A NG17 ....114 B4
Walton Rd NG5 ....148 A1
Walton St
Long Eaton NG10 ....182 B1
Sutton in A NG17 ....101 D2
Waltons La NG23 ....124 C2
Wands Cl NG25 ....136 B4
Wansbeck Cl NG7 ....222 C3
Wanstead Way NG5 ....146 C1
Wapping La DN21 ....44 B4
Warburton St NG24 ....125 D1

Ward Ave
Hucknall NG15 ....130 C1
Nottingham NG5 ....162 A2
Ward Pl NG18 ....101 F3
Ward St ➊ NG7 ....172 C4
Wardle Gr NG5 ....162 A4
Wardlow Rd DE7 ....157 F2
Wards End LE11 ....220 A2
Wareham Cl
Nottingham NG8 ....160 A2
West Bridgford NG2 ....186 A3
Warkton Cl NG9 ....183 E3
Warnadene Rd NG17 ......114 C4
Warner Pl LE11 ....220 B2
Warner St NG7 ....222 A3
Warners La ➏ LE11 ....220 A2
Warrands Cl NG25 ....136 B4
Waren Ave
Annesley NG15 ....130 B4
Nottingham NG5 ....161 D1
Warren Ave Extension
  NG9 ....182 B4
Warren Cl
Gainsborough DN21 ....15 D1
Huthwaite NG17 ....100 A1
Warren Ct NG19 ....182 B4
Warren La
Kegworth DE74 ....193 D1
Long Eaton DE74 ....203 D4
Warren Prim Sch
  NG5 ....147 D1
Warren Rd
Annesley Woodhouse
  NG17 ....115 D1
Hucknall NG15 ....145 E3
Warren The NG12 ....187 F1
Warren Way NG19 ....103 E4
Warrender Cl NG9 ....171 E1
Warrener Gr NG5 ....160 C4
Warrenhill Cl NG5 ....161 E4
Warrington Rd NG6 ....160 B4
Warser Gate NG1 ....223 F2
Warsop Cl NG8 ....159 E1
Warsop La NG21 ....117 F4
Warsop Rd NG19 ....88 B2
Warton Ave NG3 ....173 F4
Warwick Ave
Arnold NG5 ....161 F3
Beeston NG9 ....183 F4
Carlton in S81 ....25 F3
Warwick Cl
Kirkby in A NG17 ....115 E3
Saxilby LN1 ....57 D2
Warwick Dr
Mansfield NG18 ....102 C4
Shipley DE7 ....157 E2
Warwick Gdns NG12 ......187 F1
Warwick Rd
Balderton NG24 ....140 B2
Long Eaton NG10 ....194 A4
Mansfield NG18 ....102 C4
Nottingham NG5 ....161 E1
Wasdale Cl NG2 ....186 B3
Wash Pit La NG12 ....200 B4
Washdyke La NG15 ....145 F4
Washington Dr
Mansfield NG18 ....101 F3
Stapleford NG9 ....170 C1
Washington St NG3 ....24 B3
Wasnidge Cl NG3 ....223 F3
Wasnidge Wlk NG3 ....223 F4
Watch Mus* NG25 ....122 C1
Watchwood Gr NG14 ......148 C4
Watcombe Cir NG5 ....161 E1
Watcombe Rd NG5 ....161 E1
Watendlath Cl NG2 ....186 B3
Water La Carlton in S81 ....26 A3
Long Clawson LE14 ....211 F2
Mansfield NG19 ....87 D2
Newark-on-T NG24 ....124 C1
Oxton NG25 ....134 A2
Radcliffe on T NG12 ....175 F2
Retford DN22 ....39 F4
Shelford NG12 ....164 B1
South Normanton DE55 .....113 D3
Tickhill DN11 ....8 B4
Water Mdws S80 ....35 E1
Water Orton Cl NG9 ......183 D3
Waterdown Rd NG11 ......184 B1
Waterford St NG6 ....160 C3
Waterfront Ctry Pk*
  DN10 ....7 E1
Waterfurrows La
  NG12 ....164 B1
Waterhouse La NG4 ......163 D1
Waterloo Cl DE55 ....113 D4
Waterloo Cres NG7 ....222 C4
Waterloo La NG9 ....170 C3
Waterloo Prom NG7 ......222 C4
Waterloo Rd
Beeston NG9 ....184 A3
Hucknall NG15 ....131 D1
Nottingham NG7 ....222 C4
Watermeadow Cl NG19 ...88 B3
Watermeadows The
  NG10 ....193 D4
Waterside Cl
➐ Loughborough LE11 ......220 A3
Sandiacre NG10 ....182 A2
West Bridgford NG2 ....186 B3
Waterside Gdns NG7 .....172 B3
Waterslack Rd DN11 ....9 D2
Waterson Ave NG18 ......102 C3
Waterson Cl NG18 ....102 C3
Waterson Oaks NG18 .....102 C2
Waterway St NG2 ....173 E1
Waterway St W NG2 ......173 E1
Waterway The NG10 ......182 B2

Waterworks St DN21 ....24 B3
Watford Rd NG8 ....160 A1
Watkin St NG3 ....223 E4
Watkins La DN22 ....32 B3
Watnall Cres NG19 ....101 F4
Watnall Rd
Hucknall NG15 ....145 F2
Nuthall NG16 ....159 E3
Watson Ave
Mansfield NG18 ....102 B4
Nottingham NG3 ....174 A3
Watson Rd
Ilkeston DE7 ....157 E1
Worksop S80 ....35 F1
Watson St NG20 ....74 A2
Watsons La LE14 ....202 A2
Wavell Cl S81 ....35 F4
Wavell Cres DN10 ....11 D1
Waveney Cl NG5 ....162 A3
Waverley Ave
Beeston NG9 ....184 A3
Carlton NG4 ....163 D1
Waverley Rd NG18 ....102 A2
Waverley St
Long Eaton NG10 ....193 F4
Nottingham NG7 ....223 D4
Tibshelf DE55 ....99 D4
Waverley Terr NG1 ....223 D3
Waverley Way S80 ....47 D4
Waverly Cl NG17 ....115 E3
Wayford Wlk ➐ NG6 ......160 A4
Wayne Cl NG2 ....184 C1
Weardale Rd NG5 ....161 E2
Wearmouth Gdns ➎
  NG5 ....147 D1
Weaver Cl LE11 ....220 A1
Weavers Cl LE12 ....205 F2
Weavers La NG15,
  NG16 ....129 F2
Weavers The NG13 ....139 E3
Weaverthorpe Rd
  NG5 ....162 A3
Webb Rd NG8 ....172 A4
Webster Ave NG16 ....143 F1
Webster Cl NG21 ....104 A1
Weedon Cl NG3 ....174 A3
Weekday Cross NG1 ......223 E2
Weetman Ave NG20 ....74 A3
Weetman Gdns ➐ NG5 ...161 D4
Weighbridge Rd NG18 ....102 B3
Weightman Dr NG16 ......158 A4
Welbeck Ave
Carlton NG4 ....162 B1
Newark-on-T NG24 ....125 D1
Welbeck Cl
Nottingham NG3 ....223 E4
Sutton in A NG17 ....100 C3
Welbeck Cobt S80 ....46 A1
Welbeck Dr NG21 ....75 F1
Welbeck Gdns
Beeston NG9 ....182 C2
Nottingham NG3 ....162 A2
Welbeck Gr NG13 ....177 E2
Welbeck Pl NG22 ....66 A2
Welbeck Prim Sch
  NG2 ....173 E1
Welbeck Rd
Harworth DN11 ....9 D3
Long Eaton NG10 ....182 B2
Mansfield Woodhouse
  NG19 ....88 B2
Radcliffe on T NG12 ....176 A2
Retford DN22 ....39 F2
West Bridgford NG2 ....185 F4
Worksop S80 ....35 F1
Welbeck St
Creswell S80 ....58 C4
Kirkby in A NG17 ....115 E3
Mansfield NG18 ....102 A4
Market Warsop NG20 ....74 A2
Sutton in A NG17 ....100 C1
Whitwell S80 ....45 D3
Worksop S80 ....35 F2
Welbeck Wlk NG3 ....223 E4
Welby Ave NG7 ....222 B2
Welch Ave NG9 ....182 C4
Weldbank Cl NG9 ....183 D2
Welfare Cl NG20 ....72 C2
Welfitt Gr NG20 ....59 D1
Welham Cres NG5 ....162 A4
Welham Gr DN22 ....40 A4
Welham Rd DN22 ....40 A4
Well Fen La NG23 ....156 B4
Well La LE14 ....210 A1
Welland Cl
Newark-on-T NG24 ....125 D1
Worksop S80 ....35 F4
Wellcroft Cl NG18 ....101 F3
Wellesley Cl S81 ....35 E4
Wellesley Cres NG8 ......159 E1
Wellin Cl NG12 ....186 A2
Wellin Ct NG12 ....186 A2
Wellin La NG12 ....186 A2
Wellington Cir NG1 ....223 D2
Wellington Cl NG20 ....74 A2
Wellington Cres NG2 .....185 F4
Wellington Pl NG16 ......143 F1
Wellington Rd
Burton Joyce NG14 ....164 A3
➊ Newark-on-T NG24 ....140 A4
Wellington Sq
Nottingham NG7 ....222 C3
Retford DN22 ....39 F4
Wellington St
Eastwood NG16 ....143 F2
Gainsborough DN21 ....24 B4

Wellington St continued
Long Eaton NG10 ....182 B1
Loughborough LE11 ....220 B2
Nottingham NG3 ....223 E4
Retford DN22 ....39 F4
Stapleford NG9 ....182 B3
Wellington Terr NG7 .....222 C3
Wellington Villas NG7 ....222 C3
Wellow Cl NG17,
  NG19 ....101 E4
Wellow Gn NG22 ....77 E1
Wellow House Sch
  NG22 ....77 E1
Wellow Rd Eakring NG22 ..77 D2
Wellow NG22 ....77 E1
Wells Cl DN22 ....43 E3
Wells Gdns NG3 ....173 F4
Wells La DN22 ....43 E3
Wells Rd Ctr Hospl
  NG3 ....161 F1
Wells Rd The NG3 ....161 F1
Wellspring Dale NG9 .....182 C3
Welstead Ave NG8 ....160 A1
Welton Gdns NG6 ....160 A4
Welwyn Ave NG19 ....88 C2
Welwyn Rd NG8 ....171 F3
Wembley Gdns NG9 ......171 D1
Wembley Rd
Arnold NG5 ....162 A3
Langold S81 ....16 C2
Wembley St DN21 ....24 B4
Wemyss Gdns NG8 ....172 B2
Wendling Gdns NG5 ......161 D4
Wendover Dr NG8 ....160 A1
Wenham La NG17 ....99 F2
Wenlock Cl NG16 ....158 B4
Wensley Rd NG5 ....161 F3
Wensleydale Cl
Mansfield NG19 ....88 C1
Nottingham NG8 ....160 B1
Wensleydale Rd NG10 ....193 D3
Wensor Ave NG9 ....183 F4
Wentbridge Dr NG18 .....103 D2
Wentworth Cl NG19 ....88 C1
Wentworth Cnr NG24 .....139 F3
Wentworth Croft
  DE75 ....143 D2
Wentworth Ct NG16 ......158 C3
Wentworth Gn DN22 ......39 E2
Wentworth Rd
Beeston NG9 ....183 E3
Kirkby in A NG17 ....114 C4
Nottingham NG5 ....161 E2
Wentworth St DE7 ....158 A1
Wentworth Way NG12 ....186 B2
Wesley Cl
Annesley Woodhouse
  NG17 ....130 A4
Ilkeston DE7 ....157 F2
Langley Mill NG16 ....143 E2
➊ Nottingham NG5 ....161 D1
Wesley Way NG11 ....196 B3
Wesleyan Chapel Wlk
  NG9 ....182 B4
Wessex Cl S81 ....36 A3
Wessex Rd S81 ....36 A3
West Ave
Kirkby in A NG17 ....115 E2
Sandiacre NG10 ....182 A3
Stapleford NG9 ....182 C4
West Bridgford NG2 ....185 F4
West Bank Ave NG18 .....102 A4
West Bank La NG18 ....88 A1
West Bank Link NG19 ......88 A1
West Bank Mews
  DE74 ....203 E1
West Bank Wynd
  NG18 ....102 A4
West Bridgford Inf Sch The
  NG2 ....185 F4
West Bridgford Jun Sch The
  NG2 ....185 F4
West Bridgford Sch
  NG2 ....185 E3
West Brook La NG23 .....112 A3
West Burton Medieval Village
  of** DN22 ....32 C4
West Carr Rd DN22 ....39 E3
West Cl NG12 ....197 F1
West Cres
Beeston NG9 ....184 A2
West Cres NG2 ....27 E2
Westcliffe Ave NG4 ....163 D1
Edwinstowe NG21 ....76 A1
West End Beeston NG9 ....183 F3
Calverton NG14 ....148 B4
Farndon NG24 ....138 C2
Long Clawson LE14 ....211 E2
Long Whatton LE12 ....212 A2
Pinxton NG16 ....113 E2
Sutton in A NG17 ....100 C1
West End Ave NG1 ....223 D2
West End Cl NG13 ....181 D2
West End St NG9 ....182 B3

West Furlong
Cotgrave NG12 ....188 A1
Retford DN22 ....39 E4
West Gate
Long Eaton NG10 ....193 F4
15 Mansfield NG18 ......102 A4
Tickhill DN11 ....8 A3
West Gr Rd DN22 ....39 F3
West Hill
Mansfield NG18 ....102 A4
Sutton in A NG17 ....100 B3
West Hill Ave NG18 ....102 A4
West Hill Dr NG18 .....102 A4
West Hill Pk NG19 ......88 A2
West Hill Rd DN22 ......39 E2
West La
Edwinstowe NG21 ....76 A1
Girton NG23 ....82 C1
West Leake La NG11 ...204 B3
West Leake Rd LE12 ...205 E1
West Moor NG2 ....174 B2
West Moor Rd DN10 .....13 F3
**West Nottinghamshire Coll
(Chesterfield Site)**
NG18 ....102 A4
**West Nottinghamshire Coll of
F Ed** NG18 ....102 B1
West Pk Pl DN22 ....39 E3
West St Arnold NG5 ....161 F4
Harworth DN11 ....9 D3
Hucknall NG15 ....146 A4
Kimberley NG16 ....159 D2
Langley Mill NG16 ....143 D2
Misson DN10 ....4 A1
Morton DN21 ....15 D2
Nottingham NG2 ....173 F2
Retford DN22 ....39 F3
Warsop Vale NG20 ....73 E2
Whaley Thorns NG20 ....59 D2
Worksop S81 ....35 F1
West Terr
Hucknall NG15 ....146 A4
13 Ilkeston DE7 ....157 F1
West Thorpe LE12 ......217 E4
West View
Carlton in L S81 ....25 F4
West Bridgford NG2 ....185 E3
West View Rd NG4 ......174 C4
West Wells La DN10 .....12 C1
West Wlk
1 Nottingham NG1 ......173 F2
Retford DN22 ....39 E4
West Wood Est DN10 .....9 F3
Westbourne Cl
Retford DN22 ....40 A3
Sutton in A NG17 ....100 B2
Westbourne Rd
Selston NG16 ....129 D2
Sutton in A NG17 ....100 B2
Westbourne View
NG15 ....100 B2
Westbrecks La DN22 .....43 D3
Westbrook Ave NG15 ....116 C2
Westbrook Specl Sch
NG10 ....193 E4
Westbury Cl NG13 ......183 E2
Westbury Rd NG5 ....161 D1
Westby La NG16 ....158 B2
Westcliffe Ave
Carlton NG4 ....162 B2
Radcliffe on T NG12 ......176 A2
Westcroft Dr NG3 ......162 C3
Westcross Ave NG9 .....182 C4
Westdale Ave NG17 .....101 D3
Westdale Cl NG10 ......193 D3
Westdale Cres NG4 .....162 C1
Westdale Ct NG4 ....162 B1
Westdale Jun & Inf Sch
NG3 ....162 A2
Westdale La E NG4 .....162 C2
Westdale La W NG3 .....162 A2
Westdale Rd
Mansfield NG19 ....88 A1
Westwood NG16 ....128 B2
Westerdale S81 ....36 A4
Westerfield Way
NG11 ....185 D3
Westerham Cl NG8 .....171 E4
Westerham Rd NG11 ....196 A3
Westerlands NG9 ....182 C3
Western Ave
Bingham NG13 ....177 E3
Kirkby in A NG17 ....115 D2
Mansfield NG18 ....56 C2
Saxilby LN1 ....56 C2
Western Bvd NG8 ....172 B4
Western Dr NG24 ....140 C1
Western Fields NG11 ...196 A3
Western Gdns NG8 ......172 B4
Western St NG1 ....223 F3
Western Terr NG7 ......222 C2
Western Wlk DN10 ......10 A4
Westfield Cl
Mansfield NG19 ....101 F4
Sutton in A NG17 ....100 C1
Westfield Dr
Ilkeston DE7 ....157 E1
Mansfield NG19 ....101 F4
Worksop S81 ....36 A3
Westfield La
Collingham NG23 ....111 F4
Mansfield NG19 ....101 F4
Westfield Rd
Annesley Woodhouse
NG17 ....115 D1

Westfield Rd continued
Bingham NG13 ....177 E2
Retford DN22 ....39 E3
Westfield Way NG24 ....139 D2
Westfields La NG14 ....149 D2
Westgate
Southwell NG25 ....136 B4
Worksop S80 ....35 F1
Westgate St NG3 ....173 F3
Westgate View S80 ......35 F1
Westgate Inf Sch
NG5 ....160 C4
Westhay Ct NG8 ....172 B3
Westholme Gdns NG8 ...172 B3
Westhorpe NG25 ....136 B4
Westhorpe Ave NG3 ....173 F4
Westhorpe Dr NG10 ....193 E4
Westhorpe Mkt Pl
NG25 ....136 B4
Westland Ave NG15 ....145 E2
Westland Dr NG16 ......113 E2
Westleigh NG19 ....88 B3
Westleigh Rd NG8 ......159 F1
Westminster Ave
Kirkby in A NG17 ....115 E3
Stapleford NG10 ....182 B3
Westminster Cl
Nottingham NG3 ....173 F4
Worksop S81 ....36 A4
Westminster Dr NG12 ...176 C2
Westmoore Cl NG3 .....162 A2
Westmoreland Ct 16
NG5 ....161 D1
Westmorland Ct DN11 ....9 E2
Westmorland Dr S81 .....25 F4
Westmorland Way
NG16 ....128 A2
Weston Ave NG7 ....173 D4
Weston Cl Arnold NG5 ..161 F2
Sutton in A NG17 ....115 E4
Weston La NG23 ....81 E3
Weston Rd NG22,NG23 ...80 A3
Weston St DE75 ....157 D4
Westray Cl NG9 ....170 C4
Westview Ct NG4 ......174 C4
Westville Dr NG15 .....145 F2
Westville Gdns NG3 ....173 E4
Westward Ave NG9 .....184 A3
Westway
Cotgrave NG12 ....187 F1
Worksop S81 ....36 A4
Westwick Rd NG8 ......171 E3
Westwick St DE7 ....170 A3
Westwood Dr S80 ....35 D2
Westwood Inf Sch
NG16 ....128 B2
Westwood Rd NG2 ......173 F2
Wetherby Cl
Kimberley NG16 ....158 C4
Nottingham NG8 ....160 A1
Wetherlam Cl NG2 .....173 E1
**Wetlands Waterfowl
Reserve** DN22 ....29 E4
Wetsyke La NG24 ......140 C2
Whaddon Ct LE11 ......220 B1
Whaley Bridge Cl
NG18 ....103 E3
Whaley Comm S44 ....58 B2
Whaley Rd NG20 ....58 C1
**Whaley Thorns Heritage
Ctr*** NG20 ....59 D2
Whaley Thorns Prim Sch
NG20 ....59 D2
Wharf La NG12 ....175 F2
Wharf Rd
8 Mansfield NG18 ......102 A3
Ilkeston DN10 ....6 C1
Nottingham NG7 ....223 D1
Pinxton NG16 ....113 E1
Retford DN22 ....39 F3
Stanton Hill NG17 ....100 B3
Wharf St DN10 ....10 A4
Wharfdale Gdns NG18 ..103 D3
Wharfdale Rd NG10 ....193 D3
Wharfedale
Nottingham NG8 ....171 D2
Worksop S81 ....36 A4
Wharmby Ave NG19 ......87 E2
Wharncliffe Rd
Loughborough LE11 ....220 B2
Retford DN22 ....39 F2
Wharton St DN22 ....40 A3
Wharton Ct NG18 ......103 D2
Whatton Rd
Hathern LE12 ....212 C1
Kegworth DE74 ....203 E1
Whatton Rise NG5 .....161 E2
Wheat Cl NG8 ....171 E3
Wheat Croft S81 ....36 A4
Wheatacre Rd NG7 .....184 C1
Wheatcroft View
NG11 ....185 E2
Wheatfield Cres NG19 ..88 C3
Wheatfield Dr DN11 .....8 A4
Wheatfield Way NG17 ..100 C4
Wheatfields Rd NG3 ....174 A4
Wheatgrass Hill
NG25,NG25 ....122 B2
Wheatgrass Rd NG9 ....183 D3
Wheatland Dr LE11 ....220 B1
Wheatley Ave NG17 ....114 C2
Wheatley Cl
Mansfield Woodhouse
NG19 ....88 C1
Ruddington NG11 ....196 B3
Wheatley Dr NG4 ......174 B4
Wheatley Gr NG9 ......183 F2
Wheatley La NG23 .....112 A2

Wheatley Rd
Clayworth DN22 ....21 F2
Sturton le S DN22 ....32 A3
Wheatsheaf Cl NG14 ...163 F2
Wheedale Cl NG8 ....171 D2
Wheeldon St DN21 ......24 B4
Wheeler Ave NG16 .....144 A1
Wheeler Gate
Nottingham NG1 ....223 E2
Selston NG16 ....129 D1
Wheldon Ave NG4 ......162 B1
Wheldon Sch The
NG4 ....162 B1
Whernside Rd NG5 .....161 F3
Whetstone Cl NG8 .....159 E2
Whickham Ct 20 NG2 ...173 E1
Whilton Cl NG17 ....101 D3
**Whimpton Medieval Village
of*** NG22 ....67 F4
Whimsey Pk NG4 ....174 C3
Whinbush La NG14 .....133 F2
Whinfell Cl NG7 ....184 C1
Whinlatter Dr NG2 ....186 B3
Whinleys Rd DN22 ......31 D1
Whinney Bank NG19 .....88 B2
Whinney Hill NG17 ......88 B2
Whinney La NG22 ....77 E3
Whinney Moor Cl DN22 ..39 F3
Whinney Moor La DN22 ..39 F3
Whinney Moor Way
DN22 ....39 F3
Whiston Cl NG5 ....161 D3
Whitaker Cl DN22 ....29 E1
Whitbread St NG7 ......172 C4
Whitburn Rd NG9 ......182 C2
Whitby Cl NG8 ....171 D2
Whitby Cres NG5 ....162 A3
Whitby Rd
Eastwood NG16 ....144 A2
Harworth DN11 ....9 D3
Whitchurch Cl NG5 ....160 C4
Whitcombe Ct DN22 .....39 E2
Whitcombe Gdns 11
NG5 ....147 D1
White Ave S81 ....16 C2
White Furrows NG12 ...187 F1
White Hart La NG23 ...112 A4
White Hart St NG18 ...102 A4
White Hart Yd S80 ......35 F1
White House Rd DN11 ....9 E2
White Lodge Gdns
NG8 ....171 E4
**White Post Modern Farm
Ctr*** NG20 ....119 D4
White Rd NG5 ....160 C2
Whitebeam Gdns NG6 ..159 F4
Whitechapel St NG6 ...160 B1
Whitegate LE11 ....220 B3
Whitegate Prim Sch
NG11 ....195 E4
Whitegate Vale NG11 ..184 B1
Whitegates Way NG17 ...99 F1
Whitehall Ct DN22 ......39 F3
Whitehall Gdns DN22 ...39 F3
Whitehall Rd DN22 ......39 F3
Whitehead Cl DE7 ......157 F1
Whitehead Dr NG16 ....143 E4
Whitehead La NG17 ....100 C3
Whitehouse Ave LE11 ..220 B1
Whitelands NG12 ......188 A1
Whitely Cl NG9 ....182 C4
Whitemoor Ave 6 NG8 ..172 B4
Whitemoor Ct NG8 .....172 B4
Whitemoor La NG23 ...112 A2
Whitemoor Prim Sch
NG8 ....160 B1
Whitemoor Rd NG6 .....160 B1
Whitemoss Cl NG8 .....171 F2
Whites Ave NG4 ....174 A3
Whites Wood La 5
NG21 ....24 C4
Whites Wood La Prim Sch
DN21 ....24 C4
Whitestone Cl NG18 ...103 D2
Whitestub La NG22 ....106 C3
Whitewater Cl NG22 ....77 E3
Whitewater La NG22 ....63 D1
Whitewater Rd NG22 ....77 E3
Whitewates La S81 .....18 A3
Whitfield Cl NG11 .....185 D3
Whitfield St NG3 ......140 A4
Whiting Ave NG9 ......182 C1
Whitney Cl NG19 ....89 D1
Whitsun Dale S81 ....36 A4
Whittaker Rd
Beeston NG9 ....183 D2
Rainworth NG21 ....118 A4
Whittier Rd NG2 ......174 A2
Whittingham Ct NG3 ...162 A2
Whittingham Rd NG3 ...162 A2
Whittle Cl NG24 ....125 D1
Whitton Cl
1 Beeston NG9 ....183 E1
16 Nottingham NG5 ....147 D1
Ranskill DN22 ....19 D2
Whitwell Cl NG8 ....159 F1
Whitwell Prim Sch S80 ..45 D3
Whitwell Rd
Nottingham NG8 ....159 F1
Thorpe Salvin S80 ....34 A2
Whitwell S81 S80 ....45 F4
Whitworth Dr
Carlton NG4 ....163 E1
Radcliffe on T NG12 ......175 F1
Whitworth Rise NG5 ...160 C4
Whomsley Cl NG4 ......140 B4
Whyburn La NG15 ......145 E4

Whyburn Prim Sch
NG15 ....145 E4
Whyburn St NG15 ......146 B3
Whyston Ct NG15 ......145 E3
Wichnor Cl NG11 ......184 C2
Wickens Wlk NG3 ......173 F3
Wickerwood Dr NG17 ...114 C3
Wicket Gr NG7 ....222 A2
Wickstead Cl NG5 .....161 F2
Widdowson Cl NG6 .....159 F4
Wide La Hathern LE12 ..213 D1
Wymeswold LE12 ....217 E2
Wide St LE12 ....213 D1
Widecombe La NG11 ....195 E4
Widmerpool La LE12 ...217 E4
Widmerpool Rd NG12 ...207 F2
Widmerpool St NG16 ...113 E1
Wighay Rd NG15 ......131 D1
Wigley Cl NG3 ....173 F3
Wigman Rd NG8 ....171 F4
Wigsley Rd Harby NG23 ..70 B1
North Scarle LN6 ....83 E3
Wigthorpe La S81 ....26 A2
Wigwam Gr NG15 ......146 B4
Wigwam La NG15 ......146 B4
Wilberforce Rd NG19 ...87 E1
Wilcox Ave NG19 ....88 A3
Wilcox Dr NG16 ....129 D1
Wild Hill NG17 ....99 F4
Wilde Cres NG16 ......129 D3
Wilden Cres NG7 ......184 C1
Wildman St NG7 ....222 C4
Wildman Villas DN10 ...14 A1
Wilford Cl NG24 ....140 A4
Wilford Cres NG11 ....196 B4
Wilford Cres E NG2 ....173 E1
Wilford Cres W NG2 ...173 E1
Wilford Gr
Nottingham NG2 ....173 E1
West Bridgford NG2 ......185 E4
Wilford La NG2 ....185 E4
Wilford Mdws Sch
NG11 ....185 E4
Wilford Rd
Mansfield NG18 ....103 D2
Nottingham NG2 ....223 E1
West Bridgford NG11 ....185 E1
Wilford Sports Complex
NG2 ....185 E3
Wilford St NG2 ....223 E1
Wilfred Ave NG24 ......140 B2
Wilfrid Gr NG2 ....185 F2
Wilhallow La NG16 ....128 C1
Wilkins Gdns NG11 ....184 B1
Wilkinson Ave NG9 ....183 F3
Wilkinson Cl NG19 ......87 D3
Wilkinson Distribution Ctr
S80 ....35 F1
Wilkinson St NG7 ......172 C4
Willand Ct DN22 ....29 F1
Willaston Cl NG6 ......160 B2
Willbert Rd NG5 ....148 A1
Willerby Rd NG5 ......162 A3
Willersley Dr NG2 .....173 E1
Willesden Gn NG16 ....159 E2
Willetts Ct NG17 ......100 C1
Willey La NG16 ....144 A4
William & Henry Mews
LN6 ....84 B2
William Ave NG16 .....143 F1
William Booth Birthplace*
NG2 ....173 F2
William Booth Inf Sch The
NG2 ....173 F2
William Booth Rd
NG2 ....174 A2
William Bradford Cl
DN10 ....3 E1
William Cl NG4 ....175 D4
William Crane Comp Sch
NG8 ....160 A1
William Harrison Sch
DN21 ....24 C3
William Lilley Inf Sch
NG9 ....182 B3
William Old Ct 10 NG8 ..172 A3
William Sharp Comp Sch
NG8 ....171 E3
William St
Hucknall NG15 ....146 A4
Long Eaton NG10 ....182 B1
Loughborough LE11 ......220 A2
Newark-on-T NG24 ......140 A4
Saxilby LN1 ....57 D2
Williams Rd NG9 ......183 D2
Williams St S81 ....16 C2
Williamson St NG19 ...101 F4
Willingham Rd DN21 ....24 C1
Willis Rd NG24 ....139 F3
Willoughby Ave
Long Eaton NG10 ....182 B2
Nottingham NG7 ....222 B2
Willoughby Cl NG7 ......64 A1
Willoughby Ct
Mansfield NG18 ....103 D1
Nottingham NG7 ....222 B1
Willoughby Prim Sch
LE12 ....217 E4
Willoughby Rd
West Bridgford NG2 ......185 F3
Widmerpool NG12 ....208 B2
Willoughby St
Beeston NG9 ....184 A3
Cossall DE7 ....158 A1
Gainsborough DN21 ....24 B4

Willoughby St continued
Nottingham NG7 ....222 B1
Willoughby Way NG22 ...64 A1
Willow Ave
Carlton NG4 ....175 D4
Carlton in L S81 ....25 F4
Hucknall NG15 ....145 E2
Kirkby in A NG17 ....114 C3
Long Eaton NG10 ....182 B1
Mansfield Woodhouse
NG19 ....89 D1
Misterton DN10 ....6 C1
Shirebrook NG20 ....72 B3
Stapleford NG9 ....182 B3
Willow Brook NG12 ....198 A1
Willow Brook Cty Prim Sch
NG12 ....198 A1
Willow Cl
Burton Joyce NG14 ......163 F3
East Leake LE12 ....214 B4
Gainsborough DN21 ......15 D2
Radcliffe on T NG12 .....175 F1
Saxilby LN1 ....57 D2
Selston NG16 ....129 D4
South Normanton DE55 ..113 D3
Worksop S80 ....35 F1
Willow Cres
Carlton NG4 ....163 D1
Lambley NG4 ....163 E4
Sutton in A NG17 ....100 B2
Willow Ct NG16 ....129 D1
Willow Dr
Annesley Woodhouse
NG15 ....129 F3
North Wheatley DN22 ...110 C1
Willow Farm Prim Sch
NG4 ....160 A3
Willow Hill Cl NG6 ....160 A3
Willow Holt
Lowdham NG14 ....150 C1
Retford DN22 ....39 F2
Willow La Carlton NG4 ..163 D1
Mansfield NG18 ....190 A1
Willow Pool La LE12 ...213 E3
Willow Rd
Bingham NG13 ....178 A2
Carlton NG4 ....175 D4
New Balderton NG24 .....140 B3
Nottingham NG7 ....172 C1
West Bridgford NG2 .....185 F2
Willow Rise NG10 .....182 A3
Willow Tree Cl NG19 ...89 E1
Willow Wong NG14 ....163 F3
Willowbridge La NG17 ..100 B1
Willowbrook Ct 16 NG2 .173 E1
Willowdene NG12 .....188 A2
Willows The
Farndon NG24 ....139 D2
Nottingham NG8 ....172 A4
Pleasley NG19 ....87 D3
Willwell Dr NG2 ....185 E2
Wilmington Cl LE11 ....220 B1
Wilmington Gdns NG5 ..161 E3
Wilmore Way NG19 ....101 E3
Wilmot La NG9 ....183 F3
Wilmot St Ilkeston DE7 ..157 F1
Long Eaton NG10 ....193 D3
Wilne Ave NG10 ....193 D2
Wilne Rd NG10 ....193 D2
Wilsic Rd DN11 ....8 A3
Wilson Cl Arnold NG5 ..162 A3
Everton DN10 ....11 D1
Mattersey DN10 ....20 A4
Wilson Rd NG16 ....143 F1
Wilson St
Gainsborough DN21 ......15 D1
Newark-on-T NG24 ......124 C1
Pinxton NG16 ....113 E2
Radnenthwaite NG19 .....87 E1
Wilsons La NG25 ......137 F2
Wilstrorpe Com Sch
NG10 ....182 A1
Wilstrorpe Rd DE72 ...193 D4
Wilton Ave LE11 ......220 B1
Wilton Pl DE7 ....157 F1
Wilton Rd NG7 ....222 A4
Wilton St 2 Ilkeston DE7 ..157 F1
Nottingham NG6 ....160 C2
Wiltshire Ave NG16 ...128 C2
Wimbishthorpe Cl
NG13 ....181 D2
Wimbledon Dr NG16 ...159 F2
Wimbledon Rd NG5 ....161 D2
Wimborne Cl NG2 ......185 E3
Wimbourne Rd NG2 ....222 B4
Wimpole Rd NG9 ......171 E1
Winborne Cl NG19 .....101 E3
Winchester Ave NG9 ...183 F4
Winchester Cl
East Leake LE12 ....205 F1
Mansfield NG18 ....103 D2
Worksop S81 ....36 A4
Winchester Cres DE7 ..170 A4
Winchester Ct NG5 ....161 F2
Winchester Dr NG19 ....88 B3
Winchester St NG5 ....161 E2
Winchester Terr 7
NG5 ....161 E2
Winchilsea Ave NG24 ..140 A4
Windermere Ave DN11 ...9 F4
Windermere Cl
Carlton NG4 ....162 C1
West Bridgford NG2 .....186 B3
Worksop S81 ....35 F4
Windermere Gdns
NG10 ....182 A1

Windermere Rd
Beeston NG9 .... 183 E4
Hucknall NG15 .... 145 F4
Long Eaton NG10 .... 182 A1
Nottingham NG7 .... 173 D4
Windley Dr DE7 .... 157 E2
Windmill Ave NG15 .... 146 A3
Windmill Cl NG13 .... 173 F3
Windmill Ct NG12 .... 197 F1
Windmill Gr NG15 .... 146 A3
Windmill Hill 134 B3
Windmill La
Mansfield NG18 .... 102 B4
Nottingham NG2 .... 173 F3
Worksop S80 .... 47 D4
Windmill Rd LE11 .... 220 B2
Windmill View NG2 .... 174 A2
Windmill Way DE74 .... 203 D1
Windrush Cl NG9 .... 171 E1
Windsmoor Rd NG16 .... 143 E4
Windsor Ave
Newark-on-T NG24 .... 139 F3
Sutton in A NG17 .... 100 A2
Windsor Cl
Collingham NG23 .... 112 A4
Gringley on t H DN10 .... 12 C1
Hucknall NG15 .... 146 A4
Trowell NG9 .... 170 A3
Windsor Cres
Arnold NG5 .... 162 A3
Stapleford NG9 .... 182 C4
Windsor Ct
Bingham NG13 .... 177 E2
Harworth DN11 .... 9 D3
Sandiacre NG10 .... 182 A2
Windsor Dr NG20 .... 74 A2
Windsor Gdns
Carlton in L S81 .... 25 F3
Mansfield NG18 .... 102 B3
Windsor Rd
Carlton in L S81 .... 25 F3
Clipstone NG21 .... 89 E2
Mansfield NG18 .... 102 B3
Newark-on-T NG24 .... 139 F3
Retford DN22 .... 29 E1
Selston NG16 .... 129 D4
Worksop S81 .... 35 E4
Windsor St
Beeston NG9 .... 184 A3
Stapleford NG9 .... 182 C4
Windy Ridge NG20 .... 74 B2
Windyridge DN10 .... 11 E2
Wing Alley NG1 .... 223 F2
Wingate Cl NG8 .... 171 F3
Wingbourne Wlk NG6 .... 146 B3
Wingfield Ave S81 .... 36 A3
Wingfield Dr
Beeston NG9 .... 172 A1
Ilkeston DE7 .... 157 E2
Wingfield Rd NG18 .... 103 D2
Wings Dr NG15 .... 145 E2
Winifred Cres NG14 .... 163 F2
Winifred St
Hucknall NG15 .... 146 A3
Rhodesia S80 .... 35 D2
Winkburn La NG22 .... 121 F4
Winkburn Rd NG19 .... 101 F4
Winnery Cl DN11 .... 8 A4
Winrow Gdns NG6 .... 160 B2
Winscale Ave NG5 .... 161 D4
Winscale Gdns NG5 .... 161 D4
Winscombe Mount
NG11 .... 195 F4
Winsford Cl NG8 .... 160 A1
Winstanley Dr NG24 .... 140 C2
Winster Ave
Carlton NG4 .... 162 B1
Ravenshead NG15 .... 117 D2
Winster Cl NG9 .... 171 F1
Winster Gr S81 .... 35 E2
Winster Way NG10 .... 103 E3
Winston Cl Arnold NG5 .... 162 B3
Stapleford NG9 .... 182 C4
Winston Ct NG24 .... 139 F3
Winston Dr NG23 .... 153 F2
Winston Gn DN10 .... 19 F4
Winston Gr NG23 .... 30 A1
Winter Closes NG16 .... 128 C1
Winterbank Cl NG12 .... 100 B1
Winterbeck Cl NG13 .... 181 D2
Winterbourne Dr NG9 .... 170 C1
Wintern Ct DN21 .... 24 B3
Winterton Cl NG5 .... 161 F3
Winterton Rise NG5 .... 161 D4
Winthorpe Prim Sch
NG24 .... 125 E4
Winthorpe Rd
Arnold NG5 .... 162 A4
Newark-on-T NG24 .... 125 D2
Winthorpe St NG19 .... 101 E3
Wintringham Cres
NG5 .... 162 A3
Wire La DE55 .... 99 D2
Wisa Terr NG5 .... 161 E2
Wiseton Rd DN22 .... 21 E3
Wishford Ave NG7 .... 222 A1
Wisley Cl NG11 .... 185 E2
Wistow Cl NG8 .... 172 C4
Witch La NG23 .... 96 C4
Witham Cl NG24 .... 125 D1
Withern Rd NG8 .... 159 F1
Withorn Mews NG19 .... 101 F4
Witney Cl NG5 .... 160 C4
Wittering Cl NG10 .... 193 F3
Wiverton Rd
Bingham NG13 .... 177 F2
Nottingham NG7 .... 173 D4
Woburn Ave NG17 .... 115 E3

Woburn Cl NG2 .... 186 B2
Woburn Croft NG10 .... 182 A2
Woburn Gr NG22 .... 39 F2
Woburn La NG19 .... 87 E2
Woburn Pl NG19 .... 87 E2
Woburn Rd NG19 .... 87 E2
Woburn Rise NG5 .... 161 E4
Wodehouse Ave NG11 .... 195 D1
Wolds Dr NG12 .... 197 F2
Wolds Rise NG12 .... 197 F2
Wolfit Ave NG24 .... 140 C3
Wollacombe Cl NG3 .... 162 B3
Wollaton Ave NG4 .... 162 C1
Wollaton Cres NG9 .... 183 F4
Wollaton Ct NG6 .... 160 C3
Wollaton Hall (Natural
History Mus)* NG8 .... 172 A2
Wollaton Hall Dr NG8 ...... 172 B2
Wollaton Paddocks
NG8 .... 171 E2
Wollaton Rd
Beeston NG9 .... 183 F4
Kirkby in A NG17 .... 115 E3
Nottingham NG8 .... 172 B3
Wollaton St NG1 .... 223 D3
Wollaton Vale NG8 .... 171 F1
Wolsey Av NG7 .... 222 B3
Wolsey Dr NG17 .... 115 D4
Wolsey Rd NG24 .... 125 D2
Wolsey Way ⚫ LE11 .... 220 B2
Wonderland Adventure Pk*
NG22 .... 119 D4
Wong La DN10 .... 8 A4
Wood Ave Creswell S80 ...... 58 B4
Sandiacre NG10 .... 182 A3
Wood Cl NG18 .... 102 C4
Wood End Dr NG11 .... 117 D1
Wood Gate LE11 .... 220 A2
Wood Gr NG14 .... 148 C4
Wood Hill LE14 .... 218 C2
Wood La
Barkestone-le-V NG13 .... 192 B1
Beckingham DN10 .... 23 D4
Carlton NG4 .... 163 D1
Creswell S80 .... 58 B4
Egmanton NG22 .... 79 F3
Gringley on t H DN10 .... 12 C2
Grove DN22 .... 41 F2
Hucknall NG15 .... 145 F4
Kersall NG22 .... 94 A1
Kingston-on-S NG11 .... 204 C4
Market Warsop NG20 .... 73 F4
North Wheatley DN22 .... 22 B1
Shirebrook NG20 .... 72 C1
South Scarle NG23 .... 98 C3
Wood Link NG6 .... 159 F4
Wood Nook Cl NG16 .... 128 C3
Wood St Arnold NG5 .... 161 F4
Eastwood NG16 .... 144 A2
Ilkeston DE7 .... 157 F1
Mansfield NG18 .... 102 A4
Market Warsop NG20 .... 74 A3
Newark-on-T NG24 .... 140 A4
Nottingham NG7 .... 222 C3
Wood View NG12 .... 186 A2
Wood View Bsns Ctr 🄺
NG5 .... 147 D1
Woodbank Dr NG8 .... 171 E1
Woodbeck Rise DN22 .... 39 E4
Woodborough La NG5 .... 148 B2
Woodborough Rd
Mansfield NG18 .... 87 F1
Nottingham NG3, NG1 .... 161 F1
Woodborough Woods
Foundation Prim Sch
NG14 .... 149 E2
Woodbridge Ave
NG11 .... 184 C2
Woodchurch Rd NG5 .... 147 E3
Woodcoates Rd NG22 .... 67 D3
Wooden Beck Hill
DN10 .... 13 E2
Woodfield Rd
Gainsborough DN21 .... 15 F1
Nottingham NG8 .... 159 F1
Pinxton NG16 .... 113 E2
Woodford Cl NG15 .... 146 C1
Woodford Rd
Arnold NG5 .... 162 A3
Hucknall NG15 .... 146 A3
Woodgate Cl NG12 .... 187 F2
Woodgate Ct NG7 .... 222 C3
Woodgate La
Beckingham LN5 .... 142 C4
Cotgrave NG12 .... 187 E2
Woodgate Rd LE12 .... 214 B4
Woodhall Cl
⚫ Kirkby in A NG17 .... 114 C4
Mansfield NG18 .... 102 C4
Woodhall Cres NG16 .... 56 C2
Woodhall Gdns NG18 .... 102 C4
Woodhall Gn DN22 .... 39 E1
Woodhall Rd NG8 .... 172 A3
Woodhedge Dr NG3 .... 174 A4
Woodhill Ave DN21 .... 15 E1
Woodhill Rd NG23 .... 98 A1
Woodhouse Ct NG19 .... 88 B1
Woodhouse La
Carlton in L S81 .... 26 A4
Sutton in A NG17 .... 101 D4
Woodhouse Pl NG22 .... 66 A1
Woodhouse Rd NG18 .... 102 A4
Woodhouse St NG3 .... 173 F3
Woodhouse Way
NG16 .... 159 E2

Woodkirk Rd NG7 .... 184 C1
Woodland Ave
Gainsborough DN21 .... 15 D2
Huthwaite NG17 .... 99 F2
Ilkeston DE7 .... 157 E2
Worksop S80 .... 36 A1
Woodland Cl
Clipstone NG21 .... 90 A2
Cotgrave NG12 .... 187 F1
Farnsfield NG22 .... 120 A3
Radcliffe on T NG12 .... 176 A2
Woodland Cres NG18 .... 102 C2
Woodland Dr
Mansfield NG18 .... 102 C2
Nottingham NG3 .... 161 E1
Nuthall NG16 .... 159 F2
Southwell NG25 .... 121 E1
Worksop S81 .... 35 F3
Woodland Gr
Arnold NG5 .... 161 E2
Beeston NG9 .... 183 E3
Carlton NG4 .... 174 C3
Mansfield Woodhouse
NG19 .... 88 B2
Market Warsop NG20 .... 74 A2
Woodland Rd
Mansfield NG18 .... 102 C4
West Bridgford NG2 .... 173 F1
Woodland Rise NG15 .... 117 D1
Woodland View
Southwell NG25 .... 136 B4
Whaley Thorns NG20 .... 59 D2
Woodland Way NG16 .... 143 F1
Woodland Wlk NG15 .... 115 E3
Woodlands NG24 .... 125 E4
Woodlands Cl
Newark-on-T NG24 .... 139 F3
Wymeswold LE12 .... 216 B2
Woodlands Dr LE11 .... 220 A1
Woodlands Farm Cl
NG15 .... 145 E2
Woodlands Gr NG15 .... 145 E2
Woodlands Sch NG8 .... 172 A4
Woodlands The
Blyth S81 .... 18 A3
Mansfield NG18 .... 88 A1
Nottingham NG6 .... 160 B3
Whaley Thorns NG20 .... 59 D2
Woodlands Way NG17 ...... 100 B1
Woodlane Gdns NG3 .... 173 F4
Woodleigh NG12 .... 187 F1
Woodley Sq NG6 .... 146 B1
Woodley St NG11 .... 196 B4
Woodpecker Cl NG13 ...... 177 F2
Woodruff La NG22 .... 106 A3
Woods Foundry NG2 .... 173 E2
Woods La NG14 .... 148 C4
Woods La NG23 .... 153 D1
Woodsend NG14 .... 163 F2
Woodsetts La S81 .... 25 D1
Woodsford Gr NG7 .... 184 C1
Woodside
Eastwood NG16 .... 143 F2
Farnsfield NG22 .... 120 A3
Retford DN22 .... 39 E4
Sutton in A NG17 .... 100 C4
Woodside Ave
Mansfield NG18 .... 102 B2
Nuthall NG16 .... 159 D3
Radcliffe on T NG12 .... 176 A2
Woodside Cres
Ilkeston DE7 .... 157 E3
Long Eaton NG10 .... 193 D4
Woodside Dr NG5 .... 161 E4
Woodside Rd
Beeston NG9 .... 183 F4
Beeston, Chilwell NG9 .... 183 D2
Burton Joyce NG14 .... 163 E2
Radcliffe on T NG12 .... 176 A2
Ravenshead NG15 .... 116 C2
Sandiacre NG10 .... 182 A3
Shirebrook NG20 .... 72 C3
Shireoaks S81 .... 34 C4
Woodside View DN11 .... 9 D2
Woodstock Ave NG7 .... 222 A4
Woodstock Cl NG24 .... 140 B4
Woodstock Rd NG9 .... 182 C2
Woodstock St NG15 .... 146 A3
Wooston Wlk NG5 .... 148 A3
Woodthorpe Ave
Arnold NG5 .... 161 F2
Loughborough LE11 .... 220 A1
Woodthorpe Ct NG5 .... 161 F2
Woodthorpe Dr NG3 .... 161 F2
Woodthorpe Gdns
NG5 .... 161 F2
Woodthorpe Inf Sch
NG5 .... 161 F3
Woodthorpe Rd
Loughborough LE11 .... 220 A1
Nottingham NG3 .... 161 F2
Woodvale NG8 .... 171 F4
Woodview Ct NG4 .... 174 B3
Woodview Gdns NG19 .... 89 E1
Woodville Cl NG9 .... 183 E3
Woodville Rd ⚫ NG5 .... 161 E2
Woodward St NG2 .... 173 E1
Woodwards The NG24 ...... 140 B3
Woodyard La NG8 .... 172 A3
Woolliscroft Way DE7 ...... 157 E1
Woollaton St NG15 .... 146 A4
Woolmer Rd NG2 .... 173 E1
Woolpack La NG1 .... 223 F2
Woolpack St DN22 .... 40 A4
Woolsington Cl NG8 .... 159 E1
Woolsthorpe Cl ⚫ NG8 .... 172 A3

Wootton Cl
East Leake LE12 .... 205 F1
Nottingham NG8 .... 171 E4
Worcester Ave NG19 .... 88 B3
Worcester Cl
Lowdham NG14 .... 150 C1
Worksop S81 .... 36 A4
Worcester Gdns NG5 .... 161 F3
Worcester Mews NG19 ...... 88 B3
Worcester Rd NG5 .... 161 F3
Wordsworth Ave
Hucknall NG15 .... 145 E3
Mansfield Woodhouse
NG19 .... 88 A2
Sutton in A NG17 .... 100 A2
Wordsworth Dr NG24 .... 140 B3
Wordsworth Rd
Arnold NG5 .... 161 E4
Awsworth NG16 .... 158 B3
Nottingham NG7 .... 222 A4
West Bridgford NG2 .... 185 F3
Worksop Coll S80 .... 47 D4
Worksop Mus* S80 .... 35 F1
Worksop Priory CE Prim Sch
S80 .... 35 F1
Worksop Rd
Babworth DN22 .... 49 E4
Blyth S81 .... 18 A1
Cuckney NG20 .... 60 A2
Edwinstowe NG21,
NG22 .... 76 B3
Nottingham NG3 .... 173 F3
Whitwell S80 .... 45 D4
Woodsetts S81 .... 25 D1
Worksop Sta S80 .... 35 F2
World of Robin Hood The*
DN22 .... 64 A3
Worrall Ave
Arnold NG5 .... 161 F4
Long Eaton NG10 .... 182 C1
Worsborough Cl NG8 .... 101 F3
Worth St NG4 .... 174 C4
Worthington Rd NG24 ..... 140 C2
Wortley Ave NG9 .... 170 B2
Wortley Cl DE7 .... 170 A4
Wortley Hall Cl NG7 .... 172 B1
Worwood Dr NG2 .... 185 E3
Wossock La LE12 .... 204 C2
Woulds Field NG12 .... 187 F1
Wray Cl NG3 .... 173 F3
Wren Ct S81 .... 35 E4
Wrenthorpe Vale
NG11 .... 195 F4
Wright St Carlton NG4 ...... 175 D4
Newark-on-T NG24 .... 140 A4
Wright Wilson St DN22 ...... 39 F3
Wrights Orch NG12 .... 197 F1
Wrightson Cl NG17 .... 101 D2
Wroot Rd DN9 .... 1 A3
Wroughton Ct NG16 .... 144 A1
Wroxham Dr NG8 .... 171 E1
Wycar Rd NG22 .... 106 A2
Wychwood Dr NG9 .... 170 B1
Wychwood Rd NG13 .... 177 E2
Wycliffe Gr NG3 .... 161 F1
Wycliffe St NG7 .... 160 C2
Wycombe Cl NG11 .... 195 E4
Wye Gdns NG7 .... 172 B3
Wyggeston Rd NG13 .... 181 D2
Wyke La NG24 .... 138 C3
Wykeham Rd NG5 .... 162 A3
Wykes Ave NG4 .... 162 C1
Wymeswold CE Sch
LE12 .... 216 B2
Wymeswold Ind Est
LE12 .... 216 A1
Wymeswold Rd
Hoton LE12 .... 215 F1
Rempstone LE12 .... 215 F3
Wysall NG12 .... 207 F1
Wymondham Cl NG5 .... 162 A3
Wynbreck Dr NG12 .... 197 F2
Wyndale Dr NG18 .... 103 D3
Wyndham Cl NG9 .... 183 D2
Wyndham Mews NG3 ..... 173 D4
Wyndings The NG5 .... 161 F2
Wynhill Ct NG13 .... 177 E3
Wynlea Dr S81 .... 16 C2
Wynndale Dr NG5 .... 161 D2
Wynndale Prim Sch
NG5 .... 161 D3
Wynward Cl NG18 .... 103 D3
Wynwood Cl NG9 .... 183 D1
Wynwood Rd NG9 .... 183 D1
Wyrale Dr NG8 .... 159 F1
Wysall Cl NG19 .... 87 F1
Wysall La
Keyworth NG12 .... 207 E4
Wymeswold LE12 .... 216 B3
Wysall Rd Costock LE12 ... 206 C1
Keyworth NG12 .... 197 D1
Rempstone LE12 .... 215 F3
Widmerpool NG12 .... 208 A2
Wysall NG12 .... 207 F2
Wyton Cl NG5 .... 161 D3
Wyvelle Cres DE74 .... 203 E2
Wyvern Ave NG10 .... 193 E3
Wyvern Cl NG16 .... 158 A4
Wyville Cl NG7 .... 222 A3

Yeoman Ave NG6 .... 146 C2
Yeoman Cl S80 .... 36 A1
Yeoman Pk Sch NG19 ...... 88 B2
Yeoman Pk Specl Sch
S80 .... 88 B2
Yeomans Ct NG7 .... 222 C2
Yeovil Ct NG18 .... 103 D1
Yew Barrow Cl NG2 .... 186 B3
Yew Cl East Leake LE12 ... 214 B4
Yewdale Cres NG5 .... 161 E1
Yew Tree Ave
🄻 Kirkby in A NG17 .... 114 C3
Nottingham NG5 .... 161 E1
Yew Tree Cl
New Ollerton NG22 .... 77 E3
Radcliffe on T NG12 .... 175 E2
Yew Tree Dr Bawtry DN10 .. 9 F4
Huthwaite NG17 .... 99 F1
Shirebrook NG20 .... 72 B3
Yew Tree La
Carlton NG4 .... 163 D1
Nottingham NG11 .... 184 B1
Yew Tree Rd
Elkesley DN22 .... 50 A2
Hucknall NG15 .... 146 A2
New Ollerton NG22 .... 77 E3
Yew Tree Way NG24 .... 125 F1
Yewdale Cl
Nottingham NG11 .... 195 E4
West Bridgford NG2 .... 186 B3
Yonge Cl NG12 .... 175 F1
York Ave Beeston NG9 .... 182 A2
Sandiacre NG10 .... 182 A2
Westwood NG16 .... 128 A2
York Cl Carlton NG4 .... 162 C1
East Leake LE12 .... 205 E1
York Dr NG8 .... 159 E1
York Pl S81 .... 34 C4
York Rd Harworth DN11 ..... 9 D2
Long Eaton NG10 .... 182 B1
Loughborough LE11 .... 220 A2
Nottingham NG2 .... 72 C2
Tickhill DN11 .... 8 A4
York St Carlton NG4 .... 175 D4
East Markham NG22 .... 65 F4
Mansfield NG18 .... 102 A3
Nottingham NG1 .... 223 E4
Sutton in A NG17 .... 100 C2
York Terr
Market Warsop NG20 .... 74 A2
Misterton DN10 .... 7 D1
Pinxton NG16 .... 113 E1
Yorke Dr NG24 .... 125 D2
Yorke St Hucknall NG15 .. 146 A4
Mansfield Woodhouse
NG19 .... 88 B1
Young Cl NG6 .... 159 F3
Young Cres NG17 .... 101 D2
Yvonne Cres NG4 .... 174 C4

Z

Zouch Rd LE12 .... 213 D2
Zulla Rd NG3 .... 173 E4
Zulu Rd NG3 .... 160 C1

Y

Yalding Dr NG8 .... 171 E2
Yalding Gdns NG8 .... 171 E2
Yarwell Cl NG3 .... 174 B4
Yates Gdns ⚫ NG5 .... 161 D4
Yatesbury Cres NG8 ...... 171 F4

Addresses

Name and Address	Telephone	Page	Grid reference

NG	NH	NJ	NK
NM	NN	NO	NP
NR	NS	NT	NU
	NX	NY	NZ
SC	SD	SE	TA
SH	SJ	SK	TF	TG
SM	SN	SO	SP	TL	TM
SR	SS	ST	SU	TQ	TR
SW	SX	SY	SZ	TV

Any feature in this atlas can be given a unique reference to help you find the same feature on other Ordnance Survey maps of the area, or to help someone else locate you if they do not have a Street Atlas.

The grid squares in this atlas match the Ordnance Survey National Grid and are at 1 kilometre intervals. The small figures at the bottom and sides of every other grid line are the National Grid kilometre values (**00** to **99** km) and are repeated across the country every 100 km (see left).

To give a unique National Grid reference you need to locate where in the country you are. The country is divided into 100 km squares with each square given a unique two-letter reference. Use the administrative map to determine in which 100 km square a particular page of this atlas falls.

The bold letters and numbers between each grid line (**A** to **F**, **1** to **4**) are for use within a specific Street Atlas only, and when used with the page number, are a convenient way of referencing these grid squares.

Example   *The railway bridge over DARLEY GREEN RD in grid square A1*

Step 1: Identify the two-letter reference, in this example the page is in **SP**

Step 2: Identify the 1 km square in which the railway bridge falls. Use the figures in the southwest corner of this square: Eastings **17**, Northings **74**. This gives a unique reference: **SP 17 74**, accurate to 1 km.

Step 3: To give a more precise reference accurate to 100 m you need to estimate how many tenths along and how many tenths up this 1 km square the feature is. This makes the bridge about **8** tenths along and about **1** tenth up from the southwest corner.

This gives a unique reference: **SP 178 741**, accurate to 100 m.

Eastings (read from left to right along the bottom) come before Northings (read from bottom to top). If you have trouble remembering say to yourself "Along the hall, THEN up the stairs"!

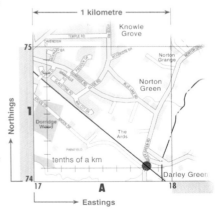

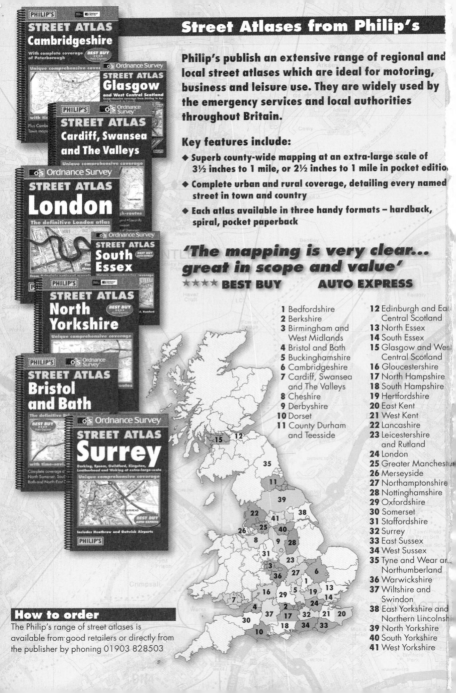